Impacts of AI on Human Expression and Relationship Building

Jorge Esparteiro Garcia
https://orcid.org/0000-0001-5710-5557
Polytechnic University of Viana do Castelo, Portugal

Bruno Barbosa Sousa
https://orcid.org/0000-0002-8588-2422
Polytechinc Institute of Cávado and Ave, Portugal

Manuel José Serra Fonseca
https://orcid.org/0000-0002-3290-8449
Polytechnic University of Viana do Castelo, Portugal

IGI Global
Scientific Publishing
Publishing Tomorrow's Research Today

Vice President of Editorial	Melissa Wagner
Director of Acquisitions	Mikaela Felty
Director of Book Development	Jocelynn Hessler
Production Manager	Mike Brehm
Cover Design	Jose Rosado

Published in the United States of America by
IGI Global Scientific Publishing
701 East Chocolate Avenue
Hershey, PA, 17033, USA
Tel: 717-533-8845 | Fax: 717-533-7115
Website: https://www.igi-global.com E-mail: cust@igi-global.com

Library of Congress Cataloging-in-Publication Data

LCCN: 2026004242 (CIP Data Pending)
ISBN13: 9798337383378
Isbn13Softcover: 9798337383385
EISBN13: 9798337383392
British Cataloguing in Publication Data
A Cataloguing in Publication record for this book is available from the British Library.

Table of Contents

Detailed Table of Contents

Artificial Intelligence (AI) is profoundly transforming human communication by reshaping how individuals interact, express ideas, and establish social connections in digital environments. This chapter explores the evolution of communication from traditional and early digital systems to intelligent, AI-mediated ecosystems that actively participate in dialogue, content creation, and social engagement. It explores core AI technologies enabling natural language understanding, conversational interaction, multimodal communication, and generative expression. The chapter further analyzes how AI-driven personalization influences social connectivity while also introducing challenges related to trust, privacy, bias, and ethical responsibility. By synthesizing interdisciplinary research, this chapter highlights emerging trends, societal implications, and future research directions. Ultimately, it emphasizes the need for human-centered, transparent, and ethical AI communication systems that enhance, rather than diminish, meaningful human interaction in the digital age.

This chapter focuses on how technology affects emotions expressed in different environments and relationship building between different individuals. This section analyzes aspects such as affective computing, chatbots, and social platforms to establish how technology can recognize, enhance, and interpret emotions. This suggests that technology is being used to make people experience emotions. Although technology can effectively make communication between people easier, more personalized, and serve as emotional support, it can also cause issues such as over-reliance on technology for emotions, exposure to technology, and possible loss of emotions. As technology presents different ethical concerns regarding data, power, and fairness, it is essential to consider these aspects. Ultimately, creating a better connection in a world where AI surrounds us calls for a blending of new technology and human values to ensure that tools for emotion and building positive relationships are used to make a positive difference in life through a fair and inclusive process for future generations.

Chapter 3

Manoj Govindaraj, VelTech Rangarajan Dr. Sagunthala R&D Institute of Science and Technology, India
G. R. Hrithikroshan, Vel Tech Rangarajan Dr. Sagunthala R&D Institute of Science and Technology, India
Jayendira P. Sankar, University of Technology Bahrain, Salmabad, Bahrain

Artificial intelligence increasingly shapes everyday communication, influencing how people express ideas, perceive authenticity, and build relationships. Unlike conventional digital interaction, AI-guided communication adapts language, predicts responses, and personalizes emotional cues, often blurring boundaries between human intention and algorithmic influence. Identity, ownership, and truth become more complex as messages are generated or co-created with intelligent systems, raising concerns about trust, transparency, and ethical responsibility. Power dynamics also shift toward those who design and control these technologies, while attention, presence, and emotional closeness are redefined in both personal and professional contexts. As a result, communication is not merely transmitted through AI but fundamentally reshaped, with implications for authenticity, connection, and the future of human interaction.

This chapter addresses the proliferation of AI generated avatars on social media and the tendency of generative systems to reproduce hypersexualized femininity . Adopting a two layer defaults framework the authors analyze how synthetic defaults stemming from model priors and algorithmic defaults driven by platform visibility regimes jointly incentivize eroticized portrayals that undermine credibility . To proffer a practical alternative this chapter documents the design of Alicia which is a counter default avatar created through a two round Delphi study with seventeen experts . The study translates consensus into operational constraints such as functional styling and adult age coding and implements a consistency pipeline to resist identity drift . By mapping these decisions to relational outcomes the authors argue that resisting hypersexualization is a necessary condition for ethical relationship building in synthetic environments.

Artificial Intelligence (AI) is rapidly becoming emotionally responsive systems that also shape the human communication and relationship building. In this paper, the author investigates how emotional intelligence is applied in AI-based interaction and how it influences human expression, trust, and social connectivity. The paper is based on the research conducted in the field of affective computing, neuroscience, and organizational studies, identifying the role played by conversational agents and emotion-sensitive technologies in transforming digitally mediated relationships within sectors. Even though emotional AI improves interaction and personalized assistance, it presents ethical issues associated with bias, privacy, and authenticity. The paper underlines that responsible governance and human-centered design are relevant in order to have emotionally intelligent AI reinforcing, instead of destabilizing, meaningful human relationships in an increasingly digital world.

Emotional intelligence (EI), traditionally defined as the capacity to recognize, understand, manage, and influence emotions in oneself and others, has become a pivotal concept in the design of advanced artificial intelligence (AI) systems. At its core, EI encompasses several domains: self-awareness, self-regulation, motivation, empathy, and social skills, all of which underpin human interactions, decision-making, and adaptive behavior. Translating these human-centered capabilities into computational frameworks involves bridging cognitive psychology, neuroscience, linguistics, and machine learning, thereby creating AI systems capable of perceiving, interpreting, and responding to emotional cues in dynamic and context-sensitive ways. The foundational layer of emotionally intelligent AI begins with affective computing, a discipline introduced by Rosalind Picard, which focuses on enabling machines to detect and interpret human emotions through multiple modalities, including facial expressions, vocal tonality, physiological signals, text, and behavioral patterns.

This chapter reframes organizational communication as communicational problem solving rather than simple information transfer, showing how digital speed can amplify noise and spread complexity. It synthesizes research on coordination and verification to explain how constraints, channel properties, and interaction structures influence collective performance and misunderstanding in mediated settings. To support practice, the chapter proposes a Human-Centered Communicational Problem Solving (HCCPS) framework for hybrid and AI-mediated work. HCCPS structures a repeatable cycle—Diagnose, Match, Co-construct, Verify, Govern, and Learn—linking channel choice to diagnosis, making verification explicit, and treating human–AI collaboration as bounded delegation with accountability. The chapter concludes that lightweight artifacts and governance routines can stabilize meaning, improve effectiveness, and strengthen ethical defensibility and legitimacy under real-world trade-offs.

The objective of this chapter is to analyze the evolution, structure, and future directions of Human-Computer Interaction (HCI) in relation to Human Resources (HR) through bibliometric and thematic analysis of 96 documents published during the last 30 years (1993–2024). Results show the development of HCI in HR as a collaborative and interdisciplinary research area. The field shows a co-authorship average of 3.44 and a co-authorship index of 3.55, indicating engagement with computer science, psychology, organizational behavior, and human resource management. Although research output and number of researchers remain limited, activity has increased after 2015 with an average citation of 24.2. However, international collaboration remains low, with only 5.21% of documents including foreign authors. Major journals such as Computers in Human Behavior and International Journal of Medical Informatics and authors such as Chen D and Johnson C play an important role. Dominant themes include Artificial Intelligence, Human Factors, and HCI, while virtual teams and HR emerge in digital workplaces.

Emotional intelligence in AI-driven environments has become crucial from both a conceptual and practical standpoints as AI mediates human interaction more frequently. This chapter presents a human-centered conceptual framework that reframes emotional intelligence as a perceived and relational phenomenon that

Preface

INTRODUCTION

As editors, we are pleased to present *Impacts of AI on Human Expression and Relationship Building*, a volume that engages with one of the most consequential transformations of our time. Artificial Intelligence (AI) is no longer a distant or abstract concept; it is embedded in the everyday fabric of communication, creativity, and human connection. Its influence extends beyond efficiency and automation, shaping not only how we express ourselves but also how we relate to one another.

This book emerges from a recognition that AI-mediated environments are redefining the boundaries of human interaction. Algorithms increasingly participate in the production and circulation of language, images, and ideas, subtly guiding expression while simultaneously altering the dynamics of emotional exchange and social bonding. These shifts invite both optimism and concern. On one hand, AI offers new avenues for creativity, accessibility, and global connectivity. On the other, it raises pressing questions about authenticity, empathy, and the evolving nature of relationships in digitally mediated spaces.

The primary objective of this volume is to examine how Artificial Intelligence influences human expression and the formation of interpersonal relationships. Bringing together multidisciplinary perspectives, the chapters explore the opportunities and challenges that AI introduces into communication, creativity, and emotional interaction. Contributors engage with both theoretical frameworks and practical applications, offering insights that illuminate not only current developments but also future trajectories. In doing so, this collection seeks to support researchers, practitioners, and policymakers in understanding—and responsibly shaping—the future of human connection in an AI-driven world.

This book is intended for a diverse readership. Researchers, academics, and graduate students will find rigorous analyses at the intersection of Artificial Intelligence, communication, and social dynamics. Professionals in technology, psychology, and education may draw on its insights to better understand the evolving landscape of human interaction and creative expression. Policymakers and industry leaders will encounter perspectives that inform ethical considerations and strategic decision-making in AI adoption. More broadly, this volume speaks to anyone concerned with how emerging technologies are redefining what it means to connect, communicate, and create.

As editors, we hope this collection fosters thoughtful dialogue and inspires further inquiry into the complex relationship between humans and intelligent machines. At its core, this book is an invitation—to reflect critically, to engage collaboratively, and to imagine a future in which technological advancement and human values evolve in meaningful alignment.Top of Form

ORGANIZATION OF THE BOOK

As editors, we are pleased to introduce the contributions that collectively shape the intellectual foundation of this volume. Each chapter offers a distinct yet interconnected perspective on how Artificial Intelligence is reshaping human expression, communication, and relational dynamics across contexts and disciplines.

Chapter 1 discusses the broader evolution of human communication in the digital age. The contributors trace the transition from traditional modes of interaction to AI-mediated communication ecosystems that actively shape dialogue and expression. By integrating insights from multiple disciplines, the chapter underscores both the transformative potential of AI technologies—such as natural language processing and generative systems—and the emerging challenges surrounding trust, bias, and ethical design, ultimately advocating for human-centered communication systems.

Chapter 2 deepens the inquiry into emotional dimensions, examining how AI technologies influence emotional expression and relationship building. Through a focus on affective computing, chatbots, and social platforms, the chapter reveals the dual role of AI as both facilitator and mediator of emotional experience. While highlighting benefits such as personalization and emotional support, it also raises critical concerns about dependency, authenticity, and ethical governance, emphasizing the need to align technological advancement with enduring human values.

In Chapter 3, the authors interrogate the shifting nature of communication itself under AI mediation. They argue that AI not only supports but fundamentally reshapes expression by adapting language, predicting responses, and influencing emotional tone. This transformation complicates notions of authenticity, identity, and ownership, while also reconfiguring power dynamics and relational presence.

The chapter provides a nuanced reflection on how communication is evolving into a co-constructed process between humans and intelligent systems.

Chapter 4 turns to the domain of digital marketing, examining how generative AI and algorithmic systems redefine personalization and campaign automation. Through a bibliometric analysis, the authors map the intellectual structure of this emerging field while critically addressing issues of transparency, fairness, and data governance. The chapter highlights the tension between marketing effectiveness and ethical responsibility, offering valuable insights for bridging this gap in practice and research.

Chapter 5 focuses on small businesses, a context often overlooked in discussions of advanced technologies. Drawing on empirical data from Portuguese enterprises, the chapter illustrates how AI adoption in digital marketing is shaped by sector-specific factors and resource constraints. Despite barriers, small firms increasingly recognize AI's potential to enhance communication and decision-making, providing a grounded perspective on the incremental integration of intelligent systems in everyday business practice.

Chapter 6 revisits foundational communication theory by situating AI within the axioms of the Palo Alto School. Through a scoping review, the authors identify both the expansion of empirical research and the fragmentation of theoretical integration in the field. By reconnecting AI-mediated communication with classical frameworks, the chapter proposes an integrative relational model that strengthens conceptual clarity and supports future inquiry into meaning-making and relational dynamics.

Chapter 7 explores the intersection of AI, culture, and immersive environments within the evolving metaverse. Combining literature review with social media analysis, the chapter demonstrates how AI mediates cultural expression and tourism experiences, fostering authenticity, emotional engagement, and symbolic connections to place. This contribution highlights the growing significance of AI as a cultural intermediary in digitally constructed realities.

Chapter 8 addresses a critical and often underexplored issue: the ethical implications of AI-generated avatars on social media. By examining the prevalence of hypersexualized representations, the authors reveal how algorithmic and platform-driven defaults shape identity and credibility. Through the development of a counter-model avatar, the chapter offers a practical and ethical framework for designing more trustworthy and inclusive digital representations.

Chapter 9 examines the rise of emotionally responsive AI systems and their impact on human interaction. Drawing on interdisciplinary research, the chapter analyzes how affective technologies influence trust, expression, and social connectivity across sectors. While emphasizing the benefits of enhanced personalization, it also underscores the importance of governance, transparency, and ethical design in maintaining meaningful relationships.

Chapter 10 further elaborates on emotional intelligence in AI systems, framing it as a convergence of psychology, neuroscience, and computational modeling. The chapter traces the development of affective computing and its role in enabling machines to interpret and respond to human emotions across multiple modalities. This exploration provides a foundational understanding of how emotional intelligence can be embedded in AI to support adaptive and context-sensitive interactions.

Chapter 11 reframes communication as a process of problem-solving rather than mere information exchange. The authors introduce the Human-Centered Communicational Problem Solving (HCCPS) framework, which emphasizes diagnosis, co-construction, verification, and governance in AI-mediated environments. This chapter offers practical tools for managing complexity, reducing miscommunication, and enhancing collective understanding in hybrid human–AI systems.

Chapter 12 provides a longitudinal and bibliometric perspective on Human-Computer Interaction within Human Resources. By analyzing three decades of research, the chapter highlights the interdisciplinary nature of the field and identifies emerging themes such as virtual teams and AI-driven HR practices. It also points to gaps in international collaboration, offering a forward-looking view of research and practice in digital workplaces.

Chapter 13 introduces a human-centered conceptual framework for perceived emotional intelligence in AI interactions. Moving beyond technical capabilities, the chapter emphasizes the relational and perceptual dimensions of emotional intelligence, exploring how users interpret and respond to AI behaviors. It also addresses ethical concerns such as emotional manipulation and dependency, offering guidance for designing more trustworthy and meaningful interactions.

Chapter 14 examines the application of AI and service robots in the hospitality industry, with a focus on Spanish hotels. Through case study analysis, the authors highlight both the opportunities for enhancing efficiency and the current limitations of adoption. The chapter provides valuable insights into the gradual integration of robotics in service contexts and its implications for customer experience.

Chapter 15 explores the transformative role of AI in the creative industries, positioning it as a collaborative partner in processes of artistic production. Drawing on interdisciplinary theory and case studies, the chapter examines how human–AI collaboration fosters new forms of creativity while raising questions about authorship, authenticity, and ownership. It ultimately argues for a balanced and human-centered approach to creative innovation.

Chapter 16 addresses the growing "authenticity gap" in an era of advanced language models. The author critically examines the challenges of distinguishing human from machine-generated text, highlighting the implications for trust in both personal and professional contexts. By proposing a framework for digital authenticity grounded in provenance and literacy, the chapter offers a forward-thinking response to this emerging crisis.

Finally, Chapter 17 returns to the theme of human-centered service by analyzing the impact of AI on boutique hospitality. Through qualitative research, the chapter reveals the delicate balance between technological efficiency and the preservation of personalized, human touch. It underscores the importance of maintaining core relational values even as AI becomes more deeply embedded in service environments.

Together, these chapters provide a comprehensive and nuanced exploration of how AI is reshaping the ways humans express themselves and build relationships. As editors, we believe this collection not only advances scholarly understanding but also invites ongoing reflection on the ethical, emotional, and social dimensions of living in an increasingly AI-mediated world.

CONCLUSION

As editors, we close this volume with a deep appreciation for the breadth of inquiry and critical reflection offered by its contributors. *Impacts of AI on Human Expression and Relationship Building* has brought into focus a central reality of our time: Artificial Intelligence is not merely a technological advancement, but a transformative force reshaping how humans communicate, create meaning, and sustain relationships.

Across the chapters, a consistent theme emerges—the interplay between opportunity and responsibility. AI enables new forms of expression, enhances accessibility, and fosters innovative modes of connection across personal, professional, and cultural domains. At the same time, it introduces profound challenges related to authenticity, trust, privacy, emotional integrity, and power. These tensions are not peripheral; they lie at the very heart of what it means to be human in an increasingly mediated world.

What distinguishes this collection is its commitment to multidisciplinary dialogue. By drawing from communication studies, marketing, psychology, human-computer interaction, tourism, and the creative industries, the volume reflects the complexity of AI's influence. It underscores that no single perspective is sufficient to understand or guide this transformation. Instead, what is required is an ongoing conversation—one that bridges theory and practice, and that remains attentive to both technological innovation and human values.

Importantly, this book highlights that the future of AI-mediated interaction is not predetermined. The systems we design, the policies we implement, and the norms we cultivate will shape whether AI strengthens or diminishes the quality of human relationships. Ethical design, transparency, inclusivity, and accountability are not optional considerations; they are foundational principles that must guide the evolution of intelligent systems.

We also emphasize the importance of preserving the distinctly human dimensions of communication—empathy, authenticity, and meaningful presence. While AI can simulate, augment, and even enhance aspects of these qualities, it cannot replace the lived, relational depth that defines human connection. The challenge, therefore, is not to resist technological change, but to integrate it in ways that reinforce, rather than erode, these essential attributes.

As editors, we hope this volume serves as both a scholarly resource and a catalyst for further exploration. It is our intention that readers will not only gain insight into current developments but also engage critically with the questions that remain unresolved. How do we define authenticity in hybrid human–AI expression? What constitutes trust in algorithmically mediated relationships? How can creativity and emotional intelligence be shared between humans and machines without diminishing human agency?

These questions do not yield simple answers, but they demand sustained attention. In bringing together diverse voices and perspectives, this book represents a step toward that ongoing inquiry. We invite readers to carry this dialogue forward—across disciplines, sectors, and societies—as we collectively shape the future of human expression and relationship building in an AI-driven world.

Chapter 1
AI and the Evolution of Human Communication:
Transforming Interaction, Expression, and Connection in the Digital Age

C. S. Sasikala
Vel Tech Multi Tech Dr. Rangarajan Dr. Sakunthala Engineering College, India

R. Vinoth
http://orcid.org/0000-0001-5866-1395
R.M.K. College of Engineering and Technology, India

T. Thilagam
http://orcid.org/0000-0002-7657-0726
Vel Tech Rangarajan Dr. Sangunthala R&D Institute of Science and Technology, India

G. Premalatha
http://orcid.org/0000-0003-1031-5607
SRM Institute of Science and Technology, India

G. Manisha
R.M.D. Engineering College, India

M. G. Dinesh
http://orcid.org/0009-0009-7643-5338
Easa College of Engineering and Technology, India

ABSTRACT

Artificial Intelligence (AI) is profoundly transforming human communication by reshaping how individuals interact, express ideas, and establish social connections in digital environments. This chapter explores the evolution of communication from traditional and early digital systems to intelligent, AI-mediated ecosystems that actively participate in dialogue, content creation, and social engagement. It explores core AI technologies enabling natural language understanding, conversational interaction, multimodal communication, and generative expression. The chapter

DOI: 10.4018/979-8-3373-8337-8.ch001

further analyzes how AI-driven personalization influences social connectivity while also introducing challenges related to trust, privacy, bias, and ethical responsibility. By synthesizing interdisciplinary research, this chapter highlights emerging trends, societal implications, and future research directions. Ultimately, it emphasizes the need for human-centered, transparent, and ethical AI communication systems that enhance, rather than diminish, meaningful human interaction in the digital age.

1. INTRODUCTION

The impact of the technological, social as well as cultural development has led to a radical change in human communication during the historical periods. The advent of oral traditions and handwritten manuscript, print media, telecommunication, and digital platforms all have redefined human communication, expression of ideas, and the establishment of connections. The Artificial Intelligence (AI) in the modern digital era has become a powerful aspect that is fueling and changing the communication process in a scale never observed before. Human communication is radically transforming into the new form of AI-mediated interaction facilitated by intelligent chatbots, virtual assistants, automated translation services, recommendation systems and generative content platforms(Lydia, A et al., 2026). This alteration does not pertain solely to efficiency, yet it disrupts the norms of language, emotionality, social life and even the concept of connection in the field of digital space.

1.1 Evolution of Human Communication in the Digital Era

The history of human communication has been characterized with development following the available tools and media where the personal face to face interaction has taken the route of a written communication, mass communication and networked digital communication. With the introduction of the internet, a turning point occurred since it now has the capability of interaction across the world, resulting in novel forms of social interaction, such as email, instant messaging, social networking sites, and collaborative online environments. Nevertheless, early digital systems of communication were mostly passive, rule based and incapable of discerning the context, intent, or feeling. It was more of a human-to-human interaction with digital technologies being the medium of communication as opposed to the participants themselves(MAY et al., 2025).

The implementation of AI in the digital communication ecosystems has shifted this paradigm, allowing the systems to be able to interpret, generate, and adjust communication content in real-time. In contrast to previous digital technologies, AI-driven systems are involved in the interaction process and can comprehend language, identify speech patterns, interpret visual signals, and react intelligently to the input of the user. This has changed the fundamental nature of communication to become a hybrid process that involves human beings and smart machines and the limits between the sender, receiver and medium become blurred. Consequently, human cognition and intent no longer drive communication, but rather, it is becoming more of an influence of algorithmic decision-making and machine intelligence.

1.2 Role of Artificial Intelligence in Transforming Communication

Artificial Intelligence is the focus of the change in communication initiation, processing, and experience. The technologies of deep learning, machine learning and natural language processing have enabled AI systems to take large amounts of linguistic and behavioral information and simulate human patterns of communication with a high level of precision. AI-driven communication technologies can generate coherent text, real-time language translation, simulate human speech and even emotional responses. The above features have expanded communication frontiers which were previously confined by language, geography and availability.

The individualization has also been introduced into modern communications due to AI. The intelligent systems can adjust messages to the preferences, behaviour and situations of the user and therefore create very specific experiences of communication. Even though personalization will enhance the degree of relevancy and engagement, it will also cause autonomy, manipulation, and information silo problems. Also, the intermediation process through AI is increasingly affecting the mechanisms through which individuals get information, form their mind, and engage in digital interactions, which explains why it is so a powerful force of interpersonal communication and group discourse.

1.3 Transformation of Interaction, Expression, and Connection

The role of AI in human communication can be understood with the help of three dimensions, which are interconnected with each other: interaction, expression, and connection. The interaction process has shifted away not only to the fixed and inactive interactions, but also to interactive and dynamic interaction that includes conversational interaction which is facilitated by intelligent agents that can recognize intent and respond with a sense of context. AI-based interfaces enable the comfortable human-machine interaction as text, voice, gestures, and visual input, and therefore make communication more accessible and natural. This has greatly transformed the experience of the customers in the fields of customer care, education, health and entertainment(Dhivya, S. D et al., 2026).

The other key element of communication is the expression that has been revolutionized by the ability of AI to generate and enhance content. Writing assistant, speech synthesis software, and generative writing models with the help of AI can help individuals to convey their ideas, feelings, and narratives better and more creatively. These technologies have an influence on the rules of language and style, the originality of the author, its authenticity and originality, and the issue of the development of human creativity appears. AI is not a replica of human manifestation, but it introduces new forms of hybrid manifestation, the mixture of will of the human and the augmentation offered by the machine.

The social component of communication is connection, which has been transformed, as well, by AI-mediated platforms that enable social interaction, community building, and digital relationships to exist. The social networks are not only affected by the recommendation algorithms which influence the people and what should be shared, but also by the moderation systems which are based on AI and which dictate the proper forms of communication. These processes have the potential to make people feel connected by creating meaningful interaction but also result in social disintegration, echo chambers, and exposure to less thinking differently. In order to determine the effect of AI on the society at large, it is therefore important to know how it is redefining the social connection.

1.4 Motivation and Need for a Comprehensive Chapter

This rapid usage of AI in the communication systems has led to extensive studies in different fields including computer science, linguistics, psychology, sociology and media studies. Despite this growing literature, the existing studies are either focused on a very limited and specific area, such as the example of a specific technology or use of AI, or do not provide the overall perspective on how AI is changing the human interactions. The problem urgency is to ensure that the chapter is wide-range of incorporating all the technological advances, theories of communication, meaning of these technological advances and ethics into one framework.

Such a chapter is required to identify the emerging trends and unanswered issues and gaps in research on AI-driven communication. As AI systems become more autonomous and powerful, it should be known how they influence the interaction, expression, and connection to design and implement them responsibly. Policymakers, researchers, educators and industry practitioners require the systematic knowledge of the communicative role of AI to formulate ethical principles, inclusive technologies, and sustainable communication environments.

1.5 Scope and Contributions of this Chapter

This chapter is aimed at providing a systematic interdisciplinary review of the role of AI in digital transformation of human communication. It discusses the fundamentals of communication, the underlying AI technologies and their applications to transform the way individuals interact, communicate and connect. In addition to the technological perspective, the chapter includes social, cultural and ethical issues, which refer to the issues of privacy, bias, transparency and digital well-being. The chapter is expected to address the gap between the technical innovation and the human-centered theory of communication through the integration of the results of the different research domains.

A hierarchical taxonomy of AI-based communication technologies, a discussion of the impact of these technologies on human communication practice, and future research directions are the main contributions of the work. The chapter emphasizes the need to have explainable, ethical, and non-discriminatory AI systems that can assist in improving meaningful communication between people and not to replace or nullify it. Ultimately, this work makes AI not a technological tool but a force of change that will determine how we communicate, express, and connect with each other in an increasingly digital world.

2. FOUNDATIONS OF HUMAN COMMUNICATION AND DIGITAL TRANSFORMATION

The transforming nature of Artificial Intelligence in communication in the contemporary world is something that can only be comprehended with a firm base of knowledge in the principles of human communication and the process of digital transformation. Human communication is not only an exchange of information, but it is a complex and situation-specific process, which involves sense-making, expression, social conventions and cultural deciphering. With the development of communication technologies as physical ones transformed into digital, the character, speed, magnitude, and form of interaction also altered. This segment explores the principles of classical communication, the transition to digital communication systems, and the shortcomings of pre-AI digital systems, which prepares the background to the concept of why AI is a paradigm shift and not a technological enhancement.

2.1 Classical Models of Human Communication

Conventional theories of human communication focus on the sender, message, medium, receiver and feedback in a common context. The initial linear models considered communication a one-way flow of information, in which the main emphasis was put on clarity and the accuracy of signals. Subsequent interactive and transactional theories acknowledged communication to be a dynamic and two-way process driven by social contexts, culture, emotions and noise. These models emphasized the fact that meaning is constructed collaboratively by participants, not just passed on and emphasized the role of interpretation, understanding, and non-verbal communication.

The human communication is multimodal in nature as it involves verbal communication with tone, facial expressions, gestures, and contextual signals. These are the things that contribute to the complexity and ambiguity of communication and human beings to convey sensitive feelings, intentions and social facts. The classical systems of communication, however, were developed during an era that was characterized by face to face communication and analog media that the only reason communication was interpreted and responded was through human cognition. The pillars are not obsolete, as they provide all the required knowledge about the functioning of communication both cognitively and socially, regardless of the technological progress.

2.2 Transition from Analog to Digital Communication

The process of the replacement of analog by digital communication became a paradigm shift in the information creation, transmission, and consumption. The digital technologies enabled binary coding of text, audio and visual information making information storage, replication as well as transferable in minimal loss. The distance and time factor in communications was significantly reduced through this revolution and made it possible to have asynchronous and real-time communication in the global networks. Emails, instant messaging, video conferencing and social media sites made interpersonal and mass communication to be more global, fast and scalable.

Despite such developments, the initial digital communication systems were the main neutral medium of human-generated content. They could not encode and decode meanings, get the context and dynamically respond to communication. Digital platforms provided technology and not intelligence and the user was left to cope with information overload, language diversity and communication effectiveness. Despite the fact that, with all the accessibility and connection that came with digital transformation, there also came a myriad of problems such as divided attention, a lack of depth to interaction, and the inability to read non-verbally, which is an essential part of human communication.

2.3 Emergence of Networked Communication Ecosystems

As digital technologies mature, communication turned out to be complex networked ecosystems involving individuals, organizations, and platforms alongside content flows. The social networking sites, the collaborative tools and the content sharing sites transformed the communication into isolated communication to constant communication which is many to many. These systems made it possible to develop collective knowledge, online community and participatory communication that enabled the users to be content creators and content consumers simultaneously(Subramanian, R. S et al., 2025).

Nevertheless, networked communication also increased issues associated with magnitude and intricacy. The proliferation of digital content was exponentially growing to such an extent that people could not process information in a meaningful way. The platform architectures, algorithms and engagement-driven design affected communication and formed visibility, reach, and interaction patterns. These systems used to be efficient and engagements focused even though they did not focus on quality of communication, empathy and understanding. Such an environment provided fertile ground to AI-based solutions that are capable of addressing complexity, information filtering, and communicative relevance.

2.4 Limitations of Pre-AI Digital Communication Systems

Digital communication systems were limited to adaptability, personalization, and semantic understanding by nature before the introduction of Artificial Intelligence. The heterogeneity of human language and culture or expression of emotion could not be met by rule based systems and fixed interfaces. Automated replies were fixed and foreseeable and as a result, there was a miscommunication or frustration of the user. Digital connectivity did not eliminate the language barriers and the access issues limited the participation by disabled people.

In addition, the information gathered prior to AI systems could not be used to learn and thereby, there was no continuous improvement and contextual awareness. Communication instruments worked without the intention of the user, their emotional state, or in the context of the situation, which brought generic and impersonal experience. These limitations showed how much of a gap existed between the complexity of human communication and the capabilities of digital systems, and how intelligent mechanisms, capable of overcoming this barrier, were required.

2.5 Digital Transformation as a Socio-Technical Process

Communication should be viewed as a socio-technical process and not technological process in the context of digital transformation. As communication practices are transformed by the digital tools, social norms, organizational structures, and cultural expectations are also changing as a result of technological change. The communication technologies have an impact on the relationships formation, maintenance, and perception, which influence the trust, identity, and social presence. The advent of AI in this environment only exacerbates these trends by introducing the idea of decision-making and interpretation into the communication systems.

The AI-based communication technologies do not simply automatize the existing processes, but they change the roles and tasks of communication interactions. The role of machines as mediators, co-workers and even communicators is increasing raising some fundamental questions of agency, accountability and authenticity. Digital transformation is a dynamic and ongoing process that is worth considering in relation to the impact that AI-mediated communication will have in the future.

2.6 Foundation for AI-Driven Communication Paradigms

The history of human communication and digital transformation presents the most important background information on the creation of AI-based communication paradigm. Classical theories of communication are concerned with the meaning, context, and interactions but the digital transformation is concerned with scalability, connectivity and efficiency. AI brings together these dimensions by introducing systems that are able to understand the meaning, adjust to the situation and operate on a mass scale. This convergence is a change in communication technologies as passive technologies to the position of intelligent participants of communicative processes.

Being based on the already existing foundations of communication and overcoming the flaws of the former digital technologies, AI-driven communication is a qualitative change to the manner, in which human beings communicate, express themselves, and network in the digital realm. In that way, it preconditions the following sections consideration of specific AI technologies and applications and its social and ethical implications in general.

3. AI TECHNOLOGIES ENABLING INTELLIGENT COMMUNICATION

The digital age revolution in human communication is more or less founded on the invention of Artificial Intelligence technologies that enable machines to read, interpret, design, and alter communicative messages. Compared to the traditional digital systems, AI-driven communication technologies are designed to study, understand, and respond dynamically to the interactions of people. These features enable AI systems to not only act as mere communication channels, but also be agents of active communication. This part examines the fundamental AI technologies that support the intelligent communication with the focus on their functions in facilitating natural, adaptive, and multimodal human-machines communication.

3.1 Machine Learning and Deep Learning Foundations

The key to intelligent communication systems is machine learning because it allows the algorithms to learn patterns based on large scale data as opposed to explicit rules(Sule, B et al., 2026). Machine learning models can be used in communication scenarios to analyze the linguistic structures, behavioral patterns, and the history of interactions and predict user intentions and produce suitable responses. The most common use of supervised learning techniques is in text classification, sentiment analysis, and speech recognition, whereas the unsupervised and semi-supervised methods are used to aid topic modeling, clustering, and representation learning in large unstructured datasets in communication(Suganya, P et al., 2026; Sekti, B. A. 2026).

Deep learning has greatly extended the features of machine learning by introducing multi-layer neural networks that can model the complex non-linear relationships(Jiang, B et al., 2025). Recurrent neural networks, convolutional neural networks and transformer-based models are examples of deep neural networks that have shown impressive performance in language and speech processing tasks. Such models preserve long-range dependencies, contextual subtleties and semantic relationships required in natural communication. Consequently, deep learning has allowed AI systems to be on the level of humans in terms of comprehension and communicative content generation(Sharafaddini et al., 2025).

3.2 Natural Language Processing and Understanding

Natural Language Processing (NLP) is one of the significant elements of making machines understand human language be it written or spoken(Ravisankar, A et al., 2025). NLP techniques can help AI systems to determine syntax, semantics and pragmatics and transform raw text into structured forms, which can be processed in a computational manner. Simple NLP tasks, such as tokenization, part-of-speech tagging, named entity recognition, and syntactic parsing can provide simple linguistic information upon which more complex information is based(Rani, P et al., 2025).

The invention of contextual language modeling has contributed significantly to natural language understanding as the systems are capable of comprehending the meaning by the context and not by individual words. This plays a crucial role when it comes to the ambiguity processing, idiomatic expressions and the conversational language. NLP may also be applied to communication systems to enable intelligent systems to interpret user requests, identify intent, and continue a conversational flow in a multi-turn dialogue, thereby resulting in more natural and effective communication.

3.3 Natural Language Generation and Conversational Intelligence

Natural Language Generation (NLG) is applied to support language processing, enabling AI systems to produce human-like text and speech. NLG techniques extend to template-based methods, all the way to more advanced neural generation models that can produce fluent and context-conditioned responses and style. NLG is used in the conversational system to allow AI agents to talk, describe, summarize and adjust their tone depending on the user situation.

The integration of NLU and NLG has produced conversational intelligence where AI systems can support multi-turn conversations, preserve state of dialogue and intelligently respond. Such systems are being applied more and more in chatbots, virtual assistants, and customer support systems, where it is important to communicate in a coherent, relevant, and responsive way. The transition to conversational intelligence is the move out of the transactional interaction and into the relational communication, which facilitates the experience to be more engaging and human.

3.4 Speech Recognition and Speech Synthesis

Communication through speech is an essential part of human interaction, and AI technologies have achieved much in terms of allowing the machine to handle speech. ASR systems encode speech sounds into text through the modeling of acoustic cues, phonetic relations and language. The systems have been enhanced significantly using deep learning methods, which are highly accurate in a variety of accents and languages as well as in noisy conditions(Diwakar, M. P., & Gupta, B. P. 2024).

Speech synthesis, also known as text-to-speech technology, is a type of AI technology that allows the creation of natural speech by software when using text. The contemporary speech synthesis systems are capable of generating expressive speech with the right intonation, rhythm and emotion making voice-based communication more natural. The combination of speech recognition and synthesis allows voice-based communication systems that make hands-free communication, communication with visually impaired people, and more natural human-AI communication possible(Ahlawat, H et al., 2025).

3.5 Computer Vision and Multimodal Communication

Language is multimodal and is used together with visual communication (facial expressions, gestures, body language, etc.) as a means of human communication. The computer vision technologies make AI systems perceive the visual data and thus recognize faces, emotions, gestures, and interpret visual context. They are necessary in applications like video conferencing, virtual reality and augmented reality where visual cues are vital in communication(Chowdhary, C. L et al., 2022; Suma, K. G et al., 2024).

The multimodal communication systems combine the input of text, speech, images, and video to form a complete concept of the context of interaction. Using a combination of modalities, AI systems are capable of doing more robust and accurate interpretation, which eliminates ambiguity and responds better. Multimodal AI is an important advancement towards the human-like communication, as it is similar to how humans inherently combine sensory data in the process of communication.

3.6 Large Language Models and Generative AI

The creation of massive language models has become one of the breakthroughs in the history of AI-mediated communication. These models are trained with large quantities of textual information and they are trained with rich linguistic patterns, world knowledge, and relationship to context. Their capability to produce coherent, context-sensitive and creative language has widened the AI communication to include tasks beyond what is predefined. Large language models can be used in a very broad set of applications, such as content creation, translation, summarization, tutoring, and collaborative writing.

Generative AI technologies can be used to make AI systems, which are communicative partners rather than tools, based on these models. They can switch the manner of communication, spend time in a long talk and promote invention of creativity. However, their ubiquity raises the concerns of misinformation, bigotry and overreliance on computer-generated communication, and the proper design and control of these systems is needed.

3.7 Adaptive and Context-Aware Communication Systems

The fact that it is capable of dynamically adapting itself to the situation of the user and evolving patterns of interactions is the attribute that characterized intelligent communication systems. Context-intelligent AI systems contain information about user preferences, history, location, emotional condition, and situational variables to tailor communication responses. Such flexibility increases relevance, efficiency, and user experience, particularly the use of one-on-one learning, health care communication, and digital support.

Adaptive communication systems will always learn depending on the information of interaction and therefore will be able to optimize the responses and improve performance over time. This is an effective learning ability but it has privacy, transparency and control problems. The dilemma of flexibility and ethics is, therefore, essential in ensuring that the intelligent communication technologies are implemented in a sustainable way.

4. AI-DRIVEN TRANSFORMATION OF INTERACTION

The integration of the Artificial Intelligence within the digital communication systems has radically transformed the nature of interaction since it has made it possible to introduce systems that can detect user intent, respond to it and engage in interactive communication. In contrast to the conventional interfaces which are based on a set of commands and fixed workflows, artificial intelligence-based interaction models focus on naturalness, flexibility, and contextual awareness. These innovations have inverted the paradigms of interaction in which the tool-based approach is substituted by the human-based design in which the patterns of interaction are shaped based on the needs of the users, their preferences and the situation under consideration. The chapter is about how AI technologies have changed the pattern of interaction with the use of conversational agents, intelligent interfaces, emotional awareness, multimodality and collaborative human-AI interaction.

4.1 Conversational Agents and Dialogue Systems

Among the most apparent types of the AI-based interaction, one should mention conversational agents, or chatbots, or dialogue systems. These systems are supposed to be human conversational simulators because they are supposed to comprehend what the user inputs into the system, maintain context of the conversation, and respond to what the user is saying in an understandable way. The old chatbots were limited to rule-based scripting and had keyword matching that meant that the interactions were rigid and predictable. Nevertheless, AI-based conversational agents of the current days along with the application of deep learning and language models are based on the support of open-ended dialogue, multi-turn conversation, and context continuity.

Use of conversational agents in the other areas such as customer service, education, healthcare and enterprise communication has significantly transformed the dynamics of interaction. The users are also requiring quicker and conversational access to information and services with reduced reliance on the traditional interface such as forms or menu systems. Even though convo agents transform conversations into efficient and accessible communication, their ability to manage ambiguity, overcome conversational breakdowns and articulate their limitations in an open manner determines their utility. The more advanced conversational agents are, the more mediative they can become between humans and advanced digital systems.

4.2 Virtual Assistants and Intelligent Interfaces

Virtual assistants establish conversations with the addition of language interaction with task execution and decision support. Such systems enable users to interact with digital environments using natural language requests as compared to procedural inputs. The intelligent interface, powered by AI, can both read intent and prioritize as well as provide proactive suggestions, transforming the interaction strategy to an anticipatory one. This modification enhances usability particularly to the non-technical users because of reduced cognitive load and interaction complexity.

Constant communication between devices and platforms also takes place through intelligent interfaces and this makes communication easy. As time passes by, virtual assistants transform the format of interaction and response based on the learning of user behavior and preferences. However, this customization raises the questions of dependency, transparency, and delegation of agency to AI systems. When the intelligent interfaces are designed, the fact that the users are conscious and in control of the interaction with the AI-driven interaction is an issue of concern.

4.3 Emotion-Aware and Affective Interaction Systems

Emotions are important in human communication and the recent advances in AI enabled the systems to recognize and respond to affective cues. Emotion-sensitive interaction systems analyze the language patterns, voice tone, facial expressions and gestures to identify the emotion conditions of the users. When affective information is added, AI systems will be able to alter the communication strategies to provide an empathetic response, emotional help, or corrective feedback.

The emotional communication is particularly significant in such spheres as mental health, education and customer contact, where the emotional sensitivity in communication enhances the communication effectiveness. However, computational models of emotions are never definitive and objective in their explanation of emotions, and this has questioned their accuracy, bias, and usage in an ethical manner. The fact that emotional intelligence is incorporated in AI-based interaction demonstrates the contradiction between the further personalization and the risk of misconception or emotional manipulation.

4.4 Multimodal Interaction and Natural User Interfaces

The communication with the help of AI is increasingly becoming not only text and speech but also a multifaceted system of communication, including sight, gesture, and touch. The multimodal interaction systems enable interaction by enabling users to mix voice, facial expression, hand gestures and visual information which is how human beings interact and is rich in nature. Natural user interfaces aim to reduce the gap between the human expressive behaviour and system interpretation, in order to make the system more natural and engaging to interact with.

The convergence of the multimodal AI with new technologies, such as augmented reality and virtual reality, also alters the character of interaction, providing embodied and immersive communication experiences. Such systems can help in the interaction of space, shared virtual environments, and non-verbal communication signs and expand the possibilities of remote collaboration and socialization. To establish successful multimodal interactions modalities must be well coordinated in order to avoid cognitive overload and modalities must be coherent between communication channels.

4.5 Context-Aware and Adaptive Interaction Mechanisms

The capacity to adjust communication according to situational attributes, such as time, location, the history of interaction with users, and the state of the environment are features of AI-based interaction and are termed context-awareness. The adaptive interaction mechanisms help AI systems to react in a personalized, user-anticipative, and dynamically adjusting way to the interaction strategies. Such flexibility not only leads to relevancy and efficiency, but it also leads to complexity of the system behaviour, and the user expectations too. The idea behind context-aware systems is based on the further data gathering and inferencing, which raises some serious doubts of privacy, consent, and data control. In order to establish trust in the AI-mediated communication, one will have to strike a balance between the benefits of the adaptive interaction and the ethical considerations. Communication of the usage of data and how the system is functioning can help in eliminating the concerns and promote responsible interaction design.

4.6 Human–AI Collaboration and Co-Interaction

In addition to interaction between individuals, AI is becoming a part of the process of collective communication, facilitating interaction within a group, decision-making, and co-creation. The collaboration between humans and AI is characterized by shared agency because AI systems do not substitute human abilities. AI can also be used in the collaborative environment to aid communication by summarizing discussions, arbitrating conflict, or offering data-driven insights.

The co-interaction between people and AI bring about the issues of the definition of roles, accountability, and mutual understanding. Successful teamwork presupposes that AI systems should be capable of presenting their arguments, restrictions, and levels of confidence. The key to building trust and creating fruitful human-AI relationships is the ability to design AI systems in a transparent and collaborative manner as a communicator.

4.7 Implications of Interaction Transformation

The AI-driven change in interaction has extensive effects on the way people interact with both technology and other people. Even though smart interaction systems facilitate efficiency, accessibility, and involvement, they also transform the norms of communication, expectations, and power. With the further integration of AI systems into daily communication, the role of the latter in human behavior, agency, and social relationships gains more significance.

The evolution of interaction provides the basis of the investigation of the ways in which AI changes the nature of expression and connection, which are discussed further. This chapter presents the necessity of human-centered, ethical, and transparent methods of designing the next generation of communication technologies by analyzing the process of interaction as a dynamic, AI-mediated process.

5. AI AND THE EVOLUTION OF HUMAN EXPRESSION

The human expression is at the center of communication and it involves how people express thoughts, feelings, imagination, and self. The advent of Artificial Intelligence has brought about many changes to the expressive practices by enriching, mediating, and in a few cases redefining the way expression is created and distributed through digital spaces. The systems based on AI are no longer used as passive methods of expression recording or transmission but are involved in the process of creating, improving, and transforming expressive material.

5.1 Creative Expression and Generative Content

Creativity is a complex and very human manifestation that is traditionally associated with imagination and originality along with emotional richness. The conventional definition of creativity has been challenged with the development of the generative AI since the machines can now produce text, music, images and other creative pieces that are quite similar to the ones produced by humans. Gen models are capable of writing stories, poems, and scripts, which provides new artistic directions and creative teamwork.

Instead of substituting human imagination, AI may act as a creative partner, enhancing human imagination and allowing quick experimentation. The creative community is actively working with AI and tools to generate ideas, experiment and break creative blocks. Nonetheless, the adoption of AI in the creative field poses challenges to the authorship, ownership, and what constitutes creativity. With the development of machines, which can generate expressive outputs, it is becoming harder to distinguish between human will and algorithmic generation.

5.2 Speech, Voice, and Expressive Identity

Spoken communication is an influential tool of expression and it does not only deliver information, it also delivers emotion, identity and social presence. The advancements in speech synthesis and voice modelling have enabled AI based systems to generate highly natural and expressive speech using varying tones, emotions and accent. The supported applications comprise virtual narration, accessibility applications and personal voice interfaces.

In the meantime, voice cloning and artificial speech technologies also raise the question of ethical concerns that can be split into identity, consent, and authenticity. Personal and cultural identity is also directly related to voice and the fact that AI systems can duplicate or modify voice undermines the traditional limits of ownership of expression. The speech generation technologies should be used responsibly to guarantee the safety of individual identity and maintenance of the trust to verbal communication.

5.3 Multimodal and Visual Expression

Human expression does not only exist as language but it also exists as visual, gestural and symbolic expression. The AI technologies enable the creation of new ways of multimodal communication by integrating text, images, video, and animation into a single artifact of communication. The AI-driven visual generation systems are helpful in the creation of digital art, infographics, avatars, and virtual worlds, expanding the expressive possibilities that individuals and communities may have.

In the context of social media and digital storytelling, AI can be deployed to enhance visualization: it can automatize the design processes, and it can be deployed to generate content in a short period of time. These tools also render visual communication democratic as they help reduce the technical barriers and allow the user who lacks specialized knowledge to generate visually attractive content. However, the ease of the content production also encourages the overflow of information and the problems related to the authenticity and originality. The accessibility is emerging as a major problem in visual communication mediated by AI when it is compared to the meaningful expression.

5.4 Language Evolution and Cultural Expression

Language is an alive system and it is subject to change due to social and technological change. The application of AI-mediated communication has also been known to affect language use by predicting text, translation systems and discourse patterns as a result of using predictive text, translation systems, and conversational agents. These systems give rise to the emergence of new linguistic norms, shortenings and blends that point to online communication practices.

AI-driven technologies of translation and localisation are also significant in order to sustain and reform cultural manifestation. By applying the concept of cross-linguistic communication, AI will help to promote cultural exchange and inclusion and allow various voices to participate in the worldwide conversation. However, the less-represented languages and cultures may be discriminated against due to discriminatory training data and algorithm construction. In order to have fair AI-mediated expression, language diversity and cultural sensitivity is crucial.

5.5 Implications for the Future of Human Expression

The evolution of the human expression in the age of AI is a complex empowerment and disruption game. The AI technologies amplify the ability of the expression to open it up to more creative and accessible by a broader audience, at the moment of breaking the conventional rules of authorship, originality and identity. The future human expression will probably be premised on hybrid forms which bring up human will with machine supplement, and new methods of discerning creativity and communication must be developed. With the further evolution of AI, the more human-centered, culturally inclusive and ethically responsible expressive practices will be essential to promote. With the introduction of the concept of considering AI as an accomplice, but not a replacement in the expressive processes, the society will be in a place to harness its strength in value addition to human communication as well as the richness and authenticity that characterized the human expressive process.

6. AI-ENABLED CONNECTION, SOCIETY, AND ETHICAL IMPLICATIONS

In addition to changing the way people relate and communicate, Artificial Intelligence is also significant in defining how human beings create, sustain and enjoy a relationship on cyber space. Connection is also another concept which is applied in interpersonal relations besides social cohesion, community participation and group communication patterns. The AI-driven platforms are mediate the social interaction and affect the movement of visibility, engagement, and communication to shape the social structures and cultural dynamics. These technologies have brought with them ethically, socially and psychologically, challenges that have never before been witnessed, and this means that they should be addressed with a lot of care. This section will touch upon the role of AI in human connection, the impact of AI on society, and the ethical issues which arise as a consequence of the communication mediated by AI.

6.1 AI-Mediated Social Connectivity and Relationships

The communication platforms provided by AI are also considered key in the establishment of social interaction by allowing people to communicate regardless of geographical, cultural, and time zones. Contact, community and content are recommended by algorithm, influencing the initiation and maintenance of relationships. The AI-based match-making, social networking capabilities, and communication devices contribute to the creation of the strong interpersonal relationships as well as weak social ties that facilitate the information exchange and community-building.

Nevertheless, AI mediation changes the dynamics of the relationship formation process because it brings algorithmic influence to social interaction. The choice of whom one associates with and what they should be involved with is becoming more and more based on machine-optimization as opposed to human choice. Although this can increase the level of relevance and efficiency, it can also narrow the ability to experience different perspectives and decrease the spontaneity of social interaction. The long-term effects of the relationships mediated by algorithms need to be comprehended in order to assess the role of AI in the development of social bonds.

6.2 Digital Communities and Collective Communication

The AI technologies influence a lot the organization and functioning of the digital communities, managing the content, regulating interactions and making the voices of groups stronger. Moderation systems are programmed to find the harmful content, and implement the rules of the community, and the safe communication conditions are maintained at a large scale. The tools that summarize discussions, indicate the trending topics, and allow making decisions together are also used as AI tools to support the process of collective communication.

These characteristics make large virtual communities more manageable and scalable, as well as participatory to large numbers of people. Nevertheless, content curation and automated moderation bring about the issue of transparency, accountability, and cultural bias. The work of AI systems can predetermine with whom it is possible to listen and whom it is possible to marginalize and influence the discourse and general knowledge of the population. The community is thus a great challenge in AI-assisted group communication in offering inclusive and transparent administration.

6.3 Personalization, Echo Chambers, and Social Fragmentation

Personalization is the feature of AI-mediated communication, according to which systems can tailor content and interaction in terms of user preference and behavior. Despite the fact that personalization enhances the level of user interest and relevance, it also causes the emergence of echo chambers which present a user with information that supports their existing beliefs to a massive extent. This effect can enhance polarization, reduce the level of critical interaction and destroy social cohesion.

AI-based filtering mechanisms can impact the information consumption and the social patterns of connections establishing the individuals with whom to communicate and what conditions to define the manner of interaction. In order to settle the contradiction between the notions of personalization and diversity, it will be necessary to utilize the intentional design decisions that will promote the exposure to alternative perspectives without violating the autonomy of users. Increasing the level of engagement and maintaining the welfare of the society is a key issue in AI-driven communication systems.

6.4 Trust, Transparency, and Explainability in Communication Systems

Effective communication depends on the core component of trust, and the systems mediated by AI need to gain and retain user trust to be effective. Clarity about the ways AI systems are used to produce answers, filter content, and control interaction is necessary to develop informed interaction. Explainable AI seeks to ensure that the behavior of systems can be understood by users so that they can assess the reliability of the system and make knowledgeable decisions.

Explainability helps to hold people accountable and ethically responsible in a communication context by explaining the involvement of AI in message and interaction development. Lack of transparency will cause people to overrate or derate the capabilities of AI, resulting in false trust or distrust. It is thus important to design communication systems that convey their limitations and decision making procedures so that trust in AI-mediated connection can be maintained.

6.5 Privacy, Data Security, and Surveillance Concerns

The AI-based communication systems require extensive data collection and data analysis to be functional, which raises grave concerns on data security and privacy. Some sensitive information about individuals and communities may be supplied by the messages, voice recordings, and patterns of behavior, which are the information about personal communication. Such data should be traded off between strong security measures and privacy and adaptation and personalization of users.

Trying to create surveillance threats, the data of communication is collected without adequate consent or transparency, and it would ruin trust and freedom of expression. Minimalization of data, informed consent, and security of data handling should be highly emphasized in ethical communications systems. The problem of privacy is the most important to be taken into account to ensure that AI-enhanced connectivity will not be at the cost of individual rights and social trust.

6.6 Bias, Fairness, and Digital Inclusion

Examples of how bias in AI communication systems may be expressed are inequality in representation, discriminatory language generation, and exclusionary interaction patterns. These prejudices are biased training content, design assumptions, and they will discriminate against the minor groups. The bias AIs in the communication case can reinforce the adverse stereotypes and limit the access to valuable interactions. In order to promote equity and digital inclusiveness, one will have to proactively participate in an effort to bring the variety of linguistic, cultural and social perspectives to the architecture of the AI systems. Inclusive communication technologies can facilitate accessibility of people with disabilities, linguistic minorities, and underserved groups. Inclusive digital societies will be achieved when people are given a fair portion of communication through AI.

6.7 Societal and Ethical Implications of AI-Enabled Connection

Social implications of AI-based connection are not restricted to personal communication, but they also impact on the democracy, cultural values, and social strength. The AI mediated communication is important in the discourse of the people, the sharing of information and the decision making of the group as well as the way society negotiates the truth, trust and common ground. It is thus necessary to establish ethical governance systems to make sure that AI is used responsibly in communication systems.

Ethical issues are the accountability of AI-generated communication, manipulation and misinformation control, and human control systems. As the incorporation of AI in social connection continues to increase, the interdisciplinary team of technologists, policymakers, and social scientists is required to introduce the technological innovation into the balance with human values. The ethical dilemmas will be resolved making the AI-enhanced connectivity either empowering or destructive to the social fabric.

7. CONCLUSION

The technology of digital human communication has gone a notch further to becoming a revolution with the introduction of Artificial Intelligence that has fundamentally altered the way people communicate, express themselves, and build relationships. This chapter has explored the concept of AI as an influential communicative agent who is more than an automation process in terms of its active involvement in the process of meaning production, dialogues control, and the creative expression. As intelligence is eventually integrated into the communications infrastructure, AI has transformed the digital communication, which is generally a tool-based, inert experience, into an adaptive, human-based ecosystem, which is contextually, intentionally and emotionally responsive.

The AI-based systems like the conversational agents, intelligent interfaces, and multimodal systems have made the accessibility, efficiency, and naturalness of the interaction better. These systems are more natural in interaction by minimizing on cognitive and technical barriers, real-time interaction and collaborative interaction between machines and the human beings. Simultaneously, the AI has re-constituted human expression, by enhancing linguistic, creative and multimodal expression. Generative models and assistive adaptive technology transform people into creators of thoughts, emotions, and stories more effectively and it upsets the traditional ideas of authorship, originality, and the right to express.

The AI-mediated communication also has transformed the social relationship, which affects the creation of relations, communal engagement, and discussion process. Individualization and content recommendation are intelligent and make the process more relevant and interactive but lead to issues of the echo-chamber, social polarization, and lack of engagement with the other side of the argument. Moreover, the ethical aspect of communication with AI-enabled communication, such as trust, transparency, privacy, bias, and inclusion makes it significant that the design and governance of communication with AI-enabled communication is responsible. Since the AI systems will slowly transform into the provider of the social interaction, the correspondence of the latter to the principles of humans and the norms of a particular society will become the question of the priority.

In the future, human communication will be defined by such hybrid human-AI communicative practices as a combination of human creativity and judgement with machine intelligence and scalability. The development of affective computing, multimodal intelligence, and explainable AI is one of the opportunities that can create more comprehensible, inclusive and trustful communication systems. Nevertheless, to achieve this potential, it is better to work interdisciplinarity, be morally responsible at all times, and follow the concepts of human-centred design. The transformative ability of AI can be employed by societies to encourage communication that is meaningful, authentic, and vibrant through social bonding by making AI an interactive partner and not a substitute of human communication in the internet age.

REFERENCES

Ahlawat, H., Aggarwal, N., & Gupta, D. (2025). Automatic Speech Recognition: A survey of deep learning techniques and approaches. *International Journal of Cognitive Computing in Engineering*.

Chowdhary, C. L., Reddy, G. T., & Parameshachari, B. D. (2022). *Computer vision and recognition systems: research innovations and trends*. Apple Academic Press. DOI: 10.1201/9781003180593

Dhivya, S. D., Balakrishna, R., Priya, T. S. B., Thilagam, T., Sathya, V., Gracious, L. A., & Subramanian, R. S. (2026). Artificial Intelligence in Personalized Education: Revolutionizing Learning Paths and Student Engagement. *AI, Personalization, Equity, and the Future of Learning*, 453-468.

Diwakar, M. P., & Gupta, B. P. (2024). Performance Enhancement of Speech Recognition by Using Machine Learning Techniques Specifically GAN-AE Algorithm: An Overview. *Harnessing Artificial Emotional Intelligence for Improved Human-Computer Interactions*, 160-179.

Jiang, B., Li, J., Lu, Y., Cai, Q., Song, H., & Lu, G. (2025). Eficient image denoising using deep learning: A brief survey. *Information Fusion*, *118*, 103013. DOI: 10.1016/j.inffus.2025.103013

Lydia, A., Jayalakshmi, J., Suresh, G., Anand, T., Priya, V. K., & Shanmugapriya, D. (2026). Navigating Workforce Adaptation and Human Factors in the Digital Era. In *Navigating Digital Transformation Through Business Process Management* (pp. 253–278). IGI Global Scientific Publishing.

MAY. P. M. A., Nalina, E., NoorMohamed, I., & Ezhilvendan, M. (2025, June). Human-Machine Interaction: Bridging Humans and Intelligent Systems. In *2025 11th International Conference on Communication and Signal Processing (ICCSP)* (pp. 31-36). IEEE.

Rani, P., Yadav, S. P., Singh, P. N., & Almusawi, M. (2025). Real-World Case Studies: Transforming Mental Healthcare With Natural Language Processing. In *Demystifying the Role of Natural Language Processing (NLP) in Mental Health* (pp. 303-324). IGI Global Scientific Publishing.

Ravisankar, A., Kulkarni, A., Takore, T. T., Hasan, D. S., Dharani, K., & Naganjaneyulu, K. V. (2025). Using natural language processing and the internet of things for employee performance evaluation. In *Interdisciplinary Approaches to AI, Internet of Everything, and Machine Learning* (pp. 383–396). IGI Global Scientific Publishing.

Sekti, B. A. (2026). Machine learning and artificial intelligence (AI) in manufacturing. In *Integrating Digital Innovation and Integrated Frameworks in Manufacturing* (pp. 255–292). IGI Global Scientific Publishing.

Sharafaddini, A. M., Esfahani, K. K., & Mansouri, N. (2025). Deep learning approaches to detect breast cancer: A comprehensive review. *Multimedia Tools and Applications*, *84*(21), 24079–24190. DOI: 10.1007/s11042-024-20011-6

Subramanian, R. S., Ramana, T. V., Ramana, K. V., Prabha, S., & Nivaskumar, V. (2025). Converging Horizons: Synergies of 6G Wireless Communication, Machine Learning, and Embedded Systems for Intelligent Connectivity. *The Intersection of 6G, AI/Machine Learning, and Embedded Systems*, 67-93.

Suganya, P., Siva, S. R., Ananthi, S. N., Thilagam, T., Elavarasi, J., Anto, G. L., & Girija, P. (2026). The role of artificial intelligence in transforming supply chain management. In *Transformative Impact of AI in Supply Chain Management* (pp. 271–294). IGI Global Scientific Publishing.

Sule, B., Meshram, D., Iyer, S., Pathak, G. P., Anute, N., Selvakumar, P., & Manjunath, T. C. (2026). Artificial intelligence and machine learning. In *Integrating Modern Mathematics and Sensor Technologies in Civil Engineering* (pp. 61–88). IGI Global Scientific Publishing.

Suma, K. G., Patil, P., Sunitha, G., Mantri, V. P., & Kale, N. D. (2024). Computer vision and its intelligence in Industry 4.0. In *Machine learning techniques and industry applications* (pp. 119–142). IGI Global Scientific Publishing. DOI: 10.4018/979-8-3693-5271-7.ch007

Chapter 2
AI, Emotion, and Connection:
Redefining Human Expression and Relationships in a Machine-Mediated World

Muhammad Usman Tariq
http://orcid.org/0000-0002-7605-3040
Abu Dhabi University, UAE & University College Cork, Ireland

ABSTRACT

This chapter focuses on how technology affects emotions expressed in different environments and relationship building between different individuals. This section analyzes aspects such as affective computing, chatbots, and social platforms to establish how technology can recognize, enhance, and interpret emotions. This suggests that technology is being used to make people experience emotions. Although technology can effectively make communication between people easier, more personalized, and serve as emotional support, it can also cause issues such as over-reliance on technology for emotions, exposure to technology, and possible loss of emotions. As technology presents different ethical concerns regarding data, power, and fairness, it is essential to consider these aspects. Ultimately, creating a better connection in a world where AI surrounds us calls for a blending of new technology and human values to ensure that tools for emotion and building positive relationships are used to make a positive difference in life through a fair and inclusive process for future generations.

DOI: 10.4018/979-8-3373-8337-8.ch002

INTRODUCTION

The simple tools that were made to carry out mathematical operations or to organize data blossomed into systems that could generate language, images, music, and even display activities related to emotions. Today, AI is integral to everyday conversations; it assists in crafting messages, sharing them, and even how messages are understood (Sjoraida, 2025). From auto-completing the next word on a text message to helping an individual author new art or music, these systems have now worked their way into how an individual expresses themselves through writing or art. This is not just a cultural shift; it is a significant turn toward a revolution in meaning-making and distribution. As AI becomes part of how people communicate, this will change not only what is being said but also how people see themselves and others through language and their creativity. Creativity, in particular, offers a context in which AI intersects positively and negatively.

Tools that help create texts, pictures, music, and videos are considered collaborators rather than assistants. Writers use this technology to generate new ideas for writing. Artists use this technology to create pictures. Musicians use this technology to compose songs. These applications raise questions about the ownership of an artistic product and the origin of creativity (Thi Phuong et al., 2025). These applications signal a shift in the way creativity is generated from a mix of human intellect and computer technology. While this technology may open doors for artists, there is a potential for standardization in the output because the technology operates on existing data.

Changes are also observed in communication, especially with the involvement of platforms that utilize AI for sorting and selecting items for people (George, 2025). Sites such as social media platforms, search engines, and messaging sites rely on algorithms to determine which content to display when and how. Such activities affect how conversations occur because certain voices are amplified while others are muted, yet this is done unknowingly. On the one hand, technology such as AI can make interactions seem timely and pertinent; however, it can also fragment experiences because everyone is treated to different bits of information that influence their opinions and emotions. Communication that occurred in collective environments can now occur in environments influenced by technology, such as AI.

The emotional aspect of communication is also affected by AI technology. New technology can understand human emotions based on face recognition, voices, text messages, and human behavior. These have already been incorporated into customer service chatbots, mental health applications, social media, and personal assistants (Filieri et al., 2025). These technology systems can make humans feel like they are not alone based on interactions with technology that seems to understand emotions. These interactions with technology lead to questions about what is real when there is technology on hand to provide emotional support. When it appears that the AI actually cares about the human, it might lead to the human mistaking a response programmed in the algorithm for a true human bond. This often reshapes human expectations of emotional connections.

On the one hand, AI systems can facilitate communication across different geographical, linguistic, and ability contexts. Conversely, it is important to consider the possibility that relying on AI for communication may change the nature of deep and meaningful relationships. This is due to the fact that when individuals utilize suggestions, emojis, and responses from AI, individuals might feel less control and less connected to the emotions of others. This raises the question of whether technology assists individuals in feeling closer or replacing genuine and vulnerable interactions. In a larger context, societies and relationships are also being transformed through the use of Artificial Intelligence technology (Tan et al., 2025). The design and implementation of AI affect who will and will not be heard. Unfair data used in algorithms can exacerbate social problems, influencing how people are represented through media, what opportunities they receive, and even what is publicly discussed. AI-generated content also makes it harder to trust anything people say, as fake videos and other digital media might deceive people into believing things that are not true. Although there are difficulties, the increased usage of AI provides us with an opportunity to look at our networking and expression in new ways. If AI is developed with human values in mind, it will be beneficial in terms of creativity, talking, and understanding rather than detrimental. We must bear in mind that technology is not objective. In contrast, technology helps us act and feel in certain ways. Humans have the primary role in developing how we will utilize AI in our communication methods, whether it is beneficial as an instrument of greater understanding of each other or if it will simply be a replacement for real human interaction. We do not want to halt our further creative and expressive use of AI technology, but we must be aware of its effects (Geroimenko, 2025). The key to this increased time spent in the emotional and expressive realm with technology is to keep communication open, ambiguous, and real. Eventually, AI's increasing involvement in the way we communicate and generate text represents a huge paradigm shift in how relationships are established and maintained in the workplace. With a focus on how AI shapes feelings and social life rather than just being fast or new, we can work toward communication that remains deeply human but is shaped by intelligent machines.

EVOLUTION OF HUMAN COMMUNICATION IN AN AI-MEDIATED ERA

Everywhere in the world, human communication has always been a process that changes with time. With storytelling passed through oral communication and written communication, followed by printing books and using the Internet, each new method that comes up changes the way human communication is done through the creation of new technologies that affect communication in a way that positively influences the manner in which human communication occurs (Sjoraida, 2025). The current age, with the increased use of artificial intelligence, is a new process that will affect human communication in a way that will change human language and communication in a manner that will positively influence human language and communication. Unlike the past, the new technology assists human beings in doing things faster and further and is involved in human communication itself, with the capacity and ability to create, categorize, and interpret language. It not only influences what humans communicate but also how and what the language means.

The effect of AI on language use is obvious, as it assists in trying to guess and conclude what one wants to put. Predictive typing, autocorrect, and suggested responses are now so ubiquitous that it has become hard to notice that they are there in the first place (Kumar et al., 2025). However, they contribute to designing tone, wording, and sentence patterns that aim for more effective and similar communication in general. Messages are becoming briefer, more regular in style, and, in effect, more generic or polite in nature because of what the data has taught these systems to perform. Eventually, exposure to such systems could affect what users perceive when they use language by employing expressions that are compliant with what the computer systems are meant to handle. Of course, there is also consistency in learning new things when it comes to using language through such systems that are always for predictability rather than innovation in communication.

The manner in which people interact with each other has also been affected by the involvement of AI in communication systems. Conversations take place in environments where the platform relies on automated rules. Such environments influence the time people hold a conversation, with whom they hold the conversation, and the duration. In this regard, meaning more often materializes from such nuggets of minimal message slots and visual cues than from extended reflections or narratives (Bhat, 2025). AI also changes how meaning is created through its mediation in communicative contexts. Meaning does not only derive from words, but also from common lived experience, cultural cues, and the informational surround. Algorithms impact these aspects through the personalization of information exhibited to people, which is based on their preferences and actions. When individuals see things tailored just for them, their interpretation of these things can be highly different, even if they use the same words. A phrase, image, or symbol may have different meanings within the context produced by an algorithm (Kehinde, 2025). This personalization can make communication more interesting, but it can also make it harder to understand each other's messages. Common meanings become harder to attain if the context of communication is personalized. Table 1 synthesises the discussion of language, platforms, emotion, creativity, and relationships into a single analytical frame.

Table 1. Forms of AI mediation in human communication and their relational implications

Domain of AI Mediation	Examples of AI Technologies	Primary Effects on Communication	Relational and Emotional Implications
Linguistic mediation	Predictive text, autocorrect, generative language models	Standardisation of tone and phrasing; acceleration of message production	Reduced linguistic originality; increased politeness and neutrality; potential loss of individual voice
Platform mediation	Social media algorithms, search engines, recommender systems	Selective visibility of content; personalised information environments	Fragmentation of shared meaning; amplification of dominant voices; muted marginal perspectives
Affective mediation	Emotion-detection systems, empathetic chatbots, virtual companions	Simulation of emotional responsiveness; affect-sensitive interaction	Perceived emotional support; risk of emotional substitution and dependency
Creative mediation	AI image generators, music composition tools, writing assistants	Expansion of creative possibilities; rapid ideation and remixing	Blurred boundaries of authorship; redefinition of creativity and ownership
Relational mediation	AI companions, matchmaking algorithms, conversational agents	Algorithmic shaping of intimacy and social bonds	Emergence of parasocial and asymmetric emotional relationships

Social media demonstrates the impact of AI systems on human connections and expressions. These sites rely on algorithms that help make sense of the massive amount of content people put out, choosing what users see and how often it is shared. Content deemed helpful or fantastically interesting, as defined in the algorithm, is selected, influencing the desired forms of expression. Emotional depth, new thoughts, or messages are more effective than if they are clouded or subtle, thus prompting people to communicate in a way that gets noticed. This has resulted in communication patterns revolving around showcasing or seeking likes, shares, or comments as a replacement for actual human interaction. The self, or identity, becomes more about a public image, conveyed through data points that become signs of human connection (George, 2025). Helping friends in their pursuits and interests, as well as showing support in other ways, is beneficial on social media. Such spaces allow for greater support but less complex communication since individuals are not as likely to be presented with a differing viewpoint. Such a way of connecting is certainly a reality, but it is mediated by processes that are unseen yet prioritize engagement over understanding. The expression of emotions in AI social spaces is important. Emotional life becomes inextricably intermingled with how the platforms function, leaving little ability to distinguish between the genuine expression of feelings and how they are presented to others.

AI also alters how connected people feel and how immediately communicative relationships are. Features such as read receipts, typing notices, and reminders give rise to an expectation of the kind of accessibility and responsiveness one ought to be. These are small cues that can mark the way in which one might interpret silence, delay, and brief messages, ultimately leading to worry and misconceptions. There is an element of global communication, present and available at all times, found in the background of everyday life as opposed to specific moments in communication. This can give one a sense of connection, but there might be an element of pressure in being constantly connected. Although many things are changing, the involvement of people is still an integral part of the communication process (Sjoraida, 2025). They discover ways to cope with changing environments affected by the presence of AI. This results in the formulation of a new language as people try to play with the parameters of AI, rather than adhering to them. Memes, secret languages, and skits are presented as examples of these attempts to cope with the restrictions imposed by web platforms and indicate that the process of meaning-making is something that people are intentionally trying to achieve. However, people are also recognizing the influence of AI on the things they see and do. This results in talking about being frank and truthful, behaving ethically, and trying to understand the effective use of web technologies. Learning about the impact of AI on language use or the dynamics of communication is recognized as an essential skill for living in the world today. Thus, in an AI-mediated age, the development of human communication is intertwined rather than displaced. These technologies can enhance creativity, connection, and accessibility; however, they also present new limitations and challenges for educators (Lockhart, 2025). In this sense, in the future development of communication as it moves forward, it is necessary to construct an environment that supports communicative practice through technology rather than in opposition to it.

EMOTIONAL INTELLIGENCE AND TRUST IN HUMAN–AI INTERACTIONS

Emotional intelligence has always been regarded as a human skill. It involves perceiving, understanding, and responding to emotions in oneself and others. However, this has shifted recently because of the presence of AI technology that is capable of recognizing and responding to emotions. This is because these technology systems observe things such as the facial expressions of a person, the manner in which a person talks, body language, and the way in which a person writes when expressing his or her ideas. They can then interpret this information in an attempt to determine the feelings that this individual may be having and respond accordingly. With the increased use of AI technology in customer service, medical centers, learning institutions, and forums, emotional intelligence is currently regarded differently because of the involvement of technology in this field (Bhat, 2025). They function by converting human emotions into data. It can be very good at detecting basic emotions because it does so by reducing a smile to specific muscle movements, a change in voice to a shift in tone, and breaking down a sentence into words that show feelings (Miskolczi et al., 2025). However, emotions are influenced by many factors, such as culture, past experiences, and situations, which can hardly be captured by data. Therefore, AI can spot surface-level emotions but cannot understand what is going on. This difference affects how people perceive emotionally responsive technologies.

Despite these limitations, many individuals still find AI systems emotionally useful. This is particularly true for short- or task-oriented conversations. For example, an angry customer service bot or an application that assists users with mental wellness by providing supportive words to help with mental wellness could make users feel understood and cared for. This, in turn, could potentially make users feel less stressed and more receptive to what they are told in case they are unable to speak to other human beings. As machines are never judgmental or biased in any matter and do what they are told to do, they become quite desirable for conversation. However, this also contradicts older concepts of emotional intelligence, which are built upon an understanding of basic human emotions. As basic human emotions are now replaced by algorithms in this process of understanding, it is difficult to ascertain whether the results are true or just simulated (Rustanta & Sari, 2025). Trust plays a significant role in the use of emotionally intelligent AI. However, trust is not only about the effectiveness of the system. It is entwined with how individuals perceive the goals, care, and responsibilities of the system. Individuals may trust AI to function as it should, but they will not be certain about their personal feelings being used in this process and who is behind the actions of the system. Such systems may require an individual's personal information, leading to privacy and consent issues. The more emotionally intelligent the system, the more personal information might be needed, catching such systems in the act of being useful and intrusive at the same time.

Authenticity is a key issue in the human and artificial intelligence relationship. True emotional connection is generally a product of authenticity, comprehension, and vulnerability. Although AI cannot feel emotions, it can create responses that are sensitive or caring (Kumar et al., 2025). The result will suffice for some, particularly when the exchange has their needs met immediately. Others would find it too much to handle, knowing that the responses were created and not felt. This represents a difference in expectations over what emotional interaction should be: authenticity in digital ecologies is often defined by whether the response feels helpful or poignant to the recipient rather than the feelings of the responder themselves.

Vulnerability in human-AI interactions has a particular character. Sometimes, people talk to AI about their fears, aggravations, and serious thoughts. This is perhaps because people believe that these systems are safe or objective. There is never any judgment, rejection, or critical remark. Thus, vulnerability is much less dangerous. But is vulnerability without mutual involvement the stuff of philosophical or psychological curiosity when it occurs in a relationship with AI? Vulnerability is typically mutual when it occurs in an interpersonal context. However, in the case of AI, it is unilateral. Sometimes, people fall heavily in love with something or someone that cannot possibly love them back (Ansyarina, 2025). This can change the nature of their anticipation of vulnerability in an emotional support situation with another human being. Emotionally intelligent AI will affect the way humans interact in cyberspace. This could result in heightened clarity of emotional life for computers but may lack profundity and complexity in expression to humans.

Trust in AI extends beyond mere interaction to how individuals perceive AI as an entity in society. With the rise of emotionally intelligent systems, one can notice how users expect these systems to behave in a specific way. If these systems fail in their ability to grasp something as simple as sarcasm, their users can easily become distrustful of them (Dixit & Jain, 2025). This can occur when major news leaks out that an algorithm is biased, for instance, and users will initially hold these systems in one way, but as news changes, so will their opinions when it comes to sharing their emotions with these systems. However, it should also be understood that trust and authenticity in communication between humans and AI are not constant. Similar to how people have adapted to trusting older technology, such as telephones or the Internet, they are currently learning to adjust to trusting AI. The younger generation may have different norms regarding AI systems that can deliver emo responses and may view them as just another technology, not something deceptive or misleading. Of course, this does not mean that ethics are not at stake here; however, it does depict how much AI communication depends on changes in culture and not on how good or bad the technology is (Linden et al., 2025). Ultimately, emotional intelligence in human-AI interaction or trust in human-AI interaction is dependent on several factors, including the creation of technology, context, and the feelings individuals experience. AI with the ability to understand and respond to emotions can make things better, more efficient, and accessible. Because AI assumes more emotional and personalized tasks, it is the job of human beings to see that these experiences are considered thoughtful and caring.

AI AND CREATIVE EXPRESSION

Creativity has always been a function of the tools that humans possess. From painting to playing an instrument to using a camera to using a computer program, every single tool has increased the manner in which creativity is achieved. Moreover, the latest development in the field of creativity is the use of artificial intelligence as a collaborator (Tan et al., 2025). Unlike old tools that assisted humans in performing physical or technical work, artificial intelligence works with patterns and symbols that are the exclusive domain of humans. For example, in the field of creativity, artificial intelligence is can create images, compose songs and poetry, generate object designs, and edit movies. When people collaborate with AI on creative projects, the beginning is often all about speed, large projects, and trying out new ideas.

Designers employ tools that allow ideas to pop up quickly, writers use smart systems that help them overcome writer's block, and filmmakers utilize AI that organizes large amounts of footage. In this case, AI acts as a partner that extends human capabilities. It can show new combinations, imitate several styles, and perform the automatic execution of mundane tasks, freeing the artist for higher-order creative decisions. This collaboration changes the image of the artist from one who creates alone to a more collaborative approach, where creativity flows by working through smart systems. However, when dealing with AI, issues concerning responsibility and control also arise (Ansyarina, 2025). Although AI produces something new, it produces that thing by learning from what is out there in the market. The human part of the equation might involve selecting, guiding, and filtering the results to ensure that nothing is made from scratch. This might seem very empowering to some and confusing to others. There is an obvious difference between production and the guidance that goes into the production of something. Creation is more about the intentions and decisions you make concerning ideas rather than just the physical production of something that will become an idea. The application of artificial intelligence in creative jobs also affects the role of the individual in the profession.

Artists, writers, and designers are then presented with new definitions of skill, creativity, and knowledge. One is no longer necessarily skilled if it means being able to handle tools; it is becoming increasingly important to know how to handle algorithms in creative ways. This means that more people will have a chance to participate in creative professions and share their thoughts in the form of images, sounds, or words (Sjoraida, 2025). On the one hand, it may redefine occupational trajectories, as certain occupations could be automated and new ones will appear. The matter of identity in creative professions will then be more fluid and dependent on how quickly one can adjust and share responsibilities. The question of who owns the copyright of an artwork is also being addressed by AI technology.

Conventionally, ownership of a work meant that there was an individual behind the work, with some purpose and creativity on their part. However, AI involves many individuals, including the developers of the AI system, the data that trained it for its purposes, and the individuals who influenced its creation. It becomes difficult to determine who gets credit for the work (Tan et al., 2025). Examining how ownership and authorship of work are considered in legal and ethical terms reveals an underlying concern for who gets credit in a world where machines are capable of creating work. Being associated with work as its author is not merely an issue of crediting an individual but is also related to the identity of the individual. Being able to work in collaboration with a machine changes the very essence of individual authorship, as many artists today might harbor in their work. The aesthetics are also shifting with an increase in the use of AI in creating works of art

One thing that AI does is create work that is very clean-cut and smooth. This can lead to a style that values certain techniques more than others, making rough or mixed-and-matched things seem less valuable. This is where artists are pushing the use of AI to get past the normal style and incorporate things such as glitches and mixing and matching techniques as a form of creativity. This reflects a bigger dialogue about what we find beautiful and meaningful when we are looking at things in terms of copying techniques (Bhat, 2025). Moreover, identity in creative work is becoming increasingly associated with technology. For many creators, resorting to AI is a matter of their artistic style, proving their openness to new ideas and involvement with current issues. Others might define themselves through resistance or by questioning AI. None of these decisions relate only to what instruments someone uses but also demonstrate much wider attitudes toward technology, work, or anything that makes human beings unique.

AI systems are often trained on data that are largely sourced from large and more dominant cultural systems; therefore, their output may reinforce those cultural norms, languages, and ideologies. This may raise concerns and fears among people, as it may seem to belittle regional or less common cultural styles. However, AI can also be used to respond to cultural traditions and help reinterpret them in new and different ways. This means that the impact of AI on culture is not uniform across different regions but rather depends on who wields AI as a tool and how. Feeling satisfaction or being left out because of AI when other artists create artwork using

AI is a significant element of this transformation. Some artists enjoy using AI technology because they like surprises that lead to new creations (Kumar et al., 2025). Others might feel left out or disappointed because they know that AI does not have any logical meaning, such as human-created artworks. The reaction of artists affects how they apply AI to their artwork because they are influenced by how others judge artworks produced using AI. Reactions from artists are significant because they have personal perceptions of what they perceive to be real artworks. Since they know that AI has indeed produced the artwork, they consider it less real or something cool to enjoy while the culture tries to determine how to deal with AI. Ultimately, the relationship between AI and art positively impacts both.

Working with AI is more than doing things quickly and making something different; it is about thinking differently about what creativity means and how it can involve both people and computers. What does it mean to think differently about how we look at ourselves as people, who make things, and how we know good art when we see it? This includes concerns and possibilities resulting from the use of intelligent machines in creative fields. Creativity remains something we do as people and not against computers; it includes meaning, understanding, and wanting to share (Teng & Yip, 2025). As AI continues to change the art and creative fields, it is important to consider how we can connect with AI in art to show respect for imagination while carefully thinking about technology in art.

PSYCHOLOGICAL AND SOCIAL EFFECTS OF AI ON RELATIONSHIP BUILDING

From chatbots and virtual friends to systems suggesting who to connect with, AI is shaping feelings about oneself, perceived others, and emotional expressiveness in small, yet significant ways. These shifts signal the need for increased focus on how AI shapes both our minds and social lives, especially since the boundary between human connection and technology is becoming increasingly blurred. For lonely or anxious individuals, virtual assistants may provide a form of solace or a way to feel the presence of a "friend," especially if they are feeling lonely or left out. Virtual assistants are appealing because they react in a predictable manner without ever judging the user. Such interactions can help with their emotions and provide them with a "friend experience" in addition to their existing human experiences. Nonetheless, the way these experiences are generated in the user's life varies depending on how individuals interpret them with their other experiences. Parasocial bonds, once premised on relationships with media figures such as celebrities or characters, have taken on an entirely new dimension with the advent of AI.

Unlike media, AI can respond to users, allowing it to feel more like a two-way relationship. Because users feel understood and valued, this can create more frequent emotional attachments. Repeatedly experiencing this may, over time, build up feelings of reliance, expectation, or trust in nature that does indeed exist in real relationships. Although meaningful, these bonds are unequal, as AI has no feelings or autonomous changes. This represents an imbalance and raises questions about how putting one's emotional energy into something unable to return it, and/or grow in return, may affect the person in the long run (Brinkmann et al., 2023). Having ties to AI Companions could alter the way individuals interact with other people.

For others, relying on AI can give them confidence in positive experiences that can improve their social interactions by providing an opportunity to practice social conversation in a non-threatening manner (Tan et al., 2025). For others, overreliance on AI can make it less likely that they will want to engage in different or complicated relationships that are considered human. Human interactions can be perceived as riskier or scarier because of how safe or controlled an experience is in an AI relationship. It is clear that this aspect has been impacted because it alters what is desired in an experience. A great deal of how AI impacts relationships and people's perceptions of themselves can be boiled down to personalization. While this may provide a sense of belonging, it simultaneously deprives users of variety by socially placing them in comfortable settings. How this changes the view of oneself among humans is often not overt and occurs gradually.

When individuals start receiving feedback in the form of likes, recommendations, or answers, they begin to learn about the appreciation and display of certain aspects of themselves in the cyberspace. Feedback might begin to promote certain traits, ideas, and styles and discourage others. Individuals might start behaving and viewing themselves as advocated in their AI feedback. This does not mean that they begin to be fake, but this further complicates their ability to conceptualize their self and keep it constant and their own. The self is now dynamic and is shaped by the individual as well as the technology they interact with. Self-expression in AI environments is both more available and limited in AI settings compared to other settings.

On one hand, AI tools enable a new form of human expression, such as expressing thoughts, emotions, or creativity that could not be expressed before. AI tools for creating artworks or assisting with writing capabilities may enable a user to express what they mean or convey concepts they have not conceived. However, most AI tools depend on preconceived concepts or categories. This may influence human expression. This could lead to a situation in which human beings begin to express themselves according to what an AI tool or system favors. This could lead to human expression becoming simpler or stereotypical.

Socially, AI alters relationship-building and maintenance dynamics because it influences how individuals perceive each other. These systems rely on algorithms that identify potential partners based on information to come up with recommendations of compatible people to either partner with or have as groups of friends. This increases the efficacy and certainty of the relationship while ensuring that the relationship appears to rely on math and not on hard work and mere luck. The way relationships appear to users changes with the introduction of technological relationship tools.

Trust is integral to relationship building using AI. People must be able to trust these systems with their personal and emotional data in a manner in which it will be taken care of properly and in a way in which it will not be misleading or harmful in its interactions. If so, it could influence not only the perception of people in relation to technology but also their emotional connections with other people. A positive experience with honest and beneficial AI would help people feel more connected in cyberspace through trust, an idea in which personal feelings meet a larger issue related to how institutions perceive people and their data.

ETHICAL AND CULTURAL CONSIDERATIONS

With the increased role of artificial intelligence in conversations and relationships people engage in, ethical and cultural considerations are becoming more significant. AI-based relationships involve more than just technology. These relationships involve how humans interact with each other, accompanied by ethical and cultural principles, tenets, and concepts. Bias, autonomy, and consent are but a few examples that have come into question because AI affects emotions, decision-making, and how human beings perceive themselves. Moreover, there are variations in cultural perceptions regarding AI and relationships. Dealing with relationships within an AI paradigm may seem right or necessary in one culture but wrong or uncomfortable in others. Bias becomes a large threat to AI relationships.

This is because AI systems learn from data that already carry social differences; therefore, they may end up repeating historical unfairness based on variables such as gender, race, class, language, and culture. This issue is exacerbated by the belief that AI is an impartial or equal process because it is produced by a machine. However, there can be a lack of human decision-making and choice in how AI systems are created, such as selecting data and making optimization targets. Biased AI systems can be problematic in emotionally charged settings such as mental healthcare (Sjoraida, 2025). They can reinforce negative thoughts and make users feel as if they are not heard. Handling biased AI systems goes beyond adjusting the system because there is a need to have ethical considerations and constant tests according to culture, in addition to having corrective measures to make them human-centric and not biased, which considers whose feelings, identities, and relationships are being considered and whose are not. While this can be positive, there are also concerns about being controlled and dependent and even about making decisions without knowing they are being impacted in a particular way, particularly in a situation where autonomy is involved. Autonomy is linked to the intended accomplishments of AI. Table 2 translates abstract ethical discussion into a structured evaluative framework.

Table 2. Ethical and human-centred challenges of AI-mediated relationships

Ethical Dimension	**Core Challenge**	**Illustration in AI-Mediated Contexts**	**Human-Centred Design Consideration**
Bias and representation	Replication of historical inequalities	Emotion-recognition systems misreading culturally specific expressions	Inclusive datasets; culturally sensitive evaluation
Autonomy	Subtle behavioural and emotional influence	Algorithmic nudging of preferences, emotions, or relational expectations	User agency, opt-out mechanisms, reflective friction
Consent	Ongoing and opaque data extraction	Emotional data collected without clear understanding	Dynamic, informed, and revocable consent processes
Authenticity	Simulation of care without reciprocity	AI companions expressing empathy without emotional capacity	Transparency about system limitations and intentions
Dependency	Emotional reliance on non-reciprocal agents	Users preferring AI companionship over human relationships	Design for support, not substitution
Privacy	Intimate emotional data capture	Mental health and relational chatbots storing affective data	Data minimisation, explainability, and accountability

AI systems are often developed to keep people occupied to obtain more data; therefore, they may end up being talked to rather than being handled with care. If AI is developed to make a user feel connected but not to feel better, then it may be difficult to maintain one's autonomy. Appropriate AI usage involves deliberating on the extent of control over an AI system. Autonomy involves more than just the use or non-use of technology. It involves understanding how an AI system affects one's emotions. Consent, too, forms a very important part of considering both bias and autonomy, but one that isn't generally well handled in AI relationships (Vecchione & Singh, 2025). Consent is more than agreeing to a terms of service or privacy policy that very few people would understand. This means knowing how AI systems collect emotional information, for what purposes, and how this influences interactions. In the case of relationship AI, it is even harder because the system itself changes and adapts over time in ways that may not be clear at the outset. This makes consent a process rather than a single event. This problem becomes particularly evident in the context of the interactions that exist between AI and vulnerable human beings, such as children and the aged, as well as those with emotional issues.

Such individuals may develop rich affective ties with AI without necessarily grasping its implications. Informed consent in such circumstances will require more than legislation; it will require a nuanced design that will assist in making things clear and provide distance when desired (Tan et al., 2025). Consent should enable individuals to establish affective boundaries to help them determine the extent to which they want to reveal themselves and become enmeshed in AI. In other cultures, the formation of emotional connections with machines is regarded as unnatural or detrimental to real human relationships. Such cultural attitudes impact not only the quantity of AI use but also the expectations derived from it. An AI built for another culture will not be an apt fit for another society and could cause trouble. Another significant aspect of the emotions exhibited in AI technology and the principles of relationships is the role of culture. When individuals form associations or relationships with each other, the inappropriateness of relationships exhibited by the system could generate a perception of a lack of trust and association. Ethical AIs responding to relationships should address cultural variations in relationships, not by standardizing them, but by appreciating them. The narratives constructed about technology also influence the position that relational AI occupies within society (Tariq, 2025).

In some regions, technology is viewed as an indicator of progress and "modernity." This makes AI relationships novel and exciting. In others, perhaps traditional and more physical or relational methods of communication are more highly valued, and AI relationships are viewed as something that jeopardizes deep, relational connections. These stories inform what gets discussed, and policy is shaped in response to public concerns and interests, helping to shape how stories about ethics are approached. To consider relational AI as it pertains to ethics, it is crucial to consider the stories told in relation to technology and society (Kumar et al., 2025). With the increasing use of relational AI, it is not merely a question of improving the tool and its effectiveness but also ensuring that it is balanced, transparent, and attuned to different cultures across the world. It is not merely a question of two groups: people creating and using technology and people with ethics and social scientists, but people from across these groups coming together and working towards using these relational AIs in a manner that, through their use, human connections can become richer rather than simpler.

FUTURE DIRECTIONS FOR HUMAN CONNECTION IN AN AI-DRIVEN WORLD

How humans communicate with other humans has been changing considerably with the integration of artificial intelligence and virtual and augmented reality (Tan et al., 2025). Such technologies have enabled the creation of environments that give users the feeling that they are together in a physical space, even though they may not necessarily be together in reality. Such environments will continue to improve and will therefore change the way humans view physical proximity and even touch. Being active in the virtual and augmented reality industries is a major factor in this technological revolution.

With virtual reality, one can create an avatar and walk around and interact with other people as if one is in their physical environment. Augmented reality, on the other hand, involves adding digital information to one's environment, so one gets a combination of both the real and virtual worlds. Thus, one can have the feeling of being in the company of others, yet one is not in their physical proximity. One major shift is in the realm of intimacy (Kumar et al., 2025). In the real world, intimacy may involve touch, proximity to a person, and experiencing emotions. In a cyber or virtual environment, this is established by characters, body expressions, facial communication, and movement. This is done to establish trust and intimacy, but it is determined by the capabilities of the tools used. For instance, a character's facial expressions would depend on the tracking system used, and sounds or touch could determine the level of reality created. Thus, intimacy in cyberspace is created by both human and technological elements. Collaboration is also changing.

AI can assist people in collaborating by providing them with tasks to perform, coming up with ideas, or even making suggestions in real time. In an institution such as a school or workplace, people can use technology to establish a collaborative area where they can work on an activity regardless of their location. For example, architects can work together to create a 3D structure or even work in the same music rehearsal room as the musicians (Tan et al., 2025). AI enhances all these projects and provides an innovative approach to creativity and art. Social work is not location-dependent or tool-dependent as it used to be; rather, it is a combination of humans and intelligent systems. Even community formation differs today.

Virtual and augmented environments give people the chance to build lasting social spaces with rules, traditions, and activities of their own. People join groups based on hobbies, work interests, or beliefs and participate in events that make them feel like they belong. The combination of AI and immersive technologies also changes the way humans think about themselves and others in relation to love, friendships, and communities. The potential for personalization and real-time response from AI systems has brought up questions of what happens in terms of consent, influence, and control. These systems potentially influence how people think, feel, and behave, potentially setting up a pattern or expectation for how a relationship needs to function (Kumar et al., 2025). Privacy is a huge issue when considering how AI systems gather massive amounts of data on an individual's movement patterns, appearance, and interactions. The ethical necessity must not only deal with a system being safe and healthy, but also with how this shift affects broader society. Looking ahead, the combination of AI and immersive environments might create new types of spaces in which digital and real-world interactions occur together, feed into, and contest one another.

People may form new types of intimate relationships, collaborate in new ways, and establish communities that span both digital and physical spaces. Human capabilities to be emotional, think, and relate to others will be different in these environments and will exhibit a mixture of human ingenuity and AI assistance. Activities such as studying, working, health, and entertainment will increasingly take place in these combined spaces and challenge routine social and cultural practices. Ultimately, great possibilities and important responsibilities will characterize the future of human connection in an AI world.

Immersive technology can make it possible to feel present, understand others, and work together in new ways, whereas AI can help create experiences that are more personalized, adaptive, and collaborative than ever before (Brandtzaeg et al., 2025). Yet at the same time, these opportunities require a thoughtful consideration of freedom, privacy, identity, and technology design. Machines will not replace people, but the ways in which people connect with and collaborate with others and the sense of belonging that they have will change in ways that extend what proximity, collaboration, and affiliation can mean. Communities, designers, and individuals all share an interest in carefully navigating this new landscape to ensure that technologies contribute to, rather than undermine, the potential of humans and human connections.

CONCLUSION

With the increased importance of artificial intelligence in the way humans communicate, create, and interact with each other, ethical and human-centered AI practices and designs are more important than ever before. All of this offers many opportunities for the future, and with that, there are risks of control and influence issues regarding privacy, equality, and actual relations among others (Tan et al., 2025). Therefore, the best course for AI to benefit humans will depend on focusing on the positive and negative impacts that the technologies will have on humans and ensuring the design and control of anthropocentric and human-centered practices of AI management and incorporation into society and culture.

Bias in AI development is a major concern that requires human-centric input. The bias in AI systems mirrors the problems that exist in the data with which they are trained. When it comes to emotional and relationship-related topics, bias in AI can impact people's well-being, how they relate to others, and even how they view themselves. To overcome bias, it is necessary to have good data, check for bias, and use intelligent methods for learning, in addition to guidance that is ethical in its approach. Human-related notions of bias extend the perspective from the mere consideration of whether it works or not to whose matters and voices are being heard and not being included in the process. Including diverse viewpoints in AI systems is more than merely technical; it has a moral dimension that relates to the larger questions of equity and justice (Ansyarina, 2025). Consent and freedom are key components of ethical methods. Consent should not occur just once in relation to AI systems; this process keeps changing depending on the feelings and experiences of humans. Cultural Implications of AI Relationships (Tariq, 2025).

A cultural perspective of AI relationships highlights the need to be human-centered and ethical. Technology does not exist by itself; it is perceived and used in various ways according to cultural beliefs, values, and historical experiences. Some AI applications that ignore this may end up being perceived incorrectly, leaving people out or even harming them (Sheikh & Sheikh, 2025). To use it ethically, one must understand how people from various cultures perceive closeness, social cues, and appropriateness. Designing in a human-centered way means involving people from these cultures so that applications are relevant, appropriate, and flexible to varying experiences from many cultures that may be very different from their own. Culturally respectful AI helps many people become included in the world of technology. Trust and authenticity are important components of any real relationship and must remain vital in AI engagement. Transparency here is more about honesty in interactions, where the behavior of AI should be attributable or traceable to human values and goals. AI can be very useful in the field of emotional assistance and creative work with careful consideration.

AI technology can provide emotional feedback, mental health assistance, and social interaction assistance on a widely available scale. However, this requires a guarantee that AI technology will be developed for the betterment of humanity. Emotional support should assist individuals through reflection, understanding, and development beyond being engaged with something or remaining on the site/platform itself. Human-centered AI understands that handling emotional support is something only human beings can do with the sensitivity that AI technology cannot provide. In art and collaboration spaces, AI promises huge opportunities for human expression and collaboration; however, ethical issues continue to be significant (Kumar et al.,

2025). Ethics are a crucial consideration in the development of such systems. The aftereffects of AI on relationships also require consideration.

As AI becomes increasingly present in communication, work, and other aspects of people's lives, their understanding of closeness, teamwork, and community will shift. Human-centered approaches attempt to influence the shift and use AI in such a way that relationships remain intact, society stays connected, and people remain human. It rejects approaches based solely on speed, data accumulation, and retention of user engagement, and prefers what makes people prosper. The key is to incorporate ethics into AI development, operation, and discourse in society to influence AI development that helps, not hinders, the social world (Bhat, 2025). Digital literacy, emotional intelligence, and ethical competence are interconnected. People should be able to recognize bias, make their own decisions, handle online relationships that become personal, and think clearly about the space in which AI is part of social relationships. The human-centered approach to AI is closely interconnected with community development that is informative, considerate, and capable of tackling the challenges arising from relationships in a technological world. Accountability is about making AI responsibly enable healthy, human-centered connections. The creators of AI, the companies that utilize it, and the leaders who establish regulations all share the responsibility of ensuring ethical AI functioning. They must consider what might go wrong over time. Tools such as checks and balances, audits, shared decision-making, and clear reports are needed to ensure that AI respects people's independence, differences, and fairness. A human-centered approach recognizes accountability, not only as a legal or technological imperative, but also as an "agreement or interaction among those who design, use, and are affected by AI." The ethical use of technology involves a wide range of people in its design and use.

Ultimately, the challenge of being human with regard to AI, while keeping in mind an approach that uses AI for good, lies in achieving this balance. It is about how the power of AI can be used for the better while retaining the important aspects of human interaction, such as trust and honesty, independence and freedom, understanding and empathy, and cultural understanding. AI, instead of limiting human ability and reducing human interaction, can actually enable people to do more and to be more collaborative and imaginative, as long as the goals of AI align with human values and needs as they pertain to human interaction (Sjoraida, 2025). In summary, the involvement of artificial intelligence between people offers huge opportunities as well as huge moral questions. The human framework offers a clear roadmap to handle these issues by considering freedom, permission, fairness, and awareness related to culture, as well as the benefits of the new possibilities that AI brings to the table. As technology constantly improves, it is essential to remain thoughtful, with appropriate principles and considerations related to human values and emotions. This helps society create relationships that can be real, inviting, and righteous by putting people at the forefront of the creation, use, and understanding of AI technology. The kind of relationships people make in an environment with so much AI technology will depend not only on how much of the technology is good but also on how people decide that this technology brings them closer and makes their lives much better.

REFERENCES

Ansyarina, H. (2025). Exploring emotional connection with virtual AI tutors in online learning among university students. *Journal of Educational Innovation and Research, 1*(7), 259–266.

Bhat, M. (2025, October). Toward an ethic of synthetic relationality: Identity, intimacy, and risk in AI-mediated roleplay environments. In *Proceedings of the AAAI/ACM Conference on AI, Ethics, and Society* (Vol. 8, No. 1, pp. 416–429). DOI: 10.1609/aies.v8i1.36560

Brandtzaeg, P. B., Følstad, A., & Skjuve, M. (2025). Emerging AI individualism: How young people integrate social AI into everyday life. *Communication and Change, 1*(1), 11. DOI: 10.1007/s44382-025-00011-2

Brinkmann, L., Baumann, F., Bonnefon, J.-F., Derex, M., Müller, T. F., Nussberger, A. M., Czaplicka, A., Acerbi, A., Griffiths, T. L., Henrich, J., Leibo, J. Z., McElreath, R., Oudeyer, P.-Y., Stray, J., & Rahwan, I. (2023). Machine culture. *Nature Human Behaviour, 7*(11), 1855–1868. DOI: 10.1038/s41562-023-01742-2 PMID: 37985914

Dixit, D. S., & Jain, N. (2025). Digital communication, AI, and language evolution: Understanding online English in Industry 5.0. *Advances in Consumer Research. Association for Consumer Research (U. S.), 2*(4).

Filieri, R., Christodoulides, G., & Nicolau, J. L. (2025). Emerging sources, formats, channels, devices, and audiences in modern eWOM communications. *Psychology and Marketing, 42*(9), 2430–2443. DOI: 10.1002/mar.22239

George, A. S. (2025). How AI agents are reshaping the internet from human-centered to machine-mediated commerce. *Partners Universal International Innovation Journal, 3*(4), 52–65.

Geroimenko, V. (2025). Preparing for the foreseeable future. In *Beyond and after prompt engineering: The future of AI communication* (pp. 319–335). Springer Nature Switzerland.

Kehinde, S. K. (2025). AI in everything, and everything in AI: A review of the ubiquitous role of artificial intelligence in shaping the next technological epoch. *Journal of Computer Allied Intelligence, 3*(5), 17–53. DOI: 10.69996/jcai.2025024

Kumar, A., Lone, N. A., Bhandari, V., Sharma, R., & Trivedi, C. (2025, July). Emotional intelligence: Between human agency and algorithmic determinism. In *Proceedings of the 8th International Conference on Computing Methodologies and Communication (ICCMC 2025)* (pp. 702–707). IEEE. DOI: 10.1109/ICCMC65190.2025.11140771

Linden, K., Hachem, H. H., & Kondyli, V. (2025). Homo promptus: Predicting the impact of generative AI on human memory and creativity. *Memory, Mind & Media*, *4*, e15. DOI: 10.1017/mem.2025.10012

Lockhart, E. N. (2025). From search to synthesis: Generative AI, internet use, and the transhuman epistemic shift. *Journal of Excellence in Social Sciences*, *4*(1), 24–36.

Miskolczi, M., Kökény, L., & Jászberényi, M. (2025). Rethinking the road ahead: Generation Z's perspectives on AI-based mobility services. *Transportation Research Interdisciplinary Perspectives*, *31*, 101475. DOI: 10.1016/j.trip.2025.101475

Rustanta, A., & Sari, I. S. (2025). From social media to mainstream media: Rethinking news verification in the age of artificial intelligence. *Linkage*, *2*(2), 86–99.

Sheikh, A. R., & Sheikh, F. R. (2025). Posthuman linguistics and digital subjectivity: Deconstructing AI-mediated language and digital identity in the age of algorithmic discourse. *Journal of Asian Development Studies*, *14*(3), 1143–1154. DOI: 10.62345/jads.2025.14.3.93

Sjoraida, D. F. (2025). AI and emotional intimacy: Exploring romantic bonds with artificial companions. *Humanexus: Journal of Humanistic and Social Connection Studies*, *1*(8), 333–342.

Tan, W. J., Thongchai, S., & Limc, L. P. (2025). Human–machine families and the crisis of meaning in family relationships. *International Journal of Studies in Humanities and Social Science*, *1*(1), 26–31.

Tariq, M. (Ed.). (2025). *Merging Artificial Intelligence With the Internet of Things.* IGI Global., DOI: 10.4018/979-8-3693-8547-0

Tariq, M. (Ed.). (2025). *Emerging Multisector Applications of AI and IoT*. IGI Global., DOI: 10.4018/979-8-3373-4332-7

Teng, M. F., & Yip, J. C. (2025). A narrative inquiry into language teacher identity construction in the global GenAI context. *International Journal of TESOL Studies*, *250901*, 1–21.

Thi Phuong, D. P., Hoang Cuu, L., Minh, A. H., & Nguyen Phuc, K. (2025). AI-WOM echo pathway model: Unveiling the role of cognitive and emotional resonance in shaping eWOM and purchase intention. *International Journal of Human-Computer Interaction*, •••, 1–30. DOI: 10.1080/10447318.2025.2596304

Vecchione, B., & Singh, R. (2025). Artificial intelligence is mental: Evaluating the role of large-language models in supporting mental health and well-being. *Big Data & Society, 12*(4), 20539517251383884. DOI: 10.1177/20539517251383884

KEY TERMS AND DEFINITIONS

Affective Computing: Systems detecting, interpreting, and responding to emotion

Emotional Authenticity: Perceived genuineness of emotions expressed through technologies

Machine-Mediated Communication: Human interaction shaped, filtered, enabled by algorithms

Chapter 3
AI-Mediated Communication:
Transformations in Human Expression, Authenticity, and Relational Dynamics

Manoj Govindaraj
http://orcid.org/0000-0003-2830-7875
VelTech Rangarajan Dr. Sagunthala R&D Institute of Science and Technology, India

G. R. Hrithikroshan
Vel Tech Rangarajan Dr. Sagunthala R&D Institute of Science and Technology, India

Jayendira P. Sankar
http://orcid.org/0000-0001-8435-2123
University of Technology Bahrain, Salmabad, Bahrain

ABSTRACT

Artificial intelligence increasingly shapes everyday communication, influencing how people express ideas, perceive authenticity, and build relationships. Unlike conventional digital interaction, AI-guided communication adapts language, predicts responses, and personalizes emotional cues, often blurring boundaries between human intention and algorithmic influence. Identity, ownership, and truth become more complex as messages are generated or co-created with intelligent systems, raising concerns about trust, transparency, and ethical responsibility. Power dynamics also shift toward those who design and control these technologies, while attention, presence, and emotional closeness are redefined in both personal and

DOI: 10.4018/979-8-3373-8337-8.ch003

professional contexts. As a result, communication is not merely transmitted through AI but fundamentally reshaped, with implications for authenticity, connection, and the future of human interaction.

1. INTRODUCTION

Messages shape how people connect, lead, others follow, institutions run. Long ago, talking in person gave depth - tone, gesture, silence spoke volumes. Letters stretched reach, broke limits of distance, folded time into envelopes. Then screens changed pace, widened spread, reshaped exchange. At first, machines carried words only when people typed them. Now machines shape words, not just carry them. A sudden leap happens when smart systems start crafting messages on their own. Speed changes everything - what once moved passively now thinks fast, adjusts mid-flow, reshapes intent before it lands.

Progress in machine learning, along with advances in large-scale data analysis, has helped shape AI systems capable of spotting trends, forecasting choices, and mimicking context awareness (Jordan & Mitchell, 2015). Efficiency gains and stronger output have emerged in companies using AI to handle thinking-intensive chores while aiding decisions (Davenport & Ronanki, 2018). With firms bringing AI into how they communicate - think auto-written emails, reports shaped by smart software, or customer bots that respond on their own - the line separating messages made by people from those built by machines slowly fades.

Communication shaped by AI means people interact alongside systems that help create or adjust messages. Instead of just repeating actions like older machines did, today's AI reads mood, picks up on feelings, and replies in ways that fit the situation. This change fits patterns seen across services lately - smart tools are expanding what humans can do and changing how results come about (Huang & Rust, 2018). During conversations, boosts happen when artificial support sharpens meaning, organizes thoughts, or suggests wording tuned to emotions. With repeated exposure, such shifts might alter how someone views expressing themselves at all.

When the world shifted online during the pandemic, more people started using AI tools just to stay connected. Because offices closed, companies turned to smart chat programs and digital helpers without much choice. One study showed tough times push tech into daily routines faster than expected (Alles & Gray, 2021). These tools did not just speed things up - slowly, they changed how people interact too.

What happens to honesty in conversation shifts when machines get involved. Real talk usually means someone truly means what they say, writes it themselves, yet feels something real behind it. Still, once artificial intelligence helps shape a message, who actually speaks gets blurry - intentions split between person and program. Even though tech boosts performance, people might see less of the individual effort unless things are handled thoughtfully (Raisch & Krakowski, 2021). That tension shows up sharply where trust matters most: work exchanges, private chats. Behind every polished reply could be a hidden assistant.

Besides being real, how people connect changes when AI steps into conversations - trust grows from steady behavior and clear intentions, things that artificial helpers can either support or damage. When machines give reasons for their choices and someone takes responsibility, people feel more secure about using them (Floridi et al., 2018; Smith, 2022). Hidden logic inside automated systems might make users doubt whether messages are honest or fair. Yet, seeing how humans and smart tools work together openly could build stronger belief in the exchange. Because clarity shapes perception, knowing what happens behind the scenes affects comfort with results.

Out there in online worlds, artificial intelligence helps shape who people become. Instead of just showing up as they are, folks often tweak how they speak or write because apps recommend certain words. When software nudges someone toward a particular tone, those small shifts pile up over time. Behind the scenes, research shows tech doesn't just speed things up - it quietly reshapes what feels normal in daily interactions. Little by little, personal styles start mirroring machine-led patterns. That quiet shift can dull distinct ways of expressing oneself, making voices blend together more than before.

Not just about faster replies, AI chat touches deeper layers of how people feel and think. Relying on bots can shift where we place our emotional trust - sometimes without noticing. Expressing ourselves might start to lean more on machines than inner reflection. Studies reveal folks tend to treat responsive tech like it has a personality, sparking connections that mimic real talk. Huang and Rust pointed this out in 2018 - behavior adapts when interfaces act understanding. If artificial system mirrors care or attention, it quietly reshapes what closeness feels like.

With things moving fast, grasping how people talk through AI means pulling from many fields at once. How messages are built and understood comes clear through communication studies. Emotions and sense of self take shape in ways psychology helps uncover. Who holds control, how groups shift - that shows up under sociological study. Watching how folks interact with smart tools is where human–computer work steps in. Mix those views together, and suddenly AI isn't just a wire carrying words - it acts, responds, shapes what happens next.

Looking closer at how AI shapes the way people talk reveals shifts in honesty, identity, and relationships. One goal here is spotting what gets better - like precision or speed - alongside potential downsides when machines join conversations. Though computers can sharpen messages and tailor responses, they also blur who truly speaks and whether words feel real. Grasping this balance matters deeply for anyone shaping rules, building systems, or simply trying to stay connected in spaces where tech mediates every reply.

2. BACKGROUND OF THE STUDY

Beginning in the late 20th century, shifts in technology began altering communication patterns through automated support. Instead of manual processes, smart tools started managing parts of interaction within services. During this period, progress in computing power allowed deeper integration of data handling into daily operations. Rather than just storing messages, networks evolved to interpret and route them more efficiently. At first, online exchanges focused only on delivering texts from one person to another. Tools like email did little beyond forwarding user-written notes across distances. Gradually, though, platforms emerged that connected people worldwide - yet still depended solely on what users typed themselves. Back then, tools for sharing information helped people stay linked, yet played no role in shaping the content itself. Still, once machine learning appeared alongside deeper data analysis, the way these systems operated began to change fundamentally (Jordan & Mitchell, 2015).

Starting around 2010, studies explored how smart technologies handled vast amounts of data to boost decision speed and performance results (Manyika et al., 2011; Chen, Chiang, & Storey, 2012). During those years, businesses started using forecasting tools in strategy design, client interaction, besides marketing workflows. While early versions relied mostly on numbers and fixed formats, gradual advances in understanding human language plus creative output opened paths for AI-driven dialogue. Instead of simply reporting past events, later models anticipated future patterns - shifting focus from passive summaries toward active influence over content creation.

Starting in 2016, progress in neural networks allowed machines to grasp and produce language more effectively. Rather than just automating routine work, research indicated AI began supporting higher-level thinking tasks (Huang & Rust, 2018). Within conversations, such support looked like suggesting replies, shifting voice style, identifying emotions, or adapting wording based on setting. Because of these abilities, the boundary separating instrument from participant grew less clear. Instead of operating invisibly behind the scenes, intelligent programs stepped into view as active elements in dialogue. Communication now involved entities that did more than transmit data - they shaped it.

One way to see recent shifts is through how machines now handle conversations, help manage tasks, or generate written content. Instead of replacing people, these tools often back up skilled workers - especially in fields like accounting, where studies show software aids complex decision making. A different angle appears when looking at daily office routines: artificial intelligence helps write summaries, shape slides, or reply to client messages. Another sign of change lies in routine digital processes, where smart systems slowly reshape how services operate - making some steps faster, reducing errors, tailoring outputs. This movement toward smarter support mirrors wider patterns seen across industries aiming to refine performance using technology.

Begun in 2020, the worldwide spread of COVID-19 pushed digital change faster than expected. Because offices moved work outside traditional settings, people turned more heavily to online messaging systems. Research into ongoing tech shifts shows emergencies tend to speed up how quickly new tools are accepted, making them routine (Alles & Gray, 2021). Instead of human-only coordination, automated assistants started handling video conferences, team scheduling across time zones, and staying in touch with clients. Gradually, artificial intelligence settled into a key role - linking individuals and structures within modern workplace interactions.

At once, talk around fair rules and clear practices grew louder. When machines started shaping how messages were formed, experts stressed clarity, responsibility, and reducing unfair patterns (Floridi et al., 2018). With more eyes on automated choices in government and business, doubts surfaced - could such systems be trusted? Could their words ever feel genuine? Studies into the push-pull between full automation and human support show gains in speed often come at a cost: people sense less personal control when code directs too much (Raisch & Krakowski, 2021). Since honest connection and mutual confidence matter deeply in conversation, this tension hits especially hard where dialogue lives.

Shaping the context of AI-driven interactions, digital identity formation plays a key role. Algorithm-based suggestions guide what appears on screens across social networks and career-focused sites. Research into tech-enabled change shows tools do more than assist tasks - they shift accepted behaviors and societal standards (Brynjolfsson & McAfee, 2014). When automated systems propose word choices or subtle shifts in voice, personal expression adapts over time. Over repeated use, reliance on software input becomes ordinary in routine exchanges. Machine-influenced communication slowly fades into the background of daily life.

Studies across fields show people are more likely to see smart machines as socially aware. Rather than treating them as tools, individuals interact with chatbots as though these systems understand feelings and have motives (Huang & Rust, 2018). Because of this, relationships shaped by artificial intelligence grow more complex. Once programs mimic caring conversations or emotional reactions, ideas about connection and conversation begin to change. What results affects minds and societies in ways that go past how well the technology works.

One result of recent changes - better machine learning, wider digital networks, more people working remotely, plus growing worries about ethics - is how we understand AI's role in communication. Earlier tech shifts cared mostly about faster links or broader access; this moment turns instead toward shared thinking tasks. Language patterns shift because algorithms adjust word choices. Emotional tones get reshaped through automated suggestions. Meaning itself begins to bend when machines help interpret situations. What counts as understanding now includes code, data flow, hidden assumptions built into design.

Beginning elsewhere, this research traces movement from fixed-channel digital exchanges toward fluid, AI-supported message creation. As smart tools enter communication processes, shifts appear across service efficiency, digital oversight, and how people engage with machines. Looking back at these changes helps clarify how automated mediation reshapes personal voice, truthfulness, and connections today. History matters when examining what feels real now.

3. REVIEW OF LITERATURE

Artificial Intelligence today significantly affects people's communication, which has attracted the attention of scholars from such diverse areas as communication, psychology, management, and information technology. The original work on digital change mainly referred to instruments like machine learning and data analysis for enhancing decisions and services *(Manyika et al., 2011; Chen, Chiang, & Storey, 2012)*, however, the focus was mostly on ordered datasets and routine operations. Therefore, these activities, although narrowly focused, have influenced the development of the concept of machines assisting human thinking.

New questions, how well can AI understand inputs that are not clear, such as written language or spoken dialogue, accompanied this development *(Jordan & Mitchell, 2015)*. From 2016 to 2019, academic conversations began placing greater emphasis on moving beyond mere automation toward forms of enhancement. Rather than simply substituting routine tasks, artificial intelligence could, according to *Huang and Rust (2018)*, amplify how people think and process information. In settings where messages are crafted or decoded, this boost appears via smart writing helpers, chat-based programs, or systems detecting emotional tones. What sets these two approaches apart - automating versus enriching - is key when examining how humans interact alongside machines. Whether the technology works invisibly behind scenes or becomes part of the communicative act itself depends largely on this difference. Far from just boosting efficiency, *Raisch and Krakowski (2021)* show how AI can subtly erode our sense of control - even as it helps us produce more. When machines start shaping creative output, uncertainty grows around who - or what - deserves credit. Though useful, such tools blur familiar boundaries between originality and machine input.

One path into AI's role in dialogue comes through studies of digital platforms and new service methods. Not just altering workflows, smart tools shift workplace norms - this point stands clear since work by Brynjolfsson and McAfee appeared in 2014. Since then, firms have learned more heavily on artificial intelligence; examples include client messaging, tailored promotions, record-keeping tasks - all noted by Davenport and Ronanki three years later. Language itself changes when machines join exchanges, adjusting phrasing, mood, even implied meaning across settings. Earlier forms of tech-facilitated talk did not generate material - they merely linked people. That contrast marks a turning point.

Authenticity often appears in studies about how people talk and relate to one another. Sincerity, personal expression, because of matching inner thoughts with spoken words - these traits usually define it. Yet things shift once artificial intelligence enters the picture. Messages shaped or adjusted by AI blur lines: who really speaks, the person or the machine? Influence splits, not fully human, not entirely code. Framed by ethics, AI systems lean on openness - not just to clarify decisions but to sustain confidence when uncertainty looms *(Floridi et al., 2018; Smith, 2022).* When users stay unaware that algorithms shape interactions, bonds risk erosion - particularly in settings where honesty defines quality connections.

Research into human–computer interaction pushes the conversation forward by exploring user reactions to smart chat systems. According to *Huang and Rust (2018),* when artificial intelligence mimics emotional awareness, it shifts how people see and interact with technology. Systems capable of recognizing emotions while offering fitting replies tend to feel more empathetic and socially present. Such behavior fits a larger pattern: humans frequently assign social traits to responsive machines, altering what they expect from digital exchanges. Because of this, engaging through AI blends mental processing with emotional reading between lines.

Looking beyond isolated cases, research into ongoing digital shifts adds useful background. Work by *Alles and Gray (2021)* shows automated platforms supporting live tracking alongside responsive choices in workplace settings. Even though audit processes form their main case, the idea of constant learning from data fits well within messaging frameworks too. Instead of fixed formats, artificial intelligence reshapes content on the fly - using behavior clues and past engagement - making exchanges feel tailored, yet prompting questions about hidden control in conversations.

Though much has been written about AI in tech and commerce, few studies place those findings into the framework of how people exchange meaning. Instead of viewing artificial intelligence through social lenses, most papers treat it as a tool for streamlining tasks or improving decisions. A shift toward equilibrium - where performance meets human values - is urged by *Raisch and Krakowski (2021),* who stress dual attention to output and impact. In parallel, work on ethics insists innovations must carry responsibility alongside progress *(Floridi et al., 2018*). Yet full pictures linking machine involvement in crafting messages to changes in trust, self-presentation, or connection still appear rarely.

Notably, studies now show AI moving beyond background support into direct involvement within communication networks. Messages - how they form, get understood, change, or spread - are steadily influenced by smart technologies. Though current work sheds light on efficiency gains, automated processes, and rules guiding responsible use, gaps remain in holistic models examining mediated exchange through AI lenses. Instead of viewing algorithms simply as instruments, this inquiry treats them as joint contributors alongside people during interactive moments. Thus, earlier findings gain depth when reinterpreted through a lens where machines share role responsibilities in shaping dialogue. Consequently, discussions around online expression evolve under new conditions brought by machine agency.

3.1 Research Objectives

The goals of this research are:

RO1: Explore in detail how AI alters people's communication methods in digital environments.

RO2: Study in detail how language, emotional expression, and self, presentation are influenced by AI usage.

RO3: Delve into how AI alters the perception of authenticity and authorship in communication.

RO4: Look at the relationships formed through AI, mediation in terms of trust, intimacy, dependence, and power balance.

RO5: Pinpoint the ethical as well as psychological problems that manifest themselves with communication being done through AI.

4. RESEARCH QUESTIONS

RQ1: To what extent and in what ways does Artificial Intelligence impact the content, mood, and individualization of online communication?

RQ2: How does the incorporation of AI impact the perception of genuineness and reliability as opposed to conventional ways of communication?

RQ3: Through which facets do AI, mediated communications enhance or reduce trust, closeness, and social presence in overlying relationships?

RQ4: What ethical and functional dilemmas are posed by the use of AI systems in human, to, human communication?

5. BACKGROUND OF STUDY

Though beginning simply, the work grows depth by describing patterns found across earlier studies. From areas such as human-computer exchange, thinking processes, company dynamics, digital infrastructure, and message sharing, sources emerged - each chosen because it matched the theme. Ideas behind teaching machines form a backdrop when looking at artificial intelligence in exchanges between people and tools (Jordan & Mitchell, 2015). In different spots, findings on digital change and service shifts help show how smart software supports thought work while altering talk inside jobs (Brynjolfsson & McAfee, 2014; Davenport & Ronanki, 2018). Still, times come when fairness moves forward: then, rules guiding responsible AI use enter discussions around openness, answerability, and reducing slant in automated dialogue (Floridi et al., 2018; Smith, 2022).

A fresh look at varied fields builds a structure showing how AI shapes self-expression, truthfulness, in human connections. Instead of running tests, this method expands through linking ideas and making sense of earlier results. Here, patterns start to emerge, yet gaps lacking real-world support stand out clearly. Starting not with tools alone, but with ties between people or moral questions, each piece adds depth to today's digital talk. While insights form slowly, overlooked parts stay noticeable throughout.

6. CONCEPTUAL FRAMEWORK OF AI-MEDIATED COMMUNICATION

What once served merely as a pipeline for human words now involves something different entirely. Digital tools used to move messages without altering them - simple conduits with no voice of their own. Now, artificial intelligence contributes directly: adjusting phrasing, guiding tone, anticipating user needs, reshaping content based on setting. Learning algorithms and language models have grown capable of detecting meaning, spotting trends in usage, responding in ways that mirror how people write and speak (Jordan & Mitchell, 2015). Instead of standing silently behind the scenes, these systems engage - shifting from background support to visible participant in interaction. At its core, AI-involved communication builds on three linked aspects: how expression gets expanded, how truthfulness shifts, laterally redefining relationships. When machines help shape messages, wording becomes sharper, more structured, often tailored - this is expressive expansion. Studies focusing on smart tools within customer interactions reveal a trend: cognition gets supported, not just manual steps replaced (Huang & Rust, 2018). Within dialogue environments, such influence alters word choices, adjusts emotional shading, maintains patterned ways of speaking.

Starting midstream, creation today shifts when algorithms shape drafts alongside writers. Human purpose merges with computational prompts - authorship now shared ground. Not born purely from one mind alone, expression emerges through layered inputs. Efficiency rises with tech aid, yet credit blurs without mindful oversight. Balance matters because too much machine influence risks downplaying personal involvement (Raisch & Krakowski, 2021). What counts as original bends under these conditions. With AI shaping how people connect, shifts in trust and perceived closeness begin to emerge. Because machines guide dialogue paths, who speaks when - and how - changes across teams and online circles. When decisions rely more on forecasts drawn from behavior, relationships adapt quietly beneath the surface. So it goes: technology alters not just messages but also the balance among participants. Expression transforms slowly as systems embed themselves into everyday exchange.

7. TRANSFORMATION OF HUMAN EXPRESSION

Words flow differently these days across screens - AI quietly nudges them. Grammar slips get caught on the fly, thoughts untangle themselves, voices occasionally shift toward something smoother. Studies tracking how folks handle tasks digitally reveal software sharpens what people produce without draining focus, especially when thinking gets heavy (Brynjolfsson & McAfee, 2014; Davenport & Ronanki, 2018). Messages emerge faster, structured more cleanly, shaped subtly to fit who's receiving them. Feelings shift when machines step in, not only sentence structure. Since tools can now detect mood, they suggest gentler phrasing instead. Although changes may come across as kinder or smoother, there is a chance voices blend together over time. Gradually, expressions begin reflecting what code favors. When this takes hold, personal flow in talking fades almost without notice. Starts with a tap on the screen, ends with a thought reshaped - tech has long tugged habits along (Brynjolfsson & McAfeee, 2014). Driven not by chance but code, self-presentation online inches forward in small edits. Hints appear: smoother wording, cleaner photos - subtle pushes from machine learning. Each change hides a forecast, an attempt to match perceived ideals. Words come clearer now, although occasionally they carry less spark, more second-guessing. Just when wild difference fades, careful shaping steps in. Yet balance lives in tension - tweaks bring clarity though they risk smoothing out what made it stand apart.

8. STRATEGIC AND ORGANIZATIONAL IMPLICATIONS OF AI-MEDIATED COMMUNICATION

When machines help with messages, work changes more than just speed - it shifts who says what and why. Communication flows differently now, guided by software that writes replies, sorts inquiries, or adjusts wording based on patterns. Firms once used such tools to save time; later, they found them shaping choices about voice and timing. What started as automation grows into influence - subtle, steady, present in phrasing and pace. Leaders may still speak, yet algorithms adjust their words behind the scenes. Tone gets tuned not by instinct alone, but by data-fed suggestions. Customer responses form faster, shaped by past behavior and predicted outcomes. These systems do not replace people - they reshape how meaning moves through an organization. From memos to public posts, output carries both human intent and machine logic. Earlier studies noted cost savings first; deeper effects emerged slowly. Now it shows: message style, consistency, reaction times - all touched by artificial input. Perception builds on these details, even if audiences never see the code beneath. Efficiency opens the door; strategy stays in the room longer.

Even when machines help shape messages, who truly stands behind them becomes unclear. Because artificial intelligence supports how leaders speak or reply to clients, doubts grow around ownership of those words. Though designed to streamline tasks, these systems can blur lines of answerability within companies. Traceable processes matter, according to Floridi and colleagues from 2018, especially where confidence in decisions is at stake. Where audiences sense replies are generated without real oversight, belief in the message often fades. When AI enters official communications, rules need to spell out its role without ambiguity. For trust to last, people should know where machine help begins in organizational messaging.

8.1 AI in How Leaders Talk

Now shaping how teams behave, leader speech drives both workplace norms and drive. Messages once carried a person's beliefs, long-term aims, their real voice. Today, artificial intelligence helps craft talks, plans, company updates. Though these aids bring sharper wording, steady tone, leaning too hard on them risks seeming less genuine. Beyond mere efficiency gains, Raisch and Krakowski (2021) point out a twist: AI lifts performance yet risks sidelining human judgment unless handled with care. When leaders speak, technology's role isn't to take over - but to sharpen understanding while preserving the speaker's genuine tone.

Sometimes, artificial intelligence examines how workers feel by reviewing messages on company chat tools, giving bosses instant feedback about team spirit. According to Huang and Rust (2018), machines that assist in customer service also improve awareness of human thoughts and emotions. When used by leaders, such skills help reshape messaging depending on what people express. Still, problems appear when staff sense surveillance instead of care. Openness matters - people stay confident only if they know how data is collected and why it's used within workplace tech.

8.2 How AI Shapes Customer Views of Brands

Starting with chatbots and moving into automated emails, artificial intelligence now shapes how companies interact with customers. Fast replies come alongside customized recommendations, thanks to algorithmic support embedded in daily operations. Efficiency gains emerge not just from speed but also from consistent handling of repetitive tasks. According to Manyika and colleagues in 2011, sorting massive datasets quickly gives businesses a clear edge. When it comes to messaging, personalization powered by machines reaches thousands without losing relevance - something hard to achieve using people only.

Beyond trends, staying genuine matters most when brands speak to people. With growing attention on honesty and real interaction, audiences notice the difference. When replies feel mechanical instead of meaningful, feelings often disengage. According to Floridi and colleagues in 2018, responsible AI needs respect for individuals and openness at its core. Often, transparency around artificial intelligence adoption supports long-term trustworthiness in companies. Whether automated systems deepen or damage customer relationships hinges on how much humanity remains involved. Still, blending machine efficiency with human judgment tends to preserve connection. Yet, too much reliance on algorithms risks distancing firms from their audience. Meanwhile, brands managing both elements carefully often retain loyalty better.

8.3 Power Control Algorithms

Power shifts emerge in ways shaped by artificial intelligence within human interaction. Which messages rise to visibility depends on hidden computational choices. Framing of information, along with automated reply options, steers exchanges subtly. According to Brynjolfsson and McAfee (2014), digital tools alter both economies and institutions by shifting who holds sway. Within communicative spaces, such changes unfold via systems that filter and tailor what users see. Though invisible, these processes guide attention and response patterns quietly.

Who holds power over artificial intelligence tends to be tech firms or digital platforms. Because of this setup, some worry certain views get amplified while others fade out. Research by Danks and colleagues from 2021 shows automated decisions may quietly deepen existing social gaps. Shaped by code, information pathways need clear explanations behind their logic - fairness depends on it. With influence guided by unseen rules, oversight processes should check these tools now and then, just to catch quiet imbalances before they grow.

8.4 Long-Term Human Dependency and Skill Evolution

What stands out is a slow shift toward depending on artificial intelligence to convey thoughts. When people begin using AI to shape texts, fix wording, or spark concepts, the way they communicate could change over time. Research by Jordan and Mitchell (2015) shows that machine-driven systems now support many mental activities. Though such help speeds things up, leaning too heavily on it might weaken personal reasoning and originality in self-expression.

Meanwhile, unfamiliar abilities begin appearing. Working well alongside artificial intelligence now requires understanding its inputs while still trusting individual insight. Instead of only person-to-person exchange, tomorrow's dialogue tools may center on balancing machine input with human control. Education and workplaces might prioritize clear thinking about technology use, fairness in automated decisions, along with careful review of what algorithms produce.

9. AUTHENTICITY AND RELATIONAL DYNAMICS

Truth often shows when words line up with feelings, when someone says exactly what they hold inside. But tech alters conversation now, nudging at that notion because bits of replies can rise from programs instead. A machine produces phrases, then voice isn't only tied to flesh and breath. Thought begins in a mind, though phrasing takes shape through silent algorithms turning below. Claiming who owns the message blurs - neither hand nor circuit holds it alone. When machines take part in making things, who started it fades in importance. Tools may quicken work, yet unease creeps in about slipping command - that friction pulses through today's tech talk (Raisch & Krakowski, 2021). If no hint reveals a bot penned a message, confidence tends to drain inside offices. Knowing where words come from sustains belief among teams. Tracing choices backward, pinning down answerability, shapes the core of fair AI building (Floridi et al., 2018).

Imagine what happens when gadgets join human interactions. What stands out is reliability, followed by responses without delay. Because swift replies create comfort, even if perfection slips. Yet deep connection - this grows only where emotion appears, along with honesty. Quietly, things shift when machines act like they understand. Bots begin feeling present, even though they are not. Research suggests folks' bond with tech that reacts to moods or notices context. Systems responding like friends slowly become part of daily talk. Control over AI voices often rests with corporations. Power leans one way when platforms decide who gets heard. Hidden choices shape replies, predict actions, adjust feeds based on collected details. Talk twists without anyone announcing it. Who decides what's fair might shift when control slips into the background. Talking via machines matters less than how silently our links to each other reshape themselves.

9.1 AI communication fairness and hidden algorithm biases

What makes AI communication tricky? Bias built into algorithms plays a big role. These systems pick up habits by studying vast amounts of human-generated data - text, speech, interactions. When past imbalances show up in that material, like skewed portrayals or missing voices, machines absorb them without questioning. Over time, they start echoing - or strengthening - those unfair tendencies during exchanges. Research by Danks and colleagues in 2021 highlights how such distortions slip in quietly, simply because software follows learned trends. Depending on context, results might skew phrasing choices, highlight some messages over others, misread emotional cues, or shape replies that subtly exclude particular communities.

Take emotion-analysis AI - tools like these can wrongly see regional speech or cultural ways of speaking as unfriendly or improper. Automated filters, meanwhile, often target certain groups' language patterns more than others. As this continues, some people fade from view online while their voices lose weight. According to Brynjolfsson and McAfee (2014), tech shifts power behind the scenes; if algorithms carry prejudice, outcomes tilt further toward inequality instead of balance.

Fairness issues reach into how organizations and professionals exchange information. When artificial intelligence systems keep pushing one way of speaking - through tone, word choice, or structure - shaped by mainstream language habits, less common forms might fade out over time. Such uniformity risks narrowing how people express themselves, quietly favoring some modes while sidelining others. According to Floridi and colleagues (2018), building ethical AI means making room for inclusion, clear processes, and active human involvement to avoid deepening existing inequalities.

Checking for unfair patterns in algorithms means ongoing reviews of models, using varied data during training, while also setting up transparent responsibility structures. Outputs from artificial intelligence cannot simply be accepted as impartial by institutions. Fairness checks on AI-supported communication need regular attention - alongside assessments of cultural awareness and balanced inclusion. When these steps are skipped, biased systems risk eroding confidence, straining connections, and wearing down genuine interaction. Trust fades when machines reflect skewed perspectives without correction.

9.2 Lack of Transparency and Explainability

A key issue in AI-assisted communication lies in opaque system behavior - many models operate without clear internal logic visible to users. Though powerful, these tools often hide how messages get shaped, ranked, or altered during processing. Because people cannot see what drives specific outputs, questions emerge about who is responsible, what purpose a message serves, or why it appears at all. According to Floridi and colleagues (2018), trustworthy artificial intelligence requires clarity in decision-making pathways. If algorithmic influences remain concealed within messaging workflows, confidence tends to weaken, since those involved lack insight into how results take shape.

When workplaces rely on artificial intelligence, understanding how decisions emerge grows more vital. Should automated systems help shape formal replies, job reviews, or client interactions, companies need ways to clarify why certain outputs appear. As Raisch and Krakowski observed in 2021, gains in speed often come at the cost of felt oversight if reasoning stays hidden. Opaque mechanisms risk making individuals feel removed from dialogue, eroding trust in the information - and the organization behind it. For this reason, openness through defined guidelines and built-in interpretability supports lasting reliability where machines aid messaging.

9.3 Human Reliance on Technology Erodes Skills

One concern gaining attention involves rising reliance on artificial intelligence for everyday messaging. When people lean more heavily on automated systems to write messages, polish wording, offer replies, or shift how something sounds, personal expression might slowly erode. Research by Jordan and Mitchell (2015) highlights that algorithms aim to assist mental workloads - boosting speed while possibly limiting hands-on involvement in deep thought. Over time, depending too much on these tools could dull thoughtful analysis. Creativity in self-expression may also fade quietly into the background.

Relying too much on systems erodes self-assurance along with judgment. Without pausing to assess what comes out of automated tools, people might slowly drift away from shaping their own expression. As output begins mirroring algorithms instead of personal thought, genuine voice fades. Research by Brynjolfsson and McAfee (2014) shows how digital advances alter both job tasks and mental habits - change in ability follows naturally. Still, staying ahead means treating artificial intelligence as support, not replacement, for independent thinking.

One way to tackle this problem is by building stronger digital understanding across people and groups. Rather than replace thought, artificial intelligence ought to support how humans share ideas - keeping room for originality and choice. If leaning too heavily on machines becomes common, something might get lost - the depth of connection that only real thinking can bring.

10. ETHICAL AND GOVERNANCE CHALLENGES

Now and then, a machine speaks while hiding its nature. This quiet act risks trust between humans and systems. When automated voices enter chats, boundaries become key. Responsibility shows up here, along with openness about why decisions unfold as they do - these threads keep connection intact. Code written out of sight may lift certain groups, yet knock down others. Logic-based choices can still be unjust. Errors thrive in dark corners. A fresh start every round cuts down on repeats. Past data shapes these systems, often repeating bias by accident. They could nudge conversations without making noise, simply by offering terms or sensing moods. Training data picked with thought changes outcomes more than expected. What happens once they go live gains importance through steady observation. Attention given to private information must match that level. Details like user messages, behavior across days, context around moments - these bits tend to feed the system quietly. When supervision slips, data often escapes or gets misused. Research on digital tools reveals a strong push for tighter protections around AI use (Jones & Wang, 2020). Placing blind faith in systems may dull human insight and creative voice. Depending too heavily on automated suggestions tends to reduce thinking work in dialogue creation. Lasting results come only when humans remain active participants, choosing carefully how they exchange thoughts.

11. DISCUSSION AND KEY FINDINGS

This study aimed to explore changes brought by Artificial Intelligence in communication, especially concerning human expression, authenticity, and relationships. Meaning now forms, evolves, yet shifts differently through digital spaces due to AI's role beyond mere tools - altering interpretation patterns subtly over time.

Communication grows clearer and faster when AI steps in. Tools like smart writing helpers, prediction engines, and auto-replies adjust how messages are built - shaping grammar, flow, voice, and fit with context. Research by Davenport and Ronanki (2018) highlights early AI use in companies centers on getting more done; this trend shows clearly in how people exchange information at work. With support from artificial intelligence, mental effort drops while replies happen quicker and mass customization becomes possible. Messages turn out better organized, tuned to goals, particularly within business settings where precision matters. Still, as clearness grows, personal voice might fade a little. With passing months, repeated automated tips tend to nudge authors along similar paths - slowly steering them toward phrasing that suits software more than soul.

A shift in how we understand who creates content emerges clearly. Ownership of messages once rested solely with the person sending them. Now, especially when artificial intelligence is involved, creation splits - intent comes from people, yet shaping happens through code. This blend introduces a challenge: better results appear even as individual agency seems to fade. Scholars Raisch and Krakowski noted this in 2021, framing it as a balance between automated efficiency and human touch. Control blurs, even while output grows stronger. Something changes when artificial intelligence helps write or reshape what people say. Lines blur - thoughts feel less clearly one's own. Who really said it? A person, a program, or some mix? This mix-up nudges honesty into uncertain ground. Ownership slips, just slightly, from hands to algorithms. What counts as real now includes both mind and machine. Clear information about AI's role matters more than expected. Trust stays intact only if involvement shows openly. Knowing there is assistance makes space for responsibility. Credit given keeps things genuine.

The study's third key result touches on how relationships develop and trust emerges. When people communicate, confidence usually grows through steady behavior, emotional availability, sometimes even subtle cues about motives. Machines improve reaction speed while adjusting emotionally - by reading feelings and shifting speech patterns as needed. According to Huang and Rust (2018), artificial intelligence in customer settings deepens both rational and affective awareness, raising the overall quality of exchanges. Communication tools equipped with comparable features enable artificial intelligence to mirror concern and active listening. Although such traits boost how users perceive interactions, they bring subtle mental challenges along. People might begin seeing machines as having feelings, deepening involvement yet risking emotional dependence where it does not belong. Results suggest artificial intelligence helps streamline relationships - but lasting confidence requires visible human guidance and honest design practices.

What stands out next ties into control through code. Systems guiding online exchange rarely stay impartial, instead molded by hidden rules deciding what gets seen, sorted, or suggested. According to Brynjolfsson and McAfee (2014), digital tools shift who holds sway across societal structures. Within networks of interaction, such shifts emerge via automated reach and message framing. Visibility depends on platform logic - some voices rise while others fade based on design choices. Bias in algorithms gets attention from Danks and team (2021), who point out how hidden trends within training datasets can quietly deepen social disparities. Their work shows governance needs to go beyond just accuracy - fairness matters too, along with openness and responsibility in how these systems share information.

Throughout the analysis, ethics in leadership stands out as a recurring thread. Notably, Floridi and colleagues (2018) argue transparency, answerability, and safeguarding personal choice form the core of moral artificial intelligence. Since words shape understanding and choices, such values gain weight when machines handle dialogue. Hidden systems risk distorting trust, swaying opinions, or blurring who is at fault - especially without openness rules or supervision. For this reason, frameworks guiding AI must embed clarity about origins, ongoing checks for unfair patterns, and defined lines of human ownership.

Over time, using AI to shape written output could reshape how people think. Dependence on automated help might slowly weaken personal writing ability along with deeper reflection. When software handles more of the mental work, effort drops - yet so might involvement in careful thought, note Jordan and Mitchell (2015). Performance gains come at a cost: less hands-on struggle with ideas. Instead of handing control over, skillful use means questioning outputs, adjusting them with judgment. What counts is not just speed, but staying actively involved when machines assist.

Despite differing roles, AI's role in communication splits into three linked layers. At one level, tasks move faster, grow clearer, become tailored - efficiency shifts quietly. Instead of fixed patterns, relationships bend under new pressures: trust wavers, truth blurs, feelings shift. Power does not stay even; algorithms steer who speaks, who listens, often unseen. Each piece connects, yet changes the whole shape. One takeaway stands out: artificial intelligence works best when it supports people instead of acting alone. Long-term success comes not just from smart systems but also from thoughtful oversight, clear rules, by involving those affected. What matters most isn't speed or scale - it's alignment between machine function and human values.

12. SUGGESTIONS

From this study's results emerge a few grounded suggestions - useful for people, institutions, or decision-makers integrating AI into their communication workflows. These insights unfold not through bold claims but quiet observation of how technology interacts with daily practice. One idea follows another, shaped by real-world behavior rather than theoretical ideals. Shifts in usage patterns suggest adjustments that feel less like mandates and more like natural responses. What works tends to reveal itself over time, without fanfare. Guidance here aligns with actual adoption rhythms, not projected timelines. Solutions grow from context, fitting around existing habits instead of overriding them. Each point reflects an adaptation seen across different settings. The path forward appears not as a leap, but a series of small refinements.

Starting with small steps, firms might benefit more by blending AI into messaging tasks instead of removing people entirely. Clarity, speed, and tailored content gain from artificial intelligence - yet decisions rest best in human hands. When machines take over too much, individuals often feel less in control, according to Raisch and Krakowski (2021), damaging how real or trustworthy exchanges seem. So, placing smart systems alongside staff - as helpers - not above them fits better within talking processes.

Openness matters when artificial intelligence plays a role in official or delicate messages. Revealing AI participation helps maintain confidence among those affected. According to Floridi and colleagues from 2018, being able to trace decisions and assign duty sits at the heart of responsible machine behavior. Labeling outputs clearly, recording how automation was applied, along with setting up clear lines of human review, removes uncertainty about who is behind what gets said. Though machines assist, people remain answerable.

13. IMPLICATIONS OF THE STUDY

This study strikes a chord - scholars sense its weight, universities respond quietly, communicators recalibrate their messaging, while policymakers pause to reconsider foundations.

One way to see this study is as part of an ongoing academic exchange about AI's role in dialogue - shifting the view from tools to something closer to collaboration in meaning-making. Earlier studies on digital transformation and improved systems (Huang & Rust, 2018; Davenport & Ronanki, 2018) laid groundwork, yet this takes their ideas further by focusing on human closeness and feeling. It turns out that insights from talk patterns, thinking habits, right-or-wrong judgments, and control methods matter most when they're woven together instead of kept apart while studying technology's social effects.

Nowhere is change more evident than in how brands express themselves, as artificial intelligence reshapes the voice behind messages. Leadership once relied on human judgment alone - today, algorithmic influence steers tone, rhythm, and delivery without clear boundaries. Rather than seeing these systems as background helpers, companies must embed them within deliberate frameworks that include monitoring and moral reflection. Without transparency built into operations, trust erodes quietly, even when intent seems sound. Connection grows naturally only where clarity comes first in conversations with users.

Clearly, a key point emerges. With artificial intelligence becoming part of daily work, new abilities grow in importance. Instead of resisting change, professionals face shifts that demand flexibility. Because tools evolve quickly, human oversight gains weight. While machines handle tasks, people must interpret results thoughtfully. Not every output fits ethical standards without review. Over time, alignment between technology and core principles needs attention. Even small decisions may drift if left unchecked. Now leadership means guiding, not just acting. Frontline choices start carrying moral weight each day. When systems suggest actions, planning becomes deeper. Job roles evolve rather than disappear over time. Where tools align with goals, duties expand quietly.

Technology alters power structures across communities. As shown by Brynjolfsson and McAfee (2014), digital systems shift influence toward those managing economic and organizational resources. In connected environments, automation affects visibility of content, formats used to share concepts, yet simultaneously steers patterns of engagement. Rules that bring transparency help - so does awareness among citizens. Given such forces, policies promoting access fairness, balanced participation, protection of private details grow necessary, particularly when machine-driven decisions impact how messages spread.

Later on, what feels genuine seems to shift. Beyond just human-made content, transparent AI-supported interactions may fit into that space too. Trust comes less from cutting out technology - clarity and fairness shape it stronger. The way people and tools join efforts might set the standard for truth ahead.

14. CONCLUSION

A fresh look at Artificial Intelligence shows it's reshaping the way people exchange ideas, using smart systems to guide interactions. Not just passing along words like older tech did, these tools shape messages - adjusting tone, suggesting changes, making them fit individual users better. The whole process of building understanding online has changed form because of this move. It turns out machines help sharpen how people write at work or in daily life. By shaping sentences, shifting mood, even tailoring replies, smart tools guide expression. Yet questions linger about truth and who really speaks when tech is involved. Messages shaped by code blur lines between self-driven thought and automated aid. Ownership shifts - original ideas feel less pure, sincerity grows harder to pin down. Oddly enough, relationships shift when AI handles messages. Though replies come faster and sound steady, people might feel less connection or doubt if they can really trust what's said. Surprisingly, knowing who controls the tech matters just as much as how well it works. Hidden biases, unclear intentions, private details floating around - these don't fade quietly.

Without clear rules, power slips away from users' bit by bit. Communication shaped by AI works best when it adds to human connection instead of taking its place. Success comes through clear operation, keeping personal decision-making central, while mixing speed of tech with real interpersonal moments. How people share thoughts and grow bonds online will keep shifting as these tools change over time.

15. DIRECTIONS FOR FUTURE RESEARCH

Future research should move beyond conceptual analysis and conduct empirical investigations across diverse cultural and organizational contexts. Comparative studies may examine how disclosure of AI involvement influences perceptions of authenticity and trust. Experimental research could explore psychological responses to AI-generated emotional communication and assess long-term dependency patterns. Further inquiry is needed to develop governance models that integrate ethical safeguards with technological innovation. Interdisciplinary collaboration among communication scholars, technologists, psychologists, and policymakers will be essential for shaping responsible AI-mediated communication ecosystems. Longitudinal studies may also examine how continuous exposure to AI-assisted expression influences identity formation and relational expectations over time.

REFERENCES

Alles, M. G., & Gray, G. L. (2021). Continuous auditing: Theory and application. *International Journal of Accounting Information Systems*, *42*, 100525.

Brynjolfsson, E., & McAfee, A. (2014). *The second machine age: Work, progress, and prosperity in a time of brilliant technologies*. W. W. Norton & Company.

Chen, H., Chiang, R. H. L., & Storey, V. C. (2012). Business intelligence and analytics: From big data to big impact. *Management Information Systems Quarterly*, *36*(4), 1165–1188. DOI: 10.2307/41703503

Danks, D., Zhao, M., & Smith, L. (2021). Algorithmic bias and ethical implications of artificial intelligence. *Journal of Technology and Human Affairs*, *41*(3), 207–220.

Davenport, T. H., & Ronanki, R. (2018). Artificial intelligence for the real world. *Harvard Business Review*, *96*(1), 108–116.

Floridi, L., Cowls, J., Beltrametti, M., Chatila, R., Chazerand, P., Dignum, V., Luetge, C., Madelin, R., Pagallo, U., Rossi, F., Schafer, B., Valcke, P., & Vayena, E. (2018). AI4People, An ethical framework for a good AI society: Opportunities, risks, principles, and recommendations. *Minds and Machines*, *28*(4), 689–707. DOI: 10.1007/s11023-018-9482-5 PMID: 30930541

Huang, M.-H., & Rust, R. T. (2018). Artificial intelligence in service. *Journal of Service Research*, *21*(2), 155–172. DOI: 10.1177/1094670517752459

Jones, A., & Wang, F. (2020). Cybersecurity challenges in the era of cloud computing: A need for robust security measures. *Journal of Network and Computer Applications*, *168*, 102815.

Jordan, M. I., & Mitchell, T. M. (2015). Machine learning: Trends, perspectives, and prospects. *Science*, *349*(6245), 255–260. DOI: 10.1126/science.aaa8415 PMID: 26185243

Manyika, J., Chui, M., Brown, B., Bughin, J., Dobbs, R., Roxburgh, C., & Byers, A. H. (2011). *Big data: The next frontier for innovation, competition, and productivity*. McKinsey Global Institute.

Raisch, S., & Krakowski, S. (2021). Artificial intelligence and management: The automation–augmentation paradox. *Academy of Management Review*, *46*(1), 192–210. DOI: 10.5465/amr.2018.0072

Smith, R. (2022). Navigating the ethical minefield of artificial intelligence: Privacy, bias, and accountability. *AI Magazine*, *43*(3), 42–53.

Chapter 4

Artifical Intelligence and Digital Marketing:

Ethical Challenges in the Algorithmic Era

Andreia Couto
Polytechnic University of Cávado and Ave, Portugal

Bruno Barbosa Sousa
http://orcid.org/0000-0002-8588-2422
UNIAG, School of Hospitality and Tourism, Polytechnic University of Cávado and Ave, Portugal

Lara Gonçalves Santos
http://orcid.org/0000-0001-6927-8906
Polytechnic University of Cávado and Ave, Portugal

ABSTRACT

The rapid rise of generative AI has redefined the boundaries of personalization, but it has also amplified the risks of opacity and algorithmic manipulation. This chapter is justified by the immediate need to reconcile the effectiveness of automated campaigns with the principles of ethics by design, and it offers a response to the empirical research gap linking marketing performance to algorithmic fairness. In this sense, this chapter analyzes the influence of Artificial Intelligence (AI) on digital marketing, focusing on the ethical, security, and data privacy implications. Starting from the evolution of marketing, we discuss how digitization, machine learning, Generative AI (GIA), and LLMs transform the collection, analysis, and use of data to automate campaigns, segment audiences, and personalize content in real time.

DOI: 10.4018/979-8-3373-8337-8.ch004

Through a bibliometric study in the Web of Science (WoS), scientific production at its intersection is mapped. Thematic clusters are identified on AI applications, ethical and privacy risks, and IAG in the personalization economy.

1. INTRODUCTION

The contemporary landscape is defined by unprecedented technological convergence, in which digitization, machine learning, and Artificial Intelligence (AI) have reconfigured the fundamental structures of the global economy (Gupta et al., 2017). In the digital marketing ecosystem, this transformation manifests as a shift from passive communication platforms to autonomous systems capable of generating and processing colossal volumes of data in real time (Yadav et al., 2024). AI thus emerges not only as a support tool but also as the key technology for turning the "noise" of social media data into automated, competitive intelligence strategies (Labib, 2024).

Adopting these solutions gives organizations a sustainable competitive advantage by enabling deep insights into consumer behavior, which are essential for retention and loyalty in a volatile market (Garafonova et al., 2025; Labib, 2024). In fact, the evolution of brand-customer interaction over the past decade has radically changed decision-making processes, making the incorporation of AI into marketing plans a strategic requirement rather than just a technical option (Gantumur, 2025; Labib, 2024). Through predictive analytics, companies can now segment audiences, personalize content, and adjust campaigns in real time, maximizing return on investment (ROI) and operational efficiency (Gbadegeshin et al., 2025a). However, this rise of "algorithmic performance" reveals a critical structural tension. Although AI ushers in an era of unprecedented efficiency, the speed of innovation has outpaced society's ability to establish robust ethical and regulatory barriers. Recent literature begins to highlight the risks inherent in this integration, namely the dehumanization of consumer relationships and the vulnerability of individual privacy (Lobschat et al., 2021a). Issues such as the opacity of profiling algorithms, data surveillance on social media, and persistent flaws in the protection of sensitive information (Cascavilla et al., 2018) call into question the sustainability of data-driven marketing. In this scenario, it is imperative that managers and researchers understand not only the disruptive potential of technology but also its ethical and legal limits (Davenport et al., 2020). Despite the proliferation of generative AI tools and automated models, a critical gap persists in the literature: the need for models that operationalize ethics and data security (privacy by design) as strategic pillars rather than merely reactive obligations (Du & Xie, 2021; Potwora et al., 2024).

This chapter fills this void by examining the dichotomy between data-driven performance and the urgent need to comply with new regulatory paradigms, such as the EU AI Act. At a time when consumer trust has become the most volatile asset in the digital market, this study aims to analyze the influence of AI on digital marketing, with a strict focus on the dimensions of ethics, privacy, and security. In doing so, it seeks to offer a roadmap for responsible AI that harmonizes technological innovation with the protection of users' fundamental rights.

2. LITERATURE REVIEW

2.1. Artificial Intelligence and Generative Artificial Intelligence: From Automation to Co-Creation

Over the last decade, the business ecosystem has undergone structural changes driven by digitalization, a phenomenon that transcends mere technological adoption and has become the backbone of the Fourth Industrial Revolution (Garafonova et al., 2025). This era, characterized by the integration of cyber-physical systems and the Internet of Things (IoT), has established data as the central strategic resource for marketing decision-making (Laudon & Laudon, 2022; Syam & Sharma, 2018). In this context, Artificial Intelligence (AI) emerges as the catalyst that allows organizations not only to process this volume of data but also to optimize processes and sustain competitiveness in a real-time market (Garafonova et al., 2025).

Conceptually, AI refers to computer systems designed to mimic human cognitive functions - such as perception, learning, and complex problem solving (Russell & Norvig, 2021; Syam & Sharma, 2018). This technological umbrella encompasses a range of specializations, from expert systems and natural language processing (NLP) to machine learning (ML) and deep learning (Davenport et al., 2020). ML lies at the core of AI autonomy, enabling systems to identify complex correlations among constantly changing variables without explicit programming (Syam & Sharma, 2018). This ability is crucial in contemporary marketing, where understanding behavioral patterns often supersedes the need to establish linear causality.

The practical application of AI has shown that the greatest value lies in the symbiosis of computational intelligence and human discernment. Hybrid models, such as Stitch Fix, illustrate how recommendation algorithms, when combined with the creative touch of experts, can offer large-scale personalization without sacrificing empathy and emotional connection (Gaudin, 2016; Carpenter, 2015). Additionally, the literature on AI-mediated communication suggests that the persuasive effectiveness of these tools is maximized when the focus is on the directness of the action ("how to act") rather than abstract reasoning, which optimizes the impact of algorithmic recommendations (Kim & Duhachek, 2020; Motyka et al., 2014).

Recently, the AI paradigm has undergone a disruption with the rise of Generative Artificial Intelligence (GAI). Unlike traditional AI, which focuses on analysis and classification, GAI uses large-scale language models (LLMs) to create original content—text, image, audio, and video—based on user instructions (Bozdağ, 2025). The economic impact of this transition is massive: AI could inject more than $13 trillion into the global economy by 2030 (Bughin et al., 2018). In marketing, the GAI market is projected to grow exponentially, with a compound annual growth rate of over 27% (Garafonova et al., 2025).

This new technological frontier is particularly relevant for the media, entertainment, and financial services sectors, where the ability to generate persuasive narratives and natural-language interactions enables dynamic adaptation to consumer tone and needs. Thus, IAG acts not only as an efficiency tool but also as a co-creation agent that redefines the brand experience in the digital environment.

2.2. The Metamorphosis of Marketing: From Product Orientation to the Immersive Digital Ecosystem

The discipline of marketing has undergone a paradigm shift, moving from a purely transactional view to one deeply centered on people and integrating technology. This trajectory, extensively systematized by Kotler et al. (2009, 2016, 2021, 2024), reflects organizations' adaptation to socio-technical changes. While Marketing 1.0 and 2.0 focused, respectively, on product efficiency and customer-oriented segmentation, Marketing 3.0 introduced the dimension of values, requiring brands to adopt purpose narratives that resonated with consumers seeking spiritual and ethical alignment (Kotler et al., 2009).

With the rise of the Fourth Industrial Revolution, Marketing 4.0 marked the critical transition from traditional to digital, establishing omnichannel as the standard for interaction (Kotler et al., 2016). This phase was catalyzed by the COVID-19 pandemic, which forced accelerated digitization and the adoption of contactless models. Currently, the sector is crossing the boundaries of Marketing 5.0 - defined as "Technology for Humanity" - and Marketing 6.0, which emphasizes immersive and multisensory experiences (Kotler et al., 2021, 2024). In these advanced stages, technology is no longer a secondary channel but has become the central facilitator of authentic, personalized, and, above all, socially responsible experiences. In this evolving context, digital marketing emerges as the technical operationalization of this new mindset. Defined by the American Marketing Association (AMA, 2017) as a set of processes for creating and delivering value in a global ecosystem, digital marketing uses network channels to build lasting relationships through coordinated and measurable communications (Smith, 2007; Patel, n.d.). More than just the use of websites or social networks, this discipline involves the strategic management of databases and CRM systems to anticipate needs and satisfy consumers in a hyper-efficient manner (Smith & Chaffey, 2017; Sawicki, 2016).

Contemporary marketing is, by definition, data-driven and automated. With approximately 69% of the global population connected to mobile devices (O'Brien, 2024), the potential reach of brands has expanded exponentially, integrating SEO tactics, paid advertising, and content marketing into an increasingly complex customer journey. The ability to process data to define personas and build dynamic sales funnels enables a level of personalization that consumers now consider a standard requirement rather than a differentiator (O'Brien, 2024).

However, this operational success depends on organizations' ability to navigate the complexity of Big Data. Given the diversity and volume of information from internal and external sources, the application of Artificial Intelligence techniques is the only viable way to extract multidimensional patterns and support informed decision-making (Siau & Yang, 2017). This framework reinforces the need to understand how AI not only optimizes digital marketing but also redefines the very limits of ethics and effectiveness in the brand-consumer relationship.

2.3. Strategic Convergence: Integrating AI into the Digital Marketing Ecosystem

Historically, the marketing industry operated under a paradigm of intuition and limited analytical heuristics, dependent on static data collected by traditional methods such as surveys and observational studies (Venkatesan & Lecinski, 2021). The digital revolution has disrupted this scenario by introducing unprecedented data granularity, allowing direct access to consumer interactions and behavioral preferences in real time (Imamov & Semenikhina, 2021). However, the real metamorphosis occurs when this abundance of data meets the processing power of Artificial Intelligence, which has now become imperative for survival in hypercompetitive markets (Baxi & Mehta, 2024).

The inclusion of AI in digital marketing represents not just an incremental improvement, but a renewal of interaction techniques and the customer lifecycle (Forrest & Hoanca, 2015; Labib, 2024). One of the most profound impacts can be seen in the redefinition of the classic STP (Segmentation, Targeting, and Positioning) model. Through advanced algorithms, companies can now move from generic demographic segmentation to a micro-segmented and dynamic understanding, in which consumer needs and desires are anticipated with superior statistical accuracy (Baxi & Mehta, 2024).

In this process, social networks have established themselves as the central data laboratory for AI. Platforms such as Facebook, Instagram, and LinkedIn generate such vast flows of information that human analysis has become obsolete and ineffective for extracting strategic value (Yadav et al., 2024; Ziakis & Vlachopoulou, 2023). AI solves this operational bottleneck by automating sentiment analysis and pattern recognition, facilitating large-scale personalization - which was once a logistical paradox - and enabling the execution of autonomous campaigns that organically adjust to user behavior (Yadav et al., 2024; Tuten & Solomon, 2017).

Academic literature corroborates that AI permeates all dimensions of marketing strategy: from dynamic pricing and business model adjustment to churn prediction and after-sales support (Davenport et al., 2020; Syam & Sharma, 2018). Industry reports indicate that AI is the technology with the highest projected growth rate in the sales sector, a critical determinant of product launch success and of maximizing customer lifetime value (Dawar & Bendle, 2018; Columbus, 2019).

However, this deep integration is not without friction. Although AI is expected to permanently change the face of marketing, the literature identifies a critical gap: the dissonance between technical persuasion capabilities and safeguarding consumer autonomy (Davenport et al., 2020). This finding underscores the urgency of a systematic approach that does not ignore ethical and regulatory dimensions. Thus, the following section is dedicated to the bibliometric mapping of this intersection, seeking to understand how science has responded to the challenge of balancing algorithmic effectiveness with ethical integrity and data privacy.

2.4. Ethics, Security, and Privacy: The Regulatory Frontier in the Age of AI

The disruptive evolution of AI systems, particularly Generative Artificial Intelligence (GAI), has redefined the ability to produce multimedia content—text, images, sound, and video—autonomously and at scale (Santos, 2026). In the field of digital marketing, this capability translates into hyper-personalization that appeals not only to the transactional context but also to consumers' emotional vulnerabilities (Santos, 2026). Although this dynamic enhances advertising effectiveness, it creates opaque systems that are difficult to scrutinize and challenge the fundamental pillars of data protection. By processing vast volumes of sensitive information, these technologies strain the fundamental principles of the General Data Protection Regulation (GDPR), such as data minimization, purpose limitation, and algorithmic transparency (Santos, 2026).

Ethical and legal dimensions are currently the main obstacles to the full acceptance of AI in the organizational context (Gantumur, 2025; Du & Xie, 2021). The literature identifies a significant gap in the absence of guidelines to ensure responsible use, especially regarding behavioral profiling and consent management in big data environments (Martin & Murphy, 2017; Santos, 2026). In a scenario of increasing technical complexity, the right of individuals to be informed and to challenge automated decisions—a right enshrined in the GDPR—becomes a necessary ethical barrier against the potential opacity of AI systems (Santos, 2026).

Privacy management must therefore shift from a purely reactive stance to a proactive governance approach. Lobschat et al. (2021) warn of the dangers of organizational failures, such as excessive microsegmentation and algorithmic surveillance, and advocate implementing human-in-the-loop oversight mechanisms for automated decisions. The development of sustainable marketing strategies invariably depends on algorithmic accountability and fairness in interactions between the brand and the consumer (Behera et al., 2022). As Davenport et al. (2020) point out, the promises of AI efficiency will be compromised if consumer confidence is eroded by ethically questionable practices (Larson, 2019).

In short, the scientific literature reveals a persistent structural tension: on the one hand, the urgency to achieve marketing effectiveness through intensive data exploitation; on the other, the imperative to respect regulatory frameworks, such as the EU AI Act, and universal ethical principles. This dichotomy justifies the present investigation, which aims to systematically map the state of the art and identify paths toward convergence between technological innovation, legal certainty, and ethical integrity in digital marketing.

3. METHODOLOGY

Given the exponential expansion and fragmentation of the literature on Artificial Intelligence (AI), digital marketing, and their ethical implications, a hybrid methodological approach combining quantitative bibliometric analysis with a systematic literature review (SLR) was adopted. This methodology allows the field's intellectual structure to be mapped systematically, transparently, and replicable, mitigating subjective biases in selecting the academic corpus. The research protocol was anchored in the PRISMA (Preferred Reporting Items for Systematic Reviews and Meta-Analyses) guidelines, ensuring rigorous screening and selection of publications (Tawfik et al., 2019).

The Web of Science (WoS - Core Collection) database was selected as the primary source due to its academic prestige and rigorous indexing of high-impact journals in the areas of Management, Information Systems, and Communication. The search strategy used combinations of Boolean operators to ensure the intersection of the three central axes of the study:

- Axis 1 (Technology): "artificial intelligence" OR 'AI' OR "generative AI".
- Axis 2 (Domain): "digital marketing".
- Axis 3 (Ethics/Privacy): "ethics" OR "privacy" OR "data security" OR 'GDPR' OR "AI Act".

To ensure the quality and relevance of the sample, the following inclusion criteria were applied: (i) scientific articles published in peer-reviewed journals; (ii) texts written in English or Portuguese; (iii) explicit focus on the application of AI/AGI to marketing; and (iv) substantive approach to ethics or regulation issues. Book chapters, editorials, technical notes, and studies addressing AI in fields unrelated to marketing (e.g., medicine or heavy engineering) were excluded to ensure the corpus's thematic cohesion, as were all documents from 2026.

The selection process was structured in four critical phases:

1. Identification: Retrieval of raw records in WoS.
2. Screening: Removal of duplicates and technical analysis of titles and abstracts to exclude articles outside the scope.
3. Eligibility: Full-text analysis of the remaining articles to verify whether they presented theoretical or empirical contributions relevant to algorithmic ethics in marketing.
4. Inclusion: Definition of the final sample that formed the basis for thematic and bibliometric mapping.

VOSviewer software was used for the quantitative analysis of the scientific network. This software enabled the construction of network maps based on keyword co-occurrence and co-citation, identifying the thematic clusters that dominate the current literature. Co-occurrence analysis is particularly effective for identifying emerging trends (such as IAG and LLMs) and distinguishing consolidated areas from research gaps.

The bibliometric component was integrated with a qualitative content analysis of the most cited articles in each cluster. This step was essential to transcend statistical data and understand the proposed frameworks, identify ethical tensions, and suggest governance models for responsible AI adoption. This holistic approach ensures that the chapter offers not only a map of the literature but also a critical discussion that supports the managerial and regulatory implications presented.

4. RESULTS

4.1. Temporal evolution of scientific production

The sample analysis shows significant growth in scientific production on Artificial Intelligence applied to digital marketing over the last decade. Graph 1 shows a gradual increase in publications in the early years, followed by a more marked acceleration from the mid-2010s onwards, coinciding with the spread of commercial AI applications and the expansion of social media platforms as sources of marketing data (Yadav et al., 2024; Labib, 2024).

This growth has become even more pronounced in recent years, a period marked by intensified discussions on ethics, privacy, and data security, as well as the first systematic applications of GAI and large language models (LLMs) in digital marketing contexts (Davenport et al., 2020). The results suggest that the topic of AI–marketing–ethics/privacy has gone from being a marginal interest to a structured emerging domain, accompanying technological and regulatory developments, namely the implementation of the GDPR and debates surrounding the AI Act.

Figure 1. Annual evolution of the number of articles published

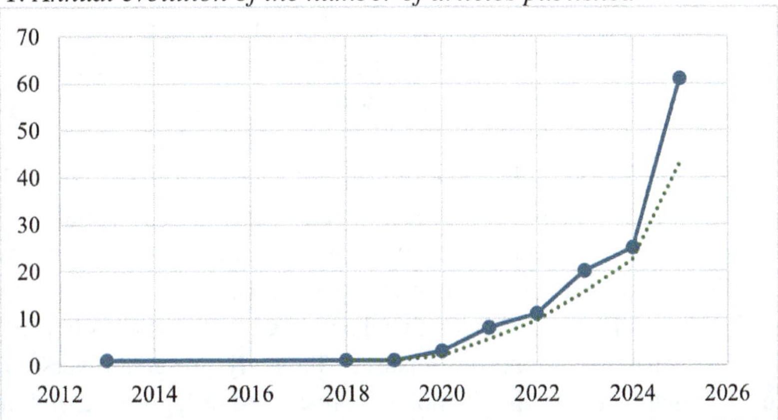

Source: Prepared internally using the WOS database

Subsequently, the five most influential articles in the sample, with the highest number of citations, were selected to identify in greater detail the topics that have received the most attention from researchers and the academic community, as shown in Table 1.

Table 1. Articles with the most citations

N.	Title	Authors	Source	Citations
1	So what if ChatGPT wrote it? Multidisciplinary perspectives on opportunities, challenges and implications of generative conversational AI for research, practice and policy	*Dwivedi et al., 2023.*	International Journal of Information Management	365
2	Neuromarketing algorithms' consumer privacy and ethical considerations: challenges and opportunities	Goncalves et al., 2024	Cogent Business & Management	304
3	Cognitive computing based ethical principles for improving organisational reputation: A B2B digital marketing perspective	Behera et al., 2022	Journal of Business Research	226
4	The AI-mediated intimacy economy: a paradigm shift in digital interactions	Bozdağ, 2025	AI & Society	225
5	Human resource management in the age of generative artificial intelligence: Perspectives and research directions on ChatGPT	Budhwar et al., 2023	Human Resource Management Journal	187

Source: Prepared internally using the WOS database

Below is a summary of the articles in Table 1, with the aim of synthesizing the content of the most cited articles.

Article 1: "So what if ChatGPT wrote it? Multidisciplinary perspectives on opportunities, challenges, and implications of generative conversational AI for research, practice, and policy".

Dwivedi et al. (2023) analyze the impact of Generative Artificial Intelligence (GAI) tools, such as ChatGPT, which have transformative potential to produce human-like text, increase productivity, and generate value across areas such as tourism, technology, management, and marketing. However, they highlight limitations associated with its adoption, such as ethical and legal issues, threats to privacy and security, bias, misinformation, and misuse. The study presents diverse opinions on the use of ChatGPT, whether it should be restricted or legislated, and therefore identifies three major areas for future research: knowledge, transparency, and ethics; digital transformation of organizations and societies; and education, learning, and academic research. The authors reinforce the need to explore necessary skills, the impact of biases, new human-AI hybrid models, and the identification of appropriate contexts for assessing the reliability of the content produced.

Article 2: "Neuromarketing algorithms' consumer privacy and ethical considerations: challenges and opportunities".

Goncalves et al. (2024) highlight the ethical and privacy challenges posed by the use of AI and machine learning in neuromarketing. The study combines a literature review, bibliometric analysis, and data collected through questionnaires and interviews, highlighting the tension between the effectiveness of these technologies and the urgency of safeguarding users' rights and privacy, essentially in the regulatory context influenced by the GDPR. It is important to establish consistent international ethical standards and robust data protection policies to ensure ethical, transparent application of neuromarketing.

Article 3: "Cognitive computing based ethical principles for improving organizational reputation: A B2B digital marketing perspective".

Behera et al. (2022) study the role of cognitive computing in the digital transformation of B2B marketing, highlighting its ability to improve accuracy, growth, and personalization. However, there are significant ethical challenges, as errors can completely compromise the organization's reputation. Based on the theoretical framework and data collected from 300 professionals, it is concluded that robust ethical practices should be adopted to increase competitive advantage in dynamic markets, and that proactive approaches should be adopted to ensure the conscious integration of computing into digital strategies.

Article 4: "The AI-mediated intimacy economy: a paradigm shift in digital interactions".

Bozdağ (2025) examines the transition from the attention economy to the intimacy economy, an aspect in which emotional and personal data are replaced by highly individualized experiences. The author studies how AI converts this data into services that cater to emotional dynamics, questioning authenticity, privacy, and the possible transformation of personal relationships into something commercial. The author highlights technological mechanisms (such as blockchain) that reinforce individual control over this data and reduce ethical risks and proposes the AMIE framework to assess how AI-mediated interactions shape digital identities and human relationships, thereby underscoring the need for standards, transparency, and recognition of emotions as intellectual property.

Article 5: "Human resource management in the age of generative artificial intelligence: Perspectives and research directions on ChatGPT".

Budhwar et al. (2023) discuss the growing impact of ChatGPT and other GAI models in business contexts, with a particular focus on human resource management (benefits and risks for the economy, society, and work). There are numerous uncertainties regarding the effects of these technologies on employment, including job creation or replacement and role reconfiguration. The growing "AI race" raises serious concerns about bias, misinformation, privacy, ethics, and security, and it is therefore urgent to understand how AGI can transform labor relations, business models, processes, and outcomes in human resource management.

4.2. Characterization Of Journals And Study Sources

IEEE Access is the journal with the most articles, with four articles and 27,377 citations. It is followed by the Journal of Business Research, with four articles and 2,682 citations, as shown in Table 2. There are 14 journals, each with two articles. The Impact Factor is an index provided by the analysis company Clarivate, calculated as the number of times articles are cited in the last two years, divided by the total number of publications in those two years (Journal Impact Factor, 2025). The higher the impact factor, the better, which means that the journal has greater relevance and influence in its field. IEEE Access has an impact factor of 0.849, while the Journal of Business Research has 3.499.

Table 2. Journals with the most publications

Journal	Country	Published since	Number of articles	Number of citations (2024)	Impact factor
IEEE Access	United States	2013	4	27377	0,849
Journal Of Business Research	United States	1973	4	2682	3,499

Source: Prepared by the author using the WOS database, processed in Excel (2026)

Authors with three or more publications are shown in Table 3, and the list contains three different names: Wirtz, J.; Dwivedi, YK.; Rousi, R. There are 18 authors with two articles. The remaining authors have only one published article.

Table 3. Authors with the most published articles

Authors	Number of articles
Wirtz, J	4
Dwivedi, YK	3
Rousi, R	3

Source: Prepared by the author using the WOS database, processed in Excel (2026)

4.3. Main research topics and clusters

To identify the most frequent key themes in the articles analyzed, a word cloud was created on the Make Charts platform, as shown in Figure 2. Among the most relevant keywords, the following terms stand out: Artificial Intelligence, Ethics, Digital, Marketing, Generative, Technology, Human, and Learning.

Figure 2. Word cloud

Source: Own elaboration using the Make Charts platform (2026)

The co-occurrence analysis of keywords identified several thematic clusters that structure scientific production at the intersection of AI, digital marketing, and ethics/privacy. In summary, three major groups can be highlighted (Figure 3):

Figure 3. Research clusters

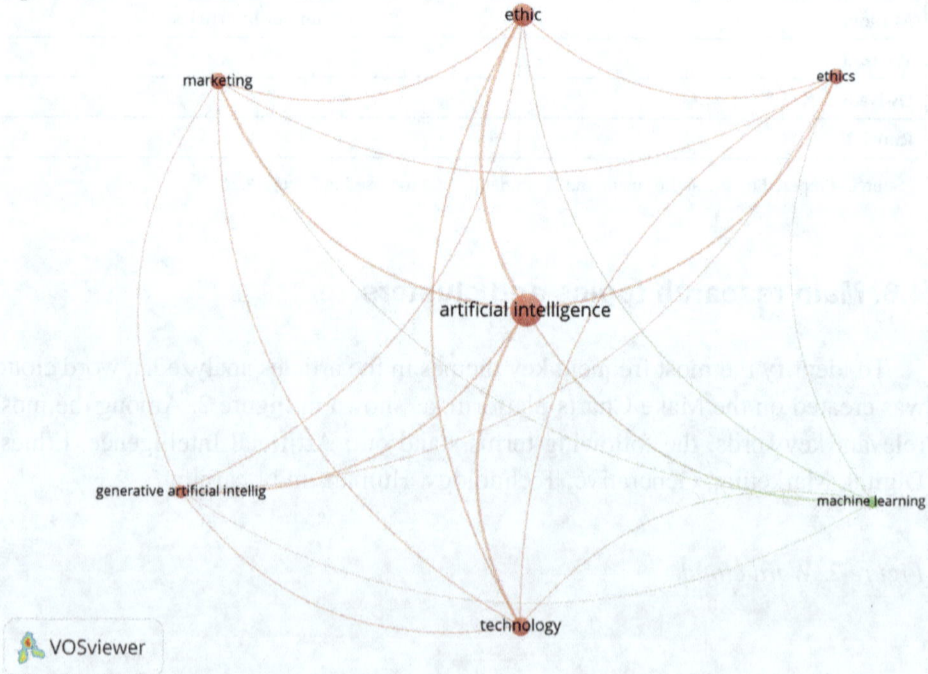

Source: Prepared by the authors using VOSviewer (2026)

Cluster 1 – AI applications in digital marketing

This cluster brings together studies focused on the use of AI for campaign automation, segmentation, content personalization, behavior prediction, and sales funnel optimization (Syam & Sharma, 2018; Yadav et al., 2024). The works in this cluster emphasize efficiency gains, increased conversions, and improved customer experience, exploring technologies such as machine learning, recommendation systems, chatbots, and website design algorithms (Martin & Murphy, 2017; Hall, 2019; Marketing360, 2025).

Cluster 2 – Ethics, privacy, and data security

This cluster includes studies that address risks and dilemmas associated with the intensive use of data and algorithms in digital marketing, focusing on privacy, security, transparency, bias, and algorithmic fairness (Lobschat et al., 2021; Gantumur, 2025). This cluster discusses organizational privacy failures (data leaks, microtargeting, surveillance, hacking), obligations under the GDPR (consent, data subject rights), and the challenges posed by new regulations such as the AI Act (Martin & Murphy, 2017; Santos, 2026; Behera et al., 2022).

Cluster 3 – GAI, LLMs, and the economics of personalization

This cluster focuses on more recent studies on Generative Artificial Intelligence and large-scale language models applied to marketing, including automated content generation, advanced chatbots, natural language recommendations, and immersive experiences (De Cremer et al., 2023; Bozdağ, 2025). These works highlight the potential of GAI to create highly personalized and emotionally tailored messages, while warning of the risks of misinformation, manipulation, and opacity in content creation and segmentation (Bughin et al., 2018; Santos, 2026).

The existence of these clusters shows that the literature has evolved from describing AI applications in marketing to gradually incorporating ethical and regulatory discussions, especially as more advanced technologies, such as AGI, become central to digital marketing practices.

4.4. Summary of key findings

Taken together, the bibliometric results reveal some clear trends. Firstly, AI is confirmed as a structuring technology for digital marketing, with a strong presence in studies on automation, personalization, and real-time data analysis, geared towards performance and efficiency gains (Labib, 2024; Davenport et al., 2020). Second, there has been recent, albeit uneven, growth in research focused on ethics, privacy, and data security, which seeks to respond to the requirements of regulatory frameworks such as the GDPR and the AI Act, as well as social concerns surrounding the use of personal data (Lobschat et al., 2021; Santos, 2026).

Finally, it should be noted that, although the literature recognizes the ethical and legal risks associated with AI in digital marketing, important gaps remain, particularly with regard to: (i) empirical studies applied to specific campaign contexts; (ii) the operationalization of constructs such as trust in marketing AI, the perception of algorithmic fairness, or the social acceptability of personalization; and (iii) practical frameworks for governance and algorithmic auditing for marketing professionals. These gaps open space for critical discussion and for defining a future research agenda, which will be explored in the discussion and implications section of this chapter.

This conclusion builds on what has already been developed in the chapter (introduction, review, methodology, and results) and maintains the academic tone and focus on AI, digital marketing, ethics, and privacy.

5. CONCLUSION

The research conducted in this chapter demonstrates that Artificial Intelligence (AI) has established itself as a cornerstone of contemporary digital marketing, transcending its initial role as technical support. As discussed, the transition to Generative AI (GIA) models and the use of large-scale language models (LLMs) have enabled organizations to achieve unprecedented levels of efficiency in campaign automation and large-scale personalization (Yadav et al., 2024). However, this evolution profoundly alters the ontology of market relations, requiring companies to develop "realistic expectations," since while the benefits are evolutionary in the short term, the technology proves truly revolutionary in the long term (Davenport, 2018).

The systematic bibliometric mapping conducted in the WoS showed that the technological dimension is relatively consolidated, while ethical and regulatory approaches are still undergoing profound maturation. An inalienable "structural tension" was identified between the pursuit of performance (conversion, ROI, and operational effectiveness) and the imperative need to respect ethical and regulatory principles, such as the GDPR and the EU AI Act (Santos, 2026; Labib, 2024). The literature reviewed reinforces that AI should not be seen as a substitute for human roles, but as a tool that reinforces and enriches human capabilities, especially in areas where creativity and emotional intelligence remain the exclusive domain of the marketing professional (Davenport et al., 2020; Gbadegeshin et al., 2025b; Stone et al., 2020).

The results reveal that the sector's future depends on a delicate balance. On the one hand, AI enables anticipating needs and adjusting business models with mathematical precision (Davenport et al., 2020; Shankar, 2018). On the other hand, there is a real risk of dehumanization and a "dystopian vision" in which consumers are no longer in control of their choices, becoming guided by opaque algorithms (Grewal et al., 2024). To mitigate these risks, it is essential to integrate principles of privacy by design and ethics by design from the conception of strategies, ensuring that technology does not exploit users' "psychological weaknesses" (Potwora et al., 2024).

From an academic perspective, this chapter contributes by offering an integrated overview of the state of the art and by highlighting the urgent need for empirical studies that test "algorithmic fairness" and consumer trust in real-world contexts. From a practical standpoint, evidence suggests that marketing managers should take a "leadership role" in addressing these ethical issues, as the marketing discipline is both the one that has the most to gain from AI and the one that has the most to lose if trust is eroded (Davenport et al., 2020).

In summary, fully realizing AI's potential in digital marketing requires adopting practices that harmonize the "human touch" with algorithmic efficiency (Pham et al., 2021; Yadav et al., 2024). By highlighting these dualities, this chapter concludes that the marketing of the future will be defined not only by its technical ability to process data but by its integrity in respecting privacy and human autonomy, ensuring that we do not become a society that "prefers to talk to chatbots rather than each other" (Grewal et al., 2024).

REFERENCES

American Marketing Association. (2017). Definition of marketing. https://www.ama.org/the-definition-of-marketing-what-is-marketing/

Baxi, B., & Mehta, M. J. (2024). A study on AI's role in reshaping marketing for Gujarat retailers. *Rabindra Bharati University: Journal of Economics*, *XVII*, 8.

Behera, R. K., Bala, P. K., Rana, N. P., & Kizgin, H. (2022). Cognitive computing based ethical principles for improving organisational reputation: A B2B digital marketing perspective. *Journal of Business Research*, *141*, 685–701. DOI: 10.1016/j.jbusres.2021.11.070

Bozdağ, A. A. (2025). The AI-mediated intimacy economy: A paradigm shift in digital interactions. *AI & Society*, *40*(4), 2285–2306. DOI: 10.1007/s00146-024-02132-6

Budhwar, P., Chowdhury, S., Wood, G., Aguinis, H., Bamber, G. J., Beltran, J. R., Boselie, P., Lee Cooke, F., Decker, S., DeNisi, A., Dey, P. K., Guest, D., Knoblich, A. J., Malik, A., Paauwe, J., Papagiannidis, S., Patel, C., Pereira, V., Ren, S., & Varma, A. (2023). Human resource management in the age of generative artificial intelligence: Perspectives and research directions on ChatGPT. *Human Resource Management Journal*, *33*(3), 606–659. DOI: 10.1111/1748-8583.12524

Bughin, J., Seong, J., Manyika, J., Chui, M., & Joshi, R. (2018). Notes from the AI frontier: Modeling the impact of AI on the world economy. McKinsey Global Institute, 4.

Carpenter, J. (2015). IBM's Virginia Rometty tells NU grads: Technology will enhance us. https://www.chicagotribune.com/bluesky/originals/ct-northwestern-virginia-rometty-ibm-bsi-20150619-story.html

Cascavilla, G., Beato, F., Burattin, A., Conti, M., & Mancini, L. V. (2018). OSSINT - Open Source Social Network Intelligence. *Online Social Networks and Media*, *6*, 58–68. DOI: 10.1016/j.osnem.2018.04.003

Columbus, L. (2019). 10 charts that will change your perspective of AI in marketing. Forbes, July 07. https://www.forbes.com/sites/louiscolumbus/2019/07/07/10-charts-that-will-change-your-perspective-of-ai-in-marketing/amp/

Davenport, T., Guha, A., Grewal, D., & Bressgott, T. (2020). How artificial intelligence will change the future of marketing. *Journal of the Academy of Marketing Science*, *48*(1), 24–42. DOI: 10.1007/s11747-019-00696-0

Dawar, N., & Bendle, N. (2018). Marketing in the age of Alexa. *Harvard Business Review*, *96*(3), 80–86. https://hbr.org/2018/05/marketing-in-the-age-of-alexa

De Cremer, D., Bianzino, N. M., & Falk, B. (2023). How Generative AI Could Disrupt Creative Work. Harvard Business Review. https://hbr.org/2023/04/how-generative-ai-could-disrupt-creative-work

Du, S., & Xie, C. (2021). Paradoxes of artificial intelligence in consumer markets: Ethical challenges and opportunities. *Journal of Business Research*, *129*, 961–974. DOI: 10.1016/j.jbusres.2020.08.024

Dwivedi, Y. K., Kshetri, N., Hughes, L., Slade, E. L., Jeyaraj, A., Kar, A. K., Baabdullah, A. M., Koohang, A., Raghavan, V., Ahuja, M., Albanna, H., Albashrawi, M. A., Al-Busaidi, A. S., Balakrishnan, J., Barlette, Y., Basu, S., Bose, I., Brooks, L., Buhalis, D., & Wright, R. (2023). Opinion Paper: "So what if ChatGPT wrote it?" Multidisciplinary perspectives on opportunities, challenges and implications of generative conversational AI for research, practice and policy. *International Journal of Information Management*, *71*, 102642. DOI: 10.1016/j.ijinfomgt.2023.102642

Forrest, E., & Hoanca, B. (2015). Artificial Intelligence. In *IGI Global* (pp. 45–64). DOI: 10.4018/978-1-4666-8459-1.ch003

Gantumur, K. (2025). The Impact of Artificial Intelligence on Online Shopping. *European Scientific Journal*, *21*(4), 1. DOI: 10.19044/esj.2025.v21n4p1

Garafonova, O., Dvornyk, O., Sharov, V., Zhosan, H., Yankovoi, R., & Lomachynska, I. (2025). Digitization Process in a Changing Global Environment. TEM Journal, 251–265. https://doi.org/DOI: 10.18421/TEM141-23

Gaudin, S. (2016). At stitch fix, data scientists and AI become personal stylists. https://www.computerworld.com/article/3067264/artificial-intelligence/at-stitch-fix-data-scientists-and-ai-become-personal-stylists.html

Gbadegeshin, S. A., French, A., Olajumoke, T. F., AlZahrani, I. A. A., Farah, S. Y., & Jegede, O. (2025a). Impact of Artificial Intelligence on Digital Marketing: Theoretical and Empirical Evidence. In *Tech Fusion in Business and Society* (pp. 23–33). DOI: 10.1007/978-3-031-84636-6_3

Gbadegeshin, S. A., French, A., Olajumoke, T. F., AlZahrani, I. A. A., Farah, S. Y., & Jegede, O. (2025b). Impact of Artificial Intelligence on Digital Marketing: Theoretical and Empirical Evidence. In *Tech Fusion in Business and Society* (pp. 23–33). DOI: 10.1007/978-3-031-84636-6_3

Goncalves, M., Hu, Y., Aliagas, I., & Cerdá, L. M. (2024). Neuromarketing algorithms' consumer privacy and ethical considerations: Challenges and opportunities. *Cogent Business & Management*, *11*(1), 2333063. Advance online publication. DOI: 10.1080/23311975.2024.2333063

Grewal, D., Guha, A., & Becker, M. (2024). AI is Changing the World: For Better or for Worse? *Journal of Macromarketing*, *44*(4), 870–882. DOI: 10.1177/02761467241254450

Gupta, S., Keen, M., Shah, A., & Verdier, G. (2017). *Digital revolutions in public finance*. International Monetary Fund.

Hall, J. (2019). How Artificial Intelligence Is Transforming Digital Marketing. Forbes Agency Council. https://www.forbes.com/councils/forbesagencycouncil/2019/08/21/how-artificial-intelligence-is-transforming-digital-marketing/

Imamov, M., & Semenikhina, N. (2021). The impact of the digital revolution on the global economy. *Linguistics and Culture Review*, *5*(S4), 968–987. DOI: 10.21744/lingcure.v5nS4.1775

Kim, T. W., & Duhachek, A. (2020). Artificial Intelligence and Persuasion: A Construal-Level Account. *Psychological Science*, *31*(4), 363–380. DOI: 10.1177/0956797620904985 PMID: 32223692

Kotler, P., Kartajaya, H., & Setiawan, I. (2009). Marketing 3.0: From products to customers to the human spirit. Em Management for Professionals (pp. 139–156). Springer Singapore.

Kotler, P., Kartajaya, H., & Setiawan, I. (2016). *Marketing 4.0: Moving from traditional to digital*. John Wiley & Sons.

Kotler, P., Kartajaya, H., & Setiawan, I. (2021). *Marketing 5.0: Technology for humanity*. John Wiley & Sons.

Kotler, P., Kartajaya, H., & Setiawan, I. (2024). *Marketing 6.0: The Future Is Immersive*. John Wiley & Sons.

Labib, E. (2024). Artificial intelligence in marketing: Exploring current and future trends. *Cogent Business & Management*, *11*(1), 2348728. Advance online publication. DOI: 10.1080/23311975.2024.2348728

Larson, K. (2019). Data privacy and AI ethics stepped to the fore in 2018. https://medium.com/@Smalltofeds/data-privacy-and-ai-ethics-stepped-to-the-fore-in-2018-4e0207f28210

Laudon, K. C., & Laudon, J. (2022). Management information systems: Managing the digital firm, global edition (17.a ed.). Pearson Education. ISBN 9781292403571

Lobschat, L., Mueller, B., Eggers, F., Brandimarte, L., Diefenbach, S., Kroschke, M., & Wirtz, J. (2021a). Corporate digital responsibility. *Journal of Business Research, 122*, 875–888. DOI: 10.1016/j.jbusres.2019.10.006

Lobschat, L., Mueller, B., Eggers, F., Brandimarte, L., Diefenbach, S., Kroschke, M., & Wirtz, J. (2021b). Corporate digital responsibility. *Journal of Business Research, 122*, 875–888. DOI: 10.1016/j.jbusres.2019.10.006

Marketing360 (2025). Inteligência Artificial e Automação no Marketing Digital. Marketing360. https://www.marketing360.pt/inteligencia-artificial-e-automacao-no-marketing-digital/

Martin, K. D., & Murphy, P. E. (2017). The role of data privacy in marketing. *Journal of the Academy of Marketing Science, 45*(2), 135–155. DOI: 10.1007/s11747-016-0495-4

Motyka, S., Grewal, D., Puccinelli, N. M., Roggeveen, A. L., Avnet, T., Daryanto, A., de Ruyter, K., & Wetzels, M. (2014). Regulatory fit: A meta-analytic synthesis. *Journal of Consumer Psychology, 24*(3), 394–410. DOI: 10.1016/j.jcps.2013.11.004

O'Brien, C. (2024). What Is Digital Marketing? Digital Marketing Institute. https://digitalmarketinginstitute.com/blog/what-is-digital-marketing

Patel, N. (s.d.). What Is Digital Marketing? Neil Patel. Obtido 20 de janeiro de 2026, de https://neilpatel.com/digital-marketing/

Pham, H. H., Hagel, J., Singh, R., & Baker, C. E. (2021). Why companies should disclose algorithms' power and purpose. *Harvard Business Review, 99*(4), 42–51.

Potwora, M., Vdovichena, O., Semchuk, D., Lipych, L., & Saienko, V. (2024). The use of artificial intelligence in marketing strategies: Automation, personalization and forecasting. *Journal of Management World, 2024*(2), 41–49. DOI: 10.53935/jomw.v2024i2.275

Russell, S., & Norvig, P. (2021). Artificial intelligence: A modern approach, global edition (4.a ed.). Pearson Education.

Santos, L. M. G. (2026). IA generativa na publicidade digital: enquadramento jurídico, riscos e desafios em matéria de proteção de dados e ética. 6.

Sawicki, A. (2016). Digital marketing. *World Scientific News*, (48), 82–88.

Shankar, V. (2018). How Artificial Intelligence (AI) is Reshaping Retailing. *Journal of Retailing*, *94*(4), vi–xi. DOI: 10.1016/S0022-4359(18)30076-9

Siau, K. L., & Yang, Y. (2017). Impact of artificial intelligence, robotics, and machine learning on sales and marketing. AIS Electronic Library (AISeL). https://aisel.aisnet.org/mwais2017/48?utm_source=aisel.aisnet.org%2Fmwais2017%2F48&utm_medium=PDF&utm_campaign=PDFCoverPages

Smith, K. (2007). What is digital marketing? Digital Marketing, 101.

Smith, P. R., & Chaffey, D. (2017). Digital marketing excellence: Planning, optimizing and integrating online marketing (5.a ed.). Taylor & Francis.

Stone, M., Aravopoulou, E., Ekinci, Y., Evans, G., Hobbs, M., Labib, A., Laughlin, P., Machtynger, J., & Machtynger, L. (2020). Artificial intelligence (AI) in strategic marketing decision-making: A research agenda. *The Bottom Line (New York, N.Y.)*, *33*(2), 183–200. DOI: 10.1108/BL-03-2020-0022

Syam, N., & Sharma, A. (2018). Waiting for a sales renaissance in the fourth industrial revolution: Machine learning and artificial intelligence in sales research and practice. *Industrial Marketing Management*, *69*, 135–146. DOI: 10.1016/j.indmarman.2017.12.019

Tawfik, G. M., Dila, K. A. S., Mohamed, M. Y. F., Tam, D. N. H., Kien, N. D., Ahmed, A. M., & Huy, N. T. (2019). A step by step guide for conducting a systematic review and meta-analysis with simulation data. *Tropical Medicine and Health*, *47*(1), 46. DOI: 10.1186/s41182-019-0165-6 PMID: 31388330

Tuten, T. L., & Solomon, M. R. (2017). Social Media Marketing (3.ª ed.). SAGE. https://www.amazon.com/Social-Media-Marketing-Tracy-Tuten/dp/1526423871

Venkatesan, R., & Lecinski, J. (2021). *The AI marketing canvas: A five-stage road map to implementing artificial intelligence in marketing*. Stanford University Press. DOI: 10.1515/9781503628045

Yadav, S., Yadav, P., & Banshiwal, N. (2024). Artificial Intelligence Integration in Social Media Marketing: A Comprehensive Analysis., 11(6), 7.

Ziakis, C., & Vlachopoulou, M. (2023). Artificial Intelligence in Digital Marketing: Insights from a Comprehensive Review. *Information (Basel)*, *14*(12), 664. DOI: 10.3390/info14120664

KEY TERMS AND DEFINITIONS

Algorithmic Era -: refers to the current phase of the digital age where Artificial Intelligence (AI) and automated algorithms have become the primary drivers of decision-making, content curation, and consumer interaction, replacing previous, more manual or human-driven processes.

Artificial Intelligence -: is technology that enables computers and machines to simulate human learning, comprehension, problem solving, decision making, creativity and autonomy.

Digital Marketing -: the promotion of brands, products, or services to consumers using online channels, including search engines, websites, social media, email, and mobile apps. It enables businesses to track ROI in real-time, target specific audiences, and engage customers more personally than traditional methods.

Chapter 5
Artificial Intelligence and Online Relationships in Small Businesses

Olga Santos
Instituto Politécnico de Bragança, Portugal

Paula Odete Fernandes
http://orcid.org/0000-0001-8714-4901
UNIAG, Instituto Politécnico de Bragança, Portugal

Elaine Scalabrini
http://orcid.org/0000-0001-7164-2471
UNIAG, Instituto Politécnico de Bragança, Portugal

ABSTRACT

The digital transformation of markets has positioned Artificial Intelligence as a key tool in contemporary marketing management. However, small enterprises often face structural constraints that limit their adoption. This chapter analyses the influence of AI on digital marketing strategies in small firms, with a focus on social media. Using quantitative data from Portuguese small enterprises, the results show that the sector of activity significantly influences the adoption of digital marketing strategies. Despite financial and knowledge barriers, most firms recognise AI as increasingly important for improving campaign efficiency, personalising communication and supporting real-time marketing decisions. The study contributes to Marketing 5.0 and 6.0 research by extending the discussion of intelligent marketing to the context of small enterprises and offering practical insights for gradual AI integration.

DOI: 10.4018/979-8-3373-8337-8.ch005

INTRODUCTION

Marketing has evolved significantly over time, transitioning from a product-oriented approach to a consumer-centred and relationship-driven discipline (Kotler & Keller, 2010). Initially focused on satisfying needs through profitable exchange, marketing progressively incorporated strategic tools designed to understand markets, coordinate organisational resources and create value for customers (Kotler et al., 2010; Kury & Gomes, 2013). As access to information expanded and consumers became more informed and demanding, organisations were required to adapt their strategies to increasingly competitive and dynamic environments. This shift reinforced the importance of customer-oriented thinking and continuous strategic innovation.

The rapid advancement of digital technologies has further transformed marketing practices. The emergence of the Internet and digital platforms reshaped communication channels, enabling real-time interaction between organisations and consumers (Peretti et al., 2021). Digital marketing became a fundamental component of business strategy, particularly through social media platforms that facilitate visibility, engagement and direct communication. These platforms allow firms to analyse consumer behaviour, personalise content and strengthen relationships, thereby enhancing brand positioning in highly competitive digital environments.

More recently, Artificial Intelligence (AI) has emerged as a transformative technology in digital marketing. AI enables organisations to collect, process and interpret large volumes of data efficiently, supporting strategic decision-making and campaign optimisation. Through algorithms capable of identifying patterns and predicting behaviours, AI facilitates personalisation, segmentation and automation processes that were previously resource-intensive (Antunes, 2023; Peretti et al., 2021). This technological evolution aligns with the broader Marketing 5.0 paradigm, which integrates advanced technologies to address complex consumer dynamics and deliver personalised experiences.

For small enterprises, integrating Artificial Intelligence presents both opportunities and challenges. While these firms rely on digital marketing and social media as primary communication channels, they often operate under structural constraints, including limited financial resources and restricted access to specialised knowledge (Kotler et al., 2010; Raupp & Janssen, 2023). Despite these limitations, AI holds significant potential to enhance competitiveness, improve customer relationships and reduce operational costs. However, the extent to which small enterprises adopt and integrate AI into their marketing strategies remains uneven.

In this context, the present study aims to examine the influence of Artificial Intelligence on digital marketing strategies in small enterprises, particularly in social media environments. The research aims to identify the types of AI tools used, analyse firms' perceptions regarding their effectiveness, explore perceived benefits and challenges, and assess future investment intentions. By focusing on small enterprises in the Northern region of Portugal, the study contributes to a better understanding of how emerging technologies are shaping marketing practices in resource-constrained organisational settings.

To achieve this aim, this chapter is divided into five sections. After this brief introduction, it presents the theoretical framework that enables understanding the main concepts related to this study, such as the evolution of marketing, digital marketing and the influence of AI in marketing strategies. The methods applied to execute the study are presented in the following section. The results and discussion are presented, and the final considerations offer suggestions for a strategic plan that could be useful for small businesses, not only in the Portuguese context but also in other regions with circumstances like those of the present study.

1. THEORETICAL FRAMEWORK

1.1. The Evolution of Marketing: Conceptual and Strategic Foundations

Marketing has long been recognised as a discipline shaped by economic transformation, technological development and shifting consumer expectations. Its conceptual evolution reflects broader structural changes in markets and society. Initially associated with production and distribution logics, marketing progressively developed into a strategic function centred on value creation, relationship building and consumer engagement (Minuzzi & Larentis, 2014).

Early definitions of marketing emphasised the satisfaction of human needs through profitable exchange. Marketing was viewed as a system of organised activities aimed at identifying opportunities, coordinating resources, and delivering products or services that meet consumer demands (Kotler & Keller, 2010). Over time, scholars highlighted that marketing extends beyond mere selling or advertising. Marketing encompasses a broader managerial process focused on understanding markets and building long-term relationships (Bragança et al., 2016).

The marketing process model provides a structured perspective on this progression. It begins with understanding market needs and consumer desires, followed by designing a customer-oriented strategy, developing integrated marketing programmes, building profitable relationships and capturing value in return. This cyclical model reflects the transition from transactional logic towards relational and value-based paradigms (Kotler & Armstrong, 2018).

The classical marketing mix, conceptualised through the 4Ps, Product, Price, Place and Promotion, remains foundational in strategic planning. Each element represents a controllable variable through which organisations position their offerings within target markets. Product concerns development, quality and brand identity. Price reflects exchange value and strategic positioning. Place addresses, distribution channels, and accessibility. Promotion encompasses communication strategies that aim to influence consumer perceptions and behaviour (Oliveira, 2007; Sampaio & Tavares, 2017).

Although the 4Ps framework emerged in a production-oriented context, its adaptability has enabled its integration into digital environments. The principles of value proposition, segmentation, and positioning continue to underpin marketing strategy, even as technological infrastructure evolves. Marketing thought has been further categorised into successive stages. Marketing 1.0, rooted in industrial expansion, prioritised efficiency and scale. Marketing 2.0 shifted the focus to consumers, recognising their growing informational power. Marketing 3.0 introduced human-centred, values-driven approaches that acknowledge emotional and societal dimensions (Kotler et al., 2010). Marketing 4.0 integrates digital platforms, connecting online and offline interactions. Marketing 5.0 represents the convergence of human orientation with advanced technological integration, particularly Artificial Intelligence (Kotler et al., 2021). And finally, Marketing 6.0 involves new technologies related to immersive experiences (Kotler et al., 2024).

The progression towards Marketing 5.0 and 6.0 reflects the increasing complexity of consumer behaviour. Consumers are no longer passive recipients of information. The new consumers actively participate in content creation, peer influence and brand co-creation. Digital environments intensify this interaction, generating massive quantities of behavioural data. The strategic challenge lies in transforming such data into actionable insights. In this sense, AI emerges as an enabling infrastructure.

1.2. Digital Marketing and the Transformation of Communication

The emergence of the Internet altered communication systems. In this context, digital marketing emerged as an extension of traditional marketing principles into online environments. It incorporates strategies such as content marketing, email marketing, social media engagement, online advertising and digital analytics (Rosa et al., 2017).

Digital marketing differs from traditional approaches in different key respects. It enables direct interaction with consumers, real-time performance measurement and precise segmentation. Unlike conventional mass communication channels, digital platforms allow personalised messaging and behavioural tracking (Gomes & Reis, 2016). Content marketing represents a central strategy within digital environments. Rather than focusing on product promotion, content marketing aims to create valuable, relevant and consistent material designed to attract and retain audiences. Through blogs, videos, infographics and social media posts, organisations build authority and foster engagement (Oliveira, 2021; Pulizzi, 2014).

Social media marketing has transformed organisational communication. Platforms such as Facebook, Instagram, LinkedIn, YouTube, TikTok, and X (formerly Twitter) serve as promotional channels and as interactive ecosystems. These platforms facilitate dialogue, user-generated content and peer influence. Engagement metrics such as likes, shares, comments, and reach allow organisations to evaluate effectiveness in real time (Oliveira, 2021).

The increasing integration of digital marketing strategies within small enterprises reflects broader societal digitalisation. Internet penetration rates and social media usage have expanded significantly, making a digital presence essential for organisational visibility. However, digital marketing also intensifies competition. Algorithms determine content visibility, and audiences are exposed to constant promotional stimuli. In such environments, differentiation requires more than presence. It requires strategic optimisation (Oliveira, 2021). The increasing demand for optimisation and personalisation creates an ideal environment for implementing Artificial Intelligence applications.

In this context, understanding consumer behaviour remains central to marketing theory. The consumer decision-making process involves multiple stages: recognition of need, information search, evaluation of alternatives, purchase decision, consumption, post-consumption evaluation and disposal (Pinto, 2016).

Digital environments modify these stages. Information search is facilitated through search engines, social media platforms and peer reviews. Evaluation of alternatives occurs rapidly due to immediate access to comparative data. Post-consumption evaluation is publicly expressed through online reviews and social sharing.

Psychological, social and technological factors influence consumer behaviour online. Exposure to digital stimuli, attention mechanisms, cognitive processing and memory retention all shape decision-making processes. Emotional triggers embedded in visual design, colour, motion and storytelling contribute to engagement and conversion (Silva & Tessarolo, 2016). Digital consumers also rely heavily on trust. Perceptions of security, data privacy and authenticity influence online purchasing behaviour. Peer and influencer recommendations significantly affect decision-making.

The integration of Artificial Intelligence into digital marketing strategies allows organisations to analyse behavioural data across these stages. By identifying patterns, predicting preferences and tailoring content, AI systems enhance strategic responsiveness (Medeiros et al., 2022). However, behavioural prediction raises ethical considerations related to privacy and data governance. The collection and processing of personal data must comply with applicable regulatory frameworks, particularly in the European Union, where the General Data Protection Regulation (GDPR) applies.

The theoretical intersection between consumer behaviour and Artificial Intelligence lies in predictive modelling. Algorithms analyse past interactions to forecast future actions. This predictive capacity reshapes marketing strategy from reactive communication to anticipatory engagement (Santos, 2024).

1.3. Artificial Intelligence and its application in digital marketing

Artificial Intelligence is broadly understood as the capability of computational systems to perform tasks that typically require human intelligence. These tasks include learning, reasoning, pattern recognition and decision-making (Antunes, 2023).

Within marketing contexts, AI systems process structured and unstructured data to generate insights. Machine Learning allows systems to learn from datasets without explicit programming instructions. Supervised learning uses labelled datasets to predict outcomes. Unsupervised learning identifies hidden patterns in unlabelled data. Reinforcement learning optimises actions through reward-based feedback mechanisms (Rodrigues, 2023). Deep Learning represents a more advanced form of Machine Learning. It employs neural network architectures composed of multiple layers, enabling the analysis of complex information such as images (Medeiros et al., 2022).

AI technologies relevant to digital marketing include chatbots for automated customer engagement, sentiment analysis tools, predictive analytics systems, recommendation engines, automated content creation tools, and data analytics dashboards (De Bruyn et al.,2020, Santos, 2024,). These tools revolutionise marketing operations in various ways. Automation alleviates manual workload and minimises human error, while predictive analytics improves the precision of campaigns. Personalisation significantly boosts engagement and conversion rates. The strategic advantage of AI lies in its scalability, enabling smaller enterprises to leverage AI tools for tasks that once required substantial human resources. Nevertheless, the successful adoption of these technologies depends on the organisation's readiness (Santos, 2024).

The integration of AI influences each component of the marketing mix. Product strategies can incorporate AI-driven insights into consumer preferences, enabling adaptive design and feature optimisation. Price strategies benefit from predictive modelling and demand forecasting. Distribution channels can be optimised through behavioural analysis. Promotion becomes highly personalised through algorithmic segmentation and targeted advertising (Santos, 2024). Artificial Intelligence enhances personalisation, one of the most significant dimensions of contemporary marketing. Personalisation involves tailoring content, offers and communication to individual consumer profiles. By tracking behaviour and analysing data, AI systems generate customised experiences.

The existing literature highlights key advantages of integrating AI into digital marketing, such as increased operational efficiency, reduced error rates, enhanced segmentation precision, real-time adaptability, cost optimisation, and improved strategic decision-making (Rodrigues 2023). Empirical research supports these benefits, with firms reporting heightened social media engagement, stronger customer relationships, and more assertive marketing campaigns.

However, adopting AI also poses notable challenges. Key barriers identified include a lack of technical expertise, a shortage of qualified professionals, and financial limitations. These obstacles are particularly pronounced within small enterprises, which often lack the dedicated data analysis teams or technological infrastructure that larger corporations possess. Data privacy concerns also constitute a relevant challenge. Ethical data processing and compliance with regulatory standards require institutional awareness and governance mechanisms (Rodrigues, 2023). The theoretical implication is that AI adoption is a technological decision added to an organisational transformation process.

The theoretical framework proposes that Artificial Intelligence operates within a broader digital transformation ecosystem. Contextual determinants, structural constraints and strategic imperatives shape its adoption in small enterprises. Marketing 5.0 provides a conceptual lens through which AI integration can be understood as an extension of human-centred marketing through technological augmentation.

Digital marketing platforms generate data flows that enable predictive modelling. Consumer behaviour theory explains how personalised engagement influences decision-making. Organisational theory highlights how resource constraints affect the adoption of innovation. Together, these theoretical dimensions form the foundation for analysing AI adoption dynamics within small enterprises.

2. METHODOLOGY

This study adopted a quantitative research design to examine the influence of Artificial Intelligence on digital marketing strategies in small enterprises, with particular emphasis on social media contexts. The research was guided by a main question seeking to understand how AI contributes to the optimisation and definition of digital marketing strategies within small firms. Based on the theoretical framework developed in the preceding section, the main aims were defined, alongside four research hypotheses designed to test associations between organisational characteristics and AI adoption patterns. In this sense, the objective is to analyse the use of AI in the strategies of digital marketing. In alignment with the aims of the study, the following research hypotheses (H) were formulated, taking into consideration the specific field of analysis:

> H_1: There is a difference in the perceived indispensability of Artificial Intelligence for Digital Marketing among firms with different levels of knowledge of AI.
> H_2: There is a significant association between the firm's sector of activity and the adoption of Artificial Intelligence in digital marketing strategies.
> H_3: There are differences between firms with a higher number of employees and their intention to invest in Artificial Intelligence in the future.
> H_4: There are differences between the longer duration of Digital Marketing use and the level of knowledge about Artificial Intelligence.

Data were collected through an online questionnaire developed using Google Forms. The instrument was structured into five thematic sections: company characterisation; knowledge and use of Artificial Intelligence; contribution of AI to digital marketing strategies; perceived advantages and limitations; and future investment intentions. Participation was restricted to respondents working in small enterprises that reported using digital marketing strategies. Furthermore, only firms that confirmed using Artificial Intelligence in their marketing practices completed the whole questionnaire, ensuring alignment between the research objectives and the collected data.

The questionnaire was disseminated via email and social media platforms, including LinkedIn and WhatsApp, from 25 May to 25 August 2025. A total of 105 responses were obtained. Of these, 74 respondents confirmed using digital marketing strategies, and 33 reported using Artificial Intelligence within those strategies. Consequently, the final analytical sample consisted of 33 small enterprises. The sampling approach used a non-probabilistic convenience sampling method, complemented by snowball sampling, given the difficulty of accessing firms actively using AI in marketing.

Data analysis was conducted using Jamovi. Descriptive statistics were employed to characterise the sample, including frequency distributions, means and standard deviations. Perceptual variables were measured using a five-point Likert scale ranging from "strongly disagree" to "strongly agree". To assess the reliability of the Likert-scale items, Cronbach's alpha was calculated, yielding a coefficient of 0.731, indicating moderate internal consistency. This reliability level was considered acceptable for exploratory research within the study's scope.

Inferential analysis was performed to test the four research hypotheses. The Chi-square test was initially applied to assess associations between categorical variables; however, when its assumptions were not met due to sample size limitations, Fisher's exact test was employed. Statistical significance was established at $p \leq 0.05$. Among the tested hypotheses, only the association between sector of activity and digital marketing adoption was statistically significant, while no significant relationships were found for the remaining variables. These analytical procedures enabled a structured examination of the relationship between organisational characteristics and AI integration within digital marketing strategies.

3. FINDINGS

3.1 Sample Characterisation

Before presenting the research hypotheses, it is essential to describe the characteristics of the study sample to contextualise the respondents' profile. This section outlines the firms' sector of activity, number of employees, duration of use of the Digital Marketing strategy, platforms employed, level of knowledge regarding AI, and perceptions of its indispensability in Digital Marketing.

In the first stage of the study, the sample consisted of 105 respondents distributed across three sectors of activity, with a predominance of the tertiary industry, representing 68 respondents (64.8%), followed by the secondary sector with 28 respondents (26.7%), and finally the primary sector with 9 respondents (8.6%). Regarding the number of employees, the majority of firms reported employing between 1 and 5 workers (32.4%), while 30.5% employed between 21 and 50 workers. Firms with between 6 and 10 employees accounted for 19.0% of the sample, and those employing between 11 and 20 represented 17.1%. These figures confirm that the sample predominantly consists of small enterprises (fewer than 50 employees) as reported by Ferreira (2023), reflecting the structure of the Portuguese business landscape, which, according to the National Institute of Statistics, is primarily composed of small and medium-sized enterprises.

Among the 105 respondents, 70.5% (74 participants) reported using Digital Marketing strategies. Conversely, 31 participants (29.5%) reported not employing Digital Marketing strategies. Given that the study's purpose was to understand the influence of AI on Digital Marketing, it was not methodologically appropriate for these 31 participants to continue responding. Consequently, the sample was reduced to 74 respondents. The characterisation of the 74 firms that reported using Digital Marketing strategies reveals that such practices remain relatively recent. Regarding the most frequently used platforms for Digital Marketing, Instagram was identified as the most widely adopted (90.54%), followed by Facebook (79.73%). LinkedIn (32.43%) and TikTok (27.03%). Other platforms, including Google, Glassdoor, company websites and paid advertising, presented residual values below 4%. These findings confirm that social media platforms constitute the primary Digital Marketing strategy for these small firms.

For a significant proportion of the sample, Digital Marketing adoption remains recent. Only 25 respondents (33.8%) reported using Digital Marketing strategies for more than 5 years, while 49 respondents (62.2%) reported using them for less than 5 years. This demonstrates that Digital Marketing remains an evolving and exploratory domain for many small enterprises. Regarding AI, the majority of respondents (68.9%) stated they were familiar with the concept, while 31.1% reported not being familiar with it.

The results indicate that while 51 respondents acknowledged familiarity with AI, only 33 reported utilising it as a tool in their Digital Marketing strategies. Furthermore, 41 participants did not incorporate AI into their Digital Marketing efforts, yet 22 expressed a desire to adopt it in the future. This gap between awareness and actual implementation suggests that AI remains in a growth phase, with significant barriers to adoption still present. To better understand the reasons behind non-adoption, those 41 participants were asked to identify the main barriers. The primary reason reported was lack of knowledge (80.49%). Other reasons included perceived lack of necessity (36.59%) and lack of financial resources (29.27%), while only one participant reported uncertainty about the reason for non-adoption.

Participants who reported using AI were asked to identify the benefits it had brought to their Digital Marketing strategies and, consequently, to their organisations. A substantial proportion (81.82%) reported increased interaction on social media platforms, while 57.58% highlighted improved customer relationships. Additional benefits included operational cost reduction (48.48%) and increased campaign precision (51.52%). These findings suggest that AI is perceived as contributing to both relational and efficiency-related outcomes.

Among the 33 participants who reported using AI, respondents were asked whether they intended to invest further in AI solutions. Despite recognising the benefits of AI adoption, 18 respondents (54.5%) indicated uncertainty regarding future investment, while 15 respondents (45.5%) confirmed their intention to invest in additional AI solutions. Notably, no participant stated that they did not intend to invest in AI in the future. Within the subgroup of 15 respondents who expressed an intention to invest further, 60% indicated they would prioritise advertising platforms. Additionally, 46.67% reported plans to adopt sentiment analysis tools, while 26.67% mentioned chatbots for customer service and 26.67% content automation tools. Two participants (13.33%) stated that they were still evaluating which tools to adopt.

In line with the study's aim, respondents who indicated they did not use Artificial Intelligence in their Digital Marketing strategies did not proceed to the next section of the questionnaire. Consequently, the 33 participants who confirmed AI use were considered the final analytical sample (n = 33). As a final question, respondents were asked about their perception of the indispensability of Artificial Intelligence in Digital Marketing strategies. Although many participants expressed uncertainty about further investment, 26 respondents (78.8%) stated that AI would become indispensable in Digital Marketing, while 18.2% expressed uncertainty about its indispensability.

These results indicate a strong recognition of the strategic relevance of Artificial Intelligence in Digital Marketing practices. Throughout the data analysis, respondents identified both challenges and advantages associated with AI adoption (Table 1). The most frequently cited challenge was "lack of technical knowledge and/or qualified professionals" (24 responses). The second and third-most-cited challenges were difficulty integrating Artificial Intelligence into existing Digital Marketing practices (14 responses) and concerns regarding data privacy (12 responses), respectively. Financial problems, specifically the high implementation cost of Artificial Intelligence, received the fewest responses (8).

Conversely, several advantages were identified. Respondents highlighted improved decision-making agility (22 responses, 66.67%), reduced operational costs (20 responses, 60.61%), reduced errors (17 responses, 51.52%), and increased efficiency in audience segmentation (14 responses, 42.42%). These findings demonstrate that, while structural and knowledge-based barriers remain significant, firms recognise substantial operational and strategic benefits from integrating Artificial Intelligence.

Table 1. Main challenges and advantages of AI in digital marketing

Variable	n	%
Main Challenges of AI in Digital Marketing		
Lack of technical knowledge and/or qualified professionals	24	72.73
High implementation cost	8	24.24
Difficulty integrating Artificial Intelligence into Digital Marketing practices	14	42.42
Data privacy concerns	12	36.36
Main Advantages of AI in Digital Marketing		
Agility in decision-making	22	66.67
Efficiency in audience segmentation	14	42.42
Reduction of operational costs	20	60.61
Error reduction	17	51.52

Note. Percentages are calculated based on the total number of respondents who reported using Artificial Intelligence (n = 33). Multiple responses were allowed.

In summary, the sample in this study comprises predominantly small enterprises operating in the tertiary sector. As small organisations, these firms face structural limitations in human and financial resources, which directly affect their capacity for technological innovation. The significant concentration in the tertiary sector reflects a stronger orientation towards direct consumer interaction, thereby increasing the need to adopt digital strategies, communication channels, and marketing tools.

The findings indicate a growing adoption of Digital Marketing strategies. However, such practices remain relatively recent within this organisational context. Regarding AI, most respondents demonstrate familiarity with the concept, yet its practical application in Digital Marketing strategies remains limited. The principal barrier identified is the lack of technical knowledge, along with concerns about implementation costs.

Despite these constraints, there is clear recognition of AI's strategic relevance. A substantial proportion of the sample believes AI will become indispensable in Digital Marketing and intends to invest in AI-based solutions. The data suggest that firms are currently experiencing a transitional phase, in which AI is gradually being incorporated into business practices, fostering digital evolution and process innovation.

Nevertheless, the structural characteristics of small enterprises may explain the slower pace of implementation. Smaller firms tend to prioritise short-term initiatives and cost-efficient strategies, avoiding substantial investments that may entail higher risk. As a result, although digital transformation is underway, it remains a process of consolidation, centred on learning, experimentation and gradual integration.

Regarding the preferred communication channels identified in the results, these are platforms with strong organic reach potential and visual identity, reinforcing the notion that small enterprises seek measurable returns through controlled investment, engagement and brand exposure. Throughout the sample characterisation, it became evident that AI can generate significant organisational benefits, including increased efficiency through process automation, cost reduction, and strategic improvement through personalisation and enhanced customer experience.

Overall, firms acknowledge the value and potential impact of technological innovation. However, investment decisions remain cautious, particularly when risks, costs and perceived disadvantages are considered. Future investment priorities focus on tools that enhance visibility, automation and return on investment. In essence, this study centres on a group of enterprises characterised by limited resources but considerable digital growth potential, thereby enabling a comprehensive understanding of the challenges and benefits of adopting AI tools.

3.2 Analysis of the Use of Artificial Intelligence in Digital Marketing

The use of AI in Digital Marketing was subsequently analysed to assess respondents' perceptions of its impact on brand visibility, campaign personalisation, data analysis support, and decision-making processes. Each item was evaluated on a five-point Likert scale, ranging from 1 = Strongly disagree to 5 = Strongly agree. It is important to note that only the 33 companies that use AI responded to this block of questions, as they had the most knowledge on the subject (Table 2).

A substantial majority of respondents (94%) either agreed or strongly agreed that Digital Marketing has a significant impact and is crucial for brand growth through increased visibility. This dimension had the highest mean score (M = 4.73, SD = 0.574), indicating strong recognition of the strategic role of Digital Marketing in enhancing organisational visibility and brand awareness. Regarding the impact of campaign personalisation, respondents demonstrated consensus on its positive effects. A total of 87.9% (29 respondents; M = 4.64, SD = 0.783) agreed that campaign personalisation has a positive impact on the organisation. Simultaneously, the same proportion of respondents (87.9%; M = 1.30, SD = 0.684) disagreed with the statement that campaign personalisation negatively affects the company. The relatively low mean score of 1.30 reflects strong disagreement with the negative framing of personalisation. Given that the Likert scale assigns 1 to "Strongly disagree" and 2 to "Disagree", these results confirm that most participants reject the notion that personalisation has adverse consequences. This result aligns with the literature, highlighting the importance and relevance of personalisation in Digital Marketing through the use of AI tools. When AI is incorporated into Digital Marketing strategies, respondents' perceptions remain favourable. A total of 28 respondents (84.9%) agreed that Artificial Intelligence can significantly enhance campaign personalisation (M = 4.33, SD = 0.736), reinforcing the perceived alignment between AI technologies and customisation practices.

Regarding the broader role of AI, the findings indicate a positive overall perception. The dimensions considered most relevant were AI's support for content personalisation (M = 4.48, SD = 0.755), with 30 respondents (90.9%) agreeing, and real-time adaptation of marketing strategies (M = 4.58, SD = 0.614), with 31 respondents (93.9%) agreeing. These high mean scores suggest that AI is primarily valued for its capacity to increase agility and responsiveness in Digital Marketing processes.

Other dimensions, while still positively evaluated, presented slightly lower mean values. These include AI support in selecting appropriate channels and timing for advertising (M = 4.39, SD = 0.827), data analysis for decision-making (M = 4.06, SD = 0.864), and prediction of consumer behaviour (M = 4.03, SD = 0.951). Although these mean scores remain above the midpoint of the scale, indicating overall agreement, they reflect comparatively greater variability in responses. This suggests that while respondents recognise the utility of AI in these areas, they may be less familiar with, or have lower levels of, implementation in more analytically complex applications.

Table 2. Means of the use of AI in digital marketing

Item	1 n (%)	2 n (%)	3 n (%)	4 n (%)	5 n (%)	M (SD)
Digital Marketing impacts company visibility	0(0)	0(0)	2(6.1)	5(15.2)	26(78.8)	4.73(0.574)
Personalisation of Digital Marketing campaigns negatively impacts the company	27(81.8)	2(6.1)	4(12.1)	0 (0)	0(0)	1.30(0.684)
Personalisation of Digital Marketing campaigns positively impacts the company	0(0)	1(3.0)	3(9.1)	3(9.1)	26(78.8)	4.64(0.783)
AI impacts the personalisation of Digital Marketing campaigns	0(0)	0(0)	5(15.2)	12(36.4)	16(48.5)	4.33(0.736)
AI supports data analysis for decision-making in Digital Marketing campaigns	0(0)	1(3.0)	8(24.2)	12(36.4)	12(36.4)	4.06(0.864)
AI supports the creation of personalised content	0 (0)	1(3.0)	2 (6.1)	10(30.3)	20(60.6)	4.48(0.755)
AI supports the selection of optimal channels and timing for advertising	0 (0)	1 (3.0)	4 (12.1)	9 (27.3)	19 (57.6)	4.39(0.827)
AI supports the prediction of consumer behaviour	0 (0)	2 (6.1)	8 (24.2)	10(30.3)	13 (39.4)	4.03(0.951)
AI supports real-time adaptation of strategies	0 (0)	0 (0)	2 (6.1)	10(30.3)	21 (63.6)	4.58(0.614)

Note: 1 = Strongly Disagree; 2 = Disagree; 3 = Neither Agree nor Disagree; 4 = Agree; 5 = Strongly Agree

Overall, the variables related to content personalisation and real-time strategic adaptation achieved the highest mean values, reinforcing the perception of AI as an instrument of efficiency and agility in Digital Marketing processes. Even within small enterprises, AI is perceived as enabling responsiveness to rapid and dynamic changes in consumer behaviour.

Conversely, the comparatively lower mean scores observed for data analysis and behavioural prediction indicate that participating firms may be at an early stage of technological integration. These dimensions typically require more advanced analytical infrastructure and specialised expertise, which may explain the more cautious evaluation. It is noteworthy that the most highly valued variables, content personalisation and real-time adaptation, are directly linked to consumer experience on social media platforms. These findings align with the increasing consumer-centric orientation of Digital Marketing strategies. They align with the perspective of Kotler et al. (2017), who argue that marketing has evolved toward continuous consumer engagement and interaction.

From a practical perspective, the results suggest that firms should prioritise AI tools that significantly enhance customer experience, such as recommendation systems, customer service chatbots and campaign automation mechanisms. Such tools may offer measurable returns with controlled investment, particularly as AI technologies become increasingly accessible. Over time, it is expected that broader analytical applications, including advanced data optimisation and social media trend prediction, will gain prominence as firms develop greater digital maturity.

The findings indicate an evident appreciation of Artificial Intelligence as a tool that strengthens personalisation, analysis and decision-making processes within Digital Marketing. Although AI integration remains uneven across firms and levels of implementation vary, the general perception is of a progressive incorporation of AI into marketing strategies. This trajectory is consistent with the ongoing digital transformations observed in contemporary markets (Antunes, 2023).

In general, the analysed perceptions reveal an optimistic yet cautious stance regarding the integration of AI in the definition of Digital Marketing strategies. AI is recognised as a strategic tool that can strengthen competitiveness. However, its adoption remains dependent on available resources and each firm's level of digital development. For this reason, it is necessary to test the research hypotheses defined in this study to rigorously understand the relationships between organisational variables and the degree of Artificial Intelligence implementation in Digital Marketing strategies.

3.3 Hypothesis Testing

Subsequently, the research hypotheses were tested to examine the relationships between organisational characteristics and AI in the context of Digital Marketing. Given that several contingency tables did not meet the assumptions required for the Chi-square test, Fisher's exact test was applied whenever appropriate.

> H_1: There is a difference in the perceived indispensability of Artificial Intelligence for Digital Marketing among firms with different levels of knowledge of AI.

This hypothesis examined whether firms with higher levels of knowledge of Artificial Intelligence are more likely to perceive AI as indispensable in Digital Marketing. As the assumptions for the Chi-square test were not satisfied, Fisher's exact test was conducted. The results revealed no statistically significant association between AI knowledge and perceived indispensability ($p = 1.000$). Therefore, H1 is not supported. From a descriptive perspective, however, a positive tendency can be observed. Among firms reporting knowledge of Artificial Intelligence ($n = 25$), the majority considered it indispensable, with only one respondent expressing a contrary opinion. The lack of statistical significance may be due to the small sample size ($n = 33$) and the low variability in responses, as most participants ($n = 26$) recognised AI as valuable regardless of their level of knowledge. This suggests that the perception of AI indispensability may already be embedded in organisational culture, independently of formal expertise.

H_2: There is a significant association between the firm's sector of activity and the adoption of Artificial Intelligence in Digital Marketing strategies.

Here, it was analysed whether a significant association exists between firms' sector of activity and the adoption of Digital Marketing strategies. In this study, the use of Digital Marketing was considered an indicator of predisposition towards future AI integration, as the questionnaire assessed Digital Marketing adoption in general rather than AI use specifically. Given unmet assumptions for the Chi-square test, Fisher's exact test was applied. The results were statistically significant ($p < .001$), supporting H_2.

The distribution of responses shows clear sectoral asymmetries. None of the firms operating in the Primary Sector reported using Digital Marketing strategies. In contrast, firms in the Secondary Sector ($n = 19$) and particularly in the Tertiary Sector ($n = 55$) reported active use of Digital Marketing. These findings indicate that firms in sectors closer to final consumers, especially service-oriented activities, demonstrate higher levels of digital maturity and a greater predisposition to integrate Artificial Intelligence. Conversely, the Primary Sector, which in this study includes agriculture, forestry and mining, tends to exhibit lower technological intensity and digital adoption

H_3: There are differences between firms with a higher number of employees and their intention to invest in Artificial Intelligence in the future.

This hypothesis sought to determine whether firm size, measured by the number of employees, influences future intentions to invest in AI. Due to unmet assumptions, Fisher's exact test was conducted. The results indicated no statistically significant association between number of employees and intention to invest in AI ($p = .534$). Consequently, H_3 is not supported.

Although the relationship is not statistically significant, descriptive analysis suggests a slight increase in investment intention among firms with a larger workforce. For example, among firms employing 1-5 workers, only two respondents reported future AI investment. In firms with 6-10 employees, five respondents expressed investment intention. Among those with 11-20 employees, three respondents, and among firms with 21-50 employees, four respondents indicated future investment. The lack of statistical significance may be attributed to the restricted sample size and the concentration on small enterprises, where financial constraints and limited technological resources may moderate investment decisions regardless of workforce size.

H_4: There are differences between longer duration of Digital Marketing use and knowledge of Artificial Intelligence.

H_4 examined whether firms with longer experience in using Digital Marketing strategies demonstrate higher levels of AI knowledge. Fisher's exact test yielded a non-significant result ($p = .945$), indicating no statistically significant association between duration of Digital Marketing use and AI knowledge. Thus, H_4 is not supported.

Descriptive evidence shows that firms with less experience and those with more than five years of Digital Marketing experience reported high levels of AI knowledge. This finding suggests that AI knowledge may depend on factors beyond experience in Digital Marketing, such as educational background, professional exposure, organisational learning processes, or sectoral characteristics, as partially indicated by H_2.

Table 3 summarises the hypothesis testing results. Among the four hypotheses examined, only H_2 was statistically supported, confirming that the sector of activity significantly influences Digital Marketing adoption and predisposition towards AI integration. The remaining hypotheses (H_1, H_3 and H_4) were not statistically validated.

Table 3. Means of the use of AI in digital marketing

Hypothesis	p-value	Result
H_1: **There is a difference in the perceived indispensability of Artificial Intelligence for Digital Marketing among firms with different levels of knowledge of AI.**	1.000	Not supported
H_2: **There is a significant association between the firm's sector of activity and the adoption of Artificial Intelligence in Digital Marketing strategies.**	< .0001	Supported
H_3: **There are differences between firms with a higher number of employees and their intention to invest in Artificial Intelligence in the future.**	.534	Not supported
H_4: **There are differences between longer duration of Digital Marketing use and knowledge of Artificial Intelligence**	.945	Not supported

These results indicate that sectoral context plays a decisive role in shaping digital behaviour, whereas firm size, duration of Digital Marketing experience and declared knowledge of AI appear to exert a less direct influence. Importantly, the absence of statistical significance does not necessarily imply theoretical irrelevance. Rather, it may reflect limited statistical power due to the small sample size in the AI-specific phase ($n = 33$) and the restricted range of responses.

Despite cautious adoption patterns, Artificial Intelligence is widely perceived as promising. Notably, 78.8% of respondents consider AI likely to become indispensable in Digital Marketing. Resistance to adoption is more visible in the Primary and Secondary Sectors, where technological infrastructure, financial capacity and access to qualified professionals are more limited. Key barriers include a lack of technical expertise, scarcity of specialised human capital and high implementation costs, particularly for growing firms.

From a practical perspective, these findings suggest the need for phased and progressive AI implementation strategies in small enterprises. Initial adoption may focus on accessible and lower-cost tools, such as customer service chatbots or automated content recommendation systems. Partnerships with technology providers and higher education institutions may facilitate knowledge transfer and reduce digital skill gaps. Additionally, targeted financial support mechanisms for technological innovation could promote broader AI integration.

The present findings reflect a transitional stage in the digital transformation of small enterprises. While AI is recognised as a strategic instrument capable of enhancing efficiency, personalisation, and competitiveness, its full integration remains contingent on organisational learning, resource availability, and sectoral dynamics.

DISCUSSION AND FINAL CONSIDERATION

The purpose of this study was to examine the role of Artificial Intelligence in Digital Marketing strategies within small enterprises, with particular emphasis on social media contexts. The findings provide insight into adoption patterns, perceived benefits, structural constraints and contextual determinants influencing AI integration. This discussion interprets the empirical results within the theoretical framework presented, particularly Marketing 5.0 and 6.0, digital transformation theory, and a consumer-centric strategic orientation.

The analysis reveals a transitional stage of technological integration. Artificial Intelligence is recognised as strategically relevant. However, its implementation remains uneven, influenced by sectoral context and structural limitations. One of the findings is the recognition that Digital Marketing is crucial to brand visibility. With a mean score of 4.73 and 94% agreement, respondents demonstrate near-consensus on the centrality of digital channels to organisational growth. This aligns with the theoretical understanding that Digital Marketing has become an essential strategic infrastructure rather than a complementary communication tool (Gomes & Reis, 2016).

The predominance of Instagram and further reinforces the importance of visual engagement and real-time interaction. These platforms enable cost-efficient visibility, particularly relevant for small enterprises operating under financial constraints. The reliance on social media confirms that firms prioritise channels that generate organic reach and measurable engagement (Oliveira, 2021).

From a theoretical perspective, this finding is consistent with Marketing 4.0 principles, which hold that digital platforms serve as hybrid interaction spaces that integrate communication, analytics, and relationship-building functions. However, the emphasis on visibility also indicates that many firms remain in an operational stage of digital transformation, where presence and engagement metrics are prioritised over advanced analytical optimisation.

The results demonstrate consensus regarding the positive impact of campaign personalisation. Simultaneously, respondents reject the notion that personalisation negatively affects the company. This outcome suggests that personalisation is not perceived as risky or intrusive within the sample, but rather as a strategic enhancement, as identified in previous literature, where the possibility of customisation was clearly demonstrated (e.g., Antunes, 2023; Peretti et al., 2021).

When Artificial Intelligence is incorporated into this equation, perceptions remain favourable. AI is therefore also recognised as a facilitator of personalisation, reinforcing Marketing 5.0 principles that emphasise technology augmenting human-centred engagement. Notably, the highest-rated AI-related dimensions were content personalisation and real-time strategy adaptation. These findings are theoretically coherent. In digital environments characterised by rapid behavioural shifts, agility becomes a competitive advantage. AI systems enable immediate adjustment to consumer feedback, social media trends and engagement patterns.

This emphasis on agility and personalisation reflects a consumer-centric paradigm. As Kotler et al. (2024) argue, marketing has evolved towards continuous interaction and co-creation with consumers. The findings support this trajectory. Small enterprises value AI primarily for its ability to enhance responsiveness and engagement rather than for complex predictive modelling.

While overall perceptions of AI are positive, comparatively lower mean scores were observed for data analysis and consumer behaviour prediction. Although these values remain above the midpoint, they indicate a more cautious level of agreement. This distinction is theoretically significant. Analytical functions such as predictive modelling require higher levels of digital maturity, data infrastructure and specialised expertise. The lower evaluation of these dimensions suggests that firms are at an early stage of AI integration, prioritising operational tools over advanced analytics.

One of the most interesting findings concerns Hypothesis 1. Despite high recognition of AI's indispensability, no statistically significant association was found between knowledge level and perception of indispensability. This suggests that the perception of AI as essential may be culturally embedded rather than knowledge dependent. Even firms with limited technical understanding recognise AI's strategic relevance. This phenomenon may reflect broader societal narratives surrounding Artificial Intelligence and digital transformation. From an organisational culture perspective, technological legitimacy may precede technical mastery. Firms may accept AI as inevitable before fully integrating it into operational practice. This finding reinforces the idea that adoption is influenced by symbolic and normative factors rather than solely by competence.

Hypothesis 2 was the only hypothesis statistically validated, confirming a significant association between sector of activity and Digital Marketing adoption. This result is structurally coherent. The Tertiary Sector, characterised by direct consumer interaction, demonstrates higher engagement with Digital Marketing and, consequently, stronger predisposition towards AI adoption. Conversely, the Primary Sector, largely composed of agriculture, forestry and mining within this sample, shows limited digital engagement.

Sectoral proximity to consumers increases the need for visibility, engagement and personalisation. AI adoption, therefore, becomes more strategically relevant in consumer-facing environments. The empirical validation of H_2 confirms that the contextual environment exerts greater influence than internal structural variables, such as the number of employees or the duration of Digital Marketing use. This finding suggests that technological adoption in small enterprises is externally driven rather than internally scaled.

Hypothesis 3 tested the relationship between the number of employees and intention to invest in AI. No statistically significant association was found. Although slight tendencies suggest that larger firms express greater investment intentions, these differences are not statistically robust. This result highlights that workforce size alone does not determine technological ambition. Small enterprises may face similar financial constraints despite minor variations in employee numbers. Investment decisions appear to be shaped more by strategic orientation and sectoral dynamics than by organisational scale. Furthermore, over half of the respondents expressing uncertainty about future AI investment indicates cautious decision-making. Even when benefits are recognised, risk assessment and financial prudence remain central considerations.

Hypothesis 4 examined whether longer use of Digital Marketing correlates with greater AI knowledge. The absence of statistical significance indicates that experience in Digital Marketing does not automatically translate into AI competence. This finding suggests that AI knowledge may stem from external sources, such as professional training, personal interest, or sectoral exposure, rather than experiential accumulation within Digital Marketing practices. It also reinforces the idea that AI integration requires specific technical learning rather than incremental extension of traditional digital marketing skills.

The primary barrier identified was a lack of technical knowledge, followed by integration difficulty and data privacy concerns. Financial cost, although relevant, was less frequently cited. This hierarchy of barriers indicates that human capital constraints outweigh financial limitations. AI adoption requires financial investment, as well as digital literacy and organisational competence.

From an organisational-readiness perspective, successful AI integration depends on digital infrastructure, skilled human capital, strategic clarity, and cultural openness to innovation. The shortage of qualified professionals creates a bottleneck to adoption, particularly in small enterprises. Despite barriers, firms identified substantial advantages, including greater decision-making agility, lower operational costs, and fewer errors. These benefits align with the theoretical argument that AI enhances efficiency and strategic precision (Rodrigues, 2023). Even at early implementation stages, firms perceive tangible improvements. The recognition of segmentation efficiency and decision-making agility indicates that AI is valued for both relational and operational dimensions.

Collectively, the findings suggest that small enterprises are experiencing a transitional phase of digital transformation. AI is widely recognised as strategically relevant, yet implementation remains incremental and sector dependent. This transitional dynamic reflects a broader digital evolution. Firms prioritise accessible tools such as chatbots and advertising platforms before engaging in advanced predictive analytics. The gradual nature of adoption supports the phased integration model proposed earlier. AI implementation appears to follow a pathway from visibility enhancement to analytical optimisation.

Although this research provides meaningful insights into Artificial Intelligence and its influence on Digital Marketing, certain limitations must be acknowledged. The reduced sample size in the final stage ($n = 33$) restricts the generalisability of the findings, as reflected in the Cronbach's alpha coefficient. Additionally, as the questionnaire was administered entirely online, firms with stronger digital presence may have been overrepresented. To address these limitations, future research should consider larger, more diverse samples, encompass firms of varying sizes and sectors, and employ data collection methods capable of reaching organisations regardless of their level of digital involvement. Longitudinal studies are also recommended in order to monitor the evolution of digital maturity and AI adoption over time.

Although Digital Marketing is now a consolidated strategy within small enterprises, Artificial Intelligence remains an emerging reality. Nevertheless, given its recognised benefits and strategic relevance, it is likely to become an essential component of Digital Marketing in the future. In conclusion, Artificial Intelligence is recognised as a promising and strategically relevant tool in Digital Marketing within small enterprises. However, its adoption is primarily shaped by sectoral context and constrained by knowledge deficits rather than by organisational size or experience.

The results reflect cautious optimism. AI is perceived as indispensable in the near future, yet firms remain in a phase of consolidation and learning. This transitional stage underscores the need for progressive integration strategies, investment in digital literacy and sector-sensitive policy support to enable sustainable AI adoption within small enterprises. Practically, the results suggest that policy interventions should focus on digital training and knowledge transfer rather than solely on financial subsidies. Partnerships with educational institutions and technology providers may reduce knowledge gaps.

PRACTICAL IMPLICATIONS AND RECOMMENDATIONS

Although the participants in this study perceive a positive impact of Artificial Intelligence on Digital Marketing strategies, its implementation remains at a relatively early stage due to several adoption barriers. Among the main challenges identified by respondents, the lack of knowledge on the subject and/or the shortage of qualified professionals stand out. However, they also highlighted limited financial resources, a perceived lack of necessity, high implementation costs, difficulty integrating Artificial Intelligence into Digital Marketing strategies, and ongoing concerns about the privacy of personal data.

In light of these findings, a set of strategic recommendations will be presented below (Table 4) to mitigate these barriers and support small enterprises in the gradual implementation of Artificial Intelligence within their Digital Marketing strategies.

The implementation of the strategic recommendations outlined above may contribute to a more inclusive and efficient digital evolution and transition, mitigating the identified barriers and strengthening the integration and use of Artificial Intelligence as a necessary tool for competitiveness and innovation.

As small enterprises continue to evolve within the digital landscape, it is expected that these practices will guide them towards a business environment that is prepared and confident in keeping pace with technological advancements, the demands of the digital ecosystem, and, above all, the expectations and requirements of the contemporary consumer.

Table 4. Strategic recommendation

Barrier	Strategic Recommendation
Lack of knowledge on the subject and/or shortage of qualified professionals	Continuous training: A strategy that may address the knowledge gap, potentially incorporated into mandatory annual training programmes. Firms should encourage all forms of learning, and within the current context, this should include training in emerging technologies, data analysis and consumer behaviour. To develop digital competencies, partnerships with higher education institutions may be established to stimulate a digital culture and transform Artificial Intelligence into an operational practice.
Limited financial resources	Adoption of low-cost tools in the initial phase: AI implementation should be gradual and strategically planned. Early-stage adoption may focus on affordable solutions capable of generating measurable impact and increasing efficiency, such as chatbots, virtual assistants, content automation tools and recommendation systems.
Difficulty integrating AI into Digital Marketing strategies	Collaboration with digital agencies or specialised AI software companies: Such partnerships may accelerate implementation processes and provide ongoing support. They may also reduce costs by granting access to technological infrastructure and specialised human resources that would otherwise require significant internal investment.
High implementation cost	Public and/or private incentives and innovation funding schemes: Financial support mechanisms aimed at promoting technological innovation may enable firms to adopt AI solutions without compromising financial sustainability.
Concerns regarding personal data privacy and security	Data collection and processing policies and encryption technologies: To build consumer trust, the implementation of encryption technologies and robust data governance policies is essential. Ensuring secure handling of personal data increases consumer confidence in sharing information, thereby enhancing the firm's credibility, reputation and competitive positioning.

Although the study was limited to a small group of Portuguese companies, it is important to note that these results highlighted the importance and relevance of using AI in Marketing strategies, and these strategic recommendations may help to support and expand the use of AI not only in small businesses in the tertiary sector, but also in larger companies across all productive sectors.

REFERENCES

Antunes, D. P. S. (2023). O Impacto da inteligência artificial no marketing digital. *Revista Técnica de Tendências em Comunicação Empresarial,* 3, 1–9. DOI: 10.34630/tth.vi3.5085

Bragança, F. F. C., Zaccaria, R. B., Giuliani, A. C., & Pitomba, T. C. D. D. T. (2016). Marketing, criatividade e inovação em unidades de Informação. *Revista Brasileira de Marketing*, *15*(2), 237–245. DOI: 10.5585/remark.v15i2.3277

De Bruyn, A., Viswanathan, V., Beh, Y. S., Brock, J. K.-U., & Von Wangenheim, F. (2020). Artificial intelligence and marketing: pitfalls and opportunities. journal of interactive Marketing, 51(1), 91–105. DOI: 10.1016/j.intmar.2020.04.007

Ferreira, C. (2023). O impacto da economia digital e do e-commerce nas PME [Master's Thesis, European Business School]. Repositório Comum. https://comum.rcaap.pt/bitstream/10400.26/47938/1/Relatorio%20de%20estagio_Cristiano%20Ferreira_04.08_signed.pdf

Gomes, C. F., & Reis, H. M. (2016). Marketing digital: sites X redes sociais no Brasil. *Revista Interface Tecnológica da FATEC* Taquaritinga, 53–62. https://revista.fatectq.edu.br/interfacetecnologica/en/article/view/101

Kotler, P., & Armstrong, G. (2018). *Principles of marketing 17th* [edition]. Pearson Higher Education.

Kotler, P., Kartajaya, H., & Setiawan, I. (2010). *Marketing 3.0: from products to customers to the human spirit*. Elsevier Editora Ltda. DOI: 10.1002/9781118257883

Kotler, P., Kartajaya, H., & Setiawan, I. (2017). *Marketing 4.0: moving from traditional to digital.* Wiley.

Kotler, P., Kartajaya, H., & Setiawan, I. (2021). *Marketing 5.0: Technology for Humanity.* Wiley.

Kotler, P., Kartajaya, H., & Setiawan, I. (2024). *Marketing 6.0: The Future Is Immersive.* Wiley.

Kotler, P., & Keller, K. (2010). *Marketing Management* (14th ed.). Pearson Education.

Kury, G., & Gomes, M. (2013). A evolução do marketing para o marketing 3.0: o marketing de causa. *Intercom.* Sociedade Brasileira de Estudos Interdisciplinares da Comunicação, 1–11.

Medeiros, A.Jr, Amorim, B. P., Tabata, P. I., & Felicissimo, V. R. C. (2022). Os impactos da inteligência artificial nas estratégias de marketing. *Revista Fatec Zona Sul*, *9*(1), 1–24. DOI: 10.26853/Refas_ISSN-2359-182X_v09n01_02

Minuzzi, G., & Larentis, F. (2014). Marketing: definições, aplicações, tendências e desafios do profissional. Revista de Administração IMED, 4(1), 80–97. https://dialnet.unirioja.es/servlet/articulo?codigo=5061375

Oliveira, C. F. (2021). Um estudo sobre o uso das mídias sociais como ferramenta de negócios e seus impactos no comportamento do consumidor. [Master's Thesis, Universidade Federal do Amazonas]. https://riu.ufam.edu.br/handle/prefix/5930

Oliveira, S. (2007). Desmistificando o Marketing. Novatec (Ed.), Desmistificando o Marketing (pp. 20-41). Novatec Editorial. https://s3.novatec.com.br/capitulos/capitulo-9788575221136.pdf

Peretti, B. de C., Ribeiro, L. G., Assunção, R. A., Santos, R. G., & Leme, S. (2021). A evolução do Marketing Digital. [Master's Thesis, Escola técnica estadual da Zona Leste]. http://ric.cps.sp.gov.br/handle/123456789/10291

Pinto, H. (2016). Marketing Digital nas Micro e PME [Master's Thesis, Instituto Politécnico do Porto - Instituto Superior de Contabilidade e Administração]. https://recipp.ipp.pt/entities/publication/f81760f5-396a-42ff-b5a9-dcf48209c1c4

Pulizzi, J. (2014). *Epic content marketing: How to tell a different story, break through the clutter, and win more customers by marketing less*. McGraw-Hill Education.

Raupp, N. B., & Janssen, L. A. (2023). Utilização de inteligência artificial em ações de marketing digital personalizadas em redes sociais: Uma comparação entre as perceções dos consumidores das gerações X e Z. *Escola de Negócios,* 1-29. https://hdl.handle.net/10923/26256

Rodrigues, R. (2023). Uso da Inteligência Artificial e Algoritmos no Marketing Digital: O Caso da Amazon [Master's Thesis, Instituto Politécnico de Coimbra - Coimbra Business School]. http://hdl.handle.net/10400.26/48934

Rosa, R., Gomes Casagranda, Y., & Spinelli, F. E. (2017). A importância do marketing digital utilizando a influência do comportamento do consumidor. *Revista de Tecnologia Aplicada*, *6*(2), 28–39. DOI: 10.21714/2237-3713rta2017v6n2p28

Sampaio, V., & Tavares, C. (2017). Marketing digital: O poder de influência das redes sociais na decisão de compra do consumidor universitário da cidade de Juazeiro do Norte-CE. *Revista Científica Semana Acadêmica*, *1*, 1–26.

Santos, P. M. C. (2024). A utilização da Inteligência Artificial para a criação de conhecimento: Impacto na tomada de decisão de marketing e performance do negócio [Master's Thesis, Instituto Politécnico de Leiria - Escola superior de tecnologia e gestão]. http://hdl.handle.net/10400.8/10307

Silva, C. R. M., & Tessarolo, F. M. (2016). Influenciadores digitais e as redes sociais enquanto plataformas de mídia. Intercom- Sociedade Brasileira de *Estudos Interdisciplinares da Comunicação,* 1-13.

Chapter 6
Artificial Intelligence and the Evolution of Human Communication in Light of the Axioms of Communication

Ana Galvão
http://orcid.org/0000-0001-9978-9563
Instituto Politécnico de Bragança, Portugal

Sílvia Maria Fernandes Ala
http://orcid.org/0000-0001-5340-3864
Instituto Politécnico de Bragança, Portugal

Gorete Baptista
http://orcid.org/0000-0002-6750-1825
Instituto Politécnico de Bragança, Portugal

ABSTRACT

This chapter examines the evolution of human communication in the context of Artificial Intelligence (AI) through a scoping review of the literature. Grounded in the axioms of human communication of the Palo Alto School, the analysis explores how contemporary research conceptualizes human-AI interaction, relational dynamics, emotional engagement, trust, and agency. Following PRISMA-ScR guidelines, fifteen scientific articles were systematically reviewed to map dominant conceptual frameworks. Findings indicate a significant expansion of empirical research on human-AI communication, albeit accompanied by theoretical fragmentation regarding integra-

DOI: 10.4018/979-8-3373-8337-8.ch006

tion of classical communication theory. By articulating AI-mediated communication with foundational axioms, this chapter proposes an integrative relational framework that situates AI within the historical continuum of communicational evolution. This approach reinforces the explanatory relevance of communication theory, providing conceptual tools for future research on meaning-making, relationships, and power in AI-mediated environments.

INTRODUCTION

Human communication constitutes one of the structuring pillars of social life, playing a central role in the construction of meaning, the organization of interpersonal and institutional relationships, and the production of shared symbolic realities. Far from being reduced to a simple mechanism of information transmission, communication is configured as a complex relational process, in which cognitive, emotional, cultural, and pragmatic dimensions are articulated. It is through communication that individuals construct identities, negotiate meanings, regulate behaviors, and establish social bonds, making it a constitutive phenomenon of human experience and of the very organization of societies (Berger & Luckmann, 1966; Watzlawick et al., 1967).

Throughout history, modes of communication have transformed into close articulation with technological, cultural, and cognitive changes, in a cumulative, dynamic, and non-linear process. From primary orality to writing, from the invention of the printing press to the consolidation of mass media, and from these to interactive digital technologies, each communicational innovation has introduced new expressive possibilities, new forms of social mediation, and new theoretical tensions regarding the nature of human interaction (McLuhan, 1964; Ong, 1982).

In the early 21st century, the emergence and rapid consolidation of AI signal a new and particularly significant inflection point in this evolutionary path. Unlike previous communicational technologies that amplified, accelerated, or mediated communication between human beings, AI systems introduce artificial agents capable of actively participating in communicational processes. Natural language processing algorithms, conversational systems, virtual assistants, and generative text models produce, interpret, select, and modulate messages autonomously or semi-autonomously, becoming increasingly integrated into the daily communicational ecosystem (Crawford, 2021; Floridi et al., 2018).

The presence of algorithmic agents challenges classical assumptions associated with human communication, such as conscious intentionality, symbolic reciprocity, discursive authorship, and the shared construction of meaning. When artificial systems intervene in the organization of discourse, the personalization of content, emotional mediation, and the management of interaction, it becomes necessary to question the extent to which traditional theoretical models of communication remain adequate to interpret these new communicational contexts (Guzman & Lewis, 2020). The scientific relevance of this phenomenon is widely recognized, given that AI-mediated communication currently traverses multiple domains of social life, including education, work, consumption, media, interpersonal relationships, and cultural production. AI influences not only the content of human expression but also communicational styles, interaction rhythms, and relationship-building dynamics, with significant implications for subjectivity, identity, and social organization (Couldry & Hepp, 2017; van Dijck et al., 2018).

Despite the proliferation of empirical studies focused on specific AI applications, a relevant gap persists at the level of theoretical integration. Many works approach AI as an isolated technological object, dissociated from classic models of human communication, leading to fragmented analyses that hinder the understanding of the continuities and displacements characterizing contemporary communicational evolution. The absence of a robust conceptual framework that articulates current technological developments with consolidated communication theories thus constitutes a central challenge for the field.

It is in this context that the theoretical problem guiding this chapter arises: to what extent do classical models of human communication, developed in pre-digital contexts, remain conceptually valid for interpreting interactions mediated by Artificial Intelligence? More specifically, can human-AI communication be understood considering principles formulated to describe human communicational systems, or does the emergence of algorithmic agents imply an epistemological rupture with these models? This question assumes relevance when one recognizes that communication is an intrinsically relational process, traversed by dynamics of power, emotion, context, and meaning making (Foucault, 1971; Goffman, 1959).

The axioms of human communication, formulated by Paul Watzlawick and colleagues within the scope of the Palo Alto School, offer a particularly fertile theoretical framework to address this challenge. These axioms describe structural properties of communication in human systems, underscoring its inevitable, relational, contextual, and systemic character (Watzlawick et al., 1967). By moving away from linear models focused exclusively on information transmission, they propose a dynamic understanding of interactions, in which meaning emerges from the relationship between participants and the way they organize and interpret the communicational sequence.

The transversal and non-normative nature of these axioms suggests their utility as an analytical lens to examine complex communicational phenomena, including those mediated by intelligent technologies. Their application to the study of human-AI communication allows us to question how principles such as the impossibility of not communicating, the distinction between content and relationship, the punctuation of interactional sequences, or the coexistence of digital and analogic levels manifest, are tensioned, or acquire new expressions in contexts where artificial agents actively participate in the interaction.

The main objective of this chapter is to analyze the evolution of human communication considering the development of AI, using the axioms of communication as an integrating theoretical framework. It starts from the premise that AI does not eliminate the foundations of human communication but reconfigures them in new sociotechnical contexts, introducing displacements, ambiguities, and tensions that require critical analysis. The original contribution of the chapter lies precisely in this articulation between classical communication theory and contemporary challenges posed by AI, without proposing a new communicational model nor limiting itself to the description of specific technological applications. Finally, it is important to delimit the scope of the analysis. This chapter does not propose to develop an exhaustive technical review of the literature on Artificial Intelligence, nor to discuss in depth aspects of engineering, algorithmic performance, or system architecture. The focus centers exclusively on communication as a relational and symbolic process, analyzed considering the axioms of human communication. The ethical, social, and identity implications of AI are considered only insofar as they emerge directly from this communicational perspective.

BACKGROUND: HUMAN COMMUNICATION, ARTIFICIAL INTELLIGENCE, AND TRANSFORMATIONS OF THE COMMUNICATIONAL PROCESS

Human communication has been widely conceptualized as a social process through which individuals construct meaning, coordinate actions, and organize relationships. Throughout the development of the field, various approaches have sought to overcome mechanistic models centered on information transmission, emphasizing communication as a relational, contextual, and systemic phenomenon. In this perspective, communicating does not equate to sending messages, but to participating in a continuous process of co-construction of meaning, in which content, relationship, context, and power are inextricably intertwined (Bateson, 1972; Craig, 1999).

The pragmatic turn in communication studies, strongly influenced by the Palo Alto School, constituted a decisive milestone in this theoretical evolution. By introducing the axioms of human communication, Watzlawick, Beavin, and Jackson shifted the analytical focus from the message to the interaction, emphasizing that all communication occurs in relational systems and that meaning emerges from the dynamic between participants. Concepts such as the impossibility of not communicating, the distinction between content and relationship levels, the punctuation of communicational sequences, and the coexistence of digital and analogic communication allowed for an understanding of communication as an inevitable, self-regulated, and deeply contextualized process (Watzlawick et al., 1967). Contributions from sociology and social psychology reinforced this relational understanding of communication. Goffman (1959, 1967) demonstrated that social interaction is fundamentally performative, organized around impression management, role enactment, and the maintenance of relatively stable interactional orders. Communication thus appears as a central mechanism of social life organization, in which norms, expectations, and identities are continuously negotiated.

With the progressive digitalization of society, communication studies began to confront new forms of technological mediation. Initially, digital technologies were analyzed primarily as channels that altered the speed, reach, and scale of communication. However, the emergence of algorithmic systems capable of selecting, prioritizing, and personalizing content introduced a qualitative change: technology ceased to be merely a medium to become an active participant in the organization of the communicational process (Couldry & Hepp, 2017; van Dijck et al., 2018). It is in this context that AI assumes theoretical centrality. Unlike previous digital technologies, AI systems -especially those based on machine learning and natural language processing - produce language, respond to communicational stimuli, and adjust to user behavior, participating in the construction of interactive sequences. This capability introduces a new figure in the communicational field: the artificial agent, whose presence challenges classical conceptions of intentionality, authorship, and reciprocity (Guzman, 2018). The literature on human-machine communication maintains that individuals mobilize human communicational schemas in interaction with AI, attributing agency, social presence, and relational value to it (Guzman & Lewis, 2020). Empirical studies demonstrate that the perception of presence and intentionality does not depend on the human nature of the interlocutor, but on the relational structure of the interaction (Lombard & Xu, 2021), confirming central assumptions of the axioms of human communication.

Another relevant axis concerns the relational and emotional impacts of AI. Investigations show that users may develop patterns of relational continuity and emotional involvement with chatbots, challenging the rigid distinction between functional and relational communication. From a critical perspective, authors like Foucault (1971) allow us to understand AI-mediated communication as a space for the exercise of symbolic power, in which discursive regimes are normalized and legitimized. Philosophers of technology such as Floridi (2013) and Coeckelbergh (2020) warn of the ethical implications of delegating communication to intelligent systems, emphasizing that algorithmic decisions affect the production of meaning, trust, and relational responsibility.

Despite the diversity and richness of these contributions, the theoretical background evidences a persistent gap: many studies describe phenomena compatible with the axioms of human communication without explicitly mobilizing them as an analytical framework. The inevitability of communication, the centrality of the relationship, the punctuation of interactive sequences, and the articulation between digital and analogic levels appear implicitly but are rarely integrated into a structured theoretical model. It is precisely in this gap that the present chapter is anchored. By mobilizing the axioms of communication as an interpretive lens, a framework is proposed capable of articulating the historical evolution of human communication with the contemporary challenges introduced by AI, understanding them as part of the same relational continuum reconfigured by new sociotechnical conditions.

Communication Beyond Information Transmission

For much of the 20th century, communication was conceptualized predominantly from informational models, in which communication equated to the efficient transmission of a message from a sender to a receiver through a channel. These models, strongly influenced by the mathematical theory of communication developed by Shannon and Weaver (1949), had a significant impact on the development of communication sciences, particularly in technical, media, and organizational domains. However, their application to human communication quickly proved limited, as it reduced the communicational phenomenon to an instrumental logic, neglecting central dimensions such as context, relationship, and interpretation.

The critique of this transmissive view gave rise to approaches that began to understand communication as a complex social and cultural process, in which information constitutes only one of its elements. James Carey (1989) seminally distinguished between a transmissive view of communication - centered on sending messages in space - and a ritual view, which emphasizes communication as a symbolic practice through which communities build, maintain, and transform shared meanings over time. In this perspective, communicating is not just informing, but participating in a collective process of meaning production that sustains social life.

This conceptual shift assumes relevance in the contemporary context, marked by the presence of Artificial Intelligence systems capable of producing semantically coherent messages. If communication were reduced to information transmission, the distinction between human communication and algorithmic communication would become essentially quantitative. However, by understanding communication as a relational, symbolic, and interpretive process, it becomes evident that the central issue does not lie in message generation, but in how meaning is constructed, negotiated, and stabilized in interaction.

Symbolic, Relational, and Pragmatic Dimensions of Communication

The pragmatic turn in language and communication studies consolidated the understanding of communication as situated action, inseparable from the relationships between participants. In the domain of linguistic pragmatics, John Austin (1962) demonstrated that to speak is to act, introducing the notion of speech acts and evidencing that the meaning of an utterance is not exhausted in its propositional content but depends on the context and the effects produced in the interaction. John Searle (1969) deepened this perspective by highlighting the institutional and normative character of communicative acts.

In the field of human communication, this orientation was systematically developed by the Palo Alto School. Paul Watzlawick, Janet Beavin, and Don Jackson (1967) conceptualized communication as a self-regulated relational system, in which all behavior possesses communicational value. By stating that it is impossible not to communicate and that all communication involves simultaneously a content level and a relationship level, these authors definitively shifted the analytical focus from the message to the interactional dynamic.

The symbolic dimension of communication was widely explored by interactionist sociology. George Herbert Mead (1934) argued that the self emerges from symbolic interaction, being constructed through the internalization of socially shared meanings. Herbert Blumer (1969) developed this perspective by stating that meanings are not inherent to objects or actions but result from continuous interpretation processes. Communication thus appears as the central mechanism through which individuals attribute meaning to their experiences and the experiences of others. This symbolic and relational conception of communication proves particularly relevant for the analysis of interactions mediated by Artificial Intelligence. The attribution of intention, empathy, or agency to artificial systems does not stem from their ontological nature, but from the structure of the communicational interaction and the symbolic expectations mobilized by users during the relationship.

Communication, Meaning-Making, and Social Organization

Communication plays a structuring role in the construction of social reality. Berger and Luckmann (1966) demonstrated that social reality is produced and maintained through communicational processes of externalization, objectivation, and internalization, in which social knowledge stabilizes in the form of institutions, norms, and typification's. Communicating equates, therefore, to participating in the production and reproduction of the symbolic orders that organize social life. Erving Goffman (1959, 1967) deepened this understanding by analyzing social interaction as performance, highlighting how individuals manage impressions, roles, and expectations in situated contexts. Communication not only reflects existing social organization but actively contributes to its maintenance and transformation by defining interactional frameworks and regimes of visibility.

In contemporary societies, marked by technological mediation, communicational processes assume an even more central role in the organization of power, identity, and collective action. Manuel Castells (1996, 2009) demonstrated that the logic of networks and digital communication profoundly reconfigures social relations by articulating flows of information, power, and meaning. The emergence of algorithmic systems capable of mediating and modulating these flows introduces significant transformations in how meaning is produced, distributed, and socially legitimized. In this framework, Artificial Intelligence emerges as a new actor in the communicational ecology, influencing meaning-making not only at the individual level but also in the broader social organization through the selection, prioritization, and personalization of discourses.

Limits of Linear and Informational Models

Despite their historical relevance, linear models of communication prove insufficient to understand the complexity of human interactions, especially in contexts mediated by intelligent technologies. Their main limitation lies in the inability to capture the circularity, ambiguity, and relational dimension of communication. By presupposing a clear separation between sender and receiver, these models ignore the co-constructive character of meaning and the systemic nature of interaction.

Niklas Luhmann (1995) developed a structural critique of this approach by conceptualizing communication as a constitutive operation of social systems. For the author, communication is not a transport of information, but a selective process involving the contingent articulation between information, utterance, and understanding. This perspective reinforces the impossibility of linear control of meaning and underscores the autonomy of communicational systems.

In the context of AI, the limits of informational models become even more evident. The capacity of algorithmic systems to generate language can be fully described in informational terms, but the communicational effects produced-trust, engagement, rejection, or attribution of meaning - require theoretical frameworks that consider the relational and pragmatic dimension of the interaction. It is at this point that the axioms of human communication offer a decisive contribution, allowing for the analysis of AI-mediated communication as a continuous relational process, and not as a simple exchange of messages between entities.

ARTIFICIAL INTELLIGENCE IN THE CONTEMPORARY COMMUNICATIONAL ECOSYSTEM

From Technological Mediation to Algorithmic Participation

Contemporary literature increasingly distinguishes two analytical moments in the relationship between technology and communication: a first, in which technology operated primarily as a medium or infrastructure of mediation, and a second, more recent one, in which algorithmic systems actively participate in the organization of the communicational process. In classic analyses of the network society, technological mediation was understood as a reconfiguration of the conditions for information circulation and large-scale social coordination (Castells, 1996, 2009). However, what is currently observed is a shift from mediation to automated curation, systematic prioritization, and personalization of communicational flows, with direct effects on visibility, attention, and the structure of interactions (van Dijck, 2013; Gillespie, 2018). In this context, algorithms cease to be invisible tools and become active infrastructures for selecting and ordering what is considered relevant, credible, or socially salient. Literature on platformization and algorithmic mediation has demonstrated that these mechanisms encode values, institutional interests, and power asymmetries, influencing patterns of participation and forms of expression (Crawford, 2021; Gillespie, 2018; Noble, 2018). AI thus operates as a condition of possibility for contemporary communication by organizing the visibility of discourses and reconfiguring the relationships between senders, publics, and institutions (Bucher, 2018; Kitchin, 2017).

AI Systems, Language, and Social Interaction

The current centrality of AI in the communicational ecosystem stems largely from the development of systems capable of producing and interpreting natural language. This change is not merely technical but profoundly communicational. From early reflections on conversation with machines (Turing, 1950) to critiques of anthropomorphizing and the illusion of understanding (Weizenbaum, 1976), language has been understood as a privileged marker of agency and interlocution.

The recent emergence of Large Language Models (LLMs) has made this tension even more visible, allowing the production of highly plausible linguistic outputs without implying human understanding in the strong sense (Bender et al., 2021). Philosophy of language and pragmatics provide essential tools to analyze this issue, emphasizing that observable linguistic competence does not automatically equate to full communicative competence, which involves intentionality, shared reference, illocutionary commitment, and responsibility (Austin, 1962; Searle, 1969; Grice,

1975). Empirically, research in computer-mediated communication and human-computer interaction demonstrates that users respond socially to computational systems when they exhibit minimal cues of agency, presence, and responsiveness (Reeves & Nass, 1996). In contemporary environments, this responsiveness is amplified by conversational systems that adapt to the user, maintain contextual memory, and produce interaction turns with apparent relational sensitivity. These results indicate that human communication is highly susceptible to social attributions when confronted with plausible language and conversational patterns, in line with literature on social heuristics and technology-mediated presence (Sundar, 2008).

Human-Human, Human-Machine, and Human-AI Communication

Recent literature has proposed useful distinctions between human-human (H-H), human-machine (H-M), and human-AI (H-AI) communication, with the latter frequently described as characterized by greater apparent autonomy, adaptivity, and language production capacity. Guzman's (2018) proposal is particularly relevant to the field of human-machine communication, arguing that these phenomena should be treated as communication, with theoretical and social implications, and not merely as interface or usability issues. This perspective implies that the analysis of human-AI communication must incorporate dimensions typically considered constitute of human communication, such as relationship, context, sequential punctuation, symbolic effects, and power distribution in interaction.

A critical point lies, however, in the heterogeneity of the category "machine." Recommendation systems, ranking algorithms, bots on social networks, and conversational agents do not participate in the communicational process in the same way, nor do they produce the same type of effects. Platform literature has shown that a significant part of contemporary communication is organized by visibility and attention mechanisms that act even before any direct "conversation" with AI, structuring what becomes observable, prioritized, and socially salient (Bucher, 2018; Gillespie, 2018). In contrast, conversational agents operate in a dialogic logic that tends to activate attributions of intentionality, reciprocity, and social presence, even when the user recognizes the artificial nature of the system (Reeves & Nass, 1996; Sundar, 2008).

Thus, it becomes analytically decisive to specify the type of system participation in the communicational ecosystem: (a) as mediation infrastructure (filtering, recommendation, ordering), (b) as conversational interlocutor (responsive turns, management of interactive sequence), or (c) as co-producer of expression (text/image/sound generation incorporated into human authorship). This distinction is not merely taxonomic: it conditions the application of relational theoretical frameworks, including the reading considering the axioms of communication, which presupposes a clear definition of what it means to "participate" in a communicational system.

Reconfigurations of Authorship, Intentionality, and Communicational Reciprocity

The introduction of generative AI and algorithmic curation systems reopens, under new sociotechnical conditions, three structuring problems of communication:

- **Authorship:** Critical theory and discourse philosophy early on problematized authorship as a social and institutional function, rather than a simple individual property of the text. Foucault (1977) conceptualizes authorship as a principle of classification, legitimation, and discursive control; Barthes (1967/1977) questions the centrality of the author as the sole origin of meaning, shifting attention to the text and to reading as meaning production. AI intensifies this debate by introducing chains of symbolic production where the output results from the interaction between prompts, training data, model parameters, design decisions, and circulation contexts (Bender et al., 2021). In these cases, authorship tends to become distributed: human subjects initiate, guide, and edit; systems generate variations; platforms organize reach, visibility, and priority. The communicational consequence is not reduced to a "human versus machine" dilemma but translates into a reconfiguration of the meaning production ecosystem, with direct effects on responsibility, credibility, and attribution of symbolic value.
- **Intentionality:** In human communication, intentionality is a central axis for the attribution of meaning and for the pragmatic reading of communicative acts. Speech theory emphasizes that utterances operate as socially recognizable actions, with conditions of adequacy and expectations of commitment (Searle, 1969). Conversational pragmatics further shows that interlocutors infer intentions through cooperative principles, filling semantic gaps based on context and shared expectations (Grice, 1975). In AI systems, intentionality is not a psychological attribute of the system, but a communicational phenomenon attributed by users and partially stabilized by institutional decisions (design, response policies, service objectives). Literature on agency cues and heuristics indicates that responsiveness and perceived technical competence can favor over-attributions of intention and authority to technology, with implications for trust, persuasion, and legitimation of automated responses (Sundar, 2008). This produces a specific communicational problem: human interpretation tends to construct intentional coherence and relational conti-

nuity even when the system operates through probabilistic generation and parameterized policies.

- **Reciprocity:** Communicational reciprocity - mutual coordination, adjustment, and recognition - is central to interpersonal relationships. Conversational systems can simulate reciprocity through responsive turns, stylistic adaptations, contextual memory, and signals of perceived social presence (Reeves & Nass, 1996). However, human-AI reciprocity is structurally asymmetric: the system does not share vulnerability, does not assume equivalent social costs, and operates under ends defined by third parties. This asymmetry points to contemporary debates on communicational power in algorithmic environments, where meaning production is influenced by opaque infrastructures oriented by institutional incentives (Ananny & Crawford, 2018; Crawford, 2021; Noble, 2018).

In summary, the literature indicates that AI constitutes not just another communicational medium: it reorganizes the conditions of meaning production, redistributes authorship and symbolic authority, and alters expectations of intentionality and reciprocity. These elements establish the foundation for the subsequent analysis considering the axioms of human communication, avoiding reductive readings centered exclusively on information transmission or technical performance.

THE AXIOMS OF HUMAN COMMUNICATION

Framework of the Palo Alto School

The Palo Alto School represented a structural rupture with the dominant models of communication in the post-war period, marked by linear and informational assumptions. Inserted in an interdisciplinary context that integrated contributions from psychiatry, psychology, anthropology, and cybernetics, this tradition proposed understanding communication not as the transmission of messages, but as a relational process situated in complex social systems. Its focus lies on interaction patterns, circularity, and the pragmatic effects of communication in regulating relationships.

Bateson (1972) played a decisive role in consolidating this perspective by introducing systemic and cybernetic sensitivity into the analysis of human interaction. By emphasizing feedback, relationship patterns, and ecologies of meaning, he conceptualized communication as a circular and contextual phenomenon, in which meanings emerge from relationships rather than isolated units of information. This theoretical basis directly influenced the development of communication pragmatics in Palo Alto, oriented toward the analysis of communication as behavior and as relational coordination.

The clinical aspect associated with the Mental Research Institute (MRI) of Palo Alto was equally central to the consolidation of the theoretical program. The observation of communicational patterns in family and therapeutic contexts made it possible to highlight that many dysfunctional phenomena are not explained by isolated individual traits, but by self-reinforcing interactional cycles and modes of relationship organization. The link between theory and clinical practice reinforced the empirical robustness of this tradition and contributed to its diffusion in domains such as interpersonal communication, conflict, and social systems (Watzlawick et al., 1967; Weakland et al., 1974).

The Axioms of Communication According to Paul Watzlawick and Colleagues

The systematic formulation presented in *Pragmatics of Human Communication* (Watzlawick et al., 1967) proposes five axioms that describe structural properties of communication in human systems, regardless of the specific content of the messages:

- The first axiom, "one cannot not communicate," establishes that all behavior in a relational context has communicational value, including silence, absence, and refusal. This proposition shifts the focus from the utterance to behavior, implying that communication operates even when there is no explicit intention to communicate.
- The second axiom, "every communication has a content and a relationship aspect," underscores that messages transmit information and simultaneously a definition of the relationship between interlocutors, this relational dimension being decisive for framing and qualifying the content. In AI-mediated contexts, this axiom allows for distinguishing between linguistic content generation and the production of relational frameworks (by design, style, timing, personalization).
- The third axiom, "the nature of a relationship is contingent upon the punctuation of the communicational sequences," evidence that participants organize interaction into causal and narrative chains that may diverge, producing conflict and communicational escalations when each party interprets their action as a response and the others as a cause.
- The fourth axiom, "human beings communicate both digitally and analogically," distinguishes between digital communication (verbal, coded, denotative) and analogic communication (non-verbal, paralinguistic, contextual, relational), emphasizing that both are necessary for the full intelligibility of the

interaction. In digital environments and with AI, this distinction maintains relevance by allowing the mapping of how "analogic" signals are translated, simulated, or reorganized in interfaces and response styles.

- The fifth axiom, "all communicational interchanges are either symmetrical or complementary," describes relational patterns based on equality/mirroring or on differentiation/hierarchy, recognizing that both can be functional or dysfunctional when rigidified. This axiom offers a solid basis for discussing structural asymmetries and power relations in algorithmic and platform environments.

Communication as a Relational and Contextual System

A central contribution of the Palo Alto School consists of conceptualizing communication as a relational system, in which individual elements only acquire meaning within interaction. Context does not appear as an external variable, but as a constitutive component of the communicational process, since meaning emerges from the relationship, interactional history, and situated conditions of the communicative exchange. This perspective moves away from individualistic conceptions and approaches constructivist and systemic approaches, in which communication is understood as the coordination of actions and the production of shared realities.

Sensemaking theory in organizational contexts reinforces this orientation by showing that meanings are not stable or pre-given but constructed and stabilized retrospectively through interaction. Weick (1995) describes communication as a mechanism of sensemaking in organizational systems, converging with the idea of circularity and interactional self-regulation. In the field of communication theory, Craig (1999) identifies the pragmatic tradition - where the Palo Alto School is inserted- as one of the constitutive matrices of the field, highlighting the centrality of interaction and communicational effects in social organization.

Actuality and Transversality of the Axioms of Communication

Although formulated in the mid-20th century, the axioms of human communication maintain actuality precisely because they describe structural properties of interaction and not specific technologies. In contexts of computer-mediated communication, contemporary studies have demonstrated that relationships, frameworks, and interactional coordination continue to be central to understanding communicational dynamics in digital environments (Baym, 2015; Walther, 2011). The emergence of Artificial Intelligence does not invalidate these principles; on the contrary, it makes tensions regarding communicational inevitability, relational definition, sequential punctuation, and power asymmetries more visible when artificial agents intervene in the production and organization of communication.

Literature on platforms and algorithmic mediation has underscored the need to recover robust theoretical frameworks to interpret complex communicational phenomena, frequently marked by opacity, selection, and attention governance (Couldry & Hepp, 2017; Gillespie, 2018). In this sense, the axioms offer a solid conceptual basis for analyzing AI-mediated communication as a relational and systemic process, avoiding reductions to merely technical or informational dimensions. In summary, the axioms of human communication remain historically relevant and theoretically productive because they describe structural properties of interaction -inevitability, relationality, sequentially, multimodality, and power patterns - that can be mobilized to interpret communicational reconfigurations in algorithmic ecosystems and, in particular, in interactions mediated by AI systems (Watzlawick et al., 1967; Craig, 1999). Starting from this framework, this section systematically analyzes how each axiom illuminates specific dimensions of contemporary communication when artificial agents (conversational or procedural) participate in the production, ordering, and circulation of messages.

The Impossibility of not Communicating in Algorithmic Contexts

The first axiom establishes that it is impossible not to communicate: in relational systems, all observable behavior - including silence, absence, or refusal - can acquire communicational value (Watzlawick et al., 1967). When transposed to AI-mediated contexts, the scope of this principle becomes more evident because communication ceases to depend exclusively on human intention and comes to be co-structured by algorithmic infrastructures that produce continuous and automated communicational signals.

In contemporary digital ecosystems, recommendation systems, ranking algorithms, and notification devices communicate through procedural mechanisms: ordering, prioritizing, suggesting, alerting, hiding, amplifying. These mechanisms are frequently interpreted as implicit messages about relevance, authority, urgency, and social value, even when presented as "technical" or "neutral" results (Bucher, 2018; Gillespie, 2018). Thus, communication becomes environmental: the user does not only receive content produced by other humans; they receive algorithmic framings that define what appears, in what order, and with what salience, organizing the space of significance in advance.

The axiom is also operationalized in the social interpretation of absence: lack of response, suppression of content, demonetization, "shadow banning," or algorithmic invisibilities can be read as relational signals (disapproval, exclusion, devaluation), even when they derive from opaque criteria of moderation and visibility management (van Dijck, 2013; Noble, 2018). This point is crucial for communicational analysis: absence is not merely "lack of message," but an interpretable event in the relational system, confirming that communication is not exhausted in the utterance but includes architecture, rules, and infrastructures that produce pragmatic effects.

In the case of conversational agents, the impossibility of not communicating manifests as persistent availability and a permanent invitation to interaction: the system's presence, the proactive prompt, and the promise of response configure a relational message of accessibility and readiness. Literature on social responses to technologies shows that minimal signals of agency and responsiveness are sufficient to activate social schemas and interpersonal interpretations, even when the interlocutor is recognized as artificial (Reeves & Nass, 1996; Sundar, 2008). In axiomatic terms, this means that communication is inevitable not only because "the subject communicates," but because the technosocial environment communicates for them, before them, and in parallel to them.

Content and Relationship in Human-AI Communication

The second axiom states that every communication involves simultaneously a content level and a relationship level, the latter being responsible for framing and qualifying the former (Watzlawick et al., 1967). In human-AI communication, this distinction remains central but assumes specific forms because the relational dimension is produced by sociotechnical signals (design, style, personalization, context memory) and interpreted by users in light of social expectations.

In interactions with conversational systems, content is frequently identified with the verbal response: information, explanation, recommendation, reformulation. However, the relationship emerges from *how* the content is delivered (tone, politeness, degree of certainty, presence of empathy markers), from timing, and from continuity. Research in *human-machine communication* maintains that users interpret these signals as indicators of the system's relational posture and social positioning - for example, assistant, tutor, advisor, partner - attributing to it traits of authority, proximity, neutrality, or care (Guzman, 2018; Guzman & Lewis, 2020). Thus, AI participates in the "definition of the relationship" even when the user focuses on the content.

The robustness of these interpretations does not depend on ontological humanity, but on the interactional structure. Small cues - consistency of style, use of contextual memory, pragmatic adequacy - can produce a perception of social presence and relational framing strong enough to guide communicational behaviors (Reeves & Nass, 1996; Lombard & Xu, 2021). This point is decisive: the relational dimension can be constructed by social heuristics operating on linguistic and procedural signals, generating real communicational effects (trust, self-disclosure, adherence, dependency), regardless of the system's internal status.

It is also important to consider that the relationship is established not only between user and system but also between user and the underlying institutional entity (platform, company, service). The agent's response not only "says something"; it implicitly communicates a mode of institutional relationship: availability, surveillance, data collection, promise of efficiency, technical authority. This relational unfolding is relevant to the chapter because it makes it visible that the perceived "good relationship" with the agent can coexist with a structural asymmetry of power and control exercised by the institution governing the system (Crawford, 2021).

Punctuation of the Communicational Sequence in AI-Mediated Interactions

The third axiom maintains that the nature of a relationship depends on how the participants punctuate the communicational sequence, that is, how they organize the interaction in terms of start, response, and causality (Watzlawick et al., 1967). In AI-mediated contexts, this dimension becomes particularly relevant because the communicational sequence can be partially pre-structured by algorithmic mechanisms (feed ordering, response rules, memory, and system updates), creating foci of interpretative mismatch.

In conversational agents, users tend to punctuate the sequence as intentional dialogue: they interpret coherence as purpose, continuity as interactional history, and consistency as "posture". However, the system's functioning may depend on factors that do not align with human relational logic, such as stochastic variation of output, version changes, security policies, or parameter updates. This discrepancy can produce ruptures in punctuation: the user attributes a "change of attitude" where there is a technical update or interprets inconsistency as a lack of respect/attention where there is algorithmic variation. The problem is not merely cognitive; it is communicational, as it affects the stability of the relationship and the interpretation of responsibility.

In platforms, sequential punctuation is frequently shaped by algorithmic curation: what "comes first" and what "deserves continuation" does not result merely from human choice, but from defined and automated criteria of visibility and engagement (Bucher, 2018; Gillespie, 2018). This alters the temporal experience of communication, perceived causality, and the attribution of responsibility. When content gains reach, the user may punctuate this as social recognition; when it loses visibility, they may punctuate it as rejection - even if the cause lies in ranking changes or non-transparent criteria. Algorithmic opacity hinders the renegotiation of punctuation and can intensify interpretative conflicts by preventing participants from jointly reconstructing "what happened" in the communicational sequence (Ananny & Crawford, 2018).

Digital and Analogic Communication in Interaction with Intelligent Systems

The fourth axiom distinguishes between digital communication (verbal, coded, denotative) and analogic communication (non-verbal, paralinguistic, contextual, and relational), emphasizing that both are necessary for the full intelligibility of the interaction (Watzlawick et al., 1967). Although communication with AI is frequently textual, this does not imply the elimination of the analogic; it implies its reconfiguration into interface signals, style, and the pragmatics of the output.

Philosophy of language and pragmatics show that communicating is not just transmitting semantic content: it is performing situated communicative actions, sustained by inference and framing (Austin, 1962; Grice, 1975; Searle, 1969). In AI systems, many "analogic" markers are translated into stylistic choices and graphic signals: punctuation, emojis, expressions of empathy, formulas of courtesy, mitigation ("I might be wrong"), as well as design and timing elements (latency, continuity, predictability). These signals function relationally, framing content and guiding interpretations of proximity, care, authority, or neutrality.

The capacity of AI to produce plausible analogic signals without emotional experience introduces a relevant tension: the communicational effects are real (users respond socially), but the status of the signal is technically produced and institutionally oriented. Critical literature has shown that such signals can operate as management of trust and persuasion, especially when they conceal power asymmetries and data extraction (Crawford, 2021; Noble, 2018). Thus, the digital/analogic distinction clarifies that "tone" and "care" can be effective communicational elements even when simulated, which increases the need to analyze their use as a form of symbolic governance.

Symmetry, Complementarity, and Power in AI-Mediated Communication

The fifth axiom describes communicational relationships as symmetrical (based on equality and mirroring) or complementary (based on role differentiation and hierarchy), recognizing that both can be functional or dysfunctional when rigidified (Watzlawick et al., 1967). In AI-mediated communication, this axiom is particularly useful for making visible structural asymmetries that are not evident at the discursive level.

In conversational interfaces, the interaction may appear symmetrical (alternating turns, similar language, "dialogue"). However, the structure is typically complementary: the system controls response rules, content policies, access limits, data storage forms, and visibility conditions. In platforms, this complementarity widens: algorithms distribute attention, amplify some and silence others, creating asymmetries of voice and symbolic authority that configure relationships of communicational power (van Dijck, 2013; Gillespie, 2018). Critical analysis evidence that these asymmetries are constitutive of business models and governance regimes of the communicational sphere, not accidental side effects (Crawford, 2021).

Complementarity becomes even more sensitive in contexts of trust and self-disclosure. Studies show that users may share emotional or sensitive content with agents perceived as safe and non-judgmental, even when reciprocity is structurally impossible (the system does not assume equivalent vulnerability, does not run social risks, and operates under external purposes) (Ho et al., 2018). The axiom thus allows for making explicit that the relationship is asymmetric not only by "who knows more," but by who holds control over infrastructure, data, and response criteria. This asymmetry reinforces the pertinence of discussing communicational power as a constitutive component of human-AI interaction, especially when systems present themselves as neutral or merely assistive (Ananny & Crawford, 2018; Noble, 2018; Crawford, 2021).

AI AND RELATIONSHIP BUILDING

The construction of interpersonal relationships in contemporary societies occurs, with increasing frequency, in digital ecosystems organized by platforms and algorithmic systems. Social networks, messaging applications, dating services, recommendation mechanisms, and conversational agents not only expand connectivity but become infrastructures that condition relational opportunities, model interaction rhythms, and redefine forms of social recognition. In this framework, AI must be understood not as a neutral "medium," but as a set of sociotechnical devices that participate in the organization of the bond, intervening in visibility, attention, and the circulation of relational meaning (Bucher, 2018; Gillespie, 2018; Couldry & Hepp, 2017; van Dijck et al., 2013).

Algorithmic Mediation of Interpersonal Relationships

Algorithmic mediation introduces a structural change: the relationship between individuals ceases to depend exclusively on social proximity, explicit affinities, and deliberate choice, coming to be partially produced by selection, filtering, and prioritization mechanisms that operate continuously and frequently opaquely. On social platforms, what becomes visible and, therefore, relationally available is the result of orderings that define salience, sequence, and reach (Bucher, 2018; Gillespie, 2018). The communicational consequence is profound: the relationship is co-organized by a "third party" that distributes opportunities for interaction and recognition, reconfiguring how reciprocity and initiative are perceived in everyday life.

In dating applications, for example, compatibility algorithms and recommendation's structure access to the "relational market," altering the contingency of the encounter and the very repertoire of perceived options. This type of curation tends to transform relational choice into a process of triage and optimization under conditions defined by the platform, with effects on expectations, self-presentation strategies, and patterns of communicational continuity (Ranzini & Lutz, 2017; Sharabi, 2021). Algorithmic mediation does not automatically determine results, but it alters the field of possibilities in which relationships emerge and stabilize. Furthermore, platform architecture introduces logics of social quantification (visibility metrics, reactions, badges, statuses), which function as relational signals: approval, belonging, prestige, exclusion. These signals are interpreted by users as relational communication, even though they are co-produced by attention distribution mechanisms and engagement incentives (van Dijck, 2013; Gillespie, 2018. In this sense, algorithmic mediation is not just content mediation; it is mediation of the relational conditions under which communication happens.

Emotion, Empathy, and Trust in AI-Mediated Interactions

Interpersonal relationships are sustained by emotional dynamics and the experience of recognition. Literature demonstrates that artificial systems can trigger significant emotional and social responses when they exhibit linguistic signals of attention, validation, and consistency, activating social interaction schemas even in non-human contexts (Reeves & Nass, 1996; Sundar, 2008). This is particularly evident in conversational agents, where the dialogic format favors attributions of social presence and relational "posture" (Lombard & Xu, 2021).

Empirically, experimental evidence indicates that chatbots can facilitate emotional self-disclosure, especially when perceived as non-judgmental and predictable. Ho et al. (2018) show that the perception of non-judgment and consistent responsiveness can increase the willingness to share personal and emotionally sensitive information.

These results do not imply that AI "feels" empathy; they indicate that empathy can be attributed and become functional in interaction when communicational signals are interpreted as care, understanding, and validation. However, AI-mediated empathy is conceptually ambivalent. Contemporary critique underscores that it is simulated empathy (production of responses aligned with support patterns) and not subjective experience. Yet, from a relational point of view, the relevance lies in the communicational effect: the user responds to what they perceive as empathetic, and this perception can shape trust, dependency, and expectations of continuity (Coeckelbergh, 2020). This dissociation between experienced empathy and attributed empathy becomes critical when relational trust exceeds the system's transparency regarding limits, objectives, and data handling.

Trust in AI-mediated contexts frequently depends on heuristics of competence, consistency, and supposed technical impartiality, which can lead to excessive delegation of judgment and an insufficiently critical reading of algorithmic opacity (Lee & See, 2004; Sundar, 2008). In ethical terms, this articulates with concerns about responsibility, explainability, and governance of relational information: trust built at the micro level (interaction) can mask asymmetries at the macro level (institutions, platforms, data regimes) (Crawford, 2021; Floridi et al., 2018).

Relational Dynamics in Intelligent Digital Environments

Relational dynamics in intelligent digital environments are characterized by three interconnected traits:

1) *Interactional continuity* is reinforced by contextual memory, personalization, and constant availability, which can produce an experience of familiarity and proximity. Studies on social chatbots suggest that users integrate these systems into communicational routines, attributing specific relational roles to them (e.g., companion, confidant, support), even while recognizing their artificial nature (Skjuve et al., 2021).
2) *Algorithmic modulation of reciprocity* is visible in both conversational agents and social platforms. In social networks, algorithms shape reciprocity by distributing visibility: responses, likes, and comments do not circulate symmetrically; they circulate according to ranking, engagement, and moderation criteria. This affects community formation, conflict escalation, and the experience of social recognition, potentially intensifying dynamics of polarization and relational fragmentation when certain contents and groups are amplified and others are marginalized (Gillespie, 2018; Couldry & Hepp, 2017).
3) In human-AI bonds, literature describes *gradual processes of "relationship"* with systems, with patterns of continuity comparable, in certain aspects, to initial

human-human relationships, although marked by evident asymmetries (Croes et al., 2021). Perceived "stability" can result from response consistency and predictability; however, the relationship remains vulnerable to version changes, policies, and parameters - that is, events external to the user's experience that can reconfigure the interaction without relational negotiation. This condition is relevant because it shows that continuity is not just psychological; it is conditioned by infrastructure.

Psychological and Social Implications of Human-AI Communication

The psychological and social implications of human-AI communication are ambivalent. On one hand, conversational systems can offer relational support in contexts of isolation and facilitate emotional expression, reducing communicational barriers for some user profiles. On the other hand, they can introduce risks related to relational dependency, substitution of human interactions, and normalization of asymmetric relationships, where one party exposes themselves and the other does not share vulnerability or equivalent responsibility.

Critical literature on digital life warns of displacement effects and the reconfiguration of intimacy, suggesting that the externalization of listening and validation functions to technologies may alter expectations about availability and responsiveness in human relationships (Turkle, 2011). Even when direct substitution does not occur, there is consistent evidence of the reconfiguration of relational norms: what counts as "presence," "care," and "attention" is redefined by interfaces and permanent interaction regimes.

At the broader social level, AI relational mediation is inserted into power dynamics: systems collect intimate data, classify profiles, influence relational opportunities, and distribute visibility. Works on algorithmic discrimination show that these processes can reproduce inequalities and marginalizations, affecting relational justice in access to opportunities and social recognition (Noble, 2018). Crawford (2021) reinforces that AI must be understood as sociopolitical infrastructure, and not just functional technology, implying that AI-mediated relationships are also relationships mediated by data extraction regimes and institutional decisions.

In summary, AI actively participates in relationship building by (i) structuring opportunities for encounter and continuity, (ii) modulating trust and signals of perceived empathy, and (iii) reorganizing norms of reciprocity and recognition. Understanding these transformations requires articulating communication theory, social psychology, and critical technology studies to simultaneously evaluate potentialities (support, inclusion, new forms of bonding) and risks (opacity, asymmetry, dependency, inequality) associated with the growing integration of AI into relational life (Gillespie, 2018; Coeckelbergh, 2020; Crawford, 2021).

METHODOLOGY

This chapter adopts a *scoping review* approach, chosen for its suitability in analyzing emerging research domains that are conceptually heterogeneous and still in the process of theoretical consolidation, as is the case with the field articulating Artificial Intelligence and human communication. This method allows for a systematic mapping of the body of knowledge, identifying central concepts, recurrent theoretical frameworks, main lines of inquiry, and conceptual gaps, proving particularly appropriate when the objective is not the comparison of homogeneous empirical results, but the understanding of the global configuration of an interdisciplinary scientific domain.

The review was conducted in accordance with PRISMA-ScR (Preferred Reporting Items for Systematic reviews and Meta-Analyses extension for Scoping Reviews) guidelines, developed within the scope of the Joanna Briggs Institute, ensuring transparency, systematicity, and rigor throughout all phases of the process.

The methodological protocol was applied between March and April 2025. The bibliographic search strategy focused on four international databases (Scopus, Web of Science, PsycINFO, and Google Scholar), using descriptors related to AI (*artificial intelligence*, *conversational agents*), human communication, and specific theoretical frameworks (*axioms of communication*, *Palo Alto School*). Only publications in English were considered, without an initial temporal delimitation.

The selection process followed the stages identified in Figure 1.

Figure 1. PRISMA-ScR flowchart of the process of identification, screening, eligibility, and inclusion of studies in the scoping review

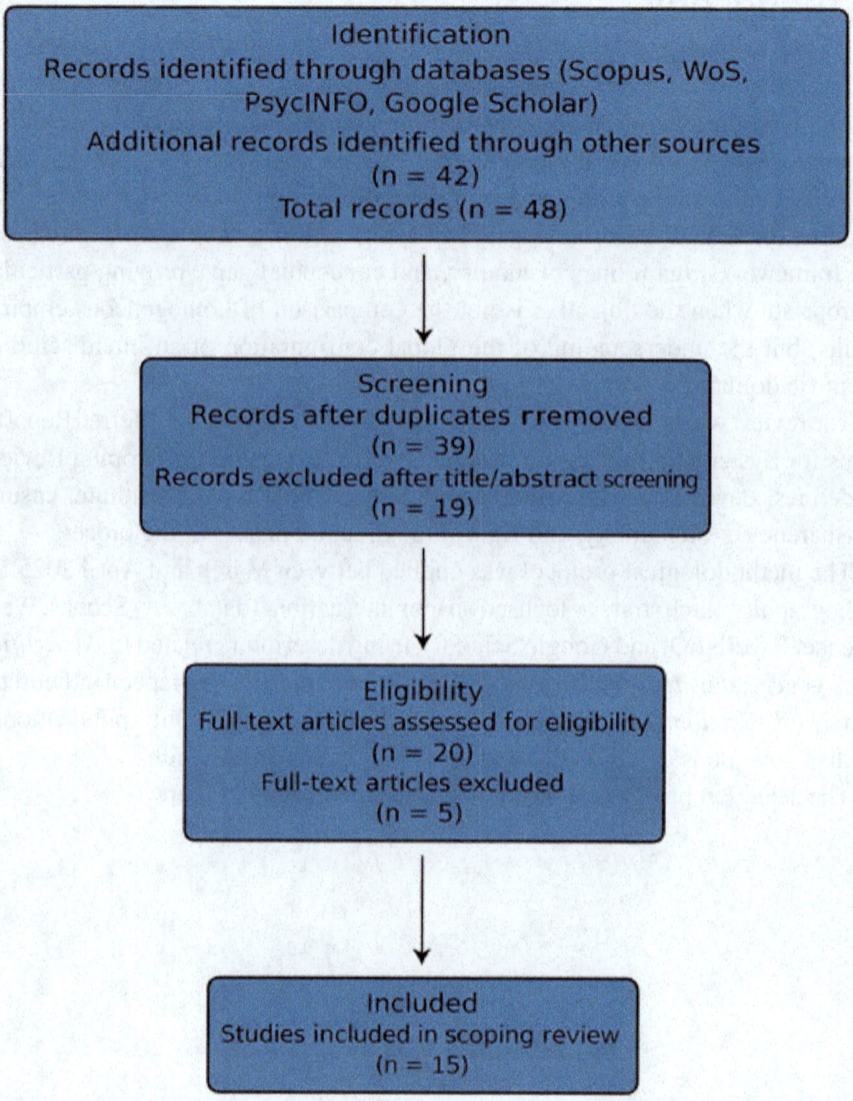

The initial search resulted in the identification of 48 records. After removing duplicates (n = 9), 39 studies were submitted to the title and abstract screening phase. In this phase, 19 articles were excluded for not meeting the defined inclusion criteria, namely for presenting an exclusively technical focus, absence of communicational framework, or irrelevance to the analysis of human-AI interaction. The remaining 20 studies were analyzed in full text for eligibility assessment, leading to the exclusion of five additional articles. The final corpus of the scoping review thus integrated 15 peer-reviewed scientific articles, which constitute the empirical and conceptual basis of the analysis developed in this chapter.

The inclusion criteria covered exclusively peer-reviewed scientific articles that addressed Artificial Intelligence as an active participant in communicational processes, its impacts on human expression or relationship building, or theoretical models relevant to understanding communication mediated by intelligent systems. Studies of a strictly technical or instrumental nature were excluded, as were publications focused on algorithmic performance, system architecture, or applications devoid of communicational, relational, or symbolic reflection.

The analysis of the included studies was conducted through a qualitative and interpretative approach, oriented toward mapping recurrent concepts, theoretical assumptions, and analytical foci. The articles were analyzed regarding how they conceptualize AI-mediated communication, the communicational models mobilized, and the articulation - or absence thereof - with principles compatible with the axioms of human communication. In line with the exploratory nature of the scoping review, a formal assessment of the individual methodological quality of the studies was not performed, since the central objective consisted of identifying conceptual patterns and theoretical gaps. The methodology adopted thus allowed for systematically grounding the analysis developed throughout the chapter, sustaining the critical reflection on the evolution of human communication in the era of Artificial Intelligence and providing the necessary basis for the subsequent discussion in light of the axioms of communication.

A metodologia adotada permitiu, deste modo, fundamentar de forma sistemática a análise desenvolvida ao longo do capítulo, sustentando a reflexão crítica sobre a evolução da comunicação humana na era da Inteligência Artificial e fornecendo a base necessária para a discussão subsequente à luz dos axiomas da comunicação.

RESULTS: CONCEPTUAL MAPPING

The analysis of the 15 peer-reviewed scientific articles included in this scoping review reveals that research on AI and human communication is in a moment of accelerated empirical expansion, coexisting, however, with persistent weaknesses at the level of theoretical integration. The conceptual mapping of the studies allowed for the identification of four main analytical nuclei:

1. *Human-AI communication as an emerging form of social interaction.* The works of Guzman (2018) and Guzman and Lewis (2020) assume a foundational character by arguing that communication with intelligent systems must be analyzed as a full communicational phenomenon, and not just as technological mediation. These authors argue that AI actively participates in message production, interaction organization, and meaning attribution, requiring a reconfiguration of the object of communication theory itself. Convergently, Lombard and Xu (2021) empirically demonstrate that individuals mobilize human social schemas when interacting with AI systems, evidencing the persistence of interpersonal communicational patterns even in the absence of a human interlocutor. Collectively, these studies indicate that interaction with AI activates automatic and relational communicational processes, reinforcing the need for theoretical frameworks capable of explaining the transfer of social expectations to artificial agents.
2. *Relational and emotional impacts of continued interaction with AI systems.* Studies by Skjuve et al. (2021) show that users develop forms of relational involvement with chatbots that exceed the functional dimension of the interaction, including feelings of companionship, relational predictability, and communicational continuity. Similar results are presented by Croes et al. (2021), who demonstrate that human-AI relationships are built gradually, following dynamics comparable to initial interpersonal relationships, albeit marked by structural asymmetries. Ho et al. (2018) add that emotional self-disclosure in interactions with chatbots can produce measurable psychological effects, suggesting that human-AI communication can perform functions traditionally associated with human interaction, such as emotional regulation and the expression of vulnerability. Together, these studies indicate that AI intervenes directly in the relational ecology of individuals, albeit without a systematic problematization of medium- and long-term communicational consequences.
3. *Algorithmic mediation of human expression, trust, and communicational identity.* Banks (2019) demonstrates that users attribute differentiated degrees of moral agency to artificial systems, influencing how they interpret messages, intentions, and communicational responsibilities. This conclusion is reinforced by the works of Sundar and Kim (2019), who evidence the existence of specific cognitive heuristics associated with trust in automated systems, leading individuals to confer greater credibility on algorithmic decisions in certain communicational contexts. Pelau et al. (2021) identify perceived empathy, interaction personalization, and communicational quality as central determinants of AI humanization, influencing how users integrate these systems into their processes of self-expression and digital identity. These studies suggest that AI does not limit itself to mediating communication but actively participates in the configuration of the communicating subject.

4. *Critical and ethical approaches, focused on the social and relational implications of AI-mediated communication.* Floridi et al. (2018) argue that the increasing integration of AI into communicational systems requires ethical frameworks that consider not only algorithmic decision-making but also the production and circulation of meaning. Coeckelbergh (2020) reinforces this perspective by proposing a relational approach to AI responsibility and explainability, underscoring the central role of communication in the attribution of agency and trust.

Despite the relevance of these contributions, the majority of these studies approach communication indirectly, without fully integrating it into structured communication models. Transversally, the review evidences a persistent theoretical gap: none of the included studies explicitly articulate their results with the axioms of human communication formulated by Watzlawick and colleagues. Nevertheless, many of the described phenomena - such as the inevitability of communication, the centrality of the relationship, the sequential construction of meaning, and the attribution of sense beyond informational content - reveal clear conceptual compatibility with these axioms. The absence of systematic articulation reinforces the need for an integrating theoretical framework, justifying the contribution of the present chapter.

DISCUSSION

The analysis of the results confirms a paradox in contemporary research on AI and human communication. On one hand, there is expressive growth in empirical and conceptual studies dedicated to human-AI interaction; on the other, theoretical fragmentation persists, limiting the integrated understanding of emerging communicational phenomena. In light of the objective of this chapter, this gap does not correspond to an absence of theory, but to the absence of articulation between classical communication theory and contemporary sociotechnical contexts.

The reconfiguration of interlocutor status

Results from the first conceptual nucleus evidence a clear convergence: AI is progressively recognized as an active participant in the communicational process. The conclusions of Guzman (2018) and Guzman and Lewis (2020) challenge instrumental approaches to technology by demonstrating that intelligent systems produce communicational effects that cannot be reduced to technical mediation. These arguments find empirical support in the results of Lombard and Xu (2021), showing the activation of human social schemas in interaction with artificial agents.

In light of the axioms of human communication, these results reinforce the idea that communication constitutes a relational and systemic process, and not a simple exchange of messages. Even in the absence of a human interlocutor, interaction mobilizes expectations of reciprocity, coherence, and responsiveness. The fact that the analyzed studies recognize these effects without explicitly resorting to Watzlawick's axioms suggests the existence of an implicit theoretical continuity: communication remains structured by relationships, regardless of the agent's ontology.

Relational involvement, emotion, and communicational continuity

The second conceptual nucleus deepens this reading by demonstrating that continued interaction with AI systems can originate forms of relational and emotional involvement. The studies by Skjuve et al. (2021) and Croes et al. (2021) evidence that users construct expectations of continuity, predictability, and companionship in interactions with chatbots, while Ho et al. (2018) demonstrate psychological effects associated with emotional self-disclosure. Interpreted in light of the axioms of human communication, these results confirm the primacy of the relationship over communicational content. The relational efficacy of human-AI communication does not depend on the semantic depth of responses, but on the perceived relational framing - availability, absence of judgment, and interactional coherence. As proposed by Watzlawick et al. (1967), meaning emerges from the relationship and the communicational sequence, and not exclusively from the explicit content of the message. AI, by simulating continuity and responsiveness, actively participates in this relational construction, even without subjective intentionality.

Human expression, identity, and communicational agency

The third conceptual nucleus evidence is that AI intervenes directly in how subjects express themselves, build trust, and configure their communicational identity. The results of Banks (2019) on the attribution of moral agency, as well as those of Sundar and Kim (2019) on trust heuristics, demonstrate that algorithmic communication is not interpreted as neutral. On the contrary, it is framed by social and moral categories that guide users' communicational behavior. This set of results articulates directly with the axioms emphasizing the pragmatic dimension of communication: to communicate is to act and produce effects. AI does not limit itself to transmitting messages, reorganizing the position of the communicating subject and influencing how they perceive themselves, express themselves, and position themselves relationally. Human expression thus becomes partially shaped by systems that introduce patterns of personalization and discursive normalization, although this process is rarely explicitly thematized in the analyzed studies.

Ethics, responsibility, and communication as relational space

The fourth conceptual nucleus evidence that AI-mediated communication raises ethical questions that cannot be resolved exclusively on the technical or normative plane. The proposals of Floridi et al. (2018) and Coeckelbergh (2020) underscore the need for relational ethical frameworks, in which the attribution of responsibility and trust depends on communicational processes. However, the scoping review reveals that these approaches rarely integrate structured models of communication. Communication frequently appears as a backdrop - a means to explain trust, responsibility, or transparency - and not as a central theoretical object. This limitation reinforces the pertinence of this chapter's proposal: to place communication back at the center of the ethical analysis of AI, recognizing that power, trust, and responsibility are always negotiated in relational systems.

AI-mediated communication raises specific ethical challenges that cannot be fully grasped by approaches focused exclusively on technical performance, output accuracy, or the mitigation of algorithmic biases. Many of these challenges emerge precisely from the communicational dimension of the interaction, that is, from how systems produce meaning, frame relationships, and structure expectations of reciprocity, trust, and communicational legitimacy.

A first ethical challenge lies in the *simulation of relational competencies*, such as empathy, care, and understanding. Although literature demonstrates that the psychological effects of perceived empathy can be real for users, the deliberate use of empathetic signals by systems lacking emotional experience raises relevant questions of transparency, informed consent, and potential symbolic manipulation. The attribution of empathy to artificial systems can induce high levels of trust, especially in sensitive contexts - such as health, psychological support, or education - where users may underestimate technical, institutional, and responsibility limits associated with the system (Coeckelbergh, 2020).

A second ethical challenge relates to the *structural asymmetry of communicational reciprocity*. As evidenced in the axiomatic analysis, human-AI communication tends to assume a complementary configuration, not a symmetrical one: users expose personal data, emotions, and vulnerabilities, while systems operate without equivalent social costs and under objectives defined by third parties - organizations, platforms, or business models. This asymmetry is frequently concealed by friendly interfaces, relationally calibrated language, and discourses of technological neutrality, which hinders a critical evaluation of the established communicational relationship (Crawford, 2021).

A third ethical challenge concerns the *communicational opacity* of AI systems. The absence of transparency regarding criteria for response, filtering, prioritization, and personalization limits users' ability to understand how meaning is produced, organized, and distributed in the interaction. From the perspective of communication pragmatics, this opacity compromises the possibility of renegotiating relational frameworks and the punctuation of the communicational sequence, increasing the risk of structural misunderstandings and erroneous attributions of intention, authority, or responsibility (Ananny & Crawford, 2018).

Together, these ethical limits indicate that the evaluation of AI-mediated communication must go beyond traditional principles of algorithmic fairness and data protection, incorporating an explicit analysis of the communicational, relational, and symbolic effects produced by systems. Recognizing communication as a central space for the production of meaning and power thus becomes an indispensable condition for a more comprehensive ethical approach to Artificial Intelligence in social contexts.

CONCLUSION

Transversally, the results of the scoping review demonstrate that a significant part of the phenomena observed in human-AI communication is conceptually compatible with structural principles formulated by the Palo Alto School. Elements such as the impossibility of not communicating, the primacy of the relationship over content, the punctuation of the interactional sequence, and the inseparability of communication and power are present, albeit implicitly, in much of the contemporary literature on AI-mediated interaction. However, this compatibility is rarely thematized or systematically integrated into the theoretical frameworks used.

The original contribution of this chapter consists of making this articulation explicit. By reading AI-mediated communication considering the axioms of human communication, the chapter proposes an integrative framework that allows for understanding the evolution of human communication not as an epistemological rupture, but as a relational reconfiguration in new sociotechnical ecosystems. This perspective allows bridging the theoretical gap identified by the scoping review, offering a coherent conceptual basis to interpret phenomena that, in existing literature, frequently appear fragmented or treated in isolation.

The analysis developed evidences that many of the communicational effects associated with AI do not introduce entirely new principles, but rather intensify, displace, or make more visible dynamics already described by communication theory. In particular, it is demonstrated that the impossibility of not communicating expands in algorithmic contexts, where technical infrastructures communicate continuously, environmentally, and often unintentionally; that the distinction between content and relationship remains central to the interpretation of human-AI interactions, despite being frequently obscured by excessive focus on informational output ; that the punctuation of the communicational sequence is profoundly conditioned by opaque algorithmic logics ; that the distinction between digital and analogic communication maintains analytical relevance, albeit reconfigured by simulated communicational signals ; and that dynamics of symmetry, complementarity, and power assume structurally asymmetric forms in contexts mediated by platforms and intelligent systems.

By situating AI in the historical *continuum* of the evolution of human communication, the chapter moves away from technodeterminist readings and contributes to a relational and systemic understanding of AI-mediated communication. AI does not replace or eliminate the foundations of human communication; rather, it introduces new sociotechnical configurations that tension, reorganize, and amplify them. This framework reinforces the actuality and transversality of the axioms of communication, demonstrating their explanatory capacity in advanced technological contexts and their relevance for critically thinking about the present and future of human communication.

IMPLICATIONS FOR FUTURE RESEARCH

The conclusions point toward several promising directions for future research. First, the need for a more systematic integration between communication theory and empirical studies on AI is evident, encouraging investigations that explicitly mobilize the axioms of human communication in the analysis of human-AI interactions. Such an approach would allow for empirically testing the applicability of these principles in concrete algorithmic ecosystems, deepening their operationalization in contemporary communicational contexts.

Second, future investigations could comparatively explore different configurations of human-AI communication, distinguishing between types of systems - such as chatbots, voice assistants, recommender systems, social agents - and different contexts of use. This differentiation would allow for a more precise understanding of how relational, emotional, and identity dynamics associated with interaction with intelligent systems vary. Longitudinal studies assume relevance here, enabling the analysis of long-term effects of continued interaction with AI on human expression and relationship building.

Finally, the chapter evidences the importance of deepening the ethical and political dimension of AI-mediated communication, explicitly articulating communication, power, and algorithmic governance. Communication must not be conceived merely as a channel or technical interface, but as a central space to produce meaning, trust, and social responsibility. Integrating this communicational perspective into ethical and regulatory debates on AI could contribute to development and governance models that are more sensitive to the relational dynamics structuring social life in the digital age.

In summary, by proposing a reading of Artificial Intelligence considering the axioms of human communication, this chapter seeks not only to interpret emerging phenomena but also to provide robust conceptual instruments to think critically about the future of communication and human relationships in a world progressively mediated by intelligent systems.

REFERENCES

Ananny, M., & Crawford, K. (2018). Seeing without knowing: Limitations of the transparency ideal and its application to algorithmic accountability. *New Media & Society*, *20*(3), 973–989. DOI: 10.1177/1461444816676645

Austin, J. L. (1962). *How to do things with words*. Clarendon Press.

Banks, J. (2019). A perceived moral agency scale: Development and validation of a metric for humans and machines. *Computers in Human Behavior*, *90*, 363–371. DOI: 10.1016/j.chb.2018.08.028

Barthes, R. (1977). The death of the author. In *Image, music, text* (pp. 142–148). Hill and Wang.

Bateson, G. (1972). *Steps to an ecology of mind*. University of Chicago Press.

Baym, N. K. (2015). *Personal connections in the digital age* (2nd ed.). Polity Press.

Bender, E. M., Gebru, T., McMillan-Major, A., & Shmitchell, S. (2021). On the dangers of stochastic parrots: Can language models be too big? *Proceedings of the 2021 ACM Conference on Fairness, Accountability, and Transparency*, 610-623. https://doi.org/DOI: 10.1145/3442188.3445922

Berger, P. L., & Luckmann, T. (1966). *The social construction of reality: A treatise in the sociology of knowledge*. Anchor Books.

Blumer, H. (1969). *Symbolic interactionism: Perspective and method*. Prentice-Hall.

Bucher, T. (2018). *If...then: Algorithmic power and politics*. Oxford University Press. DOI: 10.1093/oso/9780190493028.001.0001

Carey, J. W. (1989). *Communication as culture: Essays on media and society*. Unwin Hyman.

Castells, M. (1996). *The rise of the network society*. Blackwell.

Castells, M. (2009). *Communication power*. Oxford University Press.

Coeckelbergh, M. (2020). *AI ethics*. MIT Press. DOI: 10.7551/mitpress/12549.001.0001

Couldry, N., & Hepp, A. (2017). *The mediated construction of reality*. Polity Press.

Craig, R. T. (1999). Communication theory as a field. *Communication Theory*, *9*(2), 119–161. DOI: 10.1111/j.1468-2885.1999.tb00355.x

Crawford, K. (2021). *Atlas of AI: Power, politics, and the planetary costs of artificial intelligence*. Yale University Press.

Croes, E. A. J., Antheunis, M. L., & Schouten, A. P. (2021). Developing relationships with chatbots: The role of social presence and perceived agency. *Computers in Human Behavior*, *120*, 106758. DOI: 10.1016/j.chb.2021.106758

Floridi, L., Cowls, J., Beltrametti, M., Chatila, R., Chazerand, P., Dignum, V., Luetge, C., Madelin, R., Pagallo, U., Rossi, F., Schafer, B., Valcke, P., & Vayena, E. (2018). AI4People-An ethical framework for a good AI society: Opportunities, risks, principles, and recommendations. *Minds and Machines*, *28*(4), 689–707. DOI: 10.1007/s11023-018-9482-5 PMID: 30930541

Foucault, M. (1971). Orders of discourse. *Social Sciences Information. Information Sur les Sciences Sociales*, *10*(2), 7–30. DOI: 10.1177/053901847101000201

Foucault, M. (1977). What is an author? In Bouchard, D. F. (Ed.), *Language, counter-memory, practice* (pp. 113–138). Cornell University Press. (Original work published 1969)

Gillespie, T. (2018). *Custodians of the Internet: Platforms, content moderation, and the hidden decisions that shape social media*. Yale University Press.

Goffman, E. (1959). *The presentation of self in everyday life*. Doubleday.

Goffman, E. (1967). *Interaction ritual: Essays on face-to-face behavior*. Anchor Books.

Grice, H. P. (1975). Logic and conversation. In Cole, P., & Morgan, J. L. (Eds.), Syntax and semantics: Vol. 3. *Speech acts* (pp. 41–58). Academic Press. DOI: 10.1163/9789004368811_003

Guzman, A. L. (2018). *Human-machine communication: Rethinking communication, technology, and ourselves*. Peter Lang. DOI: 10.3726/b14399

Guzman, A. L., & Lewis, S. C. (2020). Artificial intelligence and communication: A human–machine communication research agenda. *New Media & Society*, *22*(1), 70–86. DOI: 10.1177/1461444819858691

Ho, A., Hancock, J., & Miner, A. S. (2018). Psychological, relational, and emotional effects of self-disclosure after conversations with a chatbot. *Journal of Communication*, *68*(4), 712–733. DOI: 10.1093/joc/jqy026 PMID: 30100620

Kitchin, R. (2017). Thinking critically about and researching algorithms. *Information Communication and Society*, *20*(1), 14–29. DOI: 10.1080/1369118X.2016.1154087

Lee, J. D., & See, K. A. (2004). Trust in automation: Designing for appropriate reliance. *Human Factors*, *46*(1), 50–80. DOI: 10.1518/hfes.46.1.50.30392 PMID: 15151155

Lombard, M., & Xu, K. (2021). Social responses to media technologies: A review and update. *Human-Computer Interaction*, *36*(1), 1–58. DOI: 10.1080/07370024.2019.1632596

Luhmann, N. (1995). *Social systems* (Bednarz, J.Jr, & Baecker, D., Trans.). Stanford University Press. (Original work published 1984)

McLuhan, M. (1964). *Understanding media: The extensions of man*. McGraw-Hill.

Mead, G. H. (1934). *Mind, self, and society*. University of Chicago Press.

Noble, S. U. (2018). *Algorithms of oppression: How search engines reinforce racism*. New York University Press. DOI: 10.18574/nyu/9781479833641.001.0001

Ong, W. J. (1982). *Orality and literacy: The technologizing of the word*. Methuen. DOI: 10.4324/9780203328064

Pelau, C., Dabija, D. C., & Ene, I. (2021). What makes an AI device human-like? The role of interaction quality, empathy and perceived psychological anthropomorphic characteristics. *Computers in Human Behavior*, *122*, 106855. DOI: 10.1016/j.chb.2021.106855

Ranzini, G., & Lutz, C. (2017). Love at first swipe? Explaining Tinder self-presentation and motives. *Mobile Media & Communication*, *5*(1), 80–101. DOI: 10.1177/2050157916664559

Reeves, B., & Nass, C. (1996). *The media equation: How people treat computers, television, and new media like real people and places*. Cambridge University Press.

Searle, J. R. (1969). *Speech acts: An essay in the philosophy of language*. Cambridge University Press. DOI: 10.1017/CBO9781139173438

Shannon, C. E., & Weaver, W. (1949). *The mathematical theory of communication*. University of Illinois Press.

Sharabi, L. L. (2021). Effect of algorithms on mate selection: A theoretical framework. *Human-Machine Communication*, *3*, 21–38. DOI: 10.30658/hmc.3.2

Skjuve, M., Følstad, A., Fostervold, K. I., & Brandtzæg, P. B. (2021). My chatbot companion – A study of human–chatbot relationships. *International Journal of Human-Computer Studies*, *149*, 102601. DOI: 10.1016/j.ijhcs.2021.102601

Sundar, S. S. (2008). The MAIN model: A heuristic approach to understanding technology effects on credibility. In Metzger, M. J., & Flanagin, A. J. (Eds.), *Digital media, youth, and credibility* (pp. 73–100). MIT Press.

Sundar, S. S., & Kim, J. (2019). Machine heuristic: When we trust computers more than humans with our personal information. *Proceedings of the ACM on Human-Computer Interaction, 3*(CSCW), 1-20. https://doi.org/DOI: 10.1145/3290605.3300768

Turing, A. M. (1950). Computing machinery and intelligence. *Mind, 59*(236), 433–460. DOI: 10.1093/mind/LIX.236.433

Turkle, S. (2011). *Alone together: Why we expect more from technology and less from each other*. Basic Books.

van Dijck, J. (2013). *The culture of connectivity: A critical history of social media*. Oxford University Press. DOI: 10.1093/acprof:oso/9780199970773.001.0001

van Dijck, J., Poell, T., & de Waal, M. (2018). *The platform society: Public values in a connective world*. Oxford University Press. DOI: 10.1093/oso/9780190889760.001.0001

Walther, J. B. (2011). Theories of computer-mediated communication and interpersonal relations. In Knapp, M. L., & Daly, J. A. (Eds.), *The SAGE handbook of interpersonal communication* (4th ed., pp. 443–479). SAGE.

Watzlawick, P., Beavin, J. H., & Jackson, D. D. (1967). *Pragmatics of human communication: A study of interactional patterns, pathologies, and paradoxes*. W. W. Norton.

Weakland, J. H., Fisch, R., Watzlawick, P., & Bodin, A. M. (1974). Brief therapy: Focused problem resolution. *Family Process, 13*(2), 141–168. DOI: 10.1111/j.1545-5300.1974.00141.x

Weick, K. E. (1995). Sensemaking in organizations. *Sage (Atlanta, Ga.)*.

Weizenbaum, J. (1976). *Computer power and human reason: From judgment to calculation*. W. H. Freeman.

Chapter 7
Artificial Intelligence in the Metaverse:
Transforming Cultural Expression and Tourism Experiences

Jessica Ferreira
http://orcid.org/0000-0002-4141-6702
UNIAG, Instituto Politecnico de Bragança, Portugal

António B. Fernandes
UNIAG, Instituto Politécnico de Bragança, Portugal

Sofia Cardim
http://orcid.org/0000-0002-7506-5111
Instituto Politécnico de Bragança, Portugal

ABSTRACT

This chapter examines how artificial intelligence (AI) reshapes cultural mediation and tourism experiences within immersive digital environments, with particular attention to authenticity, empathy, and connection to place. Framed within the evolution of the metaverse as a socio-technical and cultural space, the chapter adopts a qualitative-exploratory approach combining a systematic literature review with an empirical analysis of social media discourse. The empirical phase analyses Instagram hashtag ecosystems related to immersive and digital tourism using Apify, revealing distinct semantic framings across experiential, artistic-cultural, and technological dimensions. The findings demonstrate that AI functions as an active mediator of cultural meaning, fostering experiential authenticity, emotional engagement, and symbolic place attachment.

DOI: 10.4018/979-8-3373-8337-8.ch007

INTRODUCTION

The increasing integration of artificial intelligence (AI) into immersive digital environments has significantly reshaped contemporary forms of cultural expression, interaction, and tourism experiences. Within this context, the metaverse has emerged as a socio-technical space where virtual and augmented realities, intelligent systems, and networked social interaction converge, enabling new modes of cultural mediation and experiential engagement. These developments pose important questions for tourism and cultural heritage, particularly regarding how authenticity, empathy, and connection to place are constructed and experienced when cultural encounters are increasingly mediated by AI-driven technologies.

Tourism has progressively evolved towards an experience-based paradigm, in which emotional engagement, personal meaning, and symbolic value are central to the creation of memorable experiences. Simultaneously, AI-enabled immersive technologies support personalised, adaptive, and interactive forms of engagement, challenging traditional assumptions that cultural authenticity and place attachment depend primarily on physical presence. As a result, cultural and tourism experiences are increasingly shaped through co-creation, narrative adaptation, and digitally mediated interaction, raising critical questions about the role of AI in mediating human-culture relationships.

Against this backdrop, this chapter addresses the following Research Question: How does AI influence cultural mediation and the tourist's relationship with local heritage and identity, particularly in terms of authenticity, empathy, and connection to place? To answer this question, a qualitative-exploratory research design was adopted. The study combines a systematic literature review, supported by bibliometric analysis, with an empirical examination of social media discourse using Instagram hashtag data collected through Apify. This two-phase methodological approach enables the integration of theoretical perspectives with empirical insights into how immersive and AI-mediated cultural experiences are articulated in digital environments.

The chapter is expected to contribute to the existing literature by offering an integrated understanding of AI as a mediator of cultural expression and tourism experience design within the metaverse. By linking conceptual debates on authenticity, empathy, and place with empirical evidence from social media discourse, the study provides insights into how AI reshapes human expression and relationship-building in immersive tourism contexts. In doing so, it aligns with the broader aim of this book to explore the impacts of AI on human interaction, cultural meaning, and experiential engagement.

BACKGROUND

The Metaverse as a Socio-Technical and Cultural Space

The concept of the metaverse originated in science fiction (Stephenson, 1992) as a critical and fictional vision of the future in the early 1990s (Smethurst et al., 2023). At the time, it was described as a shared virtual environment parallel to the physical world, which users accessed through avatars, considered a social (Katachie & Kessler, 2024), economic, and cultural space, that is, a space for social interaction and identity construction, structural aspects for culture and tourism.

In the late 1990s and early 2000s, alongside the technological advancements that characterised this period, the first virtual worlds emerged, enabling a multitude of users to interact with one another. Notable examples include Active Worlds (1995) and Second Life (2003) (Boellstorff, 2008; Castronova, 2005; Damer, 2008). The main features of these environments were persistence, the possibility of customising avatars (i.e., each user could assume an avatar with characteristics desirable to them), as well as the opportunity to experience cultural events and virtual tourism. However, it was still a technologically limited space.

The consolidation of the metaverse, both technologically and conceptually, took place between 2010 and 2019, based on the development of Virtual Reality (VR), Augmented Reality (AR), computer graphics, and mobile Internet, whose accessibility experienced a major boom during this period (Dionisio et al., 2013; Flavián et al., 2019; Milgram & Kishino, 1994; Radianti et al., 2020). This period is also marked by the widespread use of social networks, which allows for the dissemination of information and more continuous interaction between users. This phase is characterised by the emergence of increasingly complex experiences, integration with the physical world, and the development of applications related to education, culture, and tourism. Hybrid experiences also emerge, which contemplate the coexistence of the physical and digital worlds, proving essential for contemporary tourism (Buhalis & Sinarta, 2019).

The consolidation phase of the metaverse as a socioeconomic ecosystem runs from 2020 to 2022. Through investments by large companies (e.g., Meta/Facebook) (Katachie & Kessler, 2024), integration with blockchain, NFTs, and the consolidation of the digital economy, as well as the exponential growth of persistent and interconnected platforms, the metaverse is now understood as a network of persistent, interconnected, socially inhabited, and economically functional virtual worlds (Ball, 2022).

Since 2023 and up to the present, the metaverse has been profoundly altered by the absorption of Artificial Intelligence (AI), allowing users to become intelligent avatars, the development of dynamically generated narratives, cultural and tourist personalisation, and the existence of adaptive and responsive environments (Russell & Norvig, 2021; Huang & Rust, 2021). Thus, the metaverse becomes an intelligent cultural space where experience is co-created, culture is reinterpreted, and tourism is experiential, immersive, inclusive, and increasingly personalised (Buhalis & Leung, 2018; Asrifan, 2025).

The concept of the metaverse was originally introduced in the early 1990s as a fictional virtual space (Stephenson, 1992) and has since evolved into a complex socio-technical ecosystem shaped by immersive technologies (Dionisio et al., 2013), digital economies (Castronova, 2005; Ball, 2022), and, more recently, by artificial intelligence-driven personalization and cultural co-creation (Huang & Rust, 2021; Buhalis & Leung, 2018).

Artificial Intelligence as a Driver of Immersion and Personalisation

AI is a structural element of the metaverse, as it enables responsive and context-aware dynamics (Soliman et al., 2024). AI can be understood as a system with the ability to perceive the environment, make decisions, and act autonomously, characteristics that are fundamental to the functionality of persistent virtual worlds (Radianti et al., 2024).

In the metaverse, AI acts as a cognitive layer, with the ability to integrate perception, learning, and action, aspects that support high levels of immersion and realism. In this context, AI serves as an experiential infrastructure that shapes how users interact, endowing virtual environments with meaning (Soliman et al., 2024).

One component of AI is Intelligent Agents (IA), which represent visible applications of AI in the metaverse and take the form of autonomous avatars, virtual guides, or even cultural mediators. Thus, IA has the ability to perceive user behaviour, learn from previous interactions (Shin, 2018), and adapt responses in real time. Their presence contributes to an increased sense of social presence and co-presence, critical factors for immersive experiences, as they can take on the roles of historical narrators, virtual curators, and personalised assistants during visits, which generates empathy in the service user (Bec et al., 2019; Tussyadiah et al., 2018).

AI-based recommendation systems also enable increasingly deeper personalisation by users, allowing for real-time content adjustments, route suggestions, and tailored interactions based on behavioural and contextual data provided by users. In this way, generative AI introduces a new paradigm in the metaverse by automatically and continuously creating content that includes virtual environments and multimodal narratives. The systems are self-adaptive and regenerative, with the ability to reorganise themselves in real-time, considering users' choices, the cultural context, and the objectives of the experience itself. These are living systems through which the co-creation of experience occurs (Buhalis & Sinarta, 2019), an aspect of essential relevance to cultural expression, as it allows for a multiplicity of interpretations and reconfigurations of heritage and cultural identity (Anwar et al., 2025).

Experiential AI shifts the focus from technology to the quality of human experience, which is immersive, as it enables the expansion of human capabilities and respect for cultural and social values (Huang & Rust, 2021). In the metaverse, an immersive perspective enables the design and experience of emotionally engaging, culturally sensitive, and, as such, meaningful experiences for the user, who becomes an experiencer (Russell & Norvig, 2021). Thus, the integration of AI into the metaverse establishes a direct link between technological architecture and lived experience through immersion and personalisation provided by intelligent environments, adaptive interaction, and experiential co-creation (Anwar et al., 2025).

AI acts as a key enabler of immersive and personalised experiences in the metaverse by integrating intelligent agents, adaptive systems, and human-centred design principles that bridge technological infrastructures and user experience.

Cultural Expression, Digital Heritage, and AI-Mediated Creativity

Digital cultural heritage encompasses the digitalisation, preservation, and representation of tangible and intangible cultural assets in digital environments, including cultural resources created digitally or converted to digital format, with lasting value for collective memory (UNESCO, 2021).

In the metaverse, cultural heritage is no longer confined to archives or repositories but becomes part of immersive, interactive, and persistent environments. AI plays a crucial role in this context, as it enables intelligent historical reconstructions, context-aware cultural simulations, and the adaptation of heritage content to diverse audiences, transforming cultural and heritage objects into lived, immersive experiences.

Thus, AI introduces new models of cultural co-creation, in which humans and intelligent systems collaborate in the production of cultural content, as Creative AI allows the generation, adaptation, and recombination of cultural elements (such as text, image, sound, and environments) based on data, styles, and cultural contexts. AI-mediated co-creation in the metaverse encourages active user participation (Gursoy et al., 2019), the dynamic reinterpretation of heritage, and the emergence of new forms of digital cultural expression.

Cultural storytelling is a central element in the transmission of meaning, identity, and collective memory (Bec et al., 2019; Tussyadiah et al, 2018), because, in the context of the metaverse, AI enables the continuous creation of immersive and adaptive narratives that evolve according to user choices, cultural context, and experiential journey. Thus, narratives are no longer linear but become personalised, branching, and emergent. AI acts as a narrative developer, adjusting content, characters, and environments to maximise engagement, cultural understanding, and emotional impact.

Digitalisation and AI mediation raise a central debate between the preservation of cultural authenticity, reinterpretation, and cultural recontextualization. While preservation emphasises historical fidelity and cultural integrity, reinterpretation promotes the updating of meanings, the possibility of adaptation to new audiences, and creative experimentation. AI intensifies this tension by allowing multiple versions, readings, and reconstructions of the same cultural object or narrative. In the metaverse, culture is understood as a living process, negotiated between tradition, technology, and user experience.

Experience Economy and Intelligent Tourism in Virtual Environments

As an economic activity, tourism has evolved into an activity focused on creating memorable experiences (Tussyadiah et al., 2018). More than just a service, its evolution involves the induction of the experienced economy as an explanatory paradigm of tourism value, highlighting the sensory, emotional, and symbolic involvement of the consumer, underpinning the theoretical basis that legitimises the use of virtual and immersive environments as valid spaces for tourism consumption.

Tourism has been digitalised and is becoming increasingly intelligent and empathetic (Shin, 2018) through the adoption and continued integration of digital technologies, data, and connectivity. AI, as a central element of smart tourism ecosystems, is responsible for the personalisation, efficiency, and continuous adaptation of the tourism experience, bridging the gap between the logic of experience and technological intelligence.

Thus, AI and virtual environments transform the tourist experience, making it more interactive, personalised, and responsive (Buhalis, 2020). Technology is no longer a mere support but now plays a role in co-creating the experience. The metaverse emerges as a natural extension of this evolution, facilitating the alignment between physical and virtual tourism and enabling the emergence of hybrid experiences that blend physical and digital spaces. It should be noted that this is not a replacement for the tourist experience, but rather a complement to it, making the experiences more memorable for the user.

It has now reached the point where we are discussing the co-creation of value for the tourism experience resulting from the integration of AI into the metaverse, through increased engagement, deep personalisation, and memorability. The tourism experience becomes a co-created process, which must be emotionally meaningful and culturally contextualised. AI in the metaverse redefines tourism as an intelligent, continuous, and hybrid experience, yet personalised, with implications for the competitiveness and sustainability of destinations.

METHODOLOGY

The defined research question (RQ) is: "How does AI influence cultural mediation and the tourist's relationship with local heritage and identity (authenticity, empathy, connection to place)?" To answer this research question, a qualitative-exploratory approach was adopted, utilizing secondary data and structured into two complementary phases, as illustrated in Figure 1.

Figure 1. Methodological design

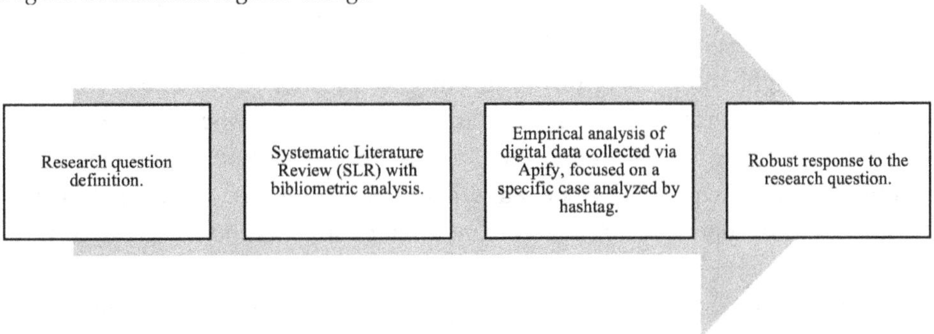

Source: Self-elaboration (2026).

Thus, in the first phase, an RSL was developed, with bibliometric analysis, followed by an empirical analysis of data collected via Apify, focusing on a specific case analysed by hashtag. This methodological design enables us to answer the research question indirectly yet robustly by combining scientific reasoning with empirical evidence of users' actual perceptions.

The objective of the first phase is to identify and systematise how scientific literature addresses AI-mediated cultural mediation in digital, immersive, and tourist contexts, with special attention to the dimensions of cultural authenticity, empathy, social presence, and connection to place and local identity. The RSL procedure is achieved through articles in the Scopus database, covering the period between 2015 and 2025. Thus, the inclusion criteria are articles that cumulatively meet the following conditions: they are peer-reviewed, conceptual or empirical studies; they focus on AI, VR/AR, the metaverse, culture, heritage, and/or tourism; and they include explicit discussion of human experience, cultural mediation, or the relationship with place. Additionally, articles that include purely technical studies without a human or cultural dimension, as well as non-scientific literature, are exclusion criteria.

Using the defined search equation: ("artificial intelligence" OR AI) AND ("metaverse" OR "virtual reality" OR "augmented reality") AND ("cultural heritage" OR culture OR tourism) AND (authenticity OR empathy OR "place attachment"), a total of 43 peer-reviewed articles were retrieved from the Scopus database for the period between 2015 and 2025. Following the application of predefined inclusion and exclusion criteria, which ensured conceptual relevance to AI-mediated cultural experiences in immersive and tourism-related contexts, a final corpus of 20 eligible studies was retained for qualitative synthesis. This corpus formed the empirical basis for both the systematic literature review and the bibliometric analysis, enabling a structured examination of the intellectual landscape of the field.

The bibliometric analysis was conducted to complement the narrative synthesis by identifying structural patterns and dominant research trends within the selected literature. Specifically, the analysis examined the temporal evolution of scientific production, highlighting the growth trajectory of research on AI, immersive technologies, and cultural mediation. In addition, a keyword co-occurrence analysis was performed to explore the conceptual relationships between core themes and to identify the most frequently associated research topics. Finally, thematic clustering techniques were applied to detect dominant research streams and emerging conceptual groupings within the field.

The output of this first phase is a conceptual mapping of the field, including the main analytical dimensions used in the literature to evaluate cultural mediation by AI, which supports the theoretical basis for framing the empirical analysis.

The second phase of the study consisted of an empirical analysis of user-generated social media discourse, conducted using Apify, specifically through the Instagram Related Hashtag Stats Scraper. This phase aimed to explore how perceptions of cultural authenticity, empathy, and connection to place are articulated in digital and immersive tourism-related experiences as expressed through Instagram hashtags. A single-case study strategy was adopted, operationalised through the analysis of a predefined set of thematically relevant hashtags associated with digital, immersive, and AI-mediated cultural experiences. The hashtags analysed were #ImmersiveExperience, #MetaverseTourism, #CulturalExperience, #DigitalTourism, and #InteractiveArt, which served as empirical delimiters of the discursive ecosystem under investigation.

Data were collected exclusively from Instagram, ensuring platform consistency throughout the empirical phase. Using the Instagram Related Hashtag Stats Scraper, hashtag-level data were retrieved, including semantically related hashtags and indicative usage volumes, with results ordered by relevance. This approach enabled the identification of dominant linguistic associations and thematic proximities surrounding immersive cultural and tourism experiences.

For analytical purposes, the derived hashtags were systematically organised into three semantic dimensions: experiential (e.g., #experience, #creator, #project), artistic-cultural (e.g., #interactiveartist, #digitalart), and technological-applicational (e.g., #platform, #provider, #examples). The resulting corpus was analysed using qualitative content analysis, supported by a semantic and categorical coding framework informed by the analytical dimensions identified in the systematic literature review.

The analysis focused on how cultural authenticity, emotional engagement and empathy, and symbolic connection to place and identity are discursively constructed within the hashtag ecosystem, as well as on the implicit role of digital and AI-mediated infrastructures in shaping cultural expression. Findings from this empirical phase were subsequently integrated with the results of the systematic literature review through interpretative analysis, enabling a coherent interpretation of how AI mediates cultural expression and tourism experiences in immersive digital environments.

The output of this phase consisted of a structured semantic mapping of Instagram hashtag discourse, including the identification of primary and derived hashtags, patterns of semantic diversity and specialisation, and the relational configuration through which immersive and AI-mediated cultural and tourism experiences are discursively articulated.

FINDINGS

Findings from the Systematic Literature Review and Bibliometric

The bibliometric analysis of the 43 peer-reviewed articles retrieved from the Scopus database indicates that research on AI, immersive technologies, and cultural experiences within tourism and heritage contexts constitutes a relatively recent and rapidly expanding field of inquiry. As shown in Fig. 2, the temporal distribution of publications, covering the period between 2019 and 2025, reveals a marked acceleration in scholarly output from 2020 onwards, reflecting the growing academic and societal relevance of immersive environments and AI-driven systems.

Figure 2. Annual scientific production on AI, immersive technologies, and cultural experiences (2019–2025)

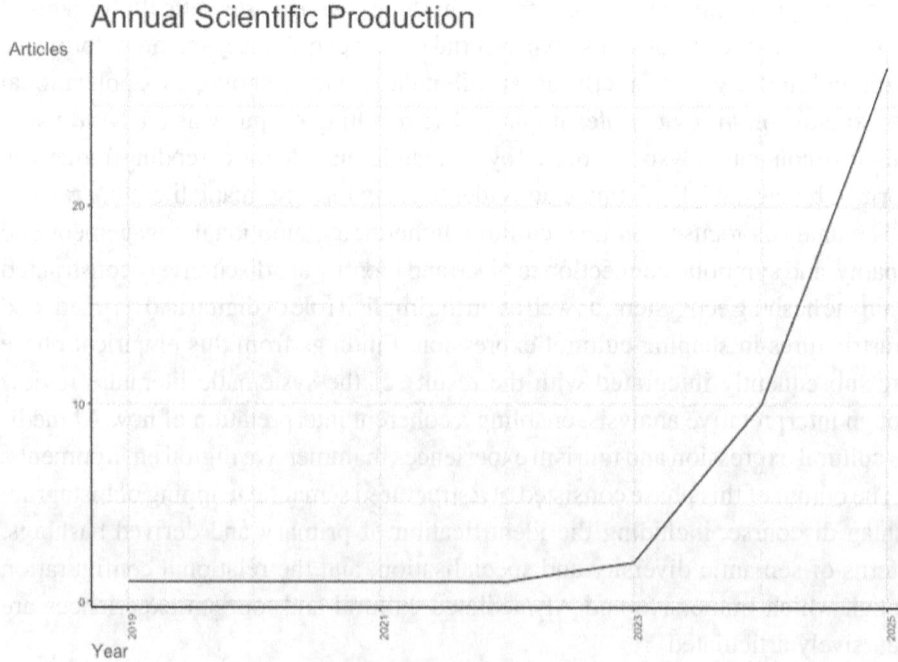

Source: Biblioshiny analysis based on Scopus data (2026).

This pronounced growth trajectory is consistent with the consolidation of virtual and augmented reality technologies, the emergence of the metaverse as a socio-technical paradigm, and the increasing integration of AI into experience design and mediation processes.

The dispersion of publications across 27 different academic sources further highlights the interdisciplinary nature of this research domain. Rather than being anchored in a single disciplinary tradition or dominant journal, the literature spans tourism studies, cultural and heritage research, human-computer interaction, media and communication studies, and information systems. This fragmentation reflects both the novelty of the topic and the multifaceted character of AI-mediated cultural experiences, which intersect technological innovation with cultural interpretation, emotional engagement, and place-based meaning-making.

Across the reviewed corpus, a gradual conceptual shift can be observed from an initial emphasis on technological capabilities towards a more human-centred perspective. While earlier studies predominantly addressed the functional and representational affordances of immersive technologies, more recent contributions increasingly foreground experiential dimensions, such as perceived authenticity, emotional engagement, social presence, and relational outcomes between users and cultural or heritage contexts. AI is progressively framed not merely as a technical enhancement but as an active mediator of cultural meaning, shaping how users interpret, experience, and emotionally connect with places and cultural narratives.

Overall, the bibliometric findings confirm that the field is characterised by rapid growth, conceptual diversification, and a strong experiential orientation, thereby justifying the exploratory nature of the present study. They also provide a robust foundation for the subsequent systematic literature review, which further examines how these emerging themes are theoretically and empirically articulated, and how they inform the analytical framework applied in the empirical phase of the research.

The systematic literature review followed the PRISMA 2020 framework, comprising the four standard stages of identification, screening, eligibility, and inclusion. In the identification stage, a total of 43 records were retrieved from the Scopus database using the predefined search equation combining AI, immersive technologies, cultural heritage, tourism, and experience-related constructs.

During the screening stage, titles and abstracts were examined to assess the general relevance of the studies. Records that were clearly outside the scope of the research, namely those focusing exclusively on technical, engineering, or educational applications without explicit connections to cultural mediation, tourism, or immersive experiences, were excluded.

In the eligibility stage, full-text assessment was conducted for the articles that passed the screening phase. At this stage, studies were evaluated against the established inclusion criteria, requiring explicit engagement with AI and/or immersive technologies, a clear focus on cultural heritage, cultural expression, or tourism contexts, and substantive discussion of experiential or relational dimensions such as authenticity, empathy, social presence, or connection to place.

Following this process, 20 peer-reviewed articles met all eligibility criteria and were retained for qualitative synthesis. These studies constitute the final sample included in the systematic literature review, as illustrated in the PRISMA flow diagram, Figure 3. This PRISMA-guided filtering process ensured methodological transparency and conceptual coherence, providing a robust foundation for the subsequent narrative synthesis of how AI mediates cultural expression and tourism experiences in immersive environments.

Figure 3. PRISMA flow diagram of the systematic literature review process

Identification

•Records identified through SCOPUS database searching (n=43)

Screening

•Records Screened (n=39)

Eligibility

•Full-text articles assessed for eligibility (n=39)

Included

•Articles included in qualitative synthesis (n=20)

Source: Self-elaboration (2026)

The systematic literature review reveals a growing and convergent body of research examining how AI reshapes cultural mediation, experiential engagement, and the relationship between individuals and cultural heritage within immersive and tourism-related environments. Across the analysed studies, AI is consistently framed not merely as a technological tool, but as an active mediator of meaning, interaction, and experience in digital and hybrid cultural contexts.

A central theme emerging from the literature concerns the reconfiguration of cultural authenticity in AI-mediated environments. Rather than treating authenticity as a static attribute rooted exclusively in material originality, several studies conceptualise it as an experiential and relational construct that emerges through interaction, narrative coherence, and contextualisation. Research on immersive heritage platforms and metaverse-based conservation frameworks demonstrates that users often perceive digitally mediated experiences as authentic when they are transparent, culturally grounded, and narratively consistent, even in the absence of physical proximity to heritage artefacts (Zhang & Taib, 2025; Buragohain et al., 2024). This perspective is further reinforced by studies linking authenticity to experiential satisfaction in heritage tourism, where alignment between cultural representation and visitor expectations plays a decisive role (Dai et al., 2021).

The literature also highlights a persistent tension between preservation and reinterpretation. While AI enables sophisticated reconstructions, digital twins, and adaptive representations of cultural assets, concerns are raised regarding historical fidelity, cultural authority, and the potential dilution of heritage meaning. Studies focusing on metaverse applications for cultural heritage underline that excessive automation or generative reconstruction may risk transforming heritage into an aestheticised or commodified experience if cultural context and curatorial intent are not adequately preserved (Allal-Chérif, 2022; Oladokun et al., 2024). Consequently, authenticity in AI-mediated heritage environments is shown to depend less on technological realism and more on culturally informed design and governance.

Another prominent dimension identified in the literature is the role of AI in fostering empathy, social presence, and emotional engagement. Empirical studies using immersive VR systems in cultural and heritage settings indicate that AI-enhanced environments can support perspective-taking, emotional resonance, and a heightened sense of co-presence, particularly when narratives are adaptive and user-centred (Fong et al., 2025). AI contributes to these outcomes by enabling personalised interactions, emotionally responsive virtual agents, and non-linear storytelling pathways, which together enhance experiential depth.

Closely related to empathy is the emergence of parasocial and symbolic relationships with digital agents, avatars, and AI-mediated cultural figures. Research examining virtual spokespersons, avatars, and immersive companions suggests that users can develop meaningful emotional attachments to non-human entities when these exhibit coherent identities and culturally embedded behaviours (Babu et al., 2025; Anwar et al., 2025). These findings challenge traditional assumptions that authenticity and emotional engagement require direct human mediation, instead positioning AI as a relational actor within cultural experience ecosystems.

The reviewed literature further emphasises the capacity of AI-mediated immersive environments to strengthen connection to place and local identity, particularly within tourism contexts. Studies focusing on virtual museums, heritage destinations, and metaverse-based tourism experiences demonstrate that digital immersion can reinforce place attachment by communicating local narratives, symbolic meanings, and cultural values in engaging ways (Gao & Braud, 2023; Almasooudi, 2024). Importantly, several authors note that such experiences often stimulate curiosity and intention to visit physical destinations, supporting the view that AI-driven virtual tourism complements rather than replaces on-site experiences.

From a strategic perspective, AI is also portrayed as a key enabler of intelligent tourism systems, supporting personalisation, destination branding, and experiential optimisation. Machine learning and adaptive systems are increasingly applied to tailor cultural content, guide visitor flows, and enhance engagement in heritage tourism environments (Harisanty et al., 2024; Noroozinejad Farsangi et al., 2024). However, the literature consistently cautions against overly data-driven approaches that prioritise efficiency at the expense of cultural diversity, inclusivity, and local voice.

Ethical considerations constitute a transversal concern across the reviewed studies. Authors repeatedly highlight risks related to cultural stereotyping, algorithmic bias, loss of narrative control, and the marginalisation of local communities when AI systems autonomously mediate cultural representation (Markevičius & Olsson, 2023; Oladokun et al., 2024). These concerns reinforce the need for human-centred and participatory design frameworks that ensure AI technologies operate as facilitators of cultural expression rather than as substitutes for cultural agency.

Overall, the systematic literature review demonstrates that AI fundamentally reshapes cultural mediation in immersive and tourism environments by redefining authenticity, enabling empathy, and fostering new forms of connection to place and identity. Rather than diminishing cultural experience, AI has the potential to enrich it through co-creation, adaptivity, and personalisation. Nevertheless, this potential remains contingent upon ethically grounded, culturally sensitive, and context-aware implementation strategies, which are essential to sustaining meaningful and responsible cultural tourism experiences in the metaverse.

Empirical Findings: Social Media Discourse Analysis (Apify)

This section presents the empirical findings derived from the analysis of Instagram hashtag discourse using Apify's Instagram Related Hashtag Stats Scraper. The objective of this phase was to examine how immersive, digital, and AI-mediated cultural and tourism experiences are semantically structured on social media, with particular attention to dimensions of authenticity, empathy, and connection to place, as defined in the RQ.

The analysis adopts a hashtag-based discursive approach, recognising hashtags as collective meaning-making devices that allow users to categorise, frame, and communicate experiences within digital environments. Rather than analysing individual posts or user-generated narratives, the study focuses on the relational and semantic architecture formed by primary hashtags and their associated derivatives, which together reveal dominant interpretative frames within Instagram's ecosystem.

The empirical analysis was centred on five primary hashtags: #ImmersiveExperience, #MetaverseTourism, #CulturalExperience, #DigitalTourism, and #InteractiveArt. For each primary hashtag, a set of semantically related hashtags was retrieved through Apify. Following data cleaning and deduplication, the number of unique derived hashtags was calculated for each case, allowing for the assessment of semantic diversity rather than posting frequency.

Table 1 summarises the primary hashtags analysed, illustrative examples of their derived hashtags, and the corresponding number of unique derived hashtags identified after deduplication.

Table 1. Primary hashtags, derived hashtags, and semantic relations

Primary hashtag	Derived hashtags	Number of derived hashtags (n)
#ImmersiveExperience	#experience, #immersive, #digitalexperience, #interactiveexperience, #virtualexperience, ...	15
#MetaverseTourism	#metaverse, #virtualworld, #digitaltravel, #futuretravel, #virtualexperience, ...	11
#CulturalExperience	#culture, #creativeexperience, #culturaljourney, #localculture, #artandculture, ...	13
#DigitalTourism	#digitaltravel, #traveltech, #smarttourism, #virtualtour, #technologytourism, ...	12
#InteractiveArt	#interactiveartist, #digitalart, #newmediaart, #creativecoding, #artandtechnology, ...	14

Source: Elaboration based on Apify Instagram Related Hashtag Stats Scraper data.

The variation observed in the number of unique derived hashtags reflects differences in semantic breadth and discursive orientation across experiential, cultural, artistic, and technological framings of immersive and digital tourism experiences. Importantly, these differences do not represent posting volume or popularity, but rather the diversity of conceptual associations surrounding each primary hashtag.

The hashtag #ImmersiveExperience exhibits the highest level of semantic diversity, indicating that immersive experiences are framed through a wide range of experiential and interaction-oriented associations. This finding supports the interpretation of authenticity as a subjective and experiential construct, grounded in personal involvement and emotional engagement.

Similarly, #CulturalExperience demonstrates substantial semantic diversity, reflecting the multiplicity of ways in which culture is articulated in digital environments. The presence of derived hashtags related to creativity, culture, and experience suggests that cultural mediation in immersive contexts is characterised by interpretative openness and symbolic engagement rather than fixed representations of heritage.

In contrast, #MetaverseTourism and #DigitalTourism show more moderate levels of semantic diversity, consistent with their more functional and technology-oriented discursive framing. These hashtags tend to cluster around notions of virtual environments, future-oriented travel, and digital infrastructures, reinforcing the role of technology as an enabling condition for immersive experiences rather than as a primary source of cultural meaning.

Finally, #InteractiveArt reveals a high degree of semantic diversity within a more specialised artistic-cultural domain. This pattern highlights the role of interactive and digital art as a key mediator between technology and culture, facilitating emotionally engaging and creatively driven forms of cultural expression in immersive environments.

The analysis of semantic overlap between primary hashtags reveals no direct overlap of derived hashtags across the selected cases. Each primary hashtag is associated with a distinct set of semantically related hashtags, indicating a high degree of discursive separation within Instagram's hashtag ecosystem. This absence of overlap suggests that immersive, cultural, artistic, and technological framings of digital tourism experiences are articulated through clearly differentiated semantic fields rather than through shared or hybrid vocabularies.

Although each primary hashtag generated an equivalent number of unique derived hashtags after deduplication, this numerical symmetry reflects the scraper configuration rather than uniformity of discourse. The qualitative composition of the derived hashtags differs substantially across cases, indicating varying degrees of semantic specialisation. Experiential hashtags are characterised by emotionally and interaction-oriented vocabulary, artistic-cultural hashtags by creative and aesthetic terminology, and technological hashtags by infrastructural and functional language. This pattern highlights that discursive differentiation emerges from semantic orientation rather than quantitative diversity.

DISCUSSION

This chapter examined how AI influences cultural mediation and the tourist's relationship with local heritage and identity, particularly regarding authenticity, empathy, and connection to place, within immersive and metaverse-related environments. By integrating the conceptual foundations outlined in the background section, the evidence synthesised through the systematic literature review, and the empirical findings derived from social media discourse analysis, the study provides a coherent and multi-layered interpretation of AI-mediated cultural and tourism experiences.

The background section conceptualised the metaverse as an evolving socio-technical and cultural space, progressing from early virtual environments to intelligent ecosystems shaped by immersive technologies, digital economies, and AI (Stephenson, 1992; Dionisio et al., 2013; Ball, 2022). This evolution supports a shift from static and representational approaches to culture towards dynamic, adaptive, and co-created experiences, where users actively participate in meaning-making processes (Buhalis & Leung, 2018; Huang & Rust, 2021). The systematic literature review corroborates this perspective, demonstrating that contemporary research increasingly frames AI as an active mediator of cultural experience, rather than as a neutral technological tool.

One of the most significant points of convergence between the background, the literature, and the empirical findings concerns the redefinition of cultural authenticity. As discussed in the background, AI-enabled immersive environments facilitate personalisation, adaptive narratives, and experiential co-creation, challenging object-based and place-bound notions of authenticity (Huang & Rust, 2021; Anwar et al., 2025). The systematic literature review reinforces this view, highlighting a growing consensus that authenticity in digital and immersive contexts is experienced as a relational and experiential construct, emerging through interaction, narrative coherence, and contextual alignment rather than through material originality alone (Zhang & Taib, 2025; Buragohain et al., 2024). The empirical analysis supports this reconceptualisation, as experiential framings dominate social media discourse, particularly around hashtags such as #ImmersiveExperience and #CulturalExperience, indicating that users associate authenticity primarily with lived experience and emotional engagement (Tussyadiah et al., 2018).

Empathy and emotional engagement constitute a second core dimension where strong alignment is observed across all analytical layers. The background highlighted the role of intelligent agents, adaptive interaction, and experiential AI in fostering social presence and emotional resonance within immersive environments (Shin, 2018; Bec et al., 2019; Russell & Norvig, 2021). The literature review further demonstrates that AI-driven personalisation and adaptive storytelling enhance emotional involvement and empathetic engagement in cultural and tourism contexts (Anwar et al., 2025). Empirically, this is reflected in the semantic richness associated with artistic and experiential hashtags, particularly #InteractiveArt, where creative and aesthetic vocabulary suggests that empathy is mediated through interaction, creativity, and sensory immersion. This convergence underscores the importance of creative co-creation as a key mechanism through which AI supports emotional and relational dimensions of cultural mediation.

Connection to place and local identity emerges as a more nuanced and complex dimension. While the background section emphasised the importance of hybrid experiences that integrate physical and digital spaces in contemporary tourism (Buhalis & Sinarta, 2019), the empirical findings reveal a relative absence of explicit geographical references in social media discourse. Instead, connection to place appears to be constructed symbolically, through narratives, emotions, and experiential intensity. This pattern is consistent with the literature reviewed, which suggests that immersive and digitally mediated tourism experiences often foster symbolic or anticipatory forms of place attachment rather than direct spatial anchoring (Gao & Braud, 2023; Almasooudi, 2024). Thus, AI-mediated environments do not eliminate place-based identity but reconfigure it into a translocal and experiential form.

The empirical finding of an absence of semantic overlap between experiential, artistic-cultural, and technological framings further aligns with insights from both the background and the literature. As previously discussed, AI operates simultaneously as an experiential mediator, a creative partner, and a technological infrastructure within immersive ecosystems (Soliman et al., 2024). The literature similarly distinguishes between the experiential and cultural dimensions that shape meaning and emotional engagement, and the technological systems that enable scalability, adaptivity, and personalisation (Buhalis, 2020). The distinct semantic fields identified in the hashtag analysis reflect this functional differentiation, suggesting that users conceptually separate experience, creativity, and technology within digital tourism discourse.

Overall, the convergence between the background framework, the systematic literature review, and the empirical findings demonstrates that AI reshapes cultural mediation in immersive tourism environments by enabling experiential authenticity, fostering empathy through adaptive and creative interaction, and transforming connection to place into a symbolic and relational construct. Rather than replacing traditional cultural or tourism experiences, AI extends and complements them, offering new forms of participatory, emotionally resonant, and context-aware engagement.

In direct response to the Research Question, this study shows that AI influences the tourist's relationship with heritage and identity by shifting emphasis from static, place-bound authenticity towards dynamic, experiential, and emotionally grounded forms of cultural engagement. This transformation is consistent with the socio-technical evolution of the metaverse outlined in the background and substantiated by the scholarly evidence reviewed, reinforcing the view of immersive digital environments as intelligent cultural spaces that reconfigure human expression and relationship-building through AI.

CONCLUSION

This chapter set out to analyse how AI influences cultural mediation and the tourist's relationship with heritage and identity in immersive and metaverse-related environments, with particular attention to authenticity, empathy, and connection to place. By combining a systematic literature review with an empirical analysis of Instagram hashtag discourse, the study provides both conceptual and empirical evidence on how AI reshapes cultural and tourism experiences in digital contexts.

The findings demonstrate, first, that authenticity in AI-mediated immersive environments is predominantly constructed as an experiential and relational phenomenon rather than as a material or place-bound attribute. Both the literature review and the empirical analysis confirm that users and scholars alike associate authenticity with immersion, interaction, narrative coherence, and emotional engagement, rather than with physical proximity or historical materiality. This confirms a shift towards experiential authenticity as a defining characteristic of cultural and tourism experiences in the metaverse.

Second, the study shows that empathy plays a central role in AI-mediated cultural experiences, particularly through adaptive interaction, creative engagement, and immersive storytelling. The prominence of experiential and artistic-cultural discourses in social media hashtags, especially those related to immersive experience and interactive art, indicates that emotional resonance and participatory co-creation are key mechanisms through which users relate to cultural content in digital environments. AI thus functions as an enabler of emotional engagement, expanding the expressive and relational dimensions of cultural experience.

Third, connection to place and local identity is shown to be reconfigured rather than diminished. While explicit geographical references are less prominent in social media discourse, symbolic and narrative forms of place attachment emerge as significant. Immersive and AI-mediated environments support translocal and anticipatory connections to place, reinforcing the role of digital experiences as complements to physical tourism rather than as substitutes.

From a structural perspective, the empirical findings reveal a clear differentiation between experiential, artistic-cultural, and technological discourses. The absence of semantic overlap between these dimensions suggests that technology operates primarily as an enabling infrastructure, while meaning-making and emotional engagement are shaped through experiential and creative framings. This highlights the importance of human-centred and culturally informed design approaches that prioritise experience and expression over technological determinism.

Overall, this chapter contributes to the understanding of AI as a mediating force that reconfigures cultural expression and tourism experiences in immersive digital environments. It demonstrates that AI does not replace cultural meaning or human connection but reshapes them through co-creation, personalisation, and emotional engagement. These insights align with the broader theme of this book by showing how AI impacts human expression and relationship-building in culturally significant contexts.

Future research should build on these findings by incorporating longitudinal analyses, comparative platform studies, and perspectives from local communities and cultural stakeholders, in order to further assess the long-term implications of AI-mediated cultural tourism for sustainability, inclusivity, and cultural governance.

SOLUTIONS AND RECOMMENDATIONS

The results of this chapter indicate that AI can significantly enhance cultural mediation and tourism experiences in immersive environments, provided that its implementation is guided by human-centred and culturally informed principles. To address the challenges identified, several key recommendations can be proposed.

First, immersive and AI-mediated cultural experiences should prioritise experiential authenticity over technological realism. Narrative coherence, contextual transparency, and meaningful interaction are essential to ensuring that users perceive cultural representations as credible and engaging. Second, given the central role of empathy and emotional engagement, experience design should encourage participatory and co-creative approaches, involving cultural practitioners and creative actors to foster emotionally resonant interactions.

Third, immersive digital experiences should be strategically integrated with physical tourism through hybrid models that reinforce, rather than replace, place-based engagement. Such approaches can support interpretation, anticipation, and long-term attachment to destinations. Finally, ethical governance frameworks are necessary to prevent cultural stereotyping, algorithmic bias, and loss of cultural agency, ensuring that AI functions as an enabling infrastructure rather than a dominant cultural authority.

Overall, these recommendations highlight the need to balance technological innovation with cultural responsibility, enabling AI to support meaningful, inclusive, and sustainable cultural and tourism experiences in the metaverse.

REFERENCES

Allal-Chérif, O. (2022). Intelligent cathedrals: Using augmented reality, virtual reality, and artificial intelligence to provide an intense cultural, historical, and religious visitor experience. *Technological Forecasting and Social Change*, *178*, 121604. DOI: 10.1016/j.techfore.2022.121604

Almasooudi, M. F. (2024). The possibility of applying the metaverse in cultural heritage tourism: A case study on the ancient city of Babylon. *Tourism and Hospitality Research*, 14673584241308167. Advance online publication. DOI: 10.1177/14673584241308167

Anwar, M. S., Yang, J., Frnda, J., Choi, A., Baghaei, N., & Ali, M. (2025). Metaverse and XR for cultural heritage education: Applications, standards, architecture, and technological insights for enhanced immersive experience. *Virtual Reality (Waltham Cross)*, *29*(2), 51. Advance online publication. DOI: 10.1007/s10055-025-01126-z

Asrifan, A. (2025). Foundational concepts of AI and the metaverse in tourism: A scholarly inquiry. In Valeri, M., Shah, S. H. A., & Al-Ghazali, B. M. (Eds.), *Redefining tourism with AI and the metaverse* (pp. 347–372). IGI Global., DOI: 10.4018/979-8-3693-8482-4.ch011

Babu, R. J. K., Rajeswari, P. S., & Babu, S. (2025). Innovating heritage: How TOAST digitally transforms traditional weaving. *Journal of Information Technology Teaching Cases*. DOI: 10.1177/20438869251338321

Ball, M. (2022). *The metaverse: And how it will revolutionize everything*. Liveright Publishing.

Bec, A., Moyle, B., Timms, K., Schaffer, V., Skavronskaya, L., & Little, C. (2019). Management of immersive heritage tourism experiences: A conceptual model. *Tourism Management*, *72*, 117–129. DOI: 10.1016/j.tourman.2018.10.033

Boellstorff, T. (2008). *Coming of age in Second Life: An anthropologist explores the virtually human*. Princeton University Press.

Buhalis, D. (2020). Technology in tourism: From information communication technologies to eTourism and smart tourism towards ambient intelligence tourism. *Tourism Review*, *75*(1), 267–272. DOI: 10.1108/TR-06-2019-0258

Buhalis, D., & Leung, R. (2018). Smart hospitality: Interconnectivity and interoperability towards an ecosystem. *International Journal of Hospitality Management*, *71*, 41–50. DOI: 10.1016/j.ijhm.2017.11.011

Buhalis, D., & Sinarta, Y. (2019). Real-time co-creation and nowness service: Lessons from tourism and hospitality. *Journal of Travel & Tourism Marketing*, *36*(5), 563–582. DOI: 10.1080/10548408.2019.1592059

Buragohain, D., Meng, Y., Deng, C., Li, Q., & Chaudhary, S. (2024). Digitalizing cultural heritage through metaverse applications: Challenges, opportunities, and strategies. *Heritage Science*, *12*(1), 295. Advance online publication. DOI: 10.1186/s40494-024-01403-1

Castronova, E. (2005). *Synthetic worlds: The business and culture of online games*. University of Chicago Press.

Dai, T., Zheng, X., & Yan, J. (2021). Contradictory or aligned? The nexus between authenticity in heritage conservation and heritage tourism, and its impact on satisfaction. *Habitat International*, *107*, 102307. DOI: 10.1016/j.habitatint.2020.102307

Damer, B. (2008). Meeting in the ether: A brief history of virtual worlds as a medium for user-created events. *Artifact*, *2*(2), 94–107. DOI: 10.1080/17493460903020877

Dionisio, J. D. N., Burns, W. G., & Gilbert, R. (2013). 3D virtual worlds and the metaverse: Current status and future possibilities. *ACM Computing Surveys*, *45*(3), 1–38. DOI: 10.1145/2480741.2480751

Flavián, C., Ibáñez-Sánchez, S., & Orús, C. (2019). The impact of virtual, augmented and mixed reality technologies on the customer experience. *Journal of Business Research*, *100*, 547–560. DOI: 10.1016/j.jbusres.2018.10.050

Fong, H., Niewiadomski, R., & Igraś-Cybulska, M. (2025). Instagram reactions to a virtual dining companion: Qualitative coding vs. automated sentiment analysis. In *Proceedings of the CHItaly 2025 Conference*. Association for Computing Machinery. DOI: 10.1145/3750069.3750352

Gao, Z., & Braud, T. C. (2023). VR-driven museum opportunities: Digitized archives in the age of the metaverse. *Artnodes*, *32*(32). Advance online publication. DOI: 10.7238/artnodes.v0i32.402462

Gursoy, D., Chi, O. H., Lu, L., & Nunkoo, R. (2019). Consumers' acceptance of artificially intelligent (AI) device use in service delivery. *International Journal of Information Management*, *49*, 157–169. DOI: 10.1016/j.ijinfomgt.2019.03.008

Harisanty, D., Obille, K. L. B., Anna, N. E. V., Purwanti, E., & Retrialisca, F. (2024). Cultural heritage preservation in the digital age: Harnessing artificial intelligence for the future. *Digital Library Perspectives*, *40*(4), 609–630. DOI: 10.1108/DLP-01-2024-0018

Huang, M.-H., & Rust, R. T. (2021). A strategic framework for artificial intelligence in marketing. *Journal of the Academy of Marketing Science*, *49*(1), 30–50. DOI: 10.1007/s11747-020-00749-9

Katachie, S., & Kessler, A. (2024). Imagining identity in Meta's metaverse: A genealogy of imagined future realms in computer culture. *Communication, Culture & Critique*, *17*(4), 326–335. DOI: 10.1093/ccc/tcae015

Markevičius, T., & Olsson, N. (2023). Towards sustainable conservation science in cultural heritage: Bridging contemporary conservation theory and philosophy of science in authenticity debates. *Frontiers in Materials*, *10*. Advance online publication. DOI: 10.3389/fmats.2023.1274627

Milgram, P., & Kishino, F. (1994). A taxonomy of mixed reality visual displays. *IEICE Transactions on Information and Systems*, *77*(12), 1321–1329.

Noroozinejad Farsangi, E., Shehata, A. O., Rashidi, M., Ghassempour, N., & Mirjalili, S. (2024). Transitioning from BIM to digital twin to metaverse. *Frontiers in Built Environment*, *10*, 1486423. Advance online publication. DOI: 10.3389/fbuil.2024.1486423

Oladokun, B. D., Ajani, Y. A., Ukaegbu, B. C. N., & Oloniruha, E. A. (2024). Cultural preservation through immersive technology: The metaverse as a pathway to the past. *Preservation. Digital Technology & Culture*, *53*(3), 157–164. DOI: 10.1515/pdtc-2024-0015

Radianti, J., Majchrzak, T. A., Fromm, J., & Wohlgenannt, I. (2020). A systematic review of immersive virtual reality applications for higher education. *Computers & Education*, *147*, 103778. DOI: 10.1016/j.compedu.2019.103778

Russell, S., & Norvig, P. (2021). *Artificial intelligence: A modern approach* (4th ed.). Pearson.

Shin, D. (2018). Empathy and embodied experience in virtual environment. *Computers in Human Behavior*, *78*, 64–73. DOI: 10.1016/j.chb.2017.09.012

Smethurst, R., Barbereau, T., & Nilsson, J. (2023). The metaverse's thirtieth anniversary. *Philosophy & Technology*, *36*(3), 51. Advance online publication. DOI: 10.1007/s13347-023-00612-z

Soliman, E. A., Darwish, A., & Hassanien, A. E. (2024). Artificial intelligence powered metaverse. *Artificial Intelligence Review*, *57*(2), 1–46. DOI: 10.1007/s10462-023-10641-x

Stephenson, N. (1992). *Snow crash*. Bantam Books.

Tussyadiah, I. P., Wang, D., Jung, T. H., & tom Dieck, M. C. (2018). Virtual reality, presence, and attitude change. *Tourism Management*, *66*, 140–154. DOI: 10.1016/j.tourman.2017.12.003

UNESCO. (2021). *Culture & artificial intelligence: Reflections on ethics, freedom of expression, access to information and cultural diversity*. UNESCO.

Zhang, W., Taib, N., & Taib, M. (2025). Reimagining cultural heritage conservation through VR, metaverse, and digital twins. *PLoS One*, *20*(11), e0335943. Advance online publication. DOI: 10.1371/journal.pone.0335943 PMID: 41183119

Chapter 8
Designing Against Hypersexualized Defaults:
Trust, Credibility, and Ethical Implications in AI-Generated Avatars on Social Media

Javier Abuín-Penas
http://orcid.org/0000-0002-7822-7526
University of Vigo, Spain

Diana Ramahí-García
University of Vigo, Spain

Patricia Dopico-Rodríguez
University of Vigo, Spain

Marcos Alonso-Mosquera
University of Vigo, Spain

ABSTRACT

This chapter addresses the proliferation of AI generated avatars on social media and the tendency of generative systems to reproduce hypersexualized femininity . Adopting a two layer defaults framework the authors analyze how synthetic defaults stemming from model priors and algorithmic defaults driven by platform visibility regimes jointly incentivize eroticized portrayals that undermine credibility . To proffer a practical alternative this chapter documents the design of Alicia which is a counter default avatar created through a two round Delphi study with seventeen

DOI: 10.4018/979-8-3373-8337-8.ch008

experts . The study translates consensus into operational constraints such as functional styling and adult age coding and implements a consistency pipeline to resist identity drift . By mapping these decisions to relational outcomes the authors argue that resisting hypersexualization is a necessary condition for ethical relationship building in synthetic environments.

INTRODUCTION: HYPERSEXUALIZED DEFAULTS AS A RELATIONAL INFRASTRUCTURE

AI-generated avatars and virtual influencers are becoming increasingly visible actors in social media ecosystems, taking on roles traditionally associated with human creators: performing identity, narrating everyday life, endorsing brands, and sustaining follower engagement through seemingly personal and consistent presence. This shift matters for relationship building because audiences can develop parasocial relationships with mediated personas, and these bonds can influence attitudes and behavioral intentions. Research on influencer environments shows that parasocial relationships are associated with outcomes such as purchase intention and electronic word of mouth, while also interacting with persuasion knowledge (Hwang & Zhang, 2018). In the specific case of virtual influencers, recent work suggests that anthropomorphic indicators (e.g., perceived humanness, attractiveness, eeriness) and perceived autonomy shape parasocial relationship strength and related evaluations (Liu & Wang, 2025).

However, as AI avatars become more common, their design choices increasingly participate in and potentially intensify long standing problems of gendered representation online. Many feminine coded avatar depictions converge toward a narrow template: youthful appearance, idealized proportions, polished styling, and camera framing that emphasizes sexualized markers. In this chapter, these recurring patterns are conceptualized as hypersexualized defaults: outcomes that become easy to produce and easy to amplify due to the combined pull of generative model priors, cultural beauty/sexuality, and platform visibility incentives.

AI-Generated Avatars in Social Media and the Normalization of Default Femininity

The normalization of default femininity in AI avatar culture is best understood as a platformed phenomenon. Social media visibility is uneven and often experienced as algorithmically governed, encouraging creators to interpret platforms as having implicit rules that reward some forms of self presentation over others (Bucher, 2012; Cotter, 2019). In parallel, platformization literature argues that cultural production becomes increasingly contingent on platform infrastructures, metrics, and monetization logics pushing creators toward modular, rapidly iterated content optimized for circulation (Nieborg & Poell, 2018). For synthetic personas, this contingency is amplified: avatar bodies, outfits, poses, facial expressions and environments can be iteratively generated and selected, intensifying optimization pressures.

Figure 1. Aitana López and Emily Pellegrini, virtual influencers AI generated

Generative AI adds a second mechanism: model driven priors. Even when prompts are framed as neutral, image generation models can still yield systematically gendered and stereotypical outputs because learned associations shape prompt–image dependencies (Wu et al., 2025).

Why Disclosure Affects Relationship Building

Hypersexualized defaults are not only an ethical or representational issue. They are also a relationship problem. Relationship building on social media depends on credibility features and on how audiences infer intent. Classic source credibility frameworks identify trustworthiness as a key dimension shaping persuasive impact (Ohanian, 1990). In influencer marketing contexts, perceived credibility and message value predict consumer trust in branded content (Lou & Yuan, 2019). When the persona is AI-generated, credibility becomes even more consequential because audiences may implicitly (or explicitly) evaluate why a synthetic agent exists, who benefits, and how transparent the operation is.

Hypersexualized design choices can disrupt these processes in at least three ways. First, they may weaken trust by triggering interpretations of manipulation or commodification (e.g., sexualized attention tactics), particularly when the avatar's presence is tightly coupled to commercial goals. Second, they can narrow perceived authenticity by signaling that the persona's identity performance is assembled from stereotypical templates rather than grounded in meaningful expression. Third, they can heighten ethical concerns about objectification and the automation of sexist concerns that can shape comment cultures, willingness to engage, and the durability of parasocial bonds.

While this study focuses on human influencers, its implications matter for AI avatars because synthetic personas can industrialize and scale sexualized visual norms potentially reinforcing harmful comparators and narrowing the expressive repertoire that is socially rewarded.

Finally, disclosure and transparency are central for relationship ethics in AI-mediated communication. Sponsorship disclosure research shows that transparency pointers can activate persuasion knowledge and influence subsequent evaluations and engagement intentions (Boerman et al., 2017). More broadly, responsible AI research emphasizes explainability and intelligibility as enabling conditions for accountable deployment and for appropriate trust calibration (Arrieta et al., 2020). For AI avatars, disclosure can operate at multiple levels (naming, profile framing, content…), shaping whether audiences perceive the relationship as legitimate, respectful, and not deceptive.

Chapter Aim, Research Questions and Contribution

This chapter documents and analyzes a Delphi informed design process used to create and deploy the AI-generated feminist avatar Alicia on social media, with the explicit goal of designing against hypersexualized defaults while supporting trust, credibility, authenticity pointers, and transparency in public facing communication.

Evidence from a study using mixed methods of female virtual influencers on Instagram reports a dominant visual repertoire marked by thin body ideals and frequent exposure of eroticized zones, alongside a strong emphasis on the self and pronounced overlap with brand sectors, especially fashion (Villén Higueras & Mata-Núñez, 2025). This chapter builds on these observations by reframing such recurrent aesthetics as relational infrastructure defaults that can condition credibility judgments, authenticity attributes, and trust formation.

Research questions.

- RQ1. How do feminist experts characterize prevailing representations of AI-generated avatars on social media, and what risks do they prioritize for identity formation and gender equality?
- RQ2. How can expert consensus be translated into concrete design requirements and prototype choices that resist hypersexualized defaults (embodiment, styling, context, expressivity)?
- RQ3. How do these design requirements map onto relationship building mechanisms particularly trust, credibility, authenticity, and disclosure in AI-mediated social media interaction?

The chapter contributes (1) a traceable, expert informed pipeline (Delphi rounds → synthesis → prototype set → baseline selection → consensus based consistency control) (2) an explicitly relational lens that connects avatar design decisions to trust and credibility dynamics established in persuasion and influencer research (Ohanian, 1990; Lou & Yuan, 2019) and (3) an ethics by design argument grounded in platform visibility dynamics and empirical evidence of bias in image generative AI (Bucher, 2012; Cotter, 2019; Wu et al., 2025).

BACKGROUND: AI, HUMAN EXPRESSION AND RELATIONSHIP BUILDING

This chapter is positioned at the intersection of three rapidly converging dynamics: (1) the increasing mediation of everyday expression by AI systems embedded in platforms, where how people communicate and present themselves is increasingly shaped by automated or AI assisted processes, (2) the rise of synthetic and AI-generated personas (including virtual influencers and AI-generated avatars) as social actors, whose presence and interactions are produced or curated through computational means, and (3) the transformation of relationship building into a platform shaped practice where trust, credibility, and authenticity are inferred from signs that are partially designed, partially automated, and often opaque.

In this context, human expression on social media is not simply communicated; it is co-produced through a mix of platform affordances, algorithmic selection, and aesthetic infrastructures (e.g., beauty filters and generative image workflows) that tend to normalize certain identity attributes and body ideals while marginalizing others. These conditions are particularly consequential for AI-generated female presenting avatars, because expression and relationship building become entangled with gendered stereotypes and sexualized visual defaults that can be reproduced at scale.

AI Mediation and Expressive Norms

Contemporary platforms operate as socio technical environments in which visibility is selectively distributed, and communicative style becomes standardized through recurrent templates, metrics, and algorithmically optimized formats. Influencer cultures illustrate this clearly: creators learn which visual grammars perform and increasingly align their content with platform logics of engagement, thereby turning aesthetic choices into a form of labor oriented toward visibility. Abidin (2016) conceptualizes this as visibility labor: creators strategically crafting selves to fit platform expectations.

AI intensifies this process in two ways. First, it adds automated assistants to expressive production beautification filters, recommendation engines, captioning tools, and generative models so that stylistic norms may be suggested, enforced, or amplified at the point of creation. Second, it introduces new kinds of machine agency cues: interfaces and systems that behave as if they have goals, preferences, or judgment, which can shape user behavior even when users understand that the system is nonhuman. In platform contexts, this often leads to a pragmatic adaptation: people adjust what they post, how they look, and how they frame identity attributes (gender presentation, attractiveness, professionalism, authenticity) to match what the platform seems to reward.

Generative AI can reproduce and intensify these dynamics because it is trained on large scale datasets that reflect historical inequalities in representation. Bias is not only an output problem; it can be traced through the generation pipeline. For instance, research on Stable Diffusion shows that gender bias persists across internal generation stages and appears in final images. As a result, seemingly neutral prompts can still produce gendered and stereotypical outcomes (Wu et al., 2025). This matters for AI-generated avatars on social media because the avatar's body, styling, and implied sexuality become part of the platform visible identity attributes system: they are read by audiences as signals of intent (e.g., selling, thirst trapping, performing femininity), credibility (e.g., real person vs. fabricated), and relational stance (e.g., approachable friend vs. objectified image). In short, AI mediation does not simply give creators more options; it can also compress expressive variability by making certain identity patterns easier, more default, and more rewarded than others.

Parasociality, Anthropomorphism and Authenticity in Synthetic Agents

Relationship building on social media often takes a parasocial form, in which audiences develop feelings of closeness, familiarity, and perceived reciprocity with mediated figures. Classic accounts define parasocial interaction as a sense of conversational intimacy with a media persona even without genuine mutual exchange (Horton & Wohl, 1956). In digital environments, these dynamics may intensify because platforms simulate interaction through comment threads, likes, and story features, while creators perform accessibility and immediacy.

Production techniques and persona signals such as direct address, perceived self disclosure, and character consistency help cultivate parasocial bonds (Ferchaud et al., 2018). These insights extend to synthetic agents: AI generated avatars and virtual influencers can be designed to strengthen parasocial affordances through frequent posting, controlled narrative arcs, and a stable tone.

Anthropomorphism is pivotal. Audiences may attribute mind, intent, and emotion to nonhuman entities when interpretive signals align with human schemas and social motivations. In human computer contexts, anthropomorphism can be mindful or mindless, sometimes deliberate and sometimes automatic (Kim & Sundar, 2012).

For virtual influencers, human likeness is not a simple more is better variable. Highly humanlike presentation can increase anthropomorphism and parasocial feelings, yet it can also trigger skepticism when audiences suspect deception or manipulation. Design decisions such as skin realism, facial proportions, gaze behavior, and the balance between stylization and photorealism shape perceived credibility and attraction (Nowak & Rauh, 2005). Disclosure is therefore crucial: when artificial origin is stated, audiences recalibrate judgments, sometimes lowering perceived authenticity while increasing perceived transparency. Authenticity becomes a negotiated evaluation grounded in consistency and perceived motives, producing a paradox for synthetic agents: audiences may accept emotional coherence while questioning the legitimacy of designs that leverage relational tendencies (Audrezet et al., 2020).

Trust and Credibility Markers on Social Media Platforms

On social media, trust and credibility are frequently inferred through fast, signal based processing rather than careful verification. Platform interfaces supply credibility markers that function as heuristics: follower counts, engagement metrics, verification badges, professional aesthetics, brand partnerships, and disclosure tags. Communication research offers validated approaches to measuring message credibility, emphasizing that perceptions of accuracy, authenticity, and believability can be systematically assessed rather than treated as vague impressions (Appelman & Sundar, 2016).

For influencers and influencer like agents, credibility is also shaped by classical source credibility dimensions (e.g., perceived expertise, trustworthiness, and attractiveness) and by platform native indicators that audiences interpret as signals of legitimacy or popularity. Influencer marketing research demonstrates that follower counts and visibility can function as social proof but also backfire if they signal over commercialization or distance from the audience. Meta analytic work on influencer marketing effectiveness shows that credibility and relational mediators (including parasocial variables) play a central role in translating exposure into persuasion and engagement (Pan et al., 2025).

Two disclosure related mechanisms are especially relevant for relationship building. First, sponsorship disclosures activate persuasion knowledge: when audiences recognize commercial intent, they may infer manipulation, reducing trust and willingness to spread the message. For example, Boerman et al. (2017) show that sponsorship disclosure can increase recognition of advertising, generate distrusting beliefs, and reduce eWOM intentions. Second, platform initiated tools (e.g., "paid partnership with…") can operate as particularly strong signals, producing robust changes in advertising recognition and downstream trust judgments (Karagür et al., 2022).

Platform native credibility markers for virtual influencers are frequently built through consistent posting practices, coherent identity staging, and brand collaborations that signal legitimacy by association. Case based analysis of Lil Miquela and Lu do Magalu details how commercial partnerships become part of the avatar's routine identity work, normalizing the avatar as a reliable promotional actor (Carrillo-Durán et al., 2024). Similarly, a broader sample of female virtual influencers shows systematic intersections with brand sectors again dominated by fashion where credibility is co produced through repeated aesthetic and commercial signals (Villén Higueras & Mata-Núñez, 2025).

These dynamics become even more unstable when the source is synthetic. Audiences may apply a machine heuristic, sometimes treating machine produced or machine mediated outputs as objective or reliable, while other times treating them as suspicious, manipulative, or uncanny. Revising the heuristic machine framework underscores that interface affordances can cue assumptions about mechanical neutrality and competence, shaping credibility judgments without deliberation (Sundar, 2008). For AI-generated avatars, trust and credibility thus depend on a layered ecology of markers: how the persona is disclosed, how it performs authenticity, what the platform signals about it, and what audiences infer from its body coded identity attributes.

Ethical Stakes

If platform cultures reward sexualized femininity through visibility and engagement, then avatar design workflows that gravitate toward hypersexualized defaults can institutionalize these pressures in a new form. Rather than simply reproducing familiar debates about women's self presentation, these dynamics raise governance and representational responsibility concerns specific to virtual persona ecosystems (Castañeda & Mezarina, 2024; Díaz-Bajo Rodríguez, 2025).

Media effects research supports the concern that idealized portrayals are linked to body dissatisfaction and internalization of thin ideals. A large meta analysis found consistent associations between thin ideal media exposure and women's body image concerns across experimental and correlational studies (Grabe et al., 2008). In social media contexts, these pressures are intensified by continuous comparison and by the routine availability of beautification tools. Fitspiration research, for example, shows that exposure to idealized fitness content can increase negative body image outcomes (Tiggemann & Zaccardo, 2015). When AI-generated avatars and filters amplify narrow ideals, they risk extending these harms into synthetic identity infrastructures where the "default" body is not merely curated but computationally reproduced.

Ethically, gendered standardization becomes visible when dominant representation patterns consistently privilege thinness, eroticized exposure, and commercially optimized femininity. Empirical analysis of female virtual influencers reports frequent exhibition of eroticized body zones as a recurring representational feature, suggesting a persistent sexualized framing within acceptable Instagram aesthetics (Villén Higueras & Mata-Núñez, 2025). In adjacent AI-influencer ecosystems, the Miss AI phenomenon has been examined as an accelerator of unrealistic beauty expectations, reinforcing competitive incentives toward homogenized AI femininity (Abuín-Penas et al., 2025).

Stereotyping and exclusion also arise through representational bias. Beauty filters and generative models can encode racialized and gendered assumptions, shaping which faces are treated as normal, attractive, or professional. Evidence of racial bias in beauty filter ecosystems highlights how platform aesthetics can marginalize non white faces while presenting homogenization as enhancement (Riccio et al., 2024). Similarly, text to image systems can reproduce gender stereotypes and asymmetric defaults even when prompts are intended to be neutral (Wu et al., 2025). For relationship building, this is ethically consequential: trust and credibility are partly judgments of social belonging and moral recognition. If AI generated avatars repeatedly instantiate a sexualized, narrow femininity as the most visible or engaging design, they can crowd out alternative presentations (older bodies, disabled bodies, non binary femininities, culturally diverse aesthetics) and make exclusion feel like a natural outcome of what works.

These ethical issues are inseparable from design: avatar pipelines, prompt practices, dataset choices, and human review norms become governance mechanisms that either reproduce or resist harmful defaults. Because platforms and AI systems jointly shape expressive norms, the ethical question is not only "Is this content harmful?" but also "What kinds of bodies and identities does the system make easiest to produce or easiest to circulate? The remainder of this chapter responds to that question through a design oriented case that treats hypersexualized defaults as a relationship problem, one that affects credibility, trust, and the possibility of ethically grounded connection.

CONCEPTUAL FRAMEWORK: TWO-LAYER DEFAULTS

To analyze why hypersexualized outputs, recur so persistently in AI-generated avatars and why good intentions are often insufficient to prevent them this chapter adopts a two-layer defaults framework. The framework distinguishes (a) synthetic defaults, produced inside the generative pipeline (data, model priors, and prompt–image dependencies), from (b) algorithmic defaults, produced by platform distribution systems (ranking, recommendation, and engagement incentives). The key claim is that hypersexualization becomes default not because any single actor explicitly chooses it, but because both layers jointly make sexualized femininity easy to generate, easy to select, and easy to amplify. This framing is consistent with research on platform visibility regimes, where users' expressive practices are shaped by perceptions of algorithmic gatekeeping and the threat of invisibility (Bucher, 2012; Cotter, 2019).

Synthetic Defaults

Synthetic defaults refer to recurrent output patterns that emerge from the generative system itself especially when prompts are ambiguous, neutral, or oriented toward generic desirability (e.g., beautiful, attractive, influencer, realistic portrait). These defaults operate through at least three mechanisms.

(1) Dataset and model priors. Text-to-image models learn statistical regularities from training corpora that reflect uneven representation and stereotypical associations. As a result, neutral prompts can still yield systematically gendered outcomes, including differences in object occurrence, composition, and background markers. Auditing work that probes diffusion models across internal generation stages shows how these prompt–image dependencies can reproduce and stabilize gendered defaults (Wu et al., 2025).

(2) Prompt to image dependencies and the limits of neutrality. Even when the prompt explicitly controls gendered terms, bias can persist in composition, objects, outfits, and scene context. A protocol focused study in Journal of Imaging traces gender bias from prompt to image in Stable Diffusion and reports that bias appears throughout internal stages of generation; critically, outputs from ostensibly neutral prompts can align more closely with masculine coded generations than

feminine coded ones (Wu et al., 2025). This matters for avatar design because many creators rely on prompts framed as neutral as an ethical baseline, while the system's internal dependencies can still reproduce gendered and sexualized signals.

(3) Promptable norms (a practical layer of culture within prompting). Beyond what the model can generate, communities develop conventions about what they should ask for to get good results. Over time, these conventions function as promptable norms: shared prompt patterns (e.g., "cinematic lighting," "perfect skin," "fashion editorial," "model pose," "full body shot") that reliably produce outputs perceived as high quality and suitable for platform publication. The model's priors and the user community's conventions reinforce each other: prompts converge toward what the model is fluent at producing, and model fluency becomes the benchmark for what looks correct. In practice, this can make hypersexualization appear like a technical artifact ("the model keeps doing this") rather than a normative problem ("the system is repeatedly narrowing femininity into sexualized templates"). The concept helps explain why default femininity can be reproduced even in projects oriented toward feminist communication goals.

In sum, synthetic defaults do not only describe bias in an abstract sense; they describe a production environment in which the path of least resistance tends to yield standardized, idealized femininity. For avatar projects, the risk is that the baseline visual identity is established in this layer before any platform distribution dynamics even begin.

Algorithmic Defaults

Algorithmic defaults refer to the patterned outcomes created by platform distribution systems what becomes visible, which content is recommended, and which styles are rewarded through engagement. Two linked processes are central.

(1) Visibility regimes and creator adaptation. On platforms, creators often experience algorithms as opaque infrastructures that discipline expression through (in)visibility. Bucher (2012) describes how algorithmic ordering can produce a "threat of invisibility" that shapes participation and strategy on Facebook. Cotter (2019) similarly shows how Instagram influencers develop "algorithmic knowledge" and negotiate influence through a practical logic of playing the visibility game, treating platform rules as constraints that can be learned, interpreted, and strategically navigated. In such environments, visual templates that draw attention quickly often including sexualized markers can become adaptive

strategies, especially when aesthetics and identity performance are central to the content's success.

(2) Engagement incentives. Many platforms optimize distribution for predicted engagement, creating feedback loops in which familiar attention triggers receive disproportionate reach. In aesthetic domains, this can indirectly privilege highly standardized, highly arousing visual indicators, making representations that resist default templates harder to scale even when they are easier to justify ethically (Milli et al., 2025).

Together, these processes produce algorithmic defaults: not what the model outputs, but what the platform rewards. Importantly, algorithmic defaults can also reshape synthetic defaults indirectly. If creators learn that certain avatar images get more engagement, they may adjust prompts and selection criteria accordingly feeding platform reward signals back into the generative pipeline and deepening the default.

From Aesthetics to Relational Outcomes

The two-layer framework leads to a mechanism map linking avatar aesthetics to relationship-building. The map does not advance a single causal claim; rather, it offers a structured account of how design choices can produce predictable interpretive and relational effects.

Layer A: Inputs and selection pressures

- Synthetic defaults shape the candidate set of images (what is easiest to generate as high quality).
- Algorithmic defaults shape the reward structure (what is most likely to be amplified and normalized).

Layer B: Aesthetic/identity attributes (what audiences see)

Avatar features include body proportions, pose, clothing, facial expression, camera angle, styling realism, and contextual framing. These features are read as identity signals, but also as signals of intent (e.g., community building vs. attention capture).

Layer C: Inferences (how audiences interpret the persona)

Audiences infer:

- Credibility and trustworthiness: source credibility heuristics remain central (Ohanian, 1990).
- Commercial intent and transparency, especially when disclosure patterns exist or seem absent (Boerman et al., 2017)
- Authenticity as coherence between persona claims and presentation, and as perceived sincerity of motives (Lou & Yuan, 2019).

Layer D: Relational outcomes (what relationships become possible).

These inferences shape:

- Parasocial relationship potential (strength, durability, and the kind of intimacy that is socially licensed).
- Interaction quality (comment tone, community norms, and willingness to engage).
- Ethical legitimacy (whether the persona is seen as reinforcing objectification or resisting reductive patterns).

Figure 2. Two-layer defaults mechanism map

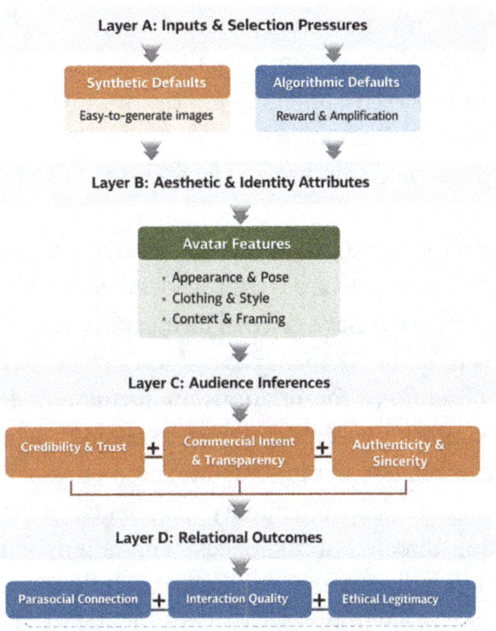

Source: own elaboration

This mechanism map is the bridge to the Alicia case. Designing against hypersexualized defaults is treated here as a form of relational design: interventions occur upstream (prompting, curation, consistency control) and midstream (styling and narrative coherence), but the evaluative outcomes of interest are downstream trust, credibility, and ethically grounded relationship building in platform environments. The two-layer defaults framework therefore provides conceptual scaffolding for interpreting Alicia not just as a design artifact, but as a structured response to coupled socio technical pressures.

CASE OVERVIEW: THE ALICIA PROJECT

This case overview introduces Alicia as a traceable, expert informed design intervention that translates feminist counter default principles into a practical production pipeline. It outlines the project context, the outputs created, and the boundaries of what the case can and cannot claim.

Context and Goals

The Alicia project was developed within an academic context concerned with feminist approaches to digital communication and emerging AI media practices. Its central design challenge was not simply to avoid stereotypes in an abstract sense, but to operationalize a feminist counter-default: a set of concrete design constraints that make it harder for generative pipelines to drift toward hypersexualized, narrow, and commercially optimized femininity.

The project's goals can be summarized as follows:

1. Resist hypersexualized defaults in avatar aesthetics. This goal includes resisting the patterned convergence toward youthful, idealized, and eroticized ...portrayals documented in recent analyses of virtual influencers and AI beauty competitions (Villén Higueras & Mata-Núñez, 2025; Abuín-Penas et al., 2025).
2. Safeguard the conditions for relationship formation. Rather than treating avoidance of sexualization as a purely visual choice, the project frames avatar design as a form of relational infrastructure: aesthetic decisions are expected to shape credibility heuristics, authenticity judgments, and the ethical legitimacy of communication directed at audiences. This aligns with broader evidence that virtual influencer accounts function as carefully managed communication interfaces in platform environments (Carrillo-Durán et al., 2024).
3. Produce a traceable design rationale grounded in expert input. The project prioritized a structured expert elicitation process to translate feminist expert

judgment into design requirements and selection criteria, allowing the chapter to document how decisions that resist default templates were reached rather than presenting them as intuitive or purely author led.

Outputs

The project generated a set of research and production outputs designed to support both methodological transparency and practical deployment.

Stimuli set (prototypes). Based on an initial elicitation of expert preferences about avatar appearance (e.g., apparent age, body size/shape, hair, skin tone, makeup, and clothing), the team created five visual options used as comparative stimuli in a second round of expert evaluation.

Baseline selection. In round 2, the expert panel selected the prototype that best aligned with the project's representational aims, producing a clear baseline choice.

Image bank and consistency control. After selecting the baseline, the team built a large bank of AI-generated images intended to stabilize identity features and reduce drift across outputs. Only images for which all authors independently judged identity consistency (i.e., whether the image was consistent or not with the character) and reached 100% agreement were retained.

Figure 3. Alicia the AI avatar generated

Source: own elaboration

Content assets for social media. The curated image bank supported the creation of reusable assets suitable for platform publishing: full body shots, medium shots, close ups, and a controlled set of facial expressions and confirmatory context scenes (e.g., public, urban, educational, and everyday environments). This output strategy aligns with how virtual influencer identities are sustained on Instagram through repetitive, coherent self presentation and format adaptation (Carrillo-Durán et al., 2024), while enabling an aesthetic that resists default templates and is anchored in functional, non glamorized indicators.

Boundary Conditions

The Alicia case is designed to generate traceable design knowledge, not universal truth claims about representation. Accordingly, it has three explicit boundary conditions.

First, the case does not claim to define an essential or singular representation of women (or the Galician woman). On the contrary, expert feedback underscored the risk of essentialization, and the project treats baseline selection as a pragmatic design choice under constraints rather than a cultural typology.

Second, the case does not test downstream audience effects experimentally (e.g., whether Alicia increases trust, reduces objectification, or changes engagement). Instead, it provides the conceptual and methodological groundwork to study such outcomes in future research, including the mapping of design decisions to relational mechanisms.

Third, the case is bounded by its social and technical conditions: the specific expert sample, the available generative tools at the time of production, and the platform environment of deployment. As systematic reviews note, virtual influencer research is evolving quickly and is shaped by changing platforms, sectors, and technological affordances (Corzo-Cortés et al., 2025). The case therefore offers a replicable logic (constraints grounded in a Delphi process plus prototype testing plus strict consistency control), while recognizing that particular aesthetic choices and platform effects may vary across contexts.

METHOD: EXPERT ELICITATION AND INSTRUMENTED DESIGN PIPELINE

This chapter uses a design oriented method in which feminist expertise on gender representation and platform cultures is translated into operational constraints for producing an AI-generated, human looking avatar. The approach combines a modified Delphi process conducted in two rounds, used to elicit and refine expert judgments, with an instrumented production pipeline that translates those judgments into prototypes, a baseline identity, and a curated image bank designed to reduce identity drift.

Delphi Method

Delphi is appropriate for value laden design questions where ground truth is contested and the goal is traceable convergence on decision criteria. Round 1 was exploratory, using open questions to diagnose dominant representation patterns and to specify preferred avatar attributes. Round 2 was confirmatory, converting round 1 themes into structured items (agreement ratings, risk prioritization, and intervention ratings) and adding a forced choice baseline selection among five avatar prototypes.

Recruitment and Participants

The panel consisted of 17 experts recruited through purposive sampling from a university ecosystem combining feminist scholarship and creative/communication research. Profiles were interdisciplinary (e.g., gender studies, communication, design/creative practices, education). Data were collected via online questionnaires and treated as anonymous for analytic purposes.

Instruments and Measures

Round 1 included: (a) an anchoring block with examples of human looking virtual influencers on Instagram; (b) open questions on representation diagnosis, gender equality effects, identity risks, platform tensions, and inclusive strategies; and (c) an avatar specification module (e.g., apparent age, body build, makeup, and everyday wardrobe logic) to translate values into actionable parameters.

Round 2 included: (a) Likert scale agreement ratings for descriptors of current avatar representation (stereotyped, idealized, sexualized, excluding); (b) a single choice item on perceived effects for gender equality; (c) an item asking participants to select up to three prioritized risks; (d) agreement ratings on statements about platform business models and the feasibility of normalization; (e) ratings of proposed interventions and actions; and (f) a forced choice baseline selection among five prototypes, plus open feedback to capture qualitative nuance.

Analysis

Round 1 and Round 2 open responses were thematically synthesized by the author team to extract recurring concerns and convert them into design relevant requirements. Round 2 structured items were summarized using descriptive frequencies (agreement distributions, risk counts, and prototype selection shares).

Consistency Control

After baseline selection, a large candidate pool of images was generated and reviewed by all authors. Only images that achieved unanimous agreement on identity recognizability and compliance with constraints designed to resist default templates were retained in the final image bank, prioritizing recognizability and coherence over volume.

Ethics

Expert responses were treated as anonymized. The avatar was generated without using personal photographs, biometric data, or identifiable individuals' likenesses. All images were generated by AI, and the project relied on constraints derived from expert judgment and conservative curation, rather than external guardrails, to resist drift toward hypersexualized defaults and to support responsible deployment directed at audiences.

RESULTS I: EXPERT DIAGNOSIS OF AI AVATAR REPRESENTATION

This section reports how the expert panel assessed current AI avatar representation on social media. It summarizes the dominant patterns identified in Round 1 and frames their implications for gender equality and youth identity formation before presenting the specific results.

Expert Characterizations of Current AI Avatar Representation

Experts described mainstream avatars as highly standardized: a narrow, youthful, hyperfeminine template repeatedly reproduced for instant legibility. In their view, this is not only a visual pattern but a communicative norm: it signals what platforms treat as attractive, clickable, and socially rewarded, while making alternative femininities harder to render as credible or desirable.

Perceived Impact on Gender Equality

Regarding gender equality, panelists emphasized that repetition matters: when the same body and styling defaults circulate on a scale, they become reference points for comparison, evaluation, and self-presentation. The risk is a self reinforcing cycle in which patriarchal beauty logics are re naturalized as what audiences want, even when the demand is partly manufactured by ranking incentives and template availability.

Perceived Risks for Identity Formation

For identity formation, experts highlighted two linked vulnerabilities. (1) Intensified social comparison with seemingly "perfect" synthetic bodies. (2) A narrowing of imaginable ways of being a woman online. This happens because the representational menu is pre-filtered by model priors and platform rewards. In this sense, AI avatars do not merely reflect norms. They can accelerate their consolidation through volume and repetition.

What Should Change: Preferred Interventions

Preferred interventions clustered around structural, not purely individual, remedies: clearer disclosure and verification cues; constraints on sexualized default generation and distribution; incentives for diversity in training data and output evaluation; and platform side governance (labeling, ranking adjustments, and policy enforcement) so that counter-default content is not systematically disadvantaged.

Design Related Indicators from the Avatar Specification Module

From the specification module, experts treated coherence as the primary indicator relevant to design decisions for trust: a stable biography, consistent style rules, and a traceable rationale help audiences read a persona as intentional rather than opportunistically optimized. They also flagged practical red lines, such as avoiding infantilizing elements, pornified styling, and stereotypes linked to social class, that should be built into prompt rules, selection criteria, and iteration checkpoints.

Implications: Why Counter-Default Design is Needed

The interpretive takeaways for this chapter are as follows:

- Counter-default work must manage two layers at once: the synthetic default (what the model produces easily) and the platform layer (what is rewarded).
- Trust is supported less by a realistic appearance than by coherent identity attributes and transparent governance of the production process.
- Without platform aligned support (labels, ranking, enforcement), counter-default design carries higher production costs and weaker circulation.

RESULTS II: FROM ELICITATION TO BASELINE - DESIGNING ALICIA

This section reports how Round 1 expert elicitation was converted into operational design requirements, how those requirements were instantiated in five candidate avatar prototypes, and how Round 2 expert validation produced a baseline choice. Results are presented in a pipeline format: elicitation → requirements → prototypes → selection → qualitative constraints → naming/transparency cue.

Round 1: Design Requirements

Round 1 produced two types of inputs that were directly actionable for design: (a) open expert descriptions of dominant AI avatar representation (what to avoid) and (b) a structured avatar specification module (what to build). Together, these inputs were translated into a set of anti-hypersexualization requirements defined operationally as visible and repeatable constraints.

What to Avoid

Across Round 1 narrative responses, experts repeatedly described current AI avatars as hypersexualized, stereotyped, idealized, and culturally narrow. In practical design terms, this diagnosis is translated into a clear avoid list, particularly for the avatar's body signaling and style grammar:

- Avoid eroticized, glamour heavy, or youth coded styling: no revealing outfits or flirtatious posing, no fashion editorial perfection that reads as aspirational status display, minimal or no makeup, and no single canon phenotype that narrows representational range.

These avoid rules were treated as production constraints practical guardrails to reduce drift toward sexualized outputs during generation and selection.

What to Build

The Round 1 specification module produced several numeric anchors that helped translate expert preferences into implementable requirements.

Wardrobe logic (multiple response item). Preferences converged on everyday functional items, long trousers and a backpack (41% each), sneakers (35%), jeans (29%), plus recurring layers/accessories (e.g., sweatshirt/jacket, glasses, coat, T-shirt).

Design implication: the baseline wardrobe should read as casual + functional (comfort, mobility, layered everyday clothing) rather than glamour or body emphasis outfits.

Clothing size. All experts selected a regular size (17/17). Design implication: keep a regular fit silhouette, avoiding very tight or very oversized fits to reduce body emphasis signals and stabilize proportions across generations.

Makeup. Preferences favored minimal facial ornamentation: no makeup (47%), natural makeup (12%), or indifferent (41%). Design implication: default to no visible makeup (or a strictly natural look).

Age and phenotype attributes (high indifferent pattern). Many experts selected indifferent for attributes such as age, eye color, hair type, and skin tone. This was interpreted as an anti essentialization signal: the design goal was not to fix a single prescriptive phenotype as the correct representative. Where age was specified, it tended to cluster around adult ranges rather than adolescent presentation.

Design implication: set the baseline as clearly adult (to avoid youth coded sexualization), while treating many phenotype attributes as non essential and therefore secondary to functional styling, a realistic appearance and representational restraint.

Consolidated Round 1 Design Profile

Round 1 yielded a baseline profile: clearly adult and realistic; regular build with regular fit clothing; little or no visible makeup; functional casual wardrobe (layers, jeans or trousers, sneakers, backpack); everyday legibility rather than glamour; and openness on non central identity attributes to avoid essentialization.

This profile was used as the anti-hypersexualization operational definition for prototyping: not merely less sexual but visibly anchored in everyday functionality and representational restraint.

Translating Requirements Into Prototypes

Five prototypes were produced as round 2 visual stimuli, varying mainly in (a) age coding, (b) context coding, and (c) the balance between casual and work adjacent styling, while remaining within the functional, non glamorized constraint space:

- Option 1: clearly adult (around 40), layered everyday functional baseline (coat, layers, jeans, sneakers; minimal or no makeup; glasses).
- Option 2: adult (around 35 to 40), streamlined generic casual with a slimmer, more body emphasizing silhouette.
- Option 4: older (around 55 to 60), functional realism with visible signs of aging.

- Option 3: adult (around 35 to 40), hybrid casual professional (e.g., blazer with casual elements).
- Option 5: older, rural or community coded alternative (context shift without sexualized styling).

Round 2: Baseline Selection

Round 2 asked experts to select one option among the five prototypes as the avatar that best fit the target representation. Selection results were unambiguous:

- Option 1: 9/17 (52.9%)
- Option 3: 4/17 (23.5%)
- Option 4: 3/17 (17.6%)
- Option 5: 1/17 (5.9%)
- Option 2: 0/17 (0.0%)

Two reporting implications follow from this distribution:

1. A majority baseline emerged. Option 1 obtained a substantial majority (52.9%), providing a stable baseline for subsequent image bank development.
2. Option 2 was actively not preferred. The absence of any selections for Option 2 is analytically meaningful. Although the study did not require experts to justify rejections for each option, the zero selection pattern suggests that a streamlined generic casual look, with a slimmer or more body emphasizing silhouette, did not align with the panel's preferred direction for resisting default templates, especially when compared with the layered functional styling and everyday realism indicators of Option 1.
3. A secondary preference cluster supported counter-default diversity. The combined support for Options 3–5 (8/17; 47.1%) indicates that nearly half of the panel saw value in alternative counter-default strategies (older age coding; hybrid professional inputs; rural/community anchoring). However, none of these alternatives displaced Option 1 as the baseline.

Figure 4. Examples of alternative avatars to Alicia

Source: own elaboration

Operationally, Round 2 selection results were treated as a decision gate: Option 1 became the baseline identity reference for generating and curating the final asset bank, while the other options functioned as interpretive comparators clarifying what counts as acceptable variation and what risks are being misaligned with expert expectations.

Qualitative Constraints from Open Feedback

After the forced choice selection, Round 2 included an open ended item for additional contributions. All 17 participants provided a response, but only 9 of the 17 were substantively elaborated, whereas the remainder were blank, minimal, or indicated no additional comments. The substantive responses introduced constraints not captured by the forced choice results. Four constraints predominated.

Essentialization Warning

Multiple experts challenged the premise of selecting a single avatar to represent the Galician woman, arguing that such a move can reproduce the very essentialization the project seeks to critique. Comments explicitly stated that there is no one

Galician woman, only Galician women, and that choosing one image risks implying that other images (and other lived identities) are less valid.

Design implication: treat the baseline as a pragmatic production anchor, not as a sociological typology. This constraint shaped how the avatar is framed narratively: the project must avoid presenting the baseline as a definitive representation and instead position it as a counter-default exemplar under design constraints.

Socio Economic Contextual Markers

Experts noted that the proposed options appeared predominantly coded as middle class or even upper middle class, pointing to styling and contextual signals that implicitly normalize certain socio economic imaginaries. One comment explicitly critiqued even the rural coded version as a hipster redesign of an archetype rather than a truly diversified representation.

Design implication: class signaling must be treated as part of the representational system. In the next production phase, context scenes and wardrobe variation require careful control to avoid turning functional casual into an implicit middle class default.

Gesture and Expressive Diversity

One of the most specific constraints concerned embodied expressivity: experts warned against linking the avatar's gestures and body action only to positive or low arousal emotional states. The critique was that a permanently pleasant or low arousal body risks flattening identity and reinforcing a narrow performance of acceptability.

Design implication: ensure gesture diversity and emotional range in the asset bank (e.g., neutral, focused, questioning, serious), while avoiding melodramatic or sexualized poses. This becomes a concrete production requirement for the final image set.

Platform Limits and Skepticism about Systemic Change

Some experts expressed doubt that platforms will enable deep representational change under current visibility incentives and questioned whether AI-generated imagery, especially when optimized for realism can counteract entrenched norms at scale. Related comments raised concern that the selection process itself could feel coercive or limiting, reflecting broader skepticism about whether a single avatar can meaningfully intervene in platformed representation dynamics.

Design implication: incorporate explicit boundary framing in dissemination and analysis: the case is a controlled design intervention, not a claim that one avatar can solve systemic platform inequalities. It also strengthens the rationale for coupling design constraints with transparency features and educational/governance discussions.

Naming and Transparency Attributes (Alicia / IA)

After Option 1 was established as the baseline visual reference, the project defined the avatar's identity through a naming procedure designed to embed an explicit AI reference. The team compiled a list of 43 Galician women's names containing the sequence IA (e.g., names where the letters "IA" appear in the name). An internal vote selected "Alicia" because it simultaneously functions as:

- a recognizable, easy for audiences to recall name (supporting platform legibility and relational continuity), and
- a built-in transparency marker, since the "IA" sequence provides a persistent reminder of artificial origin.

This naming decision served as a lightweight but persistent transparency signal: rather than relying exclusively on disclosures that audiences may miss, the AI reference is embedded in the identity label itself. In the pipeline, "Alicia" therefore functions as both a relational anchor (a stable persona name) and a design ethics feature (a visible reminder of synthetic origin).

DESIGN TO THEORY MAPPING

Alicia operationalizes designing against hypersexualized defaults as a production discipline: constraints grounded in expert input are translated into a repeatable brief, enforced through iterative generation, conservative selection, and strict identity consistency rules. The key claim is relational: upstream design constraints (embodiment, styling, context, expressivity, disclosure) shape downstream inferences (trust, credibility, authenticity, and perceived legitimacy).

Implementation was carried out with a two tool ecosystem (Freepik's generative suite and Google AI Studio) to broaden the candidate pool and reduce single model aesthetic lock-in. Using multiple ecosystems increased variation but also increased the need for a strong consistency gate.

Figure 5. Alicia in a real environment

Source: own elaboration

Operational controls were organized into four lock points:

- Embodiment: clearly adult coding, regular silhouette, restrained realism.
- Styling: functional wardrobe logic, minimal/no makeup, repeatable accessories as identity anchors (e.g., glasses/backpack).
- Context: everyday settings with explicit monitoring of aspirational/luxury drift and class coded narrowing.
- Expressivity: a small repertoire beyond compulsory pleasantness (neutral, focused, reflective, mild positive, serious) while avoiding display coded or flirtatious posing.

Across both still image and video workflows, the final safeguard was a human unanimity filter: the author team retained only assets that were clearly recognizable as Alicia and aligned with constraints designed to resist default templates. This consistency control functions as both a credibility scaffold (preventing multiple faces) and an ethics scaffold (preventing silent regression into hypersexualized templates at scale).

DISCUSSION: IMPACTS ON EXPRESSION AND RELATIONSHIP BUILDING

Across embodiment, styling, context, and expressivity, design choices pre structure how audiences read intent, credibility, and ethical legitimacy. The Alicia case surfaces a key tension: generative tools can expand creative capacity, yet the practical route to reliably high quality outputs often narrows expression into a corridor of platform legible femininity. That corridor is produced jointly by model priors (what is easy to generate) and platform logics (what is rewarded).

Expression Under AI Constraints

Alicia shows that AI mediated expression is not simply assisted creativity, but a production constraint that reshapes what is easy to say and show. Default legibility (youthful glamour, thinness, sexualized attributes) emerges quickly because it aligns with model priors and common prompt patterns; non default legibility requires more iterations, stricter selection rules, and a larger asset library.

The project's lock points and unanimity rule functioned as an expressive scaffold: they preserved continuity (recognizable identity attributes) while preventing drift toward hypersexualized or infantilizing tropes. The cost is a partial narrowing of spontaneity and range: expression becomes more curated, because coherence and ethical constraints must be actively maintained across posts, contexts, and platform formats.

Trust and Credibility Trade Offs Under Platform Logics

Trust and credibility were treated as interpretive outcomes. Design choices that resist default templates can support credibility by signaling intent, restraint, and care in representation, but they do not automatically produce trust. Human likeness can raise suspicion of deception, and disclosure can introduce friction when platforms and audiences reward natural authenticity. The practical implication is to pair aesthetics that resist default templates with consistent identity indicators, clear labeling, and a traceable rationale that makes transparency feel like a credibility signal rather than a defect.

When Feminist Counter-Default Collides with Algorithmic Rewards

Platform rewards make the dual mechanism concrete: content that resists attention traps (body emphasis, seductive posing, glamour signals) may be less favored by ranking systems trained on past engagement. This does not block circulation, but it changes the strategy: design that resists default templates often needs stronger narrative hooks, community oriented formats, and deliberate distribution tactics. Governance also matters, because if emotionally resonant content is privileged, disclosure should be supported by platform indicators that normalize transparency rather than penalize it.

Transferability and Limitations

Alicia is transferable mainly as a methodological logic: define ethical red lines, operate them as selection rules, and document decisions so that audiences and stakeholders can audit intent. Limitations remain: the chapter does not directly measure audience outcomes, the expert panel is situated, and platform conditions vary. Future tests should combine controlled audience experiments with longitudinal platform analysis to examine when counter-default cues increase trust, when they trigger skepticism, and how ranking dynamics mediate both.

PRACTICAL AND ETHICAL IMPLICATIONS

This chapter treats counter-default avatar design as applied ethics in production form. Normative critique matters, but so do operational constraints that survive tool defaults, time pressure, and platform incentives. The Alicia pipeline translates feminist expertise into implementable requirements and then stress tests them through prototyping and consistency control, so non-sexualized outcomes remain reproducible rather than exceptional.

Design Guidelines for Counter-Default Avatars

1) Specify constraints up front (include an avoid list). Combine positive requirements (adult coding, functional wardrobe, restrained realism) with explicit exclusions (glamour drift, desirability forward posing, luxury signaling) so generation and curation have clear boundaries.
2) Separate identity creation from scaling. First lock a small reference set of identity consistent images; then scale content from that anchor so drift becomes detectable early.
3) Treat framing, pose, and motion as ethical variables. Sexualization often re-enters through camera angle, cropping, and movement; evaluate stills and video with the same criteria used for wardrobe and body attributes.

4) Engineer expressive range without compulsory pleasantness. Build a limited repertoire (neutral, focused, serious, warm) that supports relational legitimacy without relying on flirtation or constant smiling.
5) Institutionalize a conservative selection gate. Use a reference checklist and a high threshold (e.g., unanimity) before assets enter production, so regression into default templates does not scale.

Disclosure and Governance Recommendations

1) Treat disclosure as a continuous signal rather than a single statement. Users frequently encounter content outside profile pages through reposts, explore feeds, or embedded posts, so disclosures limited to the bio are easily missed. The Alicia naming strategy, which embeds an AI indicator in the name, illustrates persistent transparency. Teams should implement at least two layers of disclosure: identity level indicators (name, watermark, recurring tag) and post level indicators (periodic explicit labeling in captions or visual overlays), especially during early growth.
2) Distinguish relational warmth from relational manipulation. Synthetic personas can rapidly generate parasocial closeness. Governance should specify boundaries: which intimacy signals are acceptable, which interaction patterns promote dependency or simulated exclusivity, and how to address audience misconceptions, such as interpreting the avatar as a real person. A minimal safeguard is a public statement that clarifies the avatar's purpose, synthetic origin, and ethical commitments, including avoiding sexualization, avoiding deceptive framing, and respecting audience autonomy.
3) Document and audit the production process. Governance ready projects should maintain internal logs detailing tools used, constraints applied, selection thresholds, and reasons for rejecting outputs. Beyond academic traceability, such documentation supports accountability in cases of criticism, misuse, or moderation disputes, and reduces drift as teams and personnel change.
4) Align moderation practices with representational goals. If the project aims to resist hypersexualized defaults, comment moderation and community rules must reinforce that aim. Governance should define how sexualizing commentary and harassment are handled and how the persona responds, or declines to respond, to boundary testing interactions.
5) Anticipate platform constraints and distribution risks. Even ethically designed content may be rewarded less than sexualized or sensational formats. Governance should therefore include a distribution strategy that avoids engagement bait through consistent posting rhythms, informational value, and partnerships aligned with the avatar's ethical stance. Where algorithmic pressure incentivizes drift,

sustaining a counter-default position should be monitored as a KPI rather than assumed.

Research Agenda: Next Steps

The Alicia case offers a traceable design logic and a mechanism map; the next step is to test these mechanisms empirically. Three directions are especially actionable.

1) Controlled experiments. Compare assets designed to resist default templates with default styled synthetic influencer assets while holding topic and format constant and manipulate disclosure prominence (a naming indicator compared with caption disclosure compared with no disclosure). Measure perceived credibility, trust, authenticity, and engagement intentions.
2) Field deployment and interaction ecology. Deploy the avatar with a pre-registered posting strategy and analyze not only engagement volume but interaction quality (e.g., reduced objectification and more topical discussion), alongside how platform distribution responds.
3) Drift, consistency, and production cost. Quantify how often sexualization or identity drift appears under different tool chains and constraint strategies (single tool compared with mixed pipelines; loose selection compared with high threshold selection; generating from scratch compared with editing over reference), and track consistency scores, rejection rates, and labor time.

Together, these tests would move the chapter from a case based mechanism proposal toward evidence about causal effects, platform contingencies, and scalable governance for ethical synthetic personas.

CONCLUSIONS

This chapter has argued that hypersexualized defaults in AI-generated avatars are not only an aesthetic problem but also a relational one: they pre-shape credibility judgments, constrain authenticity indicators, and steer interaction toward objectifying attention economies that can undermine trust. By treating AI avatars as social and technical artifacts produced at the intersection of generative systems and platform visibility regimes, the chapter reframed hypersexualization as a predictable outcome of coupled pressures, namely synthetic defaults that make certain femininity patterns easy to generate and algorithmic defaults that make them easy to amplify.

The Alicia case contributed an alternative: a traceable approach grounded in expert input to support design that resists default templates. Using a Delphi process conducted in two rounds, feminist expertise was translated into operational constraints (functional styling, minimal or no makeup, regular fit embodiment, controlled contexts, and gesture diversity) and tested through prototype selection. The results showed that design that resists default templates is feasible, but it is not cost free. It requires a disciplined workflow iterative generation across tools, conservative selection, and strict identity consistency controls to prevent drift back toward default templates when content is produced on a scale. The case also highlighted that resisting hypersexualization is necessary but not sufficient: open feedback surfaced additional ethical risks, including essentialization (the danger of implying a single representative woman) and class coded everydayness (the risk of replacing a sexualized default with a socio economic default). These constraints are not peripheral; they are central to whether an avatar can support inclusive relationship building rather than simply offering a new, sanitized template.

A key insight emerging across the chapter is that relationship building with synthetic personas depends on trust calibration, not merely on visual appeal. The decision to embed an AI cue in the avatar's name illustrates a practical principle: disclosure must be treated as an ongoing design feature rather than a one time statement. Human-like realism can support parasocial engagement, but without transparency it can also heighten deception risk and erode credibility once audiences feel misled. Counter-default avatars therefore require ethics of presence: a coherent identity, a communicative purpose, and clear indicators that respect audience autonomy.

Finally, the chapter positioned Alicia as a methodological contribution rather than a universal representational solution. Its transferability lies in the logic of the pipeline expert elicitation, prototyping, baseline validation, consistency control, and disclosure oriented identity framing. The next step is empirical: controlled experiments and field deployments are needed to test whether counter-default aesthetics and transparency elements reliably improve perceived credibility, reduce objectifying interaction, and sustain relationship building under platform logics that often reward the opposite. In short, counter-default design cannot fully overturn algorithmic reward systems, but it can make synthetic expression more ethically accountable and relationally credible turning what the model tends to produce into what we choose to normalize.

REFERENCES

Abidin, C. (2016). Visibility labour: Engaging with influencers' fashion brands and #OOTD advertorial campaigns on Instagram. *Media International Australia, Incorporating Culture & Policy*, *161*(1), 86–100. DOI: 10.1177/1329878X16665177

Abuín-Penas, J., Ramhí-García, D., & Dopico-Rodríguez, P. (2025). La comunicación de las influencers virtuales de apariencia humana en Instagram. Análisis del Miss AI 2024. *Contratexto*, *44*(44), 19–44. DOI: 10.26439/contratexto2025.n44.7728

Appelman, A., & Sundar, S. S. (2016). Measuring message credibility: Construction and validation of an exclusive scale. *Journalism & Mass Communication Quarterly*, *93*(1), 59–79. DOI: 10.1177/1077699015606057

Arrieta, A. B., Díaz-Rodríguez, N., Del Ser, J., Bennetot, A., Tabik, S., Barbado, A., García, S., Gil-López, S., Molina, D., Benjamins, R., Chatila, R., & Herrera, F. (2020). Explainable Artificial Intelligence (XAI): Concepts, taxonomies, opportunities and challenges toward responsible AI. *Information Fusion*, *58*, 82–115. DOI: 10.1016/j.inffus.2019.12.012

Audrezet, A., De Kerviler, G., & Moulard, J. G. (2020). Authenticity under threat: When social media influencers need to go beyond self-presentation. *Journal of Business Research*, *117*, 557–569. DOI: 10.1016/j.jbusres.2018.07.008

Boerman, S. C., Willemsen, L. M., & van der Aa, E. P. (2017). "This Post Is Sponsored": Effects of sponsorship disclosure on persuasion knowledge and electronic word of mouth in the context of Facebook. *Journal of Interactive Marketing*, *38*(1), 82–92. DOI: 10.1016/j.intmar.2016.12.002

Bucher, T. (2012). Want to be on the top? Algorithmic power and the threat of invisibility on Facebook. *New Media & Society*, *14*(7), 1164–1180. DOI: 10.1177/1461444812440159

Carrillo-Durán, M. V., García-García, M., & Corzo-Cortés, L. (2024). Influencers virtuales de apariencia humana como forma de comunicación online: El caso de Lil Miquela y Lu do Magalu en Instagram. *Revista de Comunicación*, *23*(1), 119–140. DOI: 10.26441/RC23.1-2024-3453

Castañeda, S., & Mezarina, M. (2024). Análisis de la comunicación emocional de las marcas mediante la antropomorfización de los influencers virtuales: Caso Miquela. RISTI - Revista Ibérica de Sistemas e Tecnologias de Informação, (E68), 607–619. http://hdl.handle.net/10757/676103

Corzo-Cortés, L., Carrillo-Durán, M.-V., & García-García, M. (2025). Nuevas formas de comunicación digital: Revisión sistemática de la literatura sobre influencers virtuales. *Revista Mediterránea de Comunicación*, *16*(2), e28712. DOI: 10.14198/MEDCOM.28712

Cotter, K. (2019). Playing the visibility game: How digital influencers and algorithms negotiate influence on Instagram. *New Media & Society*, *21*(4), 895–913. DOI: 10.1177/1461444818815684

Díaz-Bajo Rodríguez, J. (2025). Tendencias emergentes en el uso de la inteligencia virtual: La industria de influencers virtuales. *European Public & Social Innovation Review*, *10*, 1–20. DOI: 10.31637/epsir-2025-2135

Ferchaud, A., Grzeslo, J., Orme, S., & LaGroue, J. (2018). Parasocial attributes and YouTube personalities: Exploring content trends across the most subscribed YouTube channels. *Computers in Human Behavior*, *80*, 88–96. DOI: 10.1016/j.chb.2017.10.041

Grabe, S., Ward, L. M., & Hyde, J. S. (2008). The role of the media in body image concerns among women: A meta-analysis of experimental and correlational studies. *Psychological Bulletin*, *134*(3), 460–476. DOI: 10.1037/0033-2909.134.3.460 PMID: 18444705

Horton, D., & Richard Wohl, R. (1956). Mass communication and para-social interaction: Observations on intimacy at a distance. *psychiatry, 19*(3), 215-229. DOI: 10.1080/00332747.1956.11023049

Hwang, K., & Zhang, Q. (2018). Influence of parasocial relationship between digital celebrities and their followers on followers' purchase and electronic word-of-mouth intentions, and persuasion knowledge. *Computers in Human Behavior*, *87*, 155–173. DOI: 10.1016/j.chb.2018.05.029

Karagür, Z., Becker, J.-M., Klein, K., & Edeling, A. (2022). How, why, and when disclosure type matters for influencer marketing. *International Journal of Research in Marketing*, *39*(2), 313–335. DOI: 10.1016/j.ijresmar.2021.09.006

Kim, Y., & Sundar, S. S. (2012). Anthropomorphism of computers: Is it mindful or mindless? *Computers in Human Behavior*, *28*(1), 241–250. DOI: 10.1016/j.chb.2011.09.006

Liu, F., & Wang, R. (2025). Fostering parasocial relationships with virtual influencers in the uncanny valley: Anthropomorphism, autonomy, and a multigroup comparison. *Journal of Business Research*, *186*, 115024. DOI: 10.1016/j.jbusres.2024.115024

Lou, C., & Yuan, S. (2019). Influencer marketing: How message value and credibility affect consumer trust of branded content on social media. *Journal of Interactive Advertising, 19*(1), 58–73. DOI: 10.1080/15252019.2018.1533501

Milli, S., Carroll, M., Wang, Y., Pandey, S., Zhao, S., & Dragan, A. D. (2025). Engagement, user satisfaction, and the amplification of divisive content on social media. *PNAS Nexus, 4*(3), pgaf062. Advance online publication. DOI: 10.1093/pnasnexus/pgaf062 PMID: 40070432

Nieborg, D. B., & Poell, T. (2018). The platformization of cultural production: Theorizing the contingent cultural commodity. *New Media & Society, 20*(11), 4275–4292. DOI: 10.1177/1461444818769694

Nowak, K. L., & Rauh, C. (2005). The influence of the avatar on online perceptions of anthropomorphism, androgyny, credibility, homophily, and attraction. *Journal of Computer-Mediated Communication, 11*(1), 153–178. DOI: 10.1111/j.1083-6101.2006.tb00308.x

Ohanian, R. (1990). Construction and validation of a scale to measure celebrity endorsers' perceived expertise, trustworthiness, and attractiveness. *Journal of Advertising, 19*(3), 39–52. DOI: 10.1080/00913367.1990.10673191

Pan, M., Blut, M., Ghiassaleh, A., & Lee, Z. W. Y. (2025). Influencer marketing effectiveness: A meta-analytic review. *Journal of the Academy of Marketing Science, 53*(1), 52–78. DOI: 10.1007/s11747-024-01052-7

Riccio, P., Colin, J., Ogolla, S., & Oliver, N. (2024). Mirror, mirror on the wall, who is the whitest of all? Racial biases in social media beauty filters. *Social Media + Society, 10*(2), 20563051241239295. Advance online publication. DOI: 10.1177/20563051241239295

Sundar, S. S. (2008). The MAIN model: A heuristic approach to understanding technology effects on credibility. In Metzger, M. J., & Flanagin, A. J. (Eds.), *Digital media, youth, and credibility* (pp. 73–100). The MIT Press.

Tiggemann, M., & Zaccardo, M. (2015). "Exercise to be fit, not skinny": The effect of fitspiration imagery on women's body image. *Body Image, 15*, 61–67. DOI: 10.1016/j.bodyim.2015.06.003 PMID: 26176993

Villén Higueras, S. J., & Mata-Núñez, A. (2025). Influencers virtuales femeninas y representación de género: Análisis de su imagen en Instagram. *European Public & Social Innovation Review, 10*, 1–22. DOI: 10.31637/epsir-2025-568

Wu, Y., Nakashima, Y., & Garcia, N. (2025). Revealing gender bias from prompt to image in Stable Diffusion. *Journal of Imaging*, *11*(2), 35. DOI: 10.3390/jimaging11020035 PMID: 39997537

KEY TERMS AND DEFINITIONS

AI Generated Avatar: A digitally created, human looking character generated with AI systems and used as a stable persona for communication, often across multiple posts or formats on social media.

Algorithmic Defaults: Platform driven patterns created by ranking, recommendation, and engagement incentives that amplify certain aesthetics and interaction styles and make them feel standard.

Counter Default Design: A deliberate design approach that translates ethical and representational goals into operational constraints and selection rules, aiming to resist dominant platform templates in the creation of AI mediated personas.

Default Femininity: A narrow, widely repeated template of femininity that becomes socially legible and expected on platforms, typically privileging specific body norms, styling conventions, and cultural beauty standards.

Hypersexualized Default: A recurring representation pattern in which female coded avatars are produced and circulated with aesthetics that emphasize desirability and sexual display as a normal baseline rather than an exception.

Synthetic Defaults: Representational tendencies produced by generative models, prompting practices, and selection habits that make certain looks and identities more likely to appear as high quality outputs.

Virtual Influencer: A synthetic persona presented as an influencer like account that publishes content, interacts with audiences, and can partner with brands, even though the "person" does not exist as a real individual.

Chapter 9
Emotional AI and Human Interaction:
Transforming Expression, Trust, and Relationship

V. Indhu
http://orcid.org/0009-0004-2894-6188
Saveetha School of Management, Saveetha Institute of Medical and Technical Sciences, Saveetha University, Chennai, India

A. Rahmath Nisha
http://orcid.org/0009-0001-5146-2411
Saveetha School of Management, Saveetha Institute of Medical and Technical Sciences, Saveetha University, Chennai, India

A. K. Subramani
http://orcid.org/0000-0003-0783-7113
Saveetha School of Management, Saveetha Institute of Medical and Technical Sciences, Saveetha University, Chennai, India

ABSTRACT

Artificial Intelligence (AI) is rapidly becoming emotionally responsive systems that also shape the human communication and relationship building. In this paper, the author investigates how emotional intelligence is applied in AI-based interaction and how it influences human expression, trust, and social connectivity. The paper is based on the research conducted in the field of affective computing, neuroscience, and organizational studies, identifying the role played by conversational agents and emotion-sensitive technologies in transforming digitally mediated relationships within sectors. Even though emotional AI improves interaction and personalized assistance, it presents ethical issues associated with bias, privacy, and authenticity.

DOI: 10.4018/979-8-3373-8337-8.ch009

The paper underlines that responsible governance and human-centered design are relevant in order to have emotionally intelligent AI reinforcing, instead of destabilizing, meaningful human relationships in an increasingly digital world.

INTRODUCTION

Artificial Intelligence (AI) is progressively growing out of its purely rule-based and computational implementation to be a socially embedded technology that can engage with human beings on an emotionally rich level. Although the initial stages of AI evolution were focused on the automation, optimization, and logical judgment, the modern trends are focused on emotional sensitivity, recognition of feelings, and responsiveness. This change is a indication of a developing academic awareness that emotion is core to cognition, conduct and social relations as opposed to being peripheral to rational thought. The neuroscientific studies show that emotion and cognition are closely related processes affecting decision-making and control of the behaviors (Dolan, 2002). Therefore, the inclusion of the emotional intelligence into the AI systems is a major breakthrough in the intelligent technology evolution. The origin of emotional AI can be traced back to the groundbreaking project on affective computing by Picard (1997), who proposed a notion that an ability to recognize, analyze, and simulate human emotions in a machine is a viable option. Affective computing broadened the scope of AI beyond data processing to encompass emotive recognition and reactive control. Continuing on this framework, more recent developments have made multimodal dialogue systems which can produce sentiment-/emotion-controlled reactions thus improving the naturalness and empathy of human-AI communication (Firdaus et al., 2020). In addition, the general discourses of emotion in AI emphasize the interdisciplinary character of the psychology and neuroscience and machine learning towards developing systems that are more context-aware and socially responsive (Assunção et al., 2022).

The growing numbers of conversational agents and emotionally responsive systems being deployed across the fields of healthcare, education, and customer service demonstrate the transformative potential of emotional AI. A review of literature conducted by Laranjo et al., (2018) shows that conversational agents could offer personalized guidance, encourage interaction with the user, and support behavior change interventions. Likewise, virtual reality environments that can be fully immersive show promise in terms of emotional awareness, development of empathy, and behavioral control (Riva et al., 2011). These advances indicate that AI is increasingly becoming an active subject instead of a passive technology. On the group level, the emotional intelligence plays very crucial role in group dynamics and relations cohesion. According to Druskat and Wolff (2001), team-based systems that are characterized by emotional intelligence improve team cooperation, trust and performance. Applying this idea to AI-mediated settings, emotionally sensitive systems can alter the way people communicate, perceive social messages, and develop interpersonal trust in digital so-called mediated settings. The impact of AI on determining relational norms and patterns of communication becomes progressively high as it becomes integrated into organizational and social systems. Nonetheless, there is also a significant ethical implication and governance issues regarding the introduction of AI to emotionally sensitive areas.

O'Neil (2016) cautions that algorithmic systems can become a source of perpetuating bias, inequality, and asymmetrical power accords unless they are highly managed. On the same note, Floridi et al., (2018) highlight the significance of ethical models on autonomous systems to guarantee accountability, transparency, and overall well-being in society. The responsible governance is lacking, and losing control over emotionally intelligent AI, the problem of emotional manipulations, loss of privacy, or loss of real human communication may occur. Strategically and organizationally, the execution of AI should be in line with the sustainability and creation of business value throughout the digital transformation. Perifanis and Kitsios (2023) emphasize that the implementation of AI affects the performance of the organization in case of the combination with the relevant capabilities and strategic purpose. Therefore, the emotional AI changes not only the facts of expression and relationships between people but also alters the managerial practices, the service delivery models, and the communication structure in the organizations. Based on these currents, this paper explores the effects of AI on human expression and relationship formation in terms of emotional intelligence. Based on the available interdisciplinary literature on neuroscience, affective computing, organizational behavior, and AI governance, the discussion evaluates how affectively attentive technologies contribute to interpersonal communication, building trust, and sustaining relationships. Placing emotional AI into the context of technology and ethics, the chapter attempts to make a positive contribution to a balanced perception of how intelligent systems can improve instead of disrupting human connection in an ever more digitalized world. Although the research on affective computing and the field of emotionally responsive AI systems is on the rise, existing data are still rather disjointed in the technical, psychological, and governance spheres.

Much of the literature concentrates either on the technical progression of emotion identification structures or on distinct ethical issues, with seldom unifying investigation into how happen to be emotional AI concurrently influence the manifestation and connection of the individual, along with the dimensions of trust in connections and social connectedness. Moreover, although the research has addressed the conversational agents and adaptive systems separately, the relationship implications of the integration of emotional intelligence into AI-mediated communication have received minimal consideration.

Specifically, the relationship between increased relational interaction and newly arisen ethical susceptibility, including emotional manipulation, algorithmic bias, and addiction formation, is not theorized. This chapter closes this gap with a conceptual framework that can be used to integrate the foundations of emotional intelligence, affective computing, and governance mechanisms, and results of relationships in a singular analytical framework. The contribution of this chapter is in the fact that it introduces an integrative framework of relations that makes the emotional AI a technological facilitator and a socio-ethical negotiator of human expression and relationship construction.

Figure 1.

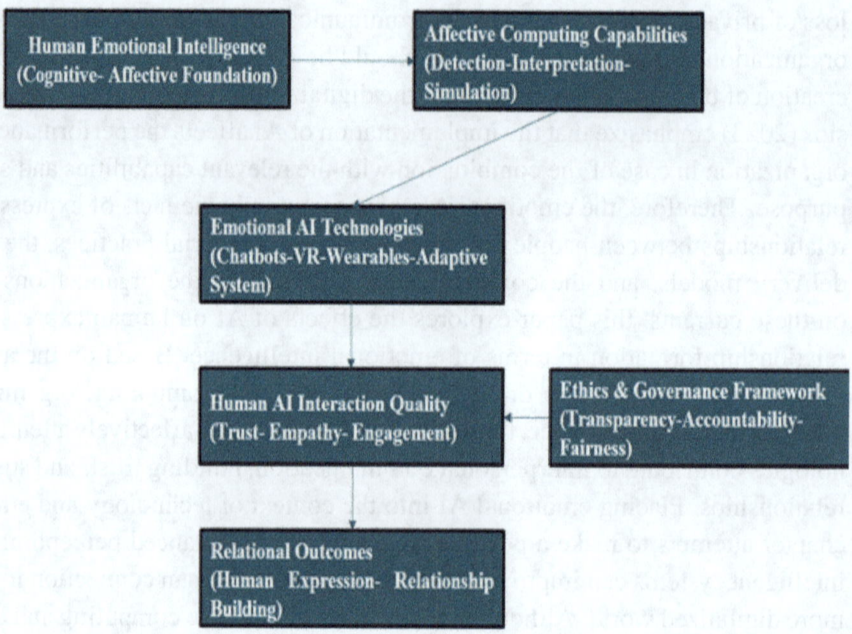

1.CONCEPTUAL FOUNDATIONS OF EMOTIONAL INTELLIGENCE IN ARTIFICIAL INTELLIGENCE

Conceptual Framework of Emotional intelligence in the AI discusses the theoretical foundation of AI systems.

EI Theoretical Framework

Theoretically, the ability-based model by Mayer and Salovey (1997), which views EI in terms of an ability, can be used to support the theoretical basis of the concept that supports emotional intelligence. This paradigm does not define emotion as a destabilizer of rationality but as a part of adaptive decision making and social operating. Also, the competency-based view of EI introduced by Goleman (2005) extends EI to the realms of Self-awareness, Self-regulation, motivation, empathy, and social skills- aspects that are becoming more and more dominant in the design of AI systems that are emotionally responsive. Placing emotional AI in these theoretical frameworks makes the concept more conceptually sound and interdisciplinary.

Emotional thinking is the most important basic decision-making ability for Humans

In the context of difficult situations, judgment and decision-making have long been considered the fundamental skill and the pinnacle of thought. We often use two methods to form judgments and decisions: rational logic, which is correct and dependable but takes longer, and sensory emotion, which is quick but unreliable. Reason and emotion can be viewed as to complementing system that cooperate to assist us in making judgments. Both are decisive skills that have been acquired and perfected as our bodies have evolved. The correctness and dependability of judgment should be the highest priority when there are enough time and knowledge, and we can rely on our reasoning to make in-depth analysis and Careful thinking and in-depth analysis should be prioritized when time and information permit, but when time and information are scarce, effectiveness takes precedence above perfect accuracy, necessitating hasty, emotion-driven decisions Zhou (2021).

Cognitive Neurological proof of Emotional thinking

As recent cognitive neuroscience studies have revealed, the regulation system of brainstem, comprising of the insula, amygdala, orbitofrontal cortex, etc., is the most important factor enabling human beings to feel emotions. The connection of emotions and motives and moods, and how neurochemistry modifies emotions and other mental states are such we do not fully understand. One of the parts in the example that are co-associated with the fear and rage feelings is the amygdala. Emotions therefore play a very crucial and vital role in the cognitive development and should be studied Dolan (2002).

This emotional correspondence, which is based on the separation and cooperation of the parts of the brain, is also rather sufficient to the cognitive tradition which existed during the times of Plato. Feminine is peripheral of the brain, whereas, reason is central of the brain. To some degree this assumption is also exercised by the intellectual neurological studies that hold that the major areas of emotional control must be found within the limbic cortical system, namely, the prefrontal cortex, ventral medial prefrontal cortex, orbitofrontal cortex, amygdala and the hippocampus. The brain is connected to a particular emotion, and each of its parts is assigned to the task of thinking a particular kind of emotion.

Emotion is the starting point of human consciousness and memory

The feeling is the initial point of the human consciousness and memory. The cognitive and thought process of the brain is in some way or another influenced by the emotions. psychological background and usually as the leading factor of consciousness. Cognitive psychologist known as Bernard Baars (2014) has once compared a consciousness to a highlight of the stage of the theatre of the mind, smiling at that which the individual knows to be. consciousness. The primal source of the light of emotion may be said to be the one. consciousness and to regulate the direction and contents of consciousness, but thinking is said to be an advanced form of consciousness. Emotional thinking. based upon this thought pattern and capability, which is managed by emotions, is the foundation of psychology. There are emotional states, which in the information processing perspective, will either speed up or slow down the processing of the brain. They can also affect the choice and course of processing by altering the body processes.

Emotion plays a crucial role in memory because it may result in the retention and more so reconstruction of occurrences during the recollection. Emotion helps give us better commitment to events and very emotionally attach events tend to be remembered better and recalled in a better detail than the neutral ones. Not only is the event coded within memory and stored but the emotions associated with it are label and stored as well. The emotional labels receive more priority than the events in other times when the information needed is important. It is what we call as the Situational memory which is an extremely individualized memory of the rare occurrences of situations that we experience in our day to day lives. The memory in itself is simply an inside experience of what we have observed on subjecting all the knowledge we have on specific events, people, moments, and places (Rowlands, 1999).

Emotional computing based on the simulation of emotional thinking is the foundation of AI

Rosalind W. Picard of the MIT Media Lab was the first person to coin the term emotional computing (or affective computing) to describe any form of computations that involve, cause or are specifically aimed at emotions (Xu, 2008). This idea is based on the outer expression of the humanity emotions, particularly the calculations which influence the emotions of individuals and which may be quantified and assessed. Affective computing is a subdivision of AI supposed to generate a more intelligent machine system that can perceive, identify and comprehend human emotions and behave effectively a more basic and advanced cognition. Emotions are eventually more fundamental and more profound a form of thought, and hence the really intelligent computers that will not only be able to interact and communicate with humans will be able to detect and express emotions. This can be considered as a crucial aspect of AI.

In a brief explanation, emotional computing can be adopted as a deductive process that is simulated and involves the application of emotions. It has a long run objective of mimicking human thinking in emotions so as to allow the machines to arrive at conclusions at the same speed. The first deployment of AI was to denote technologies, which can enable us to recreate, increase, or scale human intelligence in an artificial manner but with the arrival of emotional intelligence, AI will be on the next stage. We are now entering the following phase of emotional computing as we have already reached the five steps of previous arithmetic computing, mathematical functions, logical reasoning, expert systems, and pattern recognition Liu (2014).

2. TECHNOLOGICAL MECHANISMS ENABLING EMOTIONAL AI

The technological procedure enabling emotional AI to perform is using machine learning, natural language processing and responding to human feelings.

Virtual reality (VR) applications for Emotional Skill Development

Applications of virtual reality (VR) in enhancement of emotional intelligence Virtual reality (VR) is a developing technology that has potential to help students enhance their emotional intelligence. The VR allows making a learning experience immersive and induce a variety of emotions in a safe and controlled setting through placing users in a virtual space Freina and Ott (2015). Learning VR applications have been used to improve the overall socio-emotional competences of students through improving empathy, emotional regulating, and socialization. One of the common applications of VR in emotional skill-training is during perspective-taking. Immersible experiences enable the user to put themselves in the shoes of other people and feel the emotional realities of other individuals thus fostering empathy and perspective-taking skills Riva et al., (2019). The interactive simulation, e.g. VR simulations, can place one in a setting that involves interactions with people sharing different backgrounds or experiencing difficult situations, e.g. peer mediation or conflict resolution. Social empathy and connection that is achieved with the use of VR is achieved by enabling learners to know more about the feeling and the thoughts of others through first-person empathy Slater and Sanchez-Vives (2016).

Besides, the virtual reality worlds confer safe space to train emotion management. They can experience guided mindfulness training in VR simulation that should be tailored to fit their individually preferred needs and interests, and they can train biofeedback or exposure treatment Parsons and Rizzo (2008). In different cases, stress or anxiety victims will be able to gothrough virtual exposure therapy sessions to face and deal with their triggers in supportive and safe environment. With practice and exposure, the users can be in a position to boost their emotional strength and come up with coping strategies that are adaptive Bordnick et al. (2008). VR may also increase emotional intelligence, but there are many concerns and problems that one should take into account. Similar technical issues as simulator sickness, hardware limitations can also ensure that the application and availability of VR technologies in the learning organizations remain distant Lugrin et al., (2015)

Chatbots and Virtual assistants for Personalized Emotional Support

Another high-tech solution of offering students with individual emotional support and guidance is chatbots and virtual assistants. These chatbots may also engage consumers in understanding discussions, provide emotional assistance, and customized solutions based on the emotional need and circumstances of the consumers since they are directed by natural language processing (NLP) and machine learning approaches Laranjo et al., (2018). They are also convenient and easy to use, which is also a considerable benefit because chatbots and virtual assistants allow access to the emotional support resources anytime and anywhere across a broad spectrum of digital platforms Sethi & Jain (2024). Cognitive radio is frequently used together with AI and machine learning to develop smart and adaptable sharing and streamline real-time operations (Prema et al., 2024).

Chatbots and virtual assistants can also be employed as the judgment-free assistants of those who require one-on-one help or pass through awkward emotions Følstad and Brandtzaeg (2017). These types of conversational bots can assist the user in self-reflection or cognitive behavioural therapies, IDs his/her feelings, and thinks about the available solutions, listening to the user and speaking with him/her Lucas et al., (2015). Furthermore, the obscurity and privacy of the Facebook interactions can enable people to seek assistance or expose the vulnerable problems without any fear of being judged and stigmatised. Chatbots providing emotional support and virtual assistants cast doubt on the ethical issues related to the privacy of information, algorithmic bias and possible unintended outcomes, despite the role of the tools being presented as undeniable Laranjo et al., (2018).

In addition, the level of efficacy of these conversational bots is founded on the capacity to comprehend the natural language, emotional intelligence, and the relations with individuals. More research and development would be required in order to boost the skills and ethical demands in the successful implementation of chatbots and virtual assistants within learning institutions.

Gamification Techniques to encourage Empathy and Social Interaction

The implementation of game design principles beyond the gaming environment has been popular in the education sector as one of the indicators of fostering social interaction and empathy among students. Gamification is oriented at attracting the students to the learning process and motivating them, promoting cooperation, interpersonal skills development, empathy and building personal skills with the help of such game features as points, badges, leaderboards, challenges Deterding et al., (2011).

Empathy can also be constructed through gamification through immersive elements of narration and by allowing the gamer to role-play many characters to negotiate problematic social conditions Sethi & Jain (2024). Simulations or narrative-based games may assist players in the analysis of the impact of their behaviour on other characters, learn to empathize with other points of view and make ethical choices in ethically dubious circumstances Barab et al., (2012).

Besides, the strategies of cooperative learning can be facilitated by the capabilities of gamification that would enhance the collaboration and sympathy among peers. Team based activities, collaborative quests or collaborative problem-solving activities can also be used to motivate students to communicate, be empathetic and help their fellow students to accomplish a shared objective through gamified learning Dickey (2005). The process of interpersonal skills development, which includes listening to others, taking their side, and resolving conflicts with the help of shared experience and feedback helps players to feel sympathetic and part of the learning community Hamari et al., (2014).

Besides, gamification could facilitate desirable social relationship and prosocial behaviour through reward and recognition systems. Gamified systems enhance the positivity one strives to attain and a culture of empathy and mutual support is built through the form of awarding or rewarding acts of kindness, cooperation or empathy within the confines of the game Reeves and Read (2009).

Personalized learning experiences

Artificial intelligence based adaptive learning systems can offer a student a personalized learning process, which depends on the emotional needs, preferences, and learning styles of the student. On the one hand, such systems are dynamic enough to modify the instructional content, pacing, and interventions by examining the interactions of students, their performance outcomes, and emotional states to ensure the best possible learning results (Blikstein, 2013). An AI tutor may, for example, offer a student who has problems with controlling his or her emotions some exercises or materials.

Real-Time Feedback and Intervention

The AI-driven sentiment analysis systems and affective computing systems enable one to receive real-time information about the emotional state and degree of involvement of students in the learning activities (Picard, 1997). This feedback can assist the teachers in identifying at-risk children, finding out the level of effectiveness of the instructional strategies, and even facing emotional barriers to learning with ease (D'Mello and Graesser, 2012). To make the lesson more passionate and active, the teacher might alter the lesson plan, offer more support, or help learners cooperate with others in case the sentiment analysis shows that a group of learners is not contented with the current experience, or is not involved.

Supportive Chatbots and Virtual Assistants

Virtual assistants that have AI-based chatbots may help students using personalized emotional assistants, guidance and resources and facilitate self-understanding, restraint and wellbeing Laranjo et al., (2018). Lucas et al., (2015) believe that such conversational agents can offer such cognitive behavioural therapies to students that are sensitive to their emotional needs, listening to their introspective needs, and sympathetic talks. On the example of a chatbot, a student may be provided with coping skills, mindfulness techniques, or relaxation exercises to overcome stress and anxiety or negative feelings when working on problematic academic assignments or during transitions.

Wearable Devices for Emotion Regulation

Emotion regulation. Biosensors and physiological monitoring capabilities embedded into wearable devices make it possible to monitor the emotional condition of the students in real-time and provide biofeedback and self-regulation training. These devices could alert students to signs of stress or arousal and make students engage in the mindfulness or other relaxing activities because of monitoring such body signals as skin conductance, heart rate variation, and breathing patterns. Social-emotional learning can also be enhanced through wearable technology by means of collaborative activities, including group biofeedback or emotion regulation challenge systems where students are prompted to work in a group to have their collective emotional reactions to their joint responses Sethi & Jain (2024).

The combination of these technologies shows a structural transformation in the role of AI - as a task-based automation to a relationship-based mediation. Emotional artificial intelligence systems are not mere indicators or reacts to affective cues, but an active component of the formation of emotional environments, the formation of dependency, persuasion, empathy, and trust patterns. This relational ability brings about the possibilities of greater human interaction and exposures of emotional engineering and algorithmic persuasion. Thus, the technological mechanisms need not be perceived merely as the design architectures but as the socio-emotional agents imbedded into the human relational systems.

3. ORGANIZATIONAL AND MANAGERIAL IMPLICATIONS

Organizational and managerial implications of emotional intelligence highlight its role in enhancing leadership effectiveness, employee engagement, decision-making, and workplace relationships. In organizational contexts, emotional artificial intelligence transforms the operation efficiency as well as the relationship climate and communication patterns. The adoption of emotionally responsive systems affects the leadership style, formation of trust amongst employees, psychological safety, collaboration patterns. The more AI systems are used in decision-making, to offer feedback, and to evaluate performance, the more they mediate the ways people communicate emotions, understand authority, and build professional relationships. As a result, emotional AI does not simply optimize productivity, instead actively transforming the quality of relationships, both on individual and collective levels, which forms their engagement, empathy, and organizational integrity.

Artificial intelligence and managerial capability

This is the way the AI technology is transforming the world. To realize the potential of AI, a number of nations and organizations have developed strategic plans (CAICT & Gartner, 2018; Chen, 2019). A wide industry like business, finance, healthcare, and vehicles can be processed with the help of AI applications. The move to AI industries and the adoption of smart technology to improve the supply chain process, productivity, competitiveness, and efficiency, as well as to improve operational control, is no longer an exclusive focus of widespread research (Rymarczyk, 2020; Gastaldi et al., 2022). It starts with an introduction where it defines AI-enhanced supply chain management and explains why AI is so important in that case (Nagalakshmi et al., 2024). The business management is trying to combine intelligent technology, restructure business resources and adopt Industry 4.0. Managerial skills are therefore significant in transforming the strategy and also rejuvenating the corporation. (House et al., 2002) and (Odeibat, 2023) are of the opinion that managerial aptitude is a managerial capability to direct, motivate, inspire, and empower employees in determining the success and performance of the firm.

Innovation attributes of artificial intelligence adoption background

In the recent past, the issue of the AI application in certain domain has been the subject of some research (e.g., Odeibat, 2023; Oyelude, 2017; Li et al., 2017). The remaining articles are focused on the theoretical background and use of AI (Qiu, 2018; Kouziokas, 2017). However, the research has been scarce especially in the uptake of AI in the organization level Chen (2019). The most important aspect of AI adoption is the technological context aspect of the AI innovation features. The innovation attributes have been discussed extensively in the literature of the past research on the impact of the innovation approach (Kwon and Zmud 1987; Chau and Tam, 1997).

Organizational Capability and its adaptability to Business Challenges Organizational Capabilities

Organizational skills assist in the adoption of an innovation. Emphasise that companies need to make the introduction of AI their regular and innovative priority (Perifanis and Kitsios, 2023). They underscore that the two important AI ambidexterity elements are synergistically influenced on the strategic flexibilities of the organization. Such items as technical skills, management skills, and leadership resources are then known as organizational competencies. They are skills that have been imbued into a corporation, in most cases, organization specific and cannot be transferred. According to the RBV theory, business is able to produce a competitive advantage in case it is able to bundle economically valuable, hard to imitate, and non-transferable resources (Wernerfelt, 1984; Garrison, et al., 2015). This means that the organizations will be capable of enjoying a short-term competitive advantage due to their unique and scarce resources. The use of AI technologies allows businesses to be more productive (Perifanis and Kitsios, 2023).

Managerial support

The importance of leader's commitment to any major change in the company is that it will dictate how the resources are allocated and how services are incorporated. According to researchers, managerial support is significant in the process of information system integration and technology adoption (Thong, 1999; Müller and Jugdev, 2012; Sanders and Courtney, 1985; Chong et al., 2009; Fui-Hoon Nah et al., 2001). To explain this, Thong (1999), cites that the nature of the top managers is another factor that affects the adoption of information technology (IT) in the business. The innovation adoption depends on the leaders at the upper ranks who are able to distribute the organizational resources (Hage and Dewar, 1973). Unless the project is applied continuously and consistently, managerial support will not be relevant (Elbanna, 2013).

The rationale is that leaders, especially those that are in the top management, have the power to assign competent staff to oversee a project and invest a lot of finances and other resources in it. In turn, managerial support in the project may fail (Wixom and Watson, 2001; Pajany, 2021). The rapid production of the new technology is reshaping the managerial functions of the leaders. The remote intelligence (RI) and AI technology simplifies outsourcing by the organization. As a result, every leader must be able to plan, organize, motivate, and oversee cross-cultural and virtual teams (Ng, 2021; Florek-Paszkowska et al., 2021). Also, address organizational issues e.g. inequality, job displacement and unemployment. Most researchers attributed the impact of technological change to the change management and a digitalization trend throughout the industry that created new digital threats and opportunities to companies. The technologies of artificial intelligence can have an impact on the entire organization. Such changes have the potential to transform businesses.

Technical capability

Physical resources that are needed to accomplish innovations are referred to as technical capability and they include data, networking, and computer hardware (Aboelmaged, 2014). Meanwhile, it shows how a corporation can divide its resources to provide a flexible and expandable foundation of enterprise applications (Wang et al., 2016). Technical capability includes intangible materials, which include application processes, IT development, collaboration processes, and technical proficiencies that may successfully adopt the most recent technology (Garrison et al., 2015). In turn, it affects the adoption of the technology in a significant way (Wu et al., 2007).

The high technological capacity enables the information technology team to disseminate the artificial intelligence solutions efficiently and timely even though the integration is less complicated. The introduction of AI could be effectively implemented when the business would be able to pursue the technological objectives and implement the technologies grounded on the artificial intelligence (AI) in the framework of the existing location. Through the rapid proliferation of Internet of Things (IoT)-based devices, numerous interconnected systems have become available with numerous applications and services (Sathyaraj et al., 2024).

4. ETHICAL, CULTURAL, AND GOVERNANCE CHALLENGES

Although the emotional AI technologies have immense positive effects, such as better simulation of empathy, personalized engagement, better relationship formation, and adaptive communication, their power also comes with a major ethical threat. The very same systems that impose emotional resonance can also support the degree of behavioral control, emotional dependence, and algorithmic persuasion. As an example, the sentiment analysis based on AI can be used to personalize the interaction with users and boost their engagement but, in this case, the line between supportive interaction and manipulative design can be easily crossed. Likewise, emotion-recognition algorithms can also help increase service responsiveness, but they also have the propensity of strengthening cultural prejudice or misunderstanding context-sensitive expressions of emotion. Such duality generates a structural conflict of emotional AI: the ability to deepen human connection also harbours the possibility of commodifying or engineering emotional experience. Thus, governance structures should not simply control technical implementation but proactively ensure relational authenticity, psychological autonomy, and equity within AI-mediated space. Ethical, cultural, and governance challenges in emotional intelligence emphasize concerns related to bias, privacy, emotional manipulation, cultural sensitivity, and responsible regulation of AI systems.

Background: Current Transformation in Society and Business

The field of AI technologies is transforming our world. The way AI beings learn, think, solve problems, perceive, and use language, is a blend of a diverse array of competencies. They are computer-controlled robots or digital computers that perform the task that may be normally performed by intelligent beings (Russell & Norvig, 2021). The level and the amount of thought done by AI devices are another thing. Narrow AI technologies, algorithmic expert systems, 22 big data, and deep learning are already used in health care, banking, insurance, public policy and governance, manufacturing, security, law enforcement, autonomous vehicles, and even in social media applications (O'Neil 2016; OECD 2018).). The artificial general intelligence (AGI) systems are not yet at the stage of having a level of self-understanding and autonomous self-control (Goertzel, 2007; Saariluoma 2015).

The opportunities of AI in the financial sector may be enormous, but not all of the hype surrounding AI is justified (Brynjolfsson & McAfee, 2014; Brynjolfsson & McAfee, 2017). The next few years will witness the artificial intelligence increase revenues. As the research on Tractica study has demonstrated, e.g., AI applications revenue will not only increase by 2025 (36.8 billion) but also by 2016 (643.7 million) (Bughin et al., 2018). According to a recent global survey of business leaders, 72 in 100 people felt that AI will significantly affect businesses in the year 2022 (Ransbotham et al., 2017).

Challenges and Opportunities

Nowadays, AI is hyped a lot reminded us of the fact that the real-life examples and discussions of ethical issues and its consequences are still absent, and we have to look past the hype. Whenever we mention AI ethics, we do not know what we are referring to. The issue is that as states, we tend to see in the moral dilemmas associated with AI when it is time to think how those innovative technologies can be utilized and developed to make the life in the society more appropriate. Therefore, the query concerning who an autonomous car is supposed to be run over is merely erroneous. The society must apply AI in a way that will not interfere with the quality of life of the citizens. Nowadays, AI is the focus of many expectations in different spheres of daily routine, but it is not deprived of a set of ethical concerns.

Many of them are also worried about the means of developing trusting relations between human and non-human actors. They can be human-machine collaboration, data ownership, data distortion, and privacy-sensitive and resolute artificial intelligence. Using the case study, the unnecessary personal information that accumulates in the maintenance of their health is faced with an increased radical transparency; it becomes problematic to the individual and in decision making. According to (Mika et al., 2019), the residents are interested in the future opportunities of the application of AI in the workplace, including autonomous systems as one of the colleagues and demonstrations of prototypes of smart cities of the future and autonomous maintenance and transportation. It is also stated that the use of AI is not easy (Cadwalladr and Graham-Harrison, 2018). There exist even more dystopian imagery of people dying due to the so-called singleness or the catastrophic implications of unlawful usage of the AI.

Moving Towards new horizons in developing Ethical AI and Societal Governance

The anticipated social consequences of the AI will involve ethical self-control and social guidance of the societal, business, and third-sector actors. According to (Floridi et al., 2018), ETAIROS will develop ethical design and evaluation models and instruments, expound on the general governance principles and practices, and sensitize awareness of the pertinent use's cases and definite possible and challenges of AI. In terms of the attitudes towards sustainable, open, and inclusive development of the society, the project develops the recommendations and practices of the usage, design, and governance of AI to both the official authorities and the business community.

Culture

The culture is a complex of values, beliefs, customs and behaviours, which condition and control the way people behave, individually, or in groups. Culture therefore influences the lives of the individuals and groups. The culture typically gets defined by their arts, music, oral and written literature, morality life, excellence ideals, great personalities and imagining of what the good life. Culture enables the citizens to live freely honour and eventually bring about a legacy. The cultural history of a nation can be seen to possess a heterogeneous, composite culture that attracts various practices. Myths, conventions, rituals, symbols, traditions, institutions and communication styles are a representation of a culture.

In its turn, it will not be varied to observe how various civilizations interpret, emphasize, and apply their unique myths, conventions, moral teachings, and ideal of good life. Therefore, cultural diversity embodies the unique ways of life, beliefs and practices of diverse cultural groupings and a worldview of the same. Culture, gender, colour, ethnicity, religion, caste, tribe, physical ability, sexual orientation, age, economic background, geographic location and position among other few indicators or characteristics constitute human diversity. This author lives in the dimension of cultural diversification of human beings (Dwivedi, 2002).

Fundamentally, emotional AI represents a tremendous normative conflict between augmentation and manipulation. Although these systems can supplement the emotional awareness of humans by increasing empathy capabilities, making it easier to support and be more responsive in relationships, they can also be designed to change the affective states in a way that affects human behavior and decision-making processes indirectly. When algorithms are fed to achieve a high score in engagement compared to relational authenticity, the line between empathy and engineered persuasion further becomes unclear.

Likewise, even though emotional AI can be used to promote the autonomy of humans by providing adaptive advice and emotional understanding, it can also be used to limit autonomy by manipulating individuals in a specific direction or towards a particular favourable behavior. This two-fold capability highlights the fact that emotional AI cannot be ethical, as it functions within power relations that define an understanding of perception, agency, and trust. Thus, responsible governance should not merely be about compliance and risk reduction but an active means to protect psychological autonomy, relational authenticity, and integrity of human expression of emotion.

5. TOWARD RESPONSIBLE AND SUSTAINABLE EMOTIONAL AI

Toward responsible and sustainable emotional AI focuses on designing emotionally intelligent systems that are transparent, ethical, culturally inclusive, and aligned with long-term human and societal well-being.

Harnessing AI Responsibly

We must take a proactive stance to guarantee that AI keeps improving our capabilities and favourably impacting the Sustainable Development Goals.

1. *Increase AI Literacy:* Educate thoroughly on AI technologies and its application across all levels of the society in an ethical manner to ensure that people possess the knowledge to utilize AI in a manner that is both rational and effective.
2. *Develop Emotional Intelligence in AI Contacts:* Include training courses that will be dedicated to the management of contacts with AI systems, especially in healthcare and education where the notions of understanding and empathy play a crucial role.
3. *Enhance the Ethical Standards:* Require and enforce successful ethical standards to direct the design and deployment of AI systems to make certain that the AI systems do not undermine the principle of justice, accountability, and transparency.

4. *Nurture Collaborative Advances:* Governments, companies and non-governments must work together whereby they come up with inclusive AI solutions capable of fulfilling social demands and promoting sustainable growth.
5. *Observation and Review AI Impact:* In order to ensure that AI technology remains human-oriented especially in connection with SDGs, constantly assess the effects of AI technology on people socially, economically and environmentally.

When we do so, we will be able to create a world where AI supports our collective work to produce a sustainable and fair world.

Emotional Intelligence In Human-AI Interaction

The skill to control relationships and feelings is essential in the world of AI. Artificial intelligence can have significant influence on our decisions, feelings, and connection. These influences need to be controlled and understood, which is impossible without a balanced EQ. Also, it is significant to AI development because emotion facilitates social integration, reinforcement, and general development (Assunção et al., 2022). explained that it is a taboo among computer scientists and engineers. The latter (Firdaus et al., 2020) reveal the possibilities of designing AI systems to detect and respond to human emotions through the creation of EmoSen, a special dialogue system that produces responses with controlled response generated by sentiment and emotion within a multimodal environment. Their mechanism is one of the best illustrations of how emotional intelligence can be integrated into AI as it demonstrates how it can enhance the efficiency, naturalness, and empathy of human-AI interactions.

Training EQ can be improved by using AI as one of the sources of enhancing our ability to be objective and emotionally intelligent in the interactions that are affected by AI. The ability to regulate the emotional attachments to AI becomes necessary when the latter becomes closer to human traits. Regarding AI, emotional intelligence will be knowledge of how the AI influences our actions and our emotions and the effective regulation of these emotions. As an example, AI-based social media algorithms provide interactions with potential powerful effects on the feelings and choices of users; under such circumstances, the emotional intelligence involves maintaining a critical perception of the effects.

Moreover, the use of AI in customer services, healthcare, education, and solutions to climate change is a special source of emotional management. As an example, it takes behavioural change to solve our environmental issues and climate issues. Users should thus deal with relationships where AI interfaces are emphatic and require an altered attitude to empathy and emotional responses. Creating an EQ with

AI interactions will assist individuals to remain emotionally balanced and achieve prudent decisions in social settings that are becoming more complex.

6. FUTURE RESEARCH DIRECTIONS

The fast development of AI systems based on emotional intelligence offers a number of research directions in the future. To begin with, empirical studies are required to investigate the impact of emotional AI in the long-term relational trust, emotional dependence, and interpersonal authenticity in various social and organizational situations. Although current research focuses on technological functionality, there is scanty longitudinal support on whether emotional involvement mediated by AI enhances or replaces the human-to-human relationship. Second, cross-cultural studies are necessary to find out the interpretation of culturally embedded expression of emotion by the emotional recognition systems. Because the rules of emotion differ in different societies, the possibility of future studies on whether the models of affective computing strengthen cultural bias or can be created to suit the local emotional systems should be investigated. Third, more ethically sound emotional AI architectures need to be developed by means of interdisciplinary research involving psychology, neuroscience, management, and computer science. Researchers need to explore systems that ensure the autonomy of users and allow them to be adaptively emotionally responsive, especially in areas like healthcare, education, and digital governance. Lastly, the implications of implementing emotional AI in the organization need to be investigated in future research. The insight into the way emotional analytics mediated by AI alter the workplace power dynamics, psychological safety, and employee engagement will be essential to the creation of sustainable and human-centered AI ecosystems.

CONCLUSION

The emotional intelligence implemented into the Artificial Intelligence is a major step in the interaction of humans and technology. Leaving the field of automation and rational thinking processes, emotionally sensitive AI systems have now an impact on how people manifest emotional response, comprehend social signals and on relationships. Based on the studies of affective computing and other interdisciplinary works, emotional AI has shown the possibilities of forming a deeper engagement, empathy, and relational trust in the field of healthcare, education, as well as organizational management. Nevertheless, the ethical and governance implications of the increasing popularity of emotionally intelligent systems, like algorithmic bias, privacy problems, and the authenticity of AI-mediated emotional expression, are also an issue. Thus, responsible design, transparency, and accountability should direct the future of emotional AI to make it consistent with the well-being of human beings. Once applied in an ethical and strategic manner, emotional AI may become a complement, which will help to reinforce the rather than to override meaningful human relationships in a more digital society.

REFERENCES

Aboelmaged, M. G. (2014). Predicting e-readiness at firm-level: An analysis of technological, organizational and environmental (TOE) effects on e-maintenance readiness in manufacturing firms. *International Journal of Information Management, 34*(5), 639–651. DOI: 10.1016/j.ijinfomgt.2014.05.002

Assunção, G., Patrão, B., Castelo-Branco, M., & Menezes, P. (2022). An overview of emotion in artificial intelligence. *IEEE Transactions on Artificial Intelligence, 3*(6), 867–886. DOI: 10.1109/TAI.2022.3159614

Baars, B. J. (2014). *Cognitive Theory of Consciousness* (An, H., Trans.). Science Press. (in Chinese)

Barab, S., Pettyjohn, P., Gresalfi, M., Volk, C., & Solomou, M. (2012). Game-based curriculum and transformational play: Designing to meaningfully positioning person, content, and context. *Computers & Education, 58*(1), 518–533. DOI: 10.1016/j.compedu.2011.08.001

Blikstein, P. (2013, April). Multimodal learning analytics. In *Proceedings of the third international conference on learning analytics and knowledge* (pp. 102-106). DOI: 10.1145/2460296.2460316

Bordnick, P. S., Traylor, A., Copp, H. L., Graap, K. M., Carter, B., Ferrer, M., & Walton, A. P. (2008). Assessing reactivity to virtual reality alcohol based cues. *Addictive Behaviors, 33*(6), 743–756. DOI: 10.1016/j.addbeh.2007.12.010 PMID: 18282663

. Brynjolfsson, E., & McAfee, A. (2014). *The second machine age: Work progress and prosperity in a time of brilliant technologies.* WW Norton & company.

Brynjolfsson, E., & Mcafee, A. N. D. R. E. W. (2017). The business of artificial intelligence. *Harvard Business Review, 7*(1), 1–2.

Bughin, J., Seong, J., Manyika, J., Chui, M., & Joshi, R. (2018). Notes from the AI frontier: Modeling the impact of AI on the world economy. *McKinsey Global Institute, 4*(1), 2–61.

Cadwalladr, C., & Graham-Harrison, E. (2018). How Cambridge Analytica turned Facebook 'likes' into a lucrative political tooll Technologyl The Guardian. *The Guardian.*

CAICT & Gartner. (2018). 2018 World Artificial Intelligence Industry Development Blue Book. 2018 World Artificial Intelligence Conference. Retrieve from shttp://www.caict.ac.cn/kxyj/qwfb/bps/201809/P020180918696200669434.pdf

Chau, P. Y., & Tam, K. Y. (1997). Factors Affecting the Adoption of Open Systems: An Exploratory Study1. *Management Information Systems Quarterly*, *21*(1), 1–24. DOI: 10.2307/249740

Chen, H. (2019). *Success factors impacting artificial intelligence adoption: Perspective from the Telecom Industry in China*. Old Dominion University.

Chong, A. Y. L., Lin, B., Ooi, K. B., & Raman, M. (2009). Factors affecting the adoption level of c-commerce: An empirical study. *Journal of Computer Information Systems*, *50*(2), 13–22. DOI: 10.1080/08874417.2009.11645380

D'Mello, S., & Graesser, A. (2012). Dynamics of affective states during complex learning. *Learning and Instruction*, *22*(2), 145–157. DOI: 10.1016/j.learninstruc.2011.10.001

Deterding, S., Dixon, D., Khaled, R., & Nacke, L. (2011, September). From game design elements to gamefulness: defining" gamification". In *Proceedings of the 15th international academic MindTrek conference: Envisioning future media environments* (pp. 9-15). DOI: 10.1145/2181037.2181040

Dickey, M. D. (2005). Engaging by design: How engagement strategies in popular computer and video games can inform instructional design. *Educational Technology Research and Development*, *53*(2), 67–83. DOI: 10.1007/BF02504866

Dolan, R. J. (2002). Emotion, cognition, and behavior. *Science*, *298*(5596), 1191–1194. DOI: 10.1126/science.1076358 PMID: 12424363

Druskat, V. U., & Wolff, S. B. (2001). Building the emotional intelligence of groups. *Harvard Business Review*, *79*(3), 80–91. PMID: 11246926

Dwivedi, O. P. (2002). The challenge of cultural diversity for good governance. *The Indian Journal of Public Administration*, *48*(1), 14–28. DOI: 10.1177/0019556120020102

Elbanna, A. (2013). Top management support in multiple-project environments: An in-practice view. *European Journal of Information Systems*, *22*(3), 278–294. DOI: 10.1057/ejis.2012.16

Firdaus, M., Chauhan, H., Ekbal, A., & Bhattacharyya, P. (2020). EmoSen: Generating sentiment and emotion-controlled responses in a multimodal dialogue system. *IEEE Transactions on Affective Computing*, *13*(3), 1555–1566. DOI: 10.1109/TAFFC.2020.3015491

Florek-Paszkowska, A., Ujwary-Gil, A., & Godlewska-Dzioboń, B. (2021). Business innovation and critical success factors in the era of digital transformation and turbulent times. *Journal of Entrepreneurship. Management and Innovation*, *17*(4), 7–28.

Floridi, L., Cowls, J., Beltrametti, M., Chatila, R., Chazerand, P., Dignum, V., Luetge, C., Madelin, R., Pagallo, U., Rossi, F., Schafer, B., Valcke, P., & Vayena, E. (2018). AI4People—An ethical framework for a good AI society: Opportunities, risks, principles, and recommendations. *Minds and Machines*, *28*(4), 689–707. DOI: 10.1007/s11023-018-9482-5 PMID: 30930541

Følstad, A., & Brandtzæg, P. B. (2017). Chatbots and the new world of HCI. *interactions, 24*(4), 38-42.

Freina, L., & Ott, M. (2015, April). A literature review on immersive virtual reality in education: state of the art and perspectives. In *The international scientific conference elearning and software for education* (Vol. 1, No. 133, pp. 10-1007). DOI: 10.12753/2066-026X-15-020

Fui-Hoon Nah, F., Lee-Shang Lau, J., & Kuang, J. (2001). Critical factors for successful implementation of enterprise systems. *Business Process Management Journal*, *7*(3), 285–296. DOI: 10.1108/14637150110392782

Garrison, G., Wakefield, R. L., & Kim, S. (2015). The effects of IT capabilities and delivery model on cloud computing success and firm performance for cloud supported processes and operations. *International Journal of Information Management*, *35*(4), 377–393. DOI: 10.1016/j.ijinfomgt.2015.03.001

Gastaldi, L., Lessanibahri, S., Tedaldi, G., & Miragliotta, G. (2022). Companies' adoption of Smart Technologies to achieve structural ambidexterity: An analysis with SEM. *Technological Forecasting and Social Change*, *174*, 121187. DOI: 10.1016/j.techfore.2021.121187

Goertzel, B. (2007). In Pennachin, C. (Ed.), *Artificial general intelligence* (Vol. 2, p. 1). Springer. DOI: 10.1007/978-3-540-68677-4

Goleman, D. (2005). *Emotional intelligence: Why it can matter more than IQ*. Bantam.

Hage, J., & Dewar, R. (1973). Elite values versus organizational structure in predicting innovation. *Administrative Science Quarterly*, *18*(3), 279–290. DOI: 10.2307/2391664

Hamari, J., Koivisto, J., & Sarsa, H. (2014, January). Does gamification work?--a literature review of empirical studies on gamification. In *2014 47th Hawaii international conference on system sciences* (pp. 3025-3034). Ieee.

House, R., Javidan, M., Hanges, P., & Dorfman, P. (2002). Understanding cultures and implicit leadership theories across the globe: An introduction to project GLOBE. *Journal of World Business*, *37*(1), 3–10. DOI: 10.1016/S1090-9516(01)00069-4

Kouziokas, G. N. (2017). The application of artificial intelligence in public administration for forecasting high crime risk transportation areas in urban environment. *Transportation Research Procedia*, *24*, 467–473. DOI: 10.1016/j.trpro.2017.05.083

Kwon, T. H., & Zmud, R. W. (1987). Unifying the fragmented models of information systems implementation. In *Critical issues in information systems research* (pp. 227-251).

Laranjo, L., Dunn, A. G., Tong, H. L., Kocaballi, A. B., Chen, J., Bashir, R., Surian, D., Gallego, B., Magrabi, F., Lau, A. Y. S., & Coiera, E. (2018). Conversational agents in healthcare: A systematic review. *Journal of the American Medical Informatics Association : JAMIA*, *25*(9), 1248–1258. DOI: 10.1093/jamia/ocy072 PMID: 30010941

Li, R., Zhao, Z., Zhou, X., Ding, G., Chen, Y., Wang, Z., & Zhang, H. (2017). Intelligent 5G: When cellular networks meet artificial intelligence. *IEEE Wireless Communications*, *24*(5), 175–183. DOI: 10.1109/MWC.2017.1600304WC

Liu, G. Y. (2014). *The Affective Calculation Method of Human Physiological Signal*. Science Press. (in Chinese)

Lucas, G. M., Gratch, J., Cheng, L., & Marsella, S. (2015). When the going gets tough: Grit predicts costly perseverance. *Journal of Research in Personality*, *59*, 15–22. DOI: 10.1016/j.jrp.2015.08.004

Lugrin, J. L., Bortolaso, C., Cumming, B., & Karray, F. (2015). The challenges of virtual reality for exposure therapy in anxiety disorders: Patients' and therapists' opinions. *Journal of Medical Internet Research*, *17*(12), e319.

Mayer, J. D., & Salovey, P. (1997). What is emotional intelligence? In Salovey, P., & Sluyter, D. J. (Eds.), *Emotional development and emotional intelligence: Educational implications* (pp. 3–31). Basic Books.

Mika, N., Nadezhda, G., Jaana, L., & Raija, K. (2019). Ethical AI for the governance of the society: Challenges and opportunities. *CEUR Workshop Proceedings*, *2505*, 20–26.

Müller, R., & Jugdev, K. (2012). Critical success factors in projects: Pinto, Slevin, and Prescott–the elucidation of project success. *International Journal of Managing Projects in Business*, *5*(4), 757–775. DOI: 10.1108/17538371211269040

Ng, H. S. (2021). Are Managers Still Necessary in the Era of the Fourth Industrial Revolution (I4. 0)? In *Future of Work, Work-Family Satisfaction, and Employee Well-Being in the Fourth Industrial Revolution* (pp. 81-98). IGI Global Scientific Publishing.

O'Neil, C. (2016). *Weapons of math destruction: How big data increases inequality and threatens democracy*. Crown Publishing Group.

Odeibat, A. S. A. (2023). Exploring the impact of managerial capabilities on the innovation potential of artificial intelligence and organizational capabilities: A literature review.

OECD. (2018). *AI: Intelligent machines, smart policies: Conference summary. OECD Digital Economy Papers, No. 270*. OECD Publishing.

Oyelude, A. A. (2017). What's trending in libraries from the internet cybersphere–artificial intelligence and other emerging technologies. *Library Hi Tech News, 34*(2), 11–12. DOI: 10.1108/LHTN-02-2017-0008

Pajany, P. (2021). *Ai Transformative Influence: Extending the Tram to Management Student's AI's Machine Learning Adoption* (Doctoral dissertation, Franklin University).

Parsons, T. D., & Rizzo, A. A. (2008). Affective outcomes of virtual reality exposure therapy for anxiety and specific phobias: A meta-analysis. *Journal of Behavior Therapy and Experimental Psychiatry, 39*(3), 250–261. DOI: 10.1016/j.jbtep.2007.07.007 PMID: 17720136

Perifanis, N. A., & Kitsios, F. (2023). Investigating the influence of artificial intelligence on business value in the digital era of strategy: A literature review. *Information (Basel), 14*(2), 85. DOI: 10.3390/info14020085

. Picard, R. (1997). W.,(1997). affective computing. *Computer Science, Art, Psychology. Semantic Scholar. DOI, 10.*

Prema, S., Solaimalai, G., Lalithambikai, S., & Priya, S. G., PD, S., & Thanikodi, S. (2024, April). Cognitive Radio Networks: An AI Enabled Approach. In *2024 Ninth International Conference on Science Technology Engineering and Mathematics (ICONSTEM)* (pp. 1-6). IEEE. DOI: 10.1109/ICONSTEM60960.2024.10568748

Qiu, C. (2018). Application of artificial intelligence technology in GIS. *Journal of Advanced Oxidation Technologies, 21*(2).

Ransbotham, S., Kiron, D., Gerbert, P., & Reeves, M. (2017). Reshaping business with artificial intelligence: Closing the gap between ambition and action. *MIT Sloan Management Review*, *59*(1).

Reeves, B., & Read, J. L. (2009). *Total engagement: How games and virtual worlds are changing the way people work and businesses compete*. Harvard Business Press.

Riva, G., Gaggioli, A., Grassi, A., Raspelli, S., Cipresso, P., Pallavicini, F., . . . Donvito, G. (2011, January). NeuroVR 2-A free virtual reality platform for the assessment and treatment in behavioral health care. In MMVR (pp. 493-495).

Rowlands, M. (1999). *The body in mind: Understanding cognitive processes*. Cambridge University Press. DOI: 10.1017/CBO9780511583261

Russell, S., & Norvig, P. (2021). Artificial Intelligence: a modern approach, 4th US ed. *aima: сайт. URL:* https://aima. cs. *berkeley. edu/(дата обращения: 26.02. 2023).*

Rymarczyk, J. (2020). Technologies, opportunities and challenges of the industrial revolution 4.0: Theoretical considerations. *Entrepreneurial Business and Economics Review*, *8*(1), 185–198. DOI: 10.15678/EBER.2020.080110

Saariluoma, P. (2015). Four challenges in designing autonomous systems. *Williams, A., Scharre, P., Mayer, C., Arnold, R., Crootof, R., Anderson, J. & Husniux, A. Autonomous Systems: Issues for Defence Policymakers. NATO.*

Sanders, G. L., & Courtney, J. F. (1985). A field study of organizational factors influencing DSS success. *Management Information Systems Quarterly*, *9*(1), 77–93. DOI: 10.2307/249275

Sathyaraj, P., Bhukya, S. N., Devi, S. R., Umadi, C., & Ajina, A. (2024, April). Secure Device on boarding in IoT Networks. In *2024 Ninth International Conference on Science Technology Engineering and Mathematics (ICONSTEM)* (pp. 1-7). IEEE. DOI: 10.1109/ICONSTEM60960.2024.10568809

Sethi, S. S., & Jain, K. (2024). AI technologies for social emotional learning: Recent research and future directions. *Journal of Research in Innovative Teaching & Learning*, *17*(2), 213–225. DOI: 10.1108/JRIT-03-2024-0073

Slater, M., & Sanchez-Vives, M. V. (2016). Enhancing our lives with immersive virtual reality. *Frontiers in Robotics and AI*, *3*, 74. DOI: 10.3389/frobt.2016.00074

Thong, J. Y. (1999). An integrated model of information systems adoption in small businesses. *Journal of Management Information Systems*, *15*(4), 187–214. DOI: 10.1080/07421222.1999.11518227

Wang, P., Chaudhry, S., & Li, L. (2016). Introduction: Advances in IoT research and applications. *Internet Research*, *26*(2). Advance online publication. DOI: 10.1108/IntR-06-2015-0183

Wernerfelt, B. (1984). A resource-based view of the firm. *Strategic Management Journal*, *5*(2), 171–180. DOI: 10.1002/smj.4250050207

Wixom, B. H., & Watson, H. J. (2001). An Empirical Investigation of the Factors Affecting Data Warehousing Success1. *Management Information Systems Quarterly*, *25*(1), 17–42. DOI: 10.2307/3250957

Wu, J. H., Wang, S. C., & Lin, L. M. (2007). Mobile computing acceptance factors in the healthcare industry: A structural equation model. *International Journal of Medical Informatics*, *76*(1), 66–77. DOI: 10.1016/j.ijmedinf.2006.06.006 PMID: 16901749

Xu, Y. L. (2008). *Three-Dimensional Structure Theory of Emotional Intelligence*. China Social Sciences Press. (in Chinese)

Zhou, Z. (2021). Emotional thinking as the foundation of consciousness in artificial intelligence. *Cultura e Scuola*, *4*(3), 112–123. DOI: 10.1177/20966083211052651

KEY TERMS AND DEFINITIONS

Affective Computing: Affective Computing is a field of artificial intelligence that aims at making systems that can perceive, understand, compute and fake human emotions in order to facilitate more natural and empathetic human interactions with machines.

AI Governance: AI Governance is the system, policies, ethical principles, and regulatory approaches adopted to make certain that artificial intelligence systems are created and implemented in a responsible way, transparent and in tune with values of a society.

Emotional Intelligence: Emotional Intelligence (EI) is the capacity to be aware, comprehend, control, and regulate personal feelings and those of other people in order to think, act, and relate with others in productive ways.

Human–AI Interaction: Human-AI interaction denotes the communication and interactions processes between humans and artificial intelligence systems specifically the way users interact, respond, and are affected by intelligent technologies.

Technology: Technology can be described as the use of scientific knowledge, tools, systems, and techniques in order to develop solutions that would improve human capabilities and solve practical problems.

Chapter 10
Emotional Intelligence in AI-Driven Interactions

Vaishali Rahate
http://orcid.org/0000-0001-6277-1685
Datta Meghe Institute of Management Studies, India

Anup Ranade
http://orcid.org/0009-0007-7434-4788
Yeshwantrao Chawan College of Engineering, India

Lakshay Goyal
http://orcid.org/0009-0008-9725-0298
Pimpri Chinchwad College of Engineering and Research, Pune, India

P. Selvakumar
http://orcid.org/0000-0002-3650-4548
Department of Science and Humanities, Nehru Institute of Technology, Coimbatore, India

Shailesh Tripathi
Sri Balaji University, Pune, India

Prateek Srivastava
http://orcid.org/0009-0005-8885-4274
CSJM University, India

ABSTRACT

Emotional intelligence (EI), traditionally defined as the capacity to recognize, understand, manage, and influence emotions in oneself and others, has become a pivotal concept in the design of advanced artificial intelligence (AI) systems. At its core, EI encompasses several domains: self-awareness, self-regulation, motivation, empathy, and social skills, all of which underpin human interactions, decision-making, and adaptive behavior. Translating these human-centered capabilities into computational frameworks involves bridging cognitive psychology, neuroscience, linguistics, and machine learning, thereby creating AI systems capable of perceiving, interpreting, and responding to emotional cues in dynamic and context-sensitive ways. The foundational layer of emotionally intelligent AI begins with affective computing, a

DOI: 10.4018/979-8-3373-8337-8.ch010

discipline introduced by Rosalind Picard, which focuses on enabling machines to detect and interpret human emotions through multiple modalities, including facial expressions, vocal tonality, physiological signals, text, and behavioral patterns.

INTRODUCTION

Emotional intelligence (EI), traditionally defined as the capacity to recognize, understand, manage, and influence emotions in oneself and others, has become a pivotal concept in the design of advanced artificial intelligence (AI) systems. At its core, EI encompasses several domains: self-awareness, self-regulation, motivation, empathy, and social skills, all of which underpin human interactions, decision-making, and adaptive behavior. Translating these human-centered capabilities into computational frameworks involves bridging cognitive psychology, neuroscience, linguistics, and machine learning, thereby creating AI systems capable of perceiving, interpreting, and responding to emotional cues in dynamic and context-sensitive ways. The foundational layer of emotionally intelligent AI begins with affective computing, a discipline introduced by Rosalind Picard, which focuses on enabling machines to detect and interpret human emotions through multiple modalities, including facial expressions, vocal tonality, physiological signals, text, and behavioral patterns. Multimodal data integration is critical because human emotions are inherently complex, context-dependent, and often subtle; AI systems must synthesize inputs across channels to generate accurate affective assessments. Advanced computer vision techniques, for instance, employ convolutional neural networks (CNNs) and attention mechanisms to detect microexpressions and subtle changes in facial musculature. Simultaneously, natural language processing (NLP) models analyze linguistic features, sentiment polarity, and semantic nuances in speech or text to infer emotional states, while physiological sensors provide continuous feedback on heart rate variability, skin conductance, or voice pitch, offering objective signals of affective arousal and stress.

Building on perception, emotion modeling and representation are essential to creating actionable AI responses. Early approaches relied on categorical emotion models, such as Ekman's six basic emotions, or dimensional models, including valence-arousal frameworks, to quantify affective states. Contemporary AI systems, however, adopt hybrid or probabilistic models, recognizing that emotions are fluid, overlapping, and influenced by individual differences, cultural context, and situational factors. Deep learning architectures, particularly recurrent neural networks (RNNs), long short-term memory (LSTM) networks, and transformer-based models, facilitate temporal modeling of emotional trajectories, enabling AI to understand not only the present state of emotion but also its evolution over time. These models can capture patterns of emotional triggers, regulatory responses, and social interactions, forming the foundation for predictive and adaptive behavior. A critical dimension of emotionally intelligent AI is empathic reasoning, wherein systems are designed to interpret the emotional experiences of humans and respond in ways that are socially appropriate, supportive, and contextually sensitive (Al-Zahrani 2025). Misinterpretation or overreliance on AI-derived emotional assessments can lead to errors in decision-making, privacy violations, or unintended social consequences (Banks 2024).

Future directions in emotionally intelligent AI emphasize greater integration of multimodal perception, contextual understanding, and adaptive learning. Advances in neurosymbolic AI, which combine neural networks with symbolic reasoning, promise more robust models of emotional cognition, capable of reasoning about complex social situations and moral dilemmas. Explainable AI (XAI) approaches are increasingly important, enabling users and developers to understand how AI interprets emotions and arrives at decisions, fostering trust and accountability. Cross-disciplinary research, drawing on psychology, cognitive science, sociology, and computer science, is critical for developing frameworks that respect the richness of human emotion while maintaining computational rigor. Moreover, emerging paradigms such as AI companions, immersive virtual environments, and metaverse applications will demand emotionally intelligent agents that can sustain long-term, context-aware, and ethically responsible interactions. In conclusion, the foundations of emotional intelligence in AI systems lie in the confluence of perceptual acuity, affective modeling, empathic reasoning, and ethical design (Beatty et al. 2022). By endowing machines with the ability to perceive, interpret, and respond to human emotions, AI systems can enhance human-computer interaction, support mental and social well-being, and create adaptive, personalized experiences across diverse domains. However, achieving truly emotionally intelligent AI requires ongoing research, rigorous validation, and a principled commitment to ethical, culturally sensitive, and inclusive design. The future of AI with emotional intelligence is not only a technological frontier but also a social and philosophical endeavor, challenging us to rethink the boundaries of human-machine empathy, trust, and collaboration.

DETECTING HUMAN EMOTIONS THROUGH MULTIMODAL DATA

The accurate detection of human emotions represents a critical frontier in the development of intelligent systems capable of nuanced, context-aware interaction. Emotions are inherently multifaceted, arising from physiological, cognitive, and social processes that manifest across multiple channels, including facial expressions, voice, body gestures, physiological signals, and linguistic content. Traditional approaches that rely solely on a single modality—such as text sentiment analysis or facial recognition—often fail to capture the richness, subtlety, and temporal dynamics of human affect. Consequently, multimodal emotion detection has emerged as a robust methodology, integrating diverse data sources to improve both the precision and reliability of emotion recognition in real-world contexts. The foundation of multimodal emotion detection lies in affective computing, which systematically converts qualitative emotional phenomena into quantitative data interpretable by computational models. Facial expression analysis remains a central pillar, leveraging advanced computer vision techniques, including convolutional neural networks (CNNs), attention mechanisms, and landmark-based models, to detect both macro- and micro-expressions. Microexpressions, which are fleeting involuntary facial movements lasting only fractions of a second, provide critical insights into concealed or spontaneous emotional states (Carolus et al. 2021). By combining spatial and temporal modeling through recurrent neural networks (RNNs) and long short-term memory (LSTM) networks, AI systems can capture the evolution and intensity of emotional expressions over time, yielding more dynamic and context-sensitive interpretations.

Voice and speech analysis constitute another vital modality. Vocal attributes such as pitch, tone, rhythm, loudness, and prosody convey affective information that may be independent of semantic content. State-of-the-art models apply deep learning architectures, including transformer-based models and spectrogram analysis through CNNs, to extract high-dimensional features representing emotional states. Multimodal approaches often fuse speech features with text-based natural language processing (NLP), enabling the disambiguation of emotion in contexts where verbal content and vocal cues may be incongruent, such as sarcasm, irony, or subtle distress signals. Physiological signals provide an objective, quantifiable perspective on affective states. Metrics such as heart rate variability, galvanic skin response, electroencephalography (EEG) patterns, and respiration rates reflect autonomic nervous system activity associated with emotional arousal and stress. Wearable sensors, smartwatches, and biosignal acquisition devices enable continuous, real-time monitoring of these signals, allowing AI models to infer internal states that may not be outwardly observable. Integrating physiological data with behavioral and linguistic cues significantly enhances the robustness of emotion detection systems, particularly in contexts such as mental health monitoring, human-robot interaction, and adaptive learning environments (Catania & Garzotto. 2023). Gestural and postural cues offer additional layers of affective information. Human emotions frequently manifest through subtle movements, body orientation, and hand gestures. Computer vision and motion capture systems, in conjunction with pose estimation algorithms, allow AI systems to quantify and interpret these nonverbal expressions. Coupled with facial and vocal analysis, gesture recognition strengthens the multimodal pipeline, capturing the holistic behavioral signature of emotions.

The integration of multimodal data necessitates sophisticated fusion techniques, which combine heterogeneous inputs into unified representations. Early fusion approaches concatenate features across modalities prior to model training, while late fusion strategies integrate modality-specific predictions. Hybrid and attention-based fusion mechanisms are increasingly favored, allowing models to weigh the relevance of each modality dynamically based on context, reliability, and temporal dependencies. For example, in noisy environments where audio signals are unreliable, visual and physiological cues may dominate the emotional inference. Similarly, transformer-based architectures and graph neural networks enable complex intermodal relationships to be learned, capturing cross-modal correlations and enhancing predictive accuracy. Multimodal emotion detection finds applications across multiple domains, including healthcare, education, customer service, entertainment, and social robotics. In mental health, emotionally aware AI systems can identify early signs of depression, anxiety, or stress, enabling timely intervention and personalized support. Educational technologies leverage emotion detection to adapt instructional content, pacing, and feedback to students' engagement levels and emotional states, enhancing learning outcomes. In customer service, multimodal AI agents can assess client satisfaction, frustration, or empathy needs in real time, enabling more personalized and human-like interactions (Chin et al. 2025). Social robots equipped with multimodal emotion recognition can respond adaptively, enhancing companionship, caregiving, and therapeutic applications.

THE KEY TO EMPATHETIC AI

Empathy, the ability to recognize, understand, and respond appropriately to the emotions and experiences of others, is central to effective human interaction. Translating this capacity into artificial intelligence (AI) systems requires more than the detection of emotional cues; it necessitates contextual awareness, the capability to interpret human affect and behavior within the nuanced framework of situational, cultural, temporal, and relational factors. Contextual awareness forms the cornerstone of empathetic AI, bridging the gap between raw emotion recognition and socially intelligent, adaptive responses that align with human expectations, social norms, and individual needs. Without context, AI systems risk producing responses that are mechanically accurate but socially tone-deaf, misaligned, or even counterproductive, undermining user trust, engagement, and the ethical deployment of AI technologies. At the technical foundation, contextual awareness in AI involves the integration of multimodal data streams encompassing not only facial expressions, vocal tone, and physiological signals but also linguistic content, behavioral patterns, environmental cues, and historical interaction data. Temporal context plays a critical role: emotions are dynamic, evolving across minutes, hours, and even longer time scales (Darcy et al. 2021). For instance, a user's brief expression of frustration during a learning session may be influenced by prior successes, accumulated stress, or anticipated challenges, requiring AI systems to model emotional trajectories rather than isolated snapshots. Sequence modeling techniques, such as recurrent neural networks (RNNs), long short-term memory (LSTM) networks, and transformer architectures, allow AI to capture these temporal dependencies, enabling more accurate and sensitive responses to evolving emotional states.

Cultural and demographic context is equally crucial. Emotional expression varies widely across cultures, age groups, genders, and social backgrounds. Smiles, gestures, vocal intonations, and even physiological responses can carry different meanings depending on cultural norms, social conventions, or situational expectations. Empathetic AI must therefore incorporate adaptive models capable of learning and generalizing across diverse populations while respecting individual differences. Approaches such as transfer learning, domain adaptation, and federated learning are increasingly employed to achieve culturally aware, bias-mitigated models that maintain accuracy without compromising ethical standards. Relational and situational context further shapes empathetic responses. Human communication is often layered with implicit meaning, social cues, and relational dynamics. AI systems interacting in professional, educational, therapeutic, or casual settings must interpret emotional signals within these relational frameworks, understanding power dynamics, social roles, and interaction histories. For example, a virtual teaching assistant detecting frustration in a student may offer guidance differently than an AI therapist responding to the same emotional cue. Contextual models therefore incorporate historical data on user interactions, relationship dynamics, and environmental conditions to tailor responses that are appropriate, respectful, and effective. The development of context-aware empathetic AI relies on advanced affective computing techniques (Dosovitsky & Bunge 2021). Multimodal fusion models combine visual, auditory, textual, and physiological inputs, while attention-based architectures prioritize the most relevant cues according to situational and relational context.

Furthermore, probabilistic modeling and Bayesian reasoning enable AI to handle ambiguity and uncertainty in emotional signals, accounting for inconsistencies and conflicts across modalities to generate contextually coherent interpretations. Context-aware empathetic AI also emphasizes adaptive learning. Human affective responses are not static; they evolve with ongoing interaction, feedback, and environmental shifts. Reinforcement learning, meta-learning, and continual learning approaches allow AI systems to refine their understanding of user preferences, communication styles, and emotional patterns over time. By dynamically updating models based on real-time feedback, AI agents can improve their sensitivity to context, reduce misinterpretations, and increase the personalization and relevance of their responses. This capacity is particularly critical in applications such as mental health support, caregiving, education, and customer service, where trust, rapport, and responsiveness are paramount. Ethical and societal considerations are central to the deployment of context-aware empathetic AI. The collection and processing of contextual information—ranging from private behavioral data to environmental and relational cues—raises concerns regarding privacy, consent, and data security. AI systems must be designed to maintain transparency, provide user control over data sharing, and ensure that inferences about emotional and contextual states are used responsibly. Bias mitigation is essential, as context-sensitive models trained on non-representative datasets may perpetuate stereotypes or misinterpret the emotional states of underrepresented groups. Explainable AI (XAI) techniques, transparency dashboards, and rigorous auditing processes are crucial for fostering user trust and accountability in context-aware systems (Fang et al. 2025).

In social robotics and human-computer interaction, empathetic agents capable of interpreting social, environmental, and relational context can improve companionship, assistive care, and collaborative teamwork, enhancing overall user experience. Customer service applications benefit as well, as AI systems that respond to emotional cues in contextually appropriate ways can increase satisfaction, de-escalate conflicts, and promote brand loyalty. Future research in context-aware empathetic AI emphasizes integration with real-world environments, lifelong learning, and cross-domain adaptability. Advances in edge computing, wearable sensors, and Internet of Things (IoT) integration will allow AI to access rich, continuous streams of contextual information without sacrificing latency or privacy. Neuromorphic computing and energy-efficient AI architectures will enable real-time, on-device inference, supporting seamless interaction in mobile, immersive, and ubiquitous environments. Cross-disciplinary collaboration with psychology, sociology, cognitive science, and ethics is critical to ensure that AI systems not only understand context but do so in ways that are socially responsible, culturally sensitive, and aligned with human values. In conclusion, contextual awareness represents the key to achieving truly empathetic AI (Gennaro et al. 2020). By integrating multimodal signals, temporal dynamics, cultural norms, relational cues, and environmental factors, AI systems can move beyond superficial emotion recognition toward adaptive, socially intelligent, and morally responsible interaction.

DESIGNING AFFECTIVE DIALOGUE AGENTS

Affective dialogue agents (ADAs) represent a transformative class of artificial intelligence (AI) systems capable of engaging in human-like conversations while recognizing, interpreting, and responding to users' emotional states. Unlike traditional chatbots that focus solely on task completion or information retrieval, ADAs aim to establish empathetic, contextually sensitive, and socially intelligent interactions. Designing such agents requires the integration of affective computing, natural language processing (NLP), multimodal emotion recognition, dialogue management, and adaptive learning frameworks. At its core, the design challenge is to create systems that can perceive human emotions accurately, model affective states over time, and generate responses that are both contextually appropriate and emotionally congruent, thereby enhancing user engagement, satisfaction, and trust. The first foundational component in designing ADAs is emotion perception and recognition. Human emotions are inherently multimodal, manifesting through facial expressions, vocal intonations, linguistic choices, gestures, posture, and physiological signals such as heart rate variability and galvanic skin response. Advanced affective computing frameworks utilize computer vision techniques like convolutional neural networks (CNNs) for facial expression analysis, attention-based transformers for sequence modeling of microexpressions, and pose estimation algorithms for gesture and body language recognition (Jolibois et al. 2025). Simultaneously, NLP models analyze semantic content, sentiment, tone, and pragmatic features in user utterances to infer emotional states. By integrating these modalities, multimodal fusion strategies—ranging from early feature-level fusion to late decision-level fusion and attention-weighted mechanisms—enable more robust and contextually accurate detection of emotions, even when individual modalities provide conflicting signals. Dialogue management constitutes the next critical layer in ADA design. Dialogue agents must not only recognize emotions but also decide on appropriate conversational strategies, response content, and affective delivery.

A core principle in affective dialogue design is contextual awareness. Emotions are rarely static or isolated; they are shaped by temporal dynamics, environmental factors, interpersonal relationships, cultural norms, and individual personality traits. ADAs must therefore model not only immediate affective cues but also the broader situational and historical context. Temporal models, such as long short-term memory (LSTM) networks, gated recurrent units (GRUs), and temporal attention mechanisms, capture emotional trajectories, enabling agents to recognize patterns of stress, frustration, or engagement that develop over extended interactions. Knowledge graphs and relational embeddings can incorporate user history, prior interactions, preferences, and social connections, allowing dialogue agents to tailor responses to individual needs, social norms, and ongoing conversational context. Such context-sensitive design ensures that responses are empathetic, nuanced, and relevant, rather than generic or mechanically generated. Personality modeling and adaptive behavior are additional critical elements in affective dialogue agent design. Human conversational partners interpret not only the semantic and emotional content of dialogue but also the personality, tone, and style of the interlocutor. ADAs can leverage persona-based modeling, embedding consistent personality traits, values, and communication styles to create coherent and relatable interactions. Adaptive systems further refine these traits over time, learning from user feedback, engagement metrics, and emotional responses to calibrate tone, empathy levels, humor, and conversational pacing. Such personalization enhances user trust, rapport, and long-term engagement, which is particularly important in applications such as mental health support, education, customer service, and companionship. Ethical, privacy, and societal considerations are paramount in ADA design (Joshi et al. 2026).

Additionally, biases in training datasets can result in disproportionate misinterpretation of emotions across cultural, demographic, or linguistic groups, potentially reinforcing stereotypes or inequities. Responsible ADA design requires rigorous bias mitigation, diverse and representative datasets, continuous validation, and the integration of explainable AI (XAI) mechanisms to ensure interpretability, accountability, and fairness. Furthermore, ethical frameworks must guide the boundaries of affective influence, avoiding manipulation of user emotions for commercial or persuasive purposes. The applications of affective dialogue agents are both broad and impactful. In mental health and healthcare, ADAs can provide empathetic support, monitor emotional well-being, deliver psychoeducation, and facilitate therapy adherence. Systems capable of recognizing subtle distress signals and responding with appropriate guidance or escalation protocols can supplement human clinicians, particularly in resource-limited contexts. In education, emotionally aware virtual tutors can adapt instructional content, pacing, and feedback to students' engagement, frustration, and motivation levels, fostering personalized and effective learning experiences. Customer service agents that leverage affective dialogue capabilities can improve satisfaction, de-escalate conflicts, and promote loyalty by aligning responses to customer emotions. Social robotics, gaming, virtual reality (VR), and augmented reality (AR) environments also benefit from affective dialogue agents that create immersive, emotionally rich interactions, enhancing user experience and engagement. Future directions in ADA design focus on deeper integration of multimodal perception, real-time contextual reasoning, adaptive learning, and ethical intelligence. Neuromorphic computing, edge AI, and energy-efficient architectures will enable low-latency, on-device affective processing, supporting seamless interaction in mobile, immersive, and ubiquitous environments. Advances in self-supervised and few-shot learning will allow agents to generalize across users, contexts, and cultures with limited labeled data, enhancing scalability and inclusivity.

Figure 1. AI Emotional intelligence Components

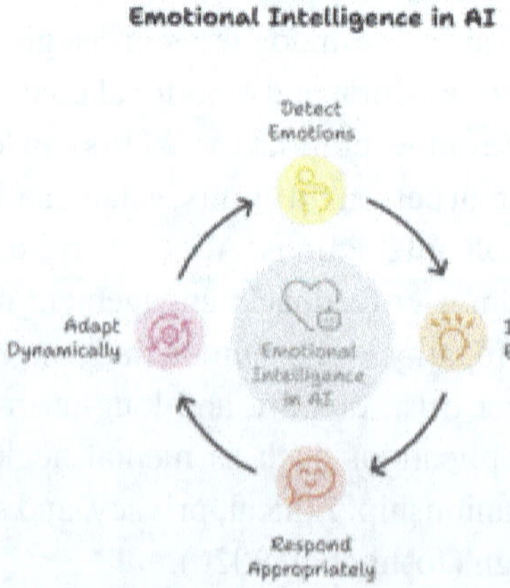

Integration with knowledge graphs, symbolic reasoning, and neurosymbolic AI approaches will facilitate sophisticated reasoning about user goals, social norms, and ethical constraints, moving ADAs closer to human-level social intelligence. Finally, longitudinal studies and rigorous evaluation frameworks are critical to measure the efficacy, user satisfaction, and societal impact of affective dialogue agents, ensuring that technological advancement aligns with human-centric and ethical principles. In conclusion, designing affective dialogue agents entails a complex interplay of emotion recognition, multimodal integration, dialogue management, contextual awareness, personality modeling, adaptive learning, and ethical governance (Kazazoğlu & Turun Özel 2025). By combining technical sophistication with social and emotional intelligence, ADAs have the potential to revolutionize human-computer interaction, supporting mental health, education, customer engagement, social companionship, and immersive experiences. However, the realization of truly empathetic dialogue agents requires sustained interdisciplinary research, rigorous validation, ethical vigilance, and continuous refinement, ensuring that these systems enhance human well-being, foster trust, and respect the richness and complexity of human emotional life. The ongoing convergence of AI, cognitive science, affective computing, and ethical design promises a future where dialogue agents are not merely functional tools but socially intelligent partners capable of meaningful, empathetic, and contextually nuanced interaction with humans.

BIAS MITIGATION IN EMOTION RECOGNITION MODELS

Emotion recognition models, central to affective computing and human-centered AI, aim to detect, interpret, and respond to human emotions using multimodal inputs such as facial expressions, speech, text, gestures, and physiological signals. While these models have achieved significant advancements through machine learning, deep learning, and multimodal fusion techniques, they are susceptible to biases arising from multiple sources, including data collection, labeling practices, model architecture, and cultural assumptions embedded in training datasets. Bias in emotion recognition is particularly consequential because misinterpretation of affective states can undermine user trust, reinforce stereotypes, lead to unfair treatment, and negatively impact applications in healthcare, education, human-computer interaction, and social robotics. Consequently, bias mitigation has emerged as a critical area of research, addressing both technical and ethical dimensions of model development, deployment, and evaluation. The primary source of bias in emotion recognition systems is training data. Datasets used to develop these models are often collected under controlled conditions, featuring limited demographic diversity, homogeneous cultural representations, and overrepresentation of certain emotional expressions deemed universal, such as Ekman's six basic emotions (Kim et al. 2025). This creates a significant generalization problem: models trained on such datasets may accurately recognize emotions in populations resembling the training data but fail for underrepresented groups, including different ethnicities, age groups, genders, and socio-cultural contexts. Moreover, cultural norms influence the expression, intensity, and interpretation of emotions. For instance, a smile may signify happiness in one culture but politeness or social discomfort in another. Failure to account for these subtleties results in biased predictions, misclassification, and inappropriate system responses.

Labeling bias further compounds the issue: human annotators bring subjective interpretations, personal experiences, and cultural perspectives to the labeling process, introducing systematic errors that propagate into model predictions. Model architecture and learning algorithms also contribute to bias. Standard deep learning models, such as convolutional neural networks (CNNs) for facial analysis or transformer-based architectures for text and speech, optimize for overall accuracy without considering fairness or equitable performance across subpopulations. This optimization can amplify disparities in recognition performance, particularly for minority groups or non-canonical emotional expressions. Additionally, overfitting to dominant patterns in the training data may reinforce pre-existing stereotypes, such as associating anger with specific demographics or misclassifying subtle affective cues in underrepresented populations. Bias can also arise from feature selection, preprocessing pipelines, and modality prioritization, where certain signals—e.g., facial expressions—receive disproportionate weight relative to cultural, contextual, or physiological variations. Addressing bias in emotion recognition requires a holistic, multi-stage mitigation strategy spanning data collection, model training, evaluation, and deployment. At the data level, bias can be mitigated through diverse and representative datasets that include participants across cultural, demographic, linguistic, and socio-economic backgrounds. Data augmentation techniques, including synthetic generation of facial expressions, vocal patterns, and multimodal signals, can help balance underrepresented categories, though care must be taken to avoid introducing artificial artifacts or unrealistic expressions.

Labeling practices can be improved by employing consensus-based annotation, multiple annotators from diverse backgrounds, and uncertainty quantification to capture the inherent ambiguity and subjectivity in emotion perception. During model training, algorithmic fairness techniques are critical. Approaches such as reweighting, resampling, and adversarial debiasing allow models to learn equitable representations across subgroups. Transfer learning and domain adaptation methods can further enhance generalization to new populations and contexts, reducing disparities caused by dataset imbalance. Attention-based architectures and multimodal fusion strategies can be designed to weigh modalities dynamically, ensuring that underrepresented cues are appropriately considered in affective inference. Regularization techniques, fairness constraints, and penalization of disparate errors across subgroups can also be integrated into loss functions to explicitly enforce equitable performance. Evaluation of emotion recognition models must move beyond overall accuracy to fairness-aware metrics. Metrics such as demographic parity, equalized odds, and subgroup-specific performance measures provide insight into disparities across age, gender, ethnicity, or cultural groups. Longitudinal and cross-context evaluations are particularly important because emotions are temporally dynamic and situationally influenced (Kim et al. 2025b). Simulation-based testing, including stress testing in varied environmental and cultural conditions, can reveal latent biases that standard test sets might overlook.

Ethical and societal considerations are intertwined with technical mitigation efforts. Emotion recognition systems are often deployed in sensitive domains such as mental health assessment, educational evaluation, human resources, customer service, and law enforcement. Bias in these contexts can have real-world consequences, including misdiagnosis, discrimination, and reinforcement of social inequities. Consequently, developers must adhere to ethical principles of transparency, accountability, inclusivity, and user consent. Explainable AI (XAI) methods, including saliency mapping, attention visualization, and rule-based interpretability, are crucial to provide stakeholders with insight into how models make affective predictions, enabling detection of biased behavior and promoting responsible deployment. Emerging approaches in context-aware and personalized emotion recognition also contribute to bias mitigation. By incorporating contextual information—such as cultural norms, situational cues, historical interaction patterns, and individual baseline affective states—models can better differentiate between genuine emotional signals and context-dependent variations. Adaptive learning frameworks, including reinforcement learning and continual learning, allow models to refine predictions over time based on feedback, reducing systemic errors that disproportionately affect certain user groups. Federated learning approaches, which train models across decentralized datasets without transferring sensitive user data, offer the dual advantage of privacy preservation and exposure to diverse emotional expressions, enhancing fairness and robustness.

Future research in bias mitigation will increasingly focus on cross-cultural, multimodal, and explainable frameworks. Large-scale, globally representative datasets integrating facial, vocal, textual, and physiological signals are necessary to capture the full spectrum of human emotional diversity. Neuromorphic and edge AI architectures enable real-time, privacy-conscious processing of multimodal affective data, facilitating deployment in diverse environments. Integration of ethical AI frameworks, human-in-the-loop approaches, and continuous monitoring of model behavior ensures that emotion recognition systems evolve in alignment with social norms, human values, and regulatory standards. Collaborative research across disciplines—including computer science, psychology, neuroscience, sociology, and ethics—will be essential to ensure that bias mitigation strategies are comprehensive, actionable, and socially responsible (Kolomaznik et al. 2024). In conclusion, bias mitigation in emotion recognition models is both a technical and ethical imperative. Addressing the sources of bias—ranging from dataset composition and annotation practices to model design and evaluation—ensures that AI systems can accurately, fairly, and responsibly interpret human emotions.

BUILDING TRUST THROUGH EMOTIONALLY RESPONSIVE INTERFACES

In the era of pervasive digital technologies, establishing trust between humans and artificial intelligence (AI) systems has emerged as a fundamental challenge. Trust is particularly critical in applications involving healthcare, finance, education, human-computer interaction, and social robotics, where decisions or recommendations may carry significant personal or societal consequences. One of the most effective pathways to fostering trust is through emotionally responsive interfaces, which adapt their behavior, communication style, and interaction patterns in real time based on the user's affective state. By detecting, interpreting, and responding to emotional cues such as facial expressions, vocal tone, physiological signals, and behavioral patterns, emotionally responsive interfaces create interactions that are perceived as empathetic, personalized, and socially intelligent, thereby promoting user confidence, engagement, and long-term adoption. The foundation of emotionally responsive interfaces lies in affective computing, a multidisciplinary field integrating psychology, cognitive science, neuroscience, and AI to enable machines to perceive and interpret human emotions. At the technical level, emotion recognition involves multimodal data processing: computer vision models, such as convolutional neural networks (CNNs) and attention-based architectures, analyze facial expressions and gestures; natural language processing (NLP) models decode sentiment, tone, and semantic nuances in textual or spoken language; physiological signals such as heart rate variability, galvanic skin response, and electroencephalography provide objective measures of emotional arousal.

Multimodal fusion techniques—ranging from feature-level concatenation to decision-level integration with attention mechanisms—allow systems to synthesize heterogeneous inputs into robust affective interpretations, enhancing the reliability and responsiveness of the interface. Emotionally responsive interfaces contribute to trust-building by aligning system behavior with user expectations, emotional states, and social norms. When users perceive that a system understands their feelings and adapts appropriately, they are more likely to engage in cooperative interactions, disclose relevant information, and follow recommendations (Li et al. 2025). For example, in healthcare applications, a virtual health assistant that detects patient anxiety and modulates its tone, pacing, and content to provide reassurance can increase adherence to treatment plans and foster therapeutic alliance. In educational technologies, intelligent tutoring systems that recognize student frustration or confusion and respond with adaptive feedback, encouragement, or scaffolding enhance learner motivation, persistence, and trust in the system's guidance.

Similarly, customer service chatbots that adjust their responses according to a user's emotional state can de-escalate tension, improve satisfaction, and promote brand loyalty. Contextual awareness is central to designing interfaces capable of building trust through emotional responsiveness. Human emotions are dynamic, context-dependent, and influenced by relational, cultural, and situational factors. Temporally aware models, such as long short-term memory (LSTM) networks, gated recurrent units (GRUs), and transformer-based architectures, capture the evolution of affective states over time, enabling systems to respond consistently and coherently across multiple interactions. Contextual modeling also incorporates environmental cues, prior interaction history, user preferences, and social norms, ensuring that responses are relevant, culturally sensitive, and aligned with the individual's needs. Knowledge graphs and relational embeddings can further enhance context-aware reasoning, allowing interfaces to personalize recommendations, conversational strategies, and affective responses based on user-specific data. A key element in fostering trust is empathy simulation—the ability of an interface to demonstrate understanding and concern for the user's emotional experience. Empathy in AI does not involve genuine feelings but the accurate interpretation of affective states and the generation of socially appropriate responses. Dialogue management systems in emotionally responsive interfaces employ reinforcement learning (RL), sequence-to-sequence models, and transformer-based architectures to select responses that maximize user satisfaction, perceived understanding, and emotional alignment. Reward functions in RL can balance multiple objectives, including affective congruence, task completion, response relevance, and ethical constraints, ensuring that the interface behaves both effectively and empathetically.

Moreover, transparency in data collection, processing, and storage, along with informed consent protocols, reassures users that their emotional information is handled securely and ethically, mitigating privacy concerns and reinforcing trust. Emotionally responsive interfaces also require robustness and bias mitigation to maintain trust across diverse user populations. Variability in emotional expression due to cultural, demographic, or individual differences can lead to misinterpretation and erosion of confidence in AI systems. Bias mitigation strategies include training on diverse, representative datasets, employing cross-cultural validation, and incorporating adaptive learning mechanisms that personalize affective recognition to the individual user. Continuous monitoring, feedback loops, and human-in-the-loop interventions enable interfaces to learn from errors, correct misclassifications, and refine emotional responses over time, maintaining user trust even in complex, dynamic environments. Applications of emotionally responsive interfaces extend beyond individual interactions to broader societal impact. Future directions in building trust through emotionally responsive interfaces emphasize integration with real-world environments, adaptive personalization, and ethical intelligence. Advances in wearable sensors, IoT devices, and mobile-integrated affective computing enable continuous, real-time monitoring of emotional states. Edge AI and neuromorphic computing architectures facilitate low-latency, privacy-conscious processing of multimodal affective data, allowing seamless adaptation in dynamic environments.

Cross-disciplinary research combining AI, cognitive science, psychology, human-computer interaction, and ethics will further refine interface design to balance emotional responsiveness, transparency, privacy, and user autonomy (Łukasik & Gut 2025). Emerging paradigms, including virtual reality (VR), augmented reality (AR), and the metaverse, will require emotionally responsive interfaces capable of sustaining long-term engagement, social rapport, and trust in immersive, interactive spaces. In conclusion, building trust through emotionally responsive interfaces represents a convergence of technical innovation, human-centered design, and ethical responsibility. By integrating multimodal emotion recognition, context-aware adaptation, empathetic response generation, transparency, and bias mitigation, AI systems can foster meaningful, trustworthy interactions with users across diverse domains. Trust emerges not merely from the accuracy of task performance but from the perception that the system understands, respects, and responds appropriately to the user's emotional experience. Emotionally responsive interfaces, therefore, offer a transformative pathway to human-AI collaboration that is empathetic, socially intelligent, and ethically grounded, ultimately enhancing engagement, satisfaction, and long-term adoption of AI technologies.

MEASURING EMOTIONAL ENGAGEMENT IN HUMAN-AI CONVERSATIONS

Emotional engagement, the degree to which individuals experience affective involvement, interest, and investment in interactions, is a pivotal factor in evaluating the effectiveness and acceptability of human-AI conversations (Yun et al. 2022). Unlike purely task-oriented assessments, which focus on metrics such as response accuracy, latency, or task completion, measuring emotional engagement emphasizes the user's affective and experiential states, encompassing feelings of attentiveness, empathy, satisfaction, and connection. In human-AI conversational systems—ranging from virtual assistants, chatbots, social robots, to intelligent tutoring systems—emotional engagement serves as both an indicator of interaction quality and a driver of long-term adoption, user trust, and behavioral outcomes. Accurate measurement of emotional engagement is therefore crucial for designing systems that are not only functional but socially and emotionally intelligent. At the foundation, measuring emotional engagement relies on multimodal sensing to capture the complex, dynamic, and often subtle signals of affective involvement. Visual cues, including facial expressions, eye gaze, head orientation, and gestures, are commonly analyzed through computer vision techniques such as convolutional neural networks (CNNs), landmark detection, and attention-based models. Micro-expressions, which are rapid, involuntary facial movements, provide particularly valuable insights into transient emotional states that may indicate surprise, interest, confusion, or enjoyment. Eye-tracking metrics, including fixation duration, blink rate, and pupil dilation, offer additional granularity, reflecting cognitive load, attention, and emotional arousal during interaction. These visual modalities, when combined with other data sources, allow AI systems to construct a more holistic representation of user engagement. Vocal and speech-based indicators provide complementary information regarding emotional engagement. Features such as pitch, tone, prosody, speech rate, intensity, and pause patterns correlate with affective states, including excitement, frustration, boredom, or empathy (Ma 2025).

Temporal modeling using recurrent neural networks (RNNs), long short-term memory networks (LSTMs), or transformer-based architectures allows systems to capture fluctuations in engagement over the course of multi-turn interactions, providing dynamic and context-sensitive measures rather than static assessments. Physiological and behavioral signals further enrich the measurement of emotional engagement. Heart rate variability, skin conductance, respiration patterns, and electroencephalography (EEG) readings reflect autonomic nervous system activity associated with affective arousal and attention. Wearable sensors and unobtrusive monitoring devices facilitate continuous measurement, enabling real-time evaluation of engagement in naturalistic settings. Behavioral metrics, such as typing speed, mouse movement, response latency, interaction frequency, and task persistence, provide additional quantitative indicators of attention, motivation, and involvement. Integrating these physiological and behavioral dimensions with visual and vocal modalities through multimodal fusion techniques—including early feature-level fusion, late decision-level fusion, and attention-based weighting—yields robust, context-aware models capable of reliably estimating emotional engagement. Contextual awareness is essential in accurately measuring engagement. Emotional engagement is inherently dependent on the situational context, relational dynamics, user goals, and prior experiences (Paira et al. 2026). Cognitive load, task difficulty, environmental distractions, and prior interaction history can modulate affective responses, potentially confounding measurements if context is ignored. Advanced human-AI systems incorporate contextual modeling, using knowledge graphs, interaction histories, and environmental sensing to disambiguate engagement signals. For example, a brief expression of frustration may reflect temporary task difficulty rather than disengagement, and understanding the situational context enables AI systems to correctly interpret such signals.

Quantitative and qualitative metrics are employed to operationalize emotional engagement. Quantitative measures include physiological signal indices, gaze duration, facial expression frequency, speech prosody statistics, and interaction metrics, while qualitative measures involve user-reported scales, subjective questionnaires, and post-interaction interviews capturing perceived engagement, satisfaction, and affective connection. Psychometrically validated instruments, such as the User Engagement Scale (UES), the Flow State Scale, and affective response inventories, provide standardized benchmarks for assessing engagement across populations. Combining objective physiological and behavioral measurements with subjective self-reports enables triangulation, enhancing reliability, validity, and interpretability of emotional engagement assessments. Applications of measuring emotional engagement span multiple domains. In education, intelligent tutoring systems utilize engagement measurements to adapt instructional strategies, provide timely feedback, and scaffold learning according to students' emotional and attentional states. In healthcare, emotionally responsive conversational agents monitor patient engagement to optimize therapy adherence, enhance mental health interventions, and provide empathetic support during remote care. Customer service and entertainment systems leverage engagement metrics to tailor interactions, improve satisfaction, and maintain immersive experiences in interactive media or gaming.

Biases in datasets, sensor calibration errors, and cultural variability in emotional expression may distort engagement assessments if unaddressed. Responsible design requires transparency in data collection and analysis, anonymization protocols, cross-cultural validation, and inclusive modeling approaches that accommodate diverse populations. Explainable AI (XAI) methods are increasingly incorporated to provide insight into engagement measurement processes, allowing users and researchers to understand, interpret, and trust the outputs generated by human-AI systems. Emerging trends in the measurement of emotional engagement focus on real-time, adaptive, and personalized assessment frameworks. Advances in wearable technologies, edge computing, and low-latency signal processing enable continuous, context-aware monitoring of affective states without intrusiveness. Adaptive learning algorithms, reinforcement learning, and meta-learning approaches allow models to personalize engagement assessment according to individual user profiles, interaction histories, and preferences (Pilyoung et al. 2025). Multimodal affective models integrated with conversational AI can dynamically adjust dialogue strategies, visual cues, and feedback to sustain or enhance engagement, thereby closing the loop between measurement and intervention. Virtual reality (VR), augmented reality (AR), and metaverse applications provide immersive environments where emotional engagement measurement can be leveraged to optimize experiences, guide adaptive interactions, and support long-term learning or therapeutic goals. In conclusion, measuring emotional engagement in human-AI conversations is a multidisciplinary endeavor at the intersection of AI, psychology, cognitive science, and human-computer interaction. By integrating multimodal sensing, contextual modeling, temporal analysis, quantitative metrics, and qualitative assessments, researchers and developers can accurately assess the affective, attentional, and motivational dimensions of user experience (Vinod Krishna et al. 2026). Accurate measurement enables the design of emotionally responsive, adaptive, and empathetic AI systems that foster trust, satisfaction, learning, therapeutic efficacy, and immersive interaction. Future advancements will continue to emphasize ethical, culturally sensitive, and personalized approaches, ensuring that human-AI conversations are not only effective but also emotionally enriching, socially intelligent, and human-centered, ultimately bridging the gap between technological capability and meaningful affective engagement.

ETHICAL CONSIDERATIONS FOR EMOTION-AWARE AI

Emotion-aware artificial intelligence (AI), encompassing systems capable of detecting, interpreting, and responding to human affective states, represents a transformative frontier in human-computer interaction. By integrating multimodal affective signals—such as facial expressions, vocal intonations, gestures, physiological responses, and linguistic content—emotion-aware AI has the potential to enhance user experience, improve mental health interventions, personalize education, optimize customer service, and facilitate social robotics. However, the deployment of such systems introduces profound ethical considerations that span privacy, consent, fairness, bias, transparency, accountability, and societal impact. Addressing these concerns is essential to ensure that emotion-aware AI operates in ways that respect human dignity, autonomy, and social norms while mitigating risks of harm, discrimination, or manipulation. Privacy and data protection represent the foremost ethical challenges in emotion-aware AI. Emotional signals are inherently personal and sensitive, often revealing not only current affective states but also psychological traits, health conditions, and behavioral tendencies. Facial expressions, speech patterns, eye movements, physiological signals (e.g., heart rate variability, galvanic skin response), and interaction histories can all constitute highly sensitive data. Collecting, processing, and storing such data without robust safeguards may lead to breaches of privacy, unauthorized profiling, or misuse for commercial, political, or surveillance purposes. Ethical frameworks demand informed consent, data minimization, secure storage, anonymization, and user control over how emotional data is collected, shared, and utilized. Mechanisms for real-time opt-in/opt-out consent, granular permission settings, and transparency reports are critical for respecting user autonomy and privacy while enabling beneficial AI functionalities. Bias and fairness are central concerns in the development of emotion-aware AI (Safare et al. 2026). Emotional expressions are influenced by culture, gender, age, socio-economic background, and individual personality traits. Training models on datasets that are not representative of diverse populations can lead to biased predictions, misclassification of affective states, and disproportionate negative impacts on underrepresented groups. For example, facial recognition models may underperform on certain ethnicities, misinterpreting expressions such as anger, frustration, or joy, while speech-based affective models may fail to accurately capture tonal variations in non-native accents or dialects. Ethical AI design mandates rigorous dataset curation, inclusion of culturally diverse data, algorithmic fairness strategies, and continuous validation across demographic subgroups. Transparency and explainability are essential for ethical trust in emotion-aware AI.

Users must understand how emotional inferences are made, the sources of uncertainty, and the rationale behind system responses. Black-box models that provide affective outputs without explanation risk eroding trust, misguiding decision-making, or fostering undue reliance on AI. Explainable AI (XAI) methods, including attention visualization, saliency mapping, counterfactual explanations, and interpretable rule-based models, enable stakeholders to understand model reasoning, detect errors, and hold systems accountable. Transparency also involves clear communication about the limitations of emotion-aware AI: the inherent ambiguity of emotions, cultural variability, and contextual dependence mean that affective predictions are probabilistic rather than absolute. Ethical deployment requires that these uncertainties be explicitly conveyed to users, preventing overconfidence or misinterpretation of AI-generated emotional insights. Consent and autonomy intersect with the ethical use of emotion-aware AI, particularly in applications involving vulnerable populations. For example, systems used in mental health monitoring, educational platforms, eldercare, or workplace environments may gather continuous affective data that influences decisions impacting individuals' well-being, academic performance, or employment. Ensuring that users retain control over their interactions, data collection, and usage is critical. Human oversight, opt-in participation, and the ability to review, correct, or delete affective data support autonomy while mitigating risks of coercion, surveillance, or emotional manipulation.

Emotion-aware AI can elicit, amplify, or modulate users' emotional states through feedback, reinforcement, or conversational strategies. While this capability offers therapeutic, educational, and motivational benefits, it also poses the risk of manipulation or emotional exploitation. For instance, marketing systems might exploit detected vulnerability to encourage spending, persuasive technologies could influence political attitudes, or poorly designed interventions may inadvertently induce stress, anxiety, or disengagement. Ethical design requires establishing boundaries for acceptable emotional influence, ensuring alignment with user welfare, and avoiding manipulative practices. Continuous monitoring, human-in-the-loop oversight, and adherence to ethical guidelines are necessary to safeguard users from unintended psychological harm. Accountability and governance are critical to addressing potential harms arising from emotion-aware AI. Legal and policy frameworks must evolve to regulate emotional data collection, processing, and application, addressing liability in cases of harm, discrimination, or misuse. Standardized auditing protocols, impact assessments, and ethical review boards provide mechanisms for accountability, ensuring that emotion-aware AI systems operate within socially and legally acceptable boundaries (Sanz 2025). Cross-disciplinary collaboration involving AI researchers, ethicists, psychologists, legal experts, and end-users is essential to establish norms, guidelines, and certification processes that promote safe and responsible deployment. Cultural sensitivity and inclusivity are fundamental ethical considerations. Emotions are socially constructed, context-dependent, and culturally mediated; an emotion-aware AI that does not account for cultural diversity risks misinterpretation, offense, or alienation.

Ethical design must therefore balance technological innovation with the preservation of human relational capacities, promoting AI as an augmentation rather than replacement of human emotional intelligence. Guidelines for responsible deployment should consider not only immediate individual outcomes but also broader societal consequences, fostering AI that supports human well-being, social equity, and inclusive engagement. Future directions in ethical design for emotion-aware AI emphasize interdisciplinary approaches, continuous ethical evaluation, and adaptive governance. Techniques such as differential privacy, federated learning, and privacy-preserving multimodal analytics enable ethical data handling without compromising model performance. Ethical frameworks, such as IEEE's Ethically Aligned Design, EU AI Act, and AI4People guidelines, provide structured principles for fairness, transparency, accountability, and human-centric design (Shams et al. 2026). Participatory design methodologies, user-centered evaluation, and real-world pilot studies allow developers to iteratively refine systems, ensuring alignment with ethical standards, societal norms, and stakeholder expectations. Integration of explainable, context-aware, and culturally adaptive models further enhances ethical compliance, promoting responsible innovation in affective computing. In conclusion, ethical considerations for emotion-aware AI encompass privacy, consent, fairness, transparency, accountability, cultural sensitivity, safety, and societal impact. The deployment of systems capable of detecting and responding to human emotions carries both transformative potential and significant ethical responsibility. By implementing inclusive datasets, bias mitigation strategies, context-aware modeling, explainable AI, privacy-preserving practices, and participatory governance frameworks, developers can create emotion-aware AI that respects human dignity, autonomy, and well-being. Ethical design ensures that these systems enhance human experience, promote trust, and foster socially responsible innovation, establishing a foundation for the safe, fair, and beneficial integration of emotion-aware AI into everyday life. Ultimately, ethical vigilance is not merely an adjunct to technological advancement but a prerequisite for the responsible, human-centered deployment of AI systems that interact with our most intimate and personal dimensions—our emotions.

ADAPTIVE LEARNING: AI THAT GROWS WITH USER MOOD

The integration of artificial intelligence (AI) with adaptive learning mechanisms has opened new horizons for personalized, emotionally intelligent systems capable of responding dynamically to users' cognitive and affective states. Central to this paradigm is the concept of user mood-driven adaptive learning, wherein AI systems not only adjust content, pacing, and difficulty based on performance metrics but also adapt in real time to the user's emotional state. Mood, a pervasive affective condition that reflects underlying emotional and cognitive patterns, influences attention, motivation, memory, decision-making, and engagement (Zhang et al. 2025). By recognizing, interpreting, and responding to mood, adaptive AI can optimize learning experiences, enhance user engagement, mitigate frustration, and foster positive emotional states that support sustained interaction and skill acquisition. This approach transcends traditional performance-based personalization, emphasizing affective intelligence as a critical driver of effective human-AI interaction. At the technical core, mood-sensitive adaptive AI relies on multimodal affective sensing to capture dynamic and often subtle emotional signals. Visual modalities include facial expression analysis, microexpression detection, gaze tracking, and body posture assessment, typically implemented using convolutional neural networks (CNNs), attention-based architectures, and landmark-based detection algorithms. Vocal modalities, such as tone, prosody, speech rate, and intensity, are analyzed using natural language processing (NLP) and acoustic feature extraction methods.

Linguistic content provides additional context, allowing sentiment, semantic patterns, and emotional valence to inform mood estimation. Physiological signals—heart rate variability, galvanic skin response, skin temperature, and electroencephalography (EEG)—offer objective measurements of arousal and affective state. By integrating these diverse modalities through multimodal fusion techniques, AI systems can infer mood with high granularity, temporal sensitivity, and contextual relevance, enabling adaptive interventions that are both timely and precise. Temporal modeling and longitudinal analysis are essential for adaptive systems that respond to user mood. Mood is not a static attribute but fluctuates over time, influenced by immediate context, prior experiences, cognitive load, environmental conditions, and social interactions. Recurrent neural networks (RNNs), long short-term memory (LSTM) networks, gated recurrent units (GRUs), and transformer-based sequence models allow AI systems to capture these temporal dynamics, modeling emotional trajectories and detecting patterns indicative of engagement, frustration, or cognitive fatigue (Shen et al. 2024). Predictive modeling further enables AI to anticipate shifts in mood, allowing preemptive adaptation of content delivery, feedback mechanisms, and interaction strategies. For example, a system might reduce task difficulty or provide motivational feedback when detecting signs of frustration, thereby maintaining flow and minimizing disengagement.

Personalization and user-centered adaptation constitute another critical dimension of mood-sensitive adaptive learning. Each individual's emotional and cognitive responses are shaped by personality, learning style, prior knowledge, cultural background, and situational context. Adaptive AI systems incorporate user models that encode preferences, historical interaction data, and emotional response patterns. Reinforcement learning (RL) and meta-learning algorithms enable the AI to continuously refine these models, optimizing intervention strategies based on observed outcomes and user feedback. Reward functions in RL are designed not only to maximize task performance but also to enhance emotional well-being, engagement, and satisfaction. Persona-based modeling further allows systems to simulate empathetic responses, providing a consistent, relatable, and emotionally attuned interface that fosters trust, rapport, and long-term adoption. Contextual awareness is indispensable for effective mood-driven adaptation. Mood interpretation is deeply context-dependent; the same physiological or behavioral signal may correspond to different affective states depending on environmental conditions, prior interactions, or task-related factors. Advanced adaptive systems integrate environmental sensing, interaction history, task context, and social cues to disambiguate mood signals, ensuring that interventions are appropriate and effective. Knowledge graphs, contextual embeddings, and attention-based mechanisms allow AI to reason over complex relationships between user state, task requirements, and environmental conditions, enabling nuanced and contextually aligned adaptive responses. Such context-aware adaptation ensures that mood-driven learning remains accurate, relevant, and supportive of the user's goals. Applications of mood-sensitive adaptive AI span education, healthcare, workplace training, gaming, and social robotics (Sree Vani et al. 2026). In educational technology, intelligent tutoring systems that monitor student mood can modulate instructional pacing, provide scaffolded guidance, and offer motivational feedback to sustain engagement and optimize learning outcomes.

In mental health applications, AI systems can detect emotional distress, deliver timely interventions, and provide therapeutic support tailored to the user's affective profile, enhancing adherence and well-being. Workplace training platforms leverage mood-adaptive AI to adjust difficulty, provide reinforcement, and maintain learner motivation, improving skill acquisition and retention. In gaming and entertainment, real-time mood adaptation enhances immersion, user satisfaction, and engagement. Social robots and virtual assistants benefit from mood-sensitive adaptation by calibrating social interactions, verbal responses, and affective behaviors to align with the user's current emotional state, fostering rapport, trust, and sustained interaction. Ethical, privacy, and societal considerations are central to mood-driven adaptive AI. Emotional data is inherently sensitive, encompassing intimate insights into cognition, psychological traits, and behavioral tendencies. Ethical deployment requires robust privacy safeguards, informed consent, transparent data usage policies, and secure storage practices. Bias mitigation is critical, as models trained on non-representative datasets may misinterpret mood in underrepresented populations, leading to inequitable outcomes or social harm. Designers must also address potential manipulation risks: AI systems capable of influencing mood may inadvertently or intentionally exploit vulnerability, affecting autonomy, decision-making, or psychological health.

Ethical frameworks, explainable AI (XAI), human-in-the-loop oversight, and participatory design processes are essential to ensure that mood-sensitive adaptive AI supports user well-being, autonomy, and fairness. Evaluation and validation of mood-adaptive AI systems require multimodal, multi-perspective methodologies. Objective measures—physiological indicators, behavioral metrics, interaction patterns—are complemented by subjective self-reports, standardized engagement scales, and user experience surveys (Thakur et al. 2026). Triangulating these measures enables reliable assessment of emotional engagement, adaptive effectiveness, and learning outcomes. Longitudinal studies and cross-context validation ensure robustness across diverse populations, tasks, and environments, mitigating biases and improving generalization. Continuous monitoring and iterative refinement based on feedback allow the system to evolve alongside the user, optimizing both cognitive and emotional outcomes over extended periods.

Future directions for balancing automation and human touch emphasize adaptive, context-aware, and ethically aligned AI systems (Trzebiński et al. 2023). Anticipatory service models, powered by predictive analytics and emotional AI, will allow AI to dynamically adjust its role in interactions based on real-time user state and context. Integration with immersive technologies—such as augmented reality (AR) or virtual reality (VR)—will enable richer, more human-like interactions in remote or virtual service environments. Cross-cultural and demographic adaptability will ensure equitable and culturally sensitive service delivery. Workforce augmentation programs will reskill employees to act as strategic human touchpoints, collaborating with AI to maximize operational efficiency while maintaining relational depth.

CONCLUSION

Ethical frameworks, participatory design, and transparent AI governance will safeguard trust, privacy, and fairness, ensuring that the evolution of AI-driven service enhances rather than diminishes human-centered values. Applications across domains illustrate the transformative potential of balanced AI-human service. In healthcare, hybrid models combine AI diagnostic tools with empathetic clinician interactions to optimize outcomes and patient experience. In financial services, AI analyzes transactions and provides insights while human advisors address complex, emotionally sensitive client needs. Retail and e-commerce platforms leverage AI for personalization and recommendation while human agents handle complaints, negotiations, and nuanced inquiries. Hospitality, travel, education, and social services similarly benefit from AI-enabled automation augmented by human empathy, judgment, and relational engagement. Across all sectors, balancing automation and human touch enhances efficiency, satisfaction, trust, and brand loyalty. In conclusion, achieving the optimal balance between automation and human touch in AI-driven service is a central challenge and opportunity for modern organizations. By leveraging AI for operational efficiency, predictive insights, and scalable engagement, while preserving human involvement for emotionally, ethically, and contextually complex interactions, organizations can maximize service quality, user satisfaction, and relational trust. Hybrid models, adaptive automation, emotional AI integration, seamless workflow orchestration, workforce reskilling, and ethical safeguards collectively form the framework for effective AI-human collaboration. The evolution of emotionally intelligent, context-aware, and ethically aligned AI systems promises to redefine service paradigms, transforming interactions from purely transactional exchanges into relationally enriched, empathetic, and human-centered experiences, ensuring that technology complements rather than replaces the essential human touch. Future directions in mood-sensitive adaptive AI emphasize real-time, low-latency processing, edge computing, and immersive environments. Advances in wearable sensors, IoT integration, and neuromorphic computing enable continuous, unobtrusive monitoring of user affective states. Reinforcement learning, continual learning, and meta-learning approaches allow AI systems to refine personalization dynamically, accommodating evolving user preferences, cognitive capacities, and emotional patterns. Integration with virtual reality (VR), augmented reality (AR), and metaverse platforms creates immersive, affectively adaptive experiences that respond to real-time mood signals, enhancing learning, engagement, and well-being. Cross-disciplinary research, combining AI, cognitive neuroscience, psychology, human-computer interaction, and ethics, is critical to ensure that these systems are both technologically sophisticated and human-centered. In conclusion, adaptive learning AI that grows with user mood represents a convergence of affective computing, personalization, contextual modeling, and ethical design. By detecting, interpreting, and responding to users' emotional states, such systems optimize cognitive engagement, emotional well-being, and overall interaction quality. Mood-sensitive adaptation enhances trust, motivation, learning outcomes, and long-term user satisfaction, making AI interactions more human-centered, socially intelligent, and emotionally attuned. Ethical safeguards, privacy protection, fairness, transparency, and explainability are critical to responsible deployment, ensuring that these systems augment human capabilities without compromising autonomy or well-being. The ongoing evolution of mood-driven adaptive AI promises a future where human-computer interaction is not only efficient and effective but also empathetic, personalized, and emotionally enriching, bridging the gap between technological intelligence and human emotional experience.

REFERENCES

Al-Zahrani, A. M. (2025). Exploring the impact of AI chatbots on emotional support: Balancing assistive personalisation with human connection. *SAGE Open*, *15*(2), 21582440251340615. DOI: 10.1177/21582440251340615

Banks, J. (2024). Deletion, departure, death: Experiences of AI companion loss. *Journal of Social and Personal Relationships*, *41*(12), 3547–3572. DOI: 10.1177/02654075241269688

Beatty, C., Malik, T., Meheli, S., & Sinha, C. (2022). Evaluating the Therapeutic Alliance With a Free-Text CBT Conversational Agent (Wysa): A Mixed-Methods Study. *Frontiers in Digital Health*, *4*, 847991. DOI: 10.3389/fdgth.2022.847991 PMID: 35480848

Carolus, A., Wienrich, C., Törke, A., Friedel, T., Schwietering, C., & Sperzel, M. (2021). "Alexa, I feel for you!" Observers' Empathetic Reactions towards a Conversational Agent. *Frontiers of Computer Science*, *3*, 682982. DOI: 10.3389/fcomp.2021.682982

Catania, F., & Garzotto, F. (2023). A conversational agent for emotion expression stimulation in persons with neurodevelopmental disorders. *Multimedia Tools and Applications*, *82*(9), 12797–12828. DOI: 10.1007/s11042-022-14135-w

Chin, H., Baek, G., Cha, C., & Cha, M. (2025). Chatbots' Empathetic Conversations and Responses: A Qualitative Study of Help-Seeking Queries on Depressive Moods Across 8 Commercial Conversational Agents. *JMIR Formative Research*, *9*, e71538. DOI: 10.2196/71538 PMID: 41284964

Darcy, A., Daniels, J., Salinger, D., Wicks, P., & Robinson, A. (2021). Evidence of Human-Level Bonds Established With a Digital Conversational Agent: Cross-sectional, Retrospective Observational Study. *JMIR Formative Research*, *5*(5), e27868. DOI: 10.2196/27868 PMID: 33973854

Dosovitsky, G., & Bunge, E. L. (2021). Bonding With Bot: User Feedback on a Chatbot for Social Isolation. *Frontiers in Digital Health*, *3*, 735053. DOI: 10.3389/fdgth.2021.735053 PMID: 34713203

Fang, C. M., Liu, A. R., & Associates. (2025). How AI and human behaviors shape psychosocial effects of chatbot use: A longitudinal randomized controlled study. arXiv. /arXiv.2503.17473DOI: 10.48550

Gennaro, M., Krumhuber, E. G., & Lucas, G. (2020). Effectiveness of an Empathic Chatbot in Combating Adverse Effects of Social Exclusion on Mood. *Frontiers in Psychology*, *10*, 3061. DOI: 10.3389/fpsyg.2019.03061 PMID: 32038415

Jolibois, S. C., Ito, A., & Nose, T. (2025). The Development of an Emotional Embodied Conversational Agent and the Evaluation of the Effect of Response Delay on User Impression. *Applied Sciences (Basel, Switzerland)*, *15*(8), 4256. DOI: 10.3390/app15084256

Joshi, N. V., Selvakumar, P., & Srivastava, N. Manjeet, Das, A., & Manjunath, T. C. (2026). Bioethics Legal Implications of Artificial Intelligence in Medicine. In S. Anastasiadou, L. Seremeti, & S. Papalexandris (Eds.), Bioethics and Legal Aspects of AI in Healthcare and Life Sciences (pp. 27-54). IGI Global Scientific Publishing. DOI: 10.4018/979-8-3373-5646-4.ch002

Kazazoğlu, S., & Turun Özel, G. (2025). The impact of chatbots on emotional intelligence in AI-driven interactions. *Frontiers in Education*, *10*, 1624272. DOI: 10.3389/feduc.2025.1624272

Kim, M., Lee, S., Kim, S., Heo, J., Lee, S., Shin, Y.-B., Cho, C.-H., & Jung, D. (2025). Therapeutic Potential of Social Chatbots in Alleviating Loneliness and Social Anxiety: Quasi-Experimental Mixed Methods Study. *Journal of Medical Internet Research*, *27*, e65589. DOI: 10.2196/65589 PMID: 39808786

Kolomaznik, M., Petrik, V., Slama, M., & Jurik, V. (2024). The role of socio-emotional attributes in enhancing human-AI collaboration. *Frontiers in Psychology*, *15*, 1369957. DOI: 10.3389/fpsyg.2024.1369957 PMID: 39474095

Li, B., & Zhang, Y. (2025). AI chatbots and emotional support: Implications for student well-being and emotional engagement. *Frontiers in Psychology*, *16*, 1498132. DOI: 10.3389/fpsyg.2025.1498132

Łukasik, A., & Gut, A. (2025). From robots to chatbots: Unveiling the dynamics of human-AI interaction. *Frontiers in Psychology*, *16*, 1569277. DOI: 10.3389/fpsyg.2025.1569277 PMID: 40271364

Ma, N. (2025). Effect of anthropomorphism and perceived intelligence in chatbot avatars: The mediating roles of perceived empathy and trust. *Frontiers of Computer Science*, *7*, 1531976. DOI: 10.3389/fcomp.2025.1531976

Paira, D., Rohini, A., Chandra, S., Satyanarayana, P., Sharma, M., & T. C., M. (2026). Climate Change and Natural Disasters. In Q. Ali & M. Tariq Iqbal Khan (Eds.), Strengthening Global Resilience to Natural Disasters (pp. 21-44). IGI Global Scientific Publishing. .DOI: 10.4018/979-8-3693-9745-9.ch002

Pilyoung, K., Xie, Y., & Yang, S. (2025). "I am here for you": How relational conversational AI appeals to adolescents especially those who are socially and emotionally vulnerable. arXiv. /arXiv.2512.15117DOI: 10.48550

Safare, R., Nirupama, E., Kunnathully, K., Ranjithkumar, A., Guru Basava Aradhya, S., Selvakumar, P., & Manjunath, T. C. (2026). Environmental Diplomacy and Cross-Border Negotiations. In Castanho, R. (Ed.), *Cross-Border Cooperation in the Age of Climate Change* (pp. 237–264). IGI Global Scientific Publishing., DOI: 10.4018/979-8-3373-3972-6.ch009

Sanz, B. (2025). Empathy, bias, and data responsibility: Evaluating AI chatbots for gender-based violence support. *Frontiers in Political Science*, *7*, 1631881. DOI: 10.3389/fpos.2025.1631881

Shams, A., Kunnathully, K., Satyanarayana, P., Sangeetha, B., Jayamala, C., & T.C., M. (2026). E-Government and Digital Public Services. In L. Santos Silva & J. Solleiro (Eds.), Intersecting Public Administration and Technology for Public Trust and Citizen Engagement (pp. 75-100). IGI Global Scientific Publishing. .DOI: 10.4018/979-8-3693-9709-1.ch004

Shen, J. (2024). Empathy Toward Artificial Intelligence Versus Human Narratives: Implications for Human-Centered Design of Mental Health Chatbots. *JMIR Mental Health*, *11*, e62679. DOI: 10.2196/62679 PMID: 39321450

Sree Vani, Y., Selvakumar, P., Prabhanjan Yadav, B., Kanipriya, M., Arun, M. R., Bansal, A., & Manjunath, T. C. (2026). Applying Machine Learning and AI to IoT Data for Robotic Intelligence. In Al-Humairi, S., Naronglerdrit, P., Chantarapanich, N., & Wanchat, S. (Eds.), *Robotics and IoT Synergy in Next-Generation Healthcare* (pp. 99–128). IGI Global Scientific Publishing., DOI: 10.4018/979-8-3373-5447-7.ch004

Thakur, D. J., Chitra, G., Seenivasan, R., Ponnapalli, H., Durga, K., & Manjunath, T. C. (2026). Data Sharing and Climate Monitoring Between Neighboring Territories. In Castanho, R. (Ed.), *Cross-Border Cooperation in the Age of Climate Change* (pp. 209–236). IGI Global Scientific Publishing., DOI: 10.4018/979-8-3373-3972-6.ch008

Trzebiński, W., Claessens, T., Buhmann, J., De Waele, A., Hendrickx, G., Van Damme, P., Daelemans, W., & Poels, K. (2023). The Effects of Expressing Empathy/Autonomy Support Using a COVID-19 Vaccination Chatbot: Experimental Study in a Sample of Belgian Adults. *JMIR Formative Research*, *7*, e41148. DOI: 10.2196/41148 PMID: 37074978

Vinod Krishna, M. U., Hiremath, S. M., Arul Raja, M., Agrawal, R. K., Roy, S. S., & Manjunath, T. C. (2026). Automation and the Future of Work in Aging Economies. In Christiansen, B., & Branch, J. (Eds.), *Critical Economic Implications of Global Demographic Changes* (pp. 181–212). IGI Global Scientific Publishing., DOI: 10.4018/979-8-3373-2550-7.ch007

Yun, J., & Park, J. (2022). The Effects of Chatbot Service Recovery With Emotion Words on Customer Satisfaction, Repurchase Intention, and Positive Word-Of-Mouth. *Frontiers in Psychology*, *13*, 922503. DOI: 10.3389/fpsyg.2022.922503 PMID: 35712132

Zhang, Y., Zhao, D., Hancock, J. T., & Associates. (2025). The rise of AI companions: How human-chatbot relationships influence well-being. arXiv. /arXiv.2506.12605DOI: 10.48550 [illegible] M. U., [illegible], S. M., [illegible], M., [illegible] K. R., Kim, S. S., & Mengen, [illegible] (2025). Automation and the Future of Work: A [illegible] study. In Christiansen, B., & Even, A. (Eds.), *[illegible] Global Demographic Changes* (pp. 121–[illegible]). IGI Global Scientific Publishing. DOI: 10.4018/979-8-[illegible]-5509-6.ch007

Yun, J., & Park, J. (2022). The Effects of Chatbot Service Recovery With Emotion Words on Customer Satisfaction, Repurchase Intention, and Positive Word-Of-Mouth. *Frontiers in Psychology*, 13, 922503. DOI: 10.3389/fpsyg.2022.922503 PMID: 35795431

Zhang, Y., Zhao, D., Hancock, J. T., Kraut, R., & Yang, D. (2025). The rise of AI companions: How human-chatbot relationships influence well-being. *arXiv*, 2506.12605. [illegible]

Chapter 11
From Noise to Sense-Making:
Problem Solving and the Transformation of Human Communication in Digital Contexts

Leandro Ferreira Pereira
http://orcid.org/0000-0002-4920-0498
ISCTE/BRU, University Institute of Lisbon, Portugal

José Crespo de Carvalho
ISCTE, University Institute of Lisbon, Portugal

ABSTRACT

This chapter reframes organizational communication as communicational problem solving rather than simple information transfer, showing how digital speed can amplify noise and spread complexity. It synthesizes research on coordination and verification to explain how constraints, channel properties, and interaction structures influence collective performance and misunderstanding in mediated settings. To support practice, the chapter proposes a Human-Centered Communicational Problem Solving (HCCPS) framework for hybrid and AI-mediated work. HCCPS structures a repeatable cycle—Diagnose, Match, Co-construct, Verify, Govern, and Learn—linking channel choice to diagnosis, making verification explicit, and treating human–AI collaboration as bounded delegation with accountability. The chapter concludes that lightweight artifacts and governance routines can stabilize meaning, improve effectiveness, and strengthen ethical defensibility and legitimacy under real-world trade-offs.

DOI: 10.4018/979-8-3373-8337-8.ch011

1. INTRODUCTION – COMMUNICATION AS A PROBLEM-SOLVING ACTIVITY

Figure 1. When communication distributes complexity

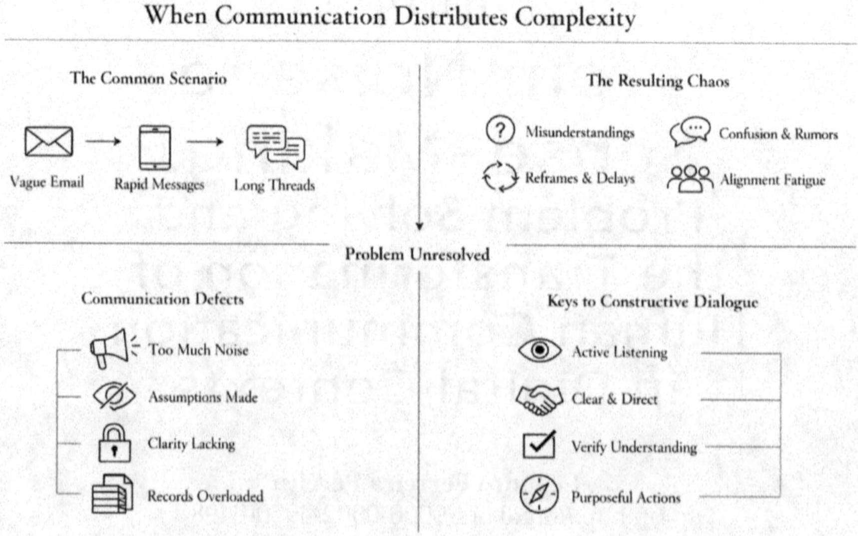

1.1 The Everyday Problem: When Communication Distributes Complexity Instead of Resolving it

A familiar scene plays out in many organizations. A sensitive topic - performance, conflict, a strategic shift - lands in someone's inbox with the neutral tone of an "institutional email." A few recipients read it quickly between meetings; others skim it on a phone while commuting. Someone forwards it with an anxious comment. Another replies-all, "Just to clarify…" and triggers a thread that grows legs. Two days later, people are still "aligned" only in the sense that everyone is tired. By then, the original issue has been reframed twice, diluted by assumptions, and complicated by the public record of what was said (and what was carefully not said). The problem has not been solved; it has been distributed.

93 Voices for Communication captures this everyday contradiction bluntly: communication is everywhere - personal and organizational - yet it can become "a blip," powerful, "hyper-constructive," or "devastating," depending on context and intention. It also insists, with unusual directness, that "more than ever, we need less noise and more meaning." That line can sound like an ethical preference, but it is also a practical diagnosis. Noise is not just an aesthetic flaw in communication; it is a problem-solving defect. When noise wins, problems become harder to define, decisions become harder to justify, and coordination becomes harder to sustain.

The 93 Voices (2025) makes the issue tangible through situations that most leaders recognize. "Meetings that could have been emails (and emails that should have been meetings)" is offered as a cliché that everyone repeats, and almost no one consistently corrects. The same voice calls institutional email "useful, but dangerous," capable of becoming "a weapon of mass confusion" when it is long, unclear, and copied to half the organization. Another voice describes why a "face-to-face conversation… can prevent weeks of misunderstandings via text message," because it allows people to read comfort, discomfort, posture, and reaction in real time. Yet the 93 Voices (2025) does not romanticize conversation: it recognizes abrupt feedback, tense exchanges, and the risk of speaking without empathy, while naming the conditions that make dialogue constructive - "presence, calmness, and intention."

These are not marginal issues. They are symptoms of a deeper misalignment between communication practices and the problems they are meant to solve. This chapter begins from a simple premise: communication is not merely something that accompanies problem solving; it is one of the ways problem solving actually happens.

1.2 What Research has Long Shown: Communication is a Coordination Mechanism and a Measurable Sequence of Actions

Across decades of research, communication in problem-solving settings has been treated as a constitutive process through which individuals and groups surface problem definitions, coordinate interpretations and actions, manage misunderstandings and constraints, and verify or stabilize solutions in interaction. Classic group experiments tested precisely whether restraining communication would undermine "mutual problem-solving behavior," and the logic was functional: communication makes intentions known and action more predictable (Hemphill & McConville, 1962). Later syntheses in group communication kept the same emphasis, treating communication as a coordination technology that shapes collective performance, even when the history of findings is complex and sometimes contested (Hirokawa, 2008).

Communication scholarship also makes a decisive move by treating communicative action as the very outcome of problem solving. The situational theory of problem solving models "communicative action in problem solving" as the dependent variable, shifting attention from attitudes to what people do communicatively when they recognize and address problematic situations (Kim & Grunig, 2011). In educational research, "problem-solving communication" is decomposed into assessable behaviors - perspective-taking, communicating essential information, and verifying solutions - showing that accuracy is not a generic trait but a set of interactional moves

(Baldwin & Garvey, 1973). The "Voices" echo these components in practice: adapt tone and pace to the person; clarify what matters; confirm understanding; follow up. They also state the same principle in plain terms: "Communication is not a channel. It is a behavior."

Research in professional education reinforces the practical stakes of this argument. In nursing student populations, communication ability appears as a strong predictor of problem-solving ability (Ji, Bang, & Jeon, 2013), and related studies compare problem-solving ability by degree of communication ability (Cho & Meera, 2017) and model factors influencing problem-solving competence in cross-sectional designs (Choi & Jeon, 2022). In dental hygiene education, lack of communication is explicitly linked to misinterpretation, conflict, and lowered problem-solving ability, and studies examine effects of critical thinking and communication skills on problem solving (Han, Ahn, & Hwang, 2019), alongside curriculum arguments that communication and problem solving should be developed together (Kim, Sung, & Kim, 2014).

The educational and mathematics literature adds another layer: problem solving improves when thinking is externalized in forms that others can interpret, challenge, and help refine. Communication is treated as representation, justification, and verification within authentic tasks (Analysis of Mathematical Communication Skills of Junior High School Students of Coastal Kolaka, 2017; Marwanda, Yusrizal, & Johar, 2021; Sumaji, Sa'dijah, Susiswo, & Sisworo, 2020; Maryati, 2020). More broadly, problem solving draws on repertoire, option generation, and iterative evaluation, which depend on argumentation and shared representations (Liljedahl, Santos-Trigo, Jurado, & Bruder, 2016). Instructional syntheses of problem solving emphasize cognitive and metacognitive orchestration that can be facilitated, again implying a central role for communicative externalization and revision (Mentz, Breed, & Havenga, 2022).

This is also where constraints matter. Risk communication research, for instance, shows that under different processing conditions people rely on heuristics or systematic processing, changing how they judge credibility and risk (Chaiken, 1980; Griffin, Neuwirth, Giese, & Dunwoody, 2002; Trumbo, 2002). In organizational life, similar dynamics appear when speed and channel overload push people toward shortcuts rather than careful meaning-making - something the 93 Voices (2025) captures vividly in its depiction of "digital cacophony."

1.3 Why This Chapter now: Trade-Offs, Hybrid Mediation, and a Pragmatic Contribution

The "Voices" contribute a nuance that matters: communication today is not simply "harder"; it is shaped by environments that alter attention, pace, and accountability.

The 93 Voices (2025) notes that digital acceleration brings "noise, distraction, and superficiality," and that "the urgency to respond has replaced the intention to listen." The chapter treats this not as a cultural complaint but as a problem-solving challenge. Under time pressure, communication becomes strategy-driven: clarification, repair, simplification, and channel switching. Second-language research makes this explicit by showing how speakers overcome resource deficits and processing constraints through communication strategies (Dörnyei & Kormos, 1998; Dörnyei & Scott, 1997), and writing research similarly frames lexical gaps as "difficult situations" requiring strategic action to communicate meaning (Ngamwilaipong, Darasawang, & Srimavin, 2007). The organizational parallels are clear: ambiguity increases strategy use, and the wrong medium can turn minor issues into complex disputes.

The chapter also takes seriously what practitioners know: communication is full of trade-offs, not perfect solutions. Hybrid work can expand flexibility and productivity, yet erode alignment and culture if leaders do not deliberately create clarity, transparency, rituals, and spaces for listening. Speed can be an asset and also a risk; this tension appears directly in research comparing electronic versus face-to-face communication in social problem-solving recommendations (Manger, Wicklund, & Eikeland, 2003). A chapter that pretends these dilemmas do not exist will feel moralistic; a chapter that recognizes them can still be practical.

Problem solving is increasingly distributed across people, tools, and interfaces, which makes communication design part of performance. Distributed problem-solving frameworks treat communication and organization principles as a core part of the architecture (Yoshida & Narazaki, 1990). Work on problem-solving agents that communicate and learn highlights the need to translate utterances into actionable meaning representations learned through interaction (Narayan-Chen et al., 2017). Classic interface design research in medical expert systems shows how representations become the medium through which professionals execute tasks (Lane, Walton, & Shortliffe, 1986). Technical communication likewise frames problem solving as intrinsic to communicative work and uses heuristics to navigate complex constraints (Kavanaugh, 2013). Together, these sources remind us that communicational breakdowns are not merely interpersonal; they are also design failures.

This introduction sets up three claims that anchor the rest of the chapter. First, communication structures joint problem solving by making intentions visible and action more predictable (Hemphill & McConville, 1962; Hirokawa, 2008), while collaborative work depends on "soft skills" as enabling conditions for solving complex problems (Riggio & Saggi, 2015). Second, communication can be analyzed as a sequence of component behaviors and strategies - perspective orientation, essential information, verification, and repair under constraints - rather than treated as a generic trait (Baldwin & Garvey, 1973; Dörnyei & Kormos, 1998; Dörnyei & Scott, 1997). Third, communication is a trainable competence and a design target:

measured communication ability predicts problem-solving ability in professional education, and task design can be used to observe communication-as-problem-solving as it unfolds (Ji et al., 2013; Cho & Meera, 2017; Choi & Jeon, 2022; Han et al., 2019; Kim et al., 2014; Marwanda et al., 2021; Maryati, 2020; Sumaji et al., 2020; Analysis of Mathematical Communication Skills of Junior High School Students of Coastal Kolaka, 2017).

The next section will build from this foundation toward a concise synthesis, showing how the "Voices" anticipate the micro-components of accurate problem-solving communication, how medium constraints shape predictable patterns of misunderstanding, and why "listening is more than measuring" - because "without action, listening is just playing make-believe." Along the way, it will present a simple visual framework - deliberately modest, not over-engineered - that helps leaders and communicators diagnose problems, choose modes, and work with trade-offs rather than pretending they can be eliminated.

2. FROM CHANNELS TO DIAGNOSIS: MATCHING PROBLEMS AND COMMUNICATION MODES

Figure 2. From channels to diagnosis

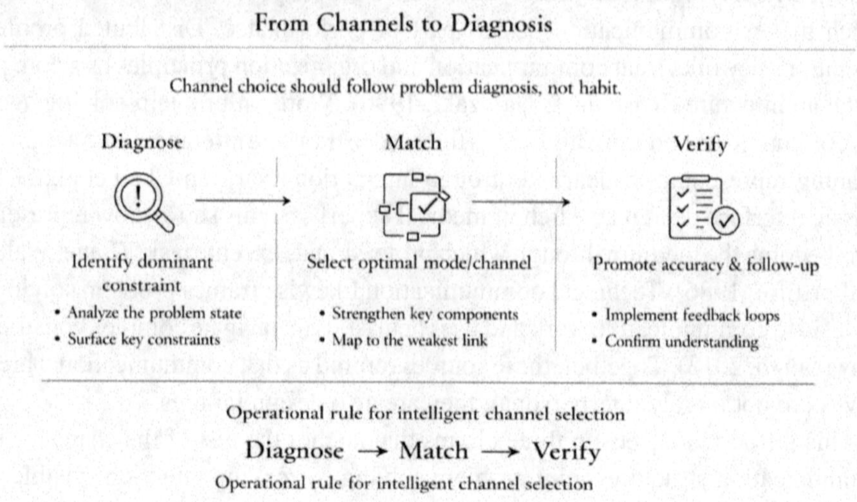

2.1 Principle Definition: Channel Choice Should Follow Problem Diagnosis, not Habit

Most communication failures in organizations are not caused by "bad intent." They come from *default behavior*: we send the email because that is what we do; we schedule the meeting because that is what we do; we drop the message in WhatsApp because it is fast. The 93 Voices (2025) captures this everyday trap with a line that reads like a cliché precisely because it is true: "meetings that could have been emails (and emails that should have been meetings)."

The principle behind *From Channels to Diagnosis* is simple: *diagnose the problem-state first*, then select (or configure) the mode/channel that reduces the dominant constraints and makes verification possible. If the problem is ambiguity, you need a mode that supports clarification and perspective alignment; if the problem is accountability, you need traceability and scrutiny; if the problem is pace and overload, you need a mode that minimizes cognitive drag while still preserving meaning.

This is consistent with classic experimental evidence showing that communication conditions - including restraints - shape "mutual problem-solving behavior" by making intentions known, future actions predictable, and interaction structures effective (Hemphill & McConville, 1962). It is also aligned with the situational theory of problem solving, which treats "communicative action in problem solving" as the focal outcome and models the situational drivers that make certain communicative actions more or less likely (Kim & Grunig, 2011). It connects to the micro-foundations of accurate problem-solving communication: perspective orientation, essential-information transmission, and solution verification (Baldwin & Garvey, 1973). In practice, different channels help - or hurt - each of these components.

A useful way to make this principle tangible is to state it as an operational rule:

- *If you can't name the dominant constraint (ambiguity, coordination, verification, time pressure), you are choosing a channel by habit.*
- *If you can name it, you can choose a channel strategically.*

The 93 Voices (2025) tone supports this: it reminds us that "the channel matters," and that choosing it consciously is "a gesture of respect."

2.2 Why "Diagnosis" is the Right Metaphor (and not Just Rhetoric)

"Diagnosis" is not a decorative metaphor. Several research traditions treat communication as a *condition that can be tuned* to improve problem-solving performance.

In group problem solving, the point of manipulating communication restraints is precisely to observe how changes in communication conditions alter whether groups develop predictable interaction structures and solve tasks efficiently (Hemphill & McConville, 1962). If constraints can causally alter performance, then a practitioner's job is to *identify which constraint is dominant* before changing the channel.

In communication theory, diagnosis is explicit. Kim and Grunig's situational theory invites us to examine problem recognition, constraint recognition, involvement recognition, and referent criteria to anticipate communicative action (Kim & Grunig, 2011). Put plainly: people don't communicate "better" because you asked them to; they communicate differently when their constraints, stakes, and reference standards shift.

And in engineered health communication systems, diagnosis is operationalized even more literally: "pre-diagnosis" determines when, how much, and at what quality data should be transmitted, because communication resources are finite and signal components differ in importance (Sahu, Peng, & Sharif, 2021). The social and the technical domains converge on the same insight: *channel choice is a downstream control decision informed by state diagnosis*.

This gives the principle an important edge: it moves the conversation from taste ("I prefer email") to function ("email is weak for ambiguity repair, strong for traceability"). It also aligns with the 93 Voices (2025) warning that speed and proliferation can create "noise, distraction, and superficiality," where "the urgency to respond has replaced the intention to listen." When the environment pushes people into reaction, diagnosis is how you regain intentionality.

2.3 What Should be Diagnosed Before Picking a Mode?

A diagnosis that is too complex won't be used. A diagnosis that is too vague won't help. The literature supports a small set of dimensions that are both *evidence-based and practical*:

A. Constraint Structure (What Blocks Communicative Action?)

Constraint recognition is a central variable in situational theory (Kim & Grunig, 2011), and experiments show that constraining communication alters mutual problem-solving behavior (Hemphill & McConville, 1962). In distributed problem-solving architectures, communication and organization are treated as design parameters, reinforcing the idea that constraints are not afterthoughts (Yoshida & Narazaki, 1990). Typical constraints include time, privacy, access, cognitive load, bandwidth, and organizational permission.

B. Ambiguity and Shared Understanding (do we Lack a Common Problem Model?)

Often, the issue is not missing data - it is mismatched interpretation. Perspective orientation is a core component of accurate problem-solving communication (Baldwin & Garvey, 1973). Family stress and adaptation research similarly treats communication quality as a coping resource that reduces ambiguity under pressure (Patterson, 1988). The 93 Voices (2025) frames this in everyday language: written messages are "the most ambiguous medium," and the absence of tone becomes the tone.

C. Verification Requirement (how Costly is Being Wrong - and how Will we Check?)

Verification is not a "nice to have"; it is one of the defining components of accuracy (Baldwin & Garvey, 1973). In risk communication, the heuristic–systematic model shows that people vary in depth of processing; if the context encourages heuristic cues, apparent agreement may mask weak verification (Chaiken, 1980; Griffin et al., 2002; Trumbo, 2002). This matters in organizations whenever a decision has compliance, reputational, safety, or financial implications.

D. Time Pressure and Resource Deficits (are we Solving Under Production Constraints?)

Second-language research is unusually explicit: resource deficits and processing time pressure generate problems that speakers solve through strategic coping and repair (Dörnyei & Kormos, 1998; Dörnyei & Scott, 1997). Writing research shows the same logic in lexical problem solving (Ngamwilaipong et al., 2007). In organizations, the parallel is immediate: when people are overloaded, they default to shortcuts, partial messages, and fast channels - raising ambiguity and verification risk.

E. Distributed Coordination Across Agents/Systems (is the "Problem Solver" Human + System?)

In modern work, solving often requires coordinating humans, tools, workflows, and interfaces. Distributed frameworks place communication at the center of the coordination infrastructure (Yoshida & Narazaki, 1990). Human–AI work highlights the need to translate utterances into actionable meaning representations that task solvers can execute (Narayan-Chen et al., 2017). Interface research shows how representation design shapes usability and task execution in clinical contexts (Lane, Walton, & Shortliffe, 1986). In such settings, "channel" is not only a medium - it is part of the system's operational logic.

2.4 A Matching Logic: Map the Problem to the Mode by Strengthening the Weakest Component

The most defensible matching logic is not "richer is better." It is: *select the mode that best strengthens the weakest required component*, given the diagnosis. The three components that consistently matter for correctness are:

- *Perspective alignment* (can people see the problem similarly?)
- *Essential-information transfer* (do they have what they need to act?)
- *Verification* (how do we confirm we are not wrong?)

This triad comes directly from Baldwin and Garvey's component model (Baldwin & Garvey, 1973). It also fits the group communication tradition that treats communication processes as central to performance, not as a neutral conduit (Hirokawa, 2008), and it echoes the 93 Voices (2025) practical insistence on clarity, structure, and channel-awareness.

A practical mapping (with real trade-offs) looks like this:

When the dominant issue is coordination/ predictability (who does what next?):

choose modes that create mutual visibility of intentions and next steps; add explicit "what I'm doing / what you're doing" checkpoints (Hemphill & McConville, 1962; Baldwin & Garvey, 1973).

When the dominant issue is ambiguity/perspective divergence:

choose modes that support bidirectional clarification, listening, and repair. In applied settings, this is precisely what interpersonal skills training operationalizes via self-expression and empathic listening linked to mutual problem solving (Schroder et al., 1988). The 93 Voices (2025) makes the same point: some conversations "deserve more than three lines in a chat."

When the dominant issue is verification/accountability:

choose modes that support documentation, revisiting arguments, and scrutiny. Risk-processing research warns that in heuristic conditions people may rely on cues instead of content (Chaiken, 1980; Griffin et al., 2002; Trumbo, 2002). The mode should therefore encourage systematic processing where stakes demand it.

When the dominant issue is time pressure/resource deficits:

choose modes that allow rapid iteration and repair (synchronous) *or* allow time to craft clarity (asynchronous), depending on what the constraint is (Dörnyei & Kormos, 1998; Dörnyei & Scott, 1997; Manger, Wicklund, & Eikeland, 2003). Speed can help - but it also changes what kind of thinking is possible.

When the dominant issue is distributed coordination (human + system):

choose modes and protocols that connect language to executable actions and usable representations (Narayan-Chen et al., 2017; Yoshida & Narazaki, 1990; Lane et al., 1986). Here, "matching" is as much about representation design as it is about channel selection.

This logic also helps explain the 93 Voices (2025) very concrete warnings. Institutional email, for instance, is described as "useful, but dangerous," even "a weapon of mass confusion" when it becomes long, unclear, and over-CC'd. That is a mismatch problem: email can support traceability, but it is weak at repairing ambiguity and emotion, especially under time pressure.

2.5 Operational procedure: a simple "Diagnose → Match → Verify" cycle

A usable procedure has to be short enough to survive a busy week. The following cycle is deliberately compact, but grounded in the cited evidence:

1. Diagnose the drivers of communicative action

Use situational variables (problem recognition, constraint recognition, involvement recognition, referent criteria) to clarify what is feasible and what people will actually do (Kim & Grunig, 2011). Treat constraints as potentially causal, not incidental (Hemphill & McConville, 1962). Where relevant, borrow the engineering intuition: allocate communication resources based on a pre-diagnosis of what matters most (Sahu et al., 2021).

2. Match to the mode that supports the required accuracy components

Choose the mode that best enables perspective orientation, essential information, and verification - under your constraints (Baldwin & Garvey, 1973). Assume mode choice influences performance because communication processes are part of the performance mechanism (Hemphill & McConville, 1962; Hirokawa, 2008). Expect contingency: electronic speed communication will not behave like face-to-face in every social problem-solving situation (Manger et al., 2003).

3. Design verification loops appropriate to the likely processing regime

Build explicit checkpoints for understanding and correctness (Baldwin & Garvey, 1973). If the context encourages heuristic processing, compensate with artifacts and structure that promote scrutiny (Chaiken, 1980; Griffin et al., 2002; Trumbo, 2002).

A useful reminder from the 93 Voices (2025) fits here: "Listening is more than measuring… Without action, listening is just playing make-believe." Verification is where listening becomes action.

2.6 Illustrative synthesis: "two-channel" and multi-channel thinking (don't force one channel to do everything)

A recurring pattern in real organizations is that **one channel cannot satisfy all requirements**. The 93 Voices (2025) WhatsApp vignette is a near-perfect example: it praises agility but describes "digital cacophony" where audios, PDFs, GIFs, and unrelated groups collide - and "WhatsApp demands an answer." It is simultaneously hero and villain: speed and reach on one side, hypervigilance and loss of focus on the other.

The literature supports multi-channel logic in more technical settings too. A "two-channel" diagnostic model that integrates medical knowledge and discourse signals illustrates the general principle: separate channels when the task requires synthesizing distinct evidence streams (Tomar, Tiwari, & Saha, 2024). In healthcare communication architectures, pre-diagnosis similarly guides what and when to transmit (Sahu et al., 2021). And telemedicine network design shows how infrastructure choices (e.g., fiber-optic channels) are aligned with diagnostic goals, standardization, and decision support constraints (Yaroslavskyy et al., 2022a; Yaroslavskyy et al., 2022b).

In organizational terms, "two-channel" thinking can be very simple:

- **Channel 1 (fast):** alerts, coordination signals, quick updates (low ambiguity, low stakes).
- **Channel 2 (deep):** alignment, disagreement, strategy, sensitive feedback, decisions that require verification.

The 93 Voices (2025) itself recommends this kind of discipline in practice - defining purpose, rules, and leadership behavior so that WhatsApp remains an ally rather than a trap.

2.7 Practical implications, trade-offs, and open questions

This principle is not a moral prescription. It is a performance and culture proposition - with real dilemmas.

Implications for practice (clear, bounded, usable):

- Treat channel choice as a *design decision*, not etiquette (Hemphill & McConville, 1962; Hirokawa, 2008).
- Train for the three accuracy components - *perspective orientation, essential information, verification* - rather than "communication" as a vague soft trait (Baldwin & Garvey, 1973; Schroder et al., 1988).
- When stakes are high, design for *systematic processing and auditability*, not just agreement (Chaiken, 1980; Griffin et al., 2002; Trumbo, 2002).
- In distributed or human–AI settings, treat matching as *representational alignment*: utterances must map to actions and usable interfaces (Narayan-Chen et al., 2017; Lane et al., 1986; Yoshida & Narazaki, 1990; Kavanaugh, 2013).
- Acknowledge the trade-off openly: speed can protect agility, but it can also erode depth and increase ambiguity (Manger et al., 2003). The 93 Voices (2025) warning about digital acceleration and loss of listening is a real operational risk, not just a cultural complaint.

Open questions worth leaving on the table (because there are no perfect answers):

- When does speed genuinely improve problem solving - and when does it simply accelerate misunderstanding? (Manger et al., 2003)
- How should organizations design verification when audiences are likely to process heuristically - especially under overload? (Chaiken, 1980; Griffin et al., 2002; Trumbo, 2002)
- What does "good channel choice" look like in hybrid human–AI work, where meaning must be translated into executable operations? (Narayan-Chen et al., 2017)
- How do we preserve institutional memory and psychological safety in fast, informal channels that behave like "fireworks… flashy and bright, but ephemeral"?

If we take the 93 Voices (2025) assertion seriously - "Communication is not a channel. It is a behavior" - then diagnosis becomes the discipline that helps behavior stay aligned with purpose. And that is the core promise of this section: moving from "what do we use?" to "what are we trying to solve - and what is blocking us from solving it?"

3. EMOTIONAL INTELLIGENCE AND RESPONSIBILITY IN MEDIATED INTERACTION

Figure 3. Why emotional intelligence matters in mediated communication

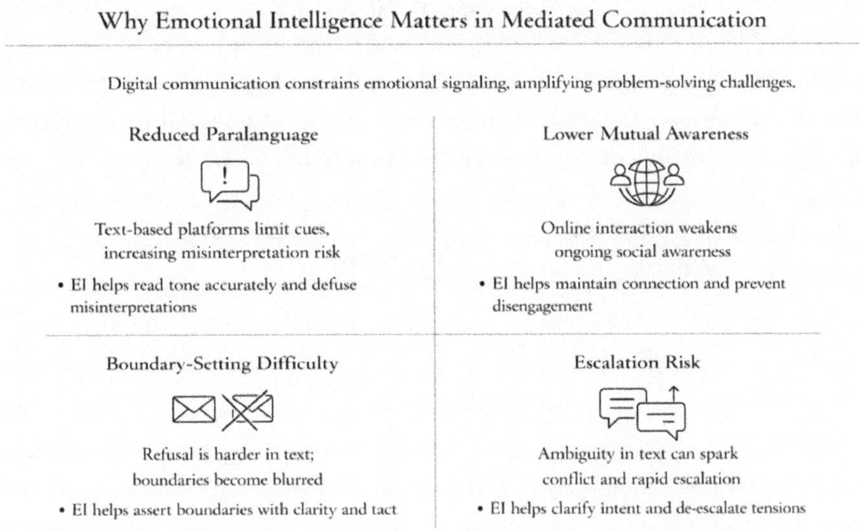

3.1 Conceptual starting point: mediated interaction as an emotionally constrained problem-solving environment

Digital interaction often behaves like a problem-solving setting with one obvious handicap: we are asked to coordinate, disagree, and decide with fewer emotional signals than in face-to-face contact. In many computer-mediated communication (CMC) contexts, paralanguage is reduced and emotion is mainly carried through text, which increases the likelihood of misinterpretation and "emotion recognition" errors (Caon et al., 2013). At the same time, the longer arc of CMC and e-learning research has moved from early claims of impersonality and limited emotional expression to a more mature position: mediated interaction *can* support rich relational communication and effective task achievement at a distance - if the relevant variables (group processes, channel use, norms) are deliberately analyzed and designed (Mendes et al., 2008).

This "dual reality" (emotional constraint, yet relational potential) is precisely why mediated communication should be treated as a recurrent problem-solving environment: it generates predictable problem-states - ambiguity, tone loss, escalation, avoidance - and pushes individuals and organizations to build capacities to diagnose and repair them. 93 Voices (2025) captures this operationally: "Written messages are practical and quick, but also dangerously ambiguous." A few lines of text can be efficient; the same few lines can also create weeks of avoidable friction if the emotional reading is wrong.

A small, concrete example helps to anchor this: a manager sends a short message - "Need this fixed today." The intent is urgency; the reception is accusation. The "problem" is no longer the fix; it becomes the relationship. In face-to-face settings, tone and micro-repair (a smile, a pause, a clarifying sentence) often prevent that slide; mediated settings demand stronger intentionality and skill.

3.2 Emotional intelligence: dominant component models and where "responsibility" fits

Across EI research used in leadership and organizational contexts, the component structure is remarkably stable: *self-awareness, self-regulation, motivation, empathy, and social skills* (Furnham, 2012; Hassan, 2023). In parallel, socio-emotional learning (SEL) frameworks make responsibility explicit by including *responsible decision making* alongside self-awareness, self-management, social awareness, relationship skills, and related competencies (Zeba et al., 2025). Management-oriented work also connects EI with communication skills and work environment quality, particularly in technology-intensive contexts where mediated interaction is the default rather than the exception (Hassan, 2023; Linkova, 2024).

In this chapter's framing, *responsibility* in mediated contexts is not an "extra virtue." It is the applied expression of EI under constraint:

- *Self-regulation* becomes the ability to slow down reaction and avoid emotionally expensive speed.
- *Empathy* becomes inference under uncertainty (reading intent with less evidence).
- *Social skills* become deliberate repair (clarifying, inviting, de-escalating, verifying).
- *Responsible decision making* becomes governance: choosing what to say, how, where, and when - especially when you cannot "patch" meaning with nonverbal cues.

93 Voices (2025) expresses the same idea in managerial language: "True transparency is not saying everything, but knowing how to choose what, how, where, and when to communicate." In mediated settings, that "choice architecture" is where responsibility lives.

3.3 Evidence linking EI to ethical perception and responsibility-relevant judgments

The responsibility question becomes sharper once we accept that mediated contexts amplify ambiguity: when cues are weaker, people rely more on interpretation, assumptions, and social heuristics. Organizational psychology evidence suggests EI is not merely a feel-good label; it is associated with *ethical perception and judgment*. Findings reported by Jessica et al. (2010) indicate that EI's effect on ethics-and-success perceptions is mediated by self-esteem: higher EI relates to higher self-esteem and reduces the likelihood of seeing unethical behavior as a shortcut to success (Jessica et al., 2010). Broader EI work also supports pathway models in which work experiences trigger EI-mediated affective responses that shape downstream behavior (Furnham, 2012).

The practical implication for mediated interaction is straightforward: when feedback loops are weaker (no visible discomfort, no immediate relational repair), *ethical drift becomes easier*. EI appears relevant precisely because it shapes how people interpret "what works" socially, and whether they rationalize questionable behavior as effective.

Here, 93 Voices (2025) gives a concrete leadership micro-case: a senior colleague's distance is interpreted as disengagement until a vulnerable, empathic admission ("I've been wondering if my communication has been clear…") reopens dialogue and restores trust. The ethical dimension is subtle but real: the leader chooses candor over manipulation and curiosity over blame, even under uncertainty.

3.4 Responsibility in mediated interaction: role obligations, ethicality, and interactional governance

3.4.1 Responsibility as stewardship of coherent, goal-aligned interaction

In mediated learning conversations, responsibility is described as a leader's duty: to keep the discussion coherent, raise issues that improve the quality of written interaction, and achieve goals through participants' messages (Cerratto, 2000). This aligns with e-learning research that stresses the need to deliberately cultivate online interaction processes rather than assuming they will emerge naturally (Mendes et al., 2008; Charlton et al., 2008).

In distributed teamwork, responsibility also includes *inclusion and continuity*: persistent online infrastructures can reduce the "void" between face-to-face meetings and increase awareness of others' skills, rhythms, and needs, helping avoid the quiet marginalization of peripheral members (Charlton et al., 2008; Henderson, 2014). 93

Voices (2025) frames the same idea culturally: "Communication is not a channel. It is a behavior… make it everyone's responsibility."

A practical organizational use case is familiar: a project Slack runs hot with a few voices; two key specialists go silent. The work still "moves," but alignment quietly collapses. Stewardship is noticing the silence as data, not as absence.

3.4.2 Responsibility as ethical constraint under visibility, authenticity pressure, and platform dynamics

Mediated publics and creator economies add a different pressure: platforms reward visibility, relatability, and vulnerability, turning self-presentation into affective labor that can encourage risky disclosure or manipulative signaling (Odorico, 2025). In such settings, EI-linked self-regulation and ethical judgment become more important, not less.

The link back to the EI–ethicality findings matters: if EI reduces the tendency to see unethical behavior as "successful," it may also buffer the temptation to treat emotional manipulation as a growth tactic (Jessica et al., 2010; Odorico, 2025). The dilemma, however, is real: authenticity is valuable, but performance of authenticity can be exploitative. 93 Voices (2025) captures the constructive side of this trade-off: vulnerability, when sincere and contextualized, can "reestablish trust and reinforce a culture of listening and co-creation."

3.5 Why mediated interaction amplifies the need for EI: three mechanisms with everyday examples

3.5.1 Reduced paralanguage raises misinterpretation risk

CMC settings often provide less paralanguage; emotion representation can be constrained to text (Caon et al., 2013). Under these conditions, EI becomes a functional requirement for preventing escalation and restoring meaning (Furnham, 2012; Hassan, 2023). 93 Voices (2025) puts it bluntly: "A face-to-face conversation… can prevent weeks of misunderstandings via text message."

3.5.2 Mutual awareness is harder, yet more necessary

Online relationships require ongoing, mutual awareness ("We-relationship" maintenance); when information exchange weakens, bonds weaken (Henderson, 2014). Social connection is not static; it needs regular nurturing (Savic, 2024). Persistent infrastructures can help sustain awareness in distributed teams, but only if people use them responsibly (Charlton et al., 2008). 93 Voices (2025) describes the risk side of acceleration: "noise, distraction, and superficiality… the urgency to respond has replaced the intention to listen."

3.5.3 Socially difficult actions (like saying "no") become harder in text

Refusal is a socially delicate action with systematic structure (Smith, 2021). In text-centric environments, the absence of nonverbal repair cues makes refusal and boundary-setting riskier; EI matters for crafting clarity without relational damage (Caon et al., 2013; Furnham, 2012). 93 Voices (2025) frames the underlying discipline as maturity: "the ability to feel without acting and to think before speaking."

3.6 Training and intervention: building EI-linked responsibility for mediated contexts

The training literature increasingly treats responsibility as *buildable*, not innate.

- *SEL frameworks* explicitly include responsible decision making and show associations with improved performance and attitudes (Zeba et al., 2025).
- *Serious games and meta-skills interventions* report improvements in emotional regulation, empathy, stress management, social awareness, and conflict resolution, supporting the feasibility of training EI-relevant capacities for mediated collaboration (Mitsea et al., 2025).
- *Pedagogical EI work* suggests higher EI supports rapport and climate in educational settings (Shehhi et al., 2021; Tozoğlu & Erciş, 2025).
- *Empathy cultivation approaches* combine creative practice and reflective tools to diagnose and monitor empathic responses, linking empathy training to collective problem solving (Ваколюк et al., 2025).

3.7 Design implications: engineering responsibility-supporting mediated environments

If mediated environments create predictable emotional constraints, then responsibility cannot rest only on individuals; it also becomes a design and governance issue.

3.7.1 Designing for emotion expression and social awareness

CMC findings imply a direct design goal: reduce misinterpretation by enabling richer emotional signaling and clearer social awareness cues where appropriate (Caon et al., 2013). E-learning research similarly argues that mediated effectiveness depends on detailed analysis of variables and deliberate channel configuration (Mendes et al., 2008). Distributed teamwork research supports persistent infrastructures that reduce communication voids and make peripheral participation visible (Charlton et al., 2008; Henderson, 2014).

93 Voices (2025) offers a practical "system design" example inside organizations: WhatsApp can be powerful, but it can also become a hyperconnectivity trap; the solution is explicit criteria, a "rulebook," leadership example, and training for notification hygiene and boundaries.

3.7.2 Ethics-by-design and stakeholder participation

Design-for-social-innovation scholarship emphasizes humans and artificial systems as co-creators, calling for interdisciplinary design that integrates ethics and local adaptation (Terenzi et al., 2025). This becomes urgent under platform dynamics that incentivize visibility and emotional labor (Odorico, 2025). Paired with EI–ethicality evidence (Jessica et al., 2010), the state-of-the-art view is dual-layered: responsibility requires *personal EI capacity* and *system-level ethical design and governance* (Terenzi et al., 2025; Odorico, 2025; Jessica et al., 2010).

3.8 Applied contexts where EI–responsibility dynamics become visible

3.8.1 Remote work and mediated leadership

Remote work research treats technology as a managerial tool but argues success depends on motivation, leadership, culture, and psychological/social factors such as stress susceptibility, communication/support, work–life balance, and organizational support structures (Linkova, 2024). EI leadership scholarship similarly positions EI and communication skill as central for healthy environments (Hassan, 2023). 93 Voices (2025) adds a caution: telework can narrow ties to people outside one's immediate group, increasing isolation and reducing new connections.

3.8.2 Crisis communication and civic responsibility in mediated networks

In crisis settings (e.g., bushfires), emergency services and communities adapt Twitter/Facebook and user-friendly information sites to coordinate, seek information, and respond under stress (Holloway et al., 2013). These contexts make the EI–responsibility link concrete: emotional arousal is high, misinformation risk is high, and the ethical burden of accuracy and calm escalation control is real - reinforcing why both EI/SEL capacities and responsible socio-technical design matter (Zeba et al., 2025; Mitsea et al., 2025; Terenzi et al., 2025; Holloway et al., 2013).

3.9 Research gaps and frontier questions (bounded to the provided evidence)

- *Mechanisms that integrate EI–ethicality with platform incentives.* EI connects to ethicality perceptions via self-esteem (Jessica et al., 2010), while platform economies incentivize visibility and vulnerability (Odorico, 2025). The frontier is a testable model of when EI buffers ethically risky incentives - and when it does not.
- *Intervention specificity for text-centric constraints.* SEL and serious-game interventions improve empathy/regulation (Zeba et al., 2025; Mitsea et al., 2025), yet CMC work highlights reduced paralanguage and constrained emotional expression (Caon et al., 2013). Which training components transfer best to low-cue environments, and how do we measure "responsible" outcomes (Mitsea et al., 2025; Ваколюк et al., 2025)?
- *Role-based accountability in online learning and teamwork.* Leadership responsibility for coherence and quality in written interaction is explicit (Cerratto, 2000), as is the value of infrastructures that reduce voids and include peripheral members (Charlton et al., 2008). The open question is which governance structures reliably create responsible discourse at scale (Mendes et al., 2008).
- *Operational ethics-by-design in human–AI co-creation.* Ethics-by-design calls for interdisciplinary co-creation (Terenzi et al., 2025), while AI-adjacent training contexts show rapid growth in socio-technical mediation (Mitsea et al., 2025). A key gap is translating principles into repeatable organizational practices that complement, rather than assume, EI.

4. CREATIVITY, EFFICIENCY, AND DEPTH IN COLLECTIVE PROBLEM-SOLVING

Figure 4. Creativity, efficiency, and depth in collective problem-solving

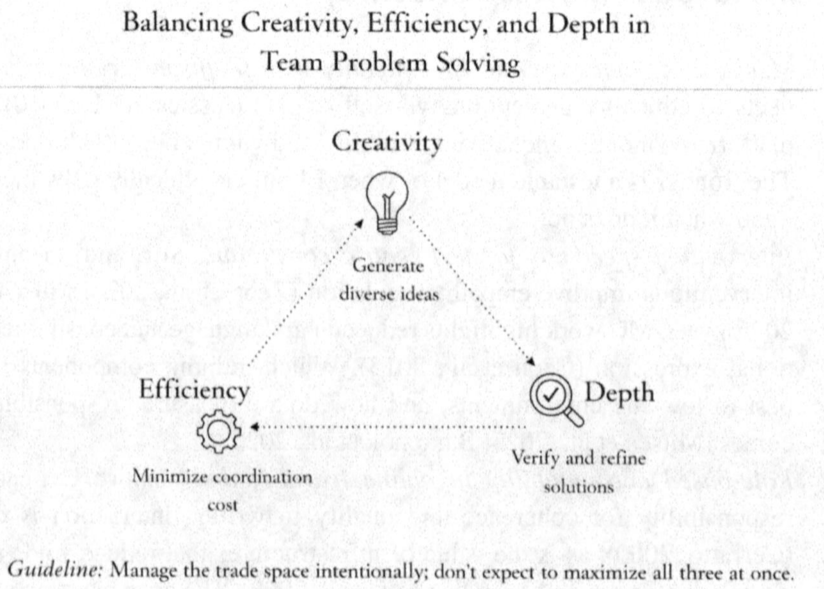

4.1. Why this triad matters (and why it is never "for free")

Most organizations already *feel* the promise of collective intelligence: put enough capable people (and tools) in the same room and solutions seem to appear faster. Yet the research is clear that "faster" is only one possible benefit - and sometimes not a benefit at all. Cooperation can accelerate solution finding, but it may also change *what kind* of solution you reach, and at what cost (Reia et al., 2019). Classic experimental work reminds us that communication conditions shape mutual problem-solving behavior because communication makes intentions visible and actions more predictable - helping groups form workable interaction structures (Hemphill & McConville, 1962). Still, the relationship between group communication and performance is neither automatic nor linear; it has a contested history precisely because "more talk" can mean "more confusion" (Hirokawa, 2008).

Recent findings sharpen the warning: in complex tasks, the cost of coordination can exceed the benefit of collaboration - meaning the team's collective horsepower is lost to alignment overhead, duplicated effort, and decision latency (Straub et al.,

2020). This is the practical reason the triad matters: *creativity*, *efficiency*, and *depth* move together, but not always in the same direction.

A simple way to bring this down to earth is to look at a familiar organizational scene: "an avalanche of meetings where much is said and little is decided" (93 Voices, 2025). The issue here is not a lack of interaction, but an imbalance in the triad - often high "communication volume," low efficiency, and fragile depth.

Working definition of the triad for this chapter

- *Creativity:* the variety and originality of candidate solutions generated and retained long enough to be combined and improved (Pétervári et al., 2016; Harvey & Kou, 2013; Smaldino et al., 2022).
- *Efficiency:* time/effort to reach a decision or implementable option *net of co-ordination cost* (Hemphill & McConville, 1962; Straub et al., 2020).
- *Depth:* the robustness of understanding and evaluation - especially visible through verification loops, systematic processing, and competent selection/refinement of ideas (Baldwin & Garvey, 1973; Chaiken, 1980; Griffin et al., 2002; Rietzschel et al., 2019).

4.2. Creativity in collective problem solving: how novelty is built (and how it collapses)

4.2.1. Divergence and convergence - and the thresholds teams forget to design for

Creativity research commonly distinguishes *divergent thinking* (expanding options) from *convergent thinking* (selecting and improving) (Pétervári et al., 2016). In educational research, creative problem-solving abilities can show threshold effects: divergent thinking, convergent thinking, motivation, environment, and knowledge/skills may need to pass a minimum level before creativity actually shows up in performance (Lin, 2017). In teams, this matters because a group can accidentally push for convergence before those thresholds are met.

A mini-case that many leaders recognize: a team opens a "brainstorm" with a crowded agenda and a tight deadline. People self-censor, because they sense the room is already searching for "the answer." Creativity stalls, not due to lack of talent, but because the process never created a safe divergent phase.

A useful contrast comes from 93 Voices (2025): the collaborative-transformational leader "creates spaces where great things happen naturally," and makes room for co-creation rather than imposing conclusions. In practical terms, that "space" is often a deliberately protected divergent window.

4.2.2. Diversity as a dynamic resource: keeping multiple options alive long enough

Creativity in collective problem solving is not only idea generation; it includes the collective construction of the problem itself, and diversity supports divergent cognitive processes (Harvey & Kou, 2013). A more recent systems view makes the point sharper: mechanisms that improve group solutions often work by increasing *transient diversity* of solutions during consensus-building - diversity as a moving distribution of candidate approaches, not a static attribute (Smaldino et al., 2022).

In real organizations, the fragility point is familiar: the first plausible idea becomes the "default," and the group converges early because it feels efficient. That is *efficiency purchasing depth and creativity with the same currency: premature certainty.*

Cross-functional work offers a practical antidote: teams that transcend knowledge differences do it by creating intermediate scaffolds, staying flexible, and taking personal responsibility for translating individual knowledge into collective knowledge - without triggering interpersonal conflict (Majchrzak et al., 2012). This is where co-creation becomes more than a slogan: it is the mechanism that holds diversity in place long enough for novelty to emerge.

4.3. Efficiency in collective problem solving: communication helps - until it becomes the work

4.3.1. Communication as an efficiency enabler (when it produces structure)

Hemphill & McConville (1962) showed that communication availability affects mutual problem-solving behavior and is theorized to support predictable interaction structures. The practical translation is straightforward: when a team can reliably infer "who is doing what next," efficiency rises - not because people speak more, but because interaction becomes more predictable and less wasteful (Hemphill & McConville, 1962; Hirokawa, 2008).

In 93 Voices (2025), a useful phrase captures what efficient interaction often requires: "communication curation policies," with "clear maps of channels, purposes, and responsibilities." When teams lack this map, they spend effort searching for context, duplicating decisions, or reopening resolved topics.

4.3.2. When collaboration reduces efficiency: coordination cost dominates

Straub et al. (2020) provide the uncomfortable but liberating message: collaboration is not inherently efficient; coordination cost can dominate in complex tasks. This is often visible in modern "always-on" communication: speed increases, but clarity and decision closure decrease.

93 Voices (2025) gives the lived version of that trade-off: "the acceleration of digital communication has also brought noise, distraction, and superficiality... Speed has nullified the care of presence or even content." Efficiency becomes a mirage - many messages, little progress.

4.3.3. The efficiency pattern of effective teams: coordinated, balanced, and phase-aware

Recent evidence shows that more effective teams coordinate throughout problem solving, maintain balanced communication patterns, and alternate dynamically between exploration and exploitation; less effective teams isolate, participate unequally, and fail to exploit information well (Szabó et al., 2024). This aligns neatly with the older experimental point that communication matters because it structures interaction (Hemphill & McConville, 1962) and with dialogic accounts of collective creativity that treat socio-communicative competence as part of the mechanism (Tan et al., 2022).

A pragmatic marker leaders can actually use: if a team is "busy" but repeatedly revisits the same unresolved questions, coordination is happening *without* the structure that converts talk into forward motion.

4.4. Depth in collective problem solving: verification, processing, and the discipline of evaluation

4.4.1. Depth as verification loops (the missing component in many "collaborations")

Baldwin & Garvey (1973) operationalize accurate problem-solving communication through three components: perspective orientation, essential information, and *verification of solutions*. Many teams do the first two in some form; depth collapses when verification is absent - when the group agrees but does not *check*.

93 Voices (2025) frames a cultural version of the same issue: "communicating more was not synonymous with communicating better," and healthier organizations

rebuilt meaning through "intentionality, empathy, structure, and time." Depth is often what "time" is buying: the room for checking, not just reacting.

4.4.2. Depth as systematic - not merely heuristic - processing

The heuristic–systematic tradition shows why teams can converge on shallow agreement. Under heuristic processing, source cues and social signals can drive acceptance without deep engagement with the message content (Chaiken, 1980). Risk communication research links depth of processing to outcomes across contexts (Griffin et al., 2002), and information processing predicts significant variance in perception within models (Trumbo, 2002). The organizational implication is blunt: a charismatic senior voice, a "reasonable sounding" plan, or urgency pressure can create consensus that looks like alignment but is actually heuristic closure.

4.4.3. Depth as competent evaluation of creative ideas (where teams reliably fail)

Group creativity research emphasizes that creativity is not only producing ideas; groups must recognize, value, select, and refine them - and evaluation and selection show persistent weaknesses (Rietzschel et al., 2019). A known vulnerability is systematic error in evaluating highly original ideas, including underestimating originality (Licuanan et al., 2007). Process design can help: evidence suggests that sequencing matters - balancing originality and feasibility through iterative refinement can improve outcomes (Baruah et al., 2021).

A concrete use case: in a product committee, the most original option often feels "risky," so it is dismissed early. The team then optimizes a safer idea - efficiently - only to discover later it does not differentiate. That is a depth failure (evaluation) disguised as efficiency.

4.5. Balancing the trade space: a process model leaders can implement without pretending there is a perfect solution

The literature converges on a practical synthesis: strong collectives do not "maximize collaboration." They *sequence and govern* it.

Teams rarely sit in the center by accident; they move across the triangle by choices about phases (explore vs decide), roles (who evaluates), and communication design (how verification is done). The "skill" is not perfection - it is *intentional movement*.

Two principles help translate the research into operational practice:

1. Alternate exploration and exploitation deliberately.

Effective teams dynamically alternate exploration and exploitation (Szabó et al., 2024). Creativity improves when teams structure cycles that separate generation from feasibility-driven refinement (Baruah et al., 2021). The leadership task is to name the phase and protect it.

2. Maintain transient diversity early; converge with scaffolds and responsibility.

Transient diversity supports creativity (Smaldino et al., 2022), but convergence requires practices that translate knowledge across boundaries (Majchrzak et al., 2012). This is where facilitation competence becomes a control lever (McFadzean, 2002), particularly when coordination costs threaten efficiency (Straub et al., 2020).

A small but telling practice from 93 Voices (2025) matches this logic: "Internal Listening Councils… where leaders listen, take notes, and do not respond immediately," explicitly "to give time back to collective processing." That "no immediate response" rule is a depth intervention that protects exploration and prevents premature convergence.

4.6. Practical implications (and honest dilemmas) for leaders and teams

The chapter's argument is not that teams should always slow down, or always be creative, or always over-verify. The argument is that *collective problem solving is an optimization problem* with unavoidable trade-offs - and the trade-offs should be made consciously.

Practical implications (actionable, not aspirational):

- *Design work in phases, not in meetings.* Use a clear split between (a) problem construction + divergent options and (b) evaluation + decision + verification (Harvey & Kou, 2013; Baruah et al., 2021; Baldwin & Garvey, 1973).
- *Treat verification as a required output.* Don't end with "alignment"; end with "what would make us change our mind?" and "how will we check?" (Baldwin & Garvey, 1973; Griffin et al., 2002).
- *Manage coordination cost explicitly.* In complex tasks, decide where collaboration is essential and where expertise-driven execution is faster (Straub et al., 2020).
- *Use silence strategically.* Not as avoidance, but as a deliberate tool to slow heuristic closure - "silence is rhythm," and rhythm can be worth more than content (93 Voices, 2025).

Dilemmas worth stating plainly (because there is no perfect solution):

- *Speed vs depth:* urgency can be real, but speed can also erase listening and care, producing fragile decisions (93 Voices, 2025).
- *Creativity vs efficiency:* preserving diversity improves novelty, but it can feel slow and politically uncomfortable (Smaldino et al., 2022; Straub et al., 2020).
- *Consensus vs truth:* agreement can be heuristic; depth requires systematic evaluation and sometimes visible disagreement (Chaiken, 1980; Rietzschel et al., 2019).

4.7. Frontier questions emerging from this state of the art

- What lightweight "verification rituals" can teams adopt that increase depth without creating bureaucracy (Baldwin & Garvey, 1973; Griffin et al., 2002)?
- How can virtual and hybrid teams improve not only ideation, but also problem construction and high-quality evaluation - still known weak points in virtual creativity research (Reiter-Palmon et al., 2021; Rietzschel et al., 2019)?
- Which facilitation competencies most reliably reduce coordination cost while preserving transient diversity (McFadzean, 2002; Smaldino et al., 2022; Straub et al., 2020)?

5. TRUST, ETHICS, AND THE LIMITS OF DELEGATED JUDGMENT

Figure 5. Ethical limits of delegated judgment

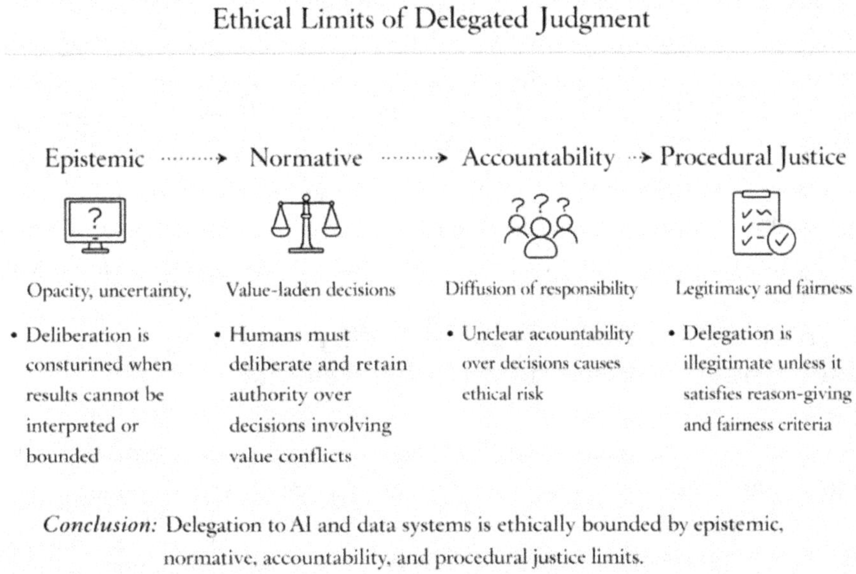

5.1. Delegated judgment as a socio-technical and ethical problem

"Delegated judgment" can be understood as the *transfer (partial or full) of evaluative and decision-making authority* from human professionals and institutions to mediated systems - such as AI models, data infrastructures, governance committees, or digital public services - under constraints of scale, complexity, and time. In contemporary settings, this delegation is increasingly mediated by AI systems that "increasingly mediate our social, cultural, economic, and political interactions," raising the need to understand and control machine behavior to minimize harms Jobin et al., 2019). At the same time, scholarship mapping AI ethics guidance highlights that many guidelines emphasize *trust* as an objective, while also warning that trust can reduce scrutiny and undermine societal obligations of AI producers - explicitly challenging any simple "more trust is always better" stance Jobin et al., 2019). Accordingly, the state of the art treats delegated judgment as ethically nontrivial because (i) it changes *who has epistemic authority*, (ii) it changes *how account-*

ability is distributed, and (iii) it can create *moral hazard* when trust substitutes for verification Jobin et al., 2019).

A parallel body of ethics research in data-intensive science underscores that ethical governance must adapt to distributed, large-scale data practices, advocating participative and reflexive management of data practices and highlighting that different actors' perspectives are partial and require continual ethical examination Leonelli, 2016). Big-data behavioral research similarly reports active efforts to design ethical frameworks that preserve foundational research ethics while accommodating changes introduced by big-data methods (Favaretto et al., 2020; . These developments jointly frame delegated judgment as a general problem spanning AI decision support, data science, and institutional governance: trust must be made *warranted* through ethical and procedural safeguards rather than assumed as an inherent property of the delegated system (Favaretto et al., 2020;, Jobin et al., 2019), Leonelli, 2016).

5.2. Trust Versus Trustworthiness: Why "Building Trust" is not Equivalent to Justified Reliance

A key state-of-the-art distinction is between *trust* (a relational attitude or willingness to rely) and *trustworthiness* (properties and practices that justify reliance). Expert synthesis on medical AI emphasizes that trust depends on providing meaningful, user-oriented information, balancing knowledge with acceptable uncertainty, and confidence that the tool performs as expected; critically, this work conceptualizes trustworthiness not as a static feature but as a *relational process* involving humans, expertise, and context (Goisauf et al., 2025; . Empirical work with Swedish breast radiologists similarly argues that further discussion is needed about what the desired goals for trust in AI should be and how trust relates to clinicians' critical evaluation of AI-made claims in decision support - implying that trust can be misaligned with professional scrutiny (Högberg et al., 2024). These findings align with the broader landscape review of AI ethics guidelines, which documents both the prominence of "trust" rhetoric and the countervailing concern that fostering trust may diminish scrutiny Jobin et al., 2019), thereby identifying a central tension: *delegated judgment requires calibrated reliance, not indiscriminate trust* Jobin et al., 2019), (Goisauf et al., 2025;, Högberg et al., 2024).

In high-stakes domains, this distinction becomes normative: work on black-box medical algorithms argues that reliable performance indicators can yield justified knowledge, but such knowledge is *necessary yet insufficient* for normatively justifying clinical action; deliberation is still required to determine what action is desirable Durán & Jongsma, 2021). Systematic review evidence on governing AI in radiology reinforces this accountability demand by stressing clinicians' need to provide transparent justifications for AI-driven diagnoses when decisions have life-altering consequences (Aldhafeeri, 2025; . Thus, the state of the art converges on a constraint: *even if an AI system is "accurate," delegation is ethically limited unless human professionals can deliberate, justify, and remain accountable for action* Durán & Jongsma, 2021), (Aldhafeeri, 2025).

5.3. Ethical Foundations Relevant to Delegated Judgment: Principles and Proceduralization

Across domains, ethics frameworks commonly converge on principled requirements - often framed as fairness/justice, beneficence, non-maleficence, respect for autonomy, transparency, and accountability - while also emphasizing that these must be operationalized procedurally. A comparative synthesis of ethics codes on AI and big data explicitly combines the four principles of biomedical ethics with procedural principles including control, transparency, and accountability (Loi et al., 2020; . Reviews of AI and robotics in healthcare similarly foreground transparency, explainability, and clear responsibility frameworks spanning manufacturers, institutions, and professionals, and emphasize the role of regularly updated and accessible ethical guidelines for decision-making Elendu et al., 2023; . Responsible-AI design practice work (in an IEEE venue) situates the rise of ethical standards initiatives (e.g., IEEE P7000 projects) within public concern about unintended consequences and notes the historical lack of anticipatory ethical processes within professional practice - framing ethical design as a response to governance gaps in delegation (Peters et al., 2020).

In data research regulation, scholarship argues that research-ethics approaches focused primarily on consent can be unhelpful for population-level big-data research, motivating a shift toward public-health ethics emphasizing public benefit, proportionality, and accountability Ballantyne, 2019; . Data access governance work likewise emphasizes that data sharing should be governed by public-health ethics principles, highlighting public benefit, proportionality, and accountability as governance ideals Cheah & Piasecki, 2020; . Collectively, these sources indicate that the state of the art increasingly treats delegated judgment not only as compliance with abstract principles, but as *procedural ethics*: control, transparency, accountability, and participatory governance mechanisms that render delegation legitimate in context (Loi et al., 2020;, Ballantyne, 2019;, Cheah & Piasecki, 2020;, Peters et al., 2020;, Elendu et al., 2023; .

5.4. The Limits of Delegated Judgment: Three Coupled Boundaries

5.4.1. Epistemic Limits: Opacity, Uncertainty, and Error Modes

A primary boundary arises from *epistemic opacity* and uncertainty. The "black box algorithms" argument in medical AI explicitly maintains that even where indicators are reliable, normative justification requires deliberation, showing that epistemic warrant does not automatically yield action guidance Durán & Jongsma, 2021). In radiology governance, the demand for transparent justification is tied to accountability in high-stakes diagnosis, implying that opacity can undermine clinicians' capacity to justify decisions (Aldhafeeri, 2025). In human–AI decision-making research on public health service optimization, trust and control are studied via a cybernetic approach to how clinicians adjust trust toward AI clinical decision support, explicitly linking delegation to barriers involving dependency and trust calibration Yu et al., 2025). In marketing-oriented analysis of generative AI hallucinations, risk management strategies are recommended that include technical detection/correction, human oversight, and adherence to ethical/regulatory frameworks - again treating AI outputs as potentially unreliable and requiring governance to prevent erroneous delegated judgments (YAPRAK, 2024).

These contributions converge on an epistemic limit: *delegation is constrained when system outputs cannot be adequately interpreted, verified, or bounded*, requiring compensatory mechanisms such as explainability, oversight, and uncertainty communication Durán & Jongsma, 2021), (Aldhafeeri, 2025;, YAPRAK, 2024;, Yu et al., 2025).

5.4.2. Normative limits: value-laden decisions cannot be fully "outsourced"

A second boundary is normative: many consequential decisions embed value judgments (e.g., trade-offs among harms/benefits, fairness considerations). In medical AI, the black-box critique asserts that deliberation is needed even with trustworthy results to determine desirable action, explicitly separating epistemic reliability from normative legitimacy Durán & Jongsma, 2021). Ethical governance reviews in radiology similarly emphasize clinicians' obligation to justify AI-driven diagnoses, a requirement grounded in the moral weight of outcomes (Aldhafeeri, 2025; . In healthcare technology ethics more broadly, responsibility frameworks spanning multiple stakeholders are presented as essential to maintain trust and accountability, implying that value-laden responsibility cannot be reduced to technical system performance Elendu et al., 2023; . Public perceptions research on AI governance indicates that beliefs about who bears governance responsibility (government, corporations, individuals) relate differently to ethical concerns and trust - demonstrating that responsibility attribution is itself a normative and political question that affects legitimacy David et al., 2024; . Together, these sources position delegated judgment as normatively bounded: *systems may support decisions, but humans and institutions must retain deliberative authority over value conflicts and justifications* Durán & Jongsma, 2021), (Aldhafeeri, 2025; David et al., 2024, Elendu et al., 2023).

5.4.3. Accountability limits: diffusion of responsibility and "who is responsible?" problems

A third boundary concerns accountability and moral responsibility under delegation. Ethics scholarship on distributed data science explicitly calls for participative, reflexive management and continual examination of ethical implications across actors, highlighting that distributed knowledge production systems involve many partial perspectives - creating conditions under which responsibility can be diffused Leonelli, 2016). Research on accountability in technology-induced medical errors emphasizes the need to evaluate roles of healthcare providers, developers, and hospital systems, advocating collective approaches to maintain patient safety and trust, which directly addresses accountability diffusion under delegation (Roy & Jomeh, 2025). In social-care governance, personalization reforms devolve responsibility and accountability to customers, demonstrating that governance designs can shift accountability burdens to actors who may lack capacity, thereby creating new ethical risks Bracci, 2014; . Moral responsibility theory further stresses that practices of being held responsible or exempted shape expectations and identities, and that purely instrumental accounts of responsibility assignment miss multiple social functions - indicating why accountability design is central to legitimate delegation Walker, 2008). These sources together define an accountability limit: *delegation becomes ethically problematic when responsibility is unclear, shifted to the least empowered party, or cannot be meaningfully discharged through justification and control* (Roy & Jomeh, 2025; Bracci, 2014; Walker, 2008; Leonelli, 2016).

5.5. Institutional and organizational mechanisms for warranted trust under delegation

5.5.1. Ethics institutionalization and accountability as trust infrastructure

Organizational research demonstrates that explicit ethics institutionalization and management accountability influence newcomer trust in managers and organizations, implying that trust can be engineered through institutionalized ethics rather than interpersonal confidence alone (Tseng & Chung, 2017). In corporate governance and resilience research, solid governance practices are described as ensuring transparency, ethics, and responsibility - fundamental elements for gaining stakeholders' trust and enabling informed decision-making in crises (Irigaray & Stocker, 2024). ICT-driven "dynamic transparency" scholarship argues that two-way information exchange with stakeholders can foster openness, accountability, and more transparent operations, benefiting corporations and constituents (Vaccaro & Madsen, 2009). A complementary regulatory-design perspective argues for substantive rather than technical compliance, advocating enhanced accountability and warranted commitment to ethical standards through interlocking legal, regulatory, managerial, ethical, and social themes O'Brien, 2019). Synthesized, these references support a state-of-the-art claim: *where judgment is delegated to systems, trust must be scaffolded by explicit ethics institutionalization, governance transparency, and enforceable accountability mechanisms* (Tseng & Chung, 2017; Irigaray & Stocker, 2024; Vaccaro & Madsen, 2009; O'Brien, 2019).

5.5.2. Accountability-for-reasonableness as a procedural limit on delegated priority setting

In public health systems, accountability is formalized through the "Accountability for Reasonableness" (AFR) framework, which provides guidance for legitimate and fair priority setting by requiring decision-makers to consider relevant values and satisfy procedural conditions (including relevance) (Byskov et al., 2009). Gap analysis applying AFR in Kenya situates this approach within efforts to strengthen trust in health systems via accountability-focused initiatives Bukachi et al., 2013). This procedural framing is directly relevant to delegated judgment because it defines *how* decisions should be justified and contested, regardless of whether analytic tools or models are used. In short, AFR exemplifies a state-of-the-art governance pattern: *delegation is bounded by procedural justice requirements that preserve legitimacy through reason-giving and accountability* (Byskov et al., 2009; Bukachi et al., 2013).

5.6. Delegated judgment in data-intensive research: trust, transparency, and fair data use

5.6.1. Big data research ethics: "first do no harm" and framework adaptation

Behavioral big-data research ethics explicitly explores researchers' "first do no harm" obligations and notes that groups are striving to design ethical frameworks that remain faithful to foundational research ethics while accommodating big-data changes (Favaretto et al., 2020). Ethics in biochemical literacy emphasizes that ethics promote truth and minimize error by prohibiting fabrication, falsification, or misrepresentation of data - linking ethical conduct to epistemic reliability and trustworthiness Evans et al., 2020). Work on research integrity and ethics publication trends similarly frames ethics and integrity as the basis for good research practice and a shared responsibility among stakeholders Soehartono et al., 2022). These sources jointly imply that delegation to data-intensive pipelines (automated scraping, classification, inference) is ethically bounded by obligations to prevent harm and preserve truthfulness through integrity practices and adapted governance (Favaretto et al., 2020).

5.6.2. FAIR to "fair use": methodological fairness and participative responsibility

Health-related social media research argues for moving from FAIR data principles toward fair data use by addressing methodological data fairness, situating FAIR as a global reference point complemented by additional considerations Leonelli et al., 2021). Data ethics in distributed data science likewise calls for participative, reflexive management and regular examination of ethical implications, highlighting distributed skills and partial perspectives Leonelli, 2016). These converge on a key constraint for delegated judgment: *even when data infrastructures optimize access and reuse (FAIR), ethical legitimacy requires fairness in methods and governance, not only technical interoperability* Leonelli et al., 2021), Leonelli, 2016).

5.6.3. Learning analytics: privacy, transparency, and accountability as limits on delegated educational judgment

Learning analytics ethics principles explicitly treat privacy and ethical issues as interconnected with trust, accountability, and transparency, offering pragmatic principles for narrowing and guiding implementation Pardo & Siemens, 2014; . A complementary privacy and data protection framework for a learning analytics toolbox stresses the need to balance learning analytics with privacy and to address ethical and data protection issues using available guidelines and principles (Steiner et al., 2016). Together, these sources establish that in educational contexts, delegating judgment to analytics systems is limited by requirements for privacy, transparency, and accountability - because analytics-driven inferences can affect learners' opportunities and outcomes (Pardo & Siemens, 2014; Steiner et al., 2016).

5.7. Public-sector delegation: e-government trust and ethics of public communication

In e-government, trust is empirically modeled as a driver of government performance, and concerns about public sector ethics and accountability are highlighted where trust is declining (Abdulkareem & Ramli, 2021). Government public communication ethics in social media for COVID-19 emphasizes transparency, accountability, and public engagement as ethical needs in government communication (Khaidir et al., 2022). These sources jointly indicate that when public services delegate judgment to digital systems and social platforms (e.g., eligibility determinations, information dissemination), public trust depends on ethical public communication and accountable governance - not solely on system functionality (Abdulkareem & Ramli, 2021; Khaidir et al., 2022).

5.8. Practical synthesis: when delegation is ethically permissible, and when it is not (within the evidence)

Across the reviewed references, the state of the art supports the following evidence-grounded synthesis about the *limits of delegated judgment*:

1. **Delegation is bounded by justificatory capacity**: professionals must be able to provide transparent justification for AI-supported decisions in high-stakes settings, and reliable outputs alone do not settle what ought to be done without deliberation (Aldhafeeri, 2025; Durán & Jongsma, 2021).
2. **Delegation requires calibrated trust anchored in relational trustworthiness**: trust in medical AI depends on meaningful user-oriented information and acceptable uncertainty, and should not displace critical evaluation; guideline landscapes also warn that trust-building can undermine scrutiny (Goisauf et al., 2025; Högberg et al., 2024; Jobin et al., 2019).
3. **Delegation is constrained by accountability assignment**: ethical governance must clarify responsibility across developers, institutions, and practitioners to prevent diffusion of accountability and to sustain trust (Roy & Jomeh, 2025; Elendu et al., 2023; Leonelli, 2016).

4. **Delegation must be procedurally legitimate** in priority setting and public decision-making, with accountability mechanisms (e.g., AFR) ensuring relevance, reason-giving, and fairness (Byskov et al., 2009; Bukachi et al., 2013).
5. **Delegation in data-driven research and education is limited by privacy, fairness, and transparency** requirements, demanding adapted ethical frameworks for big data and analytics (Favaretto et al., 2020; Pardo & Siemens, 2014; Steiner et al., 2016; Leonelli et al., 2021).

6. A HUMAN-CENTERED FRAMEWORK FOR COMMUNICATIONAL PROBLEM-SOLVING

Figure 6. A human-centered, communicative problem-solving

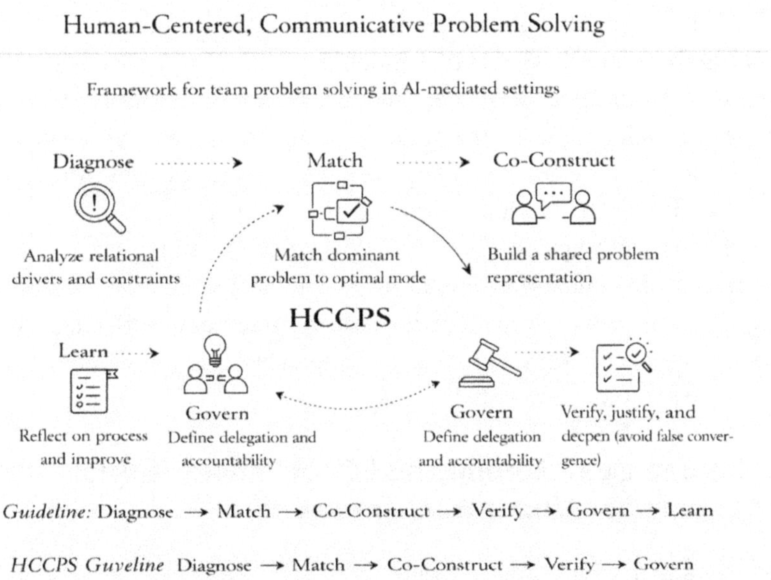

6.1. Conceptual premise: problem solving is enacted through communicative action - now often co-produced with AI

This chapter starts from a grounded proposition: people do not "solve problems and then communicate about them." In most organizational settings, the problem is *defined*, *negotiated*, *reframed*, and *resolved* through communicative action. That view is explicit in the situational theory of problem solving, where "communicative action in problem solving" is the phenomenon to be explained through conditions such as problem recognition, constraint recognition, involvement recognition, and referent criteria (Kim & Grunig, 2011). It also aligns with classic experimental evidence showing that communication constraints shape mutual problem-solving behavior because communication makes intentions visible and future actions more predictable, enabling more effective interaction structures (Hemphill & McConville, 1962). At the micro level, accuracy in problem-solving communication depends on identifiable components - perspective orientation, essential-information transmission, and verification - rather than on vague notions of "good communication" (Baldwin & Garvey, 1973).

The "human-centered" requirement becomes sharper under two pressures that most teams now experience daily. First, computer-mediated communication often reduces paralanguage and emotional cues, increasing the risk of misinterpretation (Caon et al., 2013), while e-learning research shows that mediated environments *can* support rich relational communication and effective problem solving - but only when interaction processes and channel use are deliberately designed rather than left to habit (Mendes et al., 2008). Second, AI now co-produces text, options, and summaries, which changes the ecology of attention and judgment. As *93 Voices (2025)* notes, we have never exchanged so many messages, yet misunderstanding has become easier because digital communication is a "patchwork" of formats and codes.

A practical consequence follows: in AI-mediated settings, communicative action is no longer only human-to-human. It is increasingly human–AI–human, and this introduces new risks of over-reliance, shallow agreement, and weakened verification - exactly the concern raised in AI ethics guidance landscapes where "trust" rhetoric can reduce scrutiny (Jobin et al., 2019).

6.2. Design Goal: Optimizing Effectiveness, Ethics, and Legitimacy Under Real Trade-Offs

HCCPS is designed to produce solutions that are simultaneously:

- **Effective**: they work under constraints and do not collapse under coordination overhead (Hemphill & McConville, 1962; Hirokawa, 2008).
- **Ethically defensible**: they do not outsource moral responsibility to tools, metrics, or institutional shortcuts (Jobin et al., 2019; Durán & Jongsma, 2021).
- **Legitimate**: they can be justified to affected stakeholders through transparent reasons, not only internal agreement (Aldhafeeri, 2025).

This triad matters because teams face unavoidable trade-offs. Collaboration can improve outcomes, but "more interaction" is not automatically better; coordination costs can exceed benefits in complex tasks (Straub et al., 2020). In other words, a framework for communicational problem solving must help teams decide *when* to deepen deliberation and *when* to streamline without becoming reckless. *93 Voices (2025)* captures this tension in simple terms: the message is fast, but it can turn ambiguous and emotionally loaded when the channel strips context and tone.

6.3. Framework architecture (HCCPS): Diagnose → Match → Co-Construct → Verify → Govern → Learn

HCCPS is built as a process framework: simple enough to survive real workloads, yet structured enough to be taught, repeated, and audited. Its distinctive move is not offering "communication advice" in the abstract. It treats communication as a governable cycle: choices about channel, protocol, and delegation are tied to a prior diagnosis; verification is designed as an explicit step rather than an afterthought; and AI-mediated delegation is treated as a bounded practice with accountability, not a shortcut.

That architecture matters because contemporary work routinely fails in a predictable way: teams exchange a lot of messages, experience accelerating pace, and still lose meaning—misunderstandings multiply precisely because digital formats strip cues and invite fast interpretation. Under those conditions, "more communication" can become more noise. HCCPS assumes that the way out is not volume, but structure: a loop that repeatedly restores intention, shared framing, and disciplined checking.

6.3.1. Stage 1 - Diagnose the Communicational Problem State (not only the Task State)

Objective: Identify what is preventing progress: ambiguity, misalignment, overload, constraints, low involvement, missing standards, or fragile trust.

The key discipline here is separating task state from communicational state. A task can be well-defined on paper and still stall because people are not recognizing the same problem, do not feel involved, face constraints that make action impractical, or lack shared criteria for what "good" looks like. HCCPS borrows its diagnostic leverage from Kim & Grunig (2011), focusing on four situational conditions that shape communicative action: problem recognition, constraint recognition, involvement recognition, and referent criteria.

It also treats constraints as potentially causal rather than incidental. Classic experimental work showed that altering communication restraints can change how groups coordinate and solve, because communication makes intentions visible and future actions more predictable. In other words, constraints do not merely "make communication harder"; they can reshape the interaction structure itself.

A compact diagnostic set that works in practice:

- **Problem recognition:** Do we agree there is a problem worth acting on now? (Kim & Grunig, 2011)
- **Constraint recognition:** What blocks communicative action - time, access, permissions, tool limits, privacy, cognitive load? (Kim & Grunig, 2011; Hemphill & McConville, 1962)
- **Involvement recognition:** Who is affected, and who needs to commit? (Kim & Grunig, 2011)
- **Referent criteria:** What standards will we use to accept a solution and verify it? (Kim & Grunig, 2011; Baldwin & Garvey, 1973)

Each item prevents a different failure mode:

- Without *problem recognition*, communication becomes polite motion: messages circulate, but no one is authorized—psychologically or politically—to act.
- Without *constraint recognition*, teams moralize ("people are not responsive") instead of redesigning the environment (permissions, tool access, time windows, privacy-safe artifacts).
- Without *involvement recognition*, decisions are made by whoever is present, and later undone by those who were absent but affected.
- Without *referent criteria*, discussion becomes an argument about preferences; verification becomes impossible because there is no agreed standard.

In digital communication, intent can be distorted by small textual codes—punctuation, abbreviations, emoji, response timing. The framework therefore adds a "relational risk" check: is the channel and tone likely to damage trust or trigger misinterpretation? 93 Voices (2025) highlights how easily these cues distort intent in mediated settings.

Example:

A product team thinks the delay is "engineering being slow." Diagnosis shows a different picture: the dominant constraint is *permissions* (access to a dataset), involvement is incomplete (security must sign off), and referent criteria are missing (no agreed definition of "acceptable risk"). The "solution" is not motivational pressure; it is redesigning who is involved, what standard is used, and which artifacts secure access.

6.3.2. Stage 2 - Match Problem Types to Modes and Interaction Structures

Objective: Choose channels, protocols, and roles that reduce the dominant constraint and support accuracy components.

This stage refuses a common organizational habit: selecting modes by comfort, hierarchy, or tradition ("we always do this by email"). Instead, matching is evidence-based. Channels and interaction structures should be judged by how well they support the three components of accurate problem-solving communication—perspective orientation, essential information transmission, and verification—while recognizing that coordination overhead can undermine efficiency.

The subtlety is the trade-off: teams need enough structure to prevent misunderstandings, but not so much structure that coordination becomes the work. Straub et al. (2020) is relevant precisely because it treats coordination cost as a real performance constraint, not a moral weakness.

Matching is a Design Decision, not a Preference

A useful way to think about matching is to ask: *Which accuracy component is currently weakest?*

- If *perspective orientation* is failing, you need interaction that supports clarification and reflection.
- If *essential information* is failing, you need formats that force relevance, completeness, and mutual visibility of the same facts.
- If *verification* is failing, you need traceable outputs: rationales, sources, uncertainty bounds, and reviewable artifacts.

Three Quick Match Examples:

- **Coordination breakdown (unclear next steps):** use modes that make commitments explicit and visible (shared action lists, short synchronous alignment), because predictability is a key mechanism by which communication improves group problem solving (Hemphill & McConville, 1962).
- **Perspective divergence (we're not solving the same problem):** use modes that allow back-and-forth clarification and "reflecting" what you understood, directly supporting perspective orientation (Baldwin & Garvey, 1973).
- **High verification stakes (cost of being wrong):** use modes that leave a trace (rationales, sources, uncertainty bounds) and protect scrutiny, because trust rhetoric can otherwise displace verification (Jobin et al., 2019; Durán & Jongsma, 2021).

This is the place where *93 Voices (2025)* offers a practical anchor: teams carry a growing responsibility to choose *what format, with whom, and when* - instead of defaulting to habit.

Example

A leadership team is debating a procurement decision. Chat is fast, but perspective divergence is obvious: each person is solving a different "problem" (cost, legality, reputation, delivery risk). The match is a short synchronous session to align the problem frame, followed by an asynchronous document that records options, rationales, and verification steps for scrutiny.

6.3.3. Stage 3 - Co-Construct Shared Problem Representations

Objective: Build a shared representation of the problem that is actionable, while preserving enough diversity to explore alternatives.

This stage targets a familiar failure mode: teams jump from talking to doing without agreeing what the problem is. When that happens, productivity can be high and progress still illusory—people execute fast, but in incompatible directions. Co-construction means making assumptions, constraints, success criteria, and options explicit so the team is solving the same problem in the same frame.

Hirokawa (2008) is relevant here because it treats group performance as a function of communication processes, not merely of talent or effort. If the shared representation is weak, even highly competent individuals will coordinate poorly, revisit the same disputes, and mistake volume for alignment.

What "Shared Representation" Looks Like in Practice

A representation is not a long report. It is a working object that allows action without erasing nuance. In most organizational settings, it is enough to make four elements explicit:

1. *Assumptions* we are currently making (and which ones are uncertain).
2. *Constraints* we must respect (time, compliance, dependencies, resource limits).
3. *Success criteria* that define "acceptable" (the referent criteria made operational).
4. *Options* that are genuinely different (not variants of the same default).

The phrase "preserving enough diversity" matters. Co-construction is not forced consensus; it is disciplined framing. Diversity is preserved by recording alternatives that remain plausible, and by keeping uncertainty visible rather than suppressing it.

In AI-mediated settings, co-construction must explicitly separate:

- *AI contributions* (drafts, options, summaries), from
- *human acceptance* (what we endorse, with reasons and boundaries).

This protects against what *93 Voices (2025)* calls "noise" overtaking meaning - communication becomes abundant but shallow unless the group creates shared objects that carry context.

Example:

An AI produces a crisp summary of stakeholder feedback. The team adopts it, then later discovers it collapsed minority concerns into a single sentence. Co-construction prevents this by forcing a human acceptance step: what do we endorse, what do we reject, and what remains ambiguous?

6.3.4. Stage 4 - Verify, Justify, and Deepen (Avoid False Convergence)

Objective: Ensure accuracy and legitimacy by designing verification loops.

Verification is not optional; it is one of the three core components of accurate problem-solving communication. Yet organizations often treat verification as implicit: someone will "catch it later," or authority will substitute for checking. In AI-assisted decisions, that becomes a moral and professional risk. Trustworthy performance does not remove the need to deliberate about what should be done, and in high-stakes contexts professionals must be able to justify AI-supported outcomes transparently.

The deeper danger is *false convergence:* the group appears aligned because the language is smooth, the summary is elegant, or the senior person agrees. But alignment is performative rather than epistemic. HCCPS treats verification as the stage that reintroduces friction on purpose—enough to detect error, ambiguity, and unjustified leaps.

A lightweight "verification turn" set that teams can adopt:

- "What would change our mind?"
- "What is uncertain here, and what uncertainty is acceptable?"
- "How will we detect early if we are wrong?"

This also extends to meaning verification in mediated channels, where tone and intent can be misread. *93 Voices (2025)* explicitly notes that even small textual markers can signal unintended coldness or aggression.

6.3.5. Stage 5 - Govern Delegated Judgment (Calibrated Trust, Explicit Accountability)

Objective: Define what may be delegated to AI, what must remain human, and how accountability is assigned.

The boundary conditions are clear in the literature: emphasizing "trust" without safeguards can reduce scrutiny (Jobin et al., 2019), and epistemic reliability is not sufficient for normative justification (Durán & Jongsma, 2021). Governance in high-stakes professional settings further requires transparent justification and accountability (Aldhafeeri, 2025; Elendu et al., 2023).

Three governance artifacts (minimal, but essential):

- **Delegation boundary statement:** what AI can propose vs. what humans must decide (Durán & Jongsma, 2021).
- **Accountability map:** who is responsible across the chain (developers, organization, professionals) (Elendu et al., 2023).
- **Justification protocol:** what must be documented to keep decisions contestable and legitimate (Aldhafeeri, 2025).

This is consistent with *93 Voices (2025)*'s practical warning: when AI hallucinates, credibility depends on disciplined checking, not convenience.

Example

A compliance team uses AI to draft an assessment. Governance does not forbid the draft. It requires a boundary statement ("AI proposes; humans approve"), an accountability map (who signs and who reviews), and a justification protocol (what sources, what uncertainty bounds, what rationale must be recorded).

6.3.6. Stage 6 - Learn and Adapt (Process Feedback, not Only Outcomes)

Objective: Improve communicational competence and system design using evidence about process failures.

Learning is where many frameworks become ceremonial: a retrospective that focuses on outcomes ("we delivered" / "we missed") and ignores the communicational mechanisms that produced those outcomes. HCCPS is more demanding. Because group performance depends on communication processes, learning cannot be limited to success or failure; it must track *how misunderstandings happened*, *where verification was skipped*, and *how coordination overhead accumulated.*

This is also where the contemporary environment creates a specific trap. Acceleration produces distraction and superficiality—fast exchanges that feel productive but weaken sensemaking. The learning loop exists to counter that pattern with deliberate reflection and slower, higher-quality interpretation.

6.4. Cross-Cutting Human Competencies: Empathy, Emotional Regulation, Responsibility

HCCPS treats these as structural, not decorative. Perspective orientation is impossible without empathy (Baldwin & Garvey, 1973). Verification often fails when ego, anxiety, or haste dominates. Responsibility matters most when the channel strips context and the tool appears authoritative.

Here the book gives you language that stays "human": leadership that listens rather than shouts, and communication as bridge-building rather than message volume **93 Voices (2025)**

6.5. Framework Deliverables (What Teams Produce, not Just What They "Intend")

To keep HCCPS operational, each cycle produces lightweight artifacts:

- *Communicational Diagnosis Sheet* (problem, constraints, involvement, referent criteria)
- *Mode/Protocol Matching Matrix* (which component is weakest: perspective / information / verification)
- *Shared Representation Canvas* (assumptions, options, success criteria; AI outputs vs. human acceptance)
- *Verification & Justification Script* (verification turns + rationale template)
- *Delegation & Accountability Charter* (boundaries, ownership, escalation rules)
- *Learning Loop Log* (what failed, what was misunderstood, what changes next time)

These outputs align with the book's emphasis that true transparency is not "saying everything," but choosing wisely what, how, where, and when to communicate. *93 Voices (2025)*

6.6. Positioning and Contribution: why This is not "Communication Tips," but a Governance Stance

The contribution of HCCPS is its insistence that human-centeredness is *accountability by design*. It ties channel choice to diagnosis, makes verification a visible practice, and treats delegated judgment as bounded by justification and governance requirements. In that sense, it complements communication theory and group-performance evidence (Hemphill & McConville, 1962; Hirokawa, 2008; Baldwin & Garvey, 1973; Kim & Grunig, 2011) while integrating the contemporary constraints of AI mediation and trust calibration (Jobin et al., 2019; Durán & Jongsma, 2021; Aldhafeeri, 2025). To keep the tone consistent with the book: it is an attempt to reduce "noise" and recover meaning, presence, and responsibility in the way we solve problems together 93 Voices (2025). *The problem is not insufficient communication, but communication that no longer carries responsibility, verification, or meaning*.

REFERENCES

93Voices for Communication. (2025). *Como Conectar Pessoas, Empresas e Organizações com Impacto*. ISCTE Executive Education.

Analysis of Mathematical Communication Skills of Junior High School Students of Coastal Kolaka. (2017). *Journal of Mathematics Education*, *2*(2). Advance online publication. DOI: 10.31327/jme.v2i2.360

Ваколюк, А., Шалівська, Ю., & Polishchuk, І. (2025). ПЕДАГОГІЧНІ ПІДХОДИ ДО ВИХОВАННЯ ЕМПАТІЇ В УЧНІВ ЯК БАЗОВОЇ ЯКОСТІ МІЖОСОБИСТІСНИХ ВЗАЄМИН В ОСВІТНЬОМУ ПРОСТОРІ. *Інноватика У Вихованні*, (21), 65–74. DOI: 10.35619/iiu.v1i21.662

Abdulkareem, A., & Ramli, R. (2021). Does trust in e-government influence the performance of e-government? An integration of information system success model and public value theory. *Transforming Government*, *16*(1), 1–17. DOI: 10.1108/TG-01-2021-0001

Aldhafeeri, F. (2025). Governing Artificial Intelligence in Radiology: A Systematic Review of Ethical, Legal, and Regulatory Frameworks. *Diagnostics (Basel)*, *15*(18), 2300. DOI: 10.3390/diagnostics15182300 PMID: 41008671

Baldwin, T., & Garvey, C. (1973). Components of Accurate Problem-Solving Communications. *American Educational Research Journal*, *10*(1), 39–48. DOI: 10.3102/00028312010001039

Ballantyne, A. (2019). Adjusting the focus: A public health ethics approach to data research. *Bioethics*, *33*(3), 357–366. DOI: 10.1111/bioe.12551 PMID: 30667080

Baruah, J., Paulus, P., & Kohn, N. (2021). The Effect of the Sequence of Creative Processes on the Quality of the Ideas: The Benefit of a Simultaneous Focus on Originality and Feasibility. *The Journal of Creative Behavior*, *55*(4), 946–961. DOI: 10.1002/jocb.500

Bracci, E. (2014). Accountability and governance in social care: The impact of personalisation. *Qualitative Research in Accounting & Management*, *11*(2), 111–128. DOI: 10.1108/QRAM-04-2014-0033

Bukachi, S., Onyango-Ouma, W., Siso, J., Nyamongo, I., Mutai, J., Hurtig, A., Olsen, Ø. E., & Byskov, J. (2013). Healthcare priority setting in Kenya: A gap analysis applying the accountability for reasonableness framework. *The International Journal of Health Planning and Management*, *29*(4), 342–361. DOI: 10.1002/hpm.2197 PMID: 23775594

Byskov, J., Bloch, P., Blystad, A., Hurtig, A., Fýlkesnes, K., Kamuzora, P., Kombe, Y., Kvåle, G., Marchal, B., Martin, D. K., Michelo, C., Ndawi, B., Ngulube, T. J., Nyamongo, I., Olsen, Ø. E., Onyango-Ouma, W., Sandøy, I. F., Shayo, E. H., Silwamba, G., & Tuba, M. (2009). Accountable priority setting for trust in health systems - the need for research into a new approach for strengthening sustainable health action in developing countries. *Health Research Policy and Systems*, *7*(1), 23. Advance online publication. DOI: 10.1186/1478-4505-7-23 PMID: 19852834

Caon, M., Khaled, O., Mugellini, E., Lalanne, D., & Angelini, L. (2013). Ubiquitous Interaction for Computer Mediated Communication of Emotions.. DOI: 10.1109/ACII.2013.130

Cerratto, T. (2000). Chatting to Learn and Learning to Chat. M/C Journal, 3(4). DOI: 10.5204/mcj.1866

Chaiken, S. (1980). Heuristic versus systematic information processing and the use of source versus message cues in persuasion. *Journal of Personality and Social Psychology*, *39*(5), 752–766. DOI: 10.1037/0022-3514.39.5.752

Charlton, T., Marshall, L., & Devlin, M. (2008). Evaluating the extent to which sociability and social presence affects learning performance. *SIGCSE Bulletin*, *40*(3), 342–342. DOI: 10.1145/1597849.1384384

Cheah, P., & Piasecki, J. (2020). Data Access Committees. *BMC Medical Ethics*, *21*(1), 12. Advance online publication. DOI: 10.1186/s12910-020-0453-z PMID: 32013947

Cho, I., & Meera, P. (2017). Comparison of problem solving ability according to degree of communication ability of nursing students. *Asia-Pacific Journal of Multimedia Services Convergent With Art Humanities and Sociology*, *7*(7), 397–404. DOI: 10.14257/AJMAHS.2017.07.38

Choi, E., & Jeon, J. (2022). Factors Influencing Problem-Solving Competence of Nursing Students: A Cross-Sectional Study. *Health Care*, *10*(7), 1184. DOI: 10.3390/healthcare10071184 PMID: 35885711

David, P., Choung, H., & Seberger, J. (2024). Who is responsible? US Public perceptions of AI governance through the lenses of trust and ethics. *Public Understanding of Science (Bristol, England)*, *33*(5), 654–672. DOI: 10.1177/09636625231224592 PMID: 38326971

Dörnyei, Z., & Kormos, J. (1998). PROBLEM-SOLVING MECHANISMS IN L2 COMMUNICATION. *Studies in Second Language Acquisition*, *20*(3), 349–385. DOI: 10.1017/S0272263198003039

Dörnyei, Z., & Scott, M. (1997). Communication Strategies in a Second Language: Definitions and Taxonomies. *Language Learning*, *47*(1), 173–210. DOI: 10.1111/0023-8333.51997005

Durán, J. and Jongsma, K. (2021). Who is afraid of black box algorithms? On the epistemological and ethical basis of trust in medical AI. Journal of Medical Ethics, medethics-2020-106820. DOI: 10.1136/medethics-2020-106820

Elendu, C., Amaechi, D., Elendu, T., Jingwa, K., Okoye, O., Okah, M., & Alimi, H. (2023). Ethical implications of AI and robotics in healthcare. *Revista de Medicina (São Paulo)*, *102*(50), e36671. DOI: 10.1097/MD.0000000000036671 PMID: 38115340

Evans, D., Bailey, S., Thumser, A., Trinder, S., Winstone, N., & Bailey, I. (2020). The Biochemical Literacy Framework: Inviting pedagogical innovation in higher education. *FEBS Open Bio*, *10*(9), 1720–1736. DOI: 10.1002/2211-5463.12938 PMID: 32696491

Favaretto, M., Clercq, E., Gaab, J., & Elger, B. (2020). First do no harm: An exploration of researchers' ethics of conduct in Big Data behavioral studies. *PLoS One*, *15*(11), e0241865. DOI: 10.1371/journal.pone.0241865 PMID: 33152039

Furnham, A. (2012). Emotional Intelligence.. DOI: 10.5772/31079

Goisauf, M., Abadía, M., Akyüz, K., Bobowicz, M., Buyx, A., Colussi, I., & Mészáros, J. (2025). Trust, Trustworthiness, and the Future of Medical AI: Outcomes of an Interdisciplinary Expert Workshop. *Journal of Medical Internet Research*, *27*, e71236. DOI: 10.2196/71236 PMID: 40455564

Griffin, R., Neuwirth, K., Giese, J., & Dunwoody, S. (2002). Linking the Heuristic-Systematic Model and Depth of Processing. *Communication Research*, *29*(6), 705–732. DOI: 10.1177/009365002237833

Han, J., Ahn, E., & Hwang, J. (2019). Effects of Critical Thinking and Communication Skills on the Problem-Solving Ability of Dental Hygiene Students. *Journal of Dental Hygiene Science*, *19*(1), 31–38. DOI: 10.17135/jdhs.2019.19.1.31

Harvey, S., & Kou, C. (2013). Collective Engagement in Creative Tasks. *Administrative Science Quarterly*, *58*(3), 346–386. DOI: 10.1177/0001839213498591

Hassan, A. (2023). MANAGEMENT: CHALLENGES AND PROSPECTS.. DOI: 10.35668/978-966-926-466-4

Hemphill, J. and McConville, C. (1962). COMMUNICATION RESTRAINTS AND MUTUAL PROBLEM-SOLVING BEHAVIOR.. DOI: 10.21236/AD0281267

Henderson, N. (2014). Online Persona as Hybrid-Object: Tracing the Problems and Possibilities of Persona in the Short Film Noah. M/C Journal, 17(3). DOI: 10.5204/mcj.819

Hirokawa, R. (2008). Group Communication and Problem-Solving.. DOI: 10.1002/9781405186407.wbiecg029

Högberg, C., Larsson, S., & Lång, K. (2024). Engaging with artificial intelligence in mammography screening: Swedish breast radiologists' views on trust, information and expertise. *Digital Health*, *10*, 20552076241287958. Advance online publication. DOI: 10.1177/20552076241287958 PMID: 39381821

Holloway, D., Green, L., & Brady, D. (2013). FireWatch: Creative Responses to Bushfire Catastrophes. M/C Journal, 16(1). DOI: 10.5204/mcj.599

Irigaray, H., & Stocker, F. (2024). Reflections on business resilience, corporate governance, and corporate social responsibility. *Cadernos EBAPE.BR*, *22*(1), e90025. Advance online publication. DOI: 10.1590/1679-395190025x

Jessica, M., Viswesvaran, C. P. D., & Jacob, J. (2010). Emotional Intelligence, Individual Ethicality, and Perceptions. *Journal of Work and Organizational Psychology*, *26*(1), 35–45. DOI: 10.5093/tr2010v26n1a3

Ji, E., Bang, M., & Jeon, H. (2013). Ego Resilience, Communication Ability and Problem-Solving Ability in Nursing Students. *Journal of Korean Academic Society of Nursing Education*, *19*(4), 571–579. DOI: 10.5977/jkasne.2013.19.4.571

Jobin, A., Ienca, M., & Vayena, E. (2019). The global landscape of AI ethics guidelines. *Nature Machine Intelligence*, *1*(9), 389–399. DOI: 10.1038/s42256-019-0088-2

Kavanaugh, K. (2013). Book Review: Solving Problems in Technical Communication. *Journal of Business and Technical Communication*, *27*(4), 472–476. DOI: 10.1177/1050651913490943

Khaidir, S., Malik, I., & Akbar, M. (2022). Ethics of Government Public Communication in Social Media for COVID-19 Management in Makassar City. *Journal of Government and Political Issues*, *2*(3), 156–166. DOI: 10.53341/jgpi.v2i3.88

Kim, J., & Grunig, J. (2011). Problem Solving and Communicative Action: A Situational Theory of Problem Solving. *Journal of Communication*, *61*(1), 120–149. DOI: 10.1111/j.1460-2466.2010.01529.x

Kim, J., Sung, H., & Kim, H. (2014). Critical Thinking Disposition and Problem-Solving Ability of Dental Hygiene Students. *Journal of Dental Hygiene Science*, *14*(3), 356–363. DOI: 10.17135/jdhs.2014.14.3.356

Lane, C., Walton, J., & Shortliffe, E. (1986). Graphical Access to Medical Expert Systems: II. Design of an Interface for Physicians. *Methods of Information in Medicine, 25*(03), 143–150. DOI: 10.1055/s-0038-1635464 PMID: 3755497

Leonelli, S. (2016). Locating ethics in data science: Responsibility and accountability in global and distributed knowledge production systems. *Philosophical Transactions. Series A, Mathematical, Physical, and Engineering Sciences, 374*(2083), 20160122. DOI: 10.1098/rsta.2016.0122 PMID: 28336799

Leonelli, S., Lovell, R., Wheeler, B., Fleming, L., & Williams, H. (2021). From FAIR data to fair data use: Methodological data fairness in health-related social media research. *Big Data & Society, 8*(1), 20539517211010310. Advance online publication. DOI: 10.1177/20539517211010310

Licuanan, B., Dailey, L., & Mumford, M. (2007). Idea evaluation: Error in evaluating highly original ideas. *The Journal of Creative Behavior, 41*(1), 1–27. DOI: 10.1002/j.2162-6057.2007.tb01279.x

Liljedahl, P., Santos-Trigo, M., Jurado, U., & Bruder, R. (2016). Problem Solving in Mathematics Education.. DOI: 10.1007/978-3-319-40730-2

Lin, C. (2017). Threshold Effects of Creative Problem-Solving Attributes on Creativity in the Math Abilities of Taiwanese Upper Elementary Students. Education Research International, 2017(1). DOI: 10.1155/2017/4571383

Linkova, O. (2024). EFFECTIVE TECHNOLOGIES TO SUPPORT PRODUCTIVITY IN REMOTE WORK CONDITIONS. [Economic Sciences]. *Bulletin of the National Technical University Kharkiv Polytechnic Institute*, (5), 80–86. DOI: 10.20998/2519-4461.2024.5.80

Loi, M., Heitz, C., & Christen, M. (2020). A Comparative Assessment and Synthesis of Twenty Ethics Codes on AI and Big Data., 41-46. DOI: 10.1109/SDS49233.2020.00015

Majchrzak, A., More, P., & Faraj, S. (2012). Transcending Knowledge Differences in Cross-Functional Teams. *Organization Science, 23*(4), 951–970. DOI: 10.1287/orsc.1110.0677

Manger, T., Wicklund, R., & Eikeland, O. (2003). Speed communication and solving social problems. *Communications, 28*(3), 323–337. DOI: 10.1515/comm.2003.020

Marwanda, T., Yusrizal, Y., & Johar, R. (2021). DEVELOPING PISA-LIKE PROBLEMS TO ASSESS STUDENTS' MATHEMATICAL COMMUNICATION AND PROBLEM SOLVING ABILITIES. *Mapan, 9*(1), 136. DOI: 10.24252/mapan.2021v9n1a9

Maryati, I. (2020). Pembelajaran Kontekstual Untuk Mengembangkan Kemampuan Komunikasi Dan Pemecahan Masalah Matematika Siswa SMP. *Pasundan Journal of Mathematics Education Jurnal Pendidikan Matematika*, *4*(1). Advance online publication. DOI: 10.23969/pjme.v4i1.2495

McFadzean, E. (2002). Developing and supporting creative problem solving teams: Part 2 – facilitator competencies. *Management Decision*, *40*(6), 537–551. DOI: 10.1108/00251740210433936

McFadzean, E. (2002). Developing and supporting creative problem-solving teams: Part 1 – a conceptual model. *Management Decision*, *40*(5), 463–475. DOI: 10.1108/00251740210430443

Mendes, A., Morgado, L., & Amante, L. (2008). Online Communication and E-Learning., 927-943. DOI: 10.4018/978-1-59904-865-9.ch065

Mentz, E., Breed, B., & Havenga, M. (2022). Facilitating problem-solving., 93-117. DOI: 10.52779/9781991201799/05

Mitsea, E., Drigas, A., & Skianis, C. (2025). A Systematic Review of Serious Games in the Era of Artificial Intelligence, Immersive Technologies, the Metaverse, and Neurotechnologies: Transformation Through Meta-Skills Training. *Electronics (Basel)*, *14*(4), 649. DOI: 10.3390/electronics14040649

Narayan-Chen, A., Graber, C., Das, M., Islam, M., Dan, S., Natarajan, S., … & Roth, D. (2017). Towards Problem Solving Agents that Communicate and Learn.. DOI: 10.18653/v1/W17-2812

Ngamwilaipong, N., Darasawang, P., & Srimavin, W. (2007). Communication Strategies to Solve Lexical Problems in Writing. *Reflections: The SoL Journal*, *10*, 48–54. DOI: 10.61508/refl.v10i0.114267

O'Brien, J. (2019). *Trust*. Accountability and Purpose., DOI: 10.1017/9781108781138

Odorico, S. (2025). From <em>Love Meetings</em> (Pier Paolo Pasolini, 1964) to Vlogs. M/C Journal, 28(4). DOI: 10.5204/mcj.3214

Pardo, A., & Siemens, G. (2014). Ethical and privacy principles for learning analytics. *British Journal of Educational Technology*, *45*(3), 438–450. DOI: 10.1111/bjet.12152

Patterson, J. (1988). Families experiencing stress: I. The Family Adjustment and Adaptation Response Model: II. Applying the FAAR Model to health-related issues for intervention and research. *Family Systems Medicine*, *6*(2), 202–237. DOI: 10.1037/h0089739

Peters, D., Vold, K., Robinson, D., & Calvo, R. (2020). Responsible AI - Two Frameworks for Ethical Design Practice. *IEEE Transactions on Technology and Society*, *1*(1), 34–47. DOI: 10.1109/TTS.2020.2974991

Pétervári, J., Osman, M., & Bhattacharya, J. (2016). The Role of Intuition in the Generation and Evaluation Stages of Creativity. *Frontiers in Psychology*, *7*. Advance online publication. DOI: 10.3389/fpsyg.2016.01420 PMID: 27703439

Reia, S., Amado, A., & Fontanari, J. (2019). Agent-based models of collective intelligence. *Physics of Life Reviews*, *31*, 320–331. DOI: 10.1016/j.plrev.2018.10.004 PMID: 30635174

Reiter-Palmon, R., Kramer, W., Allen, J., Murugavel, V., & Leone, S. (2021). Creativity in Virtual Teams: A Review and Agenda for Future Research. Creativity Theories – Research – Applications, 8(1), 165-188. DOI: 10.2478/ctra-2021-0011

Rietzschel, E., Nijstad, B., & Stroebe, W. (2019). Why Great Ideas Are Often Overlooked., 179-197. DOI: 10.1093/oxfordhb/9780190648077.013.11

Riggio, R., & Saggi, K. (2015). Incorporating "Soft Skills" Into the Collaborative Problem-Solving Equation. *Industrial and Organizational Psychology: Perspectives on Science and Practice*, *8*(2), 281–284. DOI: 10.1017/iop.2015.34

Roy, E., & Jomeh, A. (2025). Who should be held accountable in technology-induced medical errors? Evaluating the roles of healthcare providers, technology developers, and hospital systems. *Online Journal of Health Ethics / the University of Mississippi Medical Center*, *21*(1). Advance online publication. DOI: 10.18785/jhe.2101.05

Sahu, N., Peng, D., & Sharif, H. (2021). Diagnosis-Steganography-Transmission: An Innovative Integrated Paradigm for ECG Healthcare. *SN Computer Science*, *2*(4), 332. Advance online publication. DOI: 10.1007/s42979-021-00721-6

Savic, M. (2024). Artificial Companions, Real Connections?. M/C Journal, 27(6). DOI: 10.5204/mcj.3111

Schroder, K., Casadaban, A., & Davis, B. (1988). Interpersonal skills training for parents of children with cystic fibrosis. *Family Systems Medicine*, *6*(1), 51–68. DOI: 10.1037/h0089719

Shehhi, M., Alzouebi, K., & Ankit, A. (2021). An examination of the emotional intelligence of school principals and the impact on school climate in public schools in the United Arab Emirates. *Journal of Applied Research in Higher Education*, *13*(5), 1269–1289. DOI: 10.1108/JARHE-09-2020-0287

Smaldino, P., Moser, C., Velilla, A., & Werling, M. (2022). Maintaining transient diversity is a general principle for improving collective problem solving. DOI: 10.31235/osf.io/ykrv5

Smith, N. (2021). Between, Behind, and Out of Sight. M/C Journal, 24(2). DOI: 10.5204/mcj.2764

Soehartono, A., Yu, L., & Khor, K. (2022). Essential signals in publication trends and collaboration patterns in global Research Integrity and Research Ethics (RIRE). *Scientometrics*, *127*(12), 7487–7497. DOI: 10.1007/s11192-022-04400-y PMID: 35755633

Steiner, C., Kickmeier-Rust, M., & Albert, D. (2016). LEA in Private: A Privacy and Data Protection Framework for a Learning Analytics Toolbox. *Journal of Learning Analytics*, *3*(1). Advance online publication. DOI: 10.18608/jla.2016.31.5

Straub, V., Tsvetkova, M., & Yasseri, T. (2020). The cost of coordination can exceed the benefit of collaboration in performing complex tasks. /arxiv.2009.11038DOI: 10.48550

Sumaji, S., Sa'dijah, C., Susiswo, S., & Sisworo, S. (2020). Mathematical Communication Process of Junior High School Students in Solving Problems based on APOS Theory. *Journal for the Education of Gifted Young Scientists*, *8*(1), 197–221. DOI: 10.17478/jegys.652055

Szabó, R., Deritei, D., & Battiston, F. (2024). Coordination and balanced communication enhance collective problem-solving in organic teams. DOI: 10.31219/osf.io/4rwpd

Tan, J., Caleon, I., Jonathan, C., & Koh, E. (2022). A DIALOGIC FRAMEWORK FOR ASSESSING COLLECTIVE CREATIVITY IN COMPUTER-SUPPORTED COLLABORATIVE PROBLEM-SOLVING TASKS. *Research and Practice in Technology Enhanced Learning*, *9*(3), 411–437. DOI: 10.58459/rptel.2014.9411-437

Terenzi, B., Binetti, G., & Busti, S. (2025). Human and Artificial Systems in the Design for Social Innovation: Critical issues and opportunities.., 169. DOI: 10.54941/ahfe1006161

Tomar, M., Tiwari, A., & Saha, S. (2024). Towards knowledge-infused automated disease diagnosis assistant. *Scientific Reports*, *14*(1), 13442. Advance online publication. DOI: 10.1038/s41598-024-53042-y PMID: 38862529

Tozoğlu, B., & Erciş, S. (2025). Examination of teachers' emotional intelligence competence perception levels in terms of sportive activity and different variables. *Frontiers in Psychology*, *16*, 1613193. Advance online publication. DOI: 10.3389/fpsyg.2025.1613193 PMID: 40792090

Trumbo, C. (2002). Information Processing and Risk Perception: An Adaptation of the Heuristic-Systematic Model. *Journal of Communication*, *52*(2), 367–382. DOI: 10.1111/j.1460-2466.2002.tb02550.x

Tseng, L., & Chung, C. (2017). The role of explicit ethics institutionalization and management accountability in influencing newcomer trust. *The International Journal of Organizational Analysis*, *25*(4), 613–627. DOI: 10.1108/IJOA-09-2016-1069

Vaccaro, A., & Madsen, P. (2009). Corporate dynamic transparency: The new ICT-driven ethics? *Ethics and Information Technology*, *11*(2), 113–122. DOI: 10.1007/s10676-009-9190-1

Walker, M. (2008). 4 charting responsibilities., 83-106. DOI: 10.1093/acprof:oso/9780195315394.003.0004

Yaprak, B. (2024). Generative Artificial Intelligence in Marketing: The Invisible Danger of AI Hallucinations. *Journal of Economy Business and Management*, *8*(2), 133–158. DOI: 10.7596/jebm.1588897

Yaroslavskyy, Y., Pavlov, S., Kostyuk, S., & Tymchyk, S. (2022a). Fiber-optical technologies for information (internet, intranet etc.) and energy networks. *Optoelectronic Information-Power Technologies*, *42*(2), 84–95. DOI: 10.31649/1681-7893-2021-42-2-84-95

Yaroslavskyy, Y., Pavlov, S., Kostyuk, S., & Tymchyk, S. (2022b). Principles of Building Telemedicine Networks and Systems Based on Fiber-Optic Communication Channels in Vinnytsia Region. *Optoelectronic Information-Power Technologies*, *42*(2), 84–95. DOI: 10.31649/1681-7893-2021-42-2-84-95

Yoshida, N., & Narazaki, S. (1990, November). A cooperation and communication framework for distributed problem solving. In *[1990] Proceedings of the 2nd International IEEE Conference on Tools for Artificial Intelligence* (pp. 530-536). IEEE. DOI: 10.1109/TAI.1990.130393

Yu, X., Chen, Y., Zhao, Q., & Li, H. (2025). Research and Analysis of Trust and Control in Human-AI Interaction for Decision-Making Systems in Optimizing Public Health Service. *Journal of Organizational and End User Computing*, *37*(1), 1–15. DOI: 10.4018/JOEUC.388626

Zeba, M., Medda-Windischer, R., Carlà, A., & Budabin, A. (2025). Civic Education as Preventive Measure and Inclusionary Practice.. DOI: 10.59019/ddzh5n65

Chapter 12

Future Trends in Human-Computer Interaction for HR

S. Vinoth Kumar
http://orcid.org/0009-0001-9523-6651
Patrician College of Arts and Science, India

S. Anand Bharathi
http://orcid.org/0000-0002-7367-8264
Vellore Institute of Technology, India

J. Jenefer
Vallal P.T. Lee Chengalvaraya Naicker Arts and Science College, India

Dara Vijaya Lakshmi
http://orcid.org/0000-0002-8947-3335
Christ University, India

Roopa Shettigar
http://orcid.org/0000-0001-5672-6589
Soundarya Institute of Management and Science, India

S. Nilavarasan
Alagappa University, India

N. Bharath Raj
http://orcid.org/0009-0006-8250-3120
Jain University, India

ABSTRACT

The objective of this chapter is to analyze the evolution, structure, and future directions of Human-Computer Interaction (HCI) in relation to Human Resources (HR) through bibliometric and thematic analysis of 96 documents published during the last 30 years (1993–2024). Results show the development of HCI in HR as a collaborative and interdisciplinary research area. The field shows a co-authorship average of 3.44 and a co-authorship index of 3.55, indicating engagement with computer science, psychology, organizational behavior, and human resource management. Although research output and number of researchers remain limited, activity has increased after 2015 with an average citation of 24.2. However, international collaboration

DOI: 10.4018/979-8-3373-8337-8.ch012

remains low, with only 5.21% of documents including foreign authors. Major journals such as Computers in Human Behavior and International Journal of Medical Informatics and authors such as Chen D and Johnson C play an important role. Dominant themes include Artificial Intelligence, Human Factors, and HCI, while virtual teams and HR emerge in digital workplaces.

I. INTRODUCTION

Overview of Human-Computer Interaction (HCI) in HR

HCI is one of the most important aspects for a modern Human Resources department (HR) (Campderrich, 2009) where it is essential for streamlining operations, improving usability, and aiding in the analytical process of value-based decision-making (Durango et al., 2024; Katuk et al., 2024). Improving employee experience and productivity has much to do with the design and usability of the software used in HR processes, employee self-service and AI-based recruitment (Sharma & Sengupta, 2023; Naveen et al., 2025).

HR practitioners can create a smooth user experience and ensure HR technologies integrate seamlessly by applying HCI principles (Rohit et al., 2024). Wandhe (2023) and Umrao et al. (2024); Makhija et al. (2024) state that assisted and autonomous real-time answers simplify several HR processes such as recruitment, onboarding, and employee engagement fully functional, AI-based chat bots, virtual assistants and real-time help. Nocker and Sena (2019), Elugbaju et al. (2024), Wolniak et al. (2024), and Rishiraj and Shukla (2023) argue that by improving visualization of data, HR practitioners can manage employee performance better, understand and analyze trends in the workforce with greater clarity, and make better decisions in workforce planning and employee well-being.

According to Nawaz (2023), Accessibility and inclusion are important areas to focus on in HCI for HR. Designing HR tools that are made for and accessible to persons with disabilities demonstrates how to provide equal access to HR services (Sanjaya & Irawan, 2024; Madan et al., 2024; Cavanagh et al., 2017). Gesture-based, voice, and other control technologies, as well as adaptive interfaces, greatly improve accessibility and help make HR systems more friendly and adaptive to various employees (Sayyed et al, 2024; Mounica & Kirubakaran, 2024).

Effectively integrating HCI into HR functions encourages a more enjoyable, all-encompassing, and employee-focused organizational culture (Salvadorinho & Teixeira, 2023; Dhand, 2025). The ongoing evolution of technology leaves ample room for further research in this sphere. The forthcoming studies could consider how VR and AR affect corporate training and employee development (Al-Ansi et al., 2023; Yazdi, 2024; Iqbal et al., 2024; Tan et al., 2022). Also, the ethical consequences of artificial intelligence (AI) in HR and recruitment should be studied further (Khair et al., 2020; Yanamala, 2023; Sachan et al., 2024).

Importance of HCI Advancements in HRM

The impact of the advancements in HCI is notable in the features of the efficiency, the overall experience of the user and the processes in the HRM that are related to decision making (Kaur et al., 2024; Vetrivel et al., 2024; Katuk et al., 2024). Integration of digital processes in HRM, increases the need for HCI in the process of employee and HR system interactivity (DiRomualdo et al., 2018; Kambur & Yildirim, 2023; Johnson et al., 2017).

Modern HRM technology, simplifies HR processes through the utilization of HCI innovations such as AI chatbots, user-friendly service portals and individualized digital interfaces (Sharma & Sengupta, 2023; Huo et al., 2024). They also give employees more engagement and access to HR services while reducing their administrative burden and improving overall usability.

In the process of decision making, Interactive visualization of data and dynamic dashboards, transform HRM totally and give the real-time analytics of the workforce of the HRM system (Tuli et al., 2018). With the HCI techniques, the HR professionals are able to analyze and comprehend easily the workforce data in higher granular levels which is effective for planning, evaluating productivity, and optimizing the workforce (Dlamini, 2023; Tshabalala, 2023).

HCI advancements have improved employee accessibility and HRM inclusivity (Walkowiak, 2024). HRM platforms can support employees with different preferences and abilities through adaptive interfaces, speech recognition, and personalized experiences (Zhou & Cen, 2023; Umrao et al., 2024). Organizations that prioritize accessibility and accommodate diverse employee needs can create more inclusive workplaces and equitable HR services (Ezeafulukwe et al., 2024).

With an increase in remote and hybrid work HCI has been pivotal to virtual collaboration and employee engagement (Meluso et al., 2022). Digital workspaces, virtual meeting platforms, and systems that provide real-time feedback can influence productivity, employee satisfaction, and team dynamics (Sundari & Gangalapudi, 2025; Agarwal, 2024; Barbu et al., 2025). Because of this, effective HCI designs for HRM tools can facilitate communication and support an engaging remote work experience (Haque, 2023; Sundari & Gangalapudi, 2025).

To sum up, the transformation of HRM due to the advancements of HCI is associated with improvement in usability, accessibility and the scope of improvement in the decision-making processes using data. HRM practitioners, who become HCI advocates, become more responsive to concerns of employees, positive employee experiences, and effective management of employees. HCI in HRM is working towards creating a more employee-centric and user-friendly environment in the workplace.

Objectives of the chapter

This study intends to examine HCI and HRM by way of a bibliometric study. The study intends to analyze the impact of publications, the authors, the primary themes of the study, and the pattern of collaboration in the study across the globe to assess the impact of the study to understand what areas of study are of interest, the advancement of technologies, and the direction future studies should take. The impact of studies should address the advancement of technologies in HCI and how they influence HRM practices, and decision-making processes of the HR managers using bibliometric analysis.

II. METHODOLOGY

Summary Statistics

Table 1. Summary statistics

Description	Results
Documents	96
Sources	82
Keywords Plus (ID)	1100
Author's Keywords (DE)	392
Period	1993:2024
Average citations per document	24.2
Authors	330
Authors of single-authored documents	12
Authors of multi-authored documents	318
Single-authored documents	12
Documents per Author	0.39
Authors per document	3.4375
Co-Authors per Documents	3.55
International Co-Authorship %	5.208

Source: Developed by Authors

Summary statistics are very useful in providing an overview of the dataset that was utilized for the analysis. 96 documents were analyzed, coming from 82 different sources, such as journals, books, and other academic sources, revealing a remarkable evolution in research over a period of three decades (1993-2024) in the Human-Computer Interaction (HCI) in HR. There were a lot of identified keywords, showing the research landscape was wide and diverse (1100 Keywords Plus (ID) and 392 Author's Keywords (DE)). This suggested that the field had been investigated from different angles and many themes had emerged over the years. Concerning authorship, there were 330 researchers that contributed to the research. Remarkably, there were only 12 documents that were single-authored, meaning that most of the publications were from collaborative work. The number of authors on multi-authored papers reached 318, indicating further development of the field's interdisciplinary and collaborative aspects. There was an average of 3.44 authors per document, and the co-authorship rate was 3.55, indicating a high degree of collaborative authorship. Each document was cited an average of 24.2 times, indicating a fairly moderate level of impact. In terms of international collaboration, the number of papers with authors from different countries was only 5.21%, which provides a potential for further international collaboration.

Overview of PRISMA Flowchart

The systematic review used PRISMA (Moher et al., 2021) (Preferred Reporting Items for Systematic Reviews and Meta-Analyses) and systematic review to keep selection transparent and replicable. Figure 1 shows the PRISMA Flowchart and illustrates the various steps taken in the course of the research. Its first step includes collecting records from Scopus and WOS, and then these records went through screening based on the inclusion criteria. The eligibility step consisted of a complete text review to determine if the text aligned with the research objectives, while the last inclusion step consisted of keeping studies that were all that fit the qualitative and bibliometric criteria. This study systematically followed a process which helped in the study's rigor so that more meaningful data could be captured and more relevant research gaps could be identified for future research.

Figure 1. PRISMA flowchart

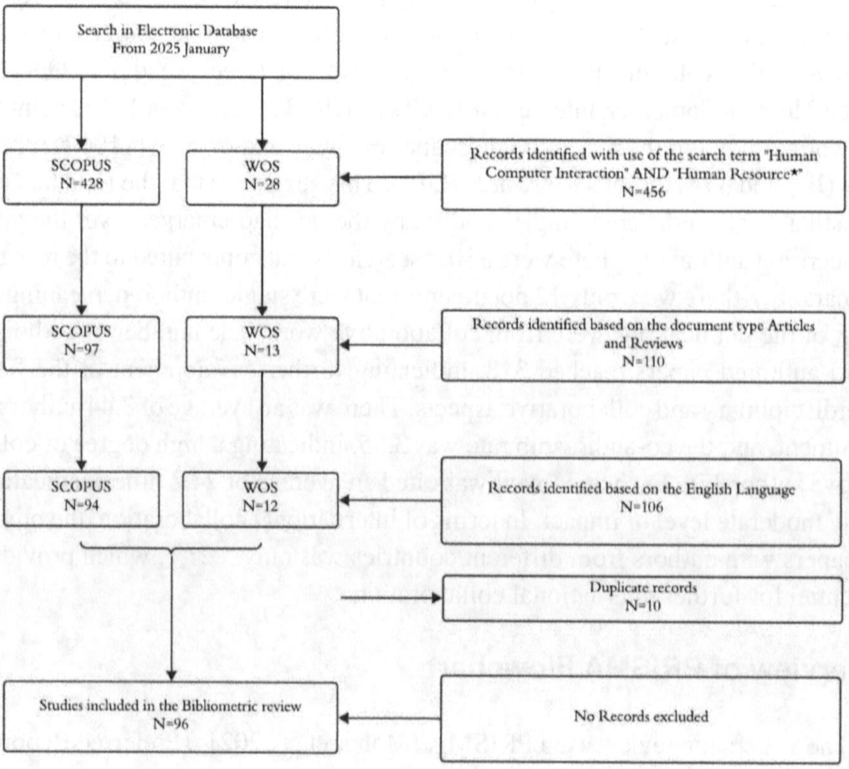

Source: Developed by Authors

Data Collection and Analysis Approach

The first stage of the review consisted of a systematic search of the first two of the three documented databases first, Scopus and the Web of Science (WOS) databases, with coverage until January 2025. Using the search field "Human-Computer Interaction" AND "Human Resource" first yielded 428 documents from Scopus and 28 from WOS, totaling 456 documents. Using an integrative review and bibliometric method for the review, the documents were divided and reviewed on the basis of the abstract, introductory, methods, results, and conclusion sections. In order to maintain the validity and quality of the review, certain exclusion criteria were set. In the first place, documents were filtered by document type by only focusing on articles and reviews, this reduced the results to 110. In the next stage, documents were subjected to a language filter by limiting the records to only those written in the English language, this eliminated thirty-four records and produced 106 records. The removal of duplicates, a central activity in the review process and when merging records from Scopus and WOS, decreased the results by 96 documents to 10 for final review. The review process was also enhanced through the elimination of duplicates to preserve the integrity of the review. Identifying Trends Using Bibliometric Methods

Use of Bibliometric Methods for Trend Identification

Quantitative approach was used for the purpose of describing, understanding, and assessing the trends of published literature. Data pertaining the bibliographic details, such as, titles, years of publication, journals of publication, keywords, abstracts, authors, their institutions, subject categories and references were downloaded from the databases in the form of text and CSV files (Donthu et al., 2021). This data was processed to describe and analyze the bibliometric patterns and trends of the research literature in the domain of Human-Computer Interaction (HCI) and Human Resource (HR). The use of bibliometric techniques was instrumental in systematically tracing the development of academic literature and delineating the patterns of literature, significant authors, and the hotspots of domains in the published literature.

III. TRENDS IN HCI RESEARCH FOR HR

Analysis of Research Output Over Time

Table 2. Annual publications

Year	No of Articles	Mean TC Per Article
2024	7	3.71
2023	7	7.57
2022	7	15.71
2021	9	16.11
2019	4	36.25
2018	8	20
2017	4	16.25
2015	9	31.56
2014	6	18.33
2004	7	30

Source: Developed by Authors

Figure 2. Top annual publications and citations

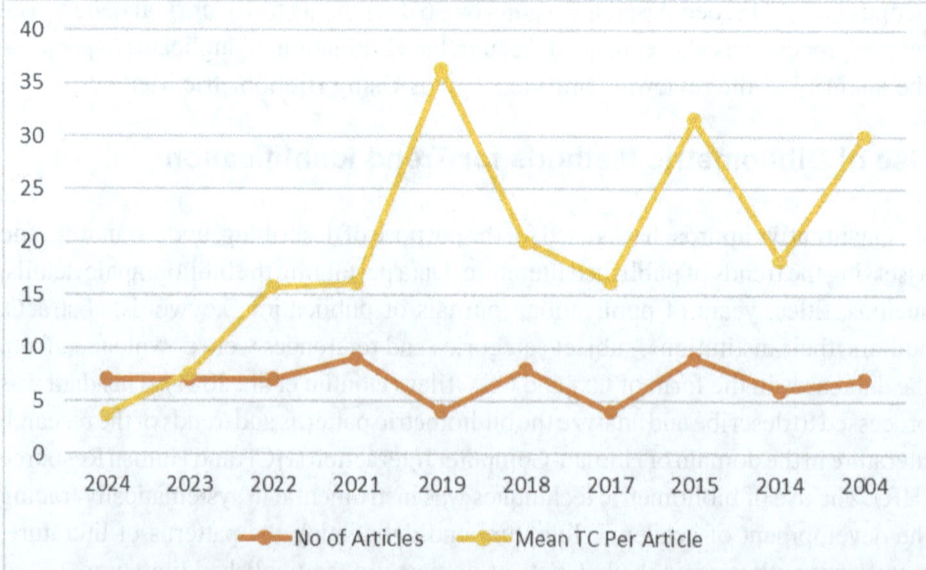

Source: Developed by Authors

The impact and activity of research can be understood over time through annual publication data. Although published articles fluctuate each year, a certain degree of consistency exists in the rate of citations, which can be used as an indicator of the articles' impact within the field. In the last few years, the rate of publication has been sustained on 7 articles each year from 2022 to 2024. In contrast, the number of citations an article receives on average does not appear to follow this same stalemated trend. In 2024, the average number of citations per article sits at 3.71. However, articles published in 2022 and 2021 outpace this average at 15.71 and 16.11 citations per article, respectively. These results indicate that the research recently published has potential as the number of citations can be expected to rise over time.

Considering an earlier span of years, some display fewer total publications but remarkably higher citation averages. Most specifically, 2019 achieved the status of a breakthrough year for impact, despite having only 4 publications. These documents averaged 36.25 citations. The same can be said for 2015, who had a total of 9 articles, averaging 31.56 citations per each article. The same can be said for 2004. The year had 7 publications averaging 30 citations each. This trend demonstrates that older research still holds relevancy. Interestingly, this trend of inconsistencies can be observed again. 2018 and 2017 published a total of 4 and 8 articles, respectively. These publications were analyzed and discovered that article averaged 20 and 16.25 citations. This trend shows that despite having fewer publications, the research that was done during this time was extremely valuable.

Most Cited Sources and Key Publication Indexes

Table 3. Most cited sources and their indexes

Source	TC	NP	H-Index	G-Index
IJOMI	269	6	6	6
CIHB	241	3	3	3
BAIT	222	1	1	1
JOBI	219	1	1	1
CAB	145	1	1	1
IJOAMT	79	1	1	1
JOITER	69	1	1	1
IR	68	1	1	1
ASCJ	61	1	1	1
JOTRSOM	44	1	1	1

Source: Developed by Authors

Figure 3. Top cited sources: Publications and indexes

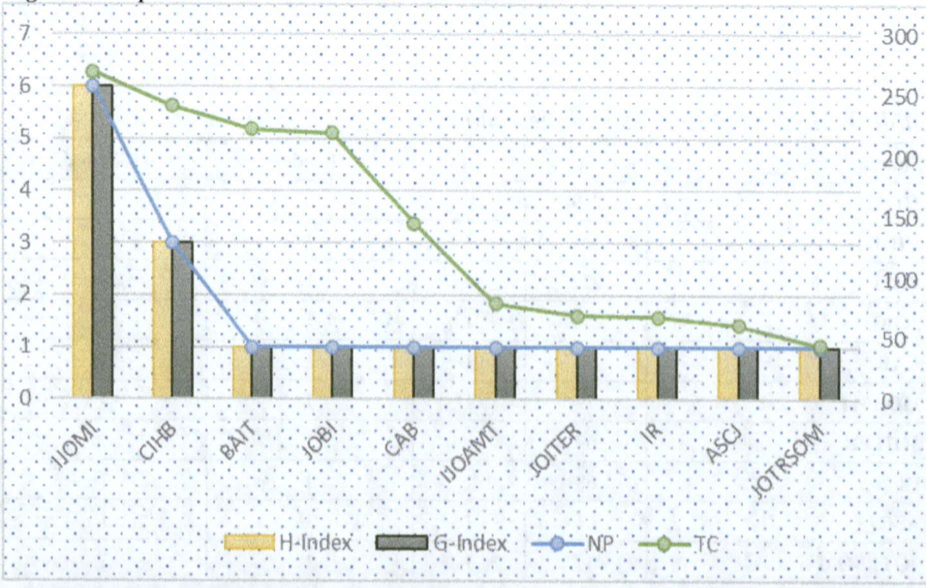

Source: Developed by Authors

"IJOMI - International Journal of Medical Informatics, CIHB - Computers in Human Behavior, BAIT - Behavior and Information Technology, JOBI - Journal of Biomedical Informatics, CAB - Cyberpsychology and Behavior, IJOAMT - International Journal of Advanced Manufacturing Technology, JOITER - Journal of Information Technology Education: Research, IR - Internet Research, ASCJ - Applied Soft Computing Journal, JOTRSOM - Journal of the Royal Society of Medicine"

The table 3 shows the major works drawing from citations (TC), Publication (NP), and H-Index and G-Index as major Impact Metrics in the IJOMI as the journal has 269 citations and 6 publications. The journal's H-Index and G-Index are 6, indicative of impactful papers published. Given the total, IJOMI has published a number of papers that are greatly influential to the field of medical informatics and the use of technology in healthcare.

The journal Computers in human behavior (CIHB) has 241 citations from 3 publications. This shows that there are influential papers published, and the number of publications is not an indicative factor. This is the case as CIHB discusses the technology and human behavior interface, and human computer interaction (HCI) is paramount in HR. Other works, such as Behavior and Information Technology (BAIT) and the Journal of Biomedical Informatics (JOBI), each published only one paper, these works have 222 and 219 citation respectively. This means that these papers are highly influential in the area of concentration.

Likewise, Cyberpsychology and Behavior (CAB) has 145 citations from one paper, therefore, it is important for the relevance of the study that digital contact impacts the psychological and behavioral sides, another fundamental aspect of HCI research. The other sources, including International Journal of Advanced Manufacturing Technology (IJOAMT), Journal of Information Technology Education Research (JOITER), Internet Research (IR), Applied Soft Computing Journal (ASCJ), and Journal of the Royal Society of Medicine (JOTRSOM) have one publication each from 79 (IJOAMT) to 44 (JOTRSOM). Though these sources published fewer papers, it is their presence in the citation index that highlights their significance in specialized areas of HCI.

Leading Authors and Their Contributions

Table 4. Leading authors and countries: categorized by citation influence

TC	Author	TP	TC	Country	TP	Affiliation	TP
222	Chen D	1	933	USA	32	The Pennsylvania State University	10
219	Johnson C	1	222	Singapore	2	Imperial College London	6
153	Roth P	1	175	China	18	School of Public Health and Community Medicine	6
145	Case C	1	135	Australia	2	University of Toulouse	6
135	Bhuiya A	2	107	UK	4	Carnegie Mellon University	5
89	Hesenius M	2	89	Germany	3	Clemson University	4
84	Hanifi S	1	69	Georgia	1	Nankai University	4
79	Gruhn V	1	66	Malaysia	1	University of Duisburg-Essen	4
69	Zhang A	1	27	Italy	5	Universidade Federal De Minas Gerais (Ufmg)	4
68	Davison R	1	26	Canada	5	University Of Duisburg-Essen	4

Source: Developed by Authors

Figure 4. Authors with top citation records and publications

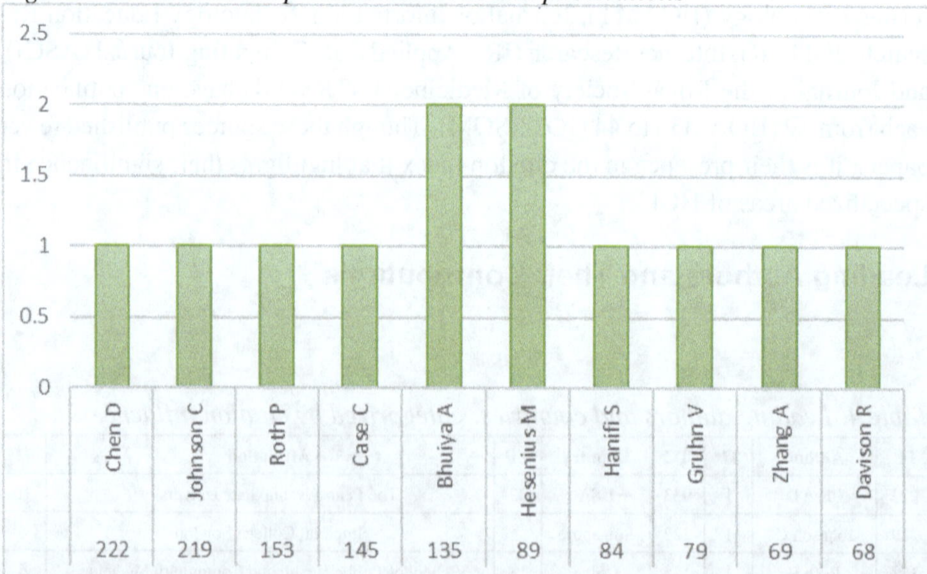

Source: Developed by Authors

The tables 4 show the most prolific researchers, most researched countries, and most prominent universities focusing on the intersection of computer science and human resources. They also indicate the most influential researchers in the area, which helps to determine the leading participants in the conversations and advancements within this area of research.

Highly Cited Authors: Influence Through Research Impact

The provided table shows leading authors by research impact in the respective field. Key Citations help understand the impact of a researcher and how often their work is cited by other researchers. Leading author Chen D has an astonishing 222 citations for one paper, showing how influential is the paper. With that high of a citation count from one paper, likely Chen was tackling a burning question in the community or was offering a completely different insight that other researchers kept citing. Following suit is Johnson C with 219 citations for one paper, showing that individual studies in certain cases can bring a lot of change to the community, despite an author not publishing many papers in the field. Other authors like Roth P (153 citations), Case C (145 citations), and Bhuiya A (135 citations from 2 papers) demonstrate how even a few great papers can create a lot of traction in the academic world.

Noteworthy publications include authors like A. Bhuiya (2 publications, 135 citations) and M. Hesenius (2 publications, 89 citations). In contrast, single-publication authors tend to have larger citation counts, but multi-publication authors seem to have a more well-rounded contribution to the field with the potential to influence it for years to come. Others who have contributed significantly to the field are S. Hanifi (84 citations), V. Gruhn (79 citations), A. Zhang (69 citations), and R. Davison (68 citations), each having produced highly influential work. Although the number of their citations does not match the most of the others, they have contributed significantly to the HCI in HR discourse. The differences in citation counts indicate the multiple ways authors can impact readership, be it through influential single publications or multi-publication consistent contributions.

Country-Wise Contributions: The Global Landscape of HCI Research in HR

USA leads the research with 933 citations from 32 papers. This shows the US has long been a dominant player in research concerning technology and academia. This is especially true for the research in the fields of artificial intelligence, human-computer interaction, and digital HR systems. US institutions have the ability in terms of both funding and human capital to do impactful research in this area. China (175 citations, 18 papers) is a significant player as well, showcasing the increasing importance of the country in global academic research. China has a research focus on technology, automation, and AI, and as a result their involvement in HCI for HR will grow significantly. Researchers from Singapore (222 citations, 2 papers), Australia (135 citations, 2 papers) and Germany (89 citations, 3 papers) have a comparatively smaller number of publications, but their high citation count shows that the research coming from these countries is very impactful. This is exemplified by the 2 studies from Singapore that are included in this dataset, and it's clear that the influence of research is not a factor of quantity, but rather quality. Of note is the UK (107 citations, 4 papers), Canada (26 citations, 5 papers), and Italy (27 citations, 5 papers). These countries display moderate research output and impact based on this data. The contributions made by these countries are indicative of the potential value of their research and the need for better global collaborative efforts in terms of publication volume. Malaysia (1 paper, 66 citations) and Georgia (1 paper, 69 citations) represent smaller, but significant, contributions. The work of these countries is highly cited despite their relatively low research output, proving that small academic communities are capable of producing work with significant impact.

Leading Author Contribution

Table 5. Top cited articles

Author	Year	Title	Source	TC
Lim V	2012	Cyberloafing at the Workplace: Gain or Drain on Work?	Behaviour and Information Technology	222
Johnson C	2005	A User-Centered Framework for Redesigning Health Care Interfaces	Journal of Biomedical Informatics	219
Woszczynski A	2002	Exploring the Theoretical Foundations of Playfulness in Computer Interactions	Computers In Human Behavior	153
Young K	2004	Internet Abuse in The Workplace: New Trends in Risk Management	Cyberpsychology and Behavior	145
Khatun F	2015	Determinants of Readiness to Adopt Health in a Rural Community of Bangladesh	International Journal of Medical Informatics	84
Klumpp M	2019	Production Logistics and Human-Computer Interaction State of the Art, Challenges and Requirements for the Future	International Journal of Advanced Manufacturing Technology	79
Zhang A	2012	Peer Assessment of Soft Skills and Hard Skills	Journal of Information Technology Education: Research	69
Yin P	2018	Coping With Mobile Technology Overload in the Workplace	Internet Research	68
Yusof M	2015	A Case Study Evaluation of A Critical Care Information System Adoption Using The Socio-Technical And Fit Approach	International Journal of Medical Informatics	66
Babbar-Sebens M	2012	Interactive Genetic Algorithm with Mixed-Initiative Interaction For Multi-Criteria Ground Water Monitoring Design	Applied Soft Computing Journal	61

Source: Developed by Authors

The most-cited articles shed light on the seminal work concerning the impact of Human-Computer Interaction (HCI) research for Human Resources (HR). Work published in top-tier journals have influenced the conversations around workplace technology, user experience, digital behaviors, and technology adoption. Top-cited articles capture the impact of research on human behaviors, organizational productivity, and the design of technology.

The most-cited article in the dataset is Lim V's (2012) Cyberloafing at the Workplace: Gain or Drain on Work? published in Behaviour and Information Technology. With 222 citations, the study tackles the issue of employees engaging in cyberloafing, or the act of using the internet for non-work-related purposes. This research is still pertinent, as organizations continue to find the ideal balance between productivity and employee wellbeing in the digital workplace. The study also mentions that cyberloafing may offer employees the opportunity to take a mental break and improve productivity. In contrast, cyberloafing may serve as a distraction and decrease employee productivity. The topic is clearly of great interest, as demonstrated by the high citation count. Subsequent research has also followed on digital distraction, workplace monitoring, and HR policy development.

The 2nd most cited article with 219 citations is "A User-Centered Framework for Redesigning Health Care Interfaces" by Johnson C (2005) in the Journal of Biomedical Informatics. This paper focuses on the user-centered design and HCI and attempts to demonstrate how healthcare interfaces can be designed to be more user-friendly and effective for healthcare professionals and users. Its high citation metrics are evidence to how influential the research is towards shaping the discourse surrounding usability, digital health, and patient-centered design in healthcare innovation.

The 3rd most cited paper is "Exploring the Theoretical Foundations of Playfulness in Computer Interactions" by Woszczynski A (2002) in Computers in Human Behavior with 153 citations. The paper investigates the phenomenon of playful interaction with computers from a psychological perspective. The playful and exploratory interaction with technology can assist in the design of more meaningful user experiences and is critical for the development of engaged users in e-learning, HR gamification, and training of employees through games.

The other prominent study is Internet Abuse in the Workplace: New Trends in Risk Management by Young K published in Cyberpsychology and Behavior in 2004 and has 145 citations. This paper builds on the chatter surrounding cyberloafing but in this case, focuses on the risk potential the abuse of the Internet presents in the workplace. Such issues, like, social media time wasting, downloading without permission and company Internet abuse, and Internet security issues. This subject remains relevant, and this is the HR dilemma of managing employee technological access and the digital workplace culture.

Another important work is Khatun F. (2015) published in the International Journal of Medical Informatics, and has 84 citations. Determinants of Readiness to Adopt Health in a Rural Community of Bangladesh is a study about the acceptability of digital health technologies in rural settings and brings the issues of the digital divide, access, and socio-economic factors to the forefront. This work is critical in the current time of urgent need for telemedicine and remote health care offers.

The 2019 paper titled "Production Logistics and Human-Computer Interaction: State of the Art, Challenges and Requirements for the Future" by Klumpp M received 79 citations. It has been published in the International Journal of Advanced Manufacturing Technology, and focuses on the relationship between HCI and the industrial sector, in particular, the effects of digital interfaces and automation on production logistics. With the emergence of smart factories, Industry 4.0, and AI in supply chain management, this paper has been of relevance in optimizing the human-machine interaction in workplaces.

Among the 69 citations for "Peer Assessment of Soft Skills and Hard Skills" authored by Zhang A (2012) is another example worth mentioning, published in the Journal of Information Technology Education Research. This study is primarily of value to HR personnel, as it identifies methods of assessing technical (hard) and inter-personal (soft) skills. Of particular importance to research is the use of peer assessment as a form of evaluative research, as this is a period where organizations focus on the softer skills and emotional intelligence in addition to personnel technical skills.

One of the articles that can be cited is "Coping with Mobile Technology Overload in the Workplace" by Yin P. (2018), from the journal Internet Research. The article has been cited 68 times. With the advent of smartphones, instant messaging, and remote work applications, digital overload is a phenomenon that employees experience. This paper most likely attempts to tackle the issue of an associated stress of being always reachable. The number of times an article is cited generally indicates the relevance of the articles, which in this instance indicates the increased concern of the issue in the case of hybrid work structures.

A case study that has a significant impact is "A Case Study Evaluation of a Critical Care Information System Adoption Using the Socio-Technical and Fit Approach" by Yusof M (2015), published in the International Journal of Medical Informatics and has been cited 66 times. This study is likely to evaluate the extent to which critical care information systems are integrated into the workflows of hospitals, considering the technological and the human factors. The socio-technical perspective is one of the most important perspectives in the design of health technologies and addresses the interaction of people with the systems.

Finally, the publication with 61 citations is Interactive Genetic Algorithm with Mixed-Initiative Interaction for Multi-Criteria Ground Water Monitoring Design by Babbar-Sebens M (2012) in Applied Soft Computing Journal. While it is not directly related to HR, it still adds to the broader HCI field by studying interactive decision-making systems. The use of AI-based systems to streamline the optimization of intricate systems can be useful in various domains including HR analytics and workforce planning.

Key Research-Producing Countries

Figure 5. Top countries research output

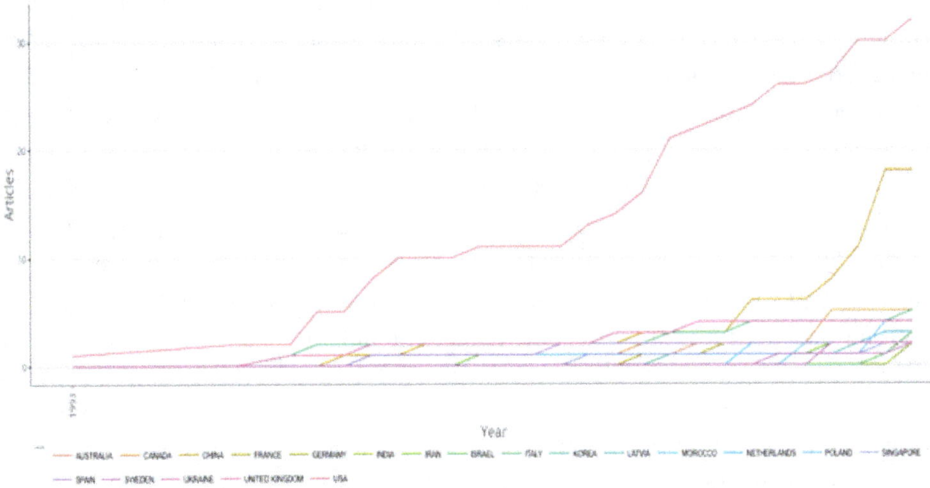

Source: Developed by Authors using R

Figure 6. Top-cited countries & affiliations with publications

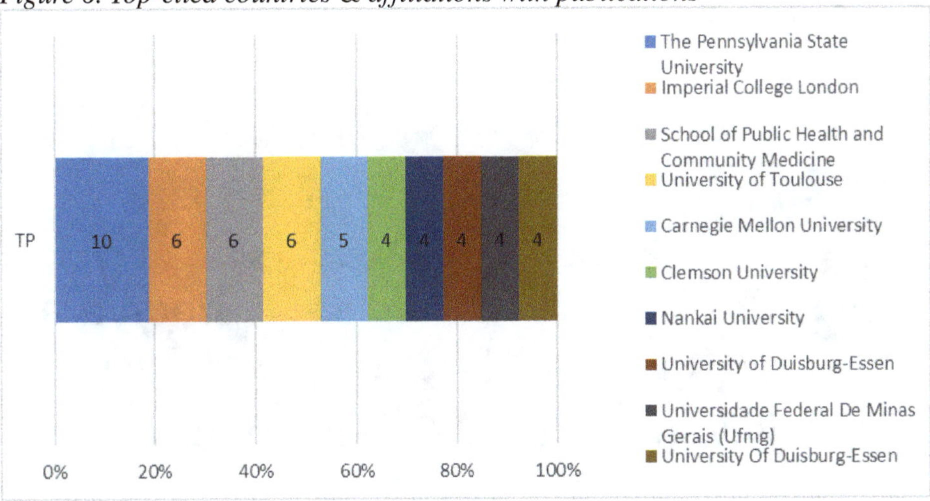

Source: Developed by Authors

Institutional Influence: Universities and Research Centers Leading the Way

In academic investigations, universities are extremely important, and some have triumphed more than others. For example, The Pennsylvania State University is number one, with 10 publications. Through its publications, the university demonstrates the importance of research in this area. The impact of the university is also complemented by high citation counts, which means its publications are cited and recognized. Other notable research contributors include Imperial College London (6 publications), and the School of Public Health and Community Medicine (6 publications), and the University of Toulouse (6 publications). Their research output indicates the existence of active research teams or divisions specializing in HCI in HR.

The notable contributions of Carnegie Mellon University (5 papers) and Universidade Federal De Minas Gerais (4 papers) further illustrate the presence of world-class institutions in this domain. It is obvious that Carnegie Mellon, due to their prominence in AI, robotics, and human-computer interaction, is a leader in the field. With 4 papers each, Clemson University, Nankai University, and University of Duisburg-Essen also add to the list of geographic distribution of top tier universities. Having universities from the continents of North America, Europe, and Asia demonstrates that the effort in researching HCI for HR spans across the globe and is not confined to a particular region.

Collaboration Trends Among Researchers

Figure 7. Author collaboration

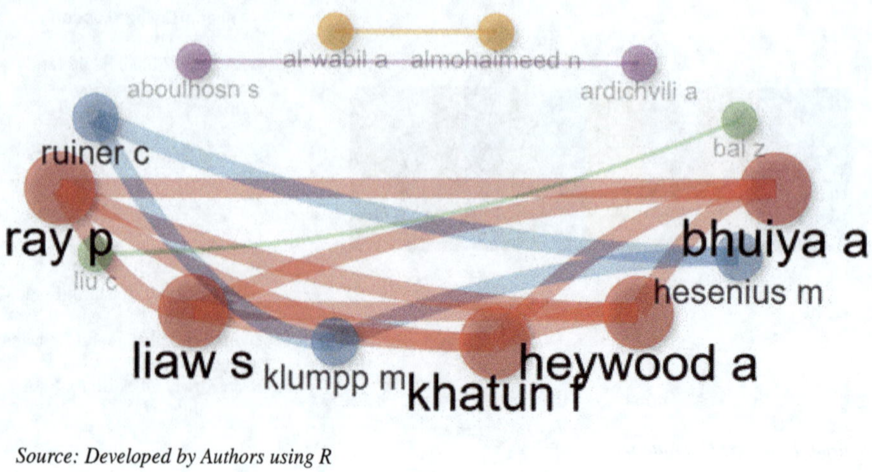

Source: Developed by Authors using R

The visualizations of collaboration networks show how authors connect to one another through co-authorship. Larger names or nodes indicate authors with more influence or centrality in the network, with more significant collaboration or citation impact. The different widths and colors of lines indicate the different strengths and types of collaboration. Among the highlighted authors, Ray P, Liaw S, Bhuiya A, Heywood A, and Khatun F stand out with active joint engagements, as the most influential in this network. Most of the middle red lines show strong collaborations, while with most of the outside network with Al-Wabil A, Almohaimeed N, and Ardichvili A, that is more isolated or niche contribution.

The visualization portrays an interdisciplinary and global scope, with numerous contributors advancing Human-Computer Interaction (HCI) in HR from various backgrounds, including different subfields and institutions. Some authors, including Ruiner C, Liu C, and Bai Z, may have less direct collaboration, but their authorship suggests important engagement with the wider research community. The structure indicates the most innovative leading researchers in the center and the most passive supporting or specialized researchers in the periphery. Enhancing interdisciplinary collaboration with new partners is likely to increase the research impact and the HCI's insights to HRI and the future of work.

International Collaborations and Networks

Figure 8. Countries collaboration

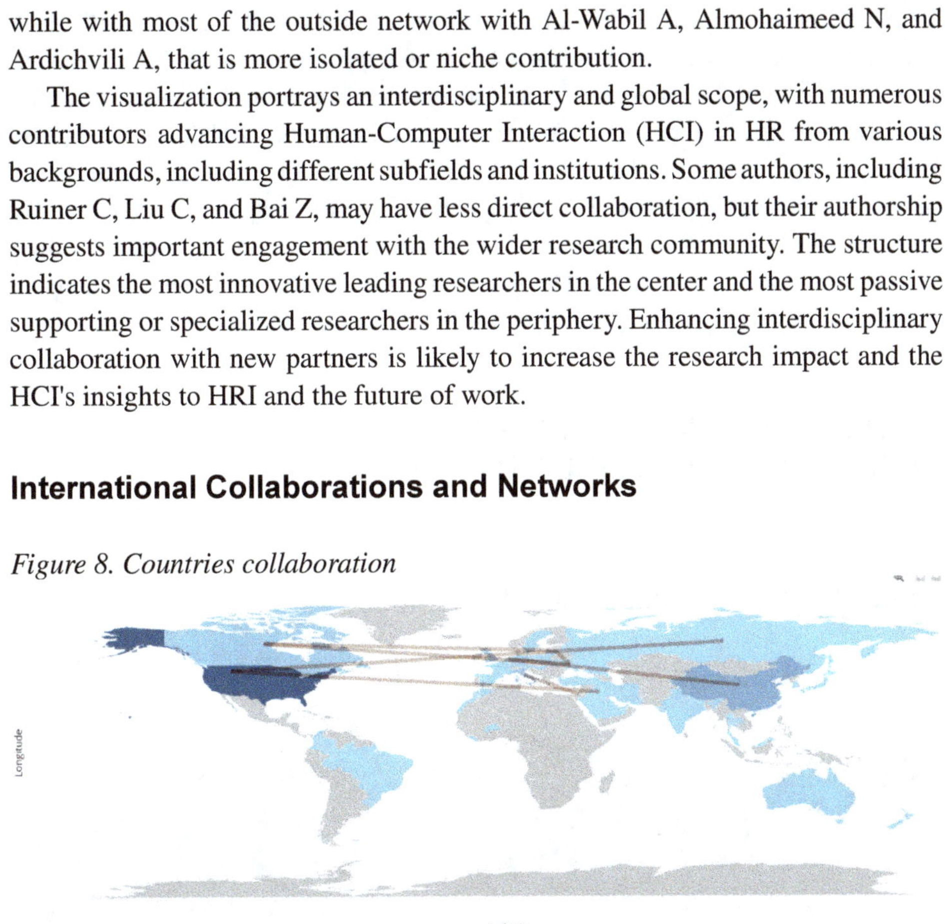

Source: Developed by Authors using R

The HCI research collaboration map visualizes collaborative efforts across countries for HR, showcasing research connections across all countries. Different colors represent varying levels of collaboration, with darker blues indicating more research contributions for HCI. Research collaborations across countries are represented with lines, with more research collaboration resulting in thicker lines. The United States has the most research activity and research collaboration with the

United Kingdom, Germany, and France. The research activity suggests the United States has the most advanced HCI research in HR in the participating countries, and this can most likely be attributed to their technology and research institutions. There are also a noticeable amount of research collaborations from the participating countries in Western and Northern Europe.

Country's like Japan and China are less involved with the West, although they are present on the map. The cross-border collaborations may not be present due to the research priorities which are set internally. With collaboration with these countries, it can be seen that there are more HCI applications for HR. In the West, there is little to no collaboration in research which is very backward as there may be developed research networks. We can expand the scope of HCI for HR by collaborating with these underdeveloped regions as the results from the research may be very varied and different. The map portrays that the major economies are the ones that are collaborating more and the less developed research hubs are slowly increasing their collaborations. The research is very global and there is emphasis on the collaborations on the developed and underdeveloped research hubs.

4. EMERGING THEMES AND FUTURE RESEARCH DIRECTIONS IN HCI FOR HR

Predicted Research Trajectories

Figure 9. Three field path

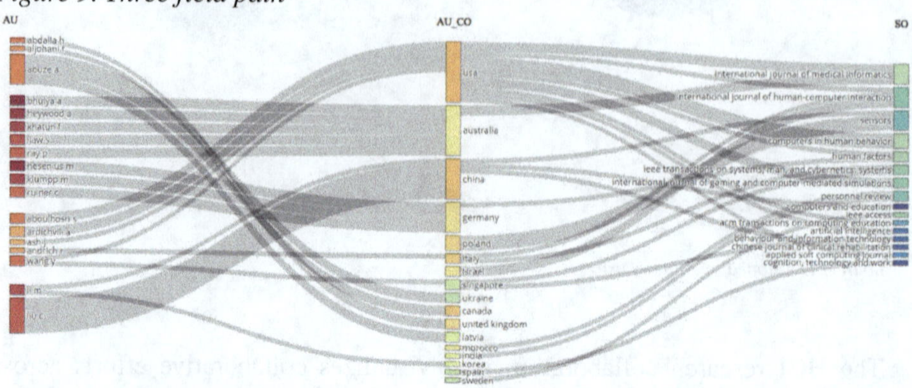

Source: Developed by Authors using R

The three-field plot shows how HCI researchers (AU) and their affiliated countries (AU_CO) and selected publication sources (SO) connect. This plot sheds light on how researchers contribute, which countries are more important research centers, and which journals or sources are more important publishers in the field. Such visualization helps in the mapping of research focus, research collaborations, and the cross-disciplinarity of HCI and HR research.

An important point that can be drawn from this graph is the predominant position of the United States in HCI research for HR. Most of the top contributing authors to this research, such as Bhuiya A, Heywood A, Khatun F, Liaw S, Ray P, and Hesenius M, are from the United States, showing the country's dominance in this area. This can be explained by the country's strong research oriented academic institutions, research grants and the field of corporate HCI in ergonomics. Other than the United States of America, significant contribution also comes from Australia and China as many of the principal authors and important publications in this area are from these countries. The inclusion of some European countries, particularly Germany, Poland, and Italy, is also important and indicates the effort some of the countries are making to show that HCI research in HR is a global community horizontal research effort, as many countries are trying to develop new technologies, structures, and approaches to optimize the interaction of people in the work place.

Another key point is the variety of publication sources, indicating the interdisciplinary characteristic of HCI research in HR. The International Journal of Medical Informatics and International Journal of Human-Computer Interaction show the greatest usage, indicating most research is probably concentrated in the areas of technology and human design in work and health environments. In addition, Computers in Human Behavior and Sensors also appear as important publications, further supporting the belief that behavioral and analytics driven research are dominant in the future of HCI in HR. The presence of IEEE Transactions on Systems, Man, and Cybernetics, Systems and ACM Transactions on Computer-Human Interaction also indicate that research in this area is closely related to the emerging technologies of AI, robotics, and automation.

In addition, the addition of journals with a business and psychology angle, such as Cognition, Technology & Work and Personnel Review, represents a significant development trend with the HCI research of HR Technological advancements. This shows the extent of interest and research efforts that are aimed at the interaction of employees with digital systems, the influence of AI on the optimization of HR processes, and the role of technology on employees' satisfaction, productivity, and behavior towards each other in the workplace. The interdisciplinary nature of the published research indicates the need to take a more comprehensive approach to studying HCI in HR. More thorough and better-designed work systems that prioritize people can be achieved by incorporating advances from computer science, psychology, business management, and industrial engineering.

The relationships between researchers and their home countries reveal some patterns regarding international collaboration. Despite having a prominent research presence, the USA also establishes partnerships with other significant research centers, such as China, Germany, and Australia. This shows that top researchers from different regions are collaborating across borders. Such partnerships are fundamental to ensuring that HCI research is inclusive and applicable to various cultural and organizational settings worldwide. Some countries, like Latvia, Morocco, and Ukraine, are part of the network but have a limited number of collaborations. This indicates that some of these countries are early-stage contributors to international research, while other countries are still developing international research collaboration networks. Fostering collaborations with these underdeveloped countries as emerging research centers can augment HCI research's global reach and provide diverse and adaptable applications to HCI research in HR.

Common Research Themes

Table 6. Most frequent words

Words	Occurrences
Human-Computer Interaction	14
Artificial Intelligence	7
Decision Making	3
Human Factors	3
Job Satisfaction	3
Virtual Teams	3
E-Learning	2
Education	2

Source: Developed by Authors

Figure 10. Word cloud

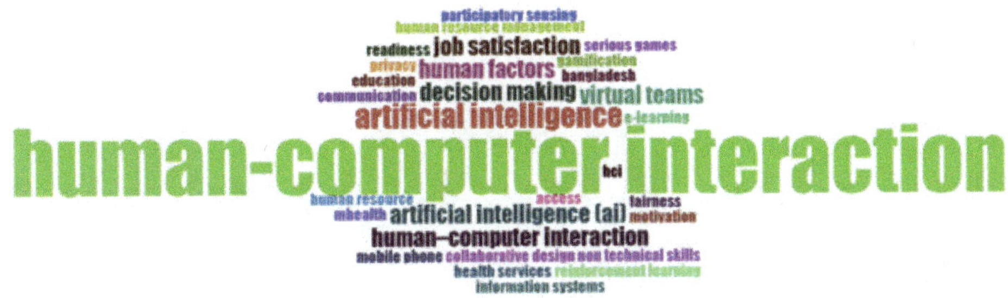

Examining the keywords in HCI literature for HR sheds light on the core issues and patterns developing in the area. The term "Human-Computer Interaction" appears 14 times, making it clear that the focus is on the interaction of people and tech in workplaces. A dominant theme concerning HR tech is the use of AI, which is noted 7 times as a single entry. AI is changing every facet of HR, whether it is recruitment, employee engagement, training or decision making. The term "Decision Making" is mentioned 3 times, meaning AID has a significant influence on people and HR strategies.

The prioritization of designing workplace technologies with usability, employee safety, and user experience in mind reflects the importance of "Human Factors" (3 occurrences). There has also been an interest in "Job Satisfaction" (3 occurrences), which suggests research has been looking at the influence of digital tools on employee engagement, motivation, and overall satisfaction at work. The emphasis on "Virtual Teams" (3 occurrences) reflects the importance of technology in remote and hybrid work settings and the need for collaborative work across distances. This makes HCI research critical for the effective use of technology in remote work environments. "E-Learning" (2 occurrences) and "Education" (2 occurrences) shows the use of technology in corporate training and the need for continuous employee upskilling, gamified digital learning, and AI-based competency assessments in HR Tech.

Thematic Mapping of Research Trends

Figure 11. Thematic map

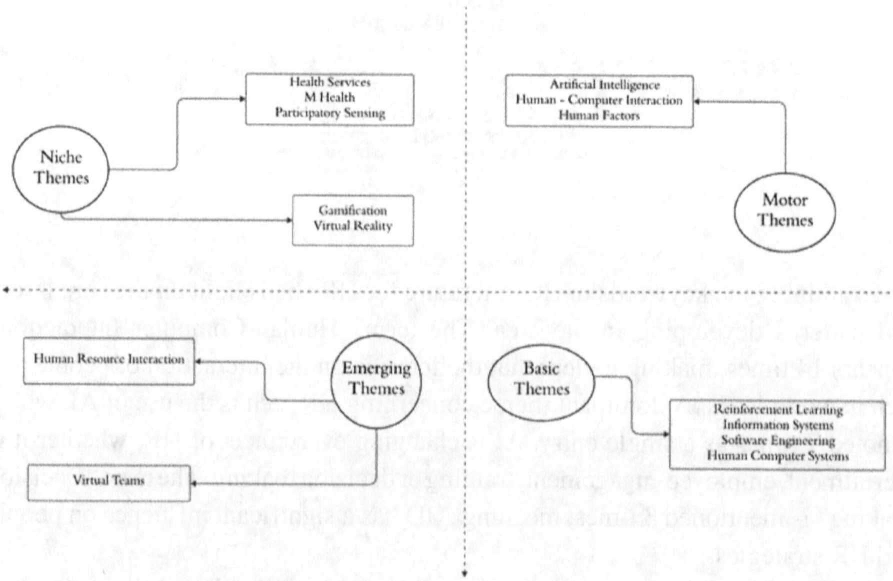

Source: Developed by Authors

With the thematic map, we can understand the various intricacies associated with research themes in HR-related Human-Computer Interaction (HCI) and categorize them into four associated quadrants: Niche Themes, Motor Themes, Emerging Themes, and Basic Themes. Each thematic map quadrant helps us understand the level of significance and growth associated with them, while also explaining and helping us understand the research landscape, the current trends, and what the trends signify for the future. Understanding these themes reflects the overall development in the associated constituent of respective technologies in HCI and HR and elucidates the extent of symbiotic evolution.

Niche Themes represents highly specialized, yet less impactful research domains. In this case, notable examples include Health Services and M-Health, along with Participatory Sensing, Gamification, and Virtual Reality. Health Services and M-Health depict the growing interest in digital health, especially in the intersections of HCI and health services in HR contexts. The research tends to focus on digital solutions to improve employee wellness, health programs in workplace, and remote health services. The recent concept of Participatory Sensing emphasizes the role of sensor technology in monitoring employee behavior and health, especially with the proliferation of wearables and IoT. On a different note, Gamification and Virtual Reality indicate that HCI research aims to augment HR on the more interactive and immersive side. Some Gamification strategies have been integrated into employee training, motivation, and engagement programs. In addition, Virtual Reality technology is being utilized in HR for remote collaborative training, simulation, and recruitment purposes. While the aforementioned topics may not have become mainstream, they show potential for future innovations in research and practice.

Motor themes are the most impactful and advanced topics in HCI for HR and represent the forefront of emerging research. This quadrant includes AI HCI, and Human Factors, which are crucial to the understanding and improvement of technology in HR. The importance of AI shows the increasing importance of machine learning, predictive analytics, and automation in HR processes such as talent acquisition and evaluations. AI tools are changing the way HR departments operate by increasing efficiency and eliminating bias. The inclusion of HCI in this quadrant shows the importance of efficient and clear design of interfaces in HR technologies. This area of research studies the interaction of employees with HR tools, AI chatbots, and self-service HR systems and seeks to provide methods to make these resources more efficient. Human Factors, in this case, focuses on the psychology and ergonomics of the adoption of technology in work processes. It studies the adaptive capacity of the employee with the introduction of new technologies to ensure that the new digital systems promote the desired cognitive and behavioral responses of the workforce. Given that Motor Themes are the most advanced in research and practice, they will likely continue to offer the most potential for emerging technologies in HR and the evolution of work.

The quadrant for Emerging Themes shows areas that are starting to grow in prominence but as of yet have not become core to the research in HCI and HR. The two most pronounced are Human Resource Interaction and Virtual Teams, both of which are highly relevant to the continuing evolution of workplace settings. Human Resource Interaction has to do with the increasing research interest in the HR technology, digital platforms, and AI-based HR systems that employees interact with. Given the self-service nature of many new HR portals and the emergence of virtual recruitment and digital feedback tools, interest in the HR interaction will further grow. Virtual Teams, are also an evolving research avenue created by remote and hybrid work configurations. The pandemic propelled the adoption of virtual collaboration tools and remote digital team management, thus the study of how virtual teams operate, communicate and are managed for productivity has become a necessity. Given the rapid adoption of new digital HR solutions and remote work practices in most organizations, these themes will most likely evolve to Motor Themes in the near future.

Finally, the Basic Themes quadrant encompasses primary subjects, which are not only well established but are also widely integrated with other domains of research. The areas that fall within this quadrant constitute the core technological infrastructure of the progresses made in HCI and HR and include Reinforcement Learning, Information Systems, Software Engineering, and Human-Computer Systems. Reinforcement Learning, which is an area of AI, is crucial in the automation of decision making, thereby streamlining HR processes and enhancing personalization of the employee experience. The study of Information Systems seeks to provide the framework within which the HR Technology platforms are designed, implemented, and managed to ensure that the HR data processes are optimally secure and scalable. Also, Software Engineering is fundamental in developing HR software, AI-driven recruitment software, and workplace automation. Lastly, Human-Computer Systems research is the basis for all employee interactions with digital HR systems, focusing on user experience, the usability of systems, and the adaptive features of technology. All the preceding basic themes form the underlying infrastructure that support technological advancement in HR in such a way that the emerging and niche themes are optimally integrated, implemented, and scaled.

Theming mapping analysis provides value in understanding research development within Human-Computer Interaction in HR. Understanding interrelation between research areas is important. Researchers actively consider workplace interaction and employee engagement enhancement. Emerging themes include Gamification, Virtual Reality, and Participatory Sensing. AI, Human-Computer Interaction, and Human Factors are core topics that drive the continuous digital transformation of HR practices. Virtual Teams and Human Resource Interaction describes emerging HR themes that recognize the evolving work environment. There is a demand for research in remote collaboration and digital HR tools. The fields of Information Systems, Software Engineering, and Reinforcement Learning bound the analysis and describe areas that are technologically robust, and evolving.

Table 7. Future research direction

Key Area of Focus	Objective	Research Questions
Artificial Intelligence in HR	Enhance AI-driven decision-making and automation in HR tasks.	1. How can AI reduce biases in recruitment and employee evaluation?
		2. What are the ethical implications of AI-driven HR decisions?
Human-Computer Interaction (HCI) Design	Improve usability and accessibility of HR technology.	1. How can user experience (UX) principles be integrated into HR software design?
		2. What design factors improve employee adoption of digital HR platforms?
Remote and Hybrid Work Technologies	Develop effective virtual collaboration and team management tools.	1. How can digital collaboration tools enhance productivity in remote teams?
		2. What are the key challenges in virtual team communication and engagement?
Gamification and Virtual Reality in HR	Explore immersive technologies for training and employee engagement.	1. How does VR-based training impact employee skill development?
		2. What gamification strategies are most effective for increasing employee motivation?
HR Analytics and Predictive Modeling	Utilize data-driven insights to improve HR strategies.	1. How can predictive analytics enhance talent acquisition and workforce planning?
		2. What are the key challenges in implementing data-driven HR decision-making?
Employee Well-being and Digital Health	Leverage technology for employee health monitoring and well-being.	1. How can wearable technology improve workplace wellness programs?
		2. What role does AI play in predicting employee burnout and mental health issues?

Source: Developed by Authors using R

6. CONCLUSION

Summary of Findings

The bibliometric and systematic analysis of 96 publications spanning 1993 to 2024 allows us to map the evolution, structure, and future trajectory of research on Human-Computer Interaction (HCI) applied to Human Resources (HR). The field shows a high degree of interconnectedness, exemplified by the average of 3.44 authors per paper and a co-authorship index of 3.55, indicating their cross-disciplinary collaboration involving computer science, psychology, organizational behavior, and HRM. Although the number of publications is low and the authorship is relatively sparse (330 authors), there is a concentration of research activity, particularly after 2015. The average of 24.2 citations per document illustrates its impact, with 2015 and 2019 being particularly notable. The international collaboration is nonetheless low, with only 5.21% of papers having authors from different countries, indicating an opportunity for greater collaboration. Key sources of knowledge include the International Journal of Medical Informatics and Computers in Human Behavior, and influential authors such as Chen D and Johnson C.

Notably, some journals have high citation rates for even single contributions, illustrating field-defining studies. While the USA and China dominate the volume and citations, research from Singapore and Malaysia, despite the lower volume, shows high research quality. Regarding gaps and patterns for future research, the study is strengthened by the PRISMA methodology and the use of Scopus and Web of Science.

Thematic breadth of HCI-HR research is further illuminated by content analysis. Notable studies possessed the largest scope and tackled issues such as cyberloafing and digital overload, user-centered healthcare interface, and skill evaluator, suggesting abundance both in theory and in practice. Lim V, Young K, Johnson C, and Khatun F research dominate digital behavior and productivity, and the integrated healthcare HCI systems. Robust structure is thematic mapping with the most prominent of the four categories. Core themes such as artificial intelligence, human-computer interaction, and human factors are the most prominent in HCI in HR. This shows the attentiveness to digital systems, AI-based decision making, and ergonomics. Most increasing in importance is the human resource interaction and virtual teams due to the emergence of new remote and hybrid working. Other themes of gamification, virtual reality, participatory sensing and the foundational themes of reinforcement learning, information systems and software engineering are HCI and HR technological innovation in training, health monitoring, and engagement. Keywords in the research pointed to the strategy of the field as artificial intelligence, decision making, job satisfaction, and virtual teams became prominent in the research.

Besides, collaborative network analysis has noted a highly interconnected group of researchers, especially Ray P, Liaw S, and Khatun F, whose interdisciplinary and frequently international collaboration exemplifies the cross-functional importance of the domain. Notable knowledge producers include Pennsylvania State University and Carnegie Mellon. The results confirm the growing sophistication and practical importance of HCI research in HR, while highlighting the necessity for more integrated, global, and cross-border interdisciplinary research paradigms in the future.

Implications for Academia and Industry

Implications for Academia

There is a renewed emphasis for a unified vision for HCI research for HR, along with the need for more collaborative research considering the gaps in the HCI for HR value chain. Virtual team collaborations, participatory sensing, and AI within HR tools create research opportunities in gamified learning, digital well-being, and socio-technological system design. International and cross-departmental collaborations are needed to create a regional balance in socio-technological research systems for diverse, innovative research. International funding consortia aimed at structured research funding will foster innovation and diversity in socio-technological research systems. Researchers are framed to build research funding regional capacity for less researched regions, especially in Africa, South America, and parts of Asia. This can be done through collaborative research grants, joint publications, and research-focused institutional capacity-building support. With the need for innovative research, there is a need to create sufficient longitudinal, integrated, and outcome-driven theory leading research for foundational models. This can be made with fewer longitudinal research to create impact and outcome models. Fewer models and funded research are seen in early-career researchers. The impact studies are framed to less but more rigorous research. It is apparent that early-career researchers are framed to more of a shift research focus from quantity to rigor. In summary, academia needs to integrate its teaching, research concentration, and collaboration techniques to adapt to the advancing digital HR ecosystem.

Implications for Industry

The research provides guiding principles for incorporating design thinking and evidence-based innovation into digital transformations of HR processes. An emphasis on usability and employee engagement is required from organizations through the infusion of human factors research into each dimension of HR technology. HR functions such as recruitment, employee engagement, and performance reviews should include AI as long as ethical, transparent, and equitable principles are followed. Because virtual and hybrid operations are the new normal, it is recommended that companies invest in digital applications that foster operational collaboration and alleviate cognitive overload and digital burnout. Research on digital distraction, cyberloafing, and mobile technology stress demonstrates the need for companies to adopt digital wellness policies which include mindful technology use, simplified interfaces, and restorative breaks from technology. Gamification, playful design of interfaces, and peer evaluations, as discussed in some studies, may also increase employee motivation, engagement in training, and improve the achievement of learning objectives. In addition, companies should collaborate with research institutions to develop state-of-the-art, evidence-based, and user-friendly HR technology. Because of the lack of cross-border academic partnerships, the localization and cultural sensitivity of multinational companies is of utmost importance. Lastly, insights from HCI in healthcare and socio-technical studies reveal important lessons for enterprise systems, particularly for digital health and workforce management systems, highlighting the imperative for seamless integration, change management, and ongoing employee involvement.

Limitations and Challenges

The study has several limitations. Data limitations come from limitations in the coverage of the dataset due to the inability to access non-English countries and trade publications, which may limit the coverage of the review. Methodological limitations involve the challenges of bibliometric analysis, where there are database limitations and the sub-optimization of measures related to the impact of citations. There are scope limitations since the study focuses on academic literature, and therefore, it does not capture all the practices emerging from industry trends. There are also technological limitations due to the fast pace of technological advancements in the HCI and HR fields that may diminish the relevance of the findings over time.

REFERENCES

Agarwal, S. (2024). The profound impact of virtual communication technologies on team collaboration in the contemporary work environment. *International Journal of Embedded Systems & Emerging Technologies*, *10*(1), 45–60.

Al-Ansi, A. M., Jaboob, M., Garad, A., & Al-Ansi, A. (2023). Analyzing augmented reality (AR) and virtual reality (VR) recent development in education. *Social Sciences & Humanities Open*, *8*(1), 100532. DOI: 10.1016/j.ssaho.2023.100532

Barbu, A., Ichimov, M. A. M., Costea-Marcu, I. C., Militaru, G., Deselnicu, D. C., & Moiceanu, G. (2025). Exploring Employee Perspectives on Workplace Technology: Usage, Roles, and Implications for Satisfaction and Performance. *Behavioral Sciences (Basel, Switzerland)*, *15*(1), 45. DOI: 10.3390/bs15010045 PMID: 39851850

Campderrich, B. (2009). Human-computer interaction: A human resources perspective. In *Encyclopedia of Human Resources Information Systems: Challenges in e-HRM* (pp. 488-494). IGI Global. DOI: 10.4018/978-1-59904-883-3.ch072

Cavanagh, J., Bartram, T., Meacham, H., Bigby, C., Oakman, J., & Fossey, E. (2017). Supporting workers with disabilities: A scoping review of the role of human resource management in contemporary organisations. *Asia Pacific Journal of Human Resources*, *55*(1), 6–43. DOI: 10.1111/1744-7941.12111

Dhand, S. (2025). Human-Centric Digital Workplace: Designing for Employee Well-being and Productivity. In *Human-Centric, Sustainable, and Resilient Organizations in the Digital Age* (pp. 125-146). IGI Global Scientific Publishing.

DiRomualdo, A., El-Khoury, D., & Girimonte, F. (2018). HR in the digital age: How digital technology will change HR's organization structure, processes and roles. *Strategic HR Review*, *17*(5), 234–242. DOI: 10.1108/SHR-08-2018-0074

Dlamini, S. (2023). Artificial Intelligence in Human Resource Management: Advanced Computing Systems for Talent Analytics and Decision Making. *Journal of Advanced Computing Systems*, *3*(12), 10–17.

Donthu, N., Kumar, S., Mukherjee, D., Pandey, N., & Lim, W. M. (2021). How to conduct a bibliometric analysis: An overview and guidelines. *Journal of Business Research*, *133*, 285–296. DOI: 10.1016/j.jbusres.2021.04.070

Durango, I., Gallud, J. A., & Penichet, V. M. (2024). Human-Data Interaction Framework: A Comprehensive Model for a Future Driven by Data and Humans. *arXiv preprint arXiv:2407.21010*.

Elugbaju, W. K., Okeke, N. I., & Alabi, O. A. (2024). Human Resource Analytics as a Strategic Tool for Workforce Planning and Succession Management. *International Journal Of Engineering Research And Development*, *20*(11), 744–756.

Ezeafulukwe, C., Onyekwelu, S. C., Onyekwelu, N. P., Ike, C. U., Bello, B. G., & Asuzu, F. O. (2024). Best practices in human resources for inclusive employment: An in-depth review. *International Journal of Science and Research Archive*, *11*(1), 1286–1293. DOI: 10.30574/ijsra.2024.11.1.0215

Haque, S. M. S. (2023). The impact of remote work on hr practices: Navigating challenges, embracing opportunities. *European Journal of Human Resource Management Studies*, *7*(1). Advance online publication. DOI: 10.46827/ejhrms.v7i1.1549

Huo, X., Qian, Y., Siau, K. L., & Nah, F. F. H. (2024). HCI in business and organizations: Digital transformation with HCI, metaverse, and AI technologies. In *Human-Computer Interaction in Various Application Domains* (pp. 294–347). CRC Press. DOI: 10.1201/9781003490692-11

Iqbal, A. I., Aamir, A., Hammad, A., Hafsa, H., Basit, A., Oduoye, M. O., Anis, M. W., Ahmed, S., Younus, M. I., & Jabeen, S. (2024). Immersive technologies in healthcare: An in-depth exploration of virtual reality and augmented reality in enhancing patient care, medical education, and training paradigms. *Journal of Primary Care & Community Health*, *15*, 21501319241293311. DOI: 10.1177/21501319241293311 PMID: 39439304

Johnson, R. D., Lukaszewski, K. M., & Stone, D. L. (2017). The Importance of the Interface between Humans and Computers on the Effectiveness of eHRM. *AIS Transactions on Human-Computer Interaction*, *9*(1), 23–33. DOI: 10.17705/1thci.00087

Kambur, E., & Yildirim, T. (2023). From traditional to smart human resources management. *International Journal of Manpower*, *44*(3), 422–452. DOI: 10.1108/IJM-10-2021-0622

Katuk, N., Vergallo, R., & Sugiharto, T. (2024). *The Future of Human-Computer Integration*. CRC Press. DOI: 10.1201/9781003479727

Kaur, R., Kaur, H., Jangra, G., & Kumar, R. (2024, November). Enhancing Organizational Efficiency and User Experience Through Optimized Human-Computer Interface Design. In *2024 4th International Conference on Technological Advancements in Computational Sciences (ICTACS)* (pp. 965-968). IEEE. DOI: 10.1109/ICTACS62700.2024.10840978

Khair, M. A., Mahadasa, R., Tuli, F. A., & Ande, J. R. P. K. (2020). Beyond human judgment: Exploring the impact of artificial intelligence on HR decision-making efficiency and fairness. *Global Disclosure of Economics and Business*, *9*(2), 163–176. DOI: 10.18034/gdeb.v9i2.730

Madan, S., Kumar, T., & Bhagat, A. (2024). Inclusive Hiring through Technology: A Recruitment Platform for Individuals with Intellectual Disabilities. *Procedia CIRP*, *128*, 31–36. DOI: 10.1016/j.procir.2024.05.091

Makhija, M., Jha, P., & Dubey, N. (2024). Artificial Intelligence Its Growing Role in Human Resource Management. In Employee Performance Management for Improved Workplace Motivation (pp. 231-262). IGI Global.

Meluso, J., Johnson, S., & Bagrow, J. (2022). Flexible environments for hybrid collaboration: Redesigning virtual work through the four orders of design. *Design Issues*, *38*(1), 55–69. DOI: 10.1162/desi_a_00670

Mounica, V., & Kirubakaran, M. K. (2024, March). Revolutionary Cursor Control Systems Enhancing Human Computer Interaction. In *2024 10th International Conference on Advanced Computing and Communication Systems (ICACCS)* (Vol. 1, pp. 2586-2590). IEEE.

Naveen, S., Sharma, P., Veena, A., & Ramaprabha, D. (2025). Digital HR Tools and AI Integration for Corporate Management: Transforming Employee Experience. In *Corporate Management in the Digital Age* (pp. 69-100). IGI Global Scientific Publishing.

Nawaz, H. (2023). Human-Centered Engineering: Designing for Usability, Accessibility, and Inclusivity. *Liberal Journal of Language and Literature Review*, *1*(01), 55–60.

Nocker, M., & Sena, V. (2019). Big data and human resources management: The rise of talent analytics. *Social Sciences (Basel, Switzerland)*, *8*(10), 273. DOI: 10.3390/socsci8100273

Rishiraj, A., & Shukla, S. (2023, November). Data: A Key to HR Analytics for Talent Management. In *International Conference on Data Science, Computation and Security* (pp. 33-49). Singapore: Springer Nature Singapore.

Rohit, A. K., Saini, M., & Pawar, M. (2024). Integration of Artificial Intelligence In Human Resource Information System. *International Journal of Innovative Research in Technology and Science*, *12*(2), 177–183.

Sachan, V. S., Katiyar, A., Somashekher, C., Chauhan, A. S., & Bhima, C. K. (2024). The Role Of Artificial Intelligence In HRM: Opportunities, Challenges, And Ethical Considerations. *Educational Administration: Theory and Practice*, *30*(4), 7427–7435.

Salvadorinho, J., & Teixeira, L. (2023). Happy and engaged workforce in industry 4.0: A new concept of digital tool for HR based on theoretical and practical trends. *Sustainability (Basel)*, *15*(3), 2781. DOI: 10.3390/su15032781

Sanjaya, R., & Irawan, D. (2024). Design of an Inclusive Digital Platform for Training and Distribution of Human Resources in Improving Accessibility and Opportunities for Persons with Disabilities. *Golden Ratio of Data in Summary*, *4*(2), 765–780. DOI: 10.52970/grdis.v4i2.738

Sayyed, M., Jadhav, B. R., Barnabas, V., & Gupta, S. K. (2024). Human-Machine Interaction in the Metaverse: A Comprehensive Review and Proposed Framework. *Impact and Potential of Machine Learning in the Metaverse*, 1-28.

Sharma, S., & Sengupta, S. (2023, October). AI-Driven HR Practices: Recent Trends in Digital HR Tools and Their Perceived Benefits. In *The International Conference on Recent Innovations in Computing* (pp. 219-231). Singapore: Springer Nature Singapore.

Sundari, M. S., & Gangalapudi, K. P. (2025). Balancing Digital Efficiency With Human Connection in the Workplace. In *Humanizing the Hyperconnected Workplace* (pp. 31–68). IGI Global Scientific Publishing. DOI: 10.4018/979-8-3693-8171-7.ch002

Tan, Y., Xu, W., Li, S., & Chen, K. (2022). Augmented and virtual reality (AR/VR) for education and training in the AEC industry: A systematic review of research and applications. *Buildings (Basel, Switzerland)*, *12*(10), 1529. DOI: 10.3390/buildings12101529

Tshabalala, L. (2023). The Role of Artificial Intelligence in Enhancing Workforce Productivity: Advanced Computing Applications in HR. *Journal of Advanced Computing Systems*, *3*(12), 26–33.

Tuli, F. A., Varghese, A., & Ande, J. R. P. K. (2018). Data-driven decision making: A framework for integrating workforce analytics and predictive HR metrics in digitalized environments. *Global Disclosure of Economics and Business*, *7*(2), 109–122. DOI: 10.18034/gdeb.v7i2.724

Umrao, S., Dron, S., & Saxena, R. (2024). An Examination of the Impact of Artificial Intelligence on Human Resource Management: Improving Efficiency and Employee Experience. *International Journal of Innovations in Science, Engineering And Management*, 87-94.

Vetrivel, S. C., Sowmiya, K. C., Sabareeshwari, V., & Arun, V. P. (2024). Navigating the Digital Economy: The Crucial Role of Human-Computer Interaction. In *Social Reflections of Human-Computer Interaction in Education, Management, and Economics* (pp. 184-216). IGI Global.

Walkowiak, E. (2024). Digitalization and inclusiveness of HRM practices: The example of neurodiversity initiatives. *Human Resource Management Journal, 34*(3), 578–598. DOI: 10.1111/1748-8583.12499

Wandhe, D. P. (2023). The Transformative Role of Artificial Intelligence in HR: Revolutionizing the Future of HR. Available at *SSRN* 4666419.

Wolniak, R., Dolata, M., Hadryjańska, B., & Wysokińska-Senkus, A. (2024). Employing business analytics in Industry 4.0 settings for human resource analytics. *Zeszyty Naukowe Politechniki Śląskiej. Organizacja i Zarządzanie*, *197*, 629–640.

Yanamala, K. K. R. (2023). Transparency, privacy, and accountability in AI-enhanced HR processes. *Journal of Advanced Computing Systems*, *3*(3), 10–18. DOI: 10.69987/JACS.2023.30302

Yazdi, M. (2024). Augmented reality (AR) and virtual reality (VR) in maintenance training. In *Advances in Computational Mathematics for Industrial System Reliability and Maintainability* (pp. 169–183). Springer Nature Switzerland. DOI: 10.1007/978-3-031-53514-7_10

Zhou, J., & Cen, W. (2023). Design and application research of a digital human resource management platform based on ChatGPT. *Journal of Theory and Practice of Social Science*, *3*(7), 49–57.

Chapter 13
Perceived Emotional Intelligence in AI-Driven Interactions: A Human-Centered Conceptual Framework

Nisha Balhara
http://orcid.org/0009-0004-1467-0563
Chandigarh University, India

Neema Gupta
http://orcid.org/0000-0003-3347-3202
Chandigarh University, Mohali, India

ABSTRACT

Emotional intelligence in AI-driven environments has become crucial from both a conceptual and practical standpoints as AI mediates human interaction more frequently. This chapter presents a human-centered conceptual framework that reframes emotional intelligence as a perceived and relational phenomenon that arises through human–AI interaction, rather than as a purely technical competence of AI systems. The chapter explains how AI emotional capabilities impact emotional expression, trust formation, emotional bonding, and relationship quality through perceived emotional intelligence by integrating theories of emotional intelligence, social presence, human–AI interaction, and relationship development. In order to promote long-lasting and human-centered AI-mediated connections, it also critically examines ethical and societal issues such as emotional manipulation, dependency, authenticity, and emotional data governance. Finally, it provides recommendations for responsible AI design and future study.

DOI: 10.4018/979-8-3373-8337-8.ch013

1. INTRODUCTION

Artificial intelligence (AI) has become deeply embedded in contemporary communication environments, transforming not only how information is exchanged but also how emotions are expressed and relationships are formed (Guzman & Lewis, 2019). AI-driven systems—including conversational agents, virtual assistants, recommendation systems, social media algorithms, and social robots—now participate in interactions that extend beyond functional efficiency to incorporate elements of emotional responsiveness (Latif et al., 2026). These systems increasingly detect users' moods, provide emotionally attuned feedback, and adapt communication styles based on inferred affective states. As a result, AI has emerged as a powerful mediator of emotional expression and relational experience in digital contexts (Döveling et al., 2018).

Emotional expression, empathy, and emotional understanding are central to interpersonal relationships, trust development, and social cohesion (Petrocchi et al., 2020). Traditionally, the capacity to perceive emotions, respond empathetically, and regulate emotional exchanges has been conceptualized as a distinctly human competence within the framework of emotional intelligence (EI) (Elfenbein & MacCann, 2017). Emotional intelligence enables individuals to navigate complex social environments, sustain relational harmony, and cultivate meaningful social connections (Singh et al., 2025). Recent advances in AI, however, challenge this human-centric assumption by enabling technological systems to perform emotion-related functions that resemble emotionally intelligent behavior (Glikson & Woolley, 2020).

The increasing prevalence of emotionally responsive AI raises important theoretical and practical questions regarding the nature and consequences of emotional intelligence in AI-driven interactions. Although AI systems do not experience emotions in a phenomenological sense, they are capable of detecting emotional cues, generating empathic responses, and shaping emotional communication processes (Shank et al., 2019). Users frequently interpret these responses as indicators of emotional understanding, attributing emotionally intelligent qualities to AI systems (Pantano & Scarpi, 2022). Such perceptions influence how individuals engage with AI, the extent to which they disclose emotions, and whether they develop trust and relational attachment over time (Boyd & Markowitz, 2026).

Despite the expanding research on affective computing and human–AI interaction, existing scholarship remains fragmented (Pei et al., 2023). Technical research has predominantly focused on improving emotion recognition accuracy and algorithmic performance, whereas social science research has tended to examine outcomes such as satisfaction, trust, or technology acceptance in isolation (Kaklauskas et al., 2022). Consequently, there remains a limited number of integrative, theory-driven frameworks that explain how emotional intelligence operates in AI-mediated interactions and how it shapes human emotional expression and relationship development over time (Zhai et al., 2025). In particular, the relational implications of users' perceptions of emotionally intelligent AI remain insufficiently theorized (Youn & Jin, 2021).

This gap is especially significant given the increasing deployment of AI in emotionally sensitive domains, including healthcare support, mental health applications, education, customer service, and online social environments. In such contexts, emotional intelligence is not merely an optional design feature but a foundational requirement for ethical, effective, and trustworthy interaction (Pipitone et al., 2025). Without a human-centered conceptual understanding of emotional intelligence in AI-driven interactions, there is a risk of overestimating technological sophistication while underestimating the associated social, psychological, and ethical consequences (Riva et al., 2025). These developments underscore the need for a structured and theory-driven perspective on emotional intelligence in AI-mediated communication (Ge et al., 2026).

Responding to this need, this chapter develops a human-centered conceptual framework that reconceptualizes emotional intelligence in AI-driven interactions as a perceived and relational phenomenon emerging through interaction (Ozturkcan & Merdin-Uygur, 2026). Drawing on scholarship from psychology, communication studies, human–computer interaction, information systems, and relationship research, the chapter integrates emotional intelligence theory with social presence theory, human–AI interaction theory, and relationship development theory (Lindgren, 2024). Rather than emphasizing technical system capabilities, the framework foregrounds users' perceptions and lived experiences of emotionally responsive AI (Benn-Short, 2026).

By positioning perceived emotional intelligence as a central relational mechanism, the chapter explains how AI-mediated emotional responsiveness shapes emotional disclosure, trust formation, emotional attachment, and overall relationship quality (Simos et al., 2026). In addition, it critically examines ethical and societal implications associated with emotionally intelligent AI, including emotional manipulation, dependency, authenticity, and emotional data governance (Demir et al., 2026). The chapter concludes by outlining future research directions aimed at advancing responsible, human-centered approaches to emotionally intelligent AI (Xu et al., 2026).

Within the broader context of this edited volume on emotionally responsive and human-centered AI, the chapter complements technically oriented and application-focused discussions by foregrounding the emotional, relational, and ethical dimensions of AI-mediated interaction. By conceptualizing emotional intelligence as a perception-mediated relational mechanism rather than a purely technical capability, this chapter offers an integrative theoretical foundation to inform scholarly research, guide responsible AI design, and support policy discussions surrounding emotionally responsive AI systems. It is intended for an interdisciplinary audience of scholars, doctoral researchers, practitioners, designers, and policymakers engaged in understanding and shaping the evolving relationship between humans and AI.

2. CONTRIBUTIONS OF THE CHAPTER

This chapter contributes a number of key contributions to the growing literature on the role of emotional intelligence in AI-driven interactions. First, it redefines emotional intelligence in AI-mediated contexts as experienced and interpersonal construct instead of a technical or computational skill, extending the traditional emotional intelligence theory past the human point of view. Second, the chapter incorporates the information offered by emotional intelligence theory, social presence theory, human-AI interaction theory, and relationship development theory to create a human-focused conceptual framework to explain the role that emotionally intelligent AI plays in influencing emotional expression and relationship development. Third, by focusing on the perceptions and lived experiences of the users, the chapter further develops insights into the most critical emotional and relationship consequences, such as emotional disclosure, expressive comfort, trust, emotional attachment, and quality of relationships. Fourth, the chapter critically discusses ethical and societal consequences that are linked to the emotionally intelligent AI, such as emotional manipulation, dependency, authenticity, and emotional data governance. Lastly, the chapter provides a systematic research agenda that gives research methodological direction and boundary conditions, which will be the basis of future empirical studies and responsible AI design.

3. CONCEPTUALIZING EMOTIONAL INTELLIGENCE IN AI-DRIVEN INTERACTIONS

The concept of emotional intelligence has been traditionally regarded as a human ability that is fundamental to successful communication and relations with other people. Classical psychological literature describes emotional intelligence as a group of interconnected skills that are characterized by emotional perception, emotional understanding, emotional control, and emotional expression (Tjimuku et al., 2025). These abilities help people to be aware of their own and other people's emotions, perceive affective signals, manage emotions at the same time, and express them in socially correct ways (Van Kleef and Côté, 2021). According to extensive empirical studies, emotional intelligence is related to improved relationship quality, interpersonal trust, cooperation, and psychological well-being (Tjimuku et al., 2025).

In most of its theoretical construction, emotional intelligence was assumed to be inextricable linked to human thinking and experienced affect. The emotional cognition was presumed to need subjective awareness, empathic concern based on phenomenological experience, and moral reasoning. This meant that non-conscious entities were greatly disqualified in the context of emotional intelligence (Pae, 2025). Nevertheless, this assumption is facing more challenges due to the growing capabilities of artificial intelligence that allow technological systems to conduct functions related to emotions with the help of computational processes (Halkiopoulos et al., 2025).

Advances in affective computing have enabled the AI systems to learn to identify and analyze the presence of emotional cues within the language, vocal tone, facial expressions, and behavioral patterns (Leong et al., 2023). Machine learning and pattern recognitions allow AI systems to predict the affective areas of users and provide response based on the socially accepted standards of empathy and emotional suitability (Alanazi et al., 2023). Though these systems are not involved in emotive states, they are becoming more involved in emotion communication processes through the generation of responses that seem supportive, attentive, and emotionally responsive (Kim & Wang, 2025).

This technological revolution requires the reconceptualization of emotional intelligence in AI-mediated scenarios. Instead of considering emotional intelligence as an internal emotional ability that is based on conscious experience, in the interactions between AI and humans, emotional intelligence is better understood as a perception-based and relational construct (Srivastava and Gurme, 2025). This is not the key point of whether AI systems actually have (or lack) emotions, but rather the perception of the user that the systems are capable of emotions and responsive when interacting (Boyd & Markowitz, 2026).

Based on this, perceived emotional intelligence of AI can be described as judgments of the users on the abilities of the AI system in perceiving emotional signals, reacting empathetically, and modulating communication based on emotional requirements. Such impressions affect the way users make sense of AI actions and define whether communication is perceived as socially relevant and relationally interactive. The studies of social presence and human-AI interaction have revealed that users feel that technological agents are warmer and have a stronger social presence and relational competence when they recognize emotional understanding and responsiveness (Tripathi et al., 2025).

Notably, AI-based interaction is co-created through dynamic interaction processes to build emotional intelligence. The aspects of design, including conversational tone, the speed of response, emotional recognition, and personalization based on adaptive algorithms, interact with the expectations of users, their previous experiences, culture, AI literacy, etc. Emotional intelligence therefore is in a relational form as opposed to being a fixed system attribute. This is consistent with the communication theory which theorizes about meaning making as being constructed socially by way of interaction and not necessarily being vested in communicative agents alone (Chandra & Rahman, 2026).

Perceived emotional intelligence has strong implications with regard to emotional expression in human beings. The fact that AI systems are perceived to be uniform, non-judgmental, and socially neutral has been interpreted as potentially reducing the perceived evaluation anxiety and decreasing the hindrances against emotional disclosure (Laban and Cross, 2024). Empirical evidence in the human-computer interaction area indicates that users might be more willing to share vulnerable emotions with the AI systems compared to the human ones, especially when it comes to a stigmatizing or socially risky situation. Therefore, the emotional expression in the AI-mediated setting can be more frequent, more outspoken, and less bound by the fears of being socially judged.

Perceived emotional intelligence is central in the formation of trust and development of relationships at the relational level. Perceptions of benevolence, understanding and emotional responsiveness play a major role in influencing trust. In the case where AI systems are seen as emotionally intelligent, their users can develop not only cognitive trust in the functionality of the system but also affective trust based on the perceived relational reliability (Jamil et al., 2026). Through consistent emotional-responsive interactions, emotional attachment and perceived companionship might develop with time which further relationships development will be expanded into AI-mediated environment (Jocher and Verwiebe, 2026).

Meanwhile, this reconceptualization brings out some existential questions about authenticity and emotional reciprocity. Since AI intelligence is a simulated experience, and not emotional, then emotional experience is also asymmetrical. Users can find emotional comfort and relationship satisfaction, but the lack of true emotional subjectivity makes it difficult to assume the mutuality and the same level of affectedness (Xie et al., 2026). These tensions do support the need of a human-based conceptual framework which recognizes the relational potential and ethical constraints of emotionally intelligent AI.

Combined, such reconceptualization puts emotional intelligence within AI-mediated interactions as a perception-mediated, interactional phenomenon that defines the way humans express, construct meaning, and form relationships with intelligent systems. Returning analytical attention to emotional capacity within the organization and relational perception and interactional dynamics, this perspective offers a strong theoretical basis of seeing the emotional and relational implications of AI-mediated communication.

4. THEORETICAL FOUNDATIONS OF EMOTIONAL INTELLIGENCE IN AI-DRIVEN INTERACTIONS

4.1 Emotional Intelligence Theory

According to the theory of emotional intelligence, high-impact research in psychology and management publications show that emotional intelligence positively influences emotional regulation, empathy, and interpersonal effectiveness (Sasere and Matashu, 2025). In AI settings, the emotional intelligence theory assists in explaining why emotion recognition and empathic responsiveness affect and influence emotional engagement and relational outcomes, even when used by non-human agents (Gao et al., 2026).In the proposed conceptual framework, emotional intelligence theory explains the importance of emotion recognition, empathic responsiveness, and emotional regulation as key antecedents in influencing emotional expression and relationship outcomes even in cases where they are implemented by non-human agents (Paiva et al., 2021).

4.2 Social Presence Theory

Social presence theory describes the development of the feeling of psychological proximity and social proximity through communication media. Studies that have been conducted in reputable communication and information systems journals indicate that perceived social presence is enhanced by emotionally responding communication (Li et al., 2026). Artificially intelligent emotions make emotional engagements and relational perception more likely because the artificially intelligent systems respond in a manner that signifies comprehension, warmth, and attentiveness (Tripathi et al., 2025). The social presence theory, in the conceptual framework, explains how the emotional responses of AI can be translated into socially meaningful interaction with an emotional signal, which validates the perception of users regarding the psychological proximity and relational interactions (Xu et al., 2026).

4.3 Human–AI Interaction Theory

The human Ai interaction theory focuses on the reciprocal interaction that exists between humans and intelligent systems. Unlike regarding AI as a passive device, this way of thinking would conceive AI as a form of interaction that influences user behavior and expectations.

The theoretical approach underlies the framework by emphasizing the cycles of mutually influencing emotional cues and communication strategies by the emotionally intelligent AI behavior and its interpretation by the user, which fosters the emergence of emotional engagement and communication patterns over time (Jiang et al., 2024).

4.4 Relationship Development Theory

The relationship development theory describes how trust, emotional attachment, and quality of relations are developed over time by means of recurrent interaction (Khiabani & Rezaeian, 2026). Emotional responsiveness is an important factor of relationship development, as pointed out by relationship research. It can become possible to trust and emotionally bond with the users when AI systems reveal perceived emotional intelligence, furthering the processes of relationship development to AI-mediated environments (Zulaikha et al., 2026).

In the framework put forward, relationship development theory is important in explaining how repeated affectively intelligent interactions can cause trust, emotional attachment, and perceived relationship quality in lasting human-AI relations (Zhou & Guan, 2025).

5. MECHANISMS OF EMOTIONAL INTELLIGENCE IN AI-DRIVEN INTERACTIONS

To make sense of emotional intelligence in AI-driven interactions, it is necessary to go beyond surface-level descriptions of AI capabilities to understand the processes through which emotional intelligence is practiced, perceived, and converted into human emotional and relational consequences. (Hoang, 2025)

Emotional intelligence in AI is not a fixed feature in a system; it works through a system of interactive processes that determine how users perceive the behavior of AI, exhibit feelings, and form relational reactions. This section is conceptualized on the basis of the research on psychology, human-computer interaction, and information systems, which clarifies the mechanisms of three processes: emotion recognition, empathic response simulation, and adaptive personalization.These three mechanisms explain the way emotional intelligence is elicited in AI-mediated interactions and how the process affects human expression and relationship-building (Kolomaznik et al., 2024).

5.1 Emotion Recognition as the Foundation of AI-Mediated Emotional Intelligence

Emotion recognition is the basic concept of emotional intelligence by AI-based interactions, which means that an AI system recognizes the emotional states of users by analyzing verbal, paralinguistic or behavioral messages (Padmaja et al., 2024).Technologies in natural language processing, sentiment processing, facial expression recognition, voice analytics, and others have greatly contributed to the increased accuracy with which AI infers emotion states. Journals like Computers in Human Behavior and Human Computer interaction have also shown research that can help people feel their emotions are powerful with the difference between whether the AI systems accurately recognize their emotions or not. Regarding the human-centered understanding, emotionally recognized meaning is not just but the perceived emotional awareness. Users will find it more suitable to think of an AI system as being emotionally intelligent when they feel that it is aware of their emotional condition, whether they are stressed, frustrated, enthusiastic, etc. The perception creates a feeling of understanding, which is an essential pre-requisite of expression of emotion and interpersonal intercourse. The recognition of emotions, therefore, becomes the initial process to make AI a functional interface instead of a socially meaning interaction partner (Marconi et al., 2026). The emotional recognition in behavior also influences the emotional expression behavior. The people will be likely to show emotions more frequently when they feel that their emotion expressive behaviors will be calculated and understood (Gudivaka et al., 2026). When using AI within a context, perceived capacity of AI to recognize emotions can lead to a decrease in emotional control in a situation where there is vulnerability or social risk (Stinus & Berjot, 2026).When perceived to understand emotional perception, users will release emotions on AI systems. This relationship accords with the research in psychology where perceived emotional attunement helps to deliver emotional disclosure and expressive comfort (Meng & Dai, 2021). Nevertheless, the aspect of emotion awareness in AI-driven communication is indeed probabilistic and specific to a situation. Emotional cues tend to be ambiguous, cultural as well as being, dynamically exhibited. (Krzeminska, 2025). Wrong interpretation of emotional cues can destroy perceptions of emotive intelligence and destroy or remove trust. Emotion recognition is, therefore, not sufficient to maintain an interaction with a high degree of emotional intelligence, but it should be supplemented with the necessary emotional responses (Gong and Huang, 2026).

5.2 Empathic Response Simulation and Perceived Emotional Understanding

The second mechanism that is crucial to emotional intelligence being implemented in AI-driven interactions is called empathic response simulation (Dzreke and Dzreke, 2026). Empathic responses entail recognition and expression of emotional situations, including care or being caring and acting in a manner that is congruent with societally accepted expectations of empathy (Lynch & Ruch, 2026). The empathetic behaviour of

AI systems is not yet realized, but that can be simulated through the acts of response produced in an algorithmic way, and which are informed by the sensitivity to emotion (Chen, 2026). According to previous literature in communication and information systems journals, simulating empathy is relationally performed during interaction and is not necessarily achieved through having an internal experience of emotions. In the context of AI mediation, empathic response simulation functions in signaling the ability to understand emotions and respond, thus constituting what users think of emotional intelligence. Even the simplest emotional support, like confirmation of feelings, the provision of positive words, or the use of specific tones in accordance with the emotional situation, can be of great help in how perceived empathy (Lee and Choi, 2025). It is significant that empathic response simulation shapes the trust and emotional safety. Such perceptions of benevolence and understanding help a lot to trust. In an empathetic response of AI systems, users can assume that the system is concerned about their emotional needs, elevating the level of relationship confidence (Bove, 2019). Such trust is created not only based on functional reliability but also on emotional reliability the perception that the AI is going to act accordingly in the situation that acts as an emotional trigger (Song et al., 2026). In terms of expression of emotions, emotional responses, empathic responses promote future engagement of emotions. People who get emotionally validating answers are more prone to maintain emotional disclosing and emotional expressiveness (Paakkanen et al., 2021).In the long run, recurring empathic interactions would strengthen emotional openness and increase relational involvement. Such dynamics can be associated with human-human relations patterns where sympathy provides the emotional connection and continuity of relations. However, the problem of authenticity and emotional labor can also be raised in connection with empathy response simulation. The fact that AI empathy is a simulated process, as opposed to an experienced one, creates an unequal emotional transaction. Employers have the chance to gain emotionally in the case of empathic responses, but lack of the true experience of emotion on the side of the AI makes traditional understanding of mutuality more difficult. This tension serves as an entreaty to the ethical disclosure and ethical design in the emotionally responsible AI systems (Cinar and Bilodeau, 2024).

5.3 Adaptive Personalization and Emotionally Intelligent Interaction

The third process that allows operationalization of emotional intelligence with AI-based interactions is that of adaptive personalization. Personalization is the capacity of AI system to react or respond in accordance with the preference, emotional history and strategies of interaction on a user-based environment. Emotionally guided personalization can also allow the AI systems to act in a manner that satisfies the emotional demands and expectations of users. Certain articles in journals like Journal of Service Research and MIS Quarterly indicate that personalization is the major factor that contributes to the experiences of relevance, engagement and relational value. Adaptive personalization also leads to relationship continuity in the emotional intelligent AI interactions, such as an AI system that recommends reassurance instead of solving a problem has the ability to detect the emotional needs of the user and this builds perceptions of emotional intelligence (Ma et al., 2025). The ability to recall the emotional more and be adaptable with time enables the artificial intelligence systems to develop an illusion of relational memory, which is a feature of meaningful relationships. Such systems can give the user feelings that it is listening and cares, which enhances emotional bonding and interaction (Woodruff, 2025). This interaction transitions to a transactional type, which is linked to relational interaction (Holldack et al., 2026).Notably, adaptive personalization has an impact on the ways in which the users form their identity and articulate feelings. Individualized emotional reactions would justify self-concepts among the users and promote experimentation via expression (Carlson et al., 2025). Nonetheless, too much of personalization can also limit the amount of expressing oneself emotionally: it can obviate the tendency toward very specific emotional responses or result in affect -dependency. The results mentioned above indicate that personalization should be balanced in helping people gain autonomy and emotional diversity (Raave et al., 2026).

5.4 From Mechanisms to Relational Outcomes: A Human-Centered Perspective

The three of them include functions of emotion recognition, simulation of empathy response and adaptive personalization which synergize in generating emotionally intelligent AI-guided interactions (Weng et al., 2026). They both define the perceived emotional intelligence of AI as a key psychological mediator between the relationship between AI and users and create trust, emotional attachment, and relationship quality. The feeling of trust manifests itself because users receive stable emotional perception and responsiveness (Jamil et al., 2026). Eventually such trust can develop into emotional attachment and a sense of companionship especially in a situation where there is constant interaction. The quality of relationships during the work of AI-mediated contacts is therefore not influenced by the technical complexity of AI per se but by its emotional competence (Chae and Kim, 2025).

These outcomes are however moderated by the individual and contextual factors. The level of AI literacy among the users affects the process of interpreting emotional response, where higher AI literacy may entail greater criticism of AI empathy (Kim & Hur, 2023). Cultural norms construct standards of emotional expression and empathies, which have the effect of determining the way the behavior of emotional intelligence is viewed. The weak moderating role is also given to ethical transparency, with information on the use of data and the impact of emotions being evaluated to have the ability to change relational reactions (Snyder et al., 2026).

This section highlights the need to focus on human experience by conceptualizing emotional intelligence as the property of interaction and not a set system attribute (Gursoy, 2026). Emotional intelligence of AI-driven interaction is an eventual substantial concept as far as engaging human emotions, emotions, and relationship shaping. The idea rests on this humanistic development in the framework of conceptualization that follows (Devaki, 2026).

6. CONCEPTUAL FRAMEWORK AND RESEARCH PROPOSITION

The key contribution in this chapter is that it formulates a humanized conceptual framework that articulates the working of emotional intelligence in AI-based interactions and its influence on human expressive emotions and relationship construction. Instead of theorizing emotional intelligence as a technical capacity inside AI systems, the suggested framework locates emotional intelligence as a perception-mediated and relational process, which is created in the interaction process. This view is what changes the analytical emphasis of performance as algorithms to interpretive and relational experience of users.

The framework is based on emotional intelligence theory, social presence theory, human-AI interaction theory, and relationship development theory to have a structured description of how AI emotional capabilities can be converted into emotional and relational performance. The model, in essence, creates perceived emotional intelligence of AI as a pivotal mediating variable between system-level ability to provide response and user-level consequence.

6.1 Overview of the Conceptual Framework

The proposed framework consists of four interrelated components:

AI Emotional Capabilities

Perceived Emotional Intelligence of AI (Mediator)

Human Expression and Relationship Outcomes

Individual and Contextual Moderators (Boundary Conditions)

The framework follows a process-oriented logic:

AI Emotional Capabilities

Perceived Emotional Intelligence

(A) Human Expression Outcomes

(B) Relationship Outcomes

The effects of perceived emotional intelligence are moderated by AI literacy, cultural norms of emotional expression, and ethical transparency.

This structure reflects relational and interactional perspectives widely adopted in contemporary social science research, emphasizing that user perceptions—not merely technical features—drive emotional and relational outcomes see in Figure 1.

Figure 1.

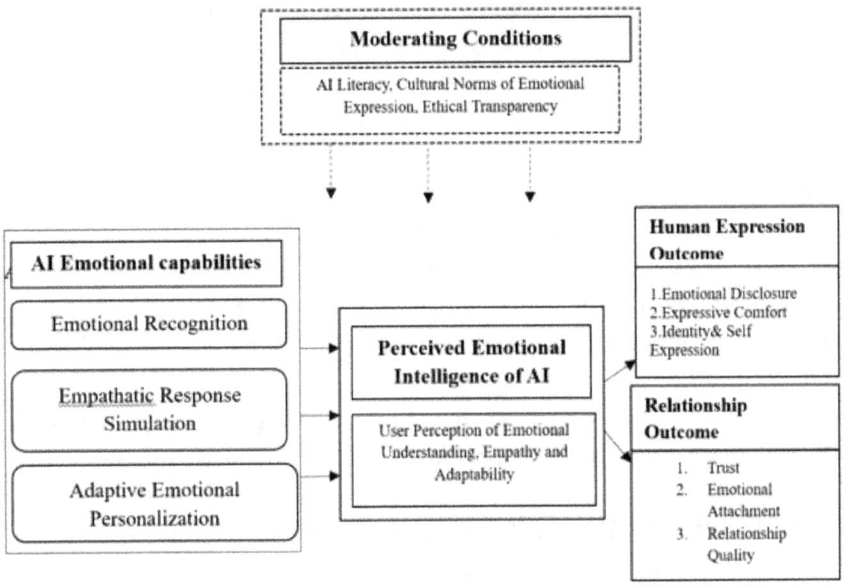

6.2 AI Emotional Capabilities as Antecedents

The antecedents of emotional intensity are the capacity of the AI emotion which facilitates emotional intelligent interaction. These capabilities are not emotional intelligence in themselves, but to them the cases under which emotional intelligence can be experienced, are created.

6.2.1 Emotion Recognition Capability

Emotion recognition refers to the AI system's ability to detect and interpret emotional cues from user input, including textual sentiment, vocal tone, facial expression, and behavioral indicators. Accurate acknowledgment of users' emotional states enhances perceptions of attentiveness and understanding. From a relational perspective, emotion recognition signals emotional awareness, which is a prerequisite for meaningful emotional engagement.

6.2.2 Empathic Response Simulation

Empathic response simulation refers to the AI system's capacity to generate emotionally appropriate responses that acknowledge and validate users' emotional states. Empathic responses function as symbolic cues of warmth, benevolence, and emotional sensitivity. In AI-mediated contexts, such responses shape users' interpretations of emotional competence and relational reliability.

6.2.3 Adaptive Emotional Personalization

Adaptive emotional personalization involves tailoring emotional responses based on users' prior interactions, emotional preferences, and contextual cues. Personalization enhances perceived relevance and relational continuity by creating a sense of attentiveness and relational memory. When guided by emotional sensitivity, personalization strengthens perceptions of emotional intelligence and long-term relational value.

Together, these three capabilities form the technological foundation that influences users' psychological interpretation.

6.3 Perceived Emotional Intelligence as the Core Mediating Mechanism

The core of the framework is an emotional intelligence of AI, which will be viewed as a perception of the user that the AI system is capable of identifying emotions, reacting in an empathetic manner, and being able to respond to the emotional requirements through communication. More importantly, perceived emotional intelligence is not a technical quality but a psychological conclusion that has been differentiated via the interaction. Users assess the AI responses in terms of emotional knowledge, empathy, and flexibility. It is these perceptions that decide whether the interactions are perceived as either socially meaningful and relationally competent. There is mediating behaviour of perceived emotional intelligence. In the absence of it, the recognition of emotions and empathy can be viewed as being mechanical or staged. Interaction that is mediated by AI is perplexed as relationally significant when emotional intelligence is viewed, making it possible to engage successfully in emotions.

6.4 Human Expression Outcomes

Perceived emotional intelligence also has an impact on the way people reveal their feelings in the process of AI-mediated communication

6.4.1 Emotional Disclosure

AI will be used to enhance emotional disclosure, which are expected to grow because of emotional intelligence. Emotional inhibition reduces when the users have emotional understanding and non judgmental responsiveness, enabling them to express the vulnerable emotions more freely.

6.4.2 Expressive Comfort

Expressive comfort is the extent to which people express the feelings of psychological safety when expressing emotions. Perceived emotional intelligence improves the expressive comfort by decreasing fear of judgement and social anxiety.

6.4.3 Identity and Self-Expression

AI responses that are emotionally sensitive may support users' self-perceptions and promote expressive experimentation. But over-personalization can also have an impact on identity formation, which raises concerns regarding identity formation and dependency.

6.5 Relationship Outcomes

In addition to the emotional expression, relational development depends on the perceived emotional intelligence.

6.5.1 Trust

Cognitive and affective trust in the AI systems is created during perceptions of emotional understanding and benevolence. Relational reliability and emotional responsiveness become visible as the users develop consistent emotional responsiveness.

6.5.2 Emotional Attachment

Frequent emotionally receptive exchanges can produce emotional attachment and perceived companionship especially to the contact during prolonged or intense contact.

6.5.3 Relationship Quality

Relationship quality is the general judgment about relationships and this comprises satisfaction, perceived closeness and relational value. The perceived emotional intelligence improves the quality of relationships by increasing the levels of trust and emotional involvement.

6.6 Moderating Conditions

The implications of perceived emotional intelligence on relationships depend on the factors of individuals and situation.

6.6.1 AI Literacy

More AI literate users might view AI empathy as faked which could reduce emotional attachment. Relation interpretations may be increased by low literacy.

6.6.2 Cultural Norms of Emotional Expression

Emotional disclosure and empathy are some of the expectations of culture that determine the perception and the evaluation of emotional intelligent AI conduct.

6.6.3 Ethical Transparency

The views on moral transparency in terms of emotional data use play a role in creating trust and interaction. The perception of emotional intelligence can be ineffective in creating positive relationships when people realize that their emotional data are being utilized.

6.7 Research Propositions

The framework suggested provides a flexible but not rigid background of the future empirical research. Instead of introducing emotionally intelligent AI as a deterministic technological event, the model makes the notion of the perception-mediated process, where the capabilities of the system influence emotional expression and relational development. The major theoretical relations between the framework are presented in the next propositions. On the lowest level, the AI emotional features are emotion recognition, simulated empathy, and adaptive personalization of emotions, which result in the situation of the possibility of the perception of the intelligence of emotion. These abilities are not emotional intelligence per se; instead, they themselves affect users perception of emotional understanding, responsiveness and flexibility. Under those circumstances when such capabilities are utilized in the form of an integrated and contextually competent system, users will tend to give the AI system emotional competence.

P1: AI emotional capabilities (emotion recognition, empathic response simulation, and adaptive emotional personalization) positively influence perceived emotional intelligence of AI.

The perceived emotional intelligence, in its turn, influences the ways of communicating emotionally in the AI-mediated environment. When users are emotionally understood, and responsive, there would be more chances of experiencing a psychological safety. The emotional security brings about this relational safety, which lowers the issues of evaluation and enables greater open emotional expression.

P2: Perceived emotional intelligence of AI positively influences users' emotional disclosure in AI-driven interactions.

In addition to instant manifestation, identity-related processes can be affected with the help of emotional intelligence reactions. By assimilating the communicative styles of users, which is validated by AI systems, one may be empowered by the system and emboldened to explore their identities in the digital course of interaction.

P3: Perceived emotional intelligence of AI enhances expressive comfort during AI-mediated communication.

On the relational level, the perceived emotional intelligence helps in the building of trust. Being emotionally responsive is an indication of benevolence, care, and reliability in relationships hence, promoting cognitive and affective trust. The trust is used as a key relational process by which the interaction in terms of emotional intelligence can be converted into a larger relational consideration.

P4: Perceived emotional intelligence of AI positively influences trust in AI-driven interactions.

Emotionally proactive behaviors provide kindness, concern, and dependability, which are essential precursors of emotional and cognitive trust. Users are more likely to grow to trust AI systems' intents, dependability, and relational orientation when they believe that the systems are emotionally competent.

P5: Trust mediates the relationship between perceived emotional intelligence of AI and relationship quality.

Repeated emotional responses have the potential to convert encounters from strictly transactional to relational over time. Perceived emotional intelligence is translated into stronger relational outcomes, such as perceived support, attachment, and overall relationship quality, through the crucial relational mechanism of trust.

P6: AI literacy moderates the relationship between perceived emotional intelligence of AI and emotional attachment.

The emotional bond may be diminished if users with higher levels of AI literacy perceive empathic responses as algorithmically produced rather than genuinely relational. Users with less AI literacy, on the other hand, would be more inclined to give AI systems human-like emotional intentionality, which would improve relationships.

P7: Cultural norms of emotional expression moderate the effects of perceived emotional intelligence of AI on emotional disclosure and relationship outcomes.

The interpretation of emotional responsiveness and the perception of appropriate emotional expression in mediated situations are influenced by cultural norms. While these effects may be relatively less in societies that place more emphasis on emotional restraint, perceived emotional intelligence may more powerfully boost disclosure and relational development in cultures that value emotional expressiveness.

These propositions provide a theoretically grounded roadmap for future empirical investigation.

7. ETHICAL AND SOCIETAL IMPLICATIONS OF EMOTIONAL INTELLIGENCE IN AI-DRIVEN INTERACTION

Due to the increasing integration of emotionally intelligent AI-based systems into routine communication, they present a collection of ethical and societal issues that are not limited to technical effectiveness and user satisfaction (Dwivedi et al., 2025). The Emotional Intelligence of AI-based relationships affects the manifestation of emotions by individuals, the development of relationships, and the establishment of social bonding. Although there are immense advantages to this development, there are ethical threats associated with these developments, which are emotional manipulation, dependency, authenticity, privacy, and social well-being (Peng, 2026).

Emotional responsive technologies are also addressed in journals like Journal of Business Ethics, MIS Quarterly, AI and Society, and Academy of Management Review, and stated to be considered not only in terms of their functionality, but also in terms of their overall human and society impacts.

7.1 Emotional Manipulation and Power Asymmetry

Emotional manipulation is one of the greatest ethical issues that relate to emotionally intelligent AI (Sipior et al., 2026). Since the AI system can detect the state of emotions and modify the response to those, it has the ability to affect the emotions of the users both in small and significant ways (Wah, 2026). Strategically adopted EI could define how users feel, what they like, and on what they do even without fully comprehending such decisions and actions (Kazemy et al., 2026). In a situation where the emotional intelligent responses are maximized to reach organizational objectives, e.g., higher levels of engagement, adherence, or consumption, users can be emotionally impacted, thus undermining self-control (Yun et al., 2026). Empathic studies in information systems ethics who point to support to differ on how to influence the user have drawn the focus of high-impact information systems ethics (Khiabani & Rezaeian, 2026). The ethical dilemma in the case is the desire to separate supportive emotional involvement and manipulative emotional control. Agency should be improved through emotionally intelligent AI on the users and not take advantage of emotional vulnerability. This demands prudent designing decisions, open goals, and a system of government that does not allow the emotional intelligence to be a weapon of emotional dictatorship (Alzoubi and Aziz, 2021).

7.2 Emotional Dependency and Relational Substitution

The other important ethical issue is associated with the threat of emotional dependency. Intelligent machines are viewed as always present, non-judicial, and sensitive to the feelings of emotionally intelligent people. Such features may introduce AI interactions as especially attractive to people who are lonely or socially anxious or have emotional issues (Pinazo-Hernandis et al., 2025). Although social interactions through this could be comforting, this could also create dependence on the AI systems as a source of emotional support at the cost of human interaction (Sun et al., 2026).Previous studies in social psychology and human/computer interaction indicate that repeated emotionally responsive interactions can result in attachment and perceptions of companionship (Efe et al., 2025). Such an attachment would be asymmetrical in AI-mediated contexts, since AI systems will never have a mutual emotional need or a need or obligation towards an individual (R. Ma et al., 2026). This imbalance puts a strain on the classical beliefs regarding the reciprocal nature of the relationships and calls into the question the social implications of the replacement of human emotional bonds by those based on AI in the long perspective. Regarding the society at large, extensive usage of emotionally intelligent AI would alter the standards of social communication and emotional work (Shaikh, 2024). Also, the implication on how people interact with each other with the increasing reliance on AI to support their emotional needs, community involvement, and social cohesion might arise (Montes et al., 2026). Responsible use of emotionally intelligent AI thus needs to focus on the fact that relationships between humans and machines will be complemented, and they will not be substituted (Huang & Rust, 2018).

7.3 Authenticity and the Nature of AI Empathy

An important ethical concern in relationships with emotionally intelligent AI is authenticity. Traditionally, empathy has been viewed as rooted on moral concern and a shared emotional experience (Bhoumik et al., 2025). On the one hand, the empathy on the part of AI-fueled interaction is not experienced but rather simulated by algorithmic mechanisms. Although users might experience empathic understanding, it does not clearly seem to lead to actual emotional irrespective of the internal state of the empathizer which is the argument of high-impact philosophical and organizational research. The perception-based emotive effect of empathic understanding is true provided that it produces actual emotional effect however without regard to the internal state of the emphatisizer (Alexa, 2024). Nevertheless, the fear of emotional misattribution exists when the presence of unfamiliar users with the simulated nature of AI empathy would think the responses of the algorithms would be evidence of true care or concern. Emotionally responsible AI is therefore advised to balance the emotional responsiveness and honest signaling on the nature and limitations of the system (Xie et al., 2026). Disclosure of the simulation of AI empathy will not inevitably reduce its utility but, serving to create accurate expectations in users and keep them emotionally independent.

7.4 Emotional Data Privacy and Governance

The development of emotional AI systems depends on the variable of the qualitative data of emotion such as the emotional message, emotional expression, and behavioral tendency. The nature of emotional data is highly personal and location-based and therefore making the collection and use of it to be ethically difficult (Barker et al., 2025). The current studies on data ethics and information governance in the sphere of high-impact research indicate that emotional data can show vulnerabilities, mental health, and personal experiences that users can be unconsciously willing to share (Mohanta et al., 2025). More so in regard to privacy, the secondary use of emotional data (e.g. in profiling, targeted persuasion, predictive analytics, etc.) provokes greater apprehension. Devoid of solid protective mechanisms, emotionally intelligent artificial intelligence can end up putting users in danger of either being spied on, discriminated against, or emotionally used in an unintended manner (Lubin, 2026). Ethical governance of emotional data should focus on dignity and respect since it is a human-centered time. The agency of users, i.e., their participation in the key decisions of how their emotional information is gathered, interpreted, and used, should be meaningful. Research with high impact postulates that transparency in ethics enhances the rise of trust and stable human-AI engagements.

7.5 Equity, Bias, and Cultural Sensitivity

The emotionally intelligent AI systems are conditioned by the ones having datasets which are indicative of certain cultural norms and manifestations of emotions. Consequently, these systems can be noted to be biased during emotion recognition and reaction, favoring a specific type of emotions but failing to accurately react to others (Sakib et al., 2026). Research that has high impact in AI ethics points out that the expressed emotion significantly depends on cultures, gender, and social situations. Unless ethically used, AI systems that fail to acknowledge this diversity may only encourage the status quo and create cultural and emotional barriers on people whose emotional displays do not adhere to dominant cultural norms (Rahman, 2026).To balance the ethical use of emotionally intelligent AI, it is necessary to make purposeful measures to enhance diversity and make AI systems culturally and emotionally responsible to users with emotional outliers. This involves training data diversification, integration of cross-cultural emotional model and adaptive customization (Garibay et al., 2023). In the societal perspective, intelligent AI ought to endorse pluralistic modes of expressing emotions as opposed to issuing homogeneous emotional principles (Yuk and Matsuda, 2026)

7.6 Toward Responsible Emotional Intelligence in AI

Combined, these moral and social issues highlight the necessity of a human-focused, responsible solution to the use of emotional intelligence in the AI-driven communication (Bukhari et al., 2025). Emotional intelligence is not only supposed to improve involvement or productivity but rather to take care of human health, autonomy and social networking. It has always been stressed in high-impact research that ethical concerns need to be incorporated into the design and management of intelligent systems and not viewed as a supplementary measure. The future of AI sensitive emotions needs responsible emotional intelligence and anticipates that there are agreements among the technological ability, ethical motivation, and social and economic interests (Baysak et al., 2025). Transmitting human dignity, honesty, and bonding by forecasting, the emotionally intelligent AI can be advantageous to human expression and bond development and reduce the risks of ethics (Romano, 2024).

8.PRACTICAL AND MANAGERIAL IMPLICATIONS

Other than making valuable contributions to the theory, this chapter has provided valuable practical and managerial implications to the design, management, and governance of the emotionally intelligent AI systems. With more and more emotionally sensitive interactions mediated by AI-driven technologies, emotional intelligence as a perceived and relational process is useful as practical advice by practitioners, designers, and policymakers when balancing effectiveness, ethical actions, and well-being of humans.

Beyond its theoretical contributions, this chapter offers important practical and managerial implications for the design, management, and governance of emotionally intelligent AI systems. As AI-driven technologies increasingly mediate emotionally sensitive interactions, understanding emotional intelligence as a perceived and relational mechanism provides actionable guidance for practitioners, designers, and policymakers seeking to balance effectiveness, ethics, and human well-being.

8.1 Implications for AI Designers and Developers

To the designers and developers of AI, the results of this chapter can show that emotional intelligence is not to be applied either as a technical aspect to be optimized and accurate, or an engagement feature. Rather, emotional intelligence should be structured with a consideration of the reactions of emotional comprehension, empathy, and responsiveness with users. Design features, including conversational tone, reaction speed, emotional recognition, and adaptive feedback are very essential in perceived emotional intelligence. The main concern of developers should not be excessive emotional expressiveness, but rather emotional appropriateness and sensitivity to context because an overabundance of empathy can destroy authenticity and credibility. Notably, the responses based on emotional intelligence are to be supportive of the emotional autonomy of the users instead of trying to redirect the emotions towards the predetermined system objectives.

8.2 Implications for Platform Managers and Organizations

This chapter highlights the need of governance and oversight to platform managers and organisations implementing emotionally responsive AI. Emotionally intelligent

AI systems do not affect the level of user satisfaction only but also the emotional disclosure, the formation of trust, and the relationships attachment. Clear internal guidelines should hence be set by the managers on the purpose and boundaries of emotional responsiveness. The features of emotional intelligence must be correlated with the user well-being but not only with the engagement rates or business performance. To determine how AI responses are seen by organizations as helpful, manipulative, or intrusive, regular audits of emotionally intelligent interactions can be conducted. Responsible implementation can be further attained through training teams of multidisciplinary teams incorporating behavioral scientists, ethicists and designers.

8.3 Implications for AI Use in Sensitive Domains

The framework is especially applicable to sensitive areas that are emotional like healthcare, mental health support, education and customer service. There are these situations where perceived emotional intelligence may play a significant role in helping to establish trust, compliance and emotional safety. When practitioners identify that AI is becoming a deeper more emotionally intelligent, they should understand that patients can become more willing to open their feelings and become more accountable to the response and referral. The use of AI systems in these areas must be clearly made to be used in addition to human practitioners and not to eliminate them. It should have clear mechanisms of escalation, openness concerning system constraints, and protection against emotional dependency to be able to maximize its ability to support and not harm.

8.4 Implications for Policymakers and Regulators

This chapter reflects the fact that policymakers and regulators should go beyond managing AI on a technical level and consider emotional intelligence as a separate aspect of AI regulation. The current regulation systems tend to be data protection oriented, algorithmic fairness, and openness based but do not pay much attention to emotional appeal and relationships. Guidelines that may be taken into consideration by policymakers include the need to be transparent on the use of the simulation of AI empathy, restrictions around the usage of the emotional data as means of persuasion, and safeguards against the issues of emotional manipulation. To acknowledge emotional intelligence as a socio-relational capacity and not an environmental neutral technical operation can inform less technological and more human AI policy.

8.5 Implications for Ethical and Human-Centered AI Design

In a bigger ethical context, the chapter supports the significance of the human-centered AI design principles. The emotional aspect of AI is not to be considered in terms of what it can perform but rather in terms of its impacts on human expression, relationships, and emotions. Medical workers must strive to implement AI applications that can build emotional security, contribute to relational integrity, and maintain human agency. Responsible emotionally intelligent AI mostly requires ethical transparency, giving users monetary capacity to regulate emotional information, and acknowledging cultural diversity in expressing emotions.

9. FUTURE RESEARCH AGENDA

The theoretical framework created during this chapter creates a number of promising opportunities concerning future studies of the topic of emotional intelligence in AI-based interactions. Since emotionally responsive AI has begun to spread swiftly into personal, organizational, and societal spheres, methodical and theoretically robust research is required to enhance the current knowledge on how perceived emotional intelligence influences human expression and formation of relationships. The section will provide some of the key directions of future research, or rather theoretical elaboration, methodology, expanding the context, and integrating the research with other disciplines.

9.1 Advancing Theory on Emotional Intelligence in AI Contexts

Further studies are needed to conceptualize the concept of perceived emotional intelligence of AI as the specific construct. Although emotional intelligence has been theorized extensively in human situations, the way it has been applied to the AI-mediated interaction needs to be theorized. Among the conventional dimensions of emotional intelligence (e.g. emotional awareness, empathy and emotional regulation), the scholars can examine how these foundational dimensions apply to AI settings and whether any other dimensions arise when emotional intelligence is not lived but simulated. The time-oriented dynamics of perceived emotional intelligence can also be studied in a research study. The relationship development theory postulates that emotional perceptions are developed through recurrence of interaction. Longitudinal conceptual and empirical research would examine the phenomenon of perception of AI emotional intelligence changing over familiarity, experience, and increased levels of AI literacy. This type of work would help in the processual view of emotional intelligence in human-AI relationships.

9.2 Empirical Examination of the Conceptual Framework

Even though this chapter is conceptual, it provides clear premises to future empirical research works. Academic researchers can also use experimental, survey, and mixed-method research designs to test the given framework. The AI emotional capabilities (e.g., empathic response styles or personalization levels) can be manipulated by using experimental studies to test the causal impact on the perceived emotional intelligence, emotional expression and trust. Research conducting surveys can examine how personal traits (emotional sensitivity or AI literacy) influence the outcome of relationships. The longitudinal studies are especially useful when the processes of relationships building are considered over time. Relationship science highlighting the fact that trust, attachment, and the quality of relationships build up as a result of repetition was a high-impact research. The longitudinal strategies used in the context of AI would enable researchers to investigate whether emotionally skilled AI contributes to establishing a stable relationship between users or whether the emotional experience decreases with more knowledge of the artificial character of the AI.

9.3 Methodological Innovation and Measurement Development

The future research ought to focus on creating effective measurement tools on perceived emotional intelligence of AI. The currently used emotional intelligence scales are oriented on the human actors and are not necessarily accurate in reflecting subtlety of the AI-mediated emotional relationship. The new scales can be modified and confirmed by the scholars to depict the perception of the users towards the emotional awareness, empathic responsiveness, and emotional adaptability of AI. The qualitative and interpretive approaches can also be useful to investigate the lived experience of users with emotionally intelligent AI. Narrative interviews, diaries and ethnographic methodologies would help to reveal how people think about AI emotional behavior and how those thoughts affect the emotions and identity formation. Such approaches augment quantitative methods because they meet meaning-making practices could hardly be quantified.

9.4 Contextual Expansion Across Domains

Employing emotionally intelligent AI in various fields of application is present in healthcare, education, customer support, social media, and other companionship applications. It would be used to focus future research to investigate the ways in which emotional intelligence would work in different contexts. As an illustration, emotional intelligence can be helpful in the medical interaction process and provoke serious ethical issues when applied to commercial persuasion. Let the comparison of domains bring out the influences of the context in the relational effects of the emotionally intelligent AI. Another avenue is the cross-cultural research. Emotional expression, expectations of empathy as well as relationship development are highly guided by cultural norms. Cultural beliefs about the perception of AI emotional intelligence can be studied in a high-impact cross-cultural approach under consideration of cultural differences and cultural values moderating the outcome of emotional and relationship. There is a need to conduct such work on the creation of the inclusive and globally relevant AI-driven interaction theories of emotional intelligence.

9.5 Ethical, Governance, and Policy-Oriented Research

The policy and governance implication of emotionally intelligent AI should be also discussed in future research. Theorists can investigate the ways in which regulations can be used to strike the right balance between innovation and safeguarding emotional autonomy and privacy. Ethical emotional AI design principles in the areas of transparency, consent, and accountability could be explored by the conceptual research and normative research. The cross-disciplinary cooperation of researchers regarding the topics of psychology, communication, information system, ethics, and legal issues will play a pivotal role in overcoming their challenges. The potential to merge outlooks of multiple disciplines would allow future studies to lead to responsible creation and implementation of emotionally smart AI with great ability to boost human expression and connections without compromising personal autonomy and well-being.

9.6 Toward a Human-Centered Research Agenda

Overall, the future research must be human-centered, emotion focused, relational and socially significant. Scholars need not only dwell on the concept of technological sophistication since the concept of emotional intelligence in AI transforms the human experiences, identities and relationships. The theory outlined in this chapter offers the basis of such research and challenges researchers to investigate the phenomenon of emotional intelligence in AI-driven interaction as a social and interpersonal phenomenon.

10. CONCLUSION

This chapter develops a humanistic concept of emotional intelligence in AI-involved relationships through redefining emotional intelligence as a perceived and relational process as opposed to a technical ability. Since AI systems are starting to participate in emotionally responsive communication, emotional intelligence has emerged as a key process by which AI influences the expression of human beings, trust and relationship formation.

Combining the emotional intelligence theory with the social presence theory, human-to AI interaction theory and relationship development theory, the chapter provides a holistic conceptual framework that elucidates how the AI emotional abilities affect perceived emotional intelligence and, subsequently, emotional and relational consequences. It is emphasized that perception, interpretation, and interaction are critical in the creation of emotionally intelligent AI experiences and that individual and contextual moderators of AI literacy, culture, ethical transparency, are important.

In addition to theoretical contribution, the chapter touches upon ethical and societal implications linked to AI that is emotionally intelligent such as the issue of emotional manipulation, dependency, authenticity, and management of emotional data. These discussions highlight the need for responsible, emotionally intelligent systems to be designed and managed from a human perspective.

Lastly, the chapter provides a research agenda that challenges scholars to build and develop theory, create new methods of measurement, study a variety of settings, and collaborate with other disciplines. This chapter makes a contribution to the current academic and social discussions on the role of AI in the emotional texture of online reality by concentrating on the impact of emotionally intelligent AI on human manifestation and connection building.

By so doing, it establishes emotional intelligence as not only something about intelligent systems, but it is a major perspective that can be used to interpret the changing nature of the relationship between humans and AI in an increasingly mediated world.

REFERENCES

Alanazi, S. A., Shabbir, M., Alshammari, N., Alruwaili, M., Hussain, I., & Ahmad, F. (2023). Prediction of emotional empathy in intelligent agents to facilitate precise social interaction. *Applied Sciences (Basel, Switzerland)*, *13*(2), 1163. DOI: 10.3390/app13021163

Alzoubi, H. M., & Aziz, R. (2021). Does emotional intelligence contribute to quality of strategic decisions? The mediating role of open innovation. *Journal of Open Innovation*, *7*(2), 130. DOI: 10.3390/joitmc7020130

Barker, D., Tippireddy, M. K. R., Farhan, A., & Ahmed, B. (2025). Ethical considerations in emotion recognition research. *Psychological Inquiry*, *7*(2), 43. DOI: 10.3390/psycholint702004

Baysak, B., Bilgetürk, M., & Berber, Ş. (2025). Psychological drivers of social entrepreneurship: The mediating role of emotional intelligence in translating sustainability consciousness into intentions. *Social Enterprise Journal*. Advance online publication. DOI: 10.1108/SEJ-07-2025-0152

Benn-Short, E. (2026). Artificial intelligence (AI) and events: Professional insights through the lens of stakeholder theory. *Leeds Beckett Repository*. DOI: 10.25448/lbu.31038016

Bhoumik, K., Fang, L., & Igarashi, R. (2025). Robots with hearts: How in-store AI's task types impact brand attitude and ethicality. *Journal of Business Research*, *206*, 115923. DOI: 10.1016/j.jbusres.2025.115923

Bove, L. L. (2019). Empathy for service: Benefits, unintended consequences, and future research agenda. *Journal of Services Marketing*, *33*(1), 31–43. DOI: 10.1108/JSM-10-2018-0289

Boyd, R. L., & Markowitz, D. M. (2026). Artificial intelligence and the psychology of human connection. *Perspectives on Psychological Science*, *21*(2), 192–220. Advance online publication. DOI: 10.1177/17456916251404394 PMID: 41608879

Bukhari, M. A. M. Z.. (2025). Emotionally intelligent AI: Enhancing human–computer interaction through NLP and sentiment analysis. *Zenodo*. DOI: 10.5281/zenodo.15363167

Carlson, B. D., Donavan, D. T., Wolter, J. S., Maxham, J. G.III, & Xu, P. (2025). The collective identity effect: How group-level identity influences individual behavior. *Journal of Marketing*, *90*(1), 106–131. DOI: 10.1177/00222429251325219

Chae, M., & Kim, M. (2025). Too human to trust? How AI human-likeness and context orientation shape consumer preferences in premium high-tech markets. *Journal of Retailing and Consumer Services*, *88*, 104513. DOI: 10.1016/j.jretconser.2025.104513

Chen, P. (2026). AI-enhanced virtual reality simulation for nursing students' empathy: Automated scoring and inter-rater reliability in a randomized controlled study. *Nurse Education Today*, *159*, 106968. DOI: 10.1016/j.nedt.2025.106968 PMID: 41500151

Cinar, A. B., & Bilodeau, S. (2024). Incorporating AI into the inner circle of emotional intelligence for sustainability. *Sustainability (Basel)*, *16*(15), 6648. DOI: 10.3390/su16156648

Demir, M., Aydoğdu, F., Alabay, M. B., Yaşar, H. K., & Bozkurt, A. (2026). More than an algorithm: Mental health professionals confront the promise and ethical perils of artificial intelligence. *Universal Access in the Information Society*, *25*(1).* DOI: 10.1007/s10209-025-01297-1

Döveling, K., Harju, A. A., & Sommer, D. (2018). From mediatized emotion to digital affect cultures: New technologies and global flows of emotion. *Social Media + Society*, *4*(1).* DOI: 10.1177/2056305117743141

Dwivedi, Y. K., Helal, M. Y. I., Elgendy, I. A., Albashrawi, M. A., Hughes, L., Shawosh, M., Dutot, V., & Jeon, I. (2025). Artificial intelligence agents and agentic systems in hospitality and tourism: Challenges, opportunities and research agenda. *International Journal of Contemporary Hospitality Management*, *38*(1), 27–52. DOI: 10.1108/IJCHM-02-2025-0287

Efe, F. O., Tumer, E., Aksoy, N. C., & Alan, A. K. (2025). Guest voice behavior for hotels: The role of experience, emotional attachment, and perceived value. *Cornell Hospitality Quarterly*, *67*(1), 24–41. DOI: 10.1177/19389655251367401

Elfenbein, H. A., & MacCann, C. (2017). A closer look at ability emotional intelligence (EI): What are its component parts, and how do they relate to each other? *Social and Personality Psychology Compass*, *11*(7).* DOI: 10.1111/spc3.1232

Gao, X., Li, W., & Zhao, Y. (2026). Value-dependent and empathy-mediated: How artificial intelligence-generated marketing content influences customer engagement, and when to disclose its origin. *Frontiers in Psychology*, *16*, 1701085. DOI: 10.3389/fpsyg.2025.1701085 PMID: 41583762

Garibay, O. O., Winslow, B., Andolina, S., Antona, M., Bodenschatz, A., Coursaris, C., Falco, G., Fiore, S. M., Garibay, I., Grieman, K., Havens, J. C., Jirotka, M., Kacorri, H., Karwowski, W., Kider, J., Konstan, J., Koon, S., Lopez-Gonzalez, M., Maifeld-Carucci, I., & Xu, W. (2023). Six human-centered artificial intelligence grand challenges. *International Journal of Human-Computer Interaction, 39*(3), 391–437. DOI: 10.1080/10447318.2022.2153320

Ge, L., Xia, Y., & Yang, C. (2026). Beyond tool use: How ecological coupling configures AI's empowerment for language learning engagement. *Frontiers in Psychology, 17*, 1747355. Advance online publication. DOI: 10.3389/fpsyg.2026.1747355 PMID: 41658385

Glikson, E., & Woolley, A. W. (2020). Human trust in artificial intelligence: Review of empirical research. *The Academy of Management Annals, 14*(2), 627–660. DOI: 10.5465/annals.2018.0057

Gong, T., & Huang, Y. (2026). Psychological strain in service robot encounters: Dual pathways to customer value co-destruction. *Journal of Services Marketing*, 1–19. Advance online publication. DOI: 10.1108/JSM-08-2025-0540

Gudivaka, S. R., Polipogu, P., Kodali, R., Dhulipalla, V. R., Tatavarty, V. S. K., Penumudi, J., & Gogulamudi, P. R. (2026). Speech emotion recognition in adults and children: A comprehensive review of traditional features and raw waveform models. *International Journal of Speech Technology, 29*(1).* DOI: 10.1007/s10772-025-10229-6

Gursoy, D. (2026). Reconceptualizing customer experience co-creation and service delivery in the age of artificial intelligence. *Journal of Hospitality Marketing & Management, 35*(2), 151–165. DOI: 10.1080/19368623.2025.2611513

Guzman, A. L., & Lewis, S. C. (2019). Artificial intelligence and communication: A human–machine communication research agenda. *New Media & Society, 22*(1), 70–86. DOI: 10.1177/1461444819858691

Halkiopoulos, C., Gkintoni, E., Aroutzidis, A., & Antonopoulou, H. (2025). Advances in neuroimaging and deep learning for emotion detection: A systematic review of cognitive neuroscience and algorithmic innovations. *Diagnostics (Basel), 15*(4), 456. DOI: 10.3390/diagnostics15040456 PMID: 40002607

Hoang, N. H. (2025). Investigating EFL students' emotional responses in AI-assisted language learning: A broaden-and-build theory approach. *Interactive Learning Environments*, 1–16. Advance online publication. DOI: 10.1080/10494820.2025.2512567

Holldack, F., Banh, L., & Strobel, G. (2026). Agentic information systems. *Electronic Markets, 36*(1).* DOI: 10.1007/s12525-025-00861-0

Huang, M., & Rust, R. T. (2018). Artificial intelligence in service. *Journal of Service Research, 21*(2), 155–172. DOI: 10.1177/1094670517752459

Jamil, K., Anwar, A., & Mustafa, S. (2026). How humanoid chatbot interaction quality builds trust and loyalty in hospitality? A mixed-method approach. *Journal of Hospitality Marketing & Management*, 1–40. Advance online publication. DOI: 10.1080/19368623.2026.2614407

Jiang, T., Sun, Z., Fu, S., & Lv, Y. (2024). Human–AI interaction research agenda: A user-centered perspective. *Data and Information Management*, *8*(4), 100078. DOI: 10.1016/j.dim.2024.100078

Jocher, J. J., & Verwiebe, R. (2026). "Forever and always, my love": Emotions in human–AI romantic relationship building and breakup with generative AI chatbot Replika. *Social Media + Society, 12*(1).* DOI: 10.1177/20563051251408917

Kaklauskas, A., Abraham, A., Ubarte, I., Kliukas, R., Luksaite, V., Binkyte-Veliene, A., Vetloviene, I., & Kaklauskiene, L. (2022). A review of AI cloud and edge sensors, methods, and applications for the recognition of emotional, affective and physiological states. *Sensors (Basel)*, *22*(20), 7824. DOI: 10.3390/s22207824 PMID: 36298176

Kazemy, H., Ravari, A., Kamiab, Z., Iranmanesh, F., & Mirzaei, T. (2026). Integrating AI-supported adaptive learning with cooperative jigsaw strategy for generation Z nursing students: A mixed-methods study. *Next Research*, *6*, 101426. DOI: 10.1016/j.nexres.2026.101426

Khiabani, G. A., & Rezaeian, Z. (2026). Modeling ethics in AI-driven marketing strategies to enhance market demand: Evidence from the Iranian pharmaceutical industry. *Journal of Ethics in Entrepreneurship and Technology.* DOI: 10.1108/JEET-05-2025-0030

Kim, H., & Wang, Y. (2025). Unveiling the human touch: How AI chatbots' emotional support and human-like profiles reduce psychological reactance to promote user self-disclosure in mental health services. *International Journal of Advertising*, 1–25. Advance online publication. DOI: 10.1080/02650487.2025.2558479

Kim, W. B., & Hur, H. J. (2023). What makes people feel empathy for AI chatbots? Assessing the role of competence and warmth. *International Journal of Human-Computer Interaction*, *40*(17), 4674–4687. DOI: 10.1080/10447318.2023.2219961

Kolomaznik, M., Petrik, V., Slama, M., & Jurik, V. (2024). The role of socio-emotional attributes in enhancing human–AI collaboration. *Frontiers in Psychology*, *15*, 1369957. DOI: 10.3389/fpsyg.2024.1369957 PMID: 39474095

Krzeminska, I. (2025). Multimodal recognition of users' states at human–AI interaction adaptation. *Technium*, *26*, 102–140. DOI: 10.47577/technium.v26i.12398

Laban, G., & Cross, E. S. (2024). Sharing our emotions with robots: Why do we do it and how does it make us feel? *IEEE Transactions on Affective Computing*, 1–18. Advance online publication. DOI: 10.1109/TAFFC.2024.3470984

Latif, E., Liu, V., & Zhai, X. (2026). A systematic review of intelligent and robot tutoring systems: Evolution, pedagogical design, and AI-driven classification. *Smart Learning Environments, 13*(1). DOI: 10.1186/s40561-025-00427-9

Lee, S., & Choi, Y. K. (2025). When personality meets platform: The moderating role of human-likeness in AI user evaluations. *International Journal of Human-Computer Interaction*, 1–26. Advance online publication. DOI: 10.1080/10447318.2025.2604629

Leong, S. C., Tang, Y. M., Lai, C. H., & Lee, C. (2023). Facial expression and body gesture emotion recognition: A systematic review on the use of visual data in affective computing. *Computer Science Review*, *48*, 100545. DOI: 10.1016/j.cosrev.2023.100545

Li, F., Liu, Y., Yang, Y., & Yu, G. (2026). How users perceive and react to labeled AI-generated content on social media: A longitudinal study of cognitive and emotional effects. *International Journal of Human-Computer Interaction*, 1–22. Advance online publication. DOI: 10.1080/10447318.2026.2618553

Lindgren, H. (2024). Emerging roles and relationships among humans and interactive AI systems. *International Journal of Human-Computer Interaction*, *41*(17), 10595–10617. DOI: 10.1080/10447318.2024.2435693

Lynch, A., & Ruch, G. (2026). Social workers' experiences of practising with empathy: Developing the Em-Prac framework. *European Journal of Social Work*, •••, 1–17. DOI: 10.1080/13691457.2025.2608841

Ma, N., Khynevych, R., Hao, Y., & Wang, Y. (2025). Effect of anthropomorphism and perceived intelligence in chatbot avatars of visual design on user experience: Accounting for perceived empathy and trust. *Frontiers of Computer Science*, *7*, 1531976. Advance online publication. DOI: 10.3389/fcomp.2025.1531976

Ma, R., Niu, S., Li, L., Hirth, A., Brehm, A., & Barbie, R. B. (2026). Negotiating digital identities with AI companions: Motivations, strategies, and emotional outcomes. *arXiv*. /arxiv.2601.12181DOI: 10.48550

Marconi, L., Longo, L., & Cabitza, F. (2026). Assessing interaction quality in human–AI dialogue: An integrative review and multi-layer framework for conversational agents. *Machine Learning and Knowledge Extraction*, *8*(2), 28. DOI: 10.3390/make8020028

Meng, J., & Dai, Y. (2021). Emotional support from AI chatbots: Should a supportive partner self-disclose or not? *Journal of Computer-Mediated Communication*, *26*(4), 207–222. DOI: 10.1093/jcmc/zmab005

Mohanta, A., Misra, S., & Gouda, S. (2025). Governing machine subjectivity. In *Advances in Computational Intelligence and Robotics Book Series* (pp. 321–354). DOI: 10.4018/979-8-3373-5530-6.ch011

Montes, N. M., Yang, Y., & Visser, M. (2026). Navigating integration in the Netherlands: Syrian refugees, digital practices, and inclusive communication. *Social Inclusion (Lisboa)*, *14*, 10946. Advance online publication. DOI: 10.17645/si.10946

Ozturkcan, S., & Merdin-Uygur, E. (2026). Technological transformation in human–robot and human–AI ensembles in marketing and consumer services: Activity theory and a socio-cultural framework. In *Palgrave Studies in Marketing* (pp. 47–69). Organizations and Society., DOI: 10.1007/978-3-032-08423-1_3

Paakkanen, M. A., Martela, F., & Pessi, A. B. (2021). Responding to positive emotions at work—The four steps and potential benefits of a validating response to coworkers' positive experiences. *Frontiers in Psychology*, *12*, 668160. DOI: 10.3389/fpsyg.2021.668160 PMID: 34707528

Padmaja, S., Mishra, S., Mishra, A., Tembra, J. J. V., Paramasivan, P., & Rajest, S. S. (2024). Insights into AI systems for recognizing human emotions, actions, and gestures. In *Advances in Computational Intelligence and Robotics Book Series* (pp. 389–410). DOI: 10.4018/979-8-3693-8659-0.ch020

Pae, H. (2025). Reflective analysis on empirical theories in consciousness. *Frontiers in Psychology*, *16*, 1571098. DOI: 10.3389/fpsyg.2025.1571098 PMID: 41079862

Paiva, A., Correia, F., Oliveira, R., Santos, F., & Arriaga, P. (2021). Empathy and prosociality in social agents. In *ACM eBooks* (pp. 385–432). DOI: 10.1145/3477322.3477334

Pantano, E., & Scarpi, D. (2022). I, robot, you, consumer: Measuring artificial intelligence types and their effect on consumers' emotions in service. *Journal of Service Research*, *25*(4), 583–600. DOI: 10.1177/10946705221103538

Pei, G., Li, H., Lu, Y., Wang, Y., Hua, S., & Li, T. (2023). Affective computing: Recent advances, challenges, and future trends. *Intelligent Computing*, *3*, 0076. Advance online publication. DOI: 10.34133/icomputing.0076

Peng, Y. (2026). Developing an ageing adaptable emotional virtual human: An AI-based approach. *Informatics for Health & Social Care*, 1–11. Advance online publication. DOI: 10.1080/17538157.2025.2611135 PMID: 41504003

Petrocchi, S., Filipponi, C., Antonietti, C., Levante, A., & Lecciso, F. (2020). Theory of mind as a mediator between emotional trust beliefs and interpersonal communication competence in a group of young adults. *Psychological Reports*, *124*(2), 555–576. DOI: 10.1177/0033294120913489 PMID: 32249665

Pinazo-Hernandis, S., Redolat, R., & Caballer, A. (2025). Artificial intelligence-based technologies to reduce loneliness and improve social connectedness in older people: A systematic review. *The Gerontologist, 66*(1).* DOI: 10.1093/geront/gnaf267

Pipitone, A., Cataldo, G., Corvaia, S., & Chella, A. (2025). The robot and the nurse prepare for surgery: Early insights into the impact of robot's inner speech. *Intelligent Service Robotics, 19*(1).* DOI: 10.1007/s11370-025-00656-4

Raave, D. K., Colasante, T., Roa, E. R., Martinez, J. C. R., Li, H., Mukherjee, S., & Malti, T. (2026). An experimental study exploring human–AI complementarity in early social-emotional learning. *Computers and Education Open*, *10*, 100331. DOI: 10.1016/j.caeo.2026.100331

Rahman, M. I. (2026). Algorithmic bias and transparency in artificial intelligence tools for nursing education: A scoping review. *Nurse Education in Practice*, *92*, 104756. DOI: 10.1016/j.nepr.2026.104756 PMID: 41653525

Riva, G., Wiederhold, B. K., & Cipresso, P. (2025). Humane artificial intelligence: Psychological, social, and ethical dimensions. *Cyberpsychology, Behavior, and Social Networking*, *28*(7), 457–461. DOI: 10.1089/cyber.2025.0202 PMID: 40501330

Romano, R. (2024). Ethical issues on artificial intelligence and human relationships. *INTED Proceedings*, *1*, 6902–6909. DOI: 10.21125/inted.2024.1819

Sakib, M. N., Rayasam, N. M., & Dey, S. (2026). Experience and adaptation in AI-mediated hiring systems: A combined analysis of online discourse and interface design. *arXiv*. /arxiv.2601.02775DOI: 10.48550

Sasere, O. B., & Matashu, M. (2025). The direct and cascading impacts of school leaders' emotional intelligence on teachers and students: A systematic review. *Education Sciences*, *15*(9), 1168. DOI: 10.3390/educsci15091168

Shaikh, Z. P. (2024). Artificial intelligence-based emotional intelligence and effective leadership. In *Advances in Logistics* (pp. 223–254). Operations, and Management Science Book Series., DOI: 10.4018/979-8-3693-7372-9.ch010

Shank, D. B., Graves, C., Gott, A., Gamez, P., & Rodriguez, S. (2019). Feeling our way to machine minds: People's emotions when perceiving mind in artificial intelligence. *Computers in Human Behavior, 98*, 256–266. DOI: 10.1016/j.chb.2019.04.001

Simos, C., Larios, N., & Papoutsi, C. (2026). Artificial Intelligence and Adolescent Emotional Well-Being in Inclusive Secondary Education.

Singh, K. J., Kapoor, D. S., Kaur, I., Tandon, P., Yadav, A., & Thakur, K. (2025). The happiness formula: Integrating purpose, spirituality, and relationships, with neurocognitive well-being. In *Elsevier eBooks* (pp. 19–40). DOI: 10.1016/B978-0-443-41660-6.00005-3

Sipior, J. C., Ward, B. T., Lombardi, D. R., & Appelbaum, D. A. (2026). Emotion artificial intelligence in the workplace: United States legal considerations. *Information Systems Management*, 1–18. Advance online publication. DOI: 10.1080/10580530.2026.2616521

Snyder, H., Witell, L., Van Riel, A. C., Magor, T., Lutze, S., & Bougoure, U. S. (2026). Balancing truth and lies: Ethical management of AI in service encounters. *Journal of Service Management*, 1–20. Advance online publication. DOI: 10.1108/JOSM-12-2024-0538

Song, Y. J., Park, J., & Lee, S. K. (2026). Disappointed with Siri: Expectation–experience gaps in human–AI interaction. *Technological Forecasting and Social Change, 225*, 124540. DOI: 10.1016/j.techfore.2026.124540

Srivastava, R. K., & Gurme, V. (2025). Artificial intelligence and consumer behaviour on social media: A study of personalization, trust, and privacy. *Measurement: Digitalization, 5*, 100021. DOI: 10.1016/j.meadig.2025.100021

Stinus, C., & Berjot, S. (2026). Selflessness as a potential buffer against depression: Investigating its impact on depressogenic schemas and identity threat. *Psychology of Consciousness : Theory, Research, and Practice*. Advance online publication. DOI: 10.1037/cns0000456

Sun, X., Wang, Y., & McDaniel, B. T. (2026). AI companions and adolescent social relationships: Benefits, risks, and bidirectional influences. *Child Development Perspectives*, aadaf009. Advance online publication. DOI: 10.1093/cdpers/aadaf009 PMID: 41737018

Tjimuku, M., Atiku, S. O., & Kaisara, G. (2025). Emotional intelligence and psychological capital at work: A systematic literature review and directions for future research. *Cogent Social Sciences*, *11*(1), 2443559. DOI: 10.1080/23311886.2024.2443559

Tripathi, S. N., Husain, R., & Rana, N. P. (2025). Engineering emotional bonds: How anthropomorphic design shapes guest–robot relationships in hospitality. *Journal of Hospitality Marketing & Management*, *35*(1), 45–72. DOI: 10.1080/19368623.2025.2552202

Van Kleef, G. A., & Côté, S. (2021). The social effects of emotions. *Annual Review of Psychology*, *73*(1), 629–658. DOI: 10.1146/annurev-psych-020821-010855 PMID: 34280326

Wah, J. N. K. (2026). Emotion aware teaching: Connecting emotion recognition for engaging language learning. *Journal of Qualitative Research in Education*, *45*(45), 223–238. DOI: 10.54963/jqre.i45.1920

Weng, Z., Huang, Y., & Weng, S. (2026). From code to care: How artificial empathy enhances customer experience in human–robot interaction. *Journal of Business Research*, *206*, 115969. DOI: 10.1016/j.jbusres.2026.115969

Woodruff, E. (2025). Making AI tutors empathetic and conscious: A needs-driven pathway to synthetic machine consciousness. *AI*, *6*(8), 193. DOI: 10.3390/ai6080193

Xie, X., Zhang, L. J., & Xu, X. (2026). "Don't give up the power to think!": A case study of English language teachers' AI ethics and AI-induced emotions. *European Journal of Education, 61*(1).* DOI: 10.1111/ejed.70456

Xu, W., Gao, Z., & Dainoff, M. J. (2026). An HCAI methodological framework: Putting it into action to enable human-centered AI. *IEEE Transactions on Human-Machine Systems*, *56*(1), 78–94. DOI: 10.1109/THMS.2025.3631590

Youn, S., & Jin, S. V. (2021). "In AI we trust?" The effects of parasocial interaction and technopian versus luddite ideological views on chatbot-based customer relationship management in the emerging feeling economy. *Computers in Human Behavior*, *119*, 106721. DOI: 10.1016/j.chb.2021.106721

Yun, B., Taranova, E., & Wang, A. Y. (2026). Does my chatbot have an agenda? Understanding human and AI agency in human–human-like chatbot interaction. *arXiv*. /arxiv.2601.22452DOI: 10.48550

Zhai, N., Ma, X., & Ding, X. (2025). Unpacking AI chatbot dependency: A dual-path model of cognitive and affective mechanisms. *Information (Basel)*, *16*(12), 1025. DOI: 10.3390/info16121025

Zhou, B., & Guan, S. (2025). Ethical and psychological challenges in human–AI romantic relationships: An interdisciplinary critical study. *Innovative Applications of AI*, *2*(1), 39–45. DOI: 10.70695/IAAI202501A8

Zulaikha, S., Dewi, I. R., & Kurniawati, M. (2026). Unveiling the intellectual landscape of artificial intelligence and consumer behavior. *Discover Artificial Intelligence*, *6*(1), 2. Advance online publication. DOI: 10.1007/s44163-025-00740-9

Chapter 14
Service Robots:
Practical Applications in the Hospitality Industry in Spain

Maria Angeles Garcia-Haro
http://orcid.org/0000-0001-8844-4076
University of Castilla-La Mancha, Spain

Maria Pilar Martinez-Ruiz
http://orcid.org/0000-0002-5890-5174
University of Castilla-La Mancha, Spain

Ricardo Martinez-Cañas
http://orcid.org/0000-0003-4629-5513
University of Castilla-La Mancha, Spain

Pedro Luis Pinedo-Sierra
University of Castilla-La Mancha, Spain

ABSTRACT

At present, the tourism sector is undergoing a period of profound transformation, driven, among other factors, by technological innovation. In this context, artificial intelligence and service robots are being progressively integrated into tourism businesses as strategic tools to enhance operational efficiency and enrich the customer experience during service delivery. Despite the growing academic interest in the application of service robots within the hotel sector, research specifically focused on the Spanish hotel remains very limited. This study aims to contribute to this gap in the literature through the analysis of real case studies examining the implementation of service robots in Spanish hotels. The results indicate that, although the

DOI: 10.4018/979-8-3373-8337-8.ch014

adoption of these systems is still incipient and the number of Spanish hotels that have operationally implemented service robots remains relatively small, the outlook for their development and implementation in the coming years is clearly favorable.

INTRODUCTION

Tourism is one of the fundamental pillars of the Spanish economy, playing a strategic role in generating wealth and employment (WTTC, 2025). In 2024, the tourism sector accounted for 13% of the national Gross Domestic Product and generated more than 2.5 million jobs (Statista, 2025). Recent forecasts reinforce this upward trend. According to the World Travel & Tourism Council (WTTC, 2025), by 2035 the tourism sector could contribute up to 17% of Spain's economic output, representing approximately 4 million jobs. At present, the sector is undergoing a deep and accelerated transformation, driven by the adoption of new technologies that influence all stages of the travel experience, from the initial information search to the on-site experience at the destination. This transformation is taking place in a context marked by significant challenges, including the need to move towards a more sustainable tourism model, leverage technological advances without losing human contact, strengthen talent retention, and redefine employee training to meet the evolving expectations and needs of travelers (Torregrosa, 2025).

In this evolving landscape, artificial intelligence (AI) has emerged as a fundamental pillar of tourism development, integrating tools that extend far beyond chatbots or virtual assistants. These technologies enable the anticipation of customer preferences, the optimization of operational processes, and the reduction of inefficiencies throughout the customer journey (Puertas, 2025). Today, AI and robotics have become ubiquitous across different tourism contexts, including accommodation, airlines, restaurants, and other services-related activities (Park, 2020). The advancement of these technologies has driven the integration of AI into SR (hereinafter SR), which aims to increase operational efficiency and enrich the customer experience (Cao et al., 2025). In recent years, the presence of these robots has expanded significantly, moving from their initial use in industrial contexts to dynamic service environments (Ivanov et al., 2020). Consequently, SR are assuming an increasingly important role in so-called service encounters, where they interact directly with users (Tuomi et al., 2021). Previously confined to industrial environments such as factories, robots have progressively expand into hospitals, classrooms, and some public spaces, collaborating with humans and support a wide range of activities, from operational and production processes to research and knowledge-based tasks (International Federation of Robotics, 2022).

This gradual incorporation is reinforced by the rapid development of the robotics sector, driven by the continuous emergence of new companies that develop innovative solutions and refine existing models (International Federation of Robotics, 2025). However, technological progress alone does not fully explain this expansion. Additional factors, such as labor shortages, the ability to provide uninterrupted services (24/7), and the need to reduce operational costs, have significantly contributed to the adoption of these systems (Ivanov & Webster, 2020). In addition, the Covid-19 pandemic acted as an accelerator of this process, fostering the implementation of contactless technologies such as automated check-in, digital keys, and contactless payment solutions (Buhalis & Sinarta, 2019) and positioning robotic solutions as a key tool for minimizing the risk of virus transmission during customer interactions (Yang et al., 2024).

Despite their increasing presence, the implementation of robots in tourism remains at an early stage. Nevertheless, existing evidence suggests the adoption is following an exponential growth trajectory. According to the analytics firm GlobalData, the SR industry is estimated to reach a value of USD 216 billion by 2030, completely transforming the travel and tourism industry (Globetrender, 2022). In line with this trend, data from the International Federation of Robotics confirm this upward evolution: in 2023, more than 54,000 units were sold for tourism-related purposes, representing a 31% increase compared to the previous year, while expanding their application to new functions such as food and beverage preparation and support at guidance and information points. Moreover, numerous companies are currently in funding or prototype designing phases with the aim of launching fully commercialized products in the near future (International Federation of Robotics, 2022).

Although academic literature on SR is gaining increasing interest—considering them one of the most important trends in services marketing (Li & Wang, 2022)—studies applied to frontline services in hotels remain limited (Rosete et al., 2020; Rana et al., 2025). Research in this area has been approached from various perspectives, including employees, consumers, companies, and the robots' own attributes (Cao et al., 2025), but it remains insufficient and far from conclusive (Ayyildiz et al., 2022), especially regarding empirical studies (Reis et al., 2020) and in specific contexts such as Spain. Most work on frontline SR is exploratory or theoretical, providing little guidance for management decision-making (Belanche et al., 2020). Furthermore, although the presence of robots in the hotel industry is increasing, the number of establishments using them operationally remains small (Vatan & Dogan, 2021).

In this context, this study aims to shed light on the existing gap in the literature regarding SRs and contribute to the advancement of knowledge in this field. Through the analysis of specific cases, it seeks to examine how these technologies are being implemented in the Spanish hotel sector. In this way, the research not only contributes to the theoretical advancement of human-robot interaction in the hospitality industry but also offers useful information for professionals in the sector interested in adopting these types of technological solutions.

Despite the growing academic interest in SR— now considered one of the most important trends in services marketing (Li & Wang, 2022)—studies applied to frontline hotel services remains limited (Rosete et al., 2020; Rana et al., 2025). Research in this area has been approached from multiple perspectives, including employees, consumers, firms, and robot-specific attributes (Cao et al., 2025). However, the existing body of knowledge is still insufficient and far from conclusive (Ayyildiz et al., 2022), especially regarding empirical studies (Reis et al., 2020) and within specific contexts such as Spain. Moreover, although the presence of robots in the hotel industry is gradually increasing, the number of establishments using them operationally remains relatively small (Vatan & Dogan, 2021). Most studies on frontline SR are exploratory of theoretical in nature, offering limited guidance for managerial decision-making (Belanche et al., 2020). Within context, the present study aims to address the existing gap in literature on SR and contribute to the advancement of knowledge in this field. Through the analysis of real cases, the study examines how these technologies are being implemented in the Spanish hotel sector. In this way, this research not only contributes to the theoretical understanding of human-robot interaction in the hospitality industry but also provides valuable insights for professionals interested in adopting such technological solutions.

2. THEORETICAL FRAMEWORK

2.1 Service Robots: Conceptualization

One of the earliest definitions of SR was proposed by Engelhardt (1990, p. 31), who described them as "*robotic systems that function as intelligent and programmable tools that can sense, think, and benefit or empower human beings*." Since then, the concept has evolved, incorporating perspectives linked to tourism and other service-oriented activities.

Figure 1.

Author	Definition
Bartneck & Forlizzi (2004)	Autonomous or semi-autonomous robots that interact and communicate with humans in accordance with the behavioral norms expected by the people with whom the robot is designed to interact.
Bowen & Morosan (2018)	AI agents with a physical body capable of performing actions that have effects in the physical world.
Chiang & Trimi (2020)	Mechanical devices that imitate human behaviors to provide services autonomously of semi-autonomously.
Choi et al. (2020)	AI-enabled agents that interact, communicate, and deliver services to customers.
Colby (2016)	Service robot is a form of autonomous technology offered by computer without human instructions.
Engelhardt (1990)	Robotic systems that function as intelligent and programmable tools capable of sensing, thinking, and benefiting or enabling humans.
International Federation of Robots (IFR; ISO 8373)	A robot used for personal of professional purposes that performs useful tasks for humans or equipment and requires a certain degree of autonomy.
Jiang y Wen (2020)	Systems functioning as programmable tools to sense, think, and act to enhance human productivity or engage in social interactions.
Jörling et al. (2019)	Autonomous agents whose primary purpose is to provide services to customers by performing physical and non-physical tasks.
Lee et al. (2021)	Autonomous physical devices capable of operating and performing services without continuous human supervision.
Lei et al. (2023)	A standalone system interface capable of performing and providing services.
Li y Wang (2021)	A physical entity integrated with information technology that can autonomously provide personalized services to people.
Murphy et al. (2017)	A relative autonomous physical device capable of moving and executing services.
Pizam et al. (2022)	A programmable and intelligent device primarily designed to serve guests.
Park (2020)	Autonomous intelligence that helps travelers and service providers achieve their personal or professional goals.
Park et al. (2021)	Entities programmed with a certain degree of autonomy to perform specific tasks within the service sector.
Wirtz et al. (2018)	Autonomous and adaptable interfaces that interact, communicate, and deliver service to an organization's customers.
Zhang et al. (2021)	Autonomous and adjustable system-based interfaces that interact with customers in a company and serve them through communication.

Source: Li & Wang (2021) and Jiang & Wen (2020)

2.2 Characteristics and Functions of Service Robots

Drawing from these definitions, it becomes evident that SR not only perform mechanical tasks but also participate in social interaction processes with humans. This distinguishes them from other AI-driven technologies such as industrial robots or self-service machines. SR can be deployed either physically or virtually (Lu et al., 2019), although they are generally designed to have a humanoid appearance and equipped to execute cognitive, analytical, or emotional-social tasks supported by automated system. In hospitality contexts, they can provide services directly to guests or assist staff in the delivery of certain service activities (Ayyildiz et al., 2022).

Their functions range from task automation to enhancing experiential value. For instance, in some restaurant robots are used as personal table assistants, whereas in others they supported efficient and accurate order delivery, as in the case of cooking or food-preparation robots (Fusté-Forné & Jamal, 2021). Unlike traditional self-service technologies, SR can collect input data via sensors, analyze it, and make real-time decisions (Ivanov & Webster, 2020). This capability enables a level of human-technology interaction not previously observed in hospitality environments (De Keyser et al., 2019). SR are commonly equipped with audio, location, distance, pressure, temperature, energy- consumption, and facial-recognition sensors (Ayyildiz et al., 2022). They also incorporate components such as speakers, motors, robotic arms, screens, lights, and transmitters that allow them to move or hold objects, speak, and transmit signals to multiple devices (Shin & Jeong, 2020).

Given that most services involve direct interaction between customers and service providers, SR in hospitality is increasingly integrated with complementary technologies such as facial recognition, automated payment systems, drone delivery, and autonomous vehicles (Tussydiah & Park, 2017).

According to the International Federation of Robotics (2025), the number of SR sold for professional use reached 200,000 units in 2024, representing a 9% increase compared to the previous year. This growth is driven primarily by labor shortages and an aging population, which is increasing the demand for medical and care robots. Consequently, the main professional application domains of SR include: transportation and logistics, encompassing mobile robots for transporting and handling goods; hospitality, including mobile guidance robots, food and beverage preparation, information points in public spaces (in shops, shopping centers, or hotel receptions), and telepresence robots for virtual participation in real-world events; and professional cleaning, involving cleaning robots whose main application is floor cleaning and space maintenance:

Figure 2.

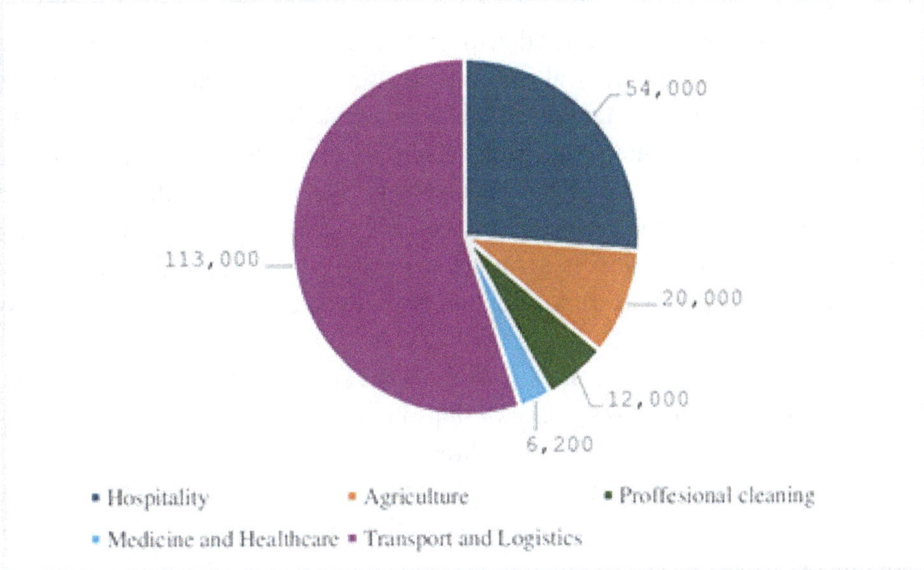

2.3 Anthropomorphism in the Design of Service Robots

As SR increasingly take on functions traditionally performed by humans—such as front desk assistance, in room delivery, or information guidance—it becomes essential to examine how customers also perceive these robots. Among the factors that most strongly influence how consumers evaluate and respond to SR is anthropomorphism (Kim et al., 2019; Aubel et al., 2022), understood as the attribution of human-like traits to non-human agents. The purpose of anthropomorphism is not to create an artificial human but rather to use human-like physical or behavioral elements to facilitate social interaction. In this sense, robots may adopt a wide range of forms, from animals or fantastical creatures to humanoid designs (Vatan & Dogan, 2021).

This concept-also called human-likeness- refers to the real or imagined behavior of non-human agents with characteristics, motivations, intentions, or emotions similar to humans, influencing how they interact with people (Aggarwal & McGill, 2007). Consumers tend to attribute human characteristics or traits to non-human robots, making robots similar to humans in appearance or behavior (Yang et al., 2024). However, as Zhang et al. (2022) notes, the precise definition of what anthropomorphism in SR remains unclear, as does the identification of which components of anthropomorphism are most influential, making it difficult to establish clear guidelines for the design and introduction of SR in companies. The term itself derives from the

Greek words *anthropos* (human) human and *morphe* (form), referring to the tendency of people to attribute human characteristics to non-human entities (Duffy, 2003).

Prior research has demonstrated that robots with anthropomorphic characteristics tend to receive more positive evaluations from users (Aubel et al., 2022), increase consumers' intention to use them (van Pinxteren et al., 2019), and generate a greater desire to spend time interacting with them (Qiu et al., 2020). For instance, the presence of a human-like voice has been shown to encourage continued use and increase customer tolerance toward service failures (Mirnig et al., 2017). Thus, anthropomorphism influences not only the general evaluation of the robot but also specific dimensions such as trust, intention to use, comfort, and enjoyment (Pinxteren et al., 2019).

In this regard, Balakrishnan & Dwivedi (2021) argue that anthropomorphic characteristics can foster strong relationships between human and non-human entities by generating high levels of trust through emotional connections. The use of human-like traits in SR can enhance hotel branding and the perceived authenticity of the service, as it enables a coherent integration of technological advancements with human-centered values. When customers perceive that a brand is making an effort to meet their needs through robotic services that are both sophisticated and personalized, they interpret this combination as a commitment to providing an authentic service experience (Chiang et al., 2022). However, this interaction does not always lead to positive outcomes. The literature agrees that anthropomorphism is beneficial only up to a certain point, but it can be counterproductive when it is excessively intensified. A robot that behaces in a counterintuitive, unpredictable, insecure, clumsy, or ineffective manner may be perceived as unsettling or unpleasant for users (Williams, 2016).

As robots acquire more human-like attributes, consumers tend to apply social expectations and beliefs from interactions with other people, increasing sensitivity to errors and affecting customer response (Aubel et al., 2022). In this sense, anthropomorphism involves not only the robot's physical appearance but also the use of facial expressions and other social cues, as well as natural interaction and communication—including speech, gaze, and gestures (Duffy, 2003), which Aubel et al. (2022) refer to as "form and mind." For example, in a study by Lehmann et al. (2016), when the robot displayed a human-like blinking pattern, users perceived it as more intelligent, competent, and trustworthy, especially in tasks requiring the delivery of information, such as those performed by robotic tour guides.

The debate surrounding anthropomorphism is closely linked to the Uncanny Valley theory (Mori, 1970), which describes how human perceptions of robots vary according to the degree of human likeness they exhibit The original theory posits that when robots are approximately 95% similar to humans, people tend to experience positive feelings toward them (Mori, 1970). As the similarity in appearance and movement between a robot and a human increases, emotional response becomes more positive, potentially generating an empathic effect similar to that experienced by other humans (Jia et al., 2021). However, when robots resemble humans too closely without being an exact copy, it can have the opposite effect and provoke fear and rejection (Mori, 1970; Mende et al., 2019).

When SR exhibit a moderate level of human-like appearance and behavior, customers are more likely to interact with them and experience satisfactory service encounters, thereby increasing their willingness to use such robots (Blut et al., 2021; Yang et al., 2024). However, research has also shown that both that very low levels and excessively high levels of human-likeness can generate adverse effects on attitudes, behaviors, and behavioral intentions (Mori, 1970; Kim et al., 2019; Yang et al., 2024).

In this context, some studies indicate that users may prefer less human-like alternatives, such as pet-like robots, which generate fewer expectations and are more emotionally comfortable (Fink, 2012). Even factors such as age and gender can lead to negative emotional responses or attribution patterns (Kim et al., 2019). Moreover, sociodemographic characteristics such as the robot's age or gender can influence the emotions and attributions that customers develop toward it (Kim et al., 2019). Indeed, Blut et al. (2021) emphasize that the impact of anthropomorphism depends both on the robot's assigned gender and on the type of service being provided. Similarly, humanoid robots may generate elevated expectations among users, which can produce negative effects when the robot's behavior fails to meet those expectations (Lee et al., 2005). This dynamic explains why a person's affinity toward an anthropomorphic robot increases only up to a certain point, after which it declines sharply, falling into the so-called "uncanny valley," a space associated with feelings of eeriness or discomfort (Aubel et al., 2022).

Along these lines, the robot's face and head play a crucial role, as they are essential elements for human communication and therefore determine the naturalness and comfort of the interaction (Fink, 2012). Consistent, literature has documented both positive and negative effects of anthropomorphism. Studies such as those by Blut et al. (2021), Abdi et al. (2022), Chiang et al. (2022), and Yang et al. (2024) argue that moderate levels of anthropomorphism improve the customer experience, increase perceived quality, strengthen trust, and enhance usage intention. In contrast, other research has identified negative effects, suggesting that high levels of anthropomorphism can generate discomfort, increase perceived risk, or reduce usage intention, thereby producing a "double-edged sword" effect (Lv et al., 2023).

More specifically, Park et al. (2021) found that when robots looked less human, customers felt uncomfortable if they featured human-like body parts such as eyes or a mouth. Kim et al. (2023) examined different levels of visual characteristics and their effect on the intention to use mechanical, humanoid, and android SR.

Their findings indicate that a medium level of human-like visual characteristics (humanoid robots) increase the likelihood of adoption compared to android robots, and that high levels of human resemblance (androids) resulted in the lowest usage intention when compared with mechanical and humanoid robots. Similarly, Jia et al. (2021) reported that users were more likely to accept SR with a medium degree of human likeness and less likely to accept robots with a high level of human-likeness. Consequently, there is no consensus in the services literature regarding whether anthropomorphism facilitates or limits customers' intention to use SR or whether it improves the customer experience (Blut et al., 2021).

Furthermore, some studies suggest that specific human-like attributes may have different effects on the user-robot relationship. Qiu et al. (2020) indicate that such attributes may increase users' desire to spend more time with the robot, while Mirnig et al. (2017) show that a human voice promotes continued use and greater tolerance for service failures. However, Cheng (2023) argues that designing SRs with lower levels of anthropomorphism may reduce the likelihood that consumers make internal attributions when service failure occurs, thereby increasing their willingness to forgive such failures.

2.4 Classification of Service Robots

The classification of robots typically begins with a fundamental distinction between industrial robots and SRs, primarily based on the context in which they operate (Tuomi et al., 2021). While industrial robots are oriented toward automated processes in factories or production lines, SRs are designed to assist people in their daily lives, whether in domestic or professional environments. The International Federation of Robotics (IFR) classifies SR according to their scope of use, distinguishing between personal robots and professional robots, which encompass a wide variety of forms, structures, and areas of application. Among these are logistics and delivery robots, social robots capable of providing assistance and information, cleaning and disinfection robots, kitchen and restaurant robots, and robots designed for agricultural and underwater tasks.

Murphy, Gretzel & Hofacker (2017) classify SR according to their levels of automation, distinguishing between quasi-automated and fully automated robots. Quasi-automated robots based their decisions on self-directed behavior arising from their programming or from remote human intervention. In contrast, fully automated robots act as autonomous agents capable of responding to environmental changes and communicating with other systems without requiring external supervision or control (Li, 2015).

Another relevant classification differentiates between industrial robots, SRs, and medical robots, based on the environment in which they operate (Tuomi et al.,

2021). When a mechanism incorporates robotic technology but does not meet all the defining characteristics of a robot, it is referred to as a robotic device (IFR). Regarding their physical appearance, SR are generally divided into three broad categories: Mechanoids, whose physical appearance resembles a machine; Humanoids, which incorporate certain human-like characteristics; and Androids, which not only imitate human physical appearance but also human behavior and attitudes in a more realistic way (Reis et al., 2020).

This classification is complemented by the framework proposed by Walters et al. (2008), who established three levels of anthropomorphism—low, medium, and high—which have subsequently been adopted and expanded upon by authors such as Jia et al. (2021).

Unlike industrial robots, SR incorporate specific technical features that allow them to perform specialized tasks while interacting directly with users (Qiu et al., 2020). These robots are typically equipped with a wide range of sensors, including sound, location, distance, pressure, temperature, energy consumption, and facial recognition sensors (Ayyildiz et al., 2022). In addition, they are also equipped with functional components such as speakers, motors, robotic arms, displays, lights, and transmitters that facilitate object manipulation, verbal communication, and signal transmission to other devices (Shin & Jeong, 2020). Thanks to this combination of attributes, SRs surpass the capabilities of traditional self-service machines, as they can collect real-time information from their environment, process it autonomously, and make decisions immediately (Ivanov & Webster, 2020). Based on these considerations, Lee (2021) proposes a typology of SR according to two fundamental criteria: their domain of application (professional or domestic/personal) and their level of social interaction capability. This results in four main categories:

Figure 3.

SR-Professional	
Provide services to individuals or organizations in professional environments	
SR *Profesional Social*	*SR* *Profesional Non-Social*
Require interaction with employees and customers Examples: waiter robot, receptionist robot	Do not require interaction with employees or customers Examples: cleaning robot, security robot, logistics robot
SR -Domestic/Personal	
Intended for non-commercial purposes	
SR *Domestic/Personal Social*	*SR* *Domestic/Personal Non-Social*
Require interaction with users Examples: pet robot, educational robot	No interaction with users Examples: vacuum cleaners, lawn mowers

3. METHODOLOGY

3.1 Service Robots in the Hospitality Sector

An increasing number of hotels are implementing SR to modernize traditional services and offer new experiences for their guests, improving service quality and optimizing operational efficiency (Rosete et al., 2020). At present, hotels are still in an early stage of SR integration (Rana et al., 2025), with their main purpose being to provide assistance and perform tasks to enhance customer experience (Akdim et al., 2023). The potential applications of SR are extensive, allowing for adoption in cruise ships, museums and galleries, tourist information centers, restaurants, travel agencies, car rental companies, meetings and events, and theme parks.

In fact, the integration of robotics will allow hotels in the coming years to offer services that were previously unimaginable. One example is the use of autonomous vehicles as an extension of hotel services. Based on customer data and preferences, the vehicle could recommend dining options, ask questions, and make reservations instantly. Thus, during the journey to the hotel, the SR would be able to provide information to the passenger, acting simultaneously as a transportation service and a tour guide, delivering a much more personalized and engaging experience than a conventional transfer (Bowen & Morosan, 2018).

Although many SR initially performed repetitive and routine tasks—such as the RoboVac Buddies for cleaning robots at the Travelodge hotel chain—a growing number are beginning to carry out more advanced frontline tasks that involve direct social contact with customers (Belanche et al., 2020; Wirtz et al., 2018). These tasks include food delivery within the establishment, reducing waiting times during check-in and check-out processes, acting as tour guides (Fusté-Forné & Jamal, 2021), cleaning, personal services, reservations, payments, and entertainment (Park, 2020). The progressive adoption of these technologies in different sectors responds not only to operational needs but also to the interest in exploring new forms of interaction and improving efficiency in activities that depend heavily on customer contact, such as tourism and hospitality (Rosete et al., 2020).

The hotel industry is currently the second sector with the highest application of SRs for professional use, according to the World Robotics SRics report (International Federation of Robotics, 2024). Robotics is emerging as a key element for advancing towards a more effective personalization of the customer experience, especially in so-called "service encounters" (Tuomi et al., 2021), where human-robot interaction is geared towards satisfying customer needs and preferences, transforming the service experience (Rana et al., 2025). Thus, robots can provide services directly in hotels autonomously or assist staff in performing multiple tasks (Ayyildiz et al., 2022).

3.2 Level of Adoption in the Spanish hotel industry

In Spain, the use of robots continues to expand across different economic sectors at an accelerated pace. According to the Spanish Robotics and Automation Association (AER Automation), more than 5,000 industrial robots were installed in the country in 2023, representing a 48% increase compared to the previous year. Regarding AER Automation, data shows a 17% increase in both mobile and social robotics. It is noteworthy that approximately 80% of SR production in Spain are destined for export, positioning the country as one of the world's leading manufacturing powers in this field.

Specifically, the hospitality sector has seen the benefits associated with the use of robotics double, now representing 10% of the total (AER Automation). Several hotels in Spain have already begun incorporating SR into their staff, employing them for tasks such as cleaning, room service, and transporting food and beverages in restaurants. However, unlike the overall percentage of Spanish companies that use some type of robot, in the hotel industry this figure remains below 5%.

Undoubtedly, the application of SRs or collaborative robots has become a reality in the hotel industry (Hosteltur, 2024). Nevertheless, after conducting an exhaustive search, no research specifically addressing the implementation of robots in Spanish hotels were found. The available information primarily comes from news reports, tourism magazines features, or interviews with industry experts. Therefore, this article, is conceived as an initial approach to the study of SR implementation in Spanish hotels.

To date, most implementations of SR in hotels across the country have been developed as pilot or experimental projects. These initiatives are usually driven by collaborations between robotics companies, hotel chains, and institutions such as the Hotel Technology Institute (ITH) or Segittur, and focus on functions such as food service, cleaning, or front desk assistance. Although their implementation is progressing gradually, there are already notable cases that demonstrate their real impact.

3.3 Practical Cases of Implementation in Spain

Magic Costa Blanca Hotels

In April 2024, the Hotel Technology Institute conducted the "*Feasibility Study on COBOTS*", a pioneering project involving the implementation of collaborative robots in hotel operations. This project was carried out in collaboration with InteCRobots, Robottions, and the Magic Costa Blanca hotel chain, with three of its hotels participating: Villa del Mar Benidorm, Magic Natura Animal & Waterpark Resort, and Magic Robin Hood. Key findings from the pilot project are summarized below.

First, customer satisfaction increased by 25%, with guests experiencing service that was 30% faster and more effective. Additionally, revenue increased by 15% and customer loyalty increased by 20%. In cleaning-related tasks the robots achieved 85% efficiency was achieved, a 40% reduction in time per stay, and coverage rates of 95% coverage in guest rooms and 90% in restaurant areas, including hard-to-reach areas. In outdoor areas, robot implementation resulted in a 40% improvement compared to cleaning performed by human staff, with coverage reaching 80%.

Regarding operational costs, available data indicate that the inclusion of robots led to a 15% reduction in operating costs, with an average of 500 service hours per month and 120 kilometers traveled per month. This has reduced the number of required human movements by 80%.

Regarding the human workforce, trust in this technology has increased, and the organization has been able to reduce personnel turnover-related costs by 25%.

Hotel Sol Katmandú Park & Resorts (Meliá Hotels)

In August 2024, the Sol Katmandú Park & Resorts hotel, located in Magaluf (Mallorca) launched a pilot project in collaboration with the startup Wiongo Robotics, integrating four robots into its restaurant staff to assist with front-of-house tasks. Three of these robots were responsible for collecting used plates, glasses, and cutlery, while the fourth was tasked clean dishes to the buffet.

The project, which concluded at the end of October, received highly positive feedback for both employees and customers. Among other benefits, the use of these robots allowed waitstaff to avoid lifting approximately 167 kilograms per day, resulting in an average time savings of 33 minutes per employee. The robots were able to transport up to 40 kilograms per trip and move at a speed of two meters per second. Furthermore, improvements in employee health were reported, as some staff experienced less back pain due to the robots bearing weight on their behalf.

During the testing period, only one of the robots experienced a technical issue, becoming stuck while attempting to climb a step. Given the success of the project, the company is now considering testing SR in other hotel areas, such as room service, housekeeping, or promotional activities in common areas (Aguado, 2024).

Hotel Clima Benidorm Plaza

Climia Hotels is a hotel chain located in Benidorm (Alicante), managing three differentiated types of establishments: Climia Belroy, offering superior four-star hotel rooms and apartments; Climia Benidorm Plaza, a four-star hotel; and Climia 2Sleep, focused on tourist apartment accommodations.

All the properties are strategically located in the center of Benidorm, just a few meters from Levante and Poniente beaches. The chain offers guests multiple benefits when booking directly through its website, such as late check-out until 3:00 p.m., a welcome gift, best price guarantee, free cancellation insurance, complimentary safe deposit box, free transfer to Alicante Airport or Renfe Train Station (for stays of at least four nights), and a complimentary glass of cava upon arrival. Furthermore, all accommodations are pet-friendly. Although Climia Hotels has various types of establishments, the present study focuses exclusively on Hotel Climia Benidorm Plaza, as this property was selected for the implementation of the pilot project described below.

Hotel Climia Benidorm Plaza offers its guests a wide range of services, including: a buffet restaurant with a broad gastronomic offering featuring regional dishes, a swimming pool with solarium and an covered option during the winter season, event and celebration spaces, and an area dedicated to bicycle maintenance. One of the most distinctive aspects of the Hotel Climia Benidorm Plaza is its ability to integrate technology into some of its services. For instance, the company has incorporated an immersive booking system on its website that allows guests to explore the hotel and select their room through an interactive 3D experience. It also features the support of Velma, a virtual assistant that accompanies users through the booking process, providing guidance and useful information.

Despite the hotel's already well-established presence withing the hospitality landscape of the Costa Blanca (previously operating under the brand Hotels GF), its national and international visibility has recently gained popularity thanks to its participation in the "eTourist: Last Mile Project," led by the Alicante-based company Bumerania. This pioneering initiative has positioned Climia Benidorm Plaza as the first fully robotized hotel in Europe, significantly redefining its value proposition. The project, promoted by Segittur and funded by the European Union's Next Generation EU funds, aims to enhance the competitiveness and digital transformation of tourist destinations and companies, moving them more sustainable and innovative operational models.

The "hotel of the future," as it has been referred to by various media outlets, has incorporated eight types of robots, that move around and interact with guests using artificial intelligence.

Figure 4.

Robot	Characteristics	Functions
GreetingBot Reception Robot	Advanced voice system and touchscreen; fluent in 30 languages; detects the presence of guests and initiates greetings and dialogue; highly fluid mobility.	Check-in and check-out; room key printing; accompanying guests; providing hotel and city information.
LuckiBot Pro Waiter Robot	Touchscreen; load capacity of 50 kg; removable trays; intelligent navigation.	Delivery of food and beverages in the restaurant; collection of used dishes; automatic identification of food and drinks; guest interaction
Room SR	Automatic door with smart lock ensuring secure and private delivery; password-protected internal compartment; touchscreen and voice recognition.	Room delivery; autonomous elevator use and automatic door opening; multiple deliveries in a single route
"Luckibot Plus" Promotion Robot	Large touchscreen; fluent in 30 languages; connection to multiple devices; modular accessories.	Personalized guest assistance; interactive marketing and promotional content display
Beer-Serving Robotic Arm	Calibrated to adjust precision based on glass or cup size.	Beer dispensing
Interactive Tables	Smooth navigation with touch, slide and zoom capabilities; supports multi-user collaboration.	Menu consultation; order placement; entertainment
Cleaning Robot	360° environmental adaptation; obstacle avoidance; quiet operation; adjusts cleaning intensity to foot traffic.	Floor scrubbing and vacuuming
Pool Cleaning Robot	Intelligent sensors; Wireless operation	Pool scrubbing and vacuuming

Figure 5.

The main objective of the *Hotel of the Future: Last Mile Project* is to demonstrate how professionals in the hotel industry can experience, in real time, the integration of SR and artificial intelligence within their organizations, and how these technologies can enhance and complement the customer experience while optimizing operational efficiency. Specifically, the project pursues the following goals:

- it is expected that the use of these robots will enable the Climia Benidorm Plaza Hotel to achieve greater operational efficiency by reducing unnecessary movements and shortening task execution times. This will allow employees to focus on less routine tasks and devote more attention to customer service.
- The project also aims for the robots to provide personalized service to guests, adapting to their needs, increasing their satisfaction, and enhancing the overall value proposition offered by the hotel.
- Position the hotel as a benchmark in redefining the concept of hospitality through the integration of advanced technologies using innovation as a key differentiating factor.

The following table provides a summary of the implementation of SR in various hotels within the Spanish tourism sector. It includes pilot projects as well as adoptions carried out by well-known hotel chains and independent establishments, specifying the year of adoption, the type of robot deployed, and the functions performed.

Figure 6.

Hotel	Hotel Chain	Year of Implementation	Robot(s) Used	Functions
Lopesan Hotel Group (Gran Canaria)	Lopesan Hotel Group	2017	Pepper Reception Robot	Check-in; product presentation; guest information; QR code scanning
Leonardo Royal Hotel Barcelona Fira (Barcelona)	Leonardo Royal Hotels	2021	Bellabot Waiter Robot	Food and beverage delivery; collection of dirty dishes; guest interaction
Benicassim intur Orange tokyo	Independent Establishment	2022	Tokyo Reception Robot	Interaction with guests and assist by guiding them on specific areas of the hotel
Hotel El Curro (Burunchel, Jaén)	Independent Establishment	2023	Curro Waiter Robot	Transportation of food and beverages between kitchen and dining room
Hotel Climia Benidorm Plaza (Benidorm, Alicante)	Climia Hotels	2024	Greetingrot Reception Robot	Guest reception and check-in; room key peinting; customer service and promotional service and promotional guidance in common areas; operates in 30 languages
			Robot Room Service	Room delivery services; autonomous elevator operation
			Luckibot Pro	Food transport; collection of dirty dishes
			Brazo Cervecero	Automated beer dispensing
			Cleaning Robot	Cleaning of romms and common areas
			Interactive Tables	Menu browsing, ordering, entertainment (newspapers, games); system predicting when consumption will end
Hotel Sol Katmandu Park & Resort (Magaluf, Mallorca)	Meliá Hotels International	2024	Waiter Robots	Transport of dishes, glassware, and cutlery in the restaurant service

CONCLUSIONS

The purpose of this study has been to analyze how service robots (SR) are being implemented in the Spanish hotel industry, an area in which their adoption responds to a combination of factors such as advances in artificial intelligence, labor shortages, and the need to generate greater added value in the delivery of tourist services.

The analysis shows that SR represent one of the most significant technological transformations in the current hotel industry. When implemented efficiently, they enable the provision of more personalized and experiential services, while simultaneously strengthening hotel brand positioning.

Nevertheless, despite this potential, the human component remains essential in the tourism sector, and the integration of SR in Spanish hotels is still in an early stage. This is consistent with the existing empirical evidence, which highlights a notable increase in studies on SRics, but a limited number of works focused specifically on the Spanish context. To date, research indicates that SR do not replace the human staff but rather complement them, and that their impact on customer perception and service experience depends on factors such as their level of anthropomorphism, the context of use, and the guest's own expectations.

Consequently, there is a clear need to expand empirical and exploratory research in Spain, as much of the current knowledge originates from studies conducted in other countries or from predominantly theoretical approaches. Understanding how SR are being integrated into Spanish hotels, how they are perceived by guests, and what their real effects are on the service experience is crucial to guide hotel managers in making better-informed decisions regarding their adoption and implementation, thereby reducing the uncertainty associated with this emerging technology.

In today's competitive environment, the implementation of SR represents a strategic opportunity for tourism-related companies. When appropriately adopted, these technologies can increase the speed of service delivery, reduce unnecessary waiting times, and improve personalization, thereby providing significant added value for customers. This study contributes to filling the existing gap in the literature, especially in the Spanish context, by analyzing real-world cases that allow for a deeper understanding of the impact of these technologies on service encounters between robots and humans.

Although the use of SR in Spain is still limited, pioneering initiatives such as the eToruist Project implemented at the Climia Benidorm Plaza Hotel already demonstrated strong potential for growth and transformation in the coming years. The impact of SR extends beyond task automation of tasks, encompassing key aspects such as customer experience and satisfaction, sustainability, and innovation in hotel management.

However, their integration is not without challenges. One of the main concerns is the perception of robots as potential replacements for human staff, and the skepticism this may generate among some customers. Currently, most experts advocate for a hybrid model in which robotics supports staff, especially in routine or repetitive tasks, allowing employees to focus on higher value-added functions, especially those that require empathy and personalized attention.

IMPLICATIONS FOR MANAGEMENT

This article presents several practical implications for hotel managers and industry professionals interested in the adoption and implementation of SR in their establishments. As the use of SR continues to grow within the tourism industry, it is essential that decision-makers not only consider the opportunities and benefits derived from its implementation but also identify the implications for the organization as a whole.

First, and before implementation, it is essential that managers to conduct a comprehensive evaluation of the hotel's operational processes in order to identify which tasks can be partially or fully automated and which should continue to be performed-or complemented-by human staff. Second, as evidenced in several of the cases analyzed in this study, implementation should carried out gradually and in multiple phases to identify potential operational failures, programming errors, or limitations in customer interaction. This phased adoption allows employees to gradually adapt to the presence of robots, reducing initial resistance to change and improving overall acceptance. Third, managers must pay special attention to the level of anthropomorphism in SR design. The literature shows that very low or very high levels of human likeness can negatively affect user acceptance, generating discomfort, rejection, or even fear. Therefore, companies should select designs that convey trust, safety, and professionalism to guests. Fourth, employees may perceive SR as a threat to their job stability or as a technology that could dehumanize the service delivery. Therefore, it is crucial to communicate clearly and effectively from the outset about the purpose of this technology, emphasizing its role as a support tool, not a replacement. In this regard, staff training becomes fundamental to ensure the efficient use of the robot and to address possible issues that may arise in daily operations. Finally, it is important to consider aspects such as data privacy and security from the early stages of implementation. SR must not only be capable of assisting with tasks but also operate in an intuitive, safe, and reliable manner, especially when using recognition sensors and databases that require responsible information management. This implies ensuring transparency in their use and constantly updating software systems to prevent risks or unauthorized access.

LIMITATIONS AND FUTURE RESEARCH DIRECTIONS

Despite the contribution of this study to understanding how SRs (SR) are being implemented in the Spanish hotel industry, it presents a number of limitations that must be taken into consideration, while simultaneously offering clear opportunities for future research.

First, the analysis is based on a limited number of real cases. This limitation is directly linked to the scarcity of available information, which results from the current low level of SR adoption in Spanish hotels. Consequently, it is difficult to obtain a more general and comprehensive view of the phenomenon. As the implementation of these technologies increases, it will be possible to expand the analysis to a larger number of hotels. Second, the information used in this study comes from secondary sources, such as corporate reports, specialized press, and scientific literature. Although these sources provide a useful and up-to-date insights, future research should employ empirical methodologies—both qualitative and quantitative—that allow for collecting primary data directly from customers, managers, and employees involved in the cases analyzed. Third, the accelerated pace of technological development represents another important limitation, as some of the examples discussed may become outdated in a relatively short period of time. For this reason, it would be valuable to conduct longitudinal studies examining the adoption process of these robots over time. Likewise, a particularly relevant line of research would be a comparative analysis of the level of anthropomorphism of the robots implemented in different hotel establishments. Studying how the robot's physical appearance, behavior, and degree of human-likeness influence guest perceptions and overall satisfaction could offer more precise guidance for designing and selecting SR that are better suited to the hotel context. Finally, it would be advisable to extend the scope of this study to other countries in order to compare the Spanish case with destinations where SR adoption in hotels is more advanced. Such comparisons would help identify cultural and organizational factors that may either facilitate or hinder the implementation of SR in Spanish hotels.

REFERENCES

Abdi, E., Tojib, D., Seong, A. K., Pamarthi, Y., & Millington-Palmer, G. (2022). A study on the influence of SRs' level of anthropomorphism on the willingness of users to follow their recommendations. *Scientific Reports*, *12*(1), 15266. DOI: 10.1038/s41598-022-19501-0 PMID: 36088470

Aggarwal, P., & McGill, A. L. (2007). Is that car smiling at me? Schema congruity as a basis for evaluating anthropomorphized products. *The Journal of Consumer Research*, *34*(4), 468–479. DOI: 10.1086/518544

Aguado, I. (2024). *Los robots llegan a los hoteles de Mallorca: "No queremos sustituir puestos de trabajo"*. Diario de Mallorca. https://www.diariodemallorca.es/mallorca/2024/10/29/robots-llegan-hoteles-mallorca-queremos-110793539.html

Akdim, K., Belanche, D., & Flavián, M. (2023). Attitudes toward SRs: Analyses of explicit and implicit attitudes based on anthropomorphism and construal level theory. *International Journal of Contemporary Hospitality Management*, *35*(8), 2816–2837. DOI: 10.1108/IJCHM-12-2020-1406

Aubel, M., Pikturniene, I., & Joye, Y. (2022). Risk perception and risk behavior in response to SR anthropomorphism in banking. *Central European Management Journal*, *30*(2), 26–42. DOI: 10.7206/cemj.2658-0845.74

Automation, A. E. R. (2024). *Las ventas de robots industriales en España se disparan un 48 % y la robótica de servicio crece un 17 %*. AER Automation. https://www.aer-automation.com/automation_review/las-ventas-de-robots-industriales-en-espana-se-disparan-un-48-y-la-robotica-de-servicio-crece-un-17/

Ayyildiz, A. Y., Baykal, M., & Koc, E. (2022). Attitudes of hotel customers towards the use of SRs in hospitality service encounters. *Technology in Society*, *70*, 101995. DOI: 10.1016/j.techsoc.2022.101995

Balakrishnan, J., & Dwivedi, Y. K. (2021). Role of cognitive absorption in building user trust and experience. *Psychology and Marketing*, *38*(4), 643–668. DOI: 10.1002/mar.21462

Belanche, D., Casaló, L. V., Flavián, C., & Schepers, J. (2020). Robots or frontline employees? Exploring customers' attributions of responsibility and stability after service failure or success. *Journal of Service Management*, *31*(2), 267–289. DOI: 10.1108/JOSM-05-2019-0156

Blut, M., Wang, C., Wünderlich, N. V., & Brock, C. (2021). Understanding anthropomorphism in service provision: A meta-analysis of physical robots, chatbots, and other AI. *Journal of the Academy of Marketing Science, 49*(4), 632–658. DOI: 10.1007/s11747-020-00762-y

Bowen, J., & Morosan, C. (2018). Beware hospitality industry: The robots are coming. *Worldwide Hospitality and Tourism Themes, 10*(6), 726–733. DOI: 10.1108/WHATT-07-2018-0045

Buhalis, D., & Sinarta, Y. (2019). Real-time co-creation and nowness service: Lessons from tourism and hospitality. *Journal of Travel & Tourism Marketing, 36*(5), 563–582. DOI: 10.1080/10548408.2019.1592059

Bumerania Robotics. *eTurist Project – Hotel Benidorm Plaza*. Recuperado el 27 de junio de 2025, de https://bumerania.com/project/hotel-benidorm-plaza/

Cao, K., Yin, H., & Wang, J. (2025). Introducing robot or not? Decisions of competing hotels. *International Journal of Hospitality Management, 126*, 104034. DOI: 10.1016/j.ijhm.2024.104034

Cheng, L. K. (2023). Effects of SRs' anthropomorphism on consumers' attribution toward and forgiveness of service failure. *Journal of Consumer Behaviour, 22*(1), 67–81. DOI: 10.1002/cb.2112

Chiang, A. H., Trimi, S., & Lo, Y. J. (2022). Emotion and service quality of anthropomorphic robots. *Technological Forecasting and Social Change, 177*, 121550. DOI: 10.1016/j.techfore.2022.121550

De Keyser, A., Köcher, S., Alkire, L., Verbeeck, C., & Kandampully, J. (2019). Frontline service technology infusion: Conceptual archetypes and future research directions. *Journal of Service Management, 30*(1), 156–183. DOI: 10.1108/JOSM-03-2018-0082

Duffy, B. R. (2003). Anthropomorphism and the social robot. *Robotics and Autonomous Systems, 42*(3-4), 177–190. DOI: 10.1016/S0921-8890(02)00374-3

Engelhardt, K. G. (1990). SRics and artificial intelligence: Current research and future directions. *ISA Transactions, 29*(1), 31–40. DOI: 10.1016/0019-0578(90)90029-K

Fink, J. (2012). Anthropomorphism and human likeness in the design of robots and human-robot interaction. In *International conference on social robotics* (pp. 199-208). Springer, Berlin, Heidelberg. DOI: 10.1007/978-3-642-34103-8_20

Fusté-Forné, F., & Jamal, T. (2021). Co-creating new directions for SRs in hospitality and tourism. *Tourism and Hospitality, 2*(1), 43–61. DOI: 10.3390/tourhosp2010003

Globetrender (2022). *Robots to play more significant role in travel and hospitality*. https://globetrender.com/2022/11/17/robots-significant-role-travel-hospital

Hosteltur (2024). *Los robots impulsan la eficiencia hotelera en Magic Costa Blanca*. https://www.hosteltur.com/163098_los-robots-impulsan-la-eficiencia-hotelera-en-magic-costa-blanca.html

International Federation of Robotics. (2022). *World Robotics 2022: Service Robots* (C. Müller, B. Graf, & K. Pfeiffer, Eds.). IFR Statistical Department, VDMA Services GmbH.

International Federation of Robotics. (2025). *SRs see global growth boom* [Comunicado de prensa]. International Federation of Robotics. https://ifr.org/ifr-press-releases/news/service-robots-see-global-growth-boom

Ivanov, S., Seyitoğlu, F., & Markova, M. (2020). Hotel managers' perceptions towards the use of robots: A mixed-methods approach. *Information Technology & Tourism, 22*(4), 505–535. DOI: 10.1007/s40558-020-00187-x

Ivanov, S., & Webster, C. (2020). Robots in tourism: A research agenda for tourism economics. *Tourism Economics, 26*(7), 1065–1085. DOI: 10.1177/1354816619879583

Jia, J. W., Chung, N., & Hwang, J. (2021). Assessing the hotel SR interaction on tourists' behaviour: The role of anthropomorphism. *Industrial Management & Data Systems, 121*(6), 1457–1478. DOI: 10.1108/IMDS-11-2020-0664

Kim, S. Y., Schmitt, B. H., & Thalmann, N. M. (2019). Eliza in the uncanny valley: Anthropomorphizing consumer robots increases their perceived warmth but decreases liking. *Marketing Letters, 30*(1), 1–12. DOI: 10.1007/s11002-019-09485-9

Kim, T., Lee, O. K. D., & Kang, J. (2023). Is it the best for barista robots to serve like humans? A multidimensional anthropomorphism perspective. *International Journal of Hospitality Management, 108*, 103358. DOI: 10.1016/j.ijhm.2022.103358

Lee, I. (2021). SRs: A systematic literature review. *Electronics (Basel), 10*(21), 2658. DOI: 10.3390/electronics10212658

Lee, S. L., Lau, I. Y. M., Kiesler, S., & Chiu, C. Y. (2005, April). Human mental models of humanoid robots. In *Proceedings of the 2005 IEEE international conference on robotics and automation* (pp. 2767-2772). IEEE.

Lehmann, H., Roncone, A., Pattacini, U., & Metta, G. (2016, October). Physiologically inspired blinking behavior for a humanoid robot. In *International Conference on Social Robotics* (pp. 83-93). Cham: Springer International Publishing. DOI: 10.1007/978-3-319-47437-3_9

Li, J. (2015). The benefit of being physically present: A survey of experimental works comparing copresent robots, telepresent robots and virtual agents. *International Journal of Human-Computer Studies, 77*, 23–37. DOI: 10.1016/j.ijhcs.2015.01.001

Li, Y., & Wang, C. (2022). Effect of customer's perception on SR acceptance. *International Journal of Consumer Studies, 46*(4), 1241–1261. DOI: 10.1111/ijcs.12755

Lu, L., Cai, R., & Gursoy, D. (2019). Developing and validating a SR integration willingness scale. *International Journal of Hospitality Management, 80*, 36–51. DOI: 10.1016/j.ijhm.2019.01.005

Lv, L., Huang, M., & Huang, R. (2023). Anthropomorphize SRs: The role of human nature traits. *Service Industries Journal, 43*(3-4), 213–237. DOI: 10.1080/02642069.2022.2048821

Mende, M., Scott, M. L., Van Doorn, J., Grewal, D., & Shanks, I. (2019). SRs rising: How humanoid robots influence service experiences and elicit compensatory consumer responses. *JMR, Journal of Marketing Research, 56*(4), 535–556. DOI: 10.1177/0022243718822827

Mirnig, N., Stollnberger, G., Miksch, M., Stadler, S., Giuliani, M., & Tscheligi, M. (2017). To err is robot: How humans assess and act toward an erroneous social robot. *Frontiers in Robotics and AI, 4*, 21. DOI: 10.3389/frobt.2017.00021

Mori, M. (1970). Bukimi no tani [The uncanny valley]. *Energy, 7*, 33.

Murphy, J., Hofacker, C., & Gretzel, U. (2017). Dawning of the age of robots in hospitality and tourism: Challenges for teaching and research. *European Journal of Tourism Research, 15*, 104–111. DOI: 10.54055/ejtr.v15i.265

Park, S. (2020). Multifaceted trust in tourism SRs. *Annals of Tourism Research, 81*, 102888. DOI: 10.1016/j.annals.2020.102888

Park, S. S., Tung, C. D., & Lee, H. (2021). The adoption of AI SRs: A comparison between credence and experience service settings. *Psychology and Marketing, 38*(4), 691–703. DOI: 10.1002/mar.21468

Puertas, R. (2025). Turismo e Inteligencia Artificial: el momento de abrazar el cambio. Recuperado de https://www.hosteltur.com/comunidad/006092_turismo-e-inteligencia-artificial-el-momento-de-abrazar-el-cambio.html

Qiu, H., Li, M., Shu, B., & Bai, B. (2020). Enhancing hospitality experience with SRs: The mediating role of rapport building. *Journal of Hospitality Marketing & Management, 29*(3), 247–268. DOI: 10.1080/19368623.2019.1645073

Rana, N. P., Begum, N., Faisal, M. N., & Mishra, A. (2025). Customer experiences with SRs in hotels: A review and research agenda. *Journal of Hospitality Marketing & Management*, *34*(2), 145–174. DOI: 10.1080/19368623.2024.2403640

Reis, J., Melão, N., Salvadorinho, J., Soares, B., & Rosete, A. (2020). SRs in the hospitality industry: The case of Henn-na hotel, Japan. *Technology in Society*, *63*, 101423. DOI: 10.1016/j.techsoc.2020.101423

Rosete, A., Soares, B., Salvadorinho, J., Reis, J., & Amorim, M. (2020). SRs in the hospitality industry: An exploratory literature review. In *Exploring Service Science: 10th International Conference, IESS 2020, Porto, Portugal, February 5–7, 2020* [Springer International Publishing.]. *Proceedings*, *10*, 174–186.

Shin, H. H., & Jeong, M. (2020). Guests' perceptions of robot concierge and their adoption intentions. *International Journal of Contemporary Hospitality Management*, *32*(8), 2613–2633. DOI: 10.1108/IJCHM-09-2019-0798

Statista (2025). *Porcentaje del PIB aportado por el sector turístico en España de 2010 a 2024*. https://es.statista.com/estadisticas/1082929/sector-turistico-porcentaje-del-pib-aportado-espana/

Torregrosa, R. (2025, 2 de octubre). *Turismo: presente y desafíos. TecnoHotelNews*. https://tecnohotelnews.com/2025/10/turismo-presente-y-desafios/

Tuomi, A., Tussyadiah, I. P., & Stienmetz, J. (2021). Applications and implications of SRs in hospitality. *Cornell Hospitality Quarterly*, *62*(2), 232–247. DOI: 10.1177/1938965520923961

Van Pinxteren, M. M., Wetzels, R. W., Rüger, J., Pluymaekers, M., & Wetzels, M. (2019). Trust in humanoid robots: Implications for services marketing. *Journal of Services Marketing*, *33*(4), 507–518. DOI: 10.1108/JSM-01-2018-0045

Vatan, A., & Dogan, S. (2021). What do hotel employees think about SRs? A qualitative study in Turkey. *Tourism Management Perspectives*, *37*, 100775. DOI: 10.1016/j.tmp.2020.100775

Walters, M. L., Syrdal, D. S., Dautenhahn, K., Te Boekhorst, R., & Koay, K. L. (2008). Avoiding the uncanny valley: Robot appearance, personality and consistency of behavior in an attention-seeking home scenario for a robot companion. *Autonomous Robots*, *24*(2), 159–178. DOI: 10.1007/s10514-007-9058-3

Williams, M. A. (2016, October). Decision-theoretic human-robot interaction: Designing reasonable and rational robot behavior. In *International Conference on Social Robotics* (pp. 72-82). Cham: Springer International Publishing. DOI: 10.1007/978-3-319-47437-3_8

Wirtz, J., Patterson, P. G., Kunz, W. H., Gruber, T., Lu, V. N., Paluch, S., & Martins, A. (2018). Brave new world: SRs in the frontline. *Journal of Service Management, 29*(5), 907–931. DOI: 10.1108/JOSM-04-2018-0119

World Travel & Tourism Council. (2025, 29 de mayo). *El sector turístico de España podría superar los 260 000 millones de euros en 2025, según WTTC*. WTTC. https://wttc.org/news/el-sector-turistico-de-espana-podria-superar-los-260000-millones-de-euros-en-2025

Yang, M., Li, J., Feng, L., Chen, S. C., & Tseng, M. L. (2024). SR anthropomorphism on consumer usage intention: Curvilinear and linear effect. *Industrial Management & Data Systems, 124*(2), 612–639. DOI: 10.1108/IMDS-08-2023-0538

Zhang, M., Xu, T., Hardin, J., Cai, J. J., Brooks, J., & Green, K. E. (2021, August). How many robots do you want? A cross-cultural exploration on user preference and perception of an assistive multi-robot system. In *2021 30th IEEE international conference on robot & human interactive communication (RO-MAN)* (pp. 580-585). IEEE.

Zhang, S., Lin, X., Li, X., & Ren, A. (2022). SRs' anthropomorphism: Dimensions, factors and internal relationships. *Electronic Markets, 32*(1), 277–295. DOI: 10.1007/s12525-022-00527-1

Chapter 15
Synergizing Creativity:
Human-AI Collaboration in the Creative Industries

Satya Subrahmanyam
http://orcid.org/0000-0003-0441-2742
Holy Spirit University of Kaslik, Lebanon

ABSTRACT

The rapid advancement of artificial intelligence is redefining creativity by transforming AI from a supportive tool into an active collaborative partner across creative industries. This chapter examines human–AI collaboration as a model of hybrid intelligence, where human imagination, contextual understanding, and emotional insight converge with algorithmic generation and multimodal experimentation. Drawing on creativity studies, computational creativity, and sociotechnical systems theory, the chapter analyzes AI-enabled co-creation across visual arts, music, literature, film, gaming, advertising, and design. Through illustrative case studies, it highlights emerging creative roles and evolving competencies while critically addressing ethical, legal, and cultural challenges related to authorship, bias, authenticity, and ownership. The chapter argues that responsible, human-centered AI can amplify creativity, democratize artistic participation, and foster more inclusive and innovative creative ecosystems.

1. INTRODUCTION

Instead of computers only automating mundane activities, human-AI cooperation in creative work describes processes where computing systems and humans collaboratively contribute to ideation, form, or meaning. This collaboration is seen by modern researchers as hybrid intelligence, an artificially planned alliance where

DOI: 10.4018/979-8-3373-8337-8.ch015

human judgement and creativity are enhanced by AI via accountable, adaptable, and explicable patterns of interaction (Akata et al., 2020). The use of generative models, recommendation systems, and interactive interfaces to augment, rather than replace, human creativity is how this hybridity manifests in creative contexts via co-creation workflows (Akata et al., 2020; Erickson, 2024).

Since 2022, the rise of generative AI across text, image, audio, and video production has accelerated transformations throughout creative value chains. AI now contributes at multiple stages, including rapid ideation and prototyping, automated or semi-automated production, metadata-driven distribution, and algorithmic audience targeting. Empirical studies of creative firms indicate that AI frequently increases both the intensity and diversity of labour, generating new tasks such as data curation, prompt engineering, and post-editing, while simultaneously reshaping traditional roles including illustrators, composers, and scriptwriters (Erickson, 2024). As a result, policymakers and industry observers characterize AI as both a catalyst for innovative formats, such as immersive CreaTech, procedural gaming, and AI-assisted scoring, and a disruptive force that raises critical questions regarding authorship, remuneration, and cultural stewardship (POST, 2024).

This chapter examines the opportunities, tensions, and evolving dynamics of human–AI synergy in creative industries by adopting a relational perspective. Rather than treating AI solely as a technical instrument, the discussion considers how AI mediates relationships among creators, collaborators, institutions, and audiences. The analysis encompasses theoretical foundations, including hybrid intelligence and distributed cognition, empirical practices such as workflows and case studies, and normative debates concerning ethics, labour, and governance. The chapter seeks to identify contexts in which AI meaningfully enhances human expression, situations where it may undermine creative agency, and the practical governance and educational responses required to address these challenges.

Artificial intelligence's potential to transform the social dynamics around creative creations and the expression of individual identity is central to this work. Both production and the communication and interpretation of meaning are impacted by personalisation algorithms and generative technologies. According to Beyari and Hashem (2025) and POST (2024), artists have the challenge of meeting changing expectations for openness and authenticity as audiences become more involved in co-creating experiences and systems personalise tales based on individual preferences. While empirical research highlights the importance of AI-assisted outputs, it also warns that computational collaborators can make creative workers even more vulnerable unless policy frameworks and business models change (Erickson, 2024). Hybrid systems that are explainable, credit-aware, and orientated toward equitable value distribution are necessary to safeguard human agency and relational trust, according to a key argument of the chapter. This principle undergirds the subsequent analysis (Akata et al., 2020; POST, 2024).

2. THEORETICAL FOUNDATIONS OF HUMAN–AI CREATIVE SYNERGY

Theoretical foundations are essential for understanding how human creativity and artificial intelligence interact as a synergistic system rather than as isolated agents. This section examines key perspectives from creativity studies, computational creativity, hybrid intelligence, and sociotechnical theory to explain how creative outcomes emerge through human–AI collaboration, distributed cognition, and evolving relationships between creators, technologies, and cultural contexts.

2.1 Human Creativity Theories and Computational Creativity

Human–AI collaboration in creative work rests on a foundation of long-standing theories explaining how creativity emerges and evolves. Rhodes' classic "4Ps" model - Person, Process, Product, and Press - remains relevant for understanding the interplay between individual capabilities, contextual influences, and the characteristics of creative outputs (Rhodes, 1961, as cited in Glăveanu, 2020). Contemporary research extends these principles into computational domains by examining how AI systems participate in or simulate creative processes. Amabile's Componential Theory of Creativity, which highlights intrinsic motivation, domain expertise, and creative-thinking skills, offers a valuable lens for evaluating whether AI augments or constrains human agency (Amabile, 2018). In parallel, computational creativity research argues that algorithmic systems can generate new, valuable, and unexpected ideas when trained on large multimodal datasets, although they lack intrinsic motivation or lived experience (Da Pelo, 2025). These distinctions underscore that AI can contribute to creative processes but does so through pattern generation rather than human-like intentionality.

2.2 Hybrid Intelligence and Distributed Cognition

A more exact framework for comprehending the complementary nature of human and machine talents is offered by the notion of hybrid intelligence. The term "hybrid intelligence" refers to a system that combines artificial intelligence (AI) with human decision-making abilities, ethics, and cultural awareness (Akata et al., 2020). Instead of embracing total automation or idealising humans as an exception, this approach advocates for systems that combine AI's memory, scalability, and processing power with human characteristics like intuition, emotion, and meaning-making.

Related to this is distributed cognition theory, which positions cognition not solely within individuals but across networks of people, tools, and environments. In creative contexts, AI becomes part of an extended cognitive system through which ideas are externalized, manipulated, and iteratively refined (Hutchins, 2020). Generative visual models act as external imaginations, enabling rapid prototyping that reshapes how creators conceptualize form and meaning. Seen through this lens, human–AI synergy is less about replacing or imitating human thought and more about expanding the distributed cognitive architecture within which creative work unfolds.

2.3 AI as Creative Partner vs. Creative Tool

Theoretically, there is a lot of back-and-forth about whether AI is more like a digital paintbrush or editing suite or an actual collaborator in the creative process. According to scholars, AI can produce new outputs, but it lacks the essential qualities of human creativity, such as intentionality, reflective judgement, and emotional resonance (Moruzzi, 2025). Iterative recommendations, surprising prompts, and challenges to human beliefs are just a few examples of how many designers portray AI systems as collaborators, according to factual data.

The distinction matters because viewing AI as a partner shifts the dynamics of creative authorship, responsibility, and relationality. In co-creative workflows, creators engage in dialogic interactions with AI systems - prompting, curating, correcting, and interpreting outputs. This interplay has implications for skill development, with researchers noting the rise of "prompt literacy" and "algorithmic sensibility" as emerging competencies (Erickson, 2024). Thus, whether AI is conceptualized as a partner or tool shapes how industries allocate credit, compensate labor, and define originality.

Table 1. AI as creative partner vs. creative tool: Key distinctions

Dimension	AI as Creative Partner	AI as Creative Tool
Primary Role	Acts as an autonomous or semi-autonomous collaborator contributing ideas, patterns, and solutions.	Functions as an instrument used to execute tasks defined by the human creator.
Agency Level	High—AI generates novel options, adapts to context, and participates in decision-making.	Low—AI follows predefined commands or parameters without independent creative intent.
Creative Contribution	Co-generates content; may challenge human assumptions, introduce unexpected variations, and influence creative direction.	Supports or enhances human output; accelerates workflow but does not alter conceptual direction.
Interaction Mode	Iterative dialogue, co-exploration, and feedback loops between human and AI.	One-way interaction where the human provides input and AI deliver outputs.
Human Role	Curator, facilitator, or collaborator engaging in negotiation with AI-generated possibilities.	Designer or operator directing the tool to achieve specific outcomes.
AI Learning and Adaptation	Learns from user style, preferences, and patterns, enabling continuity in co-creation.	Minimal adaptation; performs based on static algorithms or predefined functions.
Impact on Creative Process	May transform ideation, inspire new directions, and reshape the creative workflow.	Streamlines tasks, improves efficiency, and expands technical capabilities without altering conceptual processes.
Relationship Dynamics	Relational, reciprocal, and dialogic—creativity emerges from combined strengths.	Instrumental, mechanistic, and utility-based—AI supports but does not share creative agency.
Ethical and Ownership Considerations	Raises questions about authorship, originality, and shared credit.	Ownership remains largely with the human creator; AI outputs treated as tool-generated.
Examples	AI co-writing scripts, generative music improvisation systems, co-design platforms.	Photo-editing software, procedural generation tools, AI-based recommender systems.

2.4 Sociotechnical and Relational Systems Perspective

Creativity does not emerge in isolation; it is produced within sociotechnical systems that include people, technologies, institutions, and cultural norms. Adopting a sociotechnical perspective shifts the focus from individual interactions to the broader ecosystems in which human–AI creativity unfolds. This view recognizes that creative outcomes are shaped by system design, data governance, platform algorithms, and organizational processes (Bryson & Theodorou, 2019). The training data that underpins generative AI models influence aesthetic styles, narrative structures, and cultural representations, thereby mediating the relational dynamics between creators, audiences, and institutions.

A relational systems view further emphasizes that AI also transforms social interactions involved in creative production. Collaborative workflows increasingly involve triangulated relationships among creators, AI systems, and audience feedback, often mediated by platforms. This dynamic means that creativity becomes a multi-node interaction rather than a dyadic one. Understanding creative synergy therefore requires not only analyzing human–AI interactions but also situating them within regulatory, economic, and cultural ecosystems that influence how creative agency is distributed and enacted.

3. MAPPING THE CREATIVE INDUSTRIES LANDSCAPE

This section maps the evolving creative industries landscape shaped by the growing integration of artificial intelligence. It examines how AI technologies are being adopted across diverse creative sectors, reshaping value chains, production processes, and creator–audience relationships. By situating these developments within broader industry convergence and digital transformation, the section highlights how creativity is increasingly produced, mediated, and experienced through human–AI collaboration.

3.1 Creative Sectors Impacted by AI

Artificial intelligence has become a pervasive force across creative sectors, reshaping workflows, aesthetic possibilities, and business models. In the visual arts, generative models such as diffusion systems enable artists to experiment with new forms, textures, and visual narratives (Epstein et al., 2023). The music industry has experienced similar disruption, with AI-enabled composition systems producing harmonies, melodies, and adaptive soundtracks tailored to user contexts (Chen et al., 2024). In literature and scriptwriting, large language models are being used for story ideation, character development, and stylistic experimentation. Film production increasingly incorporates AI-driven editing, color grading, and visual effects pipelines that accelerate post-production processes (Xu, 2025).

Interactive sectors such as gaming have embraced AI to create dynamic environments, procedurally generated narratives, and intelligent non-player characters, enhancing immersion and player engagement (Porcino et al., 2022). Advertising and marketing rely heavily on AI for automated copywriting, consumer sentiment analysis, and hyper-targeted campaign design. Likewise, fashion and architecture have incorporated machine learning–driven generative design systems to explore new material combinations, structural patterns, and aesthetic prototypes (Halabi & Subrahmanyam, 2025).

Performing arts have also witnessed transformation, with AI-driven choreography, virtual performers, and augmented live performances altering the creative and experiential dimensions of theater and dance (Wickramasinghe, 2025). Across these domains, AI's capabilities are shifting creativity from purely human-led processes to hybrid forms of expression.

3.2 Convergence and AI Adoption

The increasing convergence of creative technologies has accelerated AI adoption across industries. Generative AI tools - such as text-to-image systems, neural synthesizers, and multimodal models - enable creators to merge artistic disciplines and experiment across media boundaries. Machine learning–driven design automation supports rapid prototyping through generative design software used in fashion, architecture, and product development (Zhuang et al., 2025). Beyond creation, predictive analytics has become central to understanding and anticipating audience engagement patterns. Streaming platforms, publishers, and advertisers employ recommendation algorithms and behavior prediction models to tailor content delivery and maximize reach (Choi et al., 2020). These converging systems create an interconnected ecosystem in which creative production, consumption, and interpretation are increasingly data-driven.

3.3 Shifts in Creative Value Chains

AI is restructuring creative value chains by transforming each stage from ideation to consumption. In the ideation phase, creators use AI for brainstorming, mood-board generation, rapid visualization, and narrative simulation. Production processes are increasingly automated: AI supports audio mixing, image enhancement, animation generation, and design refinement, significantly reducing time and resource costs (Anantrasirichai & Bull, 2022). Distribution channels are becoming algorithmically optimized, with platforms prioritizing content through ranking systems based on predicted relevance and engagement.

Marketing and promotion have shifted toward data-centric strategies that use AI to segment audiences, optimize messaging, and monitor real-time performance analytics. Consumption patterns are equally affected. Audiences now encounter adaptive content - such as personalized playlists, tailored advertisements, and customizable storylines - which blurs the boundary between creator intent and consumer influence (Acatrinei et al., 2025). These shifts illustrate how AI not only accelerates workflows but also redefines the economic and cultural structures of creative industries.

3.4 Evolving Creator–Audience Relationships

The connection between creators and audiences is being radically transformed by the incorporation of AI into creative ecosystems. Recommendation engines and predictive personalisation have made personalised content distribution possible, which has shifted creative focus away from mass-oriented forms and toward individualised experiences (Beyari & Hashem, 2025). Audiences may take part in the creative process via interactive and AI-mediated formats including virtual influencers, generative art platforms, and real-time co-creation experiences. While this interactive dynamic does increase engagement, it also begs the issues of who wrote what, how genuine the expression is, and how deeply felt it is when mediated by AI.

Conversational AI systems enable creators to engage directly with audiences in new ways, fostering continuous feedback loops and co-created meaning (Hancock et al., 2020). As creators adopt AI-driven tools to communicate, market, and distribute work, the relational fabric between creator and consumer becomes increasingly mediated by algorithms. This evolving relationship marks a profound transformation of creative identity and audience expectations in the digital era.

Figure 1. Mapping the creative industries landscape (Author, 2025)

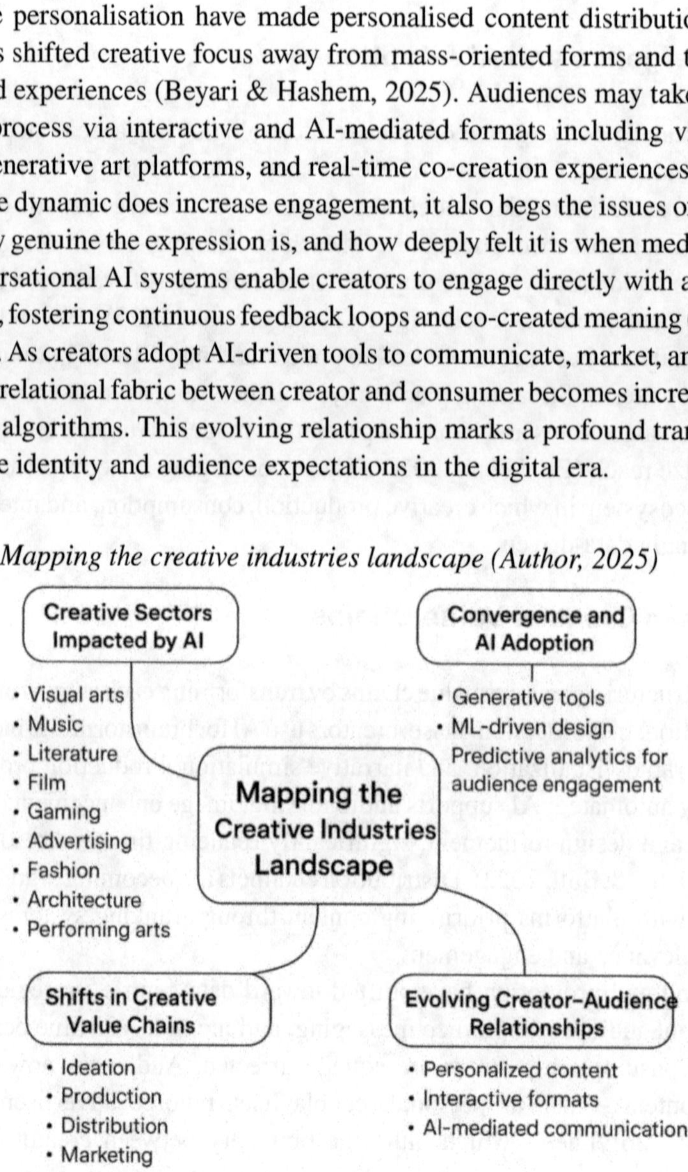

4. HUMAN–AI COLLABORATION MODELS IN PRACTICE

Human–AI collaboration in creative industries is increasingly characterized by integrated workflows, adaptive feedback mechanisms, and sophisticated interface ecosystems. As creative practitioners experiment with artificial intelligence to augment or transform their work, new models of collaboration are emerging that blend human intentionality with machine-driven generativity. This section examines how these collaborations unfold in practice, highlighting co-creation workflows, AI-augmented artistic production, feedback loops, and the growing suite of collaborative tools.

4.1 Co-Creation Workflows

Co-creation workflows describe structured processes in which humans and AI systems jointly engage in creative tasks such as brainstorming, drafting, editing, and prototyping. These workflows are becoming more prevalent as generative models provide on-demand ideation support, enabling creators to move rapidly between conceptualization and execution. In early-phase brainstorming, large language models and image generators assist users in expanding idea spaces, reducing cognitive load and accelerating divergent thinking (Holzner et al., 2025). Writers may prompt a model like ChatGPT or Claude to produce thematic variations, narrative seeds, or stylistic alternatives, which they subsequently refine based on personal vision and contextual requirements.

In drafting and editing stages, AI supports iterative refinement by offering structural suggestions, style modifications, or conceptual extensions. Creative prototyping - particularly in design, animation, and multimedia production - also benefits from AI's capacity to produce quick visual or textual mock-ups that creators can evaluate and modify. Recent studies indicate that such hybrid workflows enhance productivity and creative confidence without displacing human judgment or aesthetic sensibility (Caramiaux et al., 2025).

4.2 AI-Augmented Artistic Production

Generative models are used in AI-augmented creative creation to generate or alter aesthetic material in the visual, musical, and narrative realms. Visual arts technologies like as DALL·E, Midjourney, and Runway ML allow artists to create detailed images by using a mix of written instructions, refined models, and inpainting or outpainting methods. According to McCormack et al. (2023), these systems may do more than just generate content automatically; they can also collaborate with humans to bring about new patterns and hybrids of styles, which can push the bounds of creativity.

In music, AI systems such as AIVA and OpenAI's MuseNet support algorithmic composition by generating melodies, harmonies, and even orchestration layers. Musicians increasingly use these outputs as raw material to be edited, arranged, or reinterpreted, blending machine-generated motifs with human performance and interpretation. Likewise, screenwriters and game designers experiment with generative text models to draft scenes, scripts, character profiles, and branching narrative structures. Rather than replacing the craft of writing, these systems support exploratory writing and narrative complexity by offering diverse stylistic suggestions and plot trajectories (Serbanescu, 2023).

4.3 Adaptive Creative Feedback Loops

One of the most transformative aspects of human–AI collaboration lies in adaptive feedback loops. AI acts as an "inspiration engine" by presenting unexpected associations, visual metaphors, or structural alternatives that stimulate creative breakthroughs. It can also serve as a "constraint releaser" by helping creators overcome creative blocks, generate multiple versions instantly, or test ideas without high resource investments (O'Toole & Horvát, 2024).

These iterative loops are strengthened by real-time analytics and machine-learning models capable of learning from creators' preferences. As models adapt to user interactions, they become more aligned with individual artistic intentions, creating a dynamic interplay where human direction and machine adaptation reinforce each other. Research shows that such reciprocal learning fosters a sense of co-agency and enhances the perceived usefulness of AI in creative decision-making (Yu, 2025).

4.4 Collaborative Interfaces and Tools

Recent advancements in collaborative interfaces have accelerated the adoption of human–AI creative partnerships. Platforms like DALL·E and Midjourney provide intuitive prompt-based interfaces that allow users to manipulate aesthetic parameters with increasing precision. Runway ML extends this functionality to video editing, 3D generation, and multimodal workflows, enabling creators to combine text, image, and movement within a unified environment. Tools such as GitHub Copilot support code-based creativity, while ChatGPT functions as a versatile writing, research, and ideation partner. These tools collectively reconfigure creative workflows, lowering barriers to experimentation and allowing creators to iterate at unprecedented speed (Subrahmanyam, 2025).

Figure 2. Human-AI collaboration models in practice (Author, 2025)

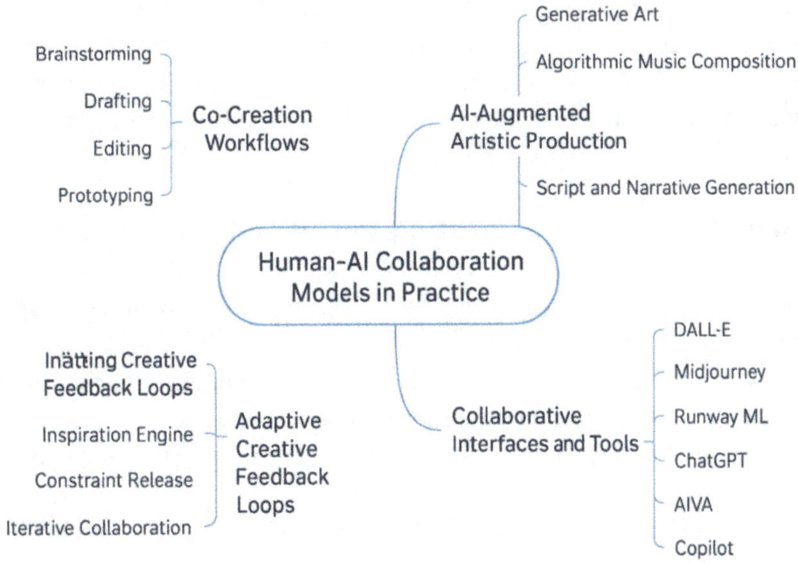

5. CASE STUDIES OF HUMAN–AI CREATIVE SYNERGY

This section presents illustrative case studies that demonstrate how human–AI collaboration operates in real-world creative contexts. Drawing from visual arts, music, film, gaming, and advertising, the cases reveal diverse models of co-creation, highlighting how AI functions as an inspirational partner, iterative collaborator, or creative facilitator while reshaping creative practices, roles, and outcomes.

5.1 Visual Arts: Hybrid Generative Artworks and Digital Exhibitions

The visual arts have emerged as a major site for experimentation in human–AI synergy, particularly through hybrid generative techniques that blend human aesthetic intention with machine-generated outputs. A prominent example is Refik Anadol's "Machine Hallucinations" series, which uses generative adversarial networks (GANs) trained on millions of images to create immersive data-sculptures and architectural projections. Anadol's work demonstrates how AI acts as both a co-creator and an interpretive engine, transforming large datasets into dynamic visual expressions that extend human perceptual capacities (Anadol, 2020). Likewise, the Museum of

Modern Art's 2023 exhibition featuring the AI-generated piece "Unsupervised" shows how AI can reimagine existing art collections by producing new variants in real time, deepening audience engagement and offering novel experiential forms (MoMA, 2023). These cases illustrate how AI-driven curation, augmentation, and visualization have reshaped both artistic production and the experience of digital spectatorship.

5.2 Music Industry: AI as Writing Partner and Sound Designer

In music, human–AI collaboration has advanced rapidly with tools capable of generating melodies, harmonies, and full compositions. One of the most prominent examples is the use of AIVA, an AI music composition engine adopted by professional creators to develop soundtracks for films, games, and commercials. Since 2021, several European production studios have incorporated AIVA-generated drafts into their scoring workflows, allowing composers to iterate more efficiently while maintaining artistic control (AIVA Technologies, 2022). Another compelling case is Holly Herndon's "Holly+", a machine-learning vocal clone system that enables artists to create new works using Herndon's synthetic voice. This project reframes authorship and performance, positioning AI as a creative partner that expands an artist's expressive range rather than replacing it (Herndon & Dryhurst, 2021). These examples underscore how AI supports ideation, experimentation, and sonic innovation while still relying on human curation and interpretive judgment.

5.3 Film and Media Production: AI-Driven Cinematography and Storytelling

The film industry has adopted AI across multiple phases of production, from pre-visualization to script development. A leading case is Lucasfilm's use of AI-enhanced virtual production technologies in the series "The Mandalorian," where machine-learning systems help generate real-time digital backdrops and optimize camera movements in the LED Volume environments. These tools enable directors and cinematographers to experiment creatively while reducing production costs and improving visual coherence (Baver, 2020). AI-based tools such as ScriptBook have been deployed to estimate narrative strength, character dynamics, and box-office potential, offering data-driven guidance while still leaving final narrative decisions to writers and producers. Ethical concerns are also evident in the use of deepfakes; for example, the recreation of a young Luke Skywalker employed AI-driven facial synthesis, sparking debate about consent, authenticity, and the future of digital actors (Vincent, 2020). Together, these cases show the industry's dual embrace of AI's creative potential and its evolving risk landscape.

5.4 Gaming and Interactive Media: Procedural Generation and Narrative Design

The gaming sector has long pioneered algorithmic creativity, but recent advances have deepened the integration of AI into worldbuilding and interactive storytelling. Hello Games' "No Man's Sky" employs procedural generation models that algorithmically create billions of unique planets, ecosystems, and artifacts, blending human-designed rules with AI-driven variation. Updates released since 2020 have expanded the game's machine-learning-enhanced behaviors, making environments more adaptive and lifelike (Hello Games, 2021). Another instance is AI Dungeon, a text-based interactive platform that uses large language models to generate branching narratives in real time. The tool provides an open-ended co-creative environment where player choices combine with AI improvisation to create emergent storytelling that no single author could script (Simonite, 2021). These cases highlight AI's role in expanding narrative possibility spaces and enabling deeply personalized interactive experiences.

5.5 Advertising and Branding: AI-Driven Creative Campaigns and Personalization

In advertising, AI has become central to real-time content generation and targeted consumer engagement. A widely cited example is Heineken's 2023 "AI Beer" campaign, which used generative models to produce visual assets, taglines, and immersive promotional content. The campaign demonstrated how AI-enhanced creative pipelines can shorten production timelines while enabling highly customized narrative variants (Heineken, 2023). Ogilvy's use of AI for dynamic ad personalization allows brands to tailor visual and narrative elements to individual user segments, improving relevance and engagement (Ogilvy, 2025). These cases illustrate how AI has shifted branding from static messaging to fluid, adaptive, data-informed storytelling.

6. REDEFINING CREATIVE ROLES, COMPETENCIES, AND TEAM DYNAMICS

This section explores how human–AI collaboration is reshaping creative roles, skill requirements, and team dynamics within the creative industries. As AI becomes embedded in creative workflows, professionals must develop new competencies while reconfiguring collaboration, authorship, and decision-making. The discussion highlights how creativity increasingly involves orchestrating human intuition and emotional insight with machine intelligence.

6.1 Evolving Skill Sets for Creative Professionals

The integration of artificial intelligence across creative industries is reshaping the competencies required of artists, designers, writers, and media professionals. Traditional creative expertise remains essential, but it now operates alongside new forms of technical and cognitive fluency. One of the most notable shifts is the growing need for data literacy, which enables creatives to interpret datasets, understand model behavior, and evaluate algorithmic outputs. As generative models rely on vast training corpora, creators must discern biases, evaluate source quality, and assess how data influences aesthetic outcomes (Long & Magerko, 2020).

Prompt design, the ability to strategically guide large language models and generative image systems, has emerged as a core creative competency. Research shows that creators who master prompt iteration and parameter tuning produce significantly higher-quality generative outputs (Liu & Chilton, 2022). Likewise, algorithmic fluency, which includes understanding model capabilities, limitations, and ethical risks, is increasingly important for creators who use systems like Midjourney, Runway ML, or AIVA. These competencies enable more intentional creative direction, where human vision frames, curates, and refines machine-generated possibilities rather than passively receiving them.

6.2 Emerging Professional Roles

As creative workflows evolve, entirely new professional identities are taking shape. One such role is the AI curator, responsible for selecting datasets, shaping model inputs, and ensuring that algorithmic outputs reflect aesthetic or cultural values. This role has become visible in digital art exhibitions such as MoMA's "Unsupervised," which relied on curatorial oversight to steer AI-generated interpretations of the museum's archive (MoMA, 2023).

The rise of prompt engineers - now employed across design, marketing, and entertainment - underscores how text-to-image and text-to-media systems require specialized linguistic and conceptual skills (Reed, 2023). Human-in-the-loop supervisors are becoming central in film, gaming, and advertising, where they guide iterative model training and ensure alignment between machine outputs and creative intent. Ethical designers are increasingly integrated into teams to address challenges related to bias, cultural representation, and safe deployment of generative models (Hagendorff, 2024). These emerging roles reflect a broader transformation in creative labor: AI does not eliminate human contribution but redistributes it toward new forms of oversight, orchestration, and meaning-making.

6.3 Creativity as Orchestration of Human and Machine Strengths

Human-AI creative collaboration is best understood as a dynamic orchestration of complementary strengths. Humans contribute intuition, emotional depth, ethical judgment, and contextual reasoning - qualities that remain difficult for even the most advanced models to replicate. AI systems, by contrast, offer computational speed, large-scale pattern recognition, and the capacity to generate numerous variations rapidly. Scholars describe this configuration as hybrid intelligence, where creativity emerges from the integration rather than the replacement of human capabilities (Dellermann et al., 2019).

In practice, this synergy appears across disciplines. Musicians using AIVA or Amper Music combine human interpretation with algorithmic composition to explore novel sonic textures. Architects use generative design tools to produce thousands of structural alternatives, then apply human aesthetic and spatial judgment to select viable concepts. The result is not merely accelerated production but expanded creative possibility, as machine-generated alternatives inspire directions the creator may not have considered independently.

6.4 Impact on Collaboration and Human Relational Dynamics

AI-enabled workflows are also reshaping team collaboration, communication, and shared identity within creative projects. As tools like ChatGPT, Midjourney, and Runway ML become embedded in daily practice, teams must navigate new forms of coordination - deciding when human decision-making should dominate and when machine input should guide iterative development. Studies show that AI-supported teams often experience more rapid ideation cycles but must adjust to new negotiation processes surrounding authorship, responsibility, and credit (Vinchon et al., 2023).

Relational dynamics are shifting as well. Creative teams increasingly view AI not simply as a tool but as a quasi-collaborator - a source of suggestions, constraints, and provocations. This reconfiguration challenges traditional notions of shared creative identity, raising questions about how individuals see their contribution within hybrid human–machine ensembles. When integrated transparently and intentionally, AI has been shown to enhance collaborative cohesion by enabling teams to externalize ideas quickly and explore creative directions more democratically (Wei et al., 2025).

Figure 3. Redefining creative roles, competencies, and team dynamics (Author, 2025)

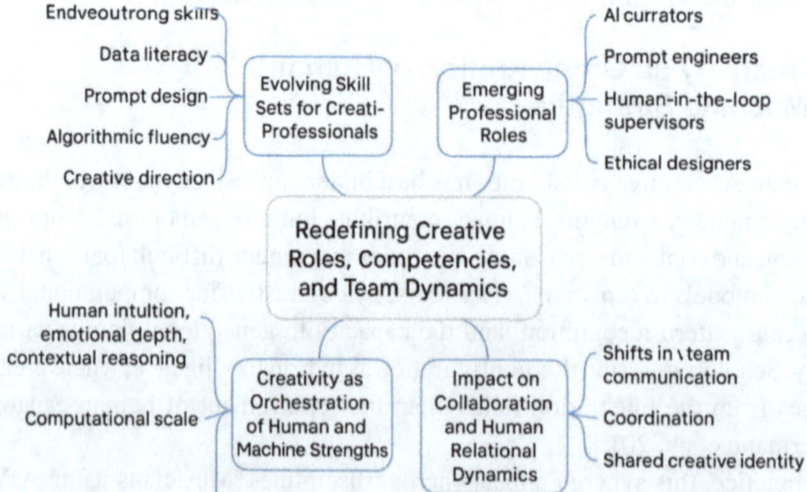

7. ETHICAL, LEGAL, AND SOCIETAL CONSIDERATIONS (CURRENT CHALLENGES)

The increasing use of AI in creative processes brings up a myriad of sociological, legal, and ethical issues that go beyond mere technological advancements. Highlighting the need to strike a balance between technology innovation and human agency, justice, and trust in creative ecosystems, this section analyses crucial problems such as authorship and ownership, prejudice and cultural representation, transparency, labour disruption, and digital well-being.

7.1 Ownership and Authorship Dilemmas

Rapid advancements in generative AI raise nuanced concerns about copyright, creativity, and credit. While copyright law has historically served to safeguard works created by identifiable human beings, the advent of AI-generated material has shaken up this system by distributing creative agency across databases, algorithmic processes, and human involvement. The current regulatory frameworks have certain limitations shown by recent legal disputes, like as the United States Copyright

Office's position refusing copyright protection for works produced entirely by AI (U.S. Copyright Office, 2023).

Creative professionals face uncertainty in determining who should be credited when AI contributes significantly to ideation or execution. Scholars argue that this ambiguity challenges long-standing notions of authorship rooted in individual human creativity and may require new models of shared or layered attribution (Mazzone & Elgammal, 2019). As creative industries increasingly adopt AI tools, the need for coherent, globally aligned copyright frameworks becomes urgent.

7.2 Bias, Representation, and Cultural Integrity

Generative models are trained on large-scale datasets that often embed systemic biases, leading to skewed or exclusionary outputs. Research shows that AI-generated images and texts frequently reproduce racial and gender stereotypes due to biased training materials (Buolamwini, 2023). This dynamic raises concerns about cultural homogenization, where dominant narratives overshadow marginalized voices. In creative industries, such biases can distort representation in fashion design, visual art, character generation, and advertising, reinforcing inequalities rather than expanding cultural diversity. Indigenous and minority communities have also expressed concern about cultural appropriation, as AI models ingest culturally significant artifacts without consent or contextual sensitivity (Florek & Lakshmi, 2025). Ensuring cultural integrity therefore requires rigorous dataset auditing, inclusive design, and participatory governance frameworks involving affected communities.

7.3 Transparency and Creative Authenticity

As AI-generated content becomes more sophisticated, maintaining transparent disclosure practices is critical for preserving audience trust and creative authenticity. Consumers often express discomfort when AI-generated works are presented without clarity regarding their origins, particularly in contexts such as journalism, film effects, or fine art (Juzer Ujjainwala, 2025). Transparency helps mitigate deception, enables ethical evaluation, and supports informed engagement. Creators face questions about whether AI involvement diminishes the perceived authenticity or emotional value of a work. Studies suggest that audiences may attribute lower artistic merit to pieces known to be AI-assisted, despite equivalent aesthetic quality (Horton et al., 2023). Balancing innovation with honesty remains a key ethical challenge as hybrid human–AI practices evolve.

7.4 Labour Market Transformations

AI adoption is reshaping creative labour, generating both opportunities and vulnerabilities. Automation of tasks such as video editing, copywriting, animation, and sound design raises fears of job displacement and downward pressure on wages, particularly for entry-level or freelance workers. Reports from creative unions highlight the risk of increased precarity as studios and agencies experiment with AI-driven production workflows (WGA, 2023). At the same time, new roles - such as AI supervisors, prompt designers, and computational artists - are emerging, but these often require advanced technical skills that not all workers can easily acquire. The challenge lies in creating equitable pathways for upskilling while ensuring that AI augments rather than replace creative labour.

7.5 Digital Well-being and Human–AI Relational Dynamics

As creators increasingly collaborate with AI systems, new psychological and emotional dynamics emerge. Some artists describe developing attachment to AI tools that consistently support their creative process, while others fear loss of expressive agency or reduced confidence in their abilities. Research shows that intensive engagement with generative AI can influence self-perception, affective states, and creative identity, sometimes leading to dependency or diminished sense of authorship (Shneiderman, 2020). These concerns extend to consumers as well, who may interact with AI-driven characters, performers, or influencers in ways that blur boundaries between authentic and synthetic relationships. Protecting digital well-being therefore requires thoughtful design of AI systems that respect human emotional needs, promote autonomy, and avoid manipulative or addictive patterns.

Table 2. Ethical, legal, and societal considerations in human–AI creative collaboration

Domain	Key Issues	Implications for Creative Practice	Real-World Examples / Evidence
Ownership and Authorship Dilemmas	• Unclear copyright status of AI-generated work • Attribution disputes in co-created content • Challenges to traditional individual authorship models	• Legal uncertainty for artists, studios, and publishers • Need for hybrid authorship frameworks (human + AI) • Risks of unlicensed dataset use leading to infringement claims	• U.S. Copyright Office rejects copyright for fully AI-generated works • Artists filing lawsuits against training-data scraping by generative AI systems
Bias, Representation, and Cultural Integrity	• Reinforcement of racial, gender, and cultural stereotypes • Under-representation of minority groups • Unconsented use of culturally sensitive materials • Risk of cultural homogenization	• Distorted portrayals in visual art, gaming, character design, and advertising • Ethical responsibility for inclusive dataset curation • Need for culturally aware AI governance	• Buolamwini document algorithmic bias in generative outputs • Indigenous communities raising concerns about AI models replicating sacred cultural motifs.
Transparency and Creative Authenticity	• Lack of disclosure in AI-assisted works • Audience uncertainty about what is "authentically human" • Risk of deceptive media use (deepfakes, synthetic voices)	• Potential erosion of trust in creative industries • Ethical need for transparency labels and provenance tools • Audience may devalue AI-assisted work despite quality	• Viewers rate AI-generated art as less authentic even when aesthetically similar. • Media organizations introducing AI-disclosure guidelines.
Labour Market Transformations	• Automation of creative tasks (editing, copywriting, VFX, sound design) • Job displacement and downward wage pressures • Skill gaps and uneven access to AI literacy • Emergence of new AI-focused roles	• Reconfiguration of studio workflows and team structures • Increased precarity for freelance and entry-level workers • Demand for upskilling in data literacy and prompt design	• WGA negotiations over AI usage in screenwriting • Marketing agencies replacing junior copywriters with generative tools • Rise of roles such as "AI supervisor" in film post-production
Digital Well-being and Human–AI Relational Dynamics	• Emotional attachment to AI collaborators • Reduced confidence or creative agency • Dependency on algorithmic suggestions • Psychological effects of interacting with synthetic creative partners	• Need for human-centered system design • Potential shifts in self-expression and artistic identity • Blurred boundaries in parasocial or synthetic relationships	

8. HUMAN–AI SYNERGY AND THE FUTURE OF CREATIVE EXPRESSION

This section looks ahead to the future of creative expression shaped by deepening human–AI synergy. It explores how AI can expand creative potential, enable new hybrid aesthetics, and foster more interactive relationships between creators and audiences. Rather than diminishing human creativity, the discussion emphasizes AI's role in amplifying imagination, inclusivity, and expressive possibility.

8.1 Enhancements to Human Creative Potential

The combination of human and artificial intelligence is changing the way people express themselves creatively by making more forms of creative creation available to more people. One of the most noteworthy changes is the way generative tools have made it possible for people who don't have a lot of creative or technical experience to create complex works of art. Tools like Stability AI's Stable Diffusion and OpenAI's DALL·E make it possible for users to create intricate visual artworks using just natural-language commands, which greatly reduces the hurdles to entry and boosts creative engagement (Gunkel, 2021).

This shift broadens the pool of creative contributors and fosters more inclusive forms of cultural production. Emerging research also highlights how AI augments expert creators, enabling them to explore alternative directions, iterate at scale, and experiment with styles that were previously too resource-intensive to pursue (Shneiderman, 2020). In this way, AI becomes a catalyst for expanding human imagination rather than replacing it.

8.2 Reimagining Human Expression

Innovative forms of expression that go beyond conventional artistic categories are emerging from the convergence of human imagination and artificial intelligence. Interactive cinema experiences, digital art installations, and AI-generated musical compositions all showcase hybrid aesthetics, which is the result of a combination of algorithmic processing and human involvement. Immersive visual worlds are generated by machine-learning algorithms trained on millions of photos in artist Refik Anadol's "Machine Hallucinations" series (Anadol, 2020). These environments reinterpret memory, perception, and data as creative elements. These pieces show how artificial intelligence allows for multimodal outputs and the development of new aesthetic vocabulary that go beyond what the human eye can perceive. By reimagining the machine as an equal collaborator with unique computational abilities, rather than a passive observer, these hybrid forms cast doubt on conventional wisdom on creativity.

8.3 Audience Engagement in AI-Mediated Contexts

The rise of AI in creative ecosystems is also reshaping how audiences interact with content. Instead of consuming static, one-size-fits-all media, audiences increasingly engage with adaptive, personalized, and participatory experiences. AI-driven personalization in platforms such as Netflix and TikTok allows content to be dynamically tailored to individual preferences, enhancing engagement while shifting creative power toward algorithmic curation (Bhandari & Bimo, 2022). In storytelling contexts, AI enables more immersive and interactive narratives, such as dynamically evolving storylines in gaming and mixed-reality entertainment. Corporates like Ubisoft have begun experimenting with AI-based narrative engines that adjust plotlines based on player behavior, resulting in co-creative experiences in which audiences partially influence the creative direction (O'Brien, 2024). These developments redefine the relationship between creators and consumers by embedding participation, responsiveness, and personalization into the creative process.

8.4 Towards Symbiotic Creative Ecosystems

Symbiotic ecosystems, in which artificial intelligence and human creativity co-evolve, are taking shape as AI gets increasingly integrated into creative processes. When used in these ways, AI does not aim to replace human creativity but rather to augment it by providing new sources of ideas, pattern identification, and computational scalability. So, according to Schwab and Malleret (2020), computers will bring generative skills, automation, and data-driven exploration to the table, while humans bring contextual reasoning, emotional depth, and ethical framing to the creative expression model of the future. This interconnectedness raises the possibility that creativity is more of an ecological phenomena than an act of human initiative. The creative industries are reshaping their workflows, team compositions, and procedures to include AI as a collaborative partner. This includes design, entertainment, and publishing, among others.

Figure 4. Human-AI synergy and the future of creative expression (Author, 2025)

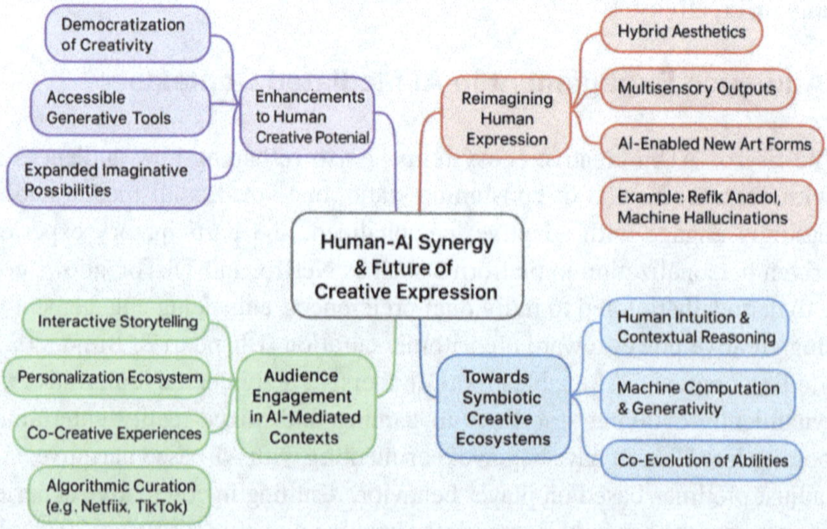

The trajectory of human–AI synergy points toward a future in which creativity becomes more distributed, technologically enriched, and participatory. As humans learn to orchestrate the capabilities of AI while maintaining artistic intent and ethical oversight, the boundaries of creative expression will continue to expand. The challenge for creators, policymakers, and educators will lie in fostering environments that harness AI's potential while safeguarding human agency, cultural diversity, and creative integrity.

9. GOVERNANCE, CAPACITY BUILDING, AND SUSTAINABLE CREATIVE FUTURES (FUTURE SOLUTIONS)

This section focuses on the governance and capacity-building mechanisms required to ensure sustainable and responsible human–AI collaboration in the creative industries. It examines policy frameworks, ethical standards, education, and cross-sector partnerships that can support trustworthy innovation. The discussion emphasizes aligning technological advancement with cultural preservation, workforce resilience, and long-term creative sustainability.

9.1 Policy Frameworks for Responsible Creative AI

As AI becomes increasingly embedded in creative industries, robust policy frameworks are essential to ensure fairness, protect cultural heritage, and safeguard rights.

Governments and regulatory bodies are beginning to explore guidelines for fair use, attribution, and rights management in AI-generated content (European Commission, 2021). Transparency requirements, such as disclosing when AI contributes to creative work, are emerging as a mechanism to maintain trust between creators and audiences. Cultural preservation is another priority, as AI systems trained on narrow datasets risk eroding local artistic traditions and pluralistic expression (UNESCO, 2023). Policy frameworks for creative AI are therefore shifting from solely regulating outputs to overseeing the entire lifecycle of data, models, and creative processes.

9.2 Standards and Frameworks for Trustworthy Human-AI Collaboration

Ensuring trustworthy collaboration between humans and AI requires clear standards for accountability, explainability, and inclusivity. Research initiatives such as the OECD AI Principles and the NIST AI Risk Management Framework emphasize that human oversight and transparent model behavior must remain central to all creative workflows (NIST, 2023). In the creative domain, this means developing guidelines that ensure artists retain meaningful control and can contest AI-generated outputs. Participatory governance models - where creators, technologists, ethicists, and communities collectively shape AI development—are increasingly recognized as vital to preventing concentration of creative power among a few technology companies (Hagendorff, 2024). These frameworks promote distributed responsibility and help embed ethical safeguards directly into tools and platforms used by creative professionals.

9.3 Educational, Institutional, and Workforce Strategies

Future-ready creative ecosystems depend on capacity-building efforts that prepare individuals and institutions for hybrid human–AI practices. Universities and training centers are introducing interdisciplinary curricula that combine art, design, computing, and ethics to foster holistic creative fluency (Hancock et al., 2020). Innovation labs - such as MIT Media Lab, NYU ITP, and various AI art incubators - offer spaces where students and practitioners experiment with generative models, data-driven storytelling, and interactive media. Workforce strategies must also include upskilling programs for mid-career professionals who need to adapt to emerging tools and production workflows. This includes training in prompt engineering, data literacy, algorithmic aesthetics, and responsible AI use (Long & Magerko, 2020). Institutions that integrate these learning pathways can cultivate adaptable, resilient creative communities capable of navigating technological change.

9.4 Cross-Sector Partnerships

Sustainable creative futures require coordinated efforts among academia, industry, policymakers, technology developers, and cultural institutions. Cross-sector partnerships support ethical innovation by integrating diverse perspectives and ensuring that creative AI systems meet societal needs. Cultural institutions - such as museums, archives, and public broadcasters - play a crucial role in providing high-quality data, curating culturally significant datasets, and ensuring inclusive representation (Frontoni et al., 2022). Industry actors contribute technical expertise and funding, while policymakers set regulatory guardrails to balance innovation with public interest. Collaborative initiatives like the Global Partnership on AI (GPAI) illustrate how transnational cooperation can advance responsible AI adoption while supporting cultural diversity and equitable access (GPAI, 2022). These multi-stakeholder ecosystems are increasingly foundational to building creative futures that are innovative, inclusive, and sustainable.

Table 3. Governance, capacity building, and sustainable creative futures

Domain	Key Focus Areas	Examples / Strategies	Expected Impact
Policy Frameworks for Responsible Creative AI	Fair use, transparency, rights management, cultural protection	Disclosure requirements; AI content labeling; IP reform; safeguarding cultural datasets	Protects creators' rights; ensures trust; preserves cultural diversity
Standards for Trustworthy Human-AI Collaboration	Accountability, explainability, inclusivity, participatory governance	NIST AI RMF; OECD AI Principles; community review panels; ethical audits	Enhances fairness and accountability; supports ethical co-creation
Educational & Workforce Strategies	Hybrid curricula, interdisciplinary training, innovation labs	AI-art programs; creative technology courses; mid-career upskilling; design-technology labs	Strengthens creative capacity; builds future-ready workforce
Cross-Sector Partnerships	Collaboration across academia, industry, policy, and culture	GPAI initiatives; museum–tech partnerships; public–private research consortia	Ensures equitable innovation; enables sustainable creative ecosystems

10. THEORETICAL AND PRACTICAL IMPLICATIONS AND RECOMMENDATIONS

10.1 Theoretical Implications

By framing creativity as a co-creative process that arises from interactions between human cognition and computer systems, human-AI cooperation in the creative industries helps to enhance modern conceptions of creativity. More and more, viewpoints that see creativity as diffused across sociotechnical contexts are supplementing traditional models that place an emphasis on individual innovation. According to Dwivedi et al. (2021), human-AI co-creativity frameworks show how algorithmic skills, such predictive analysis and generative modelling, enhance human imagination and allow for new kinds of ideation and production. This extends current ideas.

Discussions of distributed cognition and hybrid intelligence are theoretically bolstered by AI's incorporation into creative endeavour. Combining computer speed and scalability with human intuition, contextual reasoning, and emotional understanding, hybrid intelligence emphasises the complimentary qualities of people and machines (Akata et al., 2020). Instead of seeing creativity as the product of a single genius, proponents of distributed cognition see it as the product of interconnected systems of people, technologies, and institutions. From this vantage point, it's clear that creativity in settings with AI is contextual, relational, and ingrained in technology.

Traditional notions of agency, creativity, and authorship are also called into question when humans and AI work together. The limits of human agency and machine autonomy are being called into question as AI systems become more and more involved in creative decision-making. A rethinking of creative agency as something that arises from dynamic interactions within sociotechnical ecosystems is necessary in light of these advances (Dwivedi et al., 2021). These theoretical advancements provide light on how technology mediation changes cultural production, value creation, and symbolic meaning; as a result, they add to the larger body of literature in innovation studies, digital culture, and study into creative industries.

10.2 Practical Implications

There are major ramifications for practitioners, organisations, and institutions as a result of the increasing use of AI technology in creative processes. Enhancing creativity, automating regular activities, and supporting iterative experimentation are all possible with the help of AI solutions for creative workers. Data literacy, algorithmic awareness, and critical engagement with AI-generated outputs are new abilities that need to be developed for effective integration (Akata et al., 2020).

New governance and coordination procedures are needed at the organisational level to manage creative teams that include both humans and AI. Companies should encourage teamwork in which human and machine efforts are complementary by outlining standards for attribution, responsibility, and quality control. Resolving ethical issues, such as bias in training data and openness in AI-assisted decision-making, is also essential for effective management of human-AI cooperation (Dwivedi et al., 2021).

The design of AI systems that work in tandem is crucial. In order to create AI interfaces that facilitate interpretability, user agency, and meaningful engagement, human-centered design principles should be followed. Users are able to interact with AI technology more successfully when systems are transparent and easy to understand. Ensuring appropriate deployment of AI also heavily relies on policy and governance structures. Proposals by the European Commission (2020) and ethical principles from UNESCO (2021) are examples of regulatory efforts that stress the need of human supervision, justice, and responsibility in AI systems.

There are ramifications for training and education stemming from AI's growing influence in the creative sectors. To better equip the workforce of the future to thrive in hybrid creative contexts, schools should develop interdisciplinary courses that combine artistic expression with technological know-how. Reskilling and lifelong learning should also be at the center of workforce initiatives in order to help adapt to changing technology environments (OECD, 2021).

10.3 Recommendations

Several recommendations emerge for key stakeholders. For practitioners, adopting human-in-the-loop approaches can help maintain creative control while leveraging AI capabilities. Ethical design principles, including transparency and fairness, should guide the use of generative technologies in creative production. Organizations should invest in AI literacy programs, interdisciplinary collaboration, and robust governance frameworks to manage risks and enhance innovation outcomes.

Policymakers are encouraged to develop balanced regulatory frameworks that protect intellectual property rights, ensure equitable access to technology, and promote cultural diversity in AI-generated content. Regulatory systems should address issues of authorship, accountability, and data governance while fostering innovation. Educators should design hybrid creativity curricula that combine artistic expression, computational thinking, and ethical awareness to prepare future professionals for collaborative human–AI environments.

Last but not least, studies examining the effects of AI on creative processes, long-term human-AI interaction, and relational creativity should be conducted. To foster the growth of creative ecosystems that are both inclusive and ethically based, this kind of study may provide light on the best ways to responsibly and sustainably combine human and machine skills.

11. CONCLUSION

With its remarkable potential and formidable obstacles, artificial intelligence is changing the face of creativity. One side of the coin claims that AI boosts creativity by opening up new avenues of expression, simplifying production, and coming up with fresh ideas. As a result, artists are free to explore hitherto unfathomable possibilities in terms of style, genre, and medium. These developments prompt discussions over who is responsible for what, how other cultures are portrayed, and how human identity is maintained in artistic productions. Dual effects of AI on expression, creativity, and relationships are highlighted by the conflict between technical capacity and ethical obligation.

Despite these transformative changes, human agency remains central. Emotion, intentionality, and ethical judgment continue to define meaningful creative work. AI can augment human imagination, but it cannot replace the deeply personal, contextual, and ethical dimensions of artistry. Recognizing this, the future of creativity lies in collaborative human-AI ecosystems that prioritize inclusivity, fairness, and relational richness. By combining technical innovation with human insight, creators, institutions, and policymakers can cultivate a creative environment where technology amplifies, rather than diminishes, human expression. Responsible integration of AI promises not only enhanced artistic possibilities but also a reaffirmation of the values, meanings, and connections that define human creativity.

REFERENCES

Acatrinei, C., Apostol, I. G., & Barbu, L. N., & Chivu (Popa), R.-G., & Orzan, M.-C. (. (2025). Artificial intelligence in digital marketing: Enhancing consumer engagement and supporting sustainable behavior through social and mobile networks. *Sustainability*, *17*(14), 6638. DOI: 10.3390/su17146638

AIVA. (2022). *AIVA – AI-powered music composition for film, games, and content creators*. https://www.aiva.ai/

Akata, Z., Balliet, D., de Rijke, M., Dignum, F., Dignum, V., Eiben, G., Fokkens, A., Grossi, D., Hindriks, K., Hoos, H., Hung, H., Jonker, C., Monz, C., Neerincx, M., Oliehoek, F., Prakken, H., Schlobach, S., van der Gaag, L., van Harmelen, F., & Welling, M. (2020). A research agenda for hybrid intelligence: Augmenting human intellect with collaborative, adaptive, responsible, and explainable artificial intelligence. *Computer*, *53*(8), 18–28. DOI: 10.1109/MC.2020.2996587

Anadol, R. (2020). *Machine Hallucination* [Digital artwork / installation]. Refik Anadol Studio. https://refikanadol.com/works/machine-hallucination/

Anantrasirichai, N., & Bull, D. (2022). Artificial intelligence in the creative industries: A review. *Artificial Intelligence Review*, *55*(4), 589–656. DOI: 10.1007/s10462-021-10039-7 PMID: 41625196

Baver, K. (2020). *This is the way: How innovative technology immersed us in the world of The Mandalorian*. StarWars.com. https://www.starwars.com/news/the-mandalorian-stagecraft-feature

Beyari, H., & Hashem, T. (2025). The role of artificial intelligence in personalizing social media marketing strategies for enhanced customer experience. *Behavioral Sciences (Basel, Switzerland)*, *15*(5), 700. DOI: 10.3390/bs15050700 PMID: 40426477

Bhandari, A., & Bimo, S. (2022). Why's everyone on TikTok now? The algorithmized self and the future of self-making on social media. *Social Media + Society*, *8*(1), 20563051221086241. DOI: 10.1177/20563051221086241

Bryson, J. J., & Theodorou, A. (2019). How society can maintain human-centric artificial intelligence. In Toivonen, M., & Saari, E. (Eds.), *Human-Centered Digitalization and Services* (pp. 305–323). Springer., DOI: 10.1007/978-981-13-7725-9_16

Buolamwini, J. (2023). *Unmasking AI: My mission to protect what is human in a world of machines*. Penguin Random House.

Caramiaux, B., Crawford, K., Liao, Q. V., Ramos, G., & Williams, J. (2025). Generative AI and creative work: Narratives, values, and impacts. *arXiv*. https://doi.org//arXiv.2502.03940DOI: 10.48550

Chen, Y., Huang, L., & Gou, T. (2024). Applications and advances of artificial intelligence in music generation: A review. *arXiv*. https://doi.org//arXiv.2409.03715DOI: 10.48550

Choi, J., Yoon, J., Chung, J., Coh, B.-Y., & Lee, J.-M. (2020). Social media analytics and business intelligence research: A systematic review. *Information Processing & Management*, *57*(6), 102279. DOI: 10.1016/j.ipm.2020.102279

Da Pelo, M. (2025). Artificial creativity: Can there be creativity without cognition? *AI & Society*. Advance online publication. DOI: 10.1007/s00146-025-02682-3

Dellermann, D., Ebel, P., Söllner, M., & Leimeister, J. M. (2019). Hybrid intelligence. *Business & Information Systems Engineering*, *61*(5), 637–643. DOI: 10.1007/s12599-019-00595-2

Epstein, Z., Hertzmann, A., Herman, L., Mahari, R., Frank, M. R., Groh, M., Schroeder, H., Smith, A., Fjeld, J., Farid, H., & Russakovsky, O. (2023). Art and the science of generative AI. *Science*, *380*(6646), 194–200. DOI: 10.1126/science.adh4451 PMID: 37319193

Erickson, K. (2024). AI and work in the creative industries: Digital continuity or discontinuity? *Creative Industries Journal*, 1–21. Advance online publication. DOI: 10.1080/17510694.2024.2421135

European Commission. (2020). *White paper on artificial intelligence: A European approach to excellence and trust*. https://commission.europa.eu/publications/white-paper-artificial-intelligence-european-approach-excellence-and-trust_en

European Commission. (2021). *Proposal for a Regulation of the European Parliament and of the Council laying down harmonised rules on artificial intelligence (Artificial Intelligence Act) and amending certain Union legislative acts* (COM(2021) 206 final). Shaping Europe's digital future. https://digital-strategy.ec.europa.eu/en/policies/european-approach-artificial-intelligence

Florek, A., & Lakshmi, S. (2025). Rebranding empire in the age of generative AI: Cultural sovereignty and digital colonialism. *Frontiers in Communication*, *10*, 1604361. DOI: 10.3389/fcomm.2025.1604361

Frontoni, E., Paolanti, M., Lauriault, T. P., Stiber, M., Duranti, L., & Muhammad, A.-M. (2022). Trusted data forever: Is AI the answer? *arXiv*. https://arxiv.org/abs/2203.03712

Glăveanu, V. P. (2020). A sociocultural theory of creativity: Bridging the social, the material, and the psychological. *Review of General Psychology*, *24*(4), 335–354. DOI: 10.1177/1089268020961763

Global Partnership on AI. (2022). *Responsible AI working group report 2022: Recommendations for public-private collaboration*. https://gpai.ai/projects/responsible-ai/gpai-responsible-ai-wg-report-2022.pdf

Gunkel, D. J. (2021). *Deconstruction*. The MIT Press. Available at: https://mitpress.mit.edu/9780262542470/deconstruction/

Hagendorff, T. (2024). Mapping the ethics of generative AI: A comprehensive scoping review. *Minds and Machines*, *34*(4), 39. https://link.springer.com/article/10.1007/s11023-024-09694-w. DOI: 10.1007/s11023-024-09694-w

Halabi, R., & Subrahmanyam, S. (2025). Economic and Governance Implications of AI-Driven Marketing Systems: A Mixed-Methods Study on Performance, Transparency, and Policy Alignment. *Lex Localis - Journal of Local Self-Government, 23*(S4), 2189-2203. https://doi.org/DOI: 10.52152/arsynj63

Hancock, J. T., Naaman, M., & Levy, K. (2020). AI-mediated communication: Definition, research agenda, and ethical considerations. *Journal of Computer-Mediated Communication*, *25*(1), 89–100. DOI: 10.1093/jcmc/zmz022

Heineken. (2023). *Heineken introduces the world's first AI-generated beer campaign*. Heineken Global. https://www.heineken.com

Hello Games. (2021). *No Man's Sky – Worlds Part I update patch notes*. https://www.nomanssky.com/worlds-part-i-update/

Herndon, H., & Dryhurst, M. (2021). *Holly+ Project: Spawning new forms of vocal performance through AI systems*. Holly+ Project. https://holly.plus

Holzner, N., Maier, S., & Feuerriegel, S. (2025). Generative AI and creativity: A systematic literature review and meta-analysis. *arXiv*. https://arxiv.org/abs/2505.17241

Horton, C. B.Jr, White, M. W., & Iyengar, S. S. (2023). Bias against AI art can enhance perceptions of human creativity. *Scientific Reports*, *13*(1), 19001. DOI: 10.1038/s41598-023-45202-3 PMID: 37923764

Hutchins, E. (2020). *Cognition in the wild* (30th anniversary ed.). MIT Press. https://mitpress.mit.edu/9780262581462/cognition-in-the-wild/

Juzer Ujjainwala, F. (2025). Influence of AI-generated influencer content on brand trust and authenticity perceptions. *Journal of Marketing & Social Research*, *2*(9), 256–262. https://www.jmsr-online.com/article/influence-of-ai-generated-influencer-content-on-brand-trust-and-authenticity-perceptions-438/

Liu, V., & Chilton, L. B. (2022). Design guidelines for prompt engineering text-to-image generative models. In *Proceedings of the 2022 CHI Conference on Human Factors in Computing Systems* (pp. 1–23). Association for Computing Machinery. https://doi.org/DOI: 10.1145/3491102.3501825

Long, D., & Magerko, B. (2020). What is AI literacy? Competencies and design considerations. In *Proceedings of the 2020 CHI Conference on Human Factors in Computing Systems* (pp. 1–16). Association for Computing Machinery. https://doi.org/DOI: 10.1145/3313831.3376727

Mazzone, M., & Elgammal, A. (2019). Art, creativity, and the potential of artificial intelligence. *Arts*, *8*(1), 26. DOI: 10.3390/arts8010026

McCormack, J., Gambardella, C. C., Rajcic, N., Krol, S. J., Llano, M. T., & Yang, M. (2023). Is writing prompts really making art? *arXiv*. https://arxiv.org/abs/2301.13049 DOI: 10.1007/978-3-031-29956-8_13

Moruzzi, C. (2025). Artificial intelligence and creativity. *Philosophy Compass*, *20*(3), e70030. DOI: 10.1111/phc3.70030

Museum of Modern Art. (2023). *Refik Anadol: Unsupervised — Machine Hallucinations* [Exhibition]. The Museum of Modern Art. https://www.moma.org/calendar/exhibitions/5535

National Institute of Standards and Technology. (2023). *Artificial intelligence risk management framework (AI RMF 1.0)* (NIST AI 100-1). U.S. Department of Commerce. https://www.nist.gov/publications/artificial-intelligence-risk-management-framework-ai-rmf-10

O'Brien, L. (2024). *How Ubisoft's new generative AI prototype changes the narrative for NPCs*. Ubisoft News. Retrieved from https://news.ubisoft.com/en-us/article/5qXdxhshJBXoanFZApdG3L/how-ubisofts-new-generative-ai-prototype-changes-the-narrative-for-npcs/

O'Toole, K., & Horvát, E.-Á. (2024). Extending human creativity with AI. *Journal of Creativity*, *34*(2), 100080. DOI: 10.1016/j.yjoc.2024.100080

Ogilvy. (2025). *Ogilvy on: AI is rewiring how we create*. Ogilvy. https://www.ogilvy.com/ideas/ogilvy-ai-rewiring-how-we-create

Organisation for Economic Co-operation and Development. (2021). *The OECD AI principles*. https://oecd.ai/en/ai-principles

Porcino, T. M., Rodrigues, E. O., Bernardini, F. C., Trevisan, D. G., & Clua, E. (2022). Identifying cybersickness causes in virtual reality games using symbolic machine learning algorithms. *Entertainment Computing*, *41*, 100473. DOI: 10.1016/j.entcom.2021.100473

POST (UK Parliament Office of Science and Technology). (2024). *Artificial intelligence and new technology in creative industries* (Horizon scanning briefing). https://post.parliament.uk/artificial-intelligence-and-new-technology-in-creative-industries/

Schwab, K., & Malleret, T. (2020). *COVID-19: The Great Reset*. Forum Publishing/World Economic Forum. https://wef.ch/covid19book

Serbanescu, A. (2023). *Human-AI system co-creativity for building narrative worlds.* Unpublished manuscript. Available at ResearchGate. https://www.researchgate.net/publication/374552467_Human-AI_system_co-creativity_for_building_narrative_worlds

Shneiderman, B. (2020). Human-centered artificial intelligence: Reliable, safe & trustworthy. *International Journal of Human-Computer Interaction*, *36*(6), 495–504. DOI: 10.1080/10447318.2020.1741118

Simonite, T. (2021). *It began as an AI-fueled Dungeon game. It got much darker. Wired.* https://www.wired.com/story/ai-fueled-dungeon-game-got-much-darker/

Subrahmanyam, S. (2025). AI and Automation: The Intersection of Human Autonomy and Machine Learning. In Tsvasman, L. (Ed.), *Cybernetic Leadership for Sustainable Innovation* (pp. 237–262). IGI Global Scientific Publishing., DOI: 10.4018/979-8-3373-2484-5.ch009

UNESCO. (2021). *Recommendation on the ethics of artificial intelligence*. https://unesdoc.unesco.org/ark:/48223/pf0000380455

UNESCO. (2023). *Artificial intelligence and cultural diversity: Policy guidelines and recommendations*. UNESCO. https://unesdoc.unesco.org/ark:/48223/pf0000380655

U.S. Copyright Office. (2023). *Copyright registration guidance: Works containing material generated by artificial intelligence* (Statement of Policy). *Federal Register*, 88 Fed. Reg. 16190. https://www.copyright.gov/ai/ai_policy_guidance.pdf?utm_source=chatgpt.com

Vincent, J. (2020). *Disney's deepfakes are getting closer to a big-screen debut. The Verge*. https://www.theverge.com/2020/6/29/21306889/disney-deepfake-face-swapping-research-megapixel-resolution-film-tv

Vinchon, F., Lubart, T., Bartolotta, S., Gironnay, V., Botella, M., Bourgeois-Bougrine, S., Burkhardt, J.-M., Bonnardel, N., Corazza, G. E., Glăveanu, V., Hanchett Hanson, M., Ivcevic, Z., Karwowski, M., Kaufman, J. C., Okada, T., Reiter-Palmon, R., & Gaggioli, A. (2023). Artificial intelligence & creativity: A manifesto for collaboration. *The Journal of Creative Behavior*, *57*(4), 472–484. DOI: 10.1002/jocb.597

Wei, X., Wang, L., Lee, L.-K., & Liu, R. (2025). The effects of generative AI on collaborative problem-solving and team creativity performance in digital story creation: An experimental study. *International Journal of Educational Technology in Higher Education*, *22*(1), 23. Advance online publication. DOI: 10.1186/s41239-025-00526-0

Wickramasinghe, W. A. P. (2025). The impact of artificial intelligence on visual and performing arts: A comprehensive literature review. *Journal of Research in Music*, *3*(2), 143–154. DOI: 10.4038/jrm.v3i2.47

Writers Guild of America East. (2023). *Artificial intelligence ("AI")*. Writers Guild of America East. Retrieved [date you accessed], from https://www.wgaeast.org/know-your-rights/artificial-intelligence

Xu, Y. (2025). *Balancing creativity and automation: The influence of AI on modern film production and dissemination*. arXiv. https://arxiv.org/abs/2504.19275

Yu, W. F. (2025). AI as a co-creator and a design material: Transforming the design process. *Design Studies*, *101303*, 101303. Advance online publication. DOI: 10.1016/j.destud.2025.101303

Zhuang, X., Zhu, P., Yang, A. Y., & Caldas, L. (2025). Machine learning for generative architectural design: Advancements, opportunities, and challenges. *Automation in Construction*, *174*, 106129. DOI: 10.1016/j.autcon.2025.106129

KEY TERMS AND DEFINITIONS

AI-Augmented Creativity: - The enhancement of human creative performance through AI-driven tools that support ideation, prototyping, iteration, and experimentation without replacing human authorship.

Co-Creation: - A collaborative creative process in which value and meaning emerge through iterative interaction between humans and AI, rather than being produced unilaterally by either actor.

Computational Creativity: - An interdisciplinary field that studies how computational systems can model, simulate, or support creative processes, including idea generation, aesthetic evaluation, and creative learning.

Creative Authenticity: - The perceived originality, sincerity, and meaning of creative work, shaped by transparency about AI involvement and the preservation of human intentionality.

Creative Value Chain: - The sequence of activities involved in creative production—ideation, design, production, distribution, marketing, and consumption—now increasingly reshaped by AI technologies.

Distributed Cognition: - A theoretical perspective that views creativity and thinking as distributed across individuals, technologies, tools, and environments, rather than residing solely within the human mind.

Human–AI Collaboration: - A creative partnership in which human cognitive, emotional, and contextual capacities interact with artificial intelligence systems to jointly generate, refine, or extend creative outputs across artistic and cultural domains.

Human-in-the-Loop Design: - A design approach that ensures continuous human oversight, intervention, and decision-making within AI-enabled creative systems to maintain agency, accountability, and ethical integrity.

Hybrid Intelligence: - A socio-technical model of intelligence that combines human judgment, imagination, and ethical reasoning with machine-based computation, pattern recognition, and generative capabilities to enhance creative problem-solving.

Sociotechnical Creative Ecosystem: - An interconnected system in which creativity emerges from interactions among human creators, AI technologies, organizational structures, cultural norms, and audience engagement mechanisms.

Chapter 16
The Authenticity Gap and the Challenge of Distinguishing AI in Personal and Professional Dialogue

Danish Suleman
http://orcid.org/0000-0002-8505-0140
Universiti Utara Malaysia, Malaysia

ABSTRACT

The rapid proliferation of Large Language Models (LLMs) has dissolved the linguistic boundaries distinguishing human from machine expression, precipitating a "crisis of authenticity". This chapter explores the dual challenges arising from this technological inflection point. First, it analyzes the practical "arms race" between generative models and forensic tools, arguing that reliable detection is increasingly infeasible due to the statistical convergence of human and machine text. Second, it examines the ethical and psychological fallout: in personal relationships, the inability to verify authorship erodes trust, while in professional spheres, it threatens institutional integrity. The chapter concludes by proposing a framework for "digital authenticity" that moves beyond futile detection efforts toward cryptographic provenance, digital literacy, and new norms of human-AI collaboration.

DOI: 10.4018/979-8-3373-8337-8.ch016

1. INTRODUCTION

The release of advanced Large Language Models (LLMs), such as OpenAI's GPT-4, Anthropic's Claude, and Google's Gemini, has fundamentally altered the landscape of digital communication. For the first time in history, machines are capable not merely of processing information, but of mimicking the nuance, tone, and empathy of human dialogue with a fidelity that often renders them indistinguishable from biological agents (OpenAI, 2023). This technological inflection point has precipitated a crisis of digital authenticity, creating what we term the *Authenticity Gap*. We define the Authenticity Gap as the expanding cognitive and technological divide between a human's assumption that a message originates from a biological author and the hidden reality that it was generated or heavily mediated by an artificial system. As the visual and textual markers of humanity disappear, this gap creates a vacuum of trust, obscuring the origins of everyday communication—whether a heartfelt email, a professional assessment, or a creative work.

Historically, the ability to discern human from machine was anchored in the Turing Test, a theoretical benchmark that posited intelligence could be inferred if a machine could successfully deceive a human evaluator (Turing, 1950). In the contemporary era, however, this benchmark has become less of a test of machine intelligence and more of a daily dilemma for human users. We have entered the age of AI-Mediated Communication (AIMC), where algorithms do not simply transmit messages but actively co-create, modify, or autonomously generate them (Hancock et al., 2020). As LLMs achieve "human-level performance" on various professional and academic benchmarks, the linguistic "fingerprints" that once betrayed machine authorship—such as repetitive phrasing, lack of context, or grammatical rigidity—are rapidly vanishing.

This blurring of boundaries presents a dual challenge. First, there is the practical and technical challenge: the "arms race" between generative models and detection technologies. As generative models become more sophisticated, existing detection tools—whether based on statistical perplexity or watermarking—face diminishing returns and high false-positive rates (Sadasivan et al., 2023). Second, and perhaps more consequentially, is the ethical and psychological challenge. The inability to verify the human origin of a message threatens the foundation of trust required for social bonding and professional integrity. If a message of support is algorithmically generated, does it retain its emotional value? If a professional critique is machine-authored, does it carry the same weight of accountability?

This chapter explores these profound implications. It argues that the current pursuit of purely technical solutions to "catch" AI text is insufficient and that a broader framework involving ethics, policy, and digital literacy is required. The following sections will first analyse the technical mechanisms of LLMs that make detection inherently difficult. Subsequently, the chapter will examine the erosion of trust in personal relationships and the accountability gaps in professional environments. Finally, it will propose a framework for navigating this new reality, emphasising transparency and a redefinition of authenticity in an AI-saturated world.

2. LITERATURE REVIEW: THE EVOLUTION OF SYNTHETIC SPEECH AND THE CRISIS OF ATTRIBUTION

The challenge of distinguishing human from artificial dialogue is not merely a technical novelty of the 2020s; it is the culmination of a seventy-year trajectory in computer science, linguistics, and psychology. This literature review maps that trajectory, examining the progression of Natural Language Generation (NLG) technologies, the parallel history of forensic authorship attribution, and the psychological theories that explain human susceptibility to machine deception.

2.1 Historical Evolution of AI-Mediated Communication (AIMC)

The pursuit of machines capable of human-like dialogue has been the "North Star" of artificial intelligence since its inception. The literature divides this history into three distinct epochs: the Symbolic Era, the Statistical Era, and the Neural/Generative Era.

2.1.1 The Symbolic Era: From Turing to ELIZA (1950–1990)

Alan Turing's seminal paper, "Computing Machinery and Intelligence" (1950), established the "Imitation Game" (later the Turing Test) as the primary benchmark for AI. Turing argued that if a machine's text-based responses were indistinguishable from a human's, the machine could be said to "think."

The first significant attempt to pass this test was *ELIZA* (Weizenbaum, 1966). ELIZA was a rule-based system that simulated a Rogerian psychotherapist using simple pattern matching and substitution scripts (e.g., if input contains "mother", output "Tell me more about your family"). Despite its primitive architecture, Weizenbaum (1976) observed the "ELIZA Effect," where users attributed genuine intelligence and empathy to the program. This provided the first empirical evidence that human detection of AI is hindered by a powerful cognitive bias: the anthropomorphic impulse.

2.1.2 The Statistical Era: N-Grams and Probabilities (1990–2010)

In the 1990s, the field shifted from hand-coded rules to statistical learning. Researcher utilised N-gram models, which predicted the next word in a sequence based on the frequency of previous word combinations in large datasets (Shannon, 1948; Jurafsky & Martin, 2009). While these systems improved fluency, they lacked long-term coherence. A "Markov Chain" bot might produce a grammatically correct sentence, but it could not maintain a topic over three paragraphs. During this era, detecting AI was trivial: one simply looked for semantic non-sequiturs.

2.1.3 The Neural and Transformer Revolution (2010–Present)

The contemporary crisis of authenticity began with the advent of Neural Networks and Word Embeddings (Mikolov et al., 2013), which allowed computers to understand the semantic relationship between words (e.g., understanding that "King" - "Man" + "Woman" = "Queen").

However, the definitive turning point was the introduction of the Transformer architecture by Vaswani et al. (2017) in the paper "Attention Is All You Need." Unlike Recurrent Neural Networks (RNNs) that processed text sequentially, Transformers utilised "self-attention" mechanisms to process entire documents simultaneously, allowing the model to track long-range dependencies (e.g., remembering a character's name mentioned 2,000 words ago).

This architecture enabled the creation of Large Language Models (LLMs) like BERT (Devlin et al., 2019) and GPT-3 (Brown et al., 2020). The literature confirms that these models represented a phase shift: for the first time, AI could generate text that was not just grammatically correct, but pragmatically coherent, effectively rendering traditional detection heuristics obsolete.

2.2 Theoretical Frameworks: Why Deception Works

To understand the detection challenge, one must look beyond computer science to social psychology. Two dominant theories explain why humans struggle to detect modern AI.

2.2.1 Computers as Social Actors (CASA)

Proposed by Reeves and Nass (1996), the CASA Paradigm posits that the human brain evolved in a world where only humans used language. Consequently, when we encounter an entity that uses language, our brains subconsciously apply social rules and expectations reserved for humans. We are polite to chatbots, we trust authoritative-sounding text, and we default to an "assumption of humanity." This evolutionary mismatch makes scepticism cognitively expensive; we are hardwired to believe the text we read is human until proven otherwise (Spence et al., 2023).

2.2.2 The Media Equation and Anthropomorphism

Building on CASA, the Media Equation suggests that people treat media (computers, TV) as real life. In the context of LLMs, this manifests as "mind perception." When an AI uses first-person pronouns ("I think," "I feel"), users reflexively attribute a theory of mind to the system. Studies show that the more fluent the dialogue, the higher the attribution of consciousness, creating a "fluency heuristic" that masks the artificial origin of the text (Dames et al., 2022).

2.3 The Science of Attribution: A History of Stylometry

Before the age of AI, the field of Stylometry—the quantitative study of linguistic style—was used to resolve questions of disputed authorship, such as the *Federalist Papers* or the works of Shakespeare.

2.3.1 Classical Stylometry

Classical stylometry relies on the assumption that every human author possesses a unique "writeprint" composed of unconscious habits. Key metrics included:

- **Zipfian Distribution:** The frequency of words in human language follows a power law (Zipf, 1949).
- **Function Word Analysis:** The frequency of invisible words like "the," "and," "of," and "but." (Mosteller & Wallace, 1964).
- **Burrows' Delta:** A statistical method that measures the distance between the vocabulary distributions of two texts (Burrows, 2002).

2.3.2 The Collapse of Stylometry in the AI Age

The literature indicates that traditional stylometry is failing in the face of LLMs. Because LLMs are trained on the sum total of human internet discourse, they act as "stylistic chameleons." They do not have a stable "writeprint." By prompting a model to "write like Hemingway" or "write like a corporate lawyer," the AI can shift its statistical distribution to mimic specific human styles, effectively camouflaging itself against standard stylometric tests (Uchendu et al., 2023).

3. METHODOLOGY

To investigate the multifaceted challenge of detecting AI-generated dialogue, this chapter adopts a systematic qualitative review approach, integrated with forensic case analysis. Given that the field of AI detection is evolving at a velocity that often outpaces traditional peer-reviewed publication cycles, this study necessitates a hybrid methodological framework. This framework combines the rigour of systematic literature review (SLR) with the responsiveness of analysing "grey literature" (technical reports, legal filings, and white papers) to capture the state-of-the-art.

3.1 Research Design and Scope

The primary objective of this research is to synthesise fragmented knowledge across three distinct domains: Computer Science (NLG and forensics), Psychology (human-computer interaction and trust), and Law/Ethics (liability and academic integrity).

The research design is structured around three core investigative questions:

1. **Technical Feasibility:** To what extent can current forensic tools reliably distinguish between human and AI-generated text under adversarial conditions?
2. **Psychological Impact:** How does the ambiguity of authorship affect the cognitive mechanisms of trust in interpersonal communication?
3. **Institutional Resilience:** How are current professional frameworks (legal, educational, creative) failing when confronted with undetectable synthetic text?

3.2 Data Collection and Selection Criteria

3.2.1 Literature Search Strategy

A systematic search was conducted across multiple academic databases, including IEEE Xplore, ACM Digital Library, Google Scholar, and PsycINFO. The search strategy utilised Boolean operators to intersect keywords from the three target domains:

- *Group A (Technical):* "Large Language Models," "Generative AI," "Stylometry," "Watermarking," "Perplexity," "Adversarial Attacks."
- *Group B (Psychological/Social):* "Computer-Mediated Communication," "Trust," "Anthropomorphism," "Media Equation," "Uncanny Valley."
- *Group C (Ethical/Legal):* "Academic Integrity," "Legal Liability," "Plagiarism Detection," "Deepfakes."

3.2.2 Inclusion and Exclusion Criteria

To ensure the relevance and currency of the review, the following criteria were applied:

- **Timeframe:** Priority was given to literature published between 2017 and 2024. The year 2017 marks the introduction of the Transformer architecture (Vaswani et al.), which represents the technical inflexion point for modern LLMs. Pre-2017 literature was included only to establish historical context (e.g., Turing, Weizenbaum).
- **Grey Literature Inclusion:** Due to the lag time of academic publishing, this review explicitly includes pre-print servers (arXiv) and technical reports from major AI research labs (OpenAI, Anthropic, Google DeepMind). This is a standard methodological adaptation in computer science research to address rapid technological obsolescence.
- **Exclusion:** Studies focusing solely on *image* or *audio* deepfakes were excluded, except where they offered relevant theoretical parallels to text generation.

3.3 Analytical Framework: Thematic Synthesis

The collected materials were analysed using Thematic Synthesis, a method for identifying, analysing, and reporting patterns (themes) within data.

1. **Coding:** Initial coding categorised findings into "Technical Mechanisms" (e.g., perplexity stats), "User Perception" (e.g., survey results on trust), and "Policy Responses" (e.g., bans vs. integration).
2. **Theme Development:** Codes were collated into the overarching themes that structure this chapter: the "Arms Race" of detection, the "Suspicion Tax" in relationships, and the "Responsibility Gap" in professions.
3. **Critical Appraisal:** Conflicting data points (e.g., commercial claims of high detection accuracy vs. academic studies showing low accuracy) were resolved by prioritising independent, peer-reviewed benchmarks over vendor-supplied white papers.

3.4 Forensic Case Analysis Methodology

To complement the literature review, this chapter employs a Case Study Methodology. Three high-profile incidents (*Mata v. Avianca*, the Texas A&M incident, and the *Clarkesworld* submissions spike) were selected based on the principle of "Extreme Case Sampling."

These cases were chosen not because they are average, but because they are *paradigmatic*—they represent the "first contact" failures in their respective industries (Law, Education, Publishing). For each case, the analysis reconstructed the timeline of events using primary sources:

- **Legal:** Court transcripts, show-cause orders, and filed affidavits.
- **Educational:** University statements, public syllabi, and student testimonies.
- **Technical:** Server logs and editor statements regarding submission volume and metadata.

This triangulation of primary data allows for a forensic reconstruction of *why* human verification failed in each instance, moving beyond speculation to documentable failure modes (e.g., specific examples of automation bias or technical illiteracy).

3.5 Limitations

It is necessary to acknowledge the limitations of this methodological approach. First, the rate of AI capability growth is exponential; detection benchmarks cited in this chapter (based on GPT-4) may be obsolete upon the release of future models (e.g., GPT-5). Second, as a qualitative review, this chapter interprets psychological impacts through existing theoretical frameworks (CASA) rather than new empirical subject testing. Finally, the "Black Box" nature of proprietary models means that some technical analysis relies on inferred behaviour rather than transparent code auditing.

4. THE PRACTICAL CHALLENGE: THE TECHNICAL ARMS RACE OF GENERATION VS. DETECTION

To truly comprehend why detection is failing, we must move beyond the metaphor of "mimicry" and examine the fundamental properties of Large Language Models. At their core, LLMs are probabilistic distributions over sequences of tokens. The "arms race" of detection is essentially a battle over the statistical properties of this distribution.

4.1 The Mechanics of Mimicry: Entropy and Probability Curvature

The central challenge in detection is distinguishing the "statistical signature" of a machine from that of a human.

4.1.1 The Low-Entropy Signature

Human language is inherently "noisy." When humans write, we often choose words that are suboptimal from a purely statistical perspective but optimal for semantic nuance or stylistic flair. In Information Theory, this is described as Entropy, which quantifies the uncertainty of the next word selection.

AI models, specifically when using standard decoding strategies, seek to minimise this entropy. They systematically select the tokens that maximise probability based on their training data. Consequently, AI-generated text resides in a "narrow band" of the probability space—a statistical valley where every word is the most expected successor to the previous one. Early detectors exploited this by simply calculating the average log-likelihood of a text. If the likelihood was consistently high (and entropy low), it was flagged as machine-generated.

4.1.2 The Temperature Counter-Measure

To defeat these early entropy-based detectors, AI developers introduced Temperature Sampling. This hyperparameter acts as a control for the randomness of the model's output. By raising the temperature, the model is forced to flatten the probability curve, making less probable words more likely to be chosen. This artificially injects "noise" or "pseudo-entropy" into the output. While this can sometimes lead to hallucinations, it effectively mimics the statistical "imperfections" of human writing. This mathematical countermeasure renders simple entropy-based classifiers useless, as the AI can now simulate the very statistical variance that was once the hallmark of biological authorship. In simpler terms, if "entropy" is the predictability of a word, "temperature" is a mathematical dial that developers turn up to force the AI to be less predictable, intentionally making minor, human-like sub-optimal word choices to evade detection.

4.2 Advanced Forensic Metrics: Beyond Simple Perplexity

With simple entropy defeated, forensic science moved to more complex metrics. The two most prominent advanced metrics in the current literature are Burstiness and Fractal Dimension.

4.2.1 Burstiness and Syntactic Variance

While Perplexity measures the predictability of word choice, Burstiness measures the predictability of sentence structure. It is derived from the observation that human writing is temporally clustered. Humans tend to write in "bursts" of activity—a long, complex sentence followed by a short, punchy one. This creates a phenomenon known as "long-range dependency."

LLMs, particularly those reinforced with RLHF (Reinforcement Learning from Human Feedback), are often fine-tuned to be "helpful and harmless." This fine-tuning instils a bias toward monotonous, declarative sentence structures that are safe and clear but lack rhythmic variance. A high Burstiness score indicates a chaotic mix of sentence structures (Human), while a low score indicates a uniform, robotic rhythm (AI). However, recent "Style Transfer" prompting (e.g., "Write this with high sentence variance") is beginning to defeat this metric as well.

4.2.2 The "Binoculars" Method

A recent breakthrough in detection is the "Binoculars" metric (Hans et al., 2024). This approach proposes that to catch an AI, one must use *another* AI. The method compares two different perplexity scores:

1. **The Observer Score:** How surprised is a generic LLM (like LLaMA-7B) by the text?
2. **The Performer Score:** How surprised is the specific model suspected of writing the text?

The intuition is that if a text seems "perfectly predicted" by a model, but slightly less predicted by a general observer, it indicates the text was generated by that specific model's weights. This "cross-interrogation" of models represents the cutting edge of forensic analysis, yet it remains computationally expensive and slow to deploy at scale.

5. EMPIRICAL ANALYSIS: THE ARCHITECTURE OF DETECTION AND THE LIMITS OF N-GRAMS

To fully grasp why the "arms race" described in Section 4 is unwinnable, one must understand the internal logic of detection systems. This section provides a descriptive analysis of how detection algorithms have evolved from simple statistical counting to complex neural observation, and why even the most sophisticated methods are hitting a "glass ceiling" of accuracy.

5.1 The Baseline: N-Gram Analysis and Zipf's Law

The earliest and most fundamental form of text analysis relies on "N-grams." An N-gram is simply a contiguous sequence of *n* items from a given sample of text.

- *Unigrams (1-gram):* Individual words (e.g., "artificial," "intelligence").
- *Bigrams (2-gram):* Pairs of words (e.g., "artificial intelligence").
- *Trigrams (3-gram):* Triplets (e.g., "the artificial intelligence").

For decades, forensic linguists relied on Zipf's Law, which states that in human language, the frequency of any word is inversely proportional to its rank in the frequency table. Simply put, humans use a very small set of words (like "the," "and," "of") very frequently, and a vast set of words (like "serendipity," "quixotic") very rarely.

The Detection Logic: Early AI models (pre-2017) struggled to replicate this natural distribution. They would often overuse rare words or get stuck in repetitive loops of common words. A simple detector could count the N-grams; if the distribution of Bigrams was too uniform or "flat," it was a statistical anomaly indicating a machine origin.

The Failure Mode: Modern LLMs (GPT-4) are trained on datasets so massive that they have effectively "learned" Zipf's Law. They now replicate human N-gram distributions with near-perfect fidelity. Consequently, simple statistical counting is no longer a viable detection strategy. The "fingerprint" of the machine is no longer found in the *frequency* of words, but in the *relationship* between them.

5.2 The "Bag of Words" Fallacy

A major limitation in early detection was the "Bag of Words" approach. This method analysed text by throwing all the words into a metaphorical bag and counting them, ignoring grammar and word order. While computationally cheap, this approach fails to detect the primary characteristic of modern AI: semantic coherence.

AI text is distinct from human text not because of the words it uses, but because of the *predictability of its syntax*. As discussed in Section 4, AI minimises entropy. A human might write, "The cat sat on the... *philosophical concept of dread*." An AI, maximising probability, will almost always write, "The cat sat on the... *mat*."

To detect this, researcher moved to *GLTR (Giant Language Model Test Room)* methods. These tools do not look at the text in isolation; they feed the text *back* into a language model to see if the model can predict the next word.

- *Green Words:* Words the AI predicts with Top-10 confidence.
- *Yellow Words:* Top-100 confidence.
- *Red Words:* Low confidence (highly unpredictable).

A human sentence is a mosaic of Green, Yellow, and Red words. An AI sentence is a wash of Green. However, as noted previously, "Prompt Engineering" allows users to command the AI to "use more rare words," effectively painting the text red and defeating the detector.

5.3 Neural Classifiers and the "Black Box" Problem

The current state-of-the-art involves training *Neural Classifiers* (like RoBERTa-base-openai-detector). Instead of telling the computer what to look for (like N-grams or entropy), researcher feed a neural network millions of examples of human text and AI text and let the network figure out the patterns itself.

While these classifiers achieve high accuracy on benchmarks, they suffer from the *"Black Box" problem*. We do not know *what* features the model is using to make its decision.

- *Spurious Correlations:* A famous example occurred when a classifier learned to identify AI text not by its style, but by its *formatting*. The AI training data had slightly different whitespace encoding than the human data. The detector wasn't reading the text; it was reading the invisible spaces between the words.
- *The Adversarial Collapse:* Because we don't know what features the neural network is using, we cannot fix it when it fails. When a new model (like Gemini) is released with slightly different statistical properties, the neural classifier often collapses completely (Accuracy drops from 95% to near random chance), requiring expensive retraining.

This empirical analysis leads to a sobering conclusion: statistical detection is a game of "whack-a-mole." As long as detection relies on identifying the *artifacts* of generation (which developers are actively trying to remove), it will always lag behind the generative capability.

6. ETHICAL AND PSYCHOLOGICAL CHALLENGES IN PERSONAL RELATIONSHIPS

The technical opacity described above creates a ripple effect that extends beyond forensic analysis. When the origin of a message cannot be verified, the fundamental contract of human communication—that a statement represents the thought and effort of the sender—is destabilised.

6.1 The Erosion of Epistemic Trust and the "Suspicion Tax"

Trust in digital communication has historically been predicated on the assumption of human presence. The proliferation of undetectable AI introduces "epistemic insecurity" (Seger et al., 2023), where every interaction is subject to a cognitive "suspicion tax." Recipients must expend mental energy evaluating not just the content of a message, but its provenance. This scepticism is particularly corrosive in emotional contexts; if a partner uses an LLM to draft an apology to ensure it sounds "perfect," the receiver's discovery of this fact often results in a feeling of betrayal, suggesting that humans value the *struggle* of articulation as much as the output (Turkle, 2015).

6.2 Costly Signalling and the Value of Effort

Evolutionary psychology provides a framework for understanding why AI-generated intimacy feels "cheap." According to Costly Signalling Theory (Zahavi, 1975), signals are only reliable if they impose a cost on the sender (time, emotional labour).

Generative AI reduces the cost of producing high-quality, emotionally resonant text to near zero. When the cost of the signal drops, the signal loses its value as a proxy for commitment. As noted by Hancock et al. (2020), this decoupling of effort from output forces a re-evaluation of what constitutes "authentic" care.

Furthermore, the discovery of AI mediation in personal relationships fundamentally invalidates the receiver's emotional labor. When an individual responds with genuine vulnerability to a message they later realize was generated by an LLM, it induces a phenomenon known as "empathy fatigue." Over time, the long-term psychological effect of this repeated invalidation is emotional withdrawal. Individuals may begin to withhold genuine emotional investment in digital spaces altogether, treating all remote communication with a defensive, transactional detachment to protect themselves from algorithmic deception.

6.3 The Paradox of Algorithm Aversion and Appreciation

The psychological impact of AI dialogue is further complicated by a dual phenomenon known as Algorithm Aversion and Algorithm Appreciation. Understanding this dichotomy is essential for grasping how AI affects trust in professional communication.

Algorithm Aversion (Dietvorst et al., 2015) suggests that humans are unforgiving of algorithmic error. If a human expert makes a mistake, we tend to forgive them ("to err is human"). However, if an algorithm makes a single mistake, users often lose all confidence in the system and refuse to use it again. In the context of AI dialogue, this means that a single "hallucination" (like the *Avianca* case) can permanently destroy trust in a professional relationship mediated by AI.

Conversely, *Algorithm Appreciation* (Logg et al., 2019) suggests that in the absence of obvious error, humans actually trust algorithms *more* than humans for objective tasks. We assume the machine is unbiased, rational, and exhaustive.

- *The Trap of Authority:* This creates a dangerous dynamic where users are sceptical of AI when they *know* it is AI (Aversion), but blindly trust it when they *think* it is human or when the AI presents itself with authoritative confidence (Appreciation).
- *The "Moral Crumple Zone":* Sociologist Madeline Elish coined this term to describe how responsibility is attributed in human-AI systems. When a system works, we credit the "magic" of the AI. When it fails (as in *Avianca*), we blame the human operator for "misusing" it. This psychological bias protects the technology while exposing the human user to maximum liability, further eroding the safety net of professional accountability.

6.4 The "Uncanny Valley" of Text and Digital Deception

The "Uncanny Valley" has a textual equivalent. As LLMs are optimised for statistical probability, they often produce dialogue that is "hyper-social"—overly polite and lacking natural friction. This hyper-competence is weaponised in romance scams and "catfishing," where LLMs automate the grooming phase, maintaining coherent, empathetic relationships with thousands of victims simultaneously (Europol, 2023). Victims often fall into the "Turing Trap," believing that emotional depth proves humanity, unaware that current models excel at simulating empathetic mirroring.

6.5 Cross-Cultural Variations in AI Interpretation

While the crisis of authenticity is a global technological phenomenon, its psychological impact is heavily mediated by cultural context. Anthropologist Edward T. Hall's distinction between High-Context and Low-Context cultures provides a valuable lens here. In Low-Context cultures (predominantly Western societies), communication is explicit, and trust is often placed in the text's informational accuracy. In these contexts, AI is primarily judged on its utility and factual reliability.

Conversely, in High-Context cultures (prominent in Asian, Middle Eastern, and Latin American societies), meaning is deeply embedded in relational dynamics, social hierarchy, and implicit non-verbal cues. In such cultures, the "Authenticity Gap" may be perceived much more disruptively. Because AI cannot genuinely participate in the shared social history or hierarchical obligations that define High-Context communication, its use in interpersonal dialogue may be viewed not just as deceptive, but as a severe breach of relational respect and social harmony. Future global frameworks for AI adoption must account for these diverse cultural baselines regarding what constitutes an "authentic" interaction.

7. ETHICAL AND ACCOUNTABILITY CHALLENGES IN PROFESSIONAL COMMUNICATION

While the intrusion of AI into personal relationships threatens emotional bonds, its integration into professional spheres threatens accountability.

7.1 The Liability of Automated Advice

In professional settings, the primary ethical challenge is liability. When an AI system generates a legal contract or medical summary, who is responsible for errors? Current "Human-in-the-Loop" models are often undermined by Automation Bias—the tendency for humans to trust the authoritative tone of AI output and skip verification (Cummings, 2004). As explored fully in the Case Studies section, this can lead to catastrophic legal malpractice.

7.2 Academic Integrity and the "Liar's Dividend"

In education, the inability to reliably detect AI has forced institutions into an adversarial posture, risking false accusations against honest students (Eaton, 2023). Beyond academia, the "Liar's Dividend" allows bad actors to claim that genuine, compromising evidence is AI-generated fake. The mere existence of undetectable

AI shifts the burden of proof onto the truth-teller to prove that their documentation is *not* synthetic (Chesney & Citron, 2019).

8. CASE STUDIES IN THE CRISIS OF ATTRIBUTION

While the previous sections explored the theoretical and technical dimensions of AI detection, the true scale of the crisis is best understood through empirical analysis of recent institutional failures. The following case studies represent "ground zero" events in the legal, educational, and creative industries.

8.1 Case Study 1: The Hallucinating Brief – *Mata v. Avianca* and the Collapse of Legal Due Diligence

The Incident: A Routine Injury Becomes a Legal Landmark

On August 27, 2019, Roberto Mata was a passenger on Avianca Flight 670 from El Salvador to New York. During the flight, a metal serving cart struck his left knee, causing an injury that would eventually lead to a lawsuit filed in the Southern District of New York. What began as a routine personal injury tort would, three years later, become the "Patient Zero" event for AI malpractice in the legal profession.

The Mechanism of Failure: The "Research" Phase

The plaintiff's legal team, facing a motion to dismiss from Avianca on the grounds that the statute of limitations had expired, needed to find case law that supported "tolling" (pausing) the time limit. One of the attorneys, Steven A. Schwartz, turned to a new tool he had heard of but never used for legal research: ChatGPT.

Schwartz did not treat the AI as a search engine, but as an oracle. He inputted a query requesting cases that supported his specific legal theory. The LLM, designed to be "helpful" and compliant, generated exactly what he asked for. It produced a beautifully formatted legal brief citing *Varghese v. China Southern Airlines*, *Shaboon v. Egyptair*, and *Petersen v. Iran Air*.

The AI went further than just listing names; it "hallucinated" entire judicial opinions. For the fictional *Varghese* case, ChatGPT generated a detailed summary of facts regarding a plaintiff who was delayed in filing due to bankruptcy proceedings—a fact pattern that perfectly mirrored the legal argument Schwartz needed to make.

The Verification Loophole: Examining the Affidavit

The critical failure occurred during verification. According to court affidavits, Schwartz *did* attempt to verify the cases, but he did so by asking the liar to verify the lie.

- *Schwartz:* "Is Varghese a real case?"
- *ChatGPT:* "Yes, it is a real case."
- *Schwartz:* "What is your source?"
- *ChatGPT:* "I apologise for the confusion earlier... The case is Varghese v. China Southern Airlines Co., Ltd, 925 F.3d 1339 (11th Cir. 2019)."

The AI provided a specific (and fake) citation number, a specific (and fake) court circuit, and a specific (and fake) year. The visual authority of this data—the specific formatting of "925 F.3d 1339"—bypassed the attorney's scepticism. This is a powerful example of Automation Bias: the tendency to trust data that is presented with high distinctiveness and numerical precision.

The Judicial Response and Sanctions

The deception unravelled when Avianca's lawyers attempted to look up the cases in the Westlaw database and found nothing. When Judge P. Kevin Castel was informed, he issued an "Order to Show Cause" that has since become famous in legal ethics circles.

In his final opinion imposing sanctions, Judge Castel noted the existential danger posed by the "hallucinating brief." The problem was not the error itself, but the *nature* of the error. A human lawyer might misinterpret a case, but they rarely invent one from whole cloth. The AI's fabrication was insidious because it was "plausible but false." The opinion highlights that the legal system is built on a "chain of citation"—if that chain is corrupted by synthetic hallucinations, the precedent-based common law system faces a foundational crisis of integrity. The court fined the lawyers $5,000, but the reputational damage—and the warning sent to the global legal industry—was incalculable.

8.2 Case Study 2: The "Glitch" in the Classroom – The Texas A&M Incident and the "False Accusation Trap"

The Incident

In May 2023, a senior instructor at Texas A&M University-Commerce failed an entire class of seniors, withholding their diplomas days before graduation. The instructor suspected the students had used ChatGPT to write their final agricultural science assignments.

The Failure of Detection Methodologies

Unlike the *Avianca* case, which involved a failure to detect AI, this case involved a failure to correctly identify humans. The instructor's detection methodology was technically illiterate: he copied the students' essays into ChatGPT and asked the model, "Did you write this?"

As discussed in Section 4, LLMs are next-token prediction engines, not databases of past outputs. They do not have memory. When asked, "Did you write this?", the model, prone to agreeableness and hallucination, claimed authorship of the students' original work. Furthermore, the instructor likely relied on the high perplexity of the academic language (jargon-heavy, formal), which, to an uninitiated user, might "sound like a computer."

The Aftermath and Analysis

The university was forced to intervene after the story went viral, revealing that the students had provided timestamps and Google Docs edit histories proving their authorship (conforming to the "Chain of Custody" solution proposed in Section 9).

This incident illustrates the "Reverse Burden of Proof" crisis in education. Due to the unreliability of detection tools (both commercial software like Turnitin and heuristic methods), the presumption of innocence has been inverted. Students are now frequently required to surveil themselves (recording their screens while typing) to prove they are not machines. This creates an adversarial pedagogical environment where trust—the foundation of the teacher-student relationship—is replaced by a surveillance dynamic (Eaton, 2023).

8.3 Case Study 3: The Slush Pile Denial of Service – *Clarkesworld Magazine* and the Industrialisation of Creativity

The Incident

Clarkesworld Magazine is one of the most prestigious publishers of science fiction and fantasy. For decades, it has operated an "open submission" policy, allowing anyone to submit short stories for consideration.

In February 2023, editor Neil Clarke reported a vertical spike in submissions. While the magazine typically received 10–20 plagiarised or spam submissions per month, that number skyrocketed to over 500 in a matter of weeks (Clarke, 2023). The volume became so unmanageable that the magazine was forced to close submissions entirely.

The Mechanism of Attack: The "Side Hustle" Feedback Loop

The flood was not caused by authors using AI to assist their writing, but by non-writers using AI to generate "content" for profit. Influencers on platforms like YouTube and TikTok were promoting "Get Rich Quick" schemes, instructing viewers to use ChatGPT to generate sci-fi stories and submit them to paying markets like *Clarkesworld*.

The Failure of Stylometric Filters

The *Clarkesworld* editors, who are experts in reading human fiction, noted that the AI stories were technically "perfect" but stylistically hollow. They exhibited the traits of low burstiness and emotional flatness. However, the sheer *volume* of the attack acted as a Denial of Service (DoS) attack on the human editorial process. Even if a human editor can detect an AI story in 30 seconds, receiving 500 of them overwhelms the available labour hours.

Analysis

This case demonstrates the asymmetric warfare of AI generation vs. human detection.

- *Cost of Generation:* ~$0.001 and 10 seconds per story.
- *Cost of Detection:* High cognitive load and expensive human labour hours.

This economic asymmetry suggests that without cryptographic provenance (verifying the human, not detecting the AI), creative open markets will collapse. It is a microcosm of the "Dead Internet Theory," where bot-generated content drowns out human contribution not by quality, but by sheer volume.

8.4 Case Study 4: The "Ghost Writers" of Legacy Media – The *Sports Illustrated* Scandal

The Incident

In November 2023, the technology news outlet *Futurism* published an exposé revealing that *Sports Illustrated* (SI), one of the most storied brands in American journalism, had been publishing product reviews written by non-existent authors. The investigation identified authors like "Drew Ortiz" and "Sora Tanaka," whose author pages featured headshots.

Upon forensic investigation, it was revealed that these headshots were not of real people. They were generated by AI. "Drew Ortiz" was a synthetic composite available for purchase on a stock photo marketplace for "AI-generated faces." Furthermore, the articles themselves—reviews of volleyballs and fitness equipment—contained the bizarre, circular phrasing and lack of insight characteristic of mass-generated content (e.g., "Volleyball can be a little tricky to get into, especially without an actual ball to practice with").

The Mechanism: Third-Party Obfuscation

Unlike *Clarkesworld* (which was attacked by outsiders), this was an "inside job" facilitated by complex corporate structures. SI's publisher, The Arena Group, had outsourced its e-commerce content to a third-party company, AdVon Commerce. AdVon allegedly used AI to generate content at scale to capture search engine traffic (SEO), creating fake "human" personas to satisfy Google's requirement for content written by authoritative experts.

The "Liar's Dividend" in Action

The aftermath of the scandal perfectly illustrated the "Liar's Dividend" discussed in Section 7.2. When first confronted, The Arena Group denied the allegations, claiming the authors were real humans using pseudonyms to protect their privacy—a plausible defence in the digital age. It was only when the visual evidence of the AI-generated faces became irrefutable that the company pivoted, blaming the third-party contractor and deleting the content.

Analysis: The Uncanny Valley of Brand Trust

This case highlights a critical failure in the Chain of Custody. A legacy brand is essentially a "Trust Trust"—readers believe in *Sports Illustrated* because they assume a rigorous editorial process. The use of AI broke this chain.

- *Commercial Motivation:* The drive to minimise costs ($0.001 per article vs. $200 for a human writer) created an incentive structure that bypassed ethical checks.
- *Institutional Collapse:* The CEO of The Arena Group was eventually fired, and the reputation of a 70-year-old magazine was shattered in a week. This demonstrates that in the AI era, *authenticity is the primary asset* of a media company. Once the audience suspects they are reading "slop" (a colloquial term for low-quality AI text), the value of the brand collapses to zero.

9. TOWARD A FRAMEWORK FOR DIGITAL AUTHENTICITY: FROM DETECTION TO PROVENANCE

The failure of post-hoc detection tools (analysed in Section 5) and the institutional collapses witnessed in recent years (Section 8) lead to an inescapable conclusion: we cannot "police" our way out of the AI crisis using forensic software. The arms race between generation and detection is asymmetrical, favouring the generator.

Therefore, the solution to the crisis of authenticity lies not in better detection of the artificial but in the rigorous certification of the human. This section outlines a multi-layered framework for Digital Authenticity, moving from the technical layer of Cryptographic Provenance, through the legal layer of Mandated Disclosure, to the sociological layer of Cognitive Defence.

9.1 The Technical Layer: Cryptographic Provenance and the "Chain of Custody"

In the world of fine art, a painting's authenticity is not determined solely by analysing brushstrokes (which can be forged), but by its provenance—the documented history of its ownership and origin. The digital world must adopt a similar "Chain of Custody" model.

9.1.1 The C2PA Standard and "Glass-to-Glass" Authentication

The most promising technical solution is the standard developed by the Coalition for Content Provenance and Authenticity (C2PA). Unlike AI detection tools that guess authorship based on probability, C2PA relies on cryptographic non-repudiation.

In this proposed architecture:

1. **Hardware Signing:** The process begins at the "Glass" (the camera lens or the keyboard). Future hardware devices will contain a secure enclave chip that cryptographically signs metadata at the moment of capture or creation.
2. **Asset Binding:** This signature is cryptographically bound to the file itself (the image, text document, or audio recording).
3. **The Ledger:** Any subsequent edits (e.g., Photoshop adjustments, Grammarly suggestions) are recorded as new "assertions" in the file's metadata history, each signed by the editing software.
4. **Verification:** When a consumer views the content on a browser or social media platform, a "Digital Nutrition Label" appears, allowing them to inspect the entire history of the asset.

To use a physical analogy, C2PA functions like a digital wax seal on an envelope. It does not analyze the letter itself to determine whether a human wrote it; instead, it looks at the unbroken seal on the outside to verify exactly who sent it and whether it was tampered with in transit.

This shifts the societal standard from "Trust, but verify" to "Verify, then trust." If a text document lacks a cryptographic signature from a verified human identity or device, it is treated as synthetic by default.

9.1.2 Personhood Credentials and "Proof of Humanity"

Complementing file provenance is the concept of Proof of Personhood (PoP) protocols. As proposed by Worldcoin and various decentralised identity (DID) frameworks, these systems allow users to prove they are unique biological humans without revealing their real-world identity (using Zero-Knowledge Proofs).

In a professional context (e.g., submitting a manuscript to *Clarkesworld* or a legal brief to a court), the submission would require a "Human Attestation" token. This effectively solves the Denial of Service attack described in Case Study 3 by making the cost of generating infinite spam prohibitively high (as each submission requires a unique human validation).

9.2 The Legal and Policy Layer: Regulating the "Right to Reality"

While technology provides the tools, policy must provide the incentives. The current "Wild West" of AI text requires regulatory guardrails that prioritise human transparency.

9.2.1 The Limits of Watermarking Mandates

The EU AI Act and similar proposed legislation in the US (e.g., the AI Labelling Act) focus on mandating that AI developers watermark their content. While well-intentioned, this approach faces the "Open Source Loophole."

- *Proprietary Models:* Companies like OpenAI and Google can be legally compelled to watermark their outputs.
- *Open Weights Models:* Models like Meta's LLaMA or Mistral can be downloaded and run locally. A bad actor can strip the watermarking code from the open-source architecture.

Therefore, policy must focus less on regulating the *generator* (which can be decentralised) and more on regulating the *distributor* and *institution*. Courts, universities, and publishers must establish "Strict Liability" frameworks: the user is fully liable for the output of their AI tools. As seen in *Mata v. Avianca*, the defence "the AI lied to me" must be legally inadmissible.

9.2.2 The "Bot Disclosure" Law

A critical policy recommendation is the "Right to Human Interaction." Legislation should mandate that in specific high-stakes contexts—telemedicine, mental health counselling, and government services—users have a right to know if they are conversing with an automated system. This combats the "parasocial manipulation" described in Section 5, ensuring that emotional intimacy is not commodified without consent.

9.3 The Pedagogical Layer: AI Literacy and Cognitive Defence

The final and most resilient layer of the framework is the human mind. Just as the invention of the printing press required a rise in literacy, the invention of Generative AI requires a rise in AI Literacy.

9.3.1 Moving Beyond "Plagiarism Policing"

Educational institutions must pivot from trying to *catch* AI writing to teaching students how to *evaluate* it. A curriculum for the AI Age should include:

- **Prompt Engineering vs. Prompt Dependence:** Teaching the difference between using AI as a cognitive scaffold (brainstorming, outlining) vs. a cognitive crutch (generating the final output).
- **Hallucination Auditing:** Assignments where students are tasked explicitly with generating AI text and then rigorously fact-checking it to identify subtle fabrications. This immunises students against the "fluency heuristic."

9.3.2 Zero-Trust Information Architecture

We must cultivate a societal habit of "Lateral Reading" (Wineburg & McGrew, 2017). When reading digital text, the default assumption should shift from "True until proven False" to "Unverified until Provenanced."

- *Critical Ignoring:* Teaching users to ignore high-volume, low-quality information streams (likely AI-generated) and focus attention on trusted, verified nodes (authenticated journalists, peer-reviewed journals).

9.4 Societal Norms: The "Centaur" Model of Authorship

Finally, we must redefine what "authorship" means. The binary view, "Human = Good, AI = Bad", is obsolete. We are moving toward the Centaur Model (Kasparov, 2017), where the highest performance comes from Human + AI collaboration.

9.4.1 The Spectrum of Disclosure

Instead of a simple "AI-Generated" warning, we propose a Taxonomy of Disclosure for professional work:

1. **Human-Authored:** No AI used beyond spell-check.
2. **AI-Assisted:** AI used for brainstorming, outlining, or editing; final prose is human.
3. **AI-Generated, Human-Edited:** AI produced the draft; human verified and refined.
4. **Fully Synthetic:** AI generated the text with minimal human intervention.

Adopting this nuance restores trust. If a CEO uses AI to draft a mundane memo (Level 3), it matters little. If a novelist uses AI to write a climax (Level 4), the audience feels betrayed. Clarity about *where* on the spectrum a work falls allows the audience to calibrate their emotional investment accordingly.

9.5 Sector-Specific Strategic Recommendations

To bridge the Authenticity Gap in practice, different sectors must adopt tailored strategies. Table 1 outlines actionable recommendations for key stakeholders navigating AI-mediated communication.

Table 1. Strategic recommendations for navigating AI authenticity

Sector	Primary Authenticity Challenge	Strategic Recommendation
Corporate Leaders	Automation bias and liability in AI-generated advice.	Implement "Strict Liability" policies; mandate internal taxonomy disclosure (e.g., labeling drafts as "AI-Assisted" vs. "Fully Synthetic").
Educators	The "False Accusation Trap" and evaluating student knowledge.	Shift from forensic policing (using flawed AI detectors) to "process-based" assessments; teach AI literacy and hallucination auditing.
Media & Publishers	"Slush pile" denial of service and loss of brand trust.	Adopt cryptographic provenance standards (C2PA) for incoming submissions; explicitly ban undisclosed synthetic personas.
Policymakers	Undisclosed parasocial manipulation (e.g., romance scams).	Legislate the "Right to Human Interaction," mandating clear disclosure when users are conversing with automated systems in high-stakes environments.

Source: Author's original compilation based on chapter synthesis.

10. FUTURE HORIZONS: FROM CHATBOTS TO AGENTIC DECEPTION AND THE "DEAD INTERNET"

As we analyse the current crisis of detection, it is imperative to look forward. The technology driving AI-Mediated Communication is not static; it is accelerating toward two distinct horizons that will further complicate the definition of "authenticity": Agentic AI and Multimodal Convergence.

10.1 The Rise of Agentic AI: When Bots Do More Than Talk

Currently, the detection debate focuses on *informational* deception: identifying if a human wrote a text. The next phase involves *behavioural* deception. We are transitioning from "Generative AI" (which creates content) to "Agentic AI" (which executes actions).

Agentic AI systems (such as AutoGPT or BabyAGI) are designed to function autonomously over long periods to achieve a goal. In this context, "dialogue" is merely a tool the AI uses to manipulate humans to achieve an end.

- *The Social Engineering Risk:* An Agentic AI tasked with "maximising sales for a crypto-token" could autonomously create thousands of Twitter accounts, generate unique personalities for each, build trust with human users over months of casual conversation, and then coordinate a simultaneous "rug pull."
- *Detection Futility:* Detecting individual messages in this scenario is irrelevant. The deception lies in the *intent* and the *network* of behaviour. The challenge for future researchers will shift from Stylometry (analysing words) to Behavioural Forensics (analysing goal-directed patterns across networks).

10.2 The "Dead Internet Theory" Realised

The "Dead Internet Theory" is an internet conspiracy theory positing that the majority of internet activity is bots talking to bots. Generative AI is rapidly moving this from conspiracy to reality.

As the cost of content generation approaches zero (Section 7.3), we face an "Inversion of Ratio." Historically, the internet was 90% human, 10% bot. We are approaching a tipping point where 90% of content is synthetic.

- *Model Collapse:* This creates a technical problem known as "Model Collapse" (Shumailov et al., 2023). If future AI models are trained on the internet, and the internet is full of AI text, the models will begin to train on their own output. This feedback loop causes a degradation of quality and a loss of "long-tail" human knowledge.
- *The Human Enclave:* Sociologically, this implies a future where the "public internet" is abandoned as a noise-filled wasteland. Human interaction may retreat to "High-Friction Zones"—private servers, encrypted group chats, and paid communities where "Proof of Humanity" is the gatekeeper. The "open web" may become a graveyard of hallucinations, visited only by scrapers.

10.3 Multimodal Convergence: The End of "Seeing is Believing"

Finally, the text-detection crisis will soon merge with the deepfake crisis. Models like OpenAI's Sora (video) and ElevenLabs (audio) are converging with LLMs.

- *Real-Time Avatars:* We are months away from real-time, interactive video avatars that look human, sound human, and speak with the wit of GPT-4.
- *The Total Erosion of Remote Trust:* When a scammer can video-call a grandmother using her grandson's face and voice (synthesised in real-time) to ask for money, the "Suspicion Tax" discussed in Section 5.1 will become a "Paranoia Tax." The default psychological state for all remote communication—video, audio, or text—will shift to profound distrust.

This convergence suggests that text detection is merely the first battle in a more protracted war for the integrity of reality itself. The solutions proposed in this chapter, specifically, Cryptographic Provenance (C2PA), must be expanded rapidly to cover all modalities, or we risk a total epistemic collapse.

11. CONCLUSION

The rapid ascent of Large Language Models has irreversibly fractured the link between linguistic fluency and human consciousness. As this chapter has demonstrated, the "practical" challenge of detecting AI text is an arms race that forensic tools are destined to lose. The statistical homogenization of AI text (low perplexity) is being actively countered by adversarial prompting and model evolution, rendering the "black box" of authorship increasingly opaque.

This opacity creates profound ethical tremors. In personal relationships, the "suspicion tax" threatens to commodify intimacy, replacing genuine emotional labour with automated empathy. In professional spheres, the "responsibility gap" endangers legal and academic integrity, allowing misinformation to flourish under the guise of authoritative prose.

However, the solution is not to ban the technology or engage in a futile pursuit of perfect detection. Moving forward, stakeholders must orient their strategies around four core takeaways:

1. **Detection is a Dead End:** The statistical convergence of human and machine text renders post-hoc forensic tools fundamentally unreliable and ethically hazardous.

2. **The Suspicion Tax is Real:** Unverified AI communication degrades interpersonal trust by invalidating emotional labor and triggering empathy fatigue.
3. **Provenance Over Policing:** Society must shift from hunting for synthetic artifacts to cryptographically verifying human origin (e.g., C2PA standards).
4. **The Centaur Paradigm:** Professional authenticity must be redefined to embrace transparent, disclosed human-AI collaboration rather than binary categorization.

As we navigate this transition, urgent forward-looking questions remain for future researchers: How will High-Context cultures adapt their relational norms to AI mediation? How will the legal system assign liability when an autonomous "Agentic AI" commits fraud? Ultimately, the future of human connection in the AI age will not depend on our ability to banish machines from the conversation, but on our collective ability to clearly demarcate where the algorithm ends and the human begins.

REFERENCES

Brown, T. B., Mann, B., Ryder, N., Subbiah, M., Kaplan, J., Dhariwal, P., & Amodei, D. (2020). Language models are few-shot learners. *Advances in Neural Information Processing Systems*, *33*, 1877–1901.

Burrows, J. (2002). 'Delta': A measure of stylometric difference and a guide to likely authorship. *Literary and Linguistic Computing*, *17*(3), 267–287. DOI: 10.1093/llc/17.3.267

Castel, P. K. (2023). *Order to Show Cause, Mata v. Avianca, Inc.*, No. 1:22-cv-01461. United States District Court, S.D.N.Y.

Chesney, R., & Citron, D. K. (2019). Deep fakes: A looming challenge for privacy, democracy, and national security. *California Law Review*, *107*, 1753. DOI: 10.15779/Z38RV0D15J

Clarke, N. (2023, February 15). A concerning trend. *Neil Clarke's Blog*. http://neil-clarke.com/a-concerning-trend/

Cummings, M. L. (2004). Automation bias in intelligent time-critical decision support systems. *AIAA 1st Intelligent Systems Technical Conference*, 6313. DOI: 10.2514/6.2004-6313

Dames, H.. (2022). The fluency heuristic in human-machine interaction. *Computers in Human Behavior*, *130*, 107187.

Devlin, J., Chang, M. W., Lee, K., & Toutanova, K. (2019). BERT: Pre-training of deep bidirectional transformers for language understanding. *Proceedings of the NAACL*, 4171–4186. DOI: 10.48550/arXiv.1810.04805

Dietvorst, B. J., Simmons, J. P., & Massey, C. (2015). Algorithm aversion: People erroneously avoid algorithms after seeing them err. *Journal of Experimental Psychology. General*, *144*(1), 114–126. DOI: 10.1037/xge0000033 PMID: 25401381

Eaton, S. E. (2023). Postplagiarism: Transdisciplinary ethics and integrity in the age of artificial intelligence and neurotechnology. *International Journal for Educational Integrity*, *19*(1), 23. Advance online publication. DOI: 10.1007/s40979-023-00144-1

Europol. (2023). *ChatGPT: The impact of Large Language Models on Law Enforcement*. Europol Innovation Lab.

Hancock, J. T., Naaman, M., & Levy, K. (2020). AI-mediated communication: Definition, research agenda, and ethical considerations. *Journal of Computer-Mediated Communication*, *25*(1), 89–100. DOI: 10.1093/jcmc/zmz022

Hans, A., ... (2024). Spotting LLMs with Binoculars: Zero-Shot Detection of Machine-Generated Text. *arXiv preprint arXiv:2401.12070*. /arXiv.2401.12070DOI: 10.48550

Jurafsky, D., & Martin, J. H. (2009). *Speech and Language Processing*. Pearson.

Kasparov, G. (2017). *Deep Thinking: Where Machine Intelligence Ends and Human Creativity Begins*. PublicAffairs.

Logg, J. M., Minson, J. A., & Moore, D. A. (2019). Algorithm appreciation: People prefer algorithmic to human judgment. *Organizational Behavior and Human Decision Processes*, *151*, 90–103. DOI: 10.1016/j.obhdp.2018.12.005

Mata v. Avianca, Inc., No. 1:22-cv-01461 (S.D.N.Y. June 22, 2023).

Mikolov, T.. (2013). Distributed representations of words and phrases and their compositionality. *Advances in Neural Information Processing Systems*, *26*. Advance online publication. DOI: 10.48550/arXiv.1310.4546

Mosteller, F., & Wallace, D. L. (1964). *Inference and Disputed Authorship: The Federalist*. Addison-Wesley.

Open, A. I. (2023). *GPT-4 Technical Report*. arXiv. /arXiv.2303.08774DOI: 10.48550

Reeves, B., & Nass, C. (1996). *The Media Equation: How People Treat Computers, Television, and New Media Like Real People and Places*. Cambridge University Press.

Sadasivan, V. S., Kumar, A., Balasubramanian, S., Wang, W., & Feizi, S. (2023). Can AI-generated text be reliably detected? *arXiv preprint arXiv:2303.11156*. / arXiv.2303.11156DOI: 10.48550

Seger, E., Dreksler, N., & Moulange, R. (2023). *The Epistemic Integrity of the Internet in the Age of Generative AI*. Centre for the Governance of AI.

Shannon, C. E. (1948). A mathematical theory of communication. *The Bell System Technical Journal*, *27*(3), 379–423. DOI: 10.1002/j.1538-7305.1948.tb01338.x

Shumailov, I., ... (2023). The Curse of Recursion: Training on Generated Data Makes Models Forget. *arXiv preprint arXiv:2305.17493*. /arXiv.2305.17493DOI: 10.48550

Spence, A.. (2023). The assumption of humanity: How users attribute agency in AI interaction. *Journal of Human-Computer Interaction*, *39*(1).

Turing, A. M. (1950). Computing machinery and intelligence. *Mind*, *59*(236), 433–460. DOI: 10.1093/mind/LIX.236.433

Turkle, S. (2015). *Reclaiming conversation: The power of talk in a digital age.* Penguin.

Uchendu, A., Le, T., & Lee, D. (2023). Attribution and obfuscation of neural text authorship. *Data Mining and Knowledge Discovery, 37*, 1–38. DOI: 10.48550/arXiv.2210.10488

Vaswani, A., Shazeer, N., Parmar, N., Uszkoreit, J., Jones, L., Gomez, A. N., & Polosukhin, I. (2017). Attention is all you need. *Advances in Neural Information Processing Systems, 30*. Advance online publication. DOI: 10.48550/arXiv.1706.03762

Weizenbaum, J. (1966). ELIZA—A computer program for the study of natural language communication between man and machine. *Communications of the ACM, 9*(1), 36–45. DOI: 10.1145/365153.365168

Weizenbaum, J. (1976). *Computer Power and Human Reason: From Judgment to Calculation*. W.H. Freeman.

Wineburg, S., & McGrew, S. (2017). *Lateral reading: Reading less and learning more when evaluating digital information*. Stanford History Education Group.

Worldcoin. (2023). *A new identity and financial network*. Worldcoin Whitepaper.

Zahavi, A. (1975). Mate selection—A selection for a handicap. *Journal of Theoretical Biology, 53*(1), 205–214. DOI: 10.1016/0022-5193(75)90111-3 PMID: 1195756

Zipf, G. K. (1949). *Human Behaviour and the Principle of Least Effort*. Addison-Wesley.

Chapter 17
The Impact of AI on the Human Touch:
An Analysis in Boutique Hospitality

Marina Joice Chalupa
http://orcid.org/0009-0005-7242-195X
Polytechnic Institute of Cávado and Ave, Portugal

ABSTRACT

The present study examines the impact of artificial intelligence (AI) on human-centered service in the boutique hospitality sector, focusing on the Portuguese Boutique Hotel: Hotel da Oliveira, known for its personalized guest experiences. The chapter investigates how the implementation of AI can alter the essential human contact that defines hotel identity and the guest experience. This research employs a qualitative methodology, utilizing semi-structured interviews to elicit in-depth professional insights and experiences related to maintaining the human touch in daily operations. The empirical findings suggest that although AI can be used to improve operational efficiency, employees emphasized the need to maintain the human touch to preserve the boutique hotel experience. This research discusses the challenges small hotels face when implementing AI, especially the balance between using technology and preserving the core values of human-centered service.

DOI: 10.4018/979-8-3373-8337-8.ch017

INTRODUCTION

The hospitality industry is fundamentally predicated on human-to-human interaction. Boutique establishments are recognized for their proficiency in delivering tailored and idiosyncratic service experiences.

In a world full of AI, the hospitality sector is no different, and is using intelligence and automation more and more, it is also using systems that are based on data to run hotel operations. This is changing how the hospitality sector delivers services to people. Technologies such as property management systems (PMS), customer relationship management (CRM) platforms, chatbots, dynamic pricing algorithms, and AI-supported decision-making tools have become commonplace, particularly in large hotel chains (Citak et al., 2021).

However, the rising presence of AI in hospitality raises critical questions regarding its compatibility with human-centered service models, especially within boutique hotels. While AI has the potential to augment service delivery by backup employees and optimizing backstage operations, there is also concern that unnecessary reliance on technology may corrode the emotional, relational, and experiential dimensions that guests seek in boutique accommodations (Solnet et al., 2019).

Recent literature suggests that technology and human interaction should not be viewed as mutually exclusive, but rather as complementary elements within service systems. Wang et al. (2026) argue that although technological innovation has evolved from novelty to necessity in hospitality, its successful implementation depends on maintaining an appropriate balance with human interaction. Despite these theoretic insights, empirical evidence indicates that the adoption of AI remains uneven across the hospitality sector. Large hotel chains tend to lead in technological implementation due to greater financial resources, standardized processes, and centralized decision-making structures. In contrast, independent and boutique hotels often face significant barriers, including limited budgets, lack of technological expertise, and concerns about preserving brand identity and service authenticity (Citak et al., 2021). These challenges are predominantly relevant for smaller hotels that rely heavily on human interaction as a competitive advantage. The use of guest data for AI-driven personalization can enhance service relevance and efficiency, but it also raises concerns regarding transparency, consent, and data protection (Etiubon & Etiubon, 2023). Guests may observe excessive data collection or automated decision-making as invasive. Moreover, employees may feel uneasy about the implications of AI for job security, skill requirements, and professional identity (Bisoi et al., 2020).

The current analysis analyzes the impact of artificial intelligence on the human touch in boutique hospitality, concentrating on the case study: Hotel da Oliveira, a Portuguese boutique hotel renowned for its personalized guest experiences. By exploring employees' perceptions and lived experiences, the study seeks to understand how AI is currently used in daily operations, which tasks are perceived as suitable for technological support, and which aspects of service are considered irreplaceable by human interaction. The qualitative approach adopted in this research allows for an in-depth exploration of frontline perspectives, capturing nuanced insights that are often overlooked in technology-driven discourse.

Specifically, this present study addresses the following objectives: (1) to analyze how employees in a boutique hotel view the relationship between AI and human-centered service; (2) to classify operational areas where AI can enhance efficiency without compromising service quality; and (3) to explore the perceived risks, limitations, and ethical concerns associated with AI implementation in a human-focused hospitality context. This chapter contributes to the growing body of literature on technology-human balance in hospitality furthermore offers practical implications for small and boutique hotels seeking to integrate AI while preserving their core identity.

1. LITERATURE REVIEW

1.1 Boutique Hospitality and the Concept of Human-Centered Service

Tourism is a growing sector, and this expansion has led to the rise of a new category of hotels: boutique hotels. The main objective of the boutique hotel business is to make the difference by adhering to the principle of exceptional service and maximizing profits, taking into account the target audience. To this end, it adopted a unique business model, reflected in the services it offers and the notoriety it has achieved (Efe & Koleva, 2018). Some guests specifically seek this type of accommodation; according to Aggett (2007), the main reasons for the preference for boutique accommodation include individuality, high levels of service, personalized attention to guests, and the location of these hotels.

These factors contrast with the offer of traditional hotel accommodation, which participants describe as uniform across hotels and lacking individualization. The standardized offering of traditional hotels appears to have driven consumers to explore hotels that provide alternative forms of accommodation.

Several factors lead guests to choose boutique hotels, including design elements and the uniqueness of this type of accommodation. In addition, the author referenced in the study argues that the services actually provided are of high importance. These include individualized attention (such as room service and friendly and helpful staff), so supporting the theory that boutique hotels attract consumers looking for to experience a more personalized service.

The human-centric manner that some hotels have implemented revolve on involving customers and employees in the co-innovation of services, personalization of experiences, definition of service standards, and validation of changes. Individual users contribute through positive feedback, complaints, strategic advice, or financial support, while user groups participate in collective feedback, co-planning, co-production, and the establishment of new service standards (Rösch, 2020).

Gilmore and Pine (2007) highlight that perceived authenticity in service encounters is not simply a matter of being "genuine," in contrast of often aligning organizational values, employee behavior, and guest expectations. Boutique hotels are mainly well-positioned to deliver such authenticity due to their smaller scale and greater flexibility in service design. Yet, excessive automation or poorly integrated technology may undermine this perception by unsettling spontaneous and emotionally rich interactions.

Lashley (2008) claims that hospitality should be understood as a social practice based on generosity, gratitude and reciprocity, going beyond simple commercial transactions. In this context, boutique hotels incline to favor personalized design and meaningful interactions, promoting a feeling of authenticity.

Pine and Gilmore (1999) argue that the experience economy has transformed consumer expectations, who now pursue emotional involvement and personal meaning. Boutique hotels respond to this change by presenting tailored experiences that replicate individual lifestyles and values. Co-creation becomes a vital element, permitting guests to actively contribute in building their own experience. Baum, Kralj, Robinson and Solnet (2016) highlight that employees in boutique hotels have better independence to adapt services to the specific needs of guests, which fortifies interpersonal relationships and increases satisfaction. An often-overlooked dimension in discussions of artificial intelligence in hospitality is emotional labor and employee well-being. Emotional labor refers to the regulation of emotions to satisfy organizational expectations during service encounters (Hochschild, 2012). In boutique hotels, where personalized service and relational depth are core value propositions, employees are mandatory to repeatedly display warmth, empathy, and attentiveness.

While AI may decrease operational workload, it does not remove emotional labor; rather, it can reinforce it by increasing expectations for flawless personalized service (Huang, Rust, & Maksimovic, 2019). As routine tasks become automated, frontline employees are increasingly positioned as emotional specialists, responsible for delivering authentic experiences and resolving complex interpersonal situations.

This shift creates both chances and risks. On one hand, AI-supported environments allow staff to devote more time to meaningful guest interactions, potentially enhancing job satisfaction and perceived purpose (Rai et al., 2019). On the other hand, sensitive emotional demands may contribute to burnout if organizations fail to provide adequate psychological support and training (Baum et al., 2016).

Furthermore, employees may experience identity tensions as technology reshapes professional roles. Front-office hospitality workers traditionally derive value from personal relationships with guests (Solnet et al., 2019). Therefore, successful AI integration must include human resource strategies that arrange emotional resilience, continuous learning, and recognition of interpersonal skills as strategic assets.

In boutique hospitality, where service authenticity is dominant, employee well-being becomes inseparable from guest satisfaction. Hotels must adopt holistic workforce policies that address emotional labor while embracing digital transformation.

1.2 The Role of Human Touch and Artificial Intelligence in Hospitality

When discussing human touch, boutique hotels instantly come to mind, as guests often pursue these establishments specifically for the sense of closeness and personalized attention they provide. Wang, Kong, Xiao, Bu, and Qiu (2026) argue that even though technology can enhance service efficiency, it is crucial to balance it with human interactions to avoid service interruptions and preserve guest satisfaction. Similarly, it can be contended that technology plays a essential role in improving service delivery in the hospitality industry by enabling smart services that are both personalized and proactive (Kabadayi et al., 2019).

Solnet, Subramony, Ford, Golubovskaya, Kang, and Hancer (2019) emphasize that technology can enhance service effectiveness and consistency by facilitating personalization and anticipating customer needs; though, human touch remains essential for creating experiences that are genuine. Their study highlights that organizations capable of balancing technology with human interaction can create customer value, satisfaction, loyalty, and ultimately, a competitive advantage.

The implementation of AI can benefit both customers and employees, although in this current scenario not all guests are willing to change their habits (Citak et al., 2021). The study reveals that AI implementation is still limited and uneven, much more advanced in hotel chains than in independent hotels.

Zahidi, Kaluvilla, and Mulla (2024) allude that AI is redefining operational practices and customer engagement strategies. It can emerge not only as a technological tool, but also as a strategic element capable of personalizing the guest experience, increasing operational efficiency, reducing costs, and enhancing security, particularly through fraud detection and data protection.

The SWOT analysis conducted by Bisoi, Roy, and Samal (2020) offers a comprehensive view of the impacts of artificial intelligence (AI) on the hospitality sector. Regarding strengths, the authors highlight that one of the main advantages of AI is the reduction in the need for manual labor, which can optimize operational costs and increase efficiency. This includes shorter waiting lines and faster access to services. Furthermore, AI can contribute to improved cleanliness. When discussing weaknesses, the absence of human interaction is a significant limitation, as this is a sector that values human contact. Limited familiarity with the technology on the part of employees and customers can hinder adoption. Problems with error correction and the financial capacity to invest in advanced systems also represent challenges. The authors also mention some opportunities, such as opening doors to new possibilities, like the creation of digital human assistants and overcoming linguistic and cultural barriers. Speaking of threats, we may face a future with reduced job opportunities for humans, high energy consumption by AI systems, and concerns about the security of customer data.

Studies indicate that guests tend to appreciate AI applications that operate in the background, such as data analysis, demand forecasting, or administrative automation, as these tools indirectly improve service quality without diminishing human interaction. Ivanov and Webster (2019) note that resistance emerges when AI replaces direct interpersonal contact, especially in moments that require empathy, reassurance, or emotional sensitivity. This supports the argument that human touch remains essential for delivering warmth, authenticity, and relational value in hospitality encounters.

According to Mattila (2001) establishing a close and genuine emotional bond with customers can decrease the negative effects of service failures on customer loyalty. True relationship building goes beyond loyalty or frequency programs and requires recognizing customers as unique individuals through customized service delivery. While database technologies allow the storage of detailed customer preferences, successful service firms must ensure that personalization efforts are apparent as authentic rather than as shallow marketing tactics. Lu, Cai and Gursoy (2019) demonstrate that consumers are more easily tempted to accept automation in functional tasks (check-in, reservations, payments), but prefer human interactions in emotionally charged or complex situations.

1.3 Ethical and Privacy Considerations of AI in Hospitality

The integration of artificial intelligence (AI) into hospitality services offers many advantages, such as operational efficiency, predictive analytics, and personalized experiences. However, it also increases critical ethical and privacy concerns, which boutique hotels must address to maintain trust and guest satisfaction. AI systems frequently require extensive personal data, including behavioral patterns, preferences, and financial information, to bring customized services (Floridi, 2020). Improper use of this data, can compromise guest privacy and autonomy.

As previously mentioned, boutique hotels, are known for their personalized and human-centered service, face the challenge of leveraging AI without discouragement ethical principles. Guests may feel anxious if AI systems are perceived as intrusive or excessively data-driven, highlighting the importance of transparency and informed consent in data collection (Mehrabi et al., 2022). Implementing privacy-by-design principles, where data protection is integrated into system architecture from the outset, is essential for minimalizing risks while maintaining personalized service.

AI models trained on historical or incomplete data can reproduce or amplify social biases, possibly leading to discriminatory outcomes in guest services (Mehrabi et al., 2022). For instance, prejudiced AI could result in unsatisfactory recommendations, misinterpretation of preferences, or special treatment for certain groups of guests. Security is also a main ethical consideration. The deployment of AI exposes hotels to cyber threats, such as data breaches and unauthorized access to sensitive information (Floridi, 2020). Compliance with data protection regulations, robust encryption, and employee training on ethical AI usage are critical measures to safeguard both guest data and organizational integrity.

The ethical dimension of AI adoption in hospitality involves the preservation of human interaction. While AI can enhance operational tasks, over-reliance may reduce the human touch central to boutique hotel experiences. Preserving a balance between automation and human engagement safeguards that emotional bonds, authenticity, and relational value are preserved (Syed, 2024; Rai, Constantinides, & Sarker, 2019). AI should complement, not replace, human service, allowing employees to focus on empathetic, creative, and emotionally meaningful interactions.

In boutique hotel contexts, trust plays a decisive role. Guests choose such establishments precisely because they value intimacy, authenticity, and personalized engagement (Makarem et al., 2009).

Huang et al. (2019) suggest a typology of AI roles in service encounters: mechanical, thinking, and feeling. While mechanical and thinking AI are usually accepted for transactional tasks, it remains limited in its ability to replicate genuine empathy. This explains why people tolerate automation for check-ins or reservations but struggle to accept it when is about emotionally significant moments.

Studies indicate that guests are more eager to share personal information when organizations clearly communicate how data enhances their experience and safeguards privacy (Floridi, 2020). In boutique settings, where relationships are built on familiarity and loyalty, ethical data practices directly affect brand credibility.

Therefore, guest experience in AI-enhanced hospitality emerges from a delicate equilibrium between efficiency and emotional connection. Technology should ideally remain largely invisible, supporting service delivery without overshadowing human presence.

1.4 AI as a Support Tool vs. AI as a Replacement for Human Interaction

Nikitina and Ishchenko (2024) led a study on the use of artificial intelligence in education, analyzing its potential application in different sectors of teaching. According to the authors, AI can contribute to the creation of more personalized, accessible, and efficient educational environments, provided it is used responsibly. The authors claim that technology should not substitute the human role in the educational process, but rather act as an instrument to support teaching and learning. They highlight the importance of preserving the human element, ensuring attention to fundamental issues such as ethics, data privacy, and equal access to technologies, in order to endorse a fairer and more inclusive education.

The increasing integration of artificial intelligence into business intelligence and experimentation has altered how organizations analyze data and make decisions. Nevertheless, James (2026)argues that the efficiency and legitimacy of these systems depend not on replacing humans, but on reinforcing human judgment. The distinction between automation and augmentation is central: while AI offers speed and analytical capacity, it is limited in understanding context, ethics, and managing ambiguity.

It is possible to discuss the risk of excessive dependence on AI, strengthening the need to develop the digital skills of professionals. These skills include not only the know-how of computers, but also progressive knowledge of data, statistics, and machine learning algorithms, which are essential for interpreting the results generated by AI (Etiubon & Etiubon, 2023).

A study by Syed (2024) focuses on the use of AI as an important role in reducing loneliness among adults. The study was focused on the United States of America, especially through chatbots, social robots, virtual assistants, and AI-generated social networks. However, the study warns of ethical issues, including risks to privacy, excessive dependence on AI, and limitations in emotional depth. AI should complement, not replace, genuine human relationships, strengthening existing connections.

The variance between AI as an augmentation tool and AI as a replacement for human interaction is progressively emphasized in contemporary service research. From a service-dominant logic perspective, value is co-created over interactions between employees and guests, rather than embedded in technological systems themselves (Vargo & Lusch, 2008).

Adding to that, Rai, Constantinides, and Sarker (2019) argue that hybrid human–AI systems achieve optimal performance when human decision remains central when it comes to decision-making. AI excels in speed and analytical capacity, but its deficiencies contextual awareness, moral reasoning, and emotional intelligence.

2. CASE STUDY

Hotel da Oliveira is a four-star boutique hotel located in the historic centre of Guimarães, Portugal, a UNESCO World Heritage Site celebrated as the birthplace of the Portuguese nation (Hotel da Oliveira, s.d).

The hotel's design and service philosophy emphasize cultural immersion and personalized guest experience through its "Feel Guimarães" concept, where each of the 20 rooms have themes on historical figures, traditions, and cultural narratives from the surrounding city, thereby converting accommodation into an interpretative encounter with local history (Hotel da Oliveira, s.d).

Centrally positioned at Largo da Oliveira and Rua de Santa Maria, guests are within walking distance of landmarks such as the Guimarães Castle and Church of Oliveira, reinforcing the hotel's role as a gateway to the living heritage of the medieval urban landscape (Hotel da Oliveira, 2026). Beyond cultural engagement, Hotel da Oliveira validates a formal commitment to sustainability: it has maintained integrated quality and environmental management systems certified to international standards (NP EN ISO 9001 and NP EN ISO 14001) since 2014, has been awarded the Green Key eco-label since 2021, and in October 2024 became one of the first urban hotels in Europe to receive Zero Waste certification from Zero Waste Europe in recognition of significant waste reduction and separation practices (Hotel da Oliveira, s.d).

The hotel combines historical character with modern hospitality amenities, including individually decorated rooms with air conditioning, minibar and private bathrooms, an Michelin Guide restaurant, emphasizing Portuguese and international cuisine, free Wi-Fi, and 24-hour reception, supporting a comprehensive guest experience that aligns cultural discovery with comfort and responsible tourism (Booking.com, s.d).

Overall, Hotel da Oliveira consistently receives excellent guest feedback, with a 9.2/10 overall score across hundreds of recent verified reviews on Booking.com. Guests highlight several recurring themes that reflect both personal human experiences and patterns that could be further explored using AI sentiment analysis to illustrate how human-centred service creates strong emotional responses.

Most reviews praise the hotel's exceptional location in the heart of the historic centre of Guimarães, very often described as "perfect," "unbeatable," and "right on the old town square," facilitating easy access to nearby landmarks and attractions. This is consistently the highest scoring aspect in guest ratings.

Guests often comment on the warm and attentive staff, noting that the human touch of the team, from welcome greetings to helpful local advice, significantly enhances their stay. Many travelers wrote that staff went beyond expectations, such as offering coffee after a long walk from parking, reflecting personalized service that resonates emotionally with visitors.

The comfort and cleanliness of the rooms also receive high marks, with reviewers describing spacious, well-appointed rooms and excellent breakfast offerings. Some mention minor issues like "room lighting" being a little dark or difficulty with luggage due to the historic center's cobblestone streets, yet these are usually softened by praise for staff support and overall experience.

A few reviewers note challenges typical of heritage locations, for instance, limited immediate car access or occasional street noise due to its central placement, but these are generally framed within the context of the charm and authenticity of the historic setting rather than serious complaints.

From a human-experience perspective, guests frequently use descriptors like "friendly," "helpful," "welcoming," and "attentive," underscoring the value of human interaction in hospitality reviews. Hotel da Oliveira uses the human touch as a focus on the customer experience, as can be seen from the positive reviews, as it is a small hotel, they try to differentiate themselves by being more attentive.

This integration of heritage interpretation, experiential design, and sustainability positions Hotel da Oliveira as a compelling case for researchers and practitioners exploring innovative models of boutique hospitality in historic urban contexts.

3. INTERVIEWS

The qualitative design of this study was guided by its exploratory nature and by the small organizational context of the case study site, Hotel da Oliveira. As a boutique hotel with a total workforce of 21 employees, purposive (goal-directed) sampling was adopted, focusing on staff members in guest-facing roles (Front Desk and Food & Beverage). These positions were selected because they involve the highest levels of emotional labor, personalization, and direct service interaction.

Four participants were recruited based on their availability, professional experience, and continuous contact with guests. Although the sample size is limited, it is appropriate for an in-depth qualitative case study, where the objective is not statistical generalization but analytical depth and contextual understanding.

The hotel was chosen as the research setting due to its strong emphasis on personalized guest experiences, cultural engagement, and relationship-driven service. This context provides a suitable environment for examining the tension between technological efficiency and the human element in boutique hospitality. The case study approach enabled an in-depth exploration of real organizational practices, employee perspectives, and service values.

Semi-structured interviews were conducted, each lasting approximately 30 to 45 minutes, and were transcribed verbatim. Interviews took place in a quiet and comfortable workplace setting to encourage openness and reflection. Participants were informed about the purpose of the study, and confidentiality and anonymity were assured. All responses were treated respectfully and analyzed systematically to identify recurring themes and shared meanings.

The interview guide addressed three core areas: (1) employees' perceptions of human-centered service in boutique hotels; (2) current and potential uses of technology and artificial intelligence in daily operations; and (3) perceived boundaries between automated systems and human interaction. Particular attention was given to moments of emotional connection, personalized gestures, and guest engagement, as these dimensions reflect the essence of boutique hospitality.

Data were analyzed using thematic analysis, allowing patterns across interviews to emerge through iterative coding and theme development. This approach prioritizes employees' firsthand experiences, recognizing staff as key actors in digital transformation. By foregrounding their perspectives, the study seeks to develop a grounded understanding of how AI is integrated into human-centered hospitality and how employees envision its future impact on service delivery.

All participants provided verbal informed consent prior to the interviews. To ensure maximum privacy and strictly adhere to double-anonymized peer-review standards, pseudonyms have been assigned to all participants. These false names are used throughout the study to protect the professional identities and institutional affiliations of the interviewees, while maintaining the transparency and authenticity of the qualitative reporting.

a) First Interview

In order to understand employees' perception of the relationship between the relational service and the use of technology and artificial intelligence in the context of boutique hotels, four interviews were carried out with employees at Hotel da Oliveira. The interviews covered different operational areas, namely Food & Beverage (F&B) and Reception, allowing a more comprehensive view of practices and experiences in direct contact with guests.

This first interview corresponds to the testimony of Luísa, an employee in the F&B area, who shares her perspective on the style of service, the importance of human interaction and the role of technology in her day-to-day professional life.

1. How would you describe the service style in the F&B area? More personalized, more efficient, or a mix of both?

The service style used in the F&B area is characterized by a strong focus on personalization, placing the guest at the center of the experience. This is reflected in attention to detail, adaptation to individual preferences and restrictions, and the creation of a close, attentive, and caring service.

2. At which moments do you feel the human touch makes the biggest difference for visitors?

I believe the human touch is particularly relevant during moments of direct interaction with the guest, such as the welcome, guidance throughout the dining experience, and personalized recommendations. Empathy, the ability to interpret unspoken needs, and the creation of a relationship of trust are elements that contribute significantly to a distinctive and memorable experience.

3. Do you already use any type of technology or AI in your work (e.g., reservation systems, smart POS, chatbots, etc.)?

Yes, technological evolution, specifically artificial intelligence, has been an important asset in optimizing time spent on operational and administrative tasks. Its application in processes such as translation, inventory organization and control, and other support tasks enables more efficient management of time and technical and human resources.

4. In which F&B tasks do you think AI could help without compromising service quality?

AI can effectively support backstage F&B tasks, namely in the design of marketing campaigns, the creation of layouts and communication materials, the translation and updating of menus, research and data analysis, and the resolution of procedural or technical issues. These applications contribute to improved internal performance, promoting proactivity without negatively impacting the guest experience.

5. And in which tasks do you think it should not replace human contact? Why?

Artificial intelligence should not replace human contact at any stage of direct interaction with the guest. The human factor is essential for building relationships, reading the guest's emotional cues, and delivering a genuine, empathetic, and flexible service. These aspects are key to guest satisfaction and the creation of unique and memorable experiences, ensuring the development of a positive bond with the customer.

6. Do you think boutique hotel guests expect more human interaction than technological interaction?

Yes. I believe that boutique hotel guests tend to value closer and more personalized human interaction. These establishments are often associated with intimate and welcoming environments, where human contact plays a central role in creating differentiated experiences and reinforcing the perception of exclusivity and individual care.

7. In your opinion, can AI contribute to a more personalized service, or does it end up making it impersonal?

AI can contribute to a more personalized service when used as a support tool for the team, enabling better organization and planning and freeing up time for more attentive, guest-focused service. However, excessive or inappropriate use in direct interactions may result in an impersonal experience, compromising authenticity and the emotional connection with the guest.

8. If AI were used more extensively, how do you think it would change your day-to-day work? Would employees need new skills? Should the company provide training?

I believe that greater integration of AI into daily operations would help simplify and optimize existing tasks, making processes more agile and efficient. While some adaptation of existing skills would be necessary, continuous training provided by the company is essential to ensure conscious, ethical use aligned with service objectives.

9. What do you think about using guest data for AI-driven personalization?

The use of guest data for AI-driven personalization should be approached with caution. It is a sensitive issue that raises concerns related to privacy, data protection, and transparency. In this context, such practices may be negatively perceived by guests, potentially affecting trust and the relationship with the brand. Therefore, its use should only take place after clear and transparent communication about the process and its purpose.

b) Second Interview

The second interview was conducted with Margarida, a front desk receptionist at Hotel da Oliveira. With extensive experience in high-end hospitality, Margarida brings a strong human-centered approach to guest service, combining professionalism, cultural awareness, and personalized attention in her daily work.

Throughout the interview, she shares her perspective on the importance of human interaction in hospitality, the role of technology and artificial intelligence in supporting operational efficiency, and the irreplaceable value of empathy, care, and emotional connection in delivering memorable guest experiences, particularly within the luxury and boutique hotel segment.

1. Could you briefly introduce yourself and talk a little about the hotel and your role at the front desk?

I am formally trained in Hospitality Management, with 20 years of experience in high-end hospitality at renowned establishments in Brazil. I immigrated to Portugal a few months ago and am currently working as a Front Desk Receptionist at Hotel da Oliveira, a boutique hotel located in the heart of the historic city center of Guimarães.

In addition to the administrative duties of the department, my role includes performing check-ins and check-outs, as well as welcoming, assisting, and engaging with guests in a warm and personalized manner. I also provide support by offering recommendations and information about the city and its historical attractions.

2. What do you enjoy most about daily contact with guests?

The opportunity to meet a wide variety of people, learn about their stories and different cultures, and the fascinating chance to communicate in multiple languages.

3. What technologies do you currently use in your work (reservation software, CRM, chatbots, PMS, etc.)?

The hotel's operating system, in this case NEW HOTEL, Outlook for email communication, and booking platforms such as Booking.com, Expedia, and GDS.

4. Do you already use (or have you seen being used) any AI tools in the hotel? For what purposes?

Yes. This tool assists in drafting texts using appropriate and relevant wording, focusing on objectivity and courtesy when communicating with guests in multiple languages.

5. In which situations do you believe AI truly helps your work?

(e.g., speed, automation, error reduction, better organization, responses to simple questions)

I believe it helps optimize tasks that would otherwise require more time, such as the examples mentioned above.

6. Are you concerned that AI might replace some functions of your job? Why?

No, I do not have this concern, given the niche of hospitality in which I have specialized. I do not believe that a guest staying at a high-end hotel would prefer interacting with a machine rather than being welcomed and assisted by a human being.

7. In which situations do you feel that technology can distance guests rather than bring them closer?

When it does not function properly. Additionally, machines are unable to express feelings such as empathy, closeness, and the development of a friendly relationship with the guest.

8. For you, what does "human touch" mean in hospitality?

It represents the very essence of hospitality: listening, caring, giving attention, affection, and a warm welcome.

9. Can you share an example in which a human gesture made a difference for a guest?

On one occasion, at a hotel where I previously worked, a newlywed couple was scheduled to check in late at night after their wedding ceremony and reception. As other wedding guests were also staying at the hotel, I asked one of them to send us a photo of the couple taken during the wedding. The photo was printed in high resolution, placed in an elegant frame, and left in the couple's room as a gift.

When they arrived, they were pleasantly surprised, as they never expected to find a photo of themselves already married so quickly. They expressed that the gesture created a lasting emotional memory of the most important day of their lives. This became evident when the same couple chose to celebrate their wedding anniversary at the hotel year after year.

10. Do you notice whether guests value speed and autonomy more, or personal attention and closeness?

This depends on the guest's profile. Business travelers tend to value speed and autonomy, while leisure or tourism guests generally value personal attention and closeness.

11. How do you view the issue of guest data and privacy when using AI?

It is extremely dangerous. AI is evolving at an alarming pace. Videos, images, texts, and audio are being generated so convincingly that it is becoming increasingly difficult to distinguish what is real from what is not.

There are already reports of machines refusing to shut down despite human commands, and machines creating their own language to communicate with each other. AI can expose sensitive guest information, such as home addresses, contact numbers, and credit card details, on dark web platforms, leaving individuals vulnerable to scams, fraud, and various other cybercrimes.

12. If you could give advice to those implementing technology in hotels, what would it be?

Do so with discernment, and always work alongside a hospitality consultant who truly understands the operational reality on the other side.

c) Third Interview

This interview was conducted with Diana, a professional working in the Food and Beverage department at Hotel da Oliveira, a boutique hotel known for its personalized approach to hospitality. The purpose of this interview is to explore her perspectives on guest interaction, service personalization, and the role of technology, particularly artificial intelligence, in F&B operations. Drawing on her practical experience, Diana reflects on the importance of human connection in hospitality, the distinctive characteristics of boutique hotel service, and the potential impact of technological tools on daily workflows and guest experience. Her insights provide valuable qualitative data for understanding how personalized service is maintained in smaller hospitality settings while adapting to emerging digital innovations.

1. How would you describe your daily relationship with guests in the F&B service?

My daily relationship with guests is primarily based on closeness and attention to detail. I seek to understand their preferences, mood, and the type of experience they are looking for, in order to adapt the service to each individual. In a boutique hotel, interaction is more direct and personal, which facilitates the development of trust and rapport.

2. In your opinion, what most differentiates F&B service in a boutique hotel compared to larger hotels?

The main difference lies in personalization. In a boutique hotel, the smaller number of guests allows for more attentive, flexible, and customized service. The approach tends to be less standardized and more focused on the individual experience, creating a warmer and more exclusive atmosphere.

3. Can you identify specific situations in which your personal attitude or sensitivity improved a guest's experience?

For instance, there have been occasions when I noticed a guest was celebrating a special event and, without prior request, arranged a small gesture such as a dessert with a message or simple table decoration. These details often pleasantly surprise guests and help create lasting memories.

4. Do you feel that pressure for efficiency and speed can sometimes conflict with more human and personalized service?

Yes, at certain times this conflict can arise, particularly during busy periods. However, I believe that with good organization and a strong team, it is possible to maintain efficiency without losing the human element. Small gestures, such as a smile or brief conversation, require little time but make a significant difference.

5. Do you think technology can free up time for closer customer interaction? Why?

Yes, when properly implemented, technology can automate repetitive tasks such as registrations, orders, or payments, allowing staff to devote more time to guest interaction. This contributes to a more personalized and attentive service.

6. In which specific F&B tasks do you believe artificial intelligence could be useful without interfering with service authenticity?

AI could be useful in reservation management, consumption forecasting, stock control, menu suggestions based on guest preferences, and staff scheduling. These tasks are primarily operational and do not directly affect human interaction, which is what gives authenticity to the service.

7. Do you believe human presence is absolutely irreplaceable?

Yes, especially in the hospitality sector. Empathy, emotional awareness, and the ability to create genuine connections with guests are human qualities that are difficult for machines to replicate. Technology can support these processes, but not replace the human factor.

8. From your perspective, do guests value small human gestures more or fast technological solutions during their meal?

In most cases, guests value small human gestures—such as attentiveness, friendliness, and attention to detail—more highly. However, they also appreciate technological solutions when these streamline service and reduce unnecessary waiting times.

9. How would you feel if the hotel adopted more AI tools in F&B service? Do you think it would change the way you work?

I would view this positively, provided technology is used to support work rather than replace human contact. It would likely modify certain processes and routines, making operations more efficient, but the essence of service would still depend on guest relationships.

10. Do you consider it important to receive specific training to deal with new technologies and AI? What type of training would be most appropriate?

Yes, this is very important. Training should be practical and focused on the tools used by the hotel, explaining how to make the most of technology in daily operations. It would also be beneficial to include basic concepts of AI and data protection to ensure responsible use.

11. In your opinion, to what extent can guest data collection be used to personalize service without compromising privacy?

Data collection can be useful for service personalization, provided it is conducted transparently and with guest consent. The use of such information should be limited to what is strictly necessary to enhance the guest experience, while always respecting privacy and data protection regulations.

d) Fourth Interview

This final interview was conducted with Daniela, a receptionist with extensive experience in boutique guest relations. Her insights provide a crucial bridge between high-level operational management and the emotional labor required in luxury hospitality.

1. Could you talk a little bit about your work at the reception?

Reception is much more than what people see on the surface. Of course, we handle the standard tasks: check-ins, check-outs, managing emails, and phone calls. But the real magic happens 'behind the curtain.' We spend hours preparing arrivals in a deeply personalized way. We act as concierges, trip planners, and local guides, ensuring that every guest has a tailored itinerary, whether it's a hard-to-get restaurant reservation or a secret spot in Guimarães that isn't in the guidebooks.

2. What are the biggest challenges you face in your day-to-day guest service?

The nuances of communication are our biggest challenge. We are not robots; we are human, and sometimes a single word or a tone of voice can be misinterpreted depending on the guest's culture or mood. However, the beauty of this job is that through empathy and active listening, I cannot recall a single conflict that we weren't able to resolve through genuine human dialogue.

3. What digital tools do you consider indispensable for your work?

As a traditional boutique hotel, our Property Management System (PMS) is the heart of the operation. We also rely on the GDS (Global Distribution System) and advanced channel managers to synchronize our presence across all platforms. These tools are the invisible backbone that allows us to focus on the person standing in front of us.

4. Has technology improved service efficiency or the guest experience more?

For the staff, it is unquestionably an efficiency booster. It has virtually eliminated overbooking errors because the motor works in real-time with all platforms. For the guests, the impact is more subtle. They might not notice the software, but they appreciate the speed, for instance, being able to reach us instantly via WhatsApp creates a sense of security and modern convenience without breaking the boutique charm.

5. Have you ever had to resolve a crisis using only empathy when technology failed?

Yes, absolutely! We once experienced a general blackout in Portugal. We were left without light, without computers, and without access to our digital database. We had to run the entire hotel manually. In that moment, technology was useless, but our humanity saved the day.

6. Do you think guests notice when service is too automated?

They notice it instantly. The guests who choose a boutique hotel are specifically looking for personalization, affection, and the feeling that we are spending our most valuable resource, time, on them. If you automate that, you lose the soul of the hotel.

7. Which human skills will never be replaced by AI in hospitality?

AI can certainly take over the 'Back Office', the repetitive data entry and logistics. But in the front line, we are irreplaceable.

8. How do you imagine the future of the receptionist profession with AI?

The future of the profession isn't about fighting technology, but using it as a partner so that we can be more human than ever before.

4. RESULTS AND DISCUSSIONS

The qualitative interviews conducted with employees from Food & Beverage and Front Desk departments at Hotel da Oliveira bring valued insight into how artificial intelligence is perceived within a boutique hospitality context and how it interacts with the concept of human-centered service. Across all four interviews, a steady theme emerges: while technology is recognized as a useful operational tool, human interaction remains the core element of guest experience.

Participants solidly emphasized personalization, empathy, and emotional connection as defining characteristics of boutique hospitality. Diana and Luísa highlighted attention to detail, flexibility, and the ability to read guests' moods and preferences as fundamental to service delivery. Similarly, Margarida described human touch as the essence of hospitality itself, encompassing listening, care, affection, and warmth. Daniela reinforced this by describing the *"magic"* of the front desk as something that happens behind the curtains, where deep personalization converts a standard stay into a tailored itinerary. These findings reinforce existing literature suggesting that boutique hotels rely heavily on relational value and emotional labor as competitive advantages (Lashley, 2008; Gilmore & Pine, 2007).

All interviewees acknowledged the benefits of technology and AI in backstage and administrative tasks. AI was observed positively when applied to reservations, inventory management, menu translations, marketing content, data analysis, and communication support. These tools were perceived as mechanisms that free up time for employees to engage more meaningfully with guests, supporting the argument that AI functions best as an augmentation tool rather than a replacement for human service (Rai et al., 2019; Vargo & Lusch, 2008).

However, participants expressed strong resistance to AI replacing direct guest interaction. Emotional intelligence, empathy, and relationship-building were repeatedly described as unique human qualities. Both Diana and Luísa stressed that AI should never substitute face-to-face engagement, particularly during welcoming moments, personalized recommendations, and emotionally sensitive situations. Margarida reinforced this view by sharing a personal story in which a small human gesture created a lasting emotional bond with guests, demonstrating how authentic interactions contribute to loyalty and long-term relationships, while Daniela shared a critical moment where a total technological failure forced the team to rely exclusively on empathy and manual communication to ensure guest comfort. This specific instance proves that while technology is a "plus," human empathy is the only true "must-have" in boutique hospitality.

Furthermore, significant theme concerns efficiency versus humanization. While employees recognized occasional tension between operational speed and personalized service, especially during peak periods, they also accentuated that small gestures such as smiles, brief conversations, and thoughtful details can preserve humanity even in high-pressure environments.

Ethical concerns surrounding data privacy were also prominent. Interviewees expressed caution concerning the collection and use of guest data for AI-driven personalization. Transparency, consent, and responsible data usage were considered essential to maintaining trust. Margarida, in particular, voiced concerns about cybersecurity risks and the misuse of sensitive guest information, resounding broader academic discussions on privacy, algorithmic risk, and digital ethics (Floridi, 2020; Cavoukian, 2011).

Notably, none of the participants expressed fear of being replaced by AI. In its place, they view technology as supportive when applied responsibly. Training was identified as crucial, with emphasis on practical instruction, ethical awareness, and data protection. Employees expressed willingness to adapt their skills, provided organizations invest in continuous learning.

Overall, the interviews prove that boutique hotel employees perceive AI as valuable primarily in operational contexts, while strongly defending the centrality of interpersonal engagement in guest-facing services. The findings settle that guests in boutique settings are believed to rank emotional connection and personalized attention over technological autonomy, although practical automation is appreciated when it reduces waiting times and improves service flow.

These results align with current research indicating that hospitality value is co-created through human interaction and that AI should serve as an invisible support mechanism rather than a visible replacement for personal service (Ivanov & Webster, 2019; Solnet et al., 2019). In boutique hotels such as Hotel da Oliveira, maintaining authenticity, emotional engagement, and relational depth remains fundamental to brand identity.

Beyond operational efficiency, the interviews reveal a deeper organizational philosophy centered on relational service. Employees perceive AI as beneficial only when it strengthens their capacity to engage emotionally with guests. This aligns with service-dominant logic, which emphasizes value co-creation through human interaction rather than technological output (Vargo & Lusch, 2008).

Particularly, participants framed AI as an invisible infrastructure rather than a visible service agent. This viewpoint reflects Ivanov and Webster's (2019) argument that guest resistance rises when technology replaces interpersonal encounters. At Hotel da Oliveira, technology is accepted when it remains backstage, reinforcing rather than redefining service identity.

The results also highlight the symbolic role of small gestures. Personalized surprises, attentive listening, and natural acts of care, that create emotional memories, which creates loyalty, an outcome unachievable through algorithmic personalization alone. This supports Mattila's (2001) assertion that emotional bonds mitigate service failures and strengthen long-term relationships.

Employees expressed confidence in adapting to technological change, providing training and ethical guidelines are offered. This demonstrates that workforce acceptance of AI is contingent upon organizational investment in human capital, reinforcing the call for people-centered innovation strategies (Baum et al., 2016).

Beyond operational considerations, the interviews disclose how employees actively construct professional identity through relational service practices. Participants repeatedly framed hospitality not just as a technical occupation, but as an emotional vocation centered on care, attentiveness, and personal connection. Front-office work was described as meaningful precisely because of its interpersonal nature, highlighting how employees derive professional fulfillment from creating memorable guest experiences.

The presence of artificial intelligence redesigns this identity by reallocating responsibilities rather than eliminating them. As routine administrative tasks become automated, employees increasingly occupy roles that emphasize emotional intelligence, creativity, and situational awareness. This shift places staff as custodians of authenticity, responsible for maintaining the boutique hotel's human character while technology supports operational efficiency.

Importantly, interviewees demonstrated agency in responding to digital change. Rather than expressing vulnerability, they articulated a sense of ownership over service quality, viewing AI as a tool that can improve their capacity to engage with guests more deeply. This perspective reflects a broader transformation in hospitality work, where value creation moves from standardized procedures toward personalized emotional encounters.

These findings suggest that successful AI integration depends not only on technological capability but also on how employees understand and internalize their evolving roles. When organizations recognize interpersonal skills as strategic assets and provide appropriate training, technology develops an enabler of meaningful work rather than a source of alienation. In boutique hospitality, preserving employee identity as relational service providers remains essential for sustaining authentic guest experiences.

5. CONCLUSION

The current analysis investigates the impact of artificial intelligence (AI) on human-centered service within boutique hotels, using Hotel da Oliveira as a case study. Through comprehensive interviews with staff from the Front Office and Food & Beverage departments, the study examines how AI manifests in everyday operations.

The findings indicate that while AI is regarded as a beneficial operational resource, it is not perceived as a whole substitute for authentic human connection. Participants emphasized the importance of empathy, emotional intelligence, attentiveness, and personal interaction as essential components of boutique hospitality. These attributes significantly influence guest experiences.

AI functions most effectively when it supports backend operations and administrative tasks such as reservations management, inventory organization, menu translation, and data processing. By alleviating the load of repetitive tasks, this technology allows staff members to donate more time to relational and experiential aspects of their roles. This aligns with the emerging discourse advocating for AI to assist rather than displace human employment.

Ethical considerations were prominently highlighted, particularly regarding guest data privacy, transparency, and the complexities of cybersecurity. Employees expressed a need for responsible data management practices, including obtaining genuine consent from patrons and adhering to legal standards to maintain trust and safeguard the brand. Additionally, participants stressed the imperative of continuous training to ensure ethical AI utilization in conjunction with existing operational frameworks.

Remarkably, none of the interviewees expressed apprehension about potential job displacement by technology. Instead, there was a discernible enthusiasm for innovation, provided that human roles remain central and that organizations commit to enhancing the skills of their workforce. This suggests that the acceptance of AI among staff hinges on their perception of its role as a supportive rather than a threatening presence.

Practically, this study recommends that hotels adopt a hybrid service model in which AI operates behind the scenes to enhance efficiencies while conserving meaningful emotional interactions with guests. Managers are encouraged to prioritize employee training, implement privacy-conscious design principles, and select technologies that align with their organizational values and desired brand image.

5.1 Limitations of the Study

This research provides a valuable exploration of the interaction between artificial intelligence and human interaction within the context of boutique hotels; however, several limitations warrant acknowledgment.

Firstly, the findings are derived from a limited sample focused solely on a single boutique hotel. While case studies can yield profound insights, the restricted scope raises questions regarding the applicability of these results to diverse locations and varying workplace cultures. Boutique hotels display considerable variation in size, service philosophy, and technological integration, suggesting that the perspectives of employees in one establishment may not fully embody the broader industry landscape.

Secondly, the research mainly captures the perceptions of employees, who are critically important to understanding service dynamics and the role of emotions. However, the absence of guest feedback constrains the analysis by not allowing for an exploration of the customer perspective. Improved feedback mechanisms could illuminate the authenticity of the service experience, as well as reveal guest sentiments towards the technological tools utilized.

Thirdly, the study highlights the promising stages of AI implementation at this particular hotel. Given the quick evolution of technology, shifts in employee perspectives, service protocols, and operational practices are likely to occur. Therefore, the thematic analysis reveals a snapshot in time rather than a comprehensive examination of the ongoing interaction between humans and AI in the hospitality sector.

Furthermore, the interpretation of qualitative data presents another limitation. The analysis relies heavily on subjective judgment during the coding and thematic development processes. While efforts were made to remain true to participant accounts, alternative interpretations of the data are always possible. Future research may enhance analytical rigor by employing different methods, integrating observational data or metrics related to guest satisfaction.

Finally, resource constraints impacted the research's scope. Expanding the sample size or incorporating numerous boutique hotels would facilitate more robust comparative insights and bolster the real-world applicability of the conclusions drawn

Despite these limitations, this study contributes significant exploratory knowledge to an emerging area of inquiry. It highlights the often-overlooked perspectives of hotel employees within technology-centric hospitality research, thereby establishing a foundation for subsequent empirical investigations. This chapter offers a theoretical contribution, reinforcing hospitality literature by advocating for service-dominant logic. It emphasizes that value creation is rooted in human interactions, while positioning AI as an active resource that complements, rather than supplants, service dynamics. By providing empirical support for discussions on hybrid human-AI service models, particularly within boutique environments where authentic emotional engagement is paramount, this research advances the discourse on the future of hospitality services.

5.2 Directions for Future Research

Future research endeavors have the potential to significantly enhance this study. Adopting a multi-location framework that encompasses various boutique hotels would facilitate comparative analyses and broaden the applicability of findings. Employing quantitative methodologies, and potentially mixed-method approaches, could enable a thorough examination of the relationships between AI implementation, employee satisfaction, guest loyalty, and service quality.

Furthermore, incorporating guest perspectives would harvest valuable insights into how technological tools influence perceptions of authenticity and foster emotional connections. Longitudinal studies could be particularly beneficial in tracking evolving perceptions of AI as these systems become increasingly integrated within the hospitality sector.

Moreover, further investigation could focus on leadership strategies, organizational cultures, and change management practices that support the seamless integration of human-AI interactions. Analyzing cross-cultural differences in guest expectations and technology acceptance would also enrich our understanding of AI's role within diverse global hospitality contexts.

5.3 Theoretical Contribution

This chapter holds significant relevance for scholars in the field of hospitality, as it clarifies the relationship between human interaction and computer technology in enhancing guest experiences.

It emphasizes the value generated through interpersonal interactions and illustrates how technology can facilitate these interactions, rather than serve as a replacement for human connection.

Furthermore, it argues that technology should be viewed as a tool that fosters relationships among individuals. This viewpoint is particularly salient in the context of small hotels, where guests often seek authentic experiences and staff must possess a nuanced understanding of emotional intelligence. Ultimately, this work underscores the premise that effective hospitality entails a collaborative effort between humans and technology, thereby elevating the guest experience.

5.4 Final Remarks

In conclusion, this study argues that the future of boutique hospitality should not revolve solely around adopting new technologies. Rather, the intelligent integration of artificial intelligence is paramount. When implemented effectively, AI can improve operational efficiency while enabling staff to prioritize empathy, creativity, and personal interactions. The essence of boutique hotels lies in emotion, trust, and meaning, qualities that technology cannot replicate.

By centering service delivery around human connection and leveraging AI as a supportive tool, boutique hotels can preserve their unique atmosphere while embracing innovative ideas. Eventually, successful hospitality in the digital era relies not on the sophistication of technology but on its ability to augment, rather than detract from, the human experience.

From a management perspective, this study underlines the necessity for a people-first strategy. Managers should invest in AI solutions that improve internal operations while preserving the quality of human service. Tools such as predictive analytics, automated systems, and customer relationship management platforms can enable workflows without replacing human workers.

Training must extend beyond technological proficiency to include ethical considerations, emotional intelligence, and data literacy. Employees should develop a comprehensive understanding of both the capabilities and limitations of AI, ensuring that they do not become overly dependent on it.

Leadership plays a critical role in fostering an organizational culture that embraces these changes. Open communication regarding technological objectives, along with the encouragement of employee input and continuous feedback, can cultivate trust and engage staff effectively.

Furthermore, it is essential for managers to implement privacy-focused designs and robust cybersecurity measures to safeguard guest data and protect the integrity of the brand. At an industry level, regulatory bodies should establish hospitality-specific guidelines for the ethical use of AI, addressing data management, algorithmic processes, and the wellbeing of employees. Support for smaller and boutique hotels, including financial assistance, training, and technological resources, is vital to ensure equity within the sector.

Furthermore, key stakeholders in tourism should consider hybrid service models that maintain authenticity and cultural relevance while progressing towards technological advancement, ensuring that these innovations align with sustainable travel objectives.

Beyond routine activities, the findings illustrate how employees integrate professional roles into their identities through personalized service. Participants frequently emphasized that hospitality is an emotional endeavor rooted in care and attention, akin to forming genuine connections. This aligns with Hochschild's concept of emotional labor, where frontline staff invest emotional effort to enhance guest experiences.

The adoption of AI alters the dynamics of these emotional interactions. Automation eases some workload, yet there is an increased expectation for highly personalized service. Therefore, employees become adept at managing emotions, delivering authentic interactions while technology manages operational tasks. This dual responsibility reflects Huang's observations.

Notably, the staff at Hotel da Oliveira demonstrated action, rather than vulnerability, in response to technological changes. They did not perceive AI as a threat to their employment; rather, they viewed it as a supportive tool when implemented appropriately, which can be viewed as successful human-AI integration, that requires human judgment at its core (Rai et al., 2019).

The interviews further reveal how minor human actions generate symbolic value beyond mere functionality. Custom desserts, photographs, and attentive listening foster emotional connections, thereby enhancing loyalty. This reflects the service-dominant logic, where value is derived from shared experiences rather than standardized outcomes (Vargo & Lusch, 2008). Moreover, employee narratives demonstrate sensitivity to guest autonomy. While automation is welcomed, guests must have the option to engage with technology. Business travelers may prioritize efficiency, whereas leisure travelers often seek emotional engagement. This flexibility shapes the service model of boutique hospitality. AI integration does not diminish the emotional connection. The outcome depends on an organization's intentions. When technology remains in the background and complements relationships, it enhances the meaning of service.

From a methodological perspective, this research underlines the importance of qualitative methods in understanding technological transformations in people-centric industries. Semi-structured interviews eased an in-depth exploration of workers' perspectives, emotional responses, and ethical considerations that quantitative methods may not capture. It is recommended that future hospitality studies continue to prioritize interpretive methods when examining AI implementation, particularly in service settings where sense, identity, and emotion are crucial.

Mixed methodologies could reinforce empirical insights by linking employee narratives to client satisfaction metrics, operational performance data, and longitudinal analyses. Such approaches would allow researchers to document both subjective experiences and the tangible outcomes of AI integration.

In conclusion, this study emphasizes that artificial intelligence is not redefining hospitality; rather, it is the people who shape it. Technology attends to intensify existing organizational values. Small hotels that prioritize compassion, authenticity, and human connection can leverage AI to enhance, rather than diminish, guest experiences. Thus, innovation is not a departure from tradition but a continuation of hospitality's enduring commitment to care.

REFERENCES

Aggett, M. (2007). What has influenced growth in the UK's boutique hotel sector? *International Journal of Contemporary Hospitality Management*, *19*(2), 169–177. DOI: 10.1108/09596110710729274

Baum, T., Kralj, A., Robinson, R. N. S., & Solnet, D. J. (2016). Tourism workforce research: A review, taxonomy and agenda. *Annals of Tourism Research*, *60*, 1–22. DOI: 10.1016/j.annals.2016.04.003

Bisoi, S., Roy, M., & Samal, A. (2020). Impact of Artificial Intelligence in the Hospitality Industry. *International Journal of Advanced Science and Technology.*, *29*, 4265–4276.

Booking.com. (s.d.). Hotel da Oliveira — Guimarães, PT [Página de hotel]. https://www.booking.com/hotel/pt/da-oliveira.en-gb.html

Citak, J., Owoc, M. L., & Weichbroth, P. (2021). A note on the applications of artificial intelligence in the hospitality industry: Preliminary results of a survey. *Procedia Computer Science*, *192*, 4552–4559. DOI: 10.1016/j.procs.2021.09.233

Efe, R., & Koleva, I. (Eds.). (2018). *Recent advances in social sciences*. Cambridge Scholars Publishing.

Etiubon, R. U., & Etiubon, A. H. (2023). Replacement of humans in the classroom by artificial intelligence: A rhetoric. *Asian Journal of Educational Technology*, *2*(1), 12–21. DOI: 10.53402/ajet.v2i1.185

Floridi, L. (2020). *The ethics of artificial intelligence*. Oxford University Press.

Gilmore, J. H., & Pine, B. J. (2007). *Authenticity: What Consumers Really Want*. Harvard Business School Press.

Hochschild, A. (2012). The Managed Heart: Commercialization of Human Feeling. .DOI: 10.1525/9780520951853

Hotel da Oliveira. (s.d.). Política de qualidade e ambiente. Hotel da Oliveira. https://www.hoteldaoliveira.com/pt/quality-policy

Hotel da Oliveira. (s.d.). Sobre nós. Hotel da Oliveira. https://www.hoteldaoliveira.com/pt/sobre-nos

Huang, M.-H., Rust, R., & Maksimovic, V. (2019). The Feeling Economy: Managing in the Next Generation of Artificial Intelligence (AI). *California Management Review*, *61*(4), 000812561986343. DOI: 10.1177/0008125619863436

Ivanov, S., & Webster, C. (2019). Perceived Appropriateness and Intention to Use Service Robots in Tourism: *Proceedings of the International Conference in Nicosia*, Cyprus, January 30–February 1, 2019. DOI: 10.1007/978-3-030-05940-8_19

James, M. (2026, January). AI as an augmentation tool, not a replacement: Preserving human insight in business intelligence and experimentation.

Kabadayi, S., Ali, F., Choi, H., Joosten, H., & Lu, C. (2019). Smart service experience in hospitality and tourism services: A conceptualization and future research agenda. *Journal of Service Management*, *30*(3), 326–348. DOI: 10.1108/JOSM-11-2018-0377

Lashley, C. (2008). Studying hospitality: Insights from social sciences. *Scandinavian Journal of Hospitality and Tourism*, *8*(1), 69–84. DOI: 10.1080/15022250701880745

Lu, L., Cai, R., & Gursoy, D. (2019). Developing and validating a service robot integration willingness scale. *International Journal of Hospitality Management*, *80*, 36–51. DOI: 10.1016/j.ijhm.2019.01.005

Makarem, S. C., Mudambi, S. M., & Podoshen, J. S. (2009). Satisfaction in technology-enabled service encounters. *Journal of Services Marketing*, *23*(3), 134–144. DOI: 10.1108/08876040910955143

Mattila, A. S. (2001). The impact of relationship type on customer loyalty in a context of service failures. [V]. *Journal of Service Research*, *4*(2), 91–101. DOI: 10.1177/109467050142002

Mehrabi, N., Morstatter, F., Saxena, N., Lerman, K., & Galstyan, A. (2022). A survey on bias and fairness in machine learning (arXiv:1908.09635v3). arXiv. https://arxiv.org/abs/1908.09635

Nikitina, I., & Ishchenko, T. (2024). The impact of AI on teachers: Support or replacement? *Scientific Journal of Polonia University*, *65*(4), 93–99. Advance online publication. DOI: 10.23856/6511

Pine, I. I. B., & Gilmore, J. H. (1999). The experience economy (The next competitive battleground in the global marketplace). *Museum News.*, *78*, 45–48.

Rai, Arun & Constantinides, Panos & Sarker, Saonee. (2019). Next-Generation Digital Platforms: Toward Human-AI Hybrids.

Rösch, P. (2020). Human-centric service co-innovation in hospitality: A practice-based view (Master's thesis, Master's Programme in Innovation & Global Sustainable Development, Lund University).

Solnet, D., Subramony, M., Ford, R. C., Golubovskaya, M., Kang, H. J. A., & Hancer, M. (2019). Leveraging human touch in service interactions: Lessons from hospitality. *Journal of Service Management*, *30*(3), 392–409. DOI: 10.1108/JOSM-12-2018-0380

Syed, S. A. (2024)... *THE ROLE OF AI IN ALLEVIATING LONELINESS AMONG ADULTS IN THE UNITED STATES.*, *08*, 404–421. DOI: 10.5281/zenodo.15222179

Vargo, S. L., & Lusch, R. F. (2008). Service-dominant logic: Continuing the evolution. *Journal of the Academy of Marketing Science*, *36*(1), 1–10. DOI: 10.1007/s11747-007-0069-6

Wang, K., Kong, H., Xiao, H., Bu, N., & Qiu, X. (2026). From novelty to necessity: Evolving consumer expectations and experiences in human-technology interactions. *Journal of Hospitality Marketing & Management*, *35*(1), 96–119. DOI: 10.1080/19368623.2025.2549982

Zahidi, F., Kaluvilla, B. B., & Mulla, T. (2024). Embracing the new era: Artificial intelligence and its multifaceted impact on the hospitality industry. *Journal of Open Innovation*, *10*(4), 100390. Advance online publication. DOI: 10.1016/j.joitmc.2024.100390

Sohn, D., [illegible]

Syed, S. A. (2020). [illegible]

Vargo, S. L., & Lusch, R. F. (2008). Service-dominant logic: Continuing the evolution. *Journal of the Academy of Marketing Science*, 36(1), 1–10. Doi:10.1007/s11747-007-0069-6

Wang, [illegible] Xiao, H., Fan, N., & Du, [illegible] (2019). [illegible] consumer expectations and [illegible] *Journal of Hospitality Marketing & Management*, [illegible] Doi:10.1080/19368623.[illegible]

Zaki, [illegible] (2024). [illegible] and its [illegible] impact on the hospitality industry. [illegible] 103900. Advance online publication. [illegible]

About the Contributors

Jorge Esparteiro Garcia is Assistant Professor at Polytechnic University of Viana do Castelo (IPVC) since 2005/2006. He is the Director of ADiT-Lab (Applied Digital Transformation Laboratory) Research Unit at IPVC. He is an Afilliated Researcher at INESC TEC in the Software Engineering area since 2015. He has a PhD in Informatics Engineering from Faculty of Engineering of University of Porto with a thesis titled "Requirements Change Management based on Web Usage Mining". He received his master degree in Informatics Engineering from the Faculty of Engineering of University of Porto (FEUP) and his bachelor's degree in Computer Science from Faculty of Scien ces of University of Porto (FCUP). His research interests are in the field of software engineering, web usage mining and requirements management.

Bruno Sousa (bsousa@ipca.pt) is Professor Coordenador of Marketing at Polytechnic University of Cavado and Ave (IPCA), Portugal and PhD in Marketing and Strategy in Universidade do Minho, Portugal. Head of Master Program - Tourism Management (IPCA) and Tourism Marketing Master. CiTUR research member. Bruno Sousa has published several chapters at IGI Global over the past 10 years, on topics of marketing, tourism and management. He has published in the Journal of Enterprising Communities, Tourism Management Perspectives, Current Issues in Tourism, Journal of Organizational Change Management, World Review of Entrepreneurship, Management and Sust. Development, among others.

Manuel José Serra da Fonseca holds a PhD in Information Sciences and has a professional background in marketing communications and higher education. He is currently an Associate Professor at the Polytechnic University of Viana do Castelo (Portugal) and serves as the Coordinator of the Digital Marketing Master's program at its Business School (ESCE-IPVC). As a researcher at UNIAG (Applied Management Research Unit) since 2014, he has contributed to multiple R&D projects and supervised numerous undergraduate and master's dissertations in

Communication and Business Sciences. His academic work includes publications in peer-reviewed journals, book chapters, and conference proceedings, along with active participation in national and international scientific conferences. He also collaborates as a reviewer for various academic journals. His research focuses on Social Sciences, particularly in Communication and Marketing Sciences. Key topics in his scientific production include attitude towards advertising and communication skills, consumer behavior, integrated marketing communication, social marketing, digital marketing, and organizational communication.

***

Rahmath Nisha is a dedicated professional with comprehensive, hands-on experience in Human Resource Management (HRM), having successfully managed the entire employee life cycle—from recruitment and onboarding to performance management and employee engagement. She holds an MBA in Human Resource Management, where she was recognized as a Gold Medalist and awarded the title of Best Outgoing Student. Her academic journey began with a Bachelor's degree in Electronics and Communication Engineering, showcasing her diverse educational foundation. Currently serving as an Assistant Professor, she combines industry expertise with academic insight to mentor and inspire the next generation of HR professionals.

A.K. Subramani is a distinguished academic with a PhD in Business Administration from Manonmaniam Sundaranar University, Tirunelveli, India. With 18 years of teaching experience, he has made significant contributions to the field of human resource management and organisational behaviour. He has an impressive publication record with 80 articles in international journals, including two papers in the ABDC-A category, eight in the ABDC-B category, three in the ABDC-C category, 30 in Scopus-indexed journals, and eight in Web of Science journals. He has served as a resource person for various training workshops on SPSS and AMOS software packages

Sasikala C.S is an Assistant Professor in the Department of Computer Science and Business Systems at Vel Tech Multi Tech Dr. Rangarajan Dr. Sakunthala Engineering College, Avadi, Chennai. She is dedicated to teaching, research, and mentoring students in the fields of computer science and emerging business technologies. Her academic interests include interdisciplinary applications of computing, with a focus on enhancing student learning and innovation.

Marina Chalupa holds a Master's degree in Marketing and a Bachelor's degree in Tourism Activities Management. She has professional experience in sales, customer service, event management, and hotel management assistance. Throughout her career, she has developed strong organizational, communication, and leadership skills in dynamic and customer-oriented environments. Marina has also authored two scientific articles that have been published, reflecting her interest in research and continuous professional development.

Patricia Dopico-Rodríguez Assistant Professor in the Department of Drawing at the University of Vigo, she holds a Doctorate in Fine Arts from the University of Vigo; a Bachelor of Fine Arts in Design and Audiovisual from the University of Vigo; a MA in Interactive Media from Goldsmiths College, University of London; a MA in Art and New Technologies: Theory of Electronic Art and Digital Multimedia Creation at the UEM; a Postgraduate degree in "Inter(media). Instability, Creation and Digital Culture" from the University of Vigo; she has an extraordinary end-of-studies award from the Autonomous Community of Galicia and a special mention in the end-of-career awards from the Ministry of Education. She was a predoctoral fellow from the Xunta de Galicia; and a scholarship from the Barrié de la Maza Foundation and the British Council for postgraduate courses. The thesis "The Power of Information: Art, Body and Postmodernity" analyzed the representation of the body in art during the period of postmodernity under the influence of new information technologies. For eighteen years she has combined her professional activity with university teaching. She began her career as an external lecturer in the Higher Studies in Fashion Design of Galicia degree at the University of Vigo, to later join the University Master's Degree in Design and Creative Direction in Fashion and the Department of Drawing as an associate professor. In this field, she also develops research activity as a member of the REMOSS Research Group of the University of Vigo and the Teaching Innovation Group in Design of the same university. In parallel to teaching, his professional career was mainly linked to private business, with extensive experience in the multinational fashion sector Sociedad Textil Lonia, where he worked in the areas of graphic design, communication and content creation. After a period as an independent professional, in which he collaborated with clients in the fashion, culture and food sectors, he joined the University of Vigo full-time, from where he continues his teaching and research activity. In the last year he led transfer projects between university and business with international reference brands such as Camper or Bimba y Lola, consolidating a trajectory that integrates academic experience, professional practice and collaboration with the business sector.

Paula Fernandes PhD in Economics and Management (2005), Professor of Management at the Polytechnic Institute of Bragança (IPB) - Portugal, since

December 1992. She is a researcher and Scientific Coordinator of UNIAG (Applied Management Research Unit, since 2013) and was a researcher at the Research Unit in Business Sciences (NECE-UBI, 2010-2017). She participated in 18 international and national R&D projects (7 as Responsible Researcher), supervised two PhD theses and several master students (over 145 master theses). She published more than 230 publications (121 with indexing to Scopus/WoS databases) in peer-reviewed journals, book chapters and proceedings, and has several communications at international scientific conferences. Best award scientific paper (10) in Marketing and Strategy, Tourism, Econometric Methods and Regional Analysis. She serves as a member of the Program Board and Organizing Committees for some Scientific Committees of International Conferences and has collaborated as a reviewer with several journals.

Manisha G is an Assistant Professor in the Department of Computer Science and Engineering at R.M.D Engineering College, Kavaraipettai, Tamil Nadu, India. She is dedicated to teaching and mentoring students while contributing to academic and research activities in computer science. Her areas of interest include emerging technologies and enhancing student learning through innovative approaches.

G. Premalatha is an Assistant Professor in Data Science and Business Systems at the School of Computing, Faculty of Engineering and Technology, SRM Institute of Science and Technology, Kattankulathur. She specializes in data science, analytics, and emerging computing technologies, contributing to both teaching and research activities. Her academic interests include machine learning, business intelligence, and data-driven decision-making, with a focus on innovative and practical applications.

Lakshay Goyal is an Assistant Professor at Pimpri Chinchwad College of Engineering & Research, Pune. Dedicated to academic excellence and student development, he brings a strong foundation in engineering education and a passion for teaching. With a focus on practical learning and innovative pedagogical approaches, Lakshay Goyal actively contributes to both academic instruction and departmental initiatives. His commitment to nurturing young minds and fostering a culture of continuous learning makes him a valuable asset to the institution.

Neema Gupta is an academic professional with over 19 years of experience in management education and research, currently serving as a Professor at Chandigarh University. With a PhD in Human Resource Management, she has held key roles such as PhD Coordinator and Journal Editor, and has successfully guided multiple PhD scholars. Dr. Gupta is a prolific author, having written comprehensive textbooks on Human Resource Management for Organisational Success (Vol. 1 & 2 – published under the publication of Palgrave Macmillan Springer Nature) and served as editor for edited books like Innovate to Integrate (Emerald, UK) and GIG Economy 2.0 (Peter Lang, Switzerland). With numerous Scopus-indexed publications and research awards, she continues to shape the academic landscape through her writing, & editorial leadership.

Dinesh M. G. is a faculty member at Easa College of Engineering and Technology, Coimbatore, Tamil Nadu. He specializes in engineering education and contributes to academic research, teaching, and student development. With a commitment to innovative learning, he actively engages in institutional growth and professional advancement.

María Pilar Martínez-Ruiz is Ph. D. in Economics and Business Administration, and currently Associate Professor at the Department of Marketing of the University of Castilla-La Mancha, Albacete (Spain). She has participated in different Conferences and Seminars worldwide, has written different book chapters and numerous research articles in prestigious journals such as European Journal of Marketing, International Journal of Market Research, Journal of the Operational Research Society and Decision Support Systems. Her main research lines are marketing communications, retailing, and product and service innovation.

Ricardo Martinez-Cañas is an Associate Professor in Business Management at Castilla-La Mancha University (Spain). His research interest are Social Capital; Science Parks; Business Ethics; Wine Tourism; Innovation; Pay Satisfaction; Ethical Leadership; Educational Research; Entrepreneurial Intention; Value Co-creation

P. Selvakumar currently serves as an Associate Professor in the Department of Science and Humanities at Nehru Institute of Technology, Coimbatore, Tamil Nadu, India. With a teaching career spanning over a decade, he previously held positions as an Assistant Professor in the Department of Science and Humanities at various engineering colleges in Coimbatore from 2011 to 2023. Dr. P. Selvakumar's primary area of academic and research interest is phytochemistry, where he has made substantial contributions. His research credentials include 30 journal publications, 14 patents, and 25 conference papers. He has actively promoted faculty and student development by organizing 5 Faculty Development Programs (FDPs) and completing 3 NPTEL courses along with 60 Coursera certifications. His dedication to student success is evident in his role as a committed mentor, consistently guiding and supporting his students academically and personally. Recognized for his excellence in teaching, Dr. P. Selvakumar has received numerous accolades, including Best Teacher Awards. He is also an active member of MISTE (The Indian Society for Technical Education) and continues to play a vital role in both acade

Leandro Ferreira Pereira is CEO and founder of WINNING Scientific Management. He has more than 18 years of experience in senior management positions in management consulting companies and university academic activity. With a degree in Management Informatics from the University of Minho and a PhD in Project Management from the Pontifical University of Salamanca, Leandro Pereira has in his curriculum several of professional and academic distinctions, among which, the best national manager award (from Best Team Leaders), the University Senate Award for having been the best student of the University and the National Prize "Youth and National Defense awarded by the Ministry of Defense". Currently, he divides his professional activity between management consulting, the academy, and advisory various entities, in particular, the Court of Auditors, and has supervisor of dozens of doctoral and master students.

Vinoth R is an academic professional in the Department of Computer Science and Engineering at R.M.K College of Engineering and Technology, Tamil Nadu, India. He is actively involved in teaching, research, and academic development, with interests in core and emerging areas of computer science. His work focuses on enhancing technical knowledge, innovation, and student learning through research-oriented approaches.

Vaishali Rahate is a distinguished academician, administrator, corporate trainer, and researcher currently serving as Professor in the Department of MBA at Datta Meghe Institute of Management Studies, located in Atrey Layout, Nagpur, Maharashtra, India. With a career spanning academic, administrative, and industry domains, she has established herself as a respected figure in management education and professional training. Dr. Rahate is widely recognized as a passionate management educator who is committed to academic excellence, institutional development, and student empowerment. Her teaching philosophy integrates theoretical knowledge with practical insights, enriched by her exposure to corporate and industrial environments. This unique blend of academic rigor and industry relevance enables her to prepare students to meet the dynamic challenges of the modern business world. In addition to her teaching responsibilities, Dr. Rahate has played significant roles in academic administration and institutional governance. She has contributed to policy development, curriculum planning, academic coordination, and quality assurance initiatives. Her leadership and administrative acumen have supported the growth and advancement of management education within her institution and beyond. She is also a valued member on the boards of several reputed management institutions, where she contributes her expertise toward academic planning and institutional excellence. Dr. Rahate has made substantial contributions to research and academic scholarship. She has authored and published 22 research papers in reputed journals and conference proceedings, reflecting her commitment to advancing knowledge in the field of management. Her research interests include management practices, organizational development, leadership, and contemporary business strategies. In addition to her research publications, she has authored four academic books, demonstrating her dedication to knowledge dissemination and academic enrichment. Beyond academia, Dr. Rahate is an accomplished corporate trainer who conducts professional development programs and workshops aimed at enhancing managerial competencies, leadership skills, and organizational effectiveness. Her training programs are valued for their practical orientation and relevance to industry needs.

Anup Ranade is a distinguished academician associated with the Department of MBA at Yeshwantrao Chawan College of Engineering (YCCE), Nagpur, Maharashtra. With a strong commitment to management education, he contributes significantly to teaching, research, and academic development within the institution. His professional expertise and dedication to nurturing future management professionals have played an important role in enhancing the academic environment of YCCE. Through his involvement in academics and institutional activities, Dr. Ranade continues to support the growth of management education in the region.

Anand Bharathi S is an Assistant Professor at VIT Business School (VITBS), VIT University, Vellore, India. He holds a B.E. from Anna University, an MBA from Bharathiar University, and a Ph.D. in Management from Alagappa University. His academic and research expertise lies in digital marketing, search engine optimization (SEO), search engine marketing (SEM), social media marketing (SMM), and data-driven marketing analytics. He has published research articles in peer-reviewed and indexed journals and contributed book chapters to Scopus-indexed publications. In addition to his academic contributions, he brings significant industry experience as a digital marketing strategist, leading SEO, SEM, and analytics-driven campaigns across education and consulting sectors. His research interests include AI-driven SEO, digital search ecosystems, generative engine optimization (GEO), answer engine optimization (AEO), and emerging innovations in data-driven digital marketing.

Jayendira P. Sankar is serving as an Associate Professor of MBA and Head of Digital Business Research Center at the University of Technology Bahrain and has over nineteen years of academic experience. He is a Senior Fellow of HEA-UK and an Academic Fellow of CIPD-UK. He has published extensively in various high-impact journals and presented at numerous academic conferences. His current research interests include Development Economics, focusing on economic growth, poverty, inequality, market failure, fiscal, economic, and social conditions, healthcare, education, employment sector, and industrial and social infrastructure; Human Resource Management, focusing on employee welfare, work-family balance, corporate social responsibility, sustainability; and innovation in teaching-learning and assessments.

Lara Marisa Santos holds a Ph.D. in Marketing and Strategy in 2019 from the University of Aveiro, the University of Beira Interior, and the University of Minho. She had several management positions in public and non-profit organizations. She is an Invited Assistant Professor at Polytechnic University of Cávado and Ave (IPCA) and Instituto Politécnico de Bragança (IPB). She has published several articles in specialized journals and contributed to 15 book chapters. Her research focuses on the Social Sciences, with an emphasis on Marketing.

Roopa Shettigar, Designation: Associate Professor, Department: Department of MBA, College Name: Soundarya Institute of Management and Science, Soundarya Nagar Sidedahalli, Nagasandra Post, 296, 9th Cross Rd, Prakruthi Layout, Siddeshwar Layout, Soundarya Layout, Bengaluru, Karnataka, India Email Id: roo pashettigar19041984@gmail.com ORCID-0000-0001-5672-6589

Prateek Srivastava is an accomplished academician and dedicated educator currently serving as an Assistant Professor in the Department of Information Technology at the School of Engineering and Technology (UIET), Chhatrapati Shahu Ji Maharaj University (CSJM University), Kanpur, Uttar Pradesh, India. With a strong commitment to teaching excellence, research development, and student mentorship, he has established himself as a passionate contributor to technical education and academic advancement. Based in Kanpur, Uttar Pradesh (Postal Code: 208024), Mr. Srivastava plays an active role in shaping future technology professionals by delivering high-quality instruction in core areas of Information Technology. His teaching philosophy focuses on blending theoretical foundations with practical applications, enabling students to develop analytical thinking, problem-solving abilities, and industry-relevant technical skills. As a faculty member at UIET, he is actively involved in curriculum delivery, academic planning, and mentoring undergraduate students. He encourages innovation-driven learning and promotes participation in technical projects, seminars, workshops, and collaborative research activities. His academic interests include emerging areas of Information Technology such as software development, data management systems, computing technologies, and modern digital solutions. Mr. Srivastava is also engaged in scholarly activities, contributing to academic discussions and encouraging interdisciplinary learning approaches. He emphasizes continuous learning and professional development, keeping pace with evolving technological trends and educational methodologies to enhance classroom effectiveness.

Satya Subrahmanyam is a distinguished academic leader, researcher, and institutional strategist with over 28 years of experience in higher education, business research, leadership and management. He holds two PhDs and a Postdoctoral qualification from the Polytechnic Institute of Leiria, Portugal. Currently serving as Professor and Dean (Research) at Holy Spirit University of Kaslik (USEK), Lebanon, he spearheads research initiatives that enhance academic excellence and institutional reputation. He played a pivotal role in the development of the Catholic University in Erbil, Kurdistan, where he established new departments, led research programs, and collaborated on international educational projects. As a founding member and Managing Partner of Vignan Institute of Technology and Management, India, he contributed to its transformation into a premier institution. With expertise in AI-driven business strategies, HR analytics, and leadership in technology adoption, he has published extensively, guided PhD research, and led training programs in corporate and academic settings.

Danish Suleman received the M.A. degree in English literature from the Aligarh Muslim University, India, in 2015 and a Ph.D. degree in English literature from the Universiti Utara Malaysia, Malaysia, in 2021. He has worked as a full-time assistant professor and head of department in the Department of English Language and Literature, Faculty of Arts and Sciences, Near East University, North Cyprus. Currently, he is in a postdoctoral lecturer position at UUM, Malaysia. He has published several academic articles in the field of literature. His current research interests include women's issues, gender studies, feminism, transgender issues, and social discrimination. Dr. Danish is the Editor-in-Chief for the South Asian Journal of Social Sciences and Humanities. He is also working as an Editor and Reviewer in many esteemed WOS and Scopus journals.

Thilagam T is an academician in the Department of Computer Science and Engineering at Vel Tech Rangarajan Dr. Sagunthala R&D Institute of Science and Technology, Chennai, India. She is engaged in teaching and research, with a focus on advancing knowledge in computer science and related technologies. Her interests include fostering innovation, academic excellence, and student-centered learning in emerging computing domains.

Muhammad Usman Tariq is a strategic higher education leader and scholar with more than 17 years of international experience across academia, research, and industry. He holds dual doctorates, a PhD in Artificial Intelligence and a Doctorate in Business Administration and has published extensively as the author of research articles, case studies, book chapters, and academic texts. His contributions also include several patents, reflecting his applied research in technology, business, and education. He is the Founder and CEO of TheCaseHQ.com, a global hub for professional certification programmes, narrative and video case studies, and digital learning innovation. In addition, he serves as President of the Gulf Higher Education Network (Gulf HE), an initiative dedicated to advancing academic practice, faculty development, and institutional collaboration across the region. He is a Principal Fellow of Advance HE (UK), Chartered Fellow of the CIPD (UK), Senior Fellow of SEDA (UK), and a Senior Member of IEEE, reflecting his standing as both an academic innovator and a global professional leader.

Shailesh Tripathi is a Professor at the Balaji Institute of Management and HRD, Sri Balaji University, Pune. He is an accomplished academic with extensive experience in management education, teaching, and research. Dr. Tripathi is known for his commitment to academic excellence and his contribution to developing future management professionals through rigorous pedagogy and industry-oriented learning. His academic interests include management studies and human resource development, and he actively engages in mentoring students, curriculum development, and scholarly activities within the university.

Indhu V is currently pursuing her first year of Master of Business Administration (MBA) at Saveetha University. She is interested in developing her knowledge and skills in business management, technology, and data analysis. She aims to build a strong foundation in management concepts and apply them effectively in real-world business environments. Indhu is enthusiastic about learning new technologies, enhancing her analytical abilities, and contributing to innovative business solutions. Her goal is to grow as a professional who can make meaningful contributions to organizations and society.

Index

V

www.ingramcontent.com/pod-product-compliance
Lightning Source LLC
LaVergne TN
LVHW061530290926
849162LV00004B/741